BEING PROTESTANT IN REFORMATION BRITAIN

The Reformation was about ideas and power, but it was also about real human lives. Alec Ryrie provides the first comprehensive account of what it actually meant to live a Protestant life in England and Scotland between 1530 and 1640, drawing on a rich mixture of contemporary devotional works, sermons, diaries, biographies, and autobiographies to uncover the lived experience of early modern Protestantism.

Beginning from the surprisingly urgent, multifaceted emotions of Protestantism, Ryrie explores practices of prayer, of family and public worship, and of reading and writing, tracking them through the life course from childhood through conversion and vocation to the deathbed. He examines what Protestant piety drew from its Catholic predecessors and contemporaries, and grounds that piety in material realities such as posture, food, and tears.

This perspective shows us what it meant to be Protestant in the British Reformations: a meeting of intensity (a religion which sought authentic feeling above all, and which dreaded hypocrisy and hard-heartedness) with dynamism (a progressive religion, relentlessly pursuing sanctification and dreading idleness). That combination, for good or ill, gave the Protestant experience its particular quality of restless, creative zeal.

The Protestant devotional experience also shows us that this was a broad-based religion: for all the differences across time, between two countries, between men and women, and between puritans and conformists, this was recognisably a unified culture, in which common experiences and practices cut across supposed divides. Alec Ryrie shows us Protestantism, not as the preachers on all sides imagined it, but as it was really lived.

Alec Ryrie studied History and Theology at the universities of Cambridge, St Andrews, and Oxford. He is now Head of Theology and Religion and Professor of the History of Christianity at Durham University. His previous books include *The Age of Reformation* (2009), *The Sorcerer's Tale* (2008), *The Origins of the Scottish Reformation* (2006) and *The Gospel and Henry VIII* (2003).

GW00750237

Being Protestant in Reformation Britain

ALEC RYRIE

OXFORD

UNIVERSITY PRESS

OXFORD
UNIVERSITY PRESS

Great Clarendon Street, Oxford, OX2 6DP,
United Kingdom

Oxford University Press is a department of the University of Oxford.
It furthers the University's objective of excellence in research, scholarship,
and education by publishing worldwide. Oxford is a registered trade mark of
Oxford University Press in the UK and in certain other countries

First published 2013
First published in paperback 2015

Published in the United States of America by Oxford University Press
198 Madison Avenue, New York, NY 10016, United States of America

British Library Cataloguing in Publication Data
Data available

Library of Congress Cataloging in Publication Data
Data available

ISBN 978–0–19–956572–6 (Hbk.)
ISBN 978–0–19–873665–3 (Pbk.)

for Adam

The kingdome of heauen is like to a marchant man, that seketh good perles. Who having founde a perle of great price, went and solde all that he had, and bought it.

Matthew 13:45–6

Acknowledgements

This book has been in gestation for what seems like an age, and as you can see, I have laboured and at last brought forth an elephant—whether white or not, I had better not judge. What I do know is how wide a range of debts I have accumulated along the way. The seed was sown while I was reading book reviews in Bristol University Library one day in, I think, 2003. I first tried out some embryonic ideas at a conference at Magdalene College, Cambridge, the following year, and was encouraged by the response. I then left the project to its own devices for some months while I finished other things. The next growth spurt was triggered by a term's study leave granted by the University of Birmingham, and by an invitation to be a main speaker at the Ecclesiastical History Society's summer conference in 2006. A version of that lecture is now in print in the Society's 2008 volume, *Revival and Resurgence in Christian History*. I am grateful for all those early openings.

The serious work for the project began later in 2006, when I served a short-term fellowship at the Folger Shakespeare Library in Washington, DC, and so discovered the most scholarly, civilized, and delightful library on the face of the planet. I eagerly re-applied, and returned there for a long-term fellowship lasting eight glorious months in 2009. I can't adequately express my thanks to the community there (Carol Brobeck in particular), or to the community at and around St. Columba's, or—above all—to Susan and Adrian McAloon. It was during those two fellowships that the book's core ideas took shape. That second stint was made possible by my new academic home, Durham University, which allowed me two consecutive terms of research leave. On my return from that fellowship I was granted a British Academy Research Development Award, which allowed me to take a full year's study leave in 2009–10, during which time I essentially completed the research on the project. I am grateful both to the Academy and to Jonathan Willis, who stepped in to take over my teaching that year at the last minute, and did it embarrassingly, unsettlingly well. Without all this support it would have been impossible to produce anything like the book you are holding.

But the help I have received has been intellectual as well as practical—or, in one case, both: in 2007 the Arts and Humanities Research Council awarded me a 'network' grant to look into the question of worship and devotion in the early modern world. This is academic fantasy-football: the grant paid for me to assemble conferences, to which I could invite more or less any speakers I wanted, to speak on the subjects which most interested me. At the core of the 'network' were my three co-managers, Judith Maltby, Jessica Martin, and Natalie Mears: I am profoundly grateful to all of them for their practical help, intellectual resourcefulness, and, not least, their friendship during this process. Those from the wider scholarly community who participated in the network are too many to list here, but you know who you are. I was excited by the range of interest in the broad field which the network uncovered, and was set off on a series of new directions. Thank you all.

The army of volunteers and conscripts who have directly helped with the book are also too many to list. There are legions of archivists, librarians, and other custodians of remarkable objects—amongst whom I have to single out Anita Foster at Auckland Castle for special mention. Amongst the people who have answered questions, provided invaluable hints, sparked ideas, closed off blind alleys, and generally helped me to make sense of this material, are: John Barclay, Lucy Bates, Jamie Reid Baxter, Roger Bowers, Sheila Burdett, Claire Busse, Andrew Cambers, Mary Carruthers, John Coffey, Trevor Cooper, Fiona Counsell, John Craig, Leif Dixon, Hilary Elder, Liz Evenden, Tom Freeman, Anna French, Alex Gajda, Ian Green, Sasha Handley, Margaret Hannay, Hannibal Hamlin, Megan Hickerson, Peggy Kay, Erica Longfellow, Sears McGee, Elsie McKee, Paula McQuade, Aude de Mézerac-Zanetti, Meredith Neumann, Beth Quitslund, Gordon Raeburn, Joyce Ransome, Steve Roberts, Jeremy Schildt, Tom Schwanda, Ethan Shagan, Alison Shell, Cathy Shrank, David Trim, and Emily Winerock. There are many others whose names I have forgotten. There is no danger of my forgetting Eric Carlson, Douglas Davies, Carol Harrison, Kate Narveson, Alex Walsham, Micheline White, and especially Judith Maltby, who read portions of the book as it emerged and caught some of my many errors. Particular thanks, as ever, to Diarmaid MacCulloch, who helps to keep my intellectual compass calibrated, and to Peter Marshall, who does the same, and who also read the entire text for OUP (so much for anonymity). The book would have been much worse without him.

While I was finalizing the text, I heard of Patrick Collinson's death. Pat was the punning, allusive, generous, presiding genius of this field, who would have written a much better book than this, and who gave me crucial guidance and confidence at some key moments. My inner coward is relieved not to be on tenterhooks for the review he would have written, but I bitterly regret—and still can't quite believe—that he can't explain to me everything that I've missed.

Amongst less directly academic debts, I have to thank Kerry Carter, for the Divine Comedy; Scott Amos, for the University of Chicago's terrifying 'Write Your Own Academic Sentence' service; and the *New Yorker* magazine for their monthly fiction podcast, all of which helped me in my struggles to stay sane while writing. Edmundbyers, Snod's Edge, and Whittonstall have been a wonderful refuge: the word 'community' is glibly overused, but this time it is true.

My family have endured the book's long genesis patiently. My wife Victoria's unfailing support and affirmation, and my parents' steady interest, made it possible, not to mention the two children who have joined us during the process. Ben can appreciate what it means to write a book, since he has already written one, just after his fifth birthday. Adam is not quite at that stage yet, so this one's dedication is to him. When I first dreamt up this book, Victoria dubbed it my 'Big Book of Prayer', which sounds appealingly like a colouring book. Sadly for Adam, it's not nearly so much fun as that. But such as it is, it is what my family's love has made it.

Contents

List of illustrations   xiv
List of abbreviations   xv
Notes on the text   xvi

Introduction   1

I. THE PROTESTANT EMOTIONS

1. Cultivating the Affections   17
  1. Discipline and Nourish   17
  2. Hearts of Stone   20

2. Despair and Salvation   27
  1. A Culture of Despair?   27
  2. The Threat of Hell   32
  3. Emotion and Salvation   39

3. The Meaning of Mourning   49
  1. True Repentance   49
  2. How to Repent   55
  3. The End of Repentance   59

4. Desire   63
  1. The Need for Desire   63
  2. Kindling Desire   66
  3. Zeal   70

5. Joy   77
  1. Protestants and Happiness   77
  2. Enduring Joy   80
  3. Fleeting Joy   83
  4. The Paradoxes of Joy   91

II. THE PROTESTANT AT PRAYER

6. The Meaning of Prayer   99
  1. The Worth of Prayer   99
  2. Inability to Pray   102
  3. Prayer and Meditation   108

  7. **Answering Prayer**   119
     1. Why Pray?   119
     2. Worldly and Otherworldly Prayer   122
     3. Prayer and Action   127
     4. Vows and Covenants   130
     5. Experiencing Answers   140

  8. **The Practice of Prayer**   144
     1. Continuous Prayer   144
     2. Times of Prayer   147
     3. Places of Prayer   154
     4. Posture and Gesture   170
     5. Tears   187
     6. 'Humiliation'   195

  9. **Speaking to God**   200
     1. Preparation and Formality   200
     2. Words, Silence, and Groans   208
     3. Set and Extempore Prayer   214
     4. Praying in Scripture Phrase   224
     5. Common Prayer and Private Devotion   232

 10. **Prayer as Struggle**   239
     1. Persistence and Suffering   239
     2. The Armour of God   243
     3. Wrestling with God   247

III. THE PROTESTANT AND THE WORD

 11. **Reading**   259
     1. Literacy and Learning   259
     2. Protestants and their Bibles   270
     3. Protestant Books and Catholic Books   281
     4. The Book as Object   292

 12. **Writing**   298
     1. Writing the Word   298
     2. Public and Private Writing   306

IV. THE PROTESTANT IN COMPANY

 13. **The Experience of Worship**   317
     1. Public Prayer   317
     2. Baptism   329
     3. The Lord's Supper   336
     4. Experiencing the Sermon   351

14. **Prayer in the Household**   363
    1. Prescription and Practice   365
    2. Themes of Family Prayer   374
    3. Table-graces   381
    4. Conference and Fellowship   390
    5. Keeping Company with Sinners   397

V. THE PROTESTANT LIFE

15. **The Meaning of Life**   409
    1. Progress and Repentance   409
    2. Nurturing Crisis   416
    3. Aspiring to Martyrdom   422

16. **The Stages of Life**   428
    1. Childhood   428
    2. Conversion   436
    3. The Passage of Time   441
    4. Vocation   446
    5. Marking the Years   456
    6. The Deathbed   460

    Conclusion   469

Select Bibliography   476
Index   491

List of illustrations

1. John Trundle?, *Keepe within Compasse* (1619, RSTC 14898.5), title page. 155

2. John Hayward, *The sanctuarie of a troubled soule* (1602: RSTC 13003.7), sig. 2r. 165

3. Monument to Richard, Lord Rich, Felsted, Essex. 172

4. Monument to Sir Alexander Culpepper, Goudhurst, Kent. 174

5. Monument to Thomas Wylmer, Staverton, Northamptonshire. 175

6. John Hayward, *The sanctuarie of a troubled soule* (1602: RSTC 13003.7), sig. H9v. 176

7. William Hunnis, *Seuen Sobs of a Sorrowfull Soule for Sinne* (1583: RSTC 13975), sig. a4v. 179

8. *This prymer of Salysbery vse* (Rouen, 1538: RSTC 16001), sig. L2r. 181

9. Lewis Bayly, *The Practise of pietie* (1620: RSTC 1604), title page. 183

10. John Foxe, *Actes and monuments of these latter and perillous dayes* (1563: RSTC 11222), p. 1260. 184

11. *A Short Interpretation of the Lords Praier* (1627: RSTC 16823). 231

12. Overmantle, Bradninch Manor, Devon. 253

13. Lewis Bayly, *The Practise of pietie* (1620: RSTC 1604), p. 2. 264

14. Richard Day, *A Booke of Christian Prayers* (1578: RSTC 6429), sig. M1r, detail. 330

15. Richard Day, *A Booke of Christian Prayers* (1578: RSTC 6429), sig. M1v, detail. 337

16. Memorial painting to Bishop James Pilkington, Auckland Castle, County Durham. 367

17. Monument to Edward Dixon and family, Little Rollright, Oxfordshire. 368

18. Antoon Claeissins, 'Family Saying Grace', c.1585. 384

List of abbreviations

BL	British Library, London
Bod	Bodleian Library, Oxford
Forbes, 'Diary'	John Rylands Library, Manchester, English MS 958: Diary of John Forbes of Corse, 1624–48
FSL	Folger Shakespeare Library, Washington DC
Isham, 'Confessions'	Elizabeth Isham, 'My Booke of Rememberance', c. 1639, ed. Elizabeth Clarke and Erica Longfellow, at <http://www.warwick.ac.uk/english/perdita/Isham/index_bor.htm>
Isham, 'Diary'	Diary of Elizabeth Isham, 1614–48, ed. Elizabeth Clarke and Erica Longfellow, at <http://www.warwick.ac.uk/english/perdita/Isham/index_yr.htm>
LMA	London Metropolitan Archives
Mildmay, 'Meditations'	Central Library, Northampton, Northamptonshire Studies Collection: Lady Grace Mildmay's Meditations
ODNB	Oxford Dictionary of National Biography
RSTC	W. A. Jackson, J. F. Ferguson, and K. F. Pantzer (eds), *A Short-Title Catalogue of Books Printed in England, Scotland, & Ireland and of English books printed abroad 1475–1640* (2nd edn, London, 1986–91)
Saxby, 'Miscellany'	Cambridge University Library, Additional MS 3117: pious miscellany of Robert Saxby
Wing	Donald G. Wing (ed.), *Short-title catalogue of books printed in England, Scotland, Ireland, Wales, and British America . . . 1641–1700* (2nd edn, New York, 1994)
Woodford, 'Diary'	New College, Oxford MS 9502: diary of Robert Woodford, 1637–41 (unpaginated)

Notes on the text

The English language lacks an unproblematic word meaning 'a person who prays'. Throughout I use *devotee*, a late 17th-century coinage, to convey that meaning. In its later use this word frequently has connotations of fanaticism: that is not a shade of meaning which I intend.

On the use of 'we' and 'you' in place of 'one' or 'they' throughout, see p. 12.

The place of publication of all works is London unless otherwise indicated. All Biblical quotations are taken from the Geneva Bible (1560 edition), unless otherwise indicated. Where numbers of editions are indicated in a footnote, these are collated from RSTC, Wing, the English Short Title Catalogue (<http://estc.bl.uk>), and Ian Green, *Print and Protestantism in Early Modern England* (Oxford, 2000).

In quotations, some punctuation and capitalization has been amended for clarity. Thorns are rendered 'th' and yoghs 'y'. All abbreviations have been silently expanded.

Introduction

This book is about what it meant to be a Protestant in early modern Britain. More on what that question means in a moment, but first, why is it worth asking?

Christianity is an incorrigibly intellectual religion. It is grounded in books—one book above all. Christians have always taken the precise definition of doctrines immensely seriously, and they have always disagreed over those definitions, often reviling each other, and sometimes worse. This odd behaviour, which owes very little to Christianity's founder, may or may not have been good for Christians, but it has been wonderful for Christianity's historians. Doctrinal arguments leave a never-ending paper trail behind them, as theologians and polemicists hurl treatises at one another.

This was never truer than in the Reformation period. Western Christianity's great 16th-century trauma was driven by doctrinal disagreements. The modern world's materialism, pragmatism, and—to be blunt—sheer sloth makes us reluctant to accept that ideas really could matter that much to that many people, but they did. Western Christendom's last great prophet before the schism, Erasmus, argued that every Christian could and should be a theologian.[1] The Protestant reformers, in particular, made heroic efforts to realize that impossible vision, and in the process, works of doctrinal definition and controversy flew off their printing presses, an unprecedented theological blizzard which continues to buffet and to drive scholars to this day.

But in that blizzard we can lose sight of an obvious truth: Christians are more than credal statements on legs. It is true that being a Christian is usually defined primarily by conversion of some kind, that is, by giving assent—actual or implicit—to Christian doctrines; and yet converts still have lives to live. Yes, life in this world may be simply a preparation for death. In the light of eternity, it may be merely the briefest pause before one's true life begins. But that pause may still last for decades; decades which the Christian has somehow to fill and through which he or she must keep, and grow in, the faith. The questions behind this book are, first: how did early modern Protestants in Britain pass that tediously long interval between conversion and death? And second, what does the answer to the first question tell us about Protestantism?

Early modern Catholicism was full of resources consulted to address this point: from the repetition of set prayers—perhaps using an aid such as the rosary—through the annual cycle of feasts and fasts, through extraordinary acts such as

[1] Desiderius Erasmus, *Christian Humanism and the Reformation: Selected Writings*, ed. John C. Olin (New York, 1965), 100.

pilgrimages, to—in extremis—the adoption of a formal rule of life, that is, a *religion*. These actions did more than fill Catholics' days. They had merit in God's eyes, and could become a part of the work of salvation. Reformed Protestant preachers, however, dismissed all of these Catholic practices as idolatrous or, at best, futile. They insisted that neither these nor *any* human actions could have merit before God, and indeed that such pieties were barriers erected by a corrupt clergy between God and his people. Instead, humans ought to stand naked before the Creator, to be clothed in the only garment that might cover our corruption and fit us for his presence: the blood of Christ. And yet, far from wanting to abolish piety, the Protestant reformers' ambition was at heart to bring true piety to every Christian.[2]

Hence the problem: given their active distrust for ritual, ceremony, and structured pious practice, how did these Christians live out their religion? As the late, lamented Patrick Collinson observed of early modern Protestants: 'It is difficult to reconstruct regular rhythms of activity, or to answer the question once put by a child within my hearing of a certain rhinoceros in the Zoo: "But what does he do *all day?*" '[3]

I think the rhinoceros question is curious enough in itself to be worth tackling. The attempt has taught me how little we really know about some very central and obvious features of day-to-day life in the early modern past. I have repeatedly found myself asking what I thought were foolishly simple questions about what happened—for example—in churches, or around domestic dining-tables, in the 16th century. Repeatedly I have struck uncertainty, confusion, and contradictions, and done so forcefully enough to be persuaded that those problems do not exist solely in my own head. Part of what I have done in this book is simply to try to assemble answers to those mundane questions.

However, the mundane questions matter for a deeper reason. The lived experience of religion is not a detail: it is what that religion actually means to those who profess it. Protestantism was a religious force of astonishing power, which reshaped early modern Britain and through it, much of the modern world. But no religious movement, not even Reformed Protestantism, is a disembodied set of doctrines. It consists of people who have found a way of building their daily lives around it, and it is in those lives that it finds its meaning. The point of this book is that, by approaching early modern Protestantism through devotion rather than through doctrine, we can see a more rounded picture of it—and that picture throws up some surprises.

In other words, I am asking two, linked questions. What did early modern Protestants do in order to live out their religion; and what meaning did they find in those actions? And I begin with the second question, the internal one, because for Reformed Protestants the inner experience was primary. Worship must be in spirit and in truth. The struggle to achieve such a deceptively simple thing—and the harder struggle to maintain it once achieved—gave shape to the Protestant life. It is

---

[2] Scott H. Hendrix, *Recultivating the Vineyard: The Reformation Agendas of Christianisation* (Louisville, KY, 2004), 57–63.

[3] Patrick Collinson, 'Shepherds, sheepdogs and hirelings: the pastoral ministry in post-Reformation England' in W. J. Shiels and Diana Wood (eds), *The Ministry: Clerical and Lay* (Studies in Church History 26, 1989), 193.

only with that in mind that we can begin to make sense of the outward actions which that inner experience gave rise to. Thus, Part I of the book surveys the emotional landscape of early modern Protestantism, arguing along the way that it is rather richer than is often assumed, and that even bleak landscapes can have their own appeal.

With that foundation laid, the remainder of the book is, I hope, self-explanatory. Part II, the longest section of the book, considers the most fundamental and most mysterious feature of Protestant pious practice: private prayer. As well as considering what Protestants understood prayer to be, this section asks such basic questions as when, where, how long, how often, and in what postures they prayed, on the grounds that such things are an essential part of the experience of prayer. It also asks what they prayed for, what words they used—when they used words at all—and how they understood the exchange with God which prayer comprised. Prayer, for early modern Protestants, was a business less of quiet contemplation than of struggle. The zealous prayer-warrior could overcome not only sin, the world, and the Devil, but even God himself.

Part III considers one important subset of private devotion: Protestants' use of the written word, both as readers and writers. As well as exploring how such a literate religion operated in a largely illiterate society, it asks how both reading and writing functioned as pious exercises; how Protestantism was shaped by its voracious and inclusive reading habits; how books were treated in a world where they were the only sacred objects; and why so many Protestants found the experience of writing so powerful.

Part IV considers the more sociable side of Protestant devotion: formal public worship, and the—sometimes—less formal business of family and household devotions. It asks how, and whether, Protestants found spiritual succour in these practices, and how and whether those experiences were formative for their wider religious lives. It also examines the wider phenomena of the social—or anti-social—Protestant. This section of the book is deliberately the least comprehensive, since the subject is vast. I have skated over some important subjects because they have been tackled so effectively by other scholars—Sabbath observance, for example—or because I myself have written on them elsewhere—fasting and the piety of sleeping and dreaming. Other areas—such as the use of table-graces—have scarcely been touched by existing scholarship, and I have dwelled on these at a little more length.

Finally, Part V examines the Protestant life-course as a whole: not just the distinctive experiences of childhood, conversion, vocation, ageing, and death, but the meanings which were given to each stage and to the overarching narratives of their lives which Protestants assiduously constructed for themselves.

Each of these perspectives brings its own insights, I hope, but the reason I have taken such a wide-ranging approach—and produced such a long book—is to take in a broader panorama. The book's main argument is that devotional life shows us early modern British Protestantism as an *intense, dynamic,* and *broad-based* religious culture.

It was *intense* in that it sought and—often—found a particular, heightened pitch of emotional experience. Virtually all of its religious activity was aimed at cultivating this kind of intensity in some form. The focus on emotion does not mean that Protestantism was anti-intellectual; far from it. Early modern Protestants would have been puzzled by the modern assumption that intellect and emotions are opposed. Both in their theory and in their practice, the two reinforced one another. The nature of these intense emotional experiences was very varied: despair and mourning are what we might stereotypically expect, but there was also joyfulness, or mixtures of the two which are so fine-grained that they can barely be distinguished. It was the strength of these emotions, not their nature, which principally mattered. Above all, this was a search for authenticity, for the unmistakable touch of God in a believer's life. And the search for authentic intensity also focused Protestant attention onto its opposite. Hypocrisy became one of two key vices against which early modern British Protestants took their bearings.

It was this endless search for intensity which gave their religion its characteristic *dynamism*. This was a restless, progressive religion, which was nourished by crisis and starved by routine, and which therefore set out to produce regular crises for itself. Protestant lives were always in motion, and the motion was linear rather than cyclical. One reason it is hard to reconstruct 'regular rhythms' of activity is that this culture deplored rhythm. Repetition could potentially dull any pious activity into formalism—and, therefore, hypocrisy. Ease, rest, recreation, even peace: early modern Protestants learned to be suspicious of such things in this life, and if they longed for settled joy in believing, their lived experience was more staccato. Their pious lives were lives of struggle: with sin and the Devil, with the world and their own nature, and even with God. Again, this valorization of struggle and labour focused attention onto the opposing vice: idleness.

This four-cornered dance, with intensity and dynamism facing off against hypocrisy and idleness, provided the experiential matrix within which early modern British Protestants lived their lives. Most of this book is about what living in the midst of that dance entailed, but one point is worth underlining now: the exquisitely sensitive self-awareness which it required. To live this religious life was a training in self-knowledge, and especially in the treacherous, interwoven mazes of human self-deception.

Lastly, this was a *broad-based* culture: but that is a different, larger, and more controversial issue, which requires some further explanation.

*

The book's subject is Reformation-era British Protestantism: but each part of that phrase requires some clarification.

My chronological parameters are simple: from the earliest beginnings of Protestantism to 1640. The end point is an obvious one, because the jungle of Protestant exotica which spread across Britain after 1640 would need a different book. The starting point is a little more unusual, since most recent studies of early modern English Protestant culture start in around 1560. It is true that 'Protestantism' was pretty ill-defined before that date—the word itself is an anachronism for the early period—and that Protestants, or evangelicals, were pretty thin on the ground in Britain before the late 1540s at the earliest. However, those early evangelicals are absolutely fundamental for understanding their successors. They were read as authorities, imitated as models and—in many cases—treasured as martyrs. While there were some obvious shifts in Protestant religious practice across my period, the continuities are perhaps more striking. The core elements of the Protestant pious life were sketched out by William Tyndale, Hugh Latimer, and others of the first generation. In particular, they were outlined by Thomas Becon, the first English-speaking Protestant to write best-sellers, the author of the first English Protestant collection of prayers and of the first English Protestant books devoted to subjects such as prayer and fasting. Becon's work has been much derided by scholars. C. J. Stranks dismissed his books as 'harangues and lengthy statements of the obvious'; Gordon Rupp described his *Pathwaye unto praier* as 'a very stony pathway'.[4] Personally, I think this is a little harsh—Becon was no literary genius, but his work has an earnest clarity to it—but more importantly, the readers who consumed well over eighty editions of his books during the 16th century evidently disagreed. The patterns which Becon and his contemporaries sketched out were refined and added to by their successors, but not overturned. Hence my describing this whole period as the Reformation: a period of coherent, dynamic renewal, whose political manifestations were halting and uneven but whose tempo in the lives of believers remained steady and insistent. The patterns set by the earliest reformers endured at least until the Civil War era, and we will not understand the period's unity unless they are included.

My geography is also inclusive. By 'Britain' I mean the English-speaking Protestant cultures of the island of Great Britain; that is, principally of the kingdoms of Scotland and of England—with occasional reference to Anglophone Wales. The decision to tackle these two very different realms together may seem quixotic, but it is not taken lightly. The Protestant cultures of early modern England and Scotland shared a great deal.[5] Mutually comprehensible written languages gave them shared print resources, and the Scottish book-trade's dependence on London printers entangled them still further. Both countries' religious politics left each of them regularly hosting the other's exiles, and politics increasingly knotted their stories together, both before and after their crowns were united in 1603. So the comparison is close enough to be fruitful. But the two countries' Protestant cultures also remained distinct enough for the comparison to be instructive. I have found their similar-but-different quality to be useful in teasing out the meaning of what happened on both sides of the border—even if larger, more literate England inevitably contributes the bulk of the evidence.

I have been more reluctant to draw on the further-flung reaches of English-speaking Protestantism: Ireland, the continental expatriate communities, and the New World. A few of the sources coming out of those contexts are irresistibly rich,

---

[4] C. J. Stranks, *Anglican Devotion* (London, 1961), 20; Gordon Rupp, 'Protestant Spirituality in the First Age of the Reformation' in G. J. Cuming and D. Baker (eds), *Popular Belief and Practice* (Studies in Church History 8, 1972), 162.

[5] Jane Dawson, 'Anglo-Scottish Protestant culture and integration in sixteenth-century Britain' in Steven G. Ellis and Sarah Barber (eds), *Conquest and Union: fashioning a British state, 1485–1725* (New York, 1995). Cf. Tara Hamling's assessment of the two countries' religious 'common outlook': *Decorating the 'Godly' Household: Religious Art in Post-Reformation Britain* (New Haven and London, 2010), 9.

but I have tried to keep my use of them to a minimum. What England and Scotland shared was the struggle of building a universal Protestantism in a settled society. The voluntary, self-selecting, or minority nature of Protestantism in those other contexts gave it a very different flavour.

All of which raises the key question of what I mean by 'Protestantism'. My simple definition is: the mainstream Protestant cultures of England and Scotland, and in all those who were earnest in the practice of that religion. These were, at least from the mid-1540s, Reformed Protestants—or as we might say with only minor anachronism, Calvinists. They would not have used those labels for themselves, at least not until around the turn of the century, but the self-professed 'gospellers' of the 1530s and the confessed Protestants of the 1630s manifestly stand in the same tradition and would have recognized one another as brethren.[6] It is that tradition which is my subject here. So I have paid very little attention to separatists, radicals, or sectarians, and my interest in Catholicism is limited to its—substantial—influence on Protestant piety and practice.

I have also, more contentiously, largely excluded Laudians and other 17th-century prophets of ceremonial revival. I have even tried to keep Richard Hooker at arm's length, partly from a suspicion that scholars have fallen too easily for the quiet reasonableness with which he cloaked his authoritarianism. My justification for excluding this tradition is not that I doubt its Protestantism, but that it was distinct from wider Anglo-Scottish Protestant culture. Of course, to study the later 1620s and 1630s while excluding Laudian-accented voices altogether would be quixotic, and I have not done so, but I am mostly interested in those features of Laudian piety which are parallel to, or in dialogue with, the piety of the Calvinist consensus, not those which directly opposed it.

So if I am excluding separatists, Catholics, and Laudians, the suspicion must be that this is a book about puritans. It is not. My argument is that early modern Protestantism was a *broad-based* religious culture: that the division between puritan and conformist Protestants, which has been so important in English historiography, almost fades from view when examined through the lens of devotion and lived experience. The culture I am describing in this book cut across it. And given how vital devotion and lived experience are to religious identity, I am questioning how important that division is to understanding early modern England as a whole.

Undoubtedly, the Elizabethan and Jacobean church was bitterly split over a range of issues, from ceremony to governance; those splits formed the world views of generations of clerics, made and wrecked careers, and in a few cases cost lives. But while those splits certainly allow us to state that some individuals held puritan views on particular issues, that does not mean that they *were* 'puritans'. Indeed, 'puritan' is better used as an adjective than a noun. For when we look at the lived experience of religion in this period, the supposed distinction between puritan and conformist dissolves into a blurred spectrum in which even the extremes do not differ too starkly from one another.

---

[6] Peter Marshall, 'The Naming of Protestant England', *Past and Present* 214 (2012), 87–128.

Nicholas Tyacke's thesis that there was a 'Calvinist consensus' in post-Reformation England can be overplayed, but even at the doctrinal level it remains convincing. Not every mainstream theologian in Elizabethan and Jacobean England was a predestinarian—the 'consensus' was never total; but it was the water in which the English church swam. Predestinarian Reformed Protestantism was normative both for puritan agitators and for their establishment opponents. Archbishop Whitgift's strict adherence to predestination is well known, and conformist theologians were often simply looking to Zürich rather than to Geneva for inspiration. As we have become aware of this, so 'puritan', a label which was once restricted to those who actively sought to challenge the Elizabethan Settlement, has come to be applied to 'moderate puritans' who worked more or less happily within that settlement. Also, we are increasingly aware that lugubrious puritan claims to be a tiny minority were preachers' rhetoric rather than sober attempts at quantification. Even redefining puritanism as a more rebarbative and more self-consciously separate 'precisianism' does not cut it off from the wider culture which it professed to revile; nor does it undermine Alexandra Walsham's perception that 'zealous Protestantism could . . . be a popular religion'.[7]

And when we move away from divisive issues of doctrine to religious practice, the middle ground between puritanism and comformity is so thickly populated that it hardly deserves the name. As Julia Merritt has pointed out, while historians are naturally attracted to 'cantankerous, divisive and controversial figures', we should not ignore 'emollient, unifying, pastorally sensitive puritan clergymen'.[8] So we find, for example, the Jacobean cleric Richard Kilby, whose popular books were outspoken in criticizing those on both sides who were too passionate in arguments over ceremonies.[9] Indeed, there are so many individuals who resist easy categorization that the categories become suspect. Daniel Featley, for example, defender of episcopacy and opponent of Arminianism: was he a patron of puritanism or a 'contented conformist'?[10] Surely both. What of Arthur Wodenoth, who had an impeccably

[7] Alexandra Walsham, *Providence in Early Modern England* (Oxford, 1999), 325. See Nicholas Tyacke, *Anti-Calvinists: the rise of English Arminianism* (Oxford, 1987); Peter Lake, 'Calvinism and the English Church 1570–1635', *Past and Present* 114 (1986), 32–76; Peter Lake, *Moderate Puritans and the Elizabethan Church* (Cambridge, 1982); Patrick Collinson, *The Religion of Protestants* (Oxford, 1982), 189–205; Theodore Dwight Bozeman, *The Precisianist Strain: Disciplinary Religion and Antinomian Backlash in Puritanism to 1638* (Chapel Hill, NC, 2004). The classic study of English predestinarianism remains R. T. Kendall, *Calvin and English Calvinism to 1649* (Oxford, 1979). Peter White's argument for a broad if nebulous spectrum of predestinarian belief has been effectively challenged by Leif Dixon: Peter White, *Predestination, Policy and Polemic: Conflict and Consensus in the English Church from the Reformation to the Civil War* (Cambridge, 1992); Leif Dixon, 'Predestination and pastoral theology: the communication of Calvinist doctrine, c.1590–1640', shortly to be published as *Practical Predestinarians in England 1590–1640* (Farnham, Ashgate, 2013). On the ongoing attempts to define the boundaries of puritanism, see the apposite comments in Andrew Cambers, *Godly Reading: Print, Manuscript and Puritanism in England, 1580–1720* (Cambridge, 2011), 23.

[8] Julia F. Merritt, 'The pastoral tightrope: a puritan pedagogue in Jacobean London' in Thomas Cogswell et al. (eds), *Politics, Religion and Popularity in Early Stuart Britain* (Cambridge, 2002), 160.

[9] Richard Kilby, *Hallelujah. Praise yee the Lord* (1635: RSTC 14956.7), 108–9.

[10] *ODNB*; Kate Narveson, 'Piety and the genre of John Donne's Devotions', *John Donne Journal* 17 (1998), 111–12.

puritan conversion experience and then used it to argue that the existing liturgical practices of the Church of England were approved by God?[11] What of Richard Stonley, who spent whole days at prayer with his Geneva Bible, who copied that Bible's contentious marginalia into his diary, and who carefully kept a notebook of sermons, but who would not forgive his parson for the slightest deviation from the Book of Common Prayer?[12] Or take the following description of a formal fast day:

> At solemn humiliations my voyce sometimes failes me, by reason of my groans and sighs: I seldom rise from my knees, (on those days) but I see the floore watred with my Tears; And even these tears are full of comfort and pleasantness.

This could be any puritan speaking, but in fact it is Lettice Cary, patroness of a formidable Arminian salon in the 1630s.[13]

Many Protestants were both puritan and conformist. More importantly, the areas of disagreement were both relatively modest and fairly well contained. Most people did not feel the need to choose a partisan identity for themselves, even when such choices were available. With hindsight we know that this broke down in the 1640s: violence always compels people to choose sides. But it is a serious error to read those divisions back into the earlier period, when no-one knew that war would impose its sharp polarities. This is particularly true with regard to piety and devotion. As Mary Hampson Patterson's discussion of Elizabethan devotional texts observed, most such works are innocent of the controversies which have consumed so much historical attention. Trying to label them as puritan or confirmist 'feels not unlike trying to decide whether university students are "adults" or "children": they are of course a bit of both'.[14] I am not trying to jettison these labels, and in what follows I have used the P-word freely enough, but more as a tendency than a category. Many—most?—Protestants who were earnest about their religion held some puritan views; very few were puritans in any defined or exclusive sense. Likewise, as we shall see, acceptance of, and even conformity to, devotions which later puritan writers would revile spread far beyond any narrowly-defined 'Prayer-Book Protestants'. There were, indeed, people whom we could sensibly describe as Prayer-Book puritans. More to the point, as Kate Narveson has argued, early modern England—and, *a fortiori*, Scotland—'possessed a broad-based religious culture' whose unity is more striking than its many shades of variation.[15] Thus, part of this book's argument is that the puritan-conformist division has misled scholars for long enough. Its apparent prominence is a result of historians' fondness for divisive questions, and of our sources' being skewed towards polemics. From the perspective of lived religious experience, that division was simply one amongst many which criss-crossed early modern Britain's religious landscape, and neither the most clear-cut nor the

---

[11] Arthur Wodenoth, '1645, Expressions of Mr Arthur Wodenoth', ed. Harold Spencer Scott, in *The Camden Miscellany X* (Camden Society, s.3 vol. 4: 1902), 124–6.

[12] FSL MS V.a.459, esp. fos 5r, 10v, 15r, 19r, 21r, 47r, 79v.

[13] John Duncon, *The Returnes of Spiritual comfort and grief in a Devout Soul* (1648: Wing D2605), 8.

[14] Mary Hampson Patterson, *Domesticating the Reformation* (Madison, WI, 2007), 30.

[15] Kate Narveson, *Bible Readers and Lay Writers in Early Modern England* (Farnham, 2012), 4; and see following, pp. 214–24, 232–5.

most important. As Charles and Katherine George argued half a century ago, the unity of post-Reformation English religious culture is such that there is only one useful term for it: 'Protestant'.[16]

Many recent scholars have in any case passed over the word 'Puritan' in favour of terms such as 'the godly', but this has its own problems, for it inescapably implies that everyone else is ungodly, or that their Protestantism is necessarily colder. Hooker would dispute that, and for once I agree with him. Religious commitment and doctrinal views do not map neatly onto one another. If we are to follow Christopher Haigh's recent division of post-Reformation England into the godly and the profane,[17] we have to recognize that the godly, even the Protestant godly, were a diverse bunch. In this sense puritan and Arminian zeal had more in common with one another than either did with mere conformity. For this reason I prefer to think of 'earnestness' rather than 'godliness', a word with too partisan a flavour. By 'earnestness', I mean any attempt to practice Protestantism which is, or which appears to be, intended seriously—as opposed to practices engaged in cynically, for form's sake or from habit. Earnestness often tended towards puritanism, but there were other ways of being earnest about Protestantism, and they were not usually in tension with each other.

However, to use 'earnestness' as a yardstick makes plain a problem implicit in Haigh's division. As an incisive recent article by Leif Dixon notes, most English people were neither godly nor profane, but a bit of both. Such stark divisions are an artefact of preachers' rhetoric or of court processes. In reality almost everyone might recognize the importance of being earnest sometimes—at the very least, on their deathbed; but not many would keep it up without a break.[18] My interest, then, is in earnest religious behaviour wherever it may be found, and to the extent that it may be found there: both from those for whom it was a daily diet and from those who only tasted it rarely, but whose Protestantism is as important as that of their more zealous brethren.

*

A word on methods and sources. The study of religious practice is a mature and lively scholarly field, and when I embarked on this project I spent some time getting to know a little of the sociological and anthropological literature. I read some fascinating, brilliant, and, if I am honest, sometimes utterly baffling works, but I also found it difficult to see how the theories and methods which these scholars were using could be made to answer the particular questions which I wanted to ask. No doubt due to my own lumpishness, I have largely been driven back onto my training as a historian.

Still, if I am an empiricist, I hope I am not too naïve about it; we all have methodologies. One of mine is a suspicion of anachronistic abstractions, which can be an immensely useful analytical tools, but can also be a way of concealing

---

[16] Charles H. George and Katherine George, *The Protestant Mind of the English Reformation* (Princeton, 1961), introduction.

[17] Christopher Haigh, *The Plain Man's Pathways to Heaven: Kinds of Christianity in Post-Reformation England, 1570–1640* (Oxford, 2007), esp. 140–1.

[18] Leif Dixon, 'Calvinist Theology and Pastoral Reality in the Reign of King James I: the Perspective of Thomas Wilson', *Seventeenth Century* 23/2 (2008), 174–5.

meaning—or its absence—in conceptual bubble-wrap. I have tried to evade this in part through concentrating on the material reality of the past. This book repeatedly approaches Protestant piety through questions such as, what postures Protestants adopted when they prayed, how they managed their inkwells when writing sermon-notes, and whether pious children really did scrump fruit from their neighbours' orchards. I apologize if this seems simplistic. My hope is that it will keep my concepts rooted in physical reality, and prevent me from building theoretical cloud-castles.

But to build anything at all, we do need sources, and in this case that is problematic. The experience of religion is subjective and evanescent. By the act of overhearing prayer, we change its meaning. The most potent religious experiences are often left unspoken, not least because they are inexpressible. It is as if we were trying to recover the sensation of smelling a rose and all we had to work with was gardeners' account books.

I have drawn on two broad and overlapping bodies of sources: the generic and the individual. By generic sources, I mean the sermons, treatises and other works in which some Protestants—mainly, but not only, clerics—urged others at large to adopt certain pious practices or to pursue certain spiritual experiences. Scholars no longer neglect these works as they once did, but they remain an under-explored resource.[19] A huge number of such works survive in print, often echoing one another, and I have tried to ignore the siren voice which tells me I should have read them all. My sample has been guided by Ian Green's invaluable database of best- and steady selling Protestant books in early modern England, which he defines as all those which went through at least five editions in any given twenty-year period.[20] I have consulted all of the devotional works in Green's sample which were first published before 1640, in the hope that this will provide an overview of the most popular and influential devotional books of the time. I have also consulted a wide range of other early printed works which did not quite attain to Green's level of commercial success but which, in my judgement, shed some significant light on the questions addressed here. In particular, I have been more inclusive of devotional works written early in my period, or for the Scottish market, which almost never had the chance to attain the sorts of sales which Green's criteria demand.

---

[19] Brad S. Gregory, 'The "True and Zealouse Seruice of God": Robert Parsons, Edmund Bunny, and The First Booke of the Christian Exercise', *Journal of Ecclesiastical History* 45/2 (1994), 241.

[20] Ian Green, *Print and Protestantism in Early Modern England* (Oxford, 2000). Green's method has been controversial: in particular, Peter Lake and Michael Questier have lambasted his approach as skewing the field towards a cosy, consensual, and non-controversial Anglicanism. It is certainly true, as Green himself points out, that his definition of best-sellers tends to exclude newsworthy, novel and controversial books, but it is hard to see how any method other than frequency of printing can be used systematically to assess books' popularity. If this privileges establishment and consensual voices, that is because early modern states were efficient at marginalizing printed dissent, which is a significant fact in itself. In any case, it would be hard to claim that scholars of the period have been distracted from polemic by the allure of devotional works. Peter Lake with Michael Questier, *The Antichrist's Lewd Hat: Protestants, Papists and Players in Post-Reformation England* (New Haven and London, 2002), 315–31, esp. 325 n. 15.

Much of this material is simply prescriptive, but one of the surprises of research-ing this book has been how much direct testimony of actual religious experience survives. Sometimes even prescriptive texts provide this: authors who were willing to bare their souls could find themselves rewarded with lively sales. But this personal evidence also takes us beyond published devotional works. It is a com-monplace that detailed diaries were very rare before 1640, and that most of the early diaries which do survive are terse and impersonal affairs.[21] However, if we cast our net a little more widely, to include occasional journals, memoirs, and autobiograph-ical writings, a great many more lives and fragments of lives swim into view; and if we include well-informed biographies, the number jumps again. I have drawn on over forty diaries, biographies, autobiographies, and fragments to gain some kind of insight into the daily life and the lived experience of British Protestantism before 1640—in addition to the shorter fragments or narratives included in texts such as John Foxe's *Actes and Monuments* (the famous *Book of Martyrs*) or Samuel Clarke's collections of Protestant hagiography.

I have also consulted a fairly wide sample of 'commonplace books', an umbrella term for the wildly miscellaneous notebooks which were widely used to record anything which mattered to their authors: pious concerns jostle with recipes, financial matters, jokes, and all the other written detritus a life leaves behind it. That chaotic mixture is itself important testimony to the lived experience of early Protestants, whose religious concerns were woven into the everyday; but common-place books are in fact *so* miscellaneous that they provide only limited glimpses of religious life. Still, I have used them where I can.

The problems of using such material are obvious. Any sample is necessarily entirely unrepresentative.[22] More than four-fifths of my diaries or biographies are of men; fully half of them are of ministers and clerics—including all but one of the Scots.[23] Inevitably, the sources are skewed to the wealthier and more educated strata of society. Most of them tell us about the lives of pious gentry, and none of them venture lower than the craftsman, the mariner, or the jobbing lawyer. Perhaps the most important spiritual experiences of all—those of children, which shape everything that follows—are glimpsed only rarely, and then exclusively through adult eyes. Of course, the pictures which are painted even of those limited worlds are subjective at best, and at times simply dishonest. No matter. We have to work with what we have, and this book argues that what we have presents a unified and compelling picture.

*

How attractive that picture is, is another matter. Explaining recently to a friend that I was writing about Protestant piety, he asked, 'So, are you for it or against it?' Put on the spot, I wriggled and admitted, probably for it. I did not then have a chance to say any more, but here I should.

---

[21] The most famous example is *The Diary of Lady Margaret Hoby, 1599–1605*, ed. Dorothy M. Meads (1930).

[22] Elaine McKay, 'English Diarists: Gender, Geography and Occupation, 1500–1700', *History* 90/298 (2005), 191–212. Andrew Cambers is optimistic that the diaries we have are 'broadly typical' of godly culture: Cambers, *Godly reading*, 41.

[23] The exception is Archibald Johnston of Wariston.

It is now commonplace for Reformation historians to declare their own religious positions, if any. Since I have a track record of slapping religious labels onto colleagues with sometimes inappropriate gusto,[24] I should own up to where I stand. I am a believing Christian, a lay preacher in the Church of England, and within that tradition, a liberal Protestant. As such I feel both identity with and distance from my co-religionists four centuries ago; that is, I recognize that we share a common tradition, but I am well aware how profoundly alien their religion is to me, as mine would be to them.

This book was not written to defend early modern Protestantism. Rather, I am conscious of two modern views of it, and I want to quarrel with both of them. The less common but more passionately held of these views is found amongst certain evangelical Protestants, for whom the 'Puritans' remain a beacon.[25] If this is you, then I hope you will find the account I have given of early modern Protestant piety persuasive and sympathetic, but I also want to point up the tensions, shortcomings, and sometimes frankly pathological peculiarities of this form of Christianity.

But the opposite view is much more widely held nowadays: that 'Puritanism' was *entirely* pathological. When the word was coined, 'puritan' was used to mean a dour, hypocritical killjoy, and although some puritans adopted the word as a badge of pride, its negative meanings have always predominated—best summed up in H. L. Mencken's quip that puritanism is 'the haunting fear that someone, some-where, may be happy'. The stereotype is enduring, and although not many of those scholars who have actually examined puritanism would be so crude, there remains a considerable disdain for the movement. Examining the actual experience of this kind of religion, however, reveals something much richer, more intense, more coherent, and more satisfying than the stereotype allows.

In short, I am not trying to convert you, my reader, to early modern Protestant-ism. My hope is to show you why so many people did once turn to and persist in this kind of religious life; to show the experience of Protestantism from within. The only way to do this—and here is another part of my methodology—is to adopt a certain sympathy with our subjects, in the literal sense of fellow-feeling. This is why I deliberately refer, throughout, to what my texts think *you* or *we* should believe or do, rather than the easy, distancing impassivity of pronouns like *one* or *they*. It is only if we allow ourselves to feel what they felt that we can understand who they were and what they did. If all we bring to our conversation with these long-dead Protestants is our criticism of them, they will not reply. If we can restrain ourselves enough to hear them tell us what it was like to live their lives, what they gained, and what they suffered through doing so, we may learn something.

That may already seem like a pipe-dream, but there is a further complication. The people into whose lives we are trying to step had some very decided beliefs about reality. They believed that God was both transcendent and immanent, and

---

[24] Alec Ryrie, 'Britain and Ireland' in Alec Ryrie (ed.), *Palgrave Advances in the European Reformations* (Basingstoke, 2006), 124–46.

[25] For example, J. I. Packer, *A Quest for Godliness: the Puritan Vision of the Christian Life* (Wheaton, IL, 1990).

that *everything* in life, from the mundane to the miraculous, was determined by his providence. So, naturally enough, they used those beliefs to describe the world and their lives. They might—or might not—be cautious about presuming to know God's purposes, but to avoid making any reference to those purposes would be like trying to understand a farm while never mentioning the farmer.

Modern academic history, wearing its 19th-century scientific garb, plays by different rules. Historians are trained to tell our stories without any reference to supernatural agency. There are of course excellent reasons for this, from the principled—we need verifiable evidence—to the practical—if historians began to appeal to supernatural agency, then none of us would ever again agree about anything. But we pay for these advantages in condescension: the too-easy assumption that the living are right and the dead are wrong. The classic modernist approach is openly functionalist about this. So, for example, Keith Thomas argues that prayer was powerful because it helped people to concentrate, to reflect, and to screw up their courage.[26] That is certainly true, but to dismiss the possibility that it might also be powerful in other ways is only a step away from the kind of anthropology which treats religious belief as akin to obsessive-compulsive disorder.[27]

Nowadays, this kind of secularist bluntness has largely been replaced by a softer form of condescension, in which the historian routinely accepts claims to supernatural agency in the past, on the grounds that the beliefs of the people we are studying need to be taken seriously.[28] Unfortunately, as a methodological stance, believing everything is not much better than believing nothing. It rules out historians' fundamental question—'what *really* happened?'—as naïve and unanswerable, so condemning us to studying a hall of mirrors (discourse) instead. Nor does it change the powerful undertow of secular assumptions. Leigh Eric Schmidt, a historian who has wrestled with this problem at length, discerns 'narratives of suspicion' underpinning the history of religion, narratives which have an 'explanatory predeliction to take away the voices of things, to deanimate the universe through an explication of the cultural strategies by which the "sacred" is produced'.[29] And so in a careless moment we can find, for example, a first-rank historian of the Reformation explaining a dramatic healing miracle as a purely psychological event.[30]

It is easier to state this problem than to solve it. Exposing this kind of question-begging and its narratives of suspicion is a part of the battle. So is extending our historical subjects the courtesy of scepticism, by taking their attempts to describe reality seriously. For the purposes of this book, that means recognizing that when early modern Protestants prayed, they were not necessarily talking into a void. Nor,

[26] Keith Thomas, *Religion and the Decline of Magic* (1971), 175.

[27] An argument advanced in Melford E. Spiro, 'Religion: Problems of Definition and Explanation' in Michael Banton (ed.), *Anthropological Approaches to the Study of Religion* (1966), 97.

[28] An approach devastatingly analysed in Steven Justice, 'Did the Middle Ages Believe in their Miracles?', *Representations* 103 (2008), 1–29.

[29] Leigh Eric Schmidt, *Hearing Things: Religion, Illusion and the American Enlightenment* (Cambridge, MA, 2000), 33. See also the useful discussion of this problem in Philip Sheldrake, *Spirituality and History* (1991), 17–21.

[30] Ulinka Rublack, *Reformation Europe* (Cambridge, 2005), 150.

when they felt their prayers had been answered, were they necessarily deceiving themselves. This kind of approach requires all modern historians to suspend our beliefs, regardless of what those beliefs might be. That task can involve some heavy lifting, but it has its compensations, not least that the exercise itself is invigorating. It has the potential to put us on a level with men and women whose minds were as lively and subtle as ours. It can also help us to glimpse the extraordinary religious experiences which some of them claimed. It was not uncommon in the early modern period—it is not uncommon now, although we are more coy about it— for a spiritual experience of a moment's duration to alter someone's life permanently, and to linger in the memory as an enduring source of consolation or of unease.

At the heart of the Protestant experience was this 'sense of contact with something other'.[31] They spoke of engaging with—or wrestling with, in one of their favourite metaphors—a presence quite distinct from themselves, which could surprise, disturb, unnerve, frighten, comfort, or exalt. It is of course entirely appropriate for the historian to ask how those experiences were culturally constructed—as they plainly were. But if we do not at least permit the possibility that those experiences were authentic, we run the risk of belittling the experiences themselves, and of allowing the modern world's stunted spirituality to be the yardstick by which we measure the past.

One theme of this book is how similar reading is to prayer: two forms of contact with someone beyond yourself who is simultaneously present and absent. If, when we read what our early modern forebears wrote, we wish to attain a 'sense of contact' with them, we must take their sense of contact with God seriously. To evade it does violence not only to our sources, but to the men and women whose lives we are presuming to study. The words which a very, very few of them left behind are almost all that remains of them in this world. When we read them, we hold their lives in our hands, lives as real as our own. We do not always feel that responsibility heavily enough. It is in part a responsibility to be rigorous, sceptical, and perhaps even unforgiving. But before that, it is a responsibility to stand before the dust, knowing that we are dust ourselves, and to hear what it once had to say.

---

[31] Owen C. Watkins, *The Puritan Experience* (1972), 209.

PART I

THE PROTESTANT EMOTIONS

1

Cultivating the Affections

'A new heart also wil I giue you, and a new spirit wil I put within you, and I wil take away the stonie heart out of your bodye, & I wil giue you an heart of flesh.' *Ezekiel 36:26*

DISCIPLINE AND NOURISH

Here is one reading of early modern European culture. The vibrant, carnivalesque life of the later Middle Ages was assaulted, in the 16th century, by forces of order and sobriety. A 'reformation of manners' imposed austere ideals of civilized behaviour. Flamboyance gave way to restraint. It was the 'triumph of Lent' over the spirit of Carnival.[1] And Calvinism's black-clad, unsmiling shock troops were in the vanguard.

This is all true enough. And it is also true that in the modern world, Calvinists have a formidable reputation as dour, dust-dry, and emotionless. American Presbyterians cannot shake off the jibe that they are the 'frozen chosen': who needs emotion when you already know you are saved? And Scottish Calvinism's public image is made plain by the success of the *Wee Book of Calvin*,[2] in which 'Calvinism' stands for an all-embracing repression whose only emotions are gloom and a certain lugubrious malice.

Whether this is fair to modern Calvinists, I cannot say, but it was not at all true of their early modern forebears. Certainly they observed and disciplined their emotions with unusual rigour. The emotional torrent was channelled more carefully than had been the case for most medieval Christians. But channelling only makes a current swifter and deeper. Nor did early modern Protestants discipline their emotions because they wished to suppress them. Rather, they believed that the emotions—or 'affections', 'feelings' or 'passions', to use their preferred terms[3]— could be guides on the road to godliness, supports when that road became hard, and invaluable testimonies that the destination was within reach. Protestants disciplined their emotions because they knew they mattered.

[1] This is a summary, or caricature, of the argument advanced in Peter Burke, *Popular Culture in Early Modern Europe* (1978).

[2] Bill Duncan, *The Wee Book of Calvin* (2004).

[3] Gail Kern Paster et al. (eds), *Reading the Early Modern Passions: Essays in the Cultural History of Emotion* (Philadelphia, PA, 2004), 2.

Medieval Christians had done much the same; indeed, most of the emotional territory which we will survey in this chapter had been well-trodden by pious Catholic Christians for centuries.[4] The antithesis of early Protestant feeling was not medievalism, but the ancient world's suspicion or contempt for the emotions. The Greek view of the emotions as sub-intellectual had hardened by the opening of the Christian era into Stoicism, which aspired to rise above emotion altogether, and which helped to form Christian ethics. Renaissance scholars, Catholic and Protestant alike, enthusiastically revived Stoic philosophy: John Calvin's first scholarly work was on Seneca. But Renaissance Stoicism was never uncritical. While secular philosophy embraced the Stoics, Christian humanism was more likely to celebrate than to stifle the passions. Erasmus derided Stoic views on the passions as monstrous, and later Protestants—Calvin included—were outspoken in their agreement. The ideal Stoic cultivated indifference in the face of pain or loss. But for Calvin, and many others, Jesus Christ's anguish in his Passion proved not only that such feelings were legitimate, but also that suffering in Christ's service was of positive value for Christians. It taught reliance on God and compassion for others. Emotion was not a hindrance: it was a tool.[5]

This was the consensus of post-Reformation Protestants in England and Scotland. They regularly went out of their way to distance themselves from Stoicism, a Stoicism which indeed seems scarcely to have existed in their own time.[6] A few voices can be found whose praise of emotional self-discipline seems incautious. A 1629 biography of Bishop Arthur Lake praised his 'strange serenitie of minde' and his indifference to good or ill fortune. George Webbe's best-selling devotional work, *The practice of quietness,* encouraged an adamantine stillness in its readers. But even Webbe denied that he was a Stoic, albeit more because mastery over the emotions was unattainable than because it was undesirable. Others joined him in denouncing Stoic indifference as impossible. Even attempting it was dangerous, since the inevitable failure might drive Christians into despair. But generally, this denial betrayed a far more positive view of the emotions. Joseph Hall, characteristically, has the pithy adage: 'I would not bee a Stoick to haue no Passions . . . but a Christian, to order those I haue'.[7]

This went beyond the medieval, scholastic view of the emotions as appetites to be bridled, and beyond even the Aristotelian view of them as passions to be brought

[4] Susan C. Karant-Nunn, *The Reformation of Feeling: Shaping the Religious Emotions in Early Modern Germany* (Oxford, 2010), 11.

[5] Richard Strier, 'Against the Rule of Reason' in Paster et al. (eds), *Reading the Early Modern Passions,* 23–8; Karant-Nunn, *Reformation of Feeling,* 7–8; David Keck, 'Sorrow and Worship in Calvin's Geneva' in Marc R. Forster and Benjamin J. Kaplan (eds), *Piety and Family in Early Modern Europe* (Aldershot, 2005), 206–8.

[6] Ethan Shagan, *The Rule of Moderation* (Cambridge, 2011), 37.

[7] Arthur Lake, *Sermons with some religious and diuine meditations* (1629: RSTC 15134), sig. ¶5v; George Webbe, *The practise of qui[e]tnes: directing a Christian how to liue quietly in this troblesome world* (1618: RSTC 25166.3), 28–30; Gabriel Powel, *The Resolued Christian, exhorting to Resolution* (1600: RSTC 20150), 269–72; Joseph Hall, *Meditations and Vowes, Diuine and Morall* (1605: RSTC 12679.5), I. 98–9.

into harmony with the higher faculties.[8] Certainly the affections had to be disciplined, but they ought not be restrained: rather, the point was to direct and to heighten them. Preachers berated their audiences for insufficient feeling. During the plague of 1625, Arthur Hildersam tried to awaken his hearers to the horrors around them: 'None of us (I feare) are sufficiently affected'.[9] A few months earlier, the Scottish minister Gilbert Primrose had laid out a comprehensive Protestant theory of the affections from the pulpit. Christians, Primrose argued, are the gardeners of their passions: they must weed ruthlessly, but also cultivate and nurture. He denounced not only Stoicism, but also the Aristotelian view that moderate emotions were superior to excesses. 'In things which are truly good, no excesse is vicious.' The Holy Spirit, he argued, 'sanctifieth in us our naturall affections, but abolishes them not. . . . God gives them full libertie, when they come from a good cause, and aspire unto a good end.' He cited that most un-Stoic of proof texts, King David's self-abandoned joy as he danced before the Ark of the Covenant.[10]

Primrose's sermon was never reprinted, but another book on the same theme enjoyed much greater success. *A Treatise of the Affections*, by the notoriously histrionic Essex preacher William Fenner, agreed with Primrose's view. 'If the . . . Affections be fixed on their proper object, there is no danger in the excesse; God cannot be loved, or feared, &c., overmuch.' But Fenner's attack on Aristotelian orthodoxy focused on a different point. He denied that the affections belonged to the lower, animal nature, on the grounds that purely spiritual events such as shame or disgrace nevertheless stir the passions. For Fenner, therefore, emotion was an elemental spiritual force, as irresistible as hunger or gravity. It was folly to ignore it, and prudence to harness it. 'When a childe of God prayes with affection, he prayeth with force.'[11] A few years earlier, Thomas Goodwin's best-seller, *The Vanity of Thoughts Discovered,* had similarly argued that Christians should labour to inflame their passion for God: for 'such as your affections are, such necessarily must your thoughts be'. Devotion, Daniel Featley had argued a little earlier still, 'consisteth rather in the feruour of the affections, then light of the thoughts. . . . It is better felt then understood'.[12]

Far from being suspicious of the emotions, Reformed Protestants exalted them. They were too valuable and powerful to be neglected. Admittedly, in order to use that power correctly, they needed careful control, but in practice this usually meant

---

[8] Jerome Kagan, *What is Emotion? History, Measures and Meanings* (New Haven and London, 2007), 10–12. For an influential attempt to update the Aristotelian view, see Edward Reynolds, *A Treatise of the Passions and Faculties of the Soule of Man* (1640: RSTC 20938), esp. 31–41.

[9] Samuel Torshell, *The Saints Humiliation* (1633: RSTC 24142), 12; Arthur Hildersam, *The Doctrine of Fasting and Praier, and Humiliation for Sinne* (1633: RSTC 13459), 2–3, 8–10.

[10] Gilbert Primrose, *The Christian Mans Teares, And Christs Comforts* (1625: RSTC 20389), 68–9, 77–82; II Samuel 6:16–22.

[11] William Fenner, *A Treatise of the Affections; Or, The Soules Pulse* (1642: Wing F707), sig. A2v, pp. 4–5, 7 (four editions, 1641–57).

[12] Thomas Goodwin, *The Vanity of Thoughts Discovered* (1643: Wing G1264), 45 (five editions, 1637–50); Daniel Featley, *Ancilla Pietatis: Or, the Hand-Maid to Priuate Devotion* (1626: RSTC 10726), 2.

nurturing and directing them, not suppressing them. They were more alarmed by too little emotion than by too much.

Part I of this book will survey early modern Protestants' emotional landscape: the feelings to which they aspired, those which they feared, how they navigated between the two, and the emotions which they actually encountered along the way. In doing so, it picks up some of the ambitions of the late 20th-century vogue for a 'psycho-history' of religion, but I am not attempting to be psychological, still less psychoanalytical.[13] I am somewhat more informed by the early 21st-century enthusiasm for the study of the emotions in general, and of religious emotion in particular.[14] But my primary concern is less to construct a theoretical model of the Protestant emotions than to listen, and to try to discern 'what it felt like to be an early Protestant'.[15]

HEARTS OF STONE

The bane of the earnest Protestant's spiritual life was a condition variously described as dullness, hardness, heaviness, dryness, coldness, drowsiness, or deadness. This insidious malaise could creep into your heart unnoticed; its symptom was numbness, not pain. Alert Protestants learned to keep a careful watch for it, not least because—by common consent—the problem grew more acute, not less, as you matured in your faith. The never-ending battle against this listless, chilling enemy is our way into the Protestant spiritual experience.

The images chosen to describe it were significant. *Drowsiness* picked up on a host of problematic associations between sleep and spiritual malaise.[16] *Hardness* referred in general to the Biblical concept of hardness of heart, and more particularly to God's promise to the prophet Ezekiel that he would give his people hearts of flesh instead of hearts of stone.[17] The sense of being stony-hearted, blankly indifferent to God, was one which many Protestants shared, and which—in very un-Stoic fashion—they deplored in themselves. Stoniness is also implicit in talk of *dryness* and *coldness*, but these were precise images, drawn from the humours which, in the classical understanding, constituted the human body and the whole created order. Dryness and coldness were the humours of earth, heavy and lumpish. 'Why do I languish thus, drooping and dull,/As if I were all earth?' asked George Herbert, in a poem

---

[13] David Leverenz, *The Language of Puritan Feeling: An Exploration in Literature, Psychology and Social History* (New Brunswick, NJ, 1980); Charles Lloyd Cohen, *God's Caress: the psychology of Puritan religious experience* (New York, 1986).

[14] Notably Karant-Nunn, *Reformation of Feeling*; Kagan, *What is Emotion?*; Paster et al. (eds), *Reading the Early Modern Passions*; Douglas Davies, *Emotion, Identity and Religion: Hope, Reciprocity and Otherness* (Oxford, 2011).

[15] C. S. Lewis, *English Literature in the Sixteenth Century Excluding Drama* (1973), 32, cited in John Stachniewski, *The Persecutory Imagination: English Puritanism and the Literature of Religious Despair* (Oxford, 1991), 1.

[16] Alec Ryrie, 'Sleeping, waking and dreaming in Protestant piety' in Jessica Martin and Alec Ryrie (eds), *Private and Domestic Devotion in Early Modern Britain* (Farnham, 2012), 73–5.

[17] Ezekiel 11:19, 36:26.

titled *Dulnesse*.[18] They were also the humours of melancholy, the most ill-favoured of the dispositions. In Aristotelian terms, dryness was linked to tastelessness; it naturally implied barrenness. The dry heart was a dusty, stony field where nothing could grow, in which the soul's generative power had shrivelled away.

And a *cold* dryness is especially dangerous, since the sufferer is not consciously parched. The sun-baked ground's longing for rain, the deer's panting for the water, are the more hopeful spiritual states of those who know the depth of their need.[19] Dullness was characterized not by raging waters or firestorms, but by tedium. Its keynote was lassitude, and a deceptive, lulling peace, a spiritual hypothermia whose deadly progress could not be felt. Indeed, to suffer from this desiccating iciness was already to be spiritually dead, like the stone statues which Protestants despised as idols.

As the struggling cleric Samuel Rogers wrote in his diary on 28 November 1634: 'Nothing, nothing, nothing; No hearte, No prayer, Noe life, No grace, No fruitfulnesse one way as other, can be discerned'.[20] A powerful sense of *nothingness* lay beneath all these images. The Reformation era's favourite Church father, Augustine, had defined evil as nothingness, the antithesis of God. This sense of dullness, in other words, was one of the most terrible things a Christian could experience. It suggested that you were entirely cut off from God. When a little tedium began to tug on you, it was not something to be dismissed lightly; the mouth of Hell was yawning.

But the condition was ubiquitous. The struggle with it fills Rogers' diary: 'I cannot find the savor of prayer . . . oh Lord if ever then now behold dead bones; and breathe.'[21] The surviving portion of Margaret Hoby's diary begins mid-sentence, and that first, broken sentence laments her 'deadnes in praier, and . . . want of sorow for the same'. It was a theme to which she and many others would often return. John Winthrop saw his struggle with 'dead heartedness' as almost continuous.[22] Richard Baxter recalled how, in his youth,

> I wondred at the sensless hardness of my heart, that could think and talk of Sin and Hell, and Christ and Grace, of God and Heaven, with no more feeling: I cried out from day to day to God for Grace against this sensless Deadness.[23]

The peculiar horror of this condition was its pervasiveness. Every part of the Christian life might be frozen into a pallid shadow of itself. Nehemiah Wallington, who recorded his struggles with it at length, lamented how dullness had turned his

---

[18] George Herbert, *Works*, ed. F. E. Hutchinson (Oxford, 1941), 115.

[19] William Perkins, *An exposition of the Lords prayer* (1593: RSTC 19700.5), 10; 'Augustine' [ps.], *Certaine select prayers gathered out of S. Augustines meditations* (1574: RSTC 924), sigs L6v–7r; Psalm 42:1.

[20] Samuel Rogers, *The Diary of Samuel Rogers, 1634–1638*, ed. Tom Webster and Kenneth Shipps (Church of England Record Society 11: 2004), 6.

[21] Rogers, *Diary*, 26.

[22] Hoby, *Diary*, 62; John Winthrop, *Winthrop Papers, vol. I: 1498–1628* (Boston, MA, 1929), 160.

[23] Richard Baxter, *Reliquiae Baxterianae, or, Mr. Richard Baxters narrative of the most memorable passages of his life and times*, vol. I (1696: Wing B1370), 5.

prayer, his sermon-attendance, and his participation in the sacraments into sins.[24] And it was fatally easy to fall into it. As William Gouge put it, as surely as weight is drawn to the earth, so the Christian's natural tendency is to ever greater coldness, formality and faintness. 'Wherefore as fire must constantly be put vnder water to keepe it hot . . . so must wee by constant praier quicken vp our soules.'[25]

Hence one recurring theme of early modern piety: devotees who bewail their own coldness and deadness.[26] John Hayward's best-selling *Sanctvarie of a troubled soule* catches the mood:

> Woe is me wretch, what an Icie; what an yron heart haue I, that it dooth not poure forth it selfe in teares? How sleepie is my vnclean soule, that my spirites are not troubled? . . . But wherefore doe I expostulate with a dead carcase?[27]

The same sentiment can be found across the Christian spectrum, from tub-thumping puritans, through stout conformists, to Roman Catholics. It was a universal problem. Even 'the best Christians', William Perkins warned, were beset by 'their doubting and distrust, their dulnesse and deadnesse of heart'.[28] John Norden's hugely successful prayer book *A pensiue mans practise* opens with a prayer for spiritual assistance 'when we be dull'. Norden has his devotee ask 'that being of my selfe dull, I may be thereby made zealous, and whereas I am of my selfe cold, I may be thereby made feruent and faithfull'. The next prayer asks to be purged of 'all naturall dulnesse'.[29] Norden evidently felt that these were primary difficulties; his book's success may indicate that his readers agreed. Similar prayers were a fixture of most devotional works of the period. One book would have had its readers ask forgiveness for their cold prayers and deadness every Sunday; another had families confess their hearts to be 'dull and vntoward' twice daily. The most successful devotional handbook of all, Lewis Bayly's *The Practise of pietie*, had its users lament their 'dulnes of sense, and hardnes of heart' every night.[30]

[24] FSL MS V.a.436 p. 113.

[25] Edward Dering, *Godly priuate praiers, for houshoulders to meditate vppon, and to say in their famylies* (1581: RSTC 6689.2), sig. I7v; William Gouge, ΠΑΝΟΠΛΙΑ ΤΟΥ ΘΕΟΥ. *The Whole-Armor of God* (1616: RSTC 12122), 446.

[26] See, for example, Dering, *Godly priuate praiers*, sig. I1r; Thomas Bentley (ed.), *The Monument of Matrones* (1582: RSTC 1892), 440–1; William Cowper, *The triumph of a Christian* (1618: RSTC 5939), 91.

[27] John Hayward, *The sanctuarie of a troubled soule* (1602: RSTC 13003.7), 135–6.

[28] William Perkins, *A godly and learned exposition of Christs Sermon in the Mount* (Cambridge, 1608: RSTC 19722), 238.

[29] John Norden, *A pensiue mans practise, verie profitable for all persons* (1598: RSTC 18617.7), 5–9 (forty-two editions, 1584–1640).

[30] Henry Valentine, *Private Devotions, Digested into Six Letanies* (1635: RSTC 24576.3), 147–8 (eleven editions 1631–40); Michael Sparke?, *Crumms of comfort, the valley of teares, and the hill of ioy* (1627: RSTC 23015.7), sigs G5v–6r, H3r (at least twenty editions, 1623–35); Lewis Bayly, *The Practise of pietie. Directing a Christian how to walke that he may please God* (1620: RSTC 1604), 321 (over fifty editions 1612–40, with particularly frequent reprints in the 1630s); cf. 'A. F.' [Anthony Fawkener?], *A Collection of certaine Promises out of the Word of GOD* (1629: RSTC 10634.7), 13, 40–2 (six editions 1629–40).

Why should this experience be so universal? Mere human nature, which was 'dull and without all lust to pray', was at the root of it.[31] 'The nature of the earth is colde and drie', explained the ceremonialist Christopher Sutton, and 'so are earthly affections to deuotion and pietie'.[32] Sin naturally exacerbated the problem. It was Richard Rogers' experience that when he let his mind dwell over-long on worldly matters, his prayer 'began to waxe colde'; Arthur Dent described how the guilt-wracked sinner 'feeleth Lead within hym, and is all heauie'.[33] This could quickly become a downward spiral. Samuel Rogers, omitting his prayers one morning, found himself 'drooping pitifully' for the rest of the day, and observed gloomily: 'mee thinks the ice is growne thicke because it was not broken'.[34] But we should be wary of limiting ourselves to mundane explanations. For Margaret Hoby, 'Cold praier' was a judgement from God for her sins, and Nehemiah Wallington reckoned that 'when dulnes begins to come' it was because 'the Diuel so labours to lule me a sleepe'.[35] These were spiritual matters, not psychological ones.

However, if dryness and dullness were in some sense universal conditions, there was one particular spiritual blight which could fossilize them, and render a stony heart altogether impervious to God. This was *security*, a word whose resonances were thoroughly negative in our period. It was the corrupt doppelgänger of a quality which early Protestants treasured, namely *assurance*. Assurance—of which more later—is the well-grounded conviction that you are amongst the elect, and through grace, a child of God. Security is an ill-grounded conviction of the same thing. It is a presumptuous, blasé, and too-easy spiritual self-confidence—as we might say, a false sense of security. When Richard Rogers decried 'the extreeme securitie wherein we liue', this is what he meant.[36]

Security and assurance might seem hard to distinguish, but—in theory at least—they could be recognized by their fruits. 'Security', Richard Capel warned, 'will rust us, undoe us, and eate out all that good is out of us'.[37] Assurance produced earnest godliness; security produced dryness and enervating spiritual lethargy. When ministers thundered against security—and they did—they often described it as sleep: a 'pleasant, but deadly slumber which possesseth thousands in this land'.[38] Michel Sparke's *Crumms of comfort* included a prayer repenting admitting that 'I rocke my selfe in the Cradle of security'. The conceit of Thomas Tymme's

---

[31] Henry Bull, *Christian praiers and holy meditations* (1570: RSTC 4029), 8.
[32] Christopher Sutton, *Disce mori. Learne to die* (1601: RSTC 23475), 46.
[33] Arthur Dent, *A Sermon of Repentance* (1582: RSTC 6649.5), sig. B6r; M. M. Knappen (ed.), *Two Elizabethan Puritan Diaries by Richard Rogers and Samuel Ward* (Chicago, 1933), 67; cf. Winthrop, *Papers*, 166–7.
[34] Rogers, *Diary*, 68.
[35] Hoby, *Diary*, 137; FSL MS V.a.436 pp. 16–17.
[36] In Johann Habermann, *The enimie of securitie or A daily exercise of godlie meditations*, trans. Thomas Rogers (1583: RSTC 12582.6), sig. b7v.
[37] Richard Capel, *Tentations: their nature, danger, cure* (1633: RSTC 4595), 81.
[38] William Pinke, *The Tryall of a Christians syncere loue vnto Christ* (1631: RSTC 19942), II.4 (six editions, 1630–59); cf. Richard Rogers, *Seven treatises, containing such direction as is gathered out of the Holie Scriptures, leading and guiding to true happines* (1603: RSTC 21215), 121; Thomas Playfere, *The power of praier* (Cambridge, 1603: RSTC 20025), 29; John Gee, *Steps of Ascension vnto God, or, A Ladder to Heaven* (1625: RSTC 11706.4), 15.

best-selling *A siluer watch-bell* was that the book was, indeed, a watch-bell to waken sleepers from their security.[39] This was a sleep close to the sleep of death. Bayly's *Practise of pietie* warned that although despair was a sin:

> Despaire is nothing so dangerous as presumption. For wee reade not in all the Scriptures of aboue three or foure, whom roring Despaire ouerthrew: But secure Presumption hath sent millions to perdition without any noyse.[40]

Security was a silent killer, which said 'peace' when there was no peace, and took souls as they slept.

However, diagnosing spiritual dullness or 'security' was easier than treating it. Some ministers made specific suggestions, such as seeking spiritual counsel, adopting new regimes of reading or fasting, or simply turning up to more sermons.[41] But in the end, this struggle, like so many Protestant struggles, was conducted by sheer effort: effort and redoubled effort. If dullness manifested itself in a disinclination to prayer or holy duties, naturally one remedy was simply to buckle down to such duties. John Preston's best-selling sermons on prayer argued that 'a man by setting himselfe vpon the worke, shall gather a fitnesse, though he were vnfit at the first'. He compared dull Christians to labourers numbed with cold: rather than waiting until they are warm to begin work, it is only through work that they can warm up.[42] Wallington's prescription for himself in these straits—'there must be violence in prayer and violence in hearing'—vividly captures this sense of vigorous perseverence. Hayward blamed any initial 'dulnes or resistance' to religious exercises on Satanic opposition—a bracing enough idea in itself—and promised that perseverance would, through grace, render such duties 'easie and pleasant'. Others were less sunny, and perhaps more realistic. Nicholas Byfield's best-selling *Marrow of the Oracles of God* urged those afflicted by dryness to persist in prayer 'without limitation', whether or not they were granted feeling in response.[43]

Yet the attempt to squeeze feeling out of the heart by main force was both theologically dubious, and, sometimes, ineffective. Perkins wrote that the Christian who is 'hard hearted, and of a dead spirit, so as he cannot humble himselfe as he would', must simply 'be content with that grace' he has been given, and seek the virtue of humility. Elnathan Parr's popular guide to private prayer agreed that prolonging your prayers when spiritually dull was pointless. Bayly was characteristically practical:

---

[39] Sparke, *Crumms of comfort*, sig. F7v; Thomas Tymme, *A siluer watch-bell* (1605: RSTC 24421), esp. sigs *2v–3r, p. 227 (at least twenty editions, 1605–40). Sparke was the publisher of the anonymous *Crumms of comfort*, and seems likely to have been its author, or at least lead editor: I have adopted the convention of treating its words as his. *ODNB*.

[40] Bayly, *Practise of pietie*, 208.

[41] Robert Harris, *Peters enlargement upon the praryers [sic] of the Church ... The fift edition* (1627: RSTC 12842), 35; cf. Jeremiah Dyke, *A worthy communicant. Or A treatise, shewing the due order of receiving the sacrament of the Lords Supper* (1636: RSTC 7429), 492; Isham, 'Confessions', fo. 28r-v; Robert Linaker, *A comfortable treatise, for the reliefe of such as are afflicted in conscience* (1620: RSTC 15641), sigs A5r–6r.

[42] John Preston, *The Saints Daily Exercise. A Treatise concerning the whole dutie of prayer* (1629: RSTC 20251), 74–6 (nine editions 1629–35).

[43] FSL MS V.a.436 p. 111; Hayward, *Sanctuarie of a troubled soule* (1602), sigs ¶12–∴.1v; Nicholas Byfield, *The Marrow of the Oracles of God* (1619: RSTC 4219.5), 40–2 (eleven editions 1619–40).

if 'thy spirits are dull, and thy minde not apt for Prayer, and holy deuotion: striue not too much for that time', but simply redouble your zeal next time. He even provided a shortened morning prayer—less than half the length of his 'normal' text—to be used under such circumstances.[44]

Indeed, when we move from prescriptive to descriptive evidence, we find more daunted exhaustion than cheerful perseverance in the face of such spiritual drought. The Scottish devotional writer William Narne compared trying to soften a hard heart to wringing water from a stone; that is, possible, but only for God. Richard Kilby composed a prayer against stony-heartedness whose keynote is despair, and his conviction that his hypocrisy runs so deep that it is ineradicable: 'nothing can turne it'.[45] Wallington's struggle with dullness was almost daily, lamenting—to choose one example of many—on a fast day that he was 'dead and dull all the day long . . . and yet I had no power to raise up or help myselfe in this sadd condistion'.[46] Wallington would have reviled the Arminian grandee Lettice Cary, but she shared his experience. She complained that her chaplain had instructed her to be as constant and as full in her prayers 'in this my *driness*, and barrenness, as ever I was heretofore amidst my greatest *comforts*, and consolations'. Easy for him to say, but she found instead that 'the more I struggle with my disease, the more it encreaseth upon me'.[47] For all the good advice ministers could offer, the only definitive answer to such sufferers was that they must wait for God's grace.

When it came, the experience of that grace was overwhelming. When Wallington's miserable fast day was over, he suddenly broke down over his supper, and 'at that instant I did see free grace and the unconceivable love of my God in Christ in presarveing mee'.[48] The Scottish minister Robert Blair recalled a day in 1626 when he was 'exceeding dead and dull'. He began to go through the motions of praying, but once he had started he found that 'I could not end, my heart (honoured be thy Majesty!) melted so wonderfully. . . . Oh more than wonderful!'[49] With *melting*, we are suddenly in a different symbolic world. Abraham Fleming's best-selling devotional miscellany included a prayer that 'our drie and stonie harts, by the sweete dewes and showres of thy heauenlie grace, dropping downe and soking therinto, may be . . . moistened and softened', a prayer which was copied with only the lightest paraphrasing by Thomas Vicars a lifetime later to describe the experience of receiving word and sacrament.[50]

[44] William Perkins, *The first part of The cases of conscience* (Cambridge, 1604: RSTC 19668), 53; Elnathan Parr, *Abba Father: Or, a plaine and short direction concerning Priuate Prayer* (1618: RSTC 19312), 45–6 (at least five editions 1618–36); Bayly, *Practise of pietie*, 268–9, 269–74.

[45] William Narne, *The Pearle of Prayer, Most Pretious, and Powerfull* (Edinburgh, 1630: RSTC 18360), 347; Kilby, *Hallelujah*, 91–2.

[46] Nehemiah Wallington, *The Notebooks of Nehemiah Wallington, 1618–1654: A Selection*, ed. David Booy (Aldershot, 2007), 191.

[47] Duncon, *Returnes*, 27.

[48] Wallington, *Notebooks*, 191.

[49] Robert Blair, *The Life of Mr Robert Blair, Minister of St. Andrews, containing his Autobiography from 1593 to 1636*, ed. Thomas M'Crie (Edinburgh, 1848), 118.

[50] Abraham Fleming, *The diamond of deuotion* (1581: RSTC 11041), 123; Thomas Vicars, *The Grounds of that Doctrine which is according to Godlinesse* (1630: RSTC 24700), sig. B8r–v. Cf. Fawkener, *Collection of Promises*, 40–1.

Melting, softening, dew-drops: these are not symbols of joy, at least not yet. The grace which Blair and Wallington celebrated, and for which Fleming and many others prayed, was simply the grace to feel, to have the spiritual affections roused. As we shall see, the emotional experiences which followed were sometimes not at all agreeable. The spiritual life of the earnest Protestant might include profound, drawn-out misery, or sharp bouts of piercing anguish. As we explore this sometimes unpalatable territory, we should remember early Protestants' conviction that the alternative was worse. Pain is better than numbness, and broken-heartedness better than stony-heartedness, as surely as it is better to be alive than dead.

2

Despair and Salvation

'Ye haue not receiued the Spirit of bondage to feare againe: but ye haue receiued the Spirit of adopcion, whereby we crye Abba, Father.' *Romans 8:15.*

A CULTURE OF DESPAIR?

If early modern Protestantism is connected in modern imaginations with any emotional state at all, it is despair.[1] As Protestant culture put down roots by the turn of the 17th century, it supposedly bound many believers into an anguished desolation. It is customary here to mention Nehemiah Wallington, the 17th-century London woodturner who recorded his own inner life with unparalleled intimacy. Wallington's copious manuscripts have made him a favourite of scholars of the period, myself included.[2] But perhaps the best-known fact about Wallington is that, in his youth, he attempted suicide nearly a dozen times. His traumas have become symbolic of Protestantism's self-destructive emotional life.

The connection between Reformed Protestantism and despair has theological roots, in the Calvinist doctrine of predestination which had become the orthodox consensus by the later 16th century. The logic is clear. Every human being's eternal destination—Heaven or Hell—was decided before the world began by God's unalterable decree. So your deeds, prayers, and feelings cannot affect that decree at all. If you are predestined to be saved, then you *will*—at some point in your life—repent and respond to Christ's irresistible grace. As a result, you will be regenerated. You will experience grace within yourself—to some degree; and manifest it in your outward life—to some degree. If you are predestined to Hell, you may still make a show of repentance; but it is not in response to God's call, for God has not called you—at least not 'effectually' or individually. Therefore any 'conversion' will neither endure nor produce the tell-tale effects on your life. However, for a time such false conversions may look remarkably like the real thing.

So, if you become convinced that you are saved, you may fall into self-righteousness, antinomianism, or 'security'—although, as any theologian will tell you, a sense of

---

[1] John Stachniewski's polemical *The Persecutory Imagination* not only suggests that 'the majority of those who took their religion seriously . . . were consumed by despair' but even that 'the brighter side of protestantism has attracted disproportionate attention': 2, 61.

[2] Above all, see Paul S. Seaver, *Wallington's World: a puritan artisan in seventeenth-century London* (Stanford, 1985).

salvation which produces such poisonous fruits must be false. And if you
become convinced that you are damned, you may fall into despair. You are a firebrand
of God's wrath, and there is absolutely nothing you can do about it.

Actually, as a matter of strict logic, it makes no sense in this system to conclude
with certainty that you are damned. At worst, you can conclude that you have
not *yet* received your effectual calling. What you cannot know—even on your
deathbed—is whether God intends to call you at some point in the future,[3] and
Protestant theologians, like their Catholic predecessors, argued that despair is
sinful, since it presumes to overrule God's mercy. But this only made the problem
worse, by condemning the desperate for their very despair. Those tempted to think
this way could found themselves drawn to the alarming New Testament warning
that 'it is impossible that they, which . . . fall away, shulde be renued againe by
repentance': a text which was massaged into conformity with orthodoxy by theologians, but which could nevertheless easily convince those with tender consciences
that salvation was now eternally beyond their reach.[4]

Whatever the logic, by the early 17th century, large numbers of Protestants
were certainly haunted by the fear that they *might* be irrecoverably damned, and
many were—at least sometimes—absolutely convinced that they were. Wallington's suicide attempts were not terribly unusual. Suicide may seem an irrational
response to damnation—surely Hell is best postponed, even if it cannot be
avoided—but a well-established medieval and Renaissance tradition mounted a
counter-argument. Hell's punishments, while eternal, are not uniform. Worse
sinners face sharper torments. So the longer you live in sin, the worse the condemnation you earn. A quick suicide might at least cut your losses. 'Therefore', Wallington heard the tempter say to him, 'destroy thyselfe now and thy puneshment
will not be so grate in hell.'[5]

When he was in his right mind Wallington knew that this was theological
nonsense—preventing sin with sin is a losing game. However, he was not always
in his right mind, and in this at least he was not alone. Mental illness of all kinds
was widespread in all pre-modern societies, exacerbated by malnutrition, disease,
and trauma, almost always untreated, and frequently unrecognized. This problem
almost defies historical analysis, unless we wish to play the fools' game of long-
distance psychiatric diagnosis. But we can at least recognize that mental illness in
general, and depression in particular, was a part of the early modern social
landscape. As Nicholas Byfield's much-reprinted treatise on predestination argued,
some salvation-anxiety had its roots in melancholy, 'that is terrors and griefes, of
which a man can yeelde no true reason', and as such was a matter for the physician
rather than the theologian.[6] The question, of course, is how this endemic human

[3] A point made with particular clarity in Nicholas Byfield, *The Marrow of the Oracles of God* (1622: RSTC 4220.5), 'The Spirituall Touch-stone', 226; cf. Dixon, 'Predestination and pastoral theology', 258.
[4] Hebrews 6:4–6; see, for example, Winthrop, *Papers*, 157.
[5] Wallington, *Notebooks*, 35.
[6] Nicholas Byfield, *The Signes or An Essay Concerning the assurance of Gods loue, and mans saluation* (1614: RSTC 4236), 10–11 (five editions, 1617–37).

problem interacted with Calvinism. Maybe some of those plagued by depression merely used Calvinist language to rationalize or to describe their plight. That, perhaps, was the case with Archibald Johnston of Wariston, whose despair and longing to die in 1634 seems to have been chiefly a response to a wrenching bereavement.[7] But Calvinism's iron logic could at least be an additional fetter binding the depressed, or even locking otherwise healthy people into depression. The Puritan grandee Richard Rogers worried about this problem; the Laudian poet Richard Corbett mocked the way that Puritans' salvation-obsession could slide into madness. Robert Burton, the most humane writer on melancholy in this or perhaps any period, had no doubt of the connection.[8]

However, there is a real danger of exaggerating Calvinism's tendency to foment despair, due to two particular problems. First is Max Weber's brilliant and enduringly influential interpretation of what he called 'the Protestant ethic'. Weber took an uncompromisingly bleak view of predestination's psychological consequences, blaming 'its extreme inhumanity' for 'a feeling of unprecedented inner loneliness of the single individual'. He saw the Calvinist as in a state of permanent anxiety which stood at the brink of despair, and which could only be controlled—never allayed— by an unremitting regime of self-discipline. It is a powerful insight, but also an ahistorical caricature. It was Weber, above all, who created the myth of the despairing Calvinist, and we should not necessarily believe it.[9]

Secondly, we can be misled by the sources themselves. Puritan diaries often consist chiefly of obsessive self-observation and hand-wringing over the pettiest of sins. Plenty of Puritan divines wrote at enormous length about despair and salvation-anxiety, both in general and in lengthy correspondences with particular individuals. The danger lies in taking these sources at face value. Salvation-anxiety certainly produced a great deal of paper, but that does not tell us the scale of the problem. Those who were untroubled, or positively comforted, by the doctrine of predestination did not require letters or treatises to be written to ease their consciences, and so we do not now hear their voices. As to the diaries, one of the purposes of a spiritual diary was to record sin. Keeping one does not mean you are obsessed with sin, just as keeping an account-book does not mean you are obsessed with money. As Owen Watkins puts it, 'we do not get a full picture of a man from notes of this kind any more than we can judge a garden by looking through the contents of the incinerator.' In any case, even an obsession with sin does not equate to salvation-anxiety. Those who were absolutely assured of their salvation might still—*should* still—have kept a hawk's eye on their own sins, sins which could not imperil their predestined souls but which did grievously dishonour God.[10]

---

[7] *Diary of Sir Archibald Johnston of Wariston, 1632–1639*, ed. George Morison Paul (Scottish History Society, 1911), esp. 36, 42.

[8] Rogers, *Seven treatises*, 40; Richard Corbett, *The Poems of Richard Corbet*, ed. Octavius Gilchrist (1807), 244; Stachniewski, *Persecutory Imagination*, 219–53.

[9] Max Weber, *The Protestant Ethic and the Spirit of Capitalism*, tr. Talcott Parsons (1992), 104. On Weber's thesis, see below, pp. 446–56.

[10] Watkins, *Puritan Experience*, 20; Dixon, 'Predestination and pastoral theology'.

Still, for some people at least, Calvinism could be a theology of despair, a problem which was as apparent in the early 17th century as it is now. That did not discredit it, and it is worth noting why. First—and this is almost too obvious to mention—just because a doctrine is unappealing does not make it false. Calvinism—and perhaps no ideology has ever been less prone to wishful thinking—did not argue principally that predestination was nice, but that it was true. Second, and more interestingly, the Calvinist experience of despair was a subtle one. Calvinists became connoisseurs of despair, finely judging its varieties. They knew that it could be spiritually deadly, but also that it could be a valuable, even a necessary spiritual process: a hollowing-out which might in the end render the spiritual life deeper. We do not necessarily need to believe that claim, but it deserves to be taken seriously.

There is plenty of evidence of early modern Protestants suffering despair which is pathological by any measure. Theologians warned earnestly against the danger that the despairing would attempt suicide, and not without reason.[11] In some cases, again, perhaps psychological rather than theological difficulties were uppermost. With the woman whom we know as 'D.M.', who contemplated drowning herself and her newborn daughter in the 1610s, we might suspect post-natal depression. And we do not know why one of Elizabeth Isham's kinsmen was tempted to suicide, only that it did not change her view that he was 'a right honest man'.[12] In both of these cases, the potential suicides' lives were saved, and in both cases, they saw this as an act of God's grace.

That points to a wider pattern. Attempts to tie Calvinist doctrine historically to suicide are grounded more in theory and anecdote than in any systematic evidence.[13] But Calvinists may have been predisposed both to suicide 'attempts' which were not entirely in earnest, and were certainly predisposed to noticing and attributing spiritual significance to thoughts of self-harm which never came close to being enacted. Most of Wallington's attempts fall into this category; indeed, he describes them not as suicide attempts but as temptations. Some of the incidents involved consuming foodstuffs which he believed would make him sick—wine with honey, green apples, or a pint of aniseed water—unpleasant, but hardly fatal. Others were no more than thoughts: temptations to drown himself, to throw himself from a window, or to hang himself. I do not mean to minimize these incidents. They clearly disturbed him deeply, and others were more obviously dangerous: he balanced on a high ledge threatening to jump, he held a knife to his throat, and, worst of all, he drank a lethal concoction of ratsbane and beer, which might well have killed him had he not vomited it up.[14] Yet none of this adds

---

[11] Capel, *Tentations*, 335–6; Perkins, *First part of The cases of conscience*, 92–3; Thomas Shepard, *God's Plot: The Paradoxes of Puritan Piety, Being the Autobiography and Journal of Thomas Shepard*, ed. Michael McGiffert (Amherst, MA, 1972), 43.

[12] Vavasor Powell, *Spirituall Experiences, Of sundry Beleevers* (1653: Wing P3095), 33–6; Isham, 'Confessions', fo. 29v.

[13] Stachniewski, *Persecutory Imagination*, 46–52, makes such an effort; R. A. Houston, *Punishing the Dead? Suicide, Lordship, and Community in Britain, 1500–1830* (Oxford, 2010), esp. 305–12, suggests much more caution is necessary.

[14] Wallington, *Notebooks*, 32–40.

up to serious or level-headed attempts to end his life. What it does is testify to the depth of the young Wallington's anguish.

Indeed, although the suicide attempts came to an end, his suffering did not. More than a decade later, Wallington could still write

> rest comfort and quietnesse I could find none, neither day nor night at home or abrode in on rome or other, but still groning and cryings out many times, I am wearie, I am wearie of my life.... If their be any hell upon the Earth this troubeled minde and tormented contience is it.... The conscience awakened is like a beare enraged, it teares a man in pices.[15]

Unsurprisingly, some people chose a less extreme way out of this torment. According to George Gifford, already in the 1580s his Essex parishioners were grumbling that preachers were fomenting despair, whose effect was not to induce them to self-harm, but to 'bring them out of beliefe'. Richard Baxter remembered with regret how a friend of his youth, who had a weakness for drink, fell into despair at his sins: 'at last his Conscience could have no Relief or Ease but in . . . disowning the Teachers and Doctrines which had restrained him.'[16] Apostasy was more appealing than suicide.

These are the extremes, but more important, perhaps, is how normal this kind of despair was. Elizabeth Isham's comment, offhand, that 'my mother was troubled—as many are—touching predestination or falling away from grace' suggests that it was almost a routine part of the Protestant experience. The satirists agreed: Richard Corbett's caricatured Puritan was 'in dispaire/Five times a yeare'.[17] And the flourishing genre of 'conscience literature'—books written to settle the troubled consciences of those who were tempted to despair—bears witness to a readership who needed such solace. These writers set out to address those who 'feele (they say) the wrath of God kindled against their soules: and anguish of conscience most intolerable'.[18] One much-reprinted example took the form of a letter to a sufferer who had wrestled with these problems 'not only Nights and Daies, but Weekes, Moneths, and Yeeres, & yet you can find no ease nor comfort'.[19] Yet comforting such people was not easy. Simply pointing out sufferers' virtues to them did not help; they would be likely to feel themselves hypocrites. Richard Norwood discounted his teachers' breezy assurances that God loved him, on the grounds that 'I knew myself to be worse than they took me to be'. When John Winthrop was in the throes of salvation-anxiety, 'to hear others applaud mee was a dart through my liver; for still I feared I was not sound at the root'.[20]

---

[15] Wallington, *Notebooks*, 50–1.

[16] George Gifford, *A Briefe discourse of certaine points of religion, which is among the common sort of Christians, which may bee termed the Countrie Diuinitie* (1581: RSTC 11845.5), fo. 75r; Baxter, *Reliquiae Baxterianae*, 4.

[17] Isham, 'Confessions', fo. 12v; Corbett, *Poems*, 246.

[18] Rogers, *Seven treatises*, 40.

[19] Linaker, *Comfortable treatise*, 33.

[20] Richard Norwood, *The Journal of Richard Norwood, Surveyor of Bermuda*, ed. Wesley Frank Craven and Walter B. Hayward (New York, 1945), 7; Winthrop, *Papers*, 157.

To understand how early modern Protestants actually dealt with despair we need to understand why they thought it occurred. And here it is important to note that predestination's vice-like logic was not the prime suspect. It is not simply that—as we shall see—religious despair was not the exclusive property of 17th-century experimental puritans. More importantly, Protestants of all stripes blamed despair not on their doctrines but on the Devil. Martin Luther suffered from what he called *Anfechtung*, a state of despair which arose directly from a diabolical assault. And that view has consequences. First, it defines despair as pathological. As Robert Bolton put it, Satan works to keep souls either in self-satisfied 'security', or in its opposite, an appalled sense of sin which hurls them 'into the gulfe of horrour and despaire'.[21] Second, blaming the Devil also determined how despair should be fought. Seeking reassurance was all very well, but this was essentially a spiritual battle. The wise Christian does not try to reason with such 'hel-bred thoughts', Bolton argued, 'but at the very first approch, abandons and abominates them to the very pit of hell whence they came'.[22] Hence one of the stranger sub-genres of Protestant devotional writing: the dialogue between the soul and Satan, in which the soul defies the temptation to despair. One best-seller even included a 'prayer' which is actually an adjuration addressed entirely to the Devil.[23] We can only guess at what it felt like to use such a text, but we know that, for example, Elizabeth Isham made a practice of singing a particular psalm (Psalm 30) in her own battles with despair, a habit which recalls the use of psalms in exorcism.[24]

The belief that the Devil was at the root of despair had a third vital implication. Protestant theology emphasizes that Satan operates only under God's overarching sovereignty. He can tempt and deceive humanity only because God permits it, and God permits it only because it is ultimately for the best. This does not mean that temptation to despair is a good thing. But *experiencing* such temptations *may* be good, or at least necessary. It is time to consider despair as an experience which could be spiritually fruitful.

THE THREAT OF HELL

To modern eyes, one of the least appealing aspects of early modern Christianity is its readiness to preach hellfire. In the 21st century, even Christians who believe a traditional doctrine of Hell tend to tackle the subject cautiously in public. Fire-and-brimstone preaching is nowadays a specialist taste; Heaven is a better selling-point. It is important to appreciate that this is something of a departure in historic Christianity. Damnation, the Devil, and the torments of Hell were the

---

[21] Robert Bolton, *A three-fold treatise: containing the saints sure and perpetuall guide. Selfe-enriching examination. Soule-fatting fasting* (1634: RSTC 3255), III. 123–4.

[22] Robert Bolton, *A discourse about the state of true happinesse* (1611: RSTC 3228), 147.

[23] Edward Hutchins, *Davids Sling against great Goliah* (1581: RSTC 14010), 78–80, 213 (six editions 1581–1615); cf. Henry Greenwood, *A Treatise of the great and generall daye of Iudgement* (1606: RSTC 12337), sig. F1v.

[24] Isham, 'Confessions', fo. 26r.

absolute mainstays of preaching for conversion in the early modern period, for Protestants and Catholics alike. There were theological and pastoral reasons for this, to which we will come in a moment. But the first reason was that it worked.

Early modern preachers assumed that their audiences, however godless, had a vivid sense of their own sin and of Satan's malice. In modern Western societies, many more people profess to believe in God or Heaven than in the Devil or Hell. When the anti-hero of Graham Greene's *Brighton Rock* claims to doubt Heaven but to be sure of Hell, it is shockingly memorable. Three hundred years earlier that sentiment would have been almost banal. One woman, known to us as 'M.K.', concluded in her despair 'that there was no heaven, no God, no Jesus, no good Angels, onely an hell there was, and devills to carry me thither'.[25] The Scots preacher Robert Bruce, grandfather of Scots revivalism, had a knock-down argument against those who were similarly tempted to atheism. If there is no God, he asked them,

> wherefra floweth this feare and terror of conscience. This trembling and vnquietnes, quhilk gnaweth them; gif there be not a God, how is it that they are so tormented?[26]

He could assume that 'terror of conscience' was an all-but universal experience.

Perhaps Bruce was wrong about that; but certainly many earnest Protestants felt fear of damnation much more immediately and viscerally than hope for mercy. Conscience-literature existed largely to redress that balance, and to insist, as Richard Sibbes put it, that sinners need 'neuer feare to go to God'.[27] Wallington had to remind himself that God is 'not a strait handed God neither a hard Master but a louing & kind Father'; it was a comfort which early modern Christians found hard to hear. As Henry Smith, reportedly Elizabethan London's finest preacher, tells us, they had a more vivid experience:

> If there bee anie hell in this world: they which feele the worme of conscience gnawing vpon their hearts, may truely say, that they haue felt the torments of hell. Who can expresse that mans horror but himselfe? Nay, what horrors are they which he cannot expresse himselfe? Sorrowes are met in his soule as at a feast: feare, thought, & anguish, deuide his soule betweene them.[28]

Preachers must have their rhetoric, of course, and Smith was plainly trying to conjure up such feelings in his hearers as well as to describe them. But there is widespread enough testimony of such fears for us to take them seriously, for as well as being horrible to endure, they had consequences.

[25] Powell, *Spirituall Experiences*, 174.
[26] Robert Bruce, *Sermons Preached in the Kirk of Edinburgh* (Edinburgh, 1591: RSTC 3923), sig. E1v.
[27] Richard Sibbes, *The bruised reede, and smoaking flax* (1630: RSTC 22479), 26; cf. William Cowper, *A Most Comfortable and Christian Dialogue, betweene the Lord, and the Soule* (1611: RSTC 5929), 4.
[28] FSL MS V.a.436 p. 16; Henry Smith, *The Sermons of Master Henrie Smith* (1592: RSTC 22718), 900.

Where they might lead is frankly laid out for us in one of the most revealing spiritual memoirs of the period, that of Richard Norwood, an English navigator and surveyor who spent much of his life in Bermuda. It was there that he experienced a dramatic conversion in his mid-twenties, and it was there that he wrote a subtle, insightful, spiritual autobiography some twenty years later. At one point, shortly before the real crisis of his conversion, he was torn between the allure of worldly living and the fear of damnation. His problem was that piety did not fit well with his hellraising lifestyle, and 'I have no affection to heavenly things'. As such, 'I desired to shun the torments of hell but was not much affected with the joys of heaven'. It was, he wrote, as if an indebted woman were to be offered a marriage that would allow her to pay off her creditors—but to a man for whom she has no 'conjugal affection'. It was an arrangement to be embraced, but more for fear than for love.[29]

Norwood's point, when he wrote this account, was to emphasize how wrong his younger self had been: in fact, God 'fills our hearts with food and gladness'. But his youthful experience was widely shared. Both theology and experience persuaded most early modern British Protestants—not quite all of them—that fear of Hell was the most effective means of winning souls. Witness, for example, Robert Persons, the most effective Catholic critic of the Elizabethan church. Persons' greatest literary success was, for him, a sour one: his *Christian Directory* (1582) was given a light Protestant makeover and republished as *A booke of Christian exercise, appertaining to resolution* in 1584. The *Book of resolution*, as it was known, was an instant, runaway best-seller, and it remained a Protestant favourite. Its most striking feature—then and now—is its vivid, terrifying chapter on Hell. For the young Richard Baxter, who was deeply affected by the book, Persons' picture of 'the misery of the Wicked' was one its most compelling features. When the Jacobean playwright Thomas Middleton referred to the book in *A Mad World, My Masters* (1608), he singled out its chapter on Hell as the source of its power for effecting moral reform. The scurrilous pamphleteer Robert Greene ascribed his own deathbed conversion to Persons' depiction of Hell.[30]

Success brings imitation in its wake, and Persons' successors took to lacing their books liberally with brimstone, so restoring to eager Protestant readers a theme which had been prominent in medieval preaching. Another Catholic text which won a substantial Protestant readership, Jeremias Drexelius' *Considerations upon Eternitie*, was full of fearsome warnings of Hell.[31] Hayward's *Sanctvarie of a troubled soule* (at least fourteen editions from 1600–50) called its readers to repentance with a grisly description of Hell's torments. Henry Valentine's *Private*

[29] Norwood, *Journal*, 64–6.
[30] Robert Persons, *The Christian Directory (1582): The First Booke of the Christian Exercise, Appertayning to Resolution*, ed. Victor Houliston (Leiden, 1998), esp. xi–xii; Gregory, '"True and Zealouse Seruice"', esp. 259–60; Baxter, *Reliquiae Baxterianae*, 3; and see below, pp. 284–92. The chapter on Hell was actually shorter in the Protestant edition, as the whole section on Purgatory was omitted.
[31] Jeremias Drexelius, *Considerations upon Eternitie*, tr. Ralph Winterton (1632: RSTC 7235). Although there were only three editions before 1640, Drexelius' book was to run through a further eighteen editions by the 1720s.

Devotions ran through eleven editions during the 1630s; fully a quarter of this lengthy book is devoted to an alarming depiction of the day of judgement. Bayly's *Practise of pietie* contains a lengthy meditation on damnation and Hell, a passage which set in train the conversion of the twelve-year-old Elizabeth Wilkinson when she read it.[32] The title of Stephen Denison's *A three-fold Resolution* (five editions, 1603–30) is an obvious nod to Persons' book, and he devotes more than a quarter of its impressive length to a chapter on 'Hels horror'. Tymme's *A siluer watch-bell* opened with a series of chapters on death, the day of judgement, and Hell, subjects which together 'bringeth a hell in minde not to be expressed'. Not that he thought Hell was a psychological state: he provided a vivid description of the inferno, complete with volcanoes and whirlpools, although he did admit to not knowing its physical location.[33]

This sort of rhetoric was not confined to page and pulpit. Norwood remembered how, as a teenager, he had one day burned one of his fingers. A visitor to the house took it as an opportunity to warn him how much worse the fires of Hell would be. Norwood replied that 'there will be many there besides me, and I must endure it as others do'. The pious busybody did not like that at all, but it is striking that young Norwood, for all his cheeky backchat, took for granted both the reality of Hell and the fact that he was probably headed there.[34]

Yet Norwood's visitor was angry, because all this Hell-talk was not meant to engender fatalism and resignation, but repentance and conversion. Authors who dwelt on Hell invariably then turned—often at more length—to Heaven. As Henry Greenwood preached:

> There is an old saying, We must goe by the gates of Hell to Heauen: but I say more,
> We must after a sort be in Hell before euer we can be capable of Heauen: that is, in the
> hell of an ashamed, affrighted, and confounded conscience.[35]

This doctrine could be expounded in two ways. The gentler way was to use it to explain to the godly why they suffered such inner agonies. Robert Bolton comforted those who were 'stricken with sense of Gods wrath' that 'this hell vpon earth, is onely passed thorow by the heires of heauen'. Daniel Dyke, in a much-reprinted posthumous treatise, emphasized 'that the trouble of conscience is to be accounted of, as a gift', because it helps the sufferer on the way to repentance. In his hands, Hell was not quite so hellish: 'The lower ebbe, the higher tide. The deeper our descent in Humiliation, the higher our ascent in Consolation. . . . Surely after the most toylesome labour is the sweetest sleepe.'[36] We will hear a good deal more of that kind of paradox.

---

[32] Hayward, *Sanctuarie of a troubled soule* (1602), 51–64; Valentine, *Private Devotions*, 281–389; Bayly, *Practise of pietie*, 89–102; Samuel Clarke, *A Collection of the Lives of Ten Eminent Divines* (1662: Wing C4506), 515–16.

[33] John Denison, *A Three-fold Resolution, verie necessarie to saluation* (1608: RSTC 6596), 281–434; Tymme, *Siluer watch-bell* (1605), esp. 36, 71, 79–85.

[34] Norwood, *Journal*, 69.

[35] Henry Greenwood, *[Greenwoods workes]* (1616: RSTC 12327), VI.11.

[36] Bolton, *Discourse about happinesse*, 138–9; Daniel Dyke, *Two Treatises. The one, Of Repentance, The other, Of Christs Temptations* (1616: RSTC 7408), 24–5, 30–1, 33 (six editions, 1616–35).

However, it was more normal to insist that being overwhelmed by your own sin was an essential prelude to conversion.[37] As Robert Bruce told his Edinburgh congregation: 'It is not possible to you to make meikle of heaven, except you haue had some taist of hell.' Robert Linaker had Christ say that he only called those who 'are in paine, and throughly tyred with the sense and sorrow of their sinnes'. As for those sinners who do not feel such pains, 'I haue nothing to do with them'. John Dod preached that those who were 'neuer terrified nor troubled in their consciences' were lacking 'the first and principall note of true conuersion'. His own conversion, indeed, had arisen from his being overwhelmed with a sense of sin while he was ill.[38]

It is important to notice that these are not descriptions but theological claims. Dod's point was not that all conversions involved terror, but that conversions which did not were deficient. In other words, not everyone fitted this model, and partly for that reason, the consensus was beginning to crack by the end of our period. For those tempted by antinomianism in the 1630s, this was an obvious point at which to challenge orthodoxy.[39] For example, there is the teenage William Kiffin, a future Baptist minister who was already showing a certain independence of mind. 'Although I desired to mourn under the sense of my sins', as he knew he should, he could not manage it. Instead, 'I found my fears to vanish, and my heart filled with love to Jesus Christ'. It was disconcerting. Only when he heard Thomas Goodwin preach that 'the terrors of the law' might drive souls away from Christ instead of attracting them did Kiffin feel that his eyes had been opened. He concluded that 'God had not tied himself to any one way of converting a sinner'.[40] Indeed, Goodwin's account of his own conversion tells how he came to a full and overwhelming knowledge of his sins, 'yet my soul suffered not the terrors of the Almighty'. Instead, at that moment God 'created and put new life and spirit into my soul', and he parted from his sins joyfully.[41]

For every such murmur of dissent, however, there are scores of assertions of the absolute necessity of fear, and conversion narratives which demonstrate this principle in action. Some—as Kiffin tried to—embraced terror because they knew they should. The eighteen-year-old Thomas Shepard deliberately steered himself through this process, doing his best to meditate on 'the terror of God's wrath' even though that terror was difficult to translate into real abhorrence for his sins.[42] For others, however, the role of sin and fear was more visceral. Robert Bolton's conversion involved

---

[37] See, for example, Sibbes, *Bruised reede*, 13–16; Ezekiel Culverwell, *A treatise of faith* (1623: RSTC 6114), 45.

[38] Bruce, *Sermons Preached*, sig. I3r-v; Linaker, *Comfortable treatise*, 77–8; John Dod and Robert Cleaver, *Foure Godlie and Fruitful Sermons* (1611: RSTC 6938), 3–4; Samuel Clarke, *The lives of thirty-two English divines* (1677: Wing C4539), 168–9.

[39] David Como, *Blown by the Spirit: Puritanism and the emergence of an antinomian underground in pre-Civil-War England* (Stanford, 2004), 448–50.

[40] William Kiffin, *Remarkable Passages in the Life of William Kiffin: Written by Himself*, ed. William Orme (1823), 4–5, 10–11.

[41] Thomas Goodwin, *The Works of Thomas Goodwin, D.D.*, vol. II (Edinburgh, 1861), lxi.

[42] Shepard, *God's Plot*, 42.

the LORD . . . laying before him the ugly visage of his sins which lay so heavy upon him, as he roared for griefe of heart, and so affrighted him . . . he rose out of his bed in the night for very anguish of spirit.[43]

Robert Bruce had endured a similarly endless night in 1581, aged twenty-two. The Devil spelled out all his sins to him 'as vively as ever I heard anything', and so:

My conscience condemned me, and the condemnator tormented me, and made me feel the wrath of God pressing me down, as it were, to the lower hell. Yea, I was so fearfully and extremely tormented, that I would have been content to have been cast into a cauldron of hot melted lead, to have had my soul relieved of that insupportable weight.

Only when he appealed to God for mercy did relief come, with the dawn— mercifully early in a Scottish August. It was the turning-point of his life.[44]

There are many such tales from the scrupulously pious, but the threat of Hell could spark conversions wholesale as well as individually, as was the case in the revivalist preaching which swept south-west Scotland and Ulster in the late 1620s and 1630s. The minister Robert Blair summed up the experience of those converts: 'Numbers of them were at first under great terrors and deep exercise of conscience, and thereafter attained to sweet peace and strong consolation.' In one worrying case, however, an inexperienced minister could not complete the process: 'he roused up the people, and wakened them with terrors; but not understanding well the Gospel, could not settle them.'[45] Hell was not sufficient; but it was necessary.

The archetype of what this kind of preaching was supposed to achieve is found in a story told about William Perkins, the theological giant of English predestinarianism and the virtual inventor of conscience-literature. Supposedly, he once heard of a criminal, condemned to hang, who feared damnation. Perkins had the young man brought down from the gallows and prayed with him. What is striking is his prayer's theme: he dwelt at length on the condemned man's sin, and on 'the horrible and eternall punishment due for the same', reducing the man to tears. This might seem a strange comfort, but when 'he had brought him low enough even to hell gates', he changed tack, 'proceeding to the second worke of his prayer', and spoke of grace, forgiveness, and consolation. This cheered the man 'to looke beyond death with the eyes of faith [and] made him breake out into new showers of teares for joy', and he went to his death a new man, praising God.[46]

It is easy enough to see how confronting your own sin like this might work psychologically, as a minister uses the Devil and God in a pincer movement, as 'bad cop' and 'good cop'; however, it also works theologically. The paradox at Protestantism's heart is that you can attain forgiveness only when you confront the full

[43] Robert Bolton, *Mr. Boltons last and learned worke of the foure last things* (1632: RSTC 3242), sig. b5r–v.
[44] Robert Bruce, *Sermons . . . with Collections for his Life*, ed. William Cunningham (Edinburgh, 1843), 8.
[45] Blair, *Life*, 19, 70.
[46] Richard Willis, *Mount Tabor. Or Private Exercises of a Penitent Sinner* (1639: RSTC 25752), 132.

horror of your sin; you can only be redeemed when you recognize that you are beyond redemption. As Richard Sibbes put it: 'None are fitter for comfort than those that thinke themselves furthest off. . . . A holy despaire in our selves is the ground of true hope.'[47] In other words, the purpose of rubbing converts' faces in their sins was not self-loathing and misery, but liberation. As Bolton put it, once you have attained assurance and peace, you 'can heare . . . the most terrible denunciations of damnation and death against impiety and impenitency, with a pleased and ioyfull patience'.[48] You no longer need to fret about whether you deserve condemnation; you can cheerfully own that you do, and accept forgiveness instead.

Whether this would be apparent to your neighbours in the pew is another matter. 'Pleased and ioyfull patience' in the face of 'terrible denunciations' might look awfully like self-righteous hypocrisy. This was one of the standard accusations thrown at puritans in the latter part of our period, and it had some truth in it. The theology of predestination had by then become so refined that the middle ground between presumption and despair was on a knife-edge. The constant struggle to balance on it could be undignified, and the spectacle of those who fell off unattractive.

Yet what was distinctive about the later puritan experience of despair was its self-consciousness, not its nature. It is not simply that hellfire preaching was a common currency across the confessional spectrum. Despair for sin was assumed to be both a normative and ultimately a fruitful part of the Protestant experience from the very beginning; it had a pivotal place in Luther's theology. In the 1550s, Hugh Latimer described how his mentor Thomas Bilney had been racked with guilt and despair after recanting his beliefs in the 1520s, and he generalized the point. This 'agony of spirit' was, he argued, within the normal range of the Protestant experience:

> God doth cast them into hell, he hideth himself from them; but at length he bringeth them out again, and stablisheth them with a constant faith, so that they may be sure of their salvation and everlasting life. I knew once a woman that was seventeen years in such an exercise and fear, but at the length she recovered again; and God endued her with a strong and stedfast faith in the end.[49]

Latimer, importantly, was no hardline predestinarian. Despair was occasioned less by soteriological angst than by the simple ups and downs of the Christian life. A 1597 sermon apparently preached by Edward Gee described that life as voyaging through a storm; Christian souls were lifted on the billows of presumption and cast down into the gulfs of despair. It is terrifying while it lasts, but when calm weather suddenly returns, 'surely their comfort must needes be greater then if the Lord had never forsaken them at all'. The elect, Gee observed, 'oftentimes' have to endure such storms, by which God builds up their faith.[50] This was certainly William Cowper's experience. In 1595, he recalled, he wrestled with

[47] Sibbes, *Bruised reede*, 43.
[48] Robert Bolton, *A discourse about the state of true happinesse* (1618: RSTC 3230.5), 208.
[49] Hugh Latimer, *Sermons and Remains of Hugh Latimer*, ed. George Elwes Corrie (Cambridge, 1845), 51–2.
[50] FSL MS V.b.214 fos 91v–92r.

despair 'at the brinke of the pit, looking for nothing, but to be swallowed vp'. Only then did he suddenly find overwhelming relief, early one Saturday morning, an experience which 'as I trust, my soule shall neuer forget'.[51] The despair was an essential part of this experience. Plumbing the depths was a necessary prelude to scaling the heights. Seventeenth-century puritans described such experiences in more detail than other Protestants, but they did not have an exclusive lease on them.

For the last word on the subject, we can turn to Francis Rous, a puritan whose expectation of despair had nothing to do with predestination. His *The mysticall marriage* uses the analogy of a wife yearning for her absent husband to argue that God sometimes seems to abandon his children to despair. These bouts serve to pinch out any burgeoning spiritual pride, and also sharpen the heart's love for God, as absence proverbially does. There is more than an echo here of Jesuit spirituality, with its expectation of regular periods of desolation, but Rous adds an authentically Protestant note. You should not, he insists, be too patient or accepting during such episodes. Submit to God's will, yes: but 'be not patient in the absence of thine husband . . . desire his presence above all earthly joyes'.[52] The aim is not to be resigned to your fate, but to burn with desire. If absence helps to kindle those flames, the pain is worthwhile.

EMOTION AND SALVATION

As Rous' mysticism suggests, Protestants' despair was rooted in their almost narcissistic concern with their own spiritual well-being. It would be hard to exaggerate the self-conscious attention which Protestants were paying to this subject by the end of our period. One of the staples of Protestant publishing in the early 17th century was collections of signs or symptoms by which you might measure your godliness and so assess whether you were in fact among the elect. Nicholas Byfield's short book, *The Signes,* ran through five editions from 1614–37; one of the six treatises contained in his *The marrow of the oracles of God* (eleven editions from 1619–40) covers the same subject. When a second volume of the best-selling Jacobean devotional anthology, *A Garden of Spirituall Flowers,* was published, it devoted well over half its length to an 'examination and tryall of our Christian estate: whereby we may easily discerne whether we abide in the state of Nature, or the state of Grace'. Some enthusiasts prepared such lists for their own personal use. Simonds D'Ewes found so much 'comfort and reposedness of spirit' from the exercise that he persuaded his young wife to do it too.[53] Presumably, such

---

[51] William Cowper, *The Life and Death of the Reverend Father and faithfull Seruant of God, Mr. William Cowper* (1619: RSTC 5945), sig. B3r.

[52] Francis Rous, *The mysticall Marriage. Experimentall Discoveries of the heavenly Marriage betweene a Soule and her Saviour* (1631: RSTC 21342.5), 103–4, 107, 133–4, 162–3.

[53] Richard Rogers et al., *A Garden of Spirituall Flowers* (1615: RSTC 21213.3), II. sigs C6r–H5v; Simonds D'Ewes, *The Autobiography and Correspondence of Sir Simonds D'Ewes,* ed. James Orchard Halliwell, vol. I (1845), 353–4, 363; cf. Clarke, *Collection,* 303.

lists appealed to the Calvinist as medical encyclopaedias appeal to the hypochondriac. If they calmed salvation-anxiety in the short term, perhaps they exacerbated it in the long run, by affirming that it was legitimate and normal to pay such careful attention to such questions.

It is easy—and fair—enough to call this 'self-absorption', and it is equally easy to guess at its consequences.[54] Perhaps Calvinist self-obsession fostered social atomization, a redefinition of sin as exclusively inward and spiritual, and a Devil-takes-the-hindmost mentality. Or perhaps not: after all, in the Catholic world, the primary spiritual responsibility of all believers—and especially of monks and nuns—had long been to pursue their own salvation. For what it is worth, Protestant ministers regularly worried that their people were giving *insufficient* attention to their own salvation, breezily neglecting God and their own sins in favour of ephemeral trivialities like money, clothes, and food.[55] What we need to notice, however, is the logic behind this intense attention to the signs of election, a logic which, again, reaches beyond rarefied experimental puritanism.

We might expect to find Protestants' spiritual self-centredness to be balanced by God-centredness, and so to find sentiments like John Winthrop's claim, when he doubted his own salvation, that 'I found my heart still willing to justify God. Yea I was perswaded I should love him though hee should cast mee off'. This view—that your own salvation or damnation is frankly unimportant beside the glory of God—had been a theme of Luther's teaching, following a medieval tradition, but amongst English Protestants, it was extremely rare. I know of only two other examples from our period. One is Winthrop's first wife, Thomasine, who prayed on her deathbed 'that she might glorifie God, althoughe it were in hell'. Presumably one of the Winthrops taught this attitude to the other. The other exception is more revealing. The Scots Covenanter leader Archibald Johnston of Wariston kept a journal as a young man which detailed his grief and spiritual agonies following his wife's sudden death. At one point during this turmoil he remarked, 'Lord, I sould preferre thy glory to my salvation'. But importantly, he notes that voicing this sentiment immediately led to an influx of extraordinary spiritual comfort and confidence, and that led him immediately to conclude that he would definitely be saved.[56]

So perhaps early British Protestants simply could not stop thinking about their own salvation, or perhaps they were too self-aware to try to earn God's favour by pretending to be selfless. In either case, Wariston's comments point us to a deeper issue. The primary reason why early modern British Protestants paid such close attention to their emotions was that they expected to meet God in them. Emotion was a form of revelation.

[54] Peter Iver Kaufman, *Prayer, Despair and Drama: Elizabethan Introspection* (Urbana and Chicago, 1996), 7.

[55] See, for example, William Bradshaw and Arthur Hildersam, *A Direction for the weaker sort of Christians* (1609: RSTC 3510), 73; Culverwell, *Treatise of faith*, 211; Bolton, *Discourse about happinesse*, sig. *2r, p. 27.

[56] Winthrop, *Papers*, 158, 169; Wariston, *Diary*, 109; Timothy George, *Theology of the Reformers* (Nashville, 1988), 78.

This was no novelty. As William Christian has pointed out, medieval Spanish Christians saw emotions—especially strong, unexpected, or unexplained emotions—as 'a form of obscure communication ... messages to be deciphered', even 'a test for their spiritual condition'.[57] Protestants who agreed could and did cite medieval sources to support them,[58] but their doctrine of predestination added a further wrinkle. Feelings might provide testimony on a whole range of subjects, but in particular they could provide unparalleled evidence—perhaps the only true evidence—of election and of salvation.

An experiential, emotional form of Protestantism is often seen as a 17th- and 18th-century innovation, a move towards a 'religion of the heart' which grounded its claims to truth in subjective personal experience,[59] but there is a real continuity with Protestantism's earliest days. The evangelicals whom Thomas More mocked as teaching 'feeling faith' did not oppose 'head' to 'heart' as their great-grandchildren would begin to, but they certainly regarded their own affections and passions as vital sources of data about God's work in their lives. By William Perkins' time, this was a jaded truism—indeed, a truism which Perkins disliked: 'it is a propertie of them that doe indeed beleeue, to iudge their estate by feeling'.[60] The essential point had been made by Edward Dering in the 1570s, amongst many others. Praying 'to feele in heart spirituall comfortes and Faith', Dering pointed out that we are unable to conjure up such feelings for ourselves. 'It is', he therefore admitted to God, 'thy meere worke.' Vavasor Powell was simply expanding on this when he argued in the 1650s that 'inward sense and feeling' was 'a Copy written by the Spirit of God upon the hearts of beleevers'. Or as Thomas Goodwin put it, God speaks to his children by placing 'impressions in their own hearts'.[61]

In other words, Protestants' attention to their own feelings was not mere narcissism. It was in those feelings, perhaps more than anywhere else other than in Scripture itself, that God might speak to them. The comparison with Scripture should not be forced: these are Reformed Protestants, not Quakers, and they would have been appalled by any suggestion that their feelings were an *independent* source of authority. Rather, it was through a careful reading of their feelings that they could judge how the universal revelation of Scripture applied to them personally. Christians who were inattentive to their own feelings were wilfully deaf to the voice of God.

In a post-Freudian age, we are accustomed to finding naturalistic explanations for unexpected and unexplained emotions. However, this early modern view of the

---

[57] William A. Christian, Jr, 'Provoked Religious Weeping in Early Modern Spain' in John Corrigan (ed.), *Religion and Emotion: Approaches and Interpretation* (Oxford, 2004), 34, 39–40.

[58] Johann Gerhard, *The meditations of Iohn Gerhard*, tr. Ralph Winterton (Cambridge, 1627: RSTC 11772), 232.

[59] An argument made powerfully in Ted A. Campbell, *The Religion of the Heart: a Study of European Religious Life in the Seventeenth and Eighteenth Centuries* (Columbia, SC, 1991), esp. 2–3, 16–17, 64.

[60] Kaufman, *Prayer, Despair and Drama*, 19–20; William Perkins, *How to live, and that well* (1611: RSTC 19729), 57.

[61] Dering, *Godly priuate praiers*, sigs H8r-v (eight editions, 1574–81); Powell, *Spirituall Experiences*, sigs A2v–3r; Thomas Goodwin, *The Returne of Prayers* (1641: Wing G1253A), sig. a1v, p. 39 (four editions, 1636–8).

emotions was not a crude God-of-the-gaps theory, which ascribed unexplained phenomena to God *faute de mieux*. After all, in a tradition which was sceptical of miracles, how else could God be expected to speak to humanity? And did not the Devil do exactly the same thing, subtly slipping deceits or violently thrusting temptations into the mind, making the human psyche an arena for spiritual contest?[62] The ultimate reason for believing that some feelings and affections were divinely inspired was, however, simply that the experience of them was too startling and overwhelming to make any other explanation plausible.

Here we are at the edge of where history can take us: all we can do is acknowledge the experience of those convinced that they had heard, as Leigh Eric Schmidt puts it, 'a voice that was within but also beyond the self'.[63] The people who had these experiences found them indescribable. To put them into words was to strip them of what made them powerful. In the 1640s, Peter Sterry said that he could no more explain the qualitative difference between natural and divinely inspired feelings 'than I can convey the difference between Salt and Sugar; to him, who hath never tasted sweet or sharp', but that image does at least suggest the sense of surprise and of the unexpected that runs through these accounts, as vivid as tasting salt and finding it sweet on the tongue. Christopher Sutton's experience of meditation was that 'so many vnlooked for motiues to loue God do occur . . . as they may seeme . . . infallible testimonies of grace present'. Another prayer of Dering's admitted having felt God's power work 'so mightilie' within him 'that of force wee are driuen to acknowledge that it is thy working in vs, and not wee our selues'.[64] This might be the discovery of unexpected strength, as when those facing martyrdom found themselves 'able to bear more than we thought we could have done'. It might be a change of life: John Preston described Christ turning 'the very rudder of the heart, so that a mans course is to a quite contrary point of the compasse'. Or it might simply be the shock of the unexpected. Nicholas Byfield claimed that the elect are 'oftentimes on a sudden surprised with strange impressions', whether of fear or love for God. Robert Bolton's awareness 'of being mastered, guided and gouerned . . . against the violent bent of his owne inclination' is calmer but no less sharply delineated.[65]

A few witnesses dwelt on this subject at greater length. Thomas Goodwin ascribed his conversion to a promise which God 'let fall into my heart'. It was 'but a gentle sound, yet it made a noise over my whole heart, and filled and possessed all the faculties of my whole soul'. What makes this example intriguing is that Goodwin self-consciously scrutinized this experience in order to establish

---

[62] Perkins, *First part of The cases of conscience*, 150–2; Richard Kilby, *The Burthen of a Loaden Conscience* (1635: RSTC 14594.3), 9.

[63] Schmidt, *Hearing Things*, 54.

[64] Geoffrey F. Nuttall, *The Holy Spirit in Puritan Faith and Experience* (Oxford, 1946), 139; Christopher Sutton, *Disce viuere. Learne to liue* (1602: RSTC 23483), 3; Dering, *Godly priuate praiers*, sig. H6r.

[65] John Bradford, 'An exhortacion to the carienge of Chrystes crosse', in Miles Coverdale, *Remains of Myles Coverdale*, ed. George Pearson (Cambridge, 1846) (where misattributed to Coverdale), 246; John Preston, *Three Sermons vpon the Sacrament of the Lords Supper* (1631: RSTC 20281), 29–30; Byfield, *Marrow of the Oracles* (1622), 172–3; Bolton, *Discourse about happinesse*, 104.

Despair and Salvation 43

whether or not it was of divine origin. He concluded that it was, not only because it was consonant with Scripture, but because through it 'I found . . . the works of the devil to be dissolved in my heart . . . my will melted and softened, and of a stone made flesh'. What was more, it lasted. He compared it to fire-fighting: he was familiar with the effort of conscience which could contain and damp down a blaze of temptation, but he had never before experienced the sudden dousing of grace which quenched it once and for all.[66]

The fullest and least cautious claims for experience of this kind come from Scottish Protestants, often much less reticent about invoking supernatural experience than their English brethren. Cowper returned to the theme repeatedly, straining to find language vivid enough to describe the experience of God's presence. 'No man hath felt so sensibly a showre of raine descending on his body, as the childe of God will feele, when the shower of grace descends on his soule.' We perceive this presence 'by inward & glorious feelings', which produce 'a suddaine change of the whole man'. He described his own experience of being confined in darkness and fear when God sent him experiences which transformed him:

> the Lord made them suddainely to breake out like sparkles of light sent from his own throne of grace, bringing with them light, peace, and ioy, which in a moment remoued the former feares.

He characterized God as saying to the believer: 'Canst thou deny that I haue filled thy heart with my ioyes, and made thy tongue burst out in glorying speeches? . . . Canst thou deny but that thou hast felt my power working in thy soule?'[67] To those who shared this experience, its nature was, indeed, undeniable.

Some Scots revivalists went further, and used such feelings as a direct guide to action. Robert Blair, wondering whether he should accept the hospitality some new friends had offered, 'met unexpectedly with so sweet a peace, and so great a joy of spirit' that he concluded it was God's will he should accept.[68] David Dickson, a minister who had been deprived of his living for nonconformity, spent some days wrestling with the question of whether he should compromise, insisting that he required 'clearness and light from God' to make his decision. It did not come until he set off to return to his old parish. He had scarcely travelled a mile when 'his soul was filled with such joy and approbation from God of his faithfullness, that he scarcely ever had the like in all his life'. He took it as proof that he would be restored to his parish without compromising, as indeed he was.[69] In 1571 the fourteen-year-old James Melville, worried that his father would prevent him from going to university, was running an errand when suddenly 'the Lord steirit upe an extraordinar motion in my hart', causing him to fall to his knees in prayer then and there, in the open. When he had poured out his prayer, he rose 'with joy and grait

---

[66] Goodwin, *Works*, II. lxii–lxiv.
[67] Cowper, *Triumph*, 70–1, 92–3; Cowper, *Most Comfortable Dialogue*, sig. A4v, pp. 7, 19.
[68] Blair, *Life*, 54; cf. Bruce, *Sermons . . . with Collections*, 135.
[69] W. K. Tweedie (ed.), *Select Biographies Edited for the Wodrow Society, vol. I* (Edinburgh, 1845), 318.

contentment in hart', trusting—correctly—that this meant his ambition would be fulfilled.[70]

Such finely tuned use of the emotions as guidance was exceptional, and a good many Protestants, especially in England, would have raised an eyebrow at it. They were ready to see God's hand at work in their affections, but they did not believe that he communicated particularly subtly or specifically in this way. If God spoke to them in their affections, on the whole he did so with a single message: encouragement and assurance.

'Assurance' is a term with a precise meaning in Reformed Protestantism: the God-given conviction that you are predestined to salvation and eternal life.[71] The idea that you might know this with certainty has been a controversial element of Protestantism from the beginning, and it remains so amongst scholars who are keen to emphasize the anxiety and insecurity which the doctrine of predestination could breed. There is no doubt that theological reasoning cannot get you from a general doctrine of predestination to personal assurance, but assurance did not come through theological reasoning. It was grounded equally in experience, an experience of God's grace through which he used your feelings to show you your true spiritual status. We attain assurance, Henry Scudder taught, 'by immediate witnesse and suggestion'; Perkins called it a 'practical syllogism', deduced from the major premise of the Gospel and the minor of the Spirit's direct testimony.[72] So this was neither illogical nor unreasonable, but it transcended reason. Assurance could not be attained, it could only be given, and when it was given, it was given through the emotions.

The experience of receiving assurance in this way was widespread, overpowering, and apparently almost inexpressible. The word 'unspeakable' was often used. James Montagu, a future bishop, preached in 1603 that we know we are assured as a lamb knows its mother, and that the feeling 'is knowne to them that have it . . . The spirit like fyre, still ascendeth, like a steele toucht with the magnet, turnes northward'. Francis Rous said that 'one taste of it wil tell thee more, than all that is or can be said. The true knowledge of the sweetnes of God is gotten by tasting, and therefore taste first.'[73] That image of *sweetness* was widely used. The diary of the Scottish episcopalian John Forbes of Corse is full of claims that, in prayer, 'I received from him a sweet & lucid influence of spirituall & heavenlie consolation, love, joy, peace, & assurance'. For Robert Linaker assurance was 'such sweete comfort, as no worldly ioy could be like vnto it'.[74]

---

[70] James Melville, *The Autobiography and Diary of Mr James Melvill*, ed. Robert Pitcairn (Edinburgh, 1842), 24.

[71] Joel R. Beeke, *Assurance of Faith: Calvin, English Puritanism and the Dutch Second Reformation* (New York, 1991).

[72] Henry Scudder, *The Christians daily walke in holy securitie and peace* (1628: RSTC 22116), 690–1; Beeke, *Assurance of Faith*, 107–16.

[73] John Manningham, *The Diary of John Manningham of the Middle Temple, 1602–1603*, ed. Robert Parker Sorlie (Hanover, NH, 1976), 230; Rous, *Mysticall Marriage*, 54.

[74] Forbes, 'Diary', 45; Linaker, *Comfortable treatise*, 27; cf. FSL MS V.a.248 fo. 7r. On sweetness, see below, pp. 89–90.

The suddenness is as important as the sweetness. It could be dynamic and sharp-edged. If it was light, it was 'celestiall flashes, irradiations and inward testimonies of the spirit'. The feelings at work were 'fervent and stirring . . . with groanes and sighs, and strong cries'. Robert Linaker invoked the Biblical image of the 'Spirit crying in your heart, Abba Father'. 'It makes our faith liuely', Cowper wrote, 'our loue feruent, our zeale burning, and our prayer earnest.' It is life: 'a daily rising in my inner man, to newnesse of life'.[75] It is liberation and unburdening: assurance was very often described as 'release', and those who could not find it lamented that 'we feele no release at all'.[76] Henry Burton experienced such a transformation the night before his sentencing for sedition in 1637, when in prayer, 'I was filled with a mighty spirit of courage and resolution, wherewith I was carried up farre above my selfe, even as it were upon Eagles wings'. Burton was an experienced enough hand to be familiar with such feelings, but asked God 'to keep up my spirits at this height' throughout his ordeal.[77]

That last request shows us another important aspect of assurance: it was often fleeting. Henry Greenwood denied that there was 'any one of gods elect, that feeleth his loue at al tymes alike'.[78] George Herbert, in a poem called *The Glimpse*, put symbolic figures on the problem: he lamented that God gave him 'for many weeks of lingring pain and smart/But one half houre of comfort to my heart'.[79] Such feelings could not be summoned—neither in theory (God is sovereign, after all) nor in practice. The best that you could do was, indeed, to pray for them. Michael Sparke's popular *Crumms of comfort* was vividly direct on the subject:

> Come sweet Christ, let mee finde comfort, let mee feele some taste, let me feele some touch, let my heart be prepared, touch my heart. . . . Let mee haue some feeling, some taste, some sent, some glimmering of thy glorious presence.[80]

Apparently that was all he dared to hope.

Prayers like this—and there are many more—tell us that while these feelings may have been elusive, they were also widespread enough to be normative. Devotional writers appealed to them as a near-universal experience. It was one of the key arguments in conscience-literature. 'Had you euer any assurance of saluation in all your life? . . . Did you euer feele the power of true Repentance in your soule?' asked Robert Linaker—evidently expecting that most readers could answer yes.[81] John

[75] Pinke, *Tryall of a Christians loue*, II.10; Bolton, *Three-fold treatise*, II.167; Linaker, *Comfortable treatise*, 24; Cowper, *Triumph*, 70; John Brinsley, *The True Watch, and Rule of Life* (1608: RSTC 3775.5), 150.

[76] Dering, *Godly priuate praiers*, sig. I2v. Cf. William Prid, *The Glasse of Vaine-glorie* (1600: RSTC 931), sig. G5v (this prayer appears in fifth and subsequent editions); Rogers, *Seven treatises*, 40; Thomas Tymme, *A siluer watch-bell* (1606: RSTC 24422), 288 (this passage appears in third and subsequent editions). Tymme's prayer was copied (unacknowledged) in Sparke, *Crumms of comfort*, although Sparke changed the word 'release' to 'reliefe': sig. B5v.

[77] Henry Burton, *A narration of the life of Mr. Henry Burton* (1643: Wing B6169A), 12.

[78] Greenwood, *Treatise of . . . Iudgement*, sig. F2v.

[79] Herbert, *Works*, 154.

[80] Sparke, *Crumms of comfort*, sigs C11r, E8v.

[81] Linaker, *Comfortable treatise*, 25; cf., for example, Powel, *Resolued Christian*, 290–1; James Melville, *A Spirituall Propine of a Pastour to his People* (Edinburgh, 1598: RSTC 17816), 41.

Brinsley's much-reprinted *The True Watch, and Rule of Life* suggested an 'experiment' in which he invited readers to judge his doctrines by 'whether we can finde any sound comfort in our prayers', evidently assuming they could.[82] Bayly similarly dared readers who doubted the value of confessing their sins to 'trie this, and tel me whether thou shalt not finde more ease in thy conscience, then can be expressed in words'.[83] The emotions could become the basis for a version of Pascal's wager: doubters should at least test the waters of emotional revelation, since they had nothing to lose.

Unfortunately, it did not always work. If you could not give a confident 'yes' to Linaker's question, did that mean that you were unregenerate? It was all very well to encourage believers to observe their own emotions, and certainly some believers were spurred to renewed repentance by noticing the 'couldnesse' or 'deadlinesse' of their feelings.[84] But if your troubled feelings were not balanced by a periodic sense of assurance, while people around you spoke blithely of the inner sweetness which the Spirit had granted them—then despair could return with a vengeance.

We know this was a widespread problem, because so many devotional writers addressed it. Their standard solution was advanced by Richard Greenham in the 1570s. Greenham comforted a believer troubled by a lack of godly emotions, saying that 'wee must distinguish between gods spirit and his graces in us, for his spirit may live in us when his graces seem dead in us'. Like a gravely ill person, our souls may outwardly appear to be dead while the spark is in fact still alive. Greenham, practical pastor that he was,

> said to one that for want of feeling was loath to pray. you must not tarry to pray til you find feeling, but . . . pray on and continue in a praier of faith though not of feeling.

Greenham ascribed his principle, 'wee hold christ by faith and not by feeling', to John Foxe, the martyrologist, and certainly some of Foxe's heroic tales illustrated this point. Thomas Hudson, burned in 1558, went to the stake in 'great dolour and griefe . . . for lacke of feeling of hys Christ', but knelt and prayed by the pyre, 'and then rose he with great ioy, as a man new chaunged euen from death to life'. The similar tale of Robert Glover was later cited by both Gabriel Powel and Lewis Bayly. In Bayly's retelling, Glover 'could haue no comfortable feeling till he came to the sight of the stake; and then cryed out, and clapped his hands for ioy to his friends', explaining that at that moment he had been granted 'the feeling ioy of Faith and the holy Ghost'.[85]

The point was twofold. Firstly, as Bayly put it, 'the truest faith hath oftentimes the least feeling': emotion was no index to true faithfulness. Emotion merely made

[82] Brinsley, *True Watch* (1608), 161 (at least twelve editions 1606–37); cf. Robert Persons, *A booke of Christian exercise, appertaining to resolution*, ed. Edmund Bunny (1584: RSTC 19355), 206.

[83] Bayly, *Practise of pietie*, 766.

[84] Winthrop, *Papers*, 205; Kilby, *Hallelujah*, 110–11.

[85] Kenneth L. Parker and Eric J. Carlson, *'Practical Divinity': the Works and Life of Revd Richard Greenham* (Aldershot, 1998), 164, 189, 237; John Foxe, *The ecclesiasticall history contaynyng the Actes and monuments* (1570: RSTC 11223), 1891, 2233; Powel, *Resolued Christian*, 288–90; Bayly, *Practise of pietie*, 698.

it *easier* to be faithful, and therefore—and secondly—'it is a better faith to beleeue without feeling, then with feeling'.[86] If, like Glover, you found your faith unsupported by your emotions, it was an invitation from God to show your true mettle. As Francis Rous argued, unless feeling were sometimes withdrawn, the Christian could never truly show faith.[87] William Perkins returned to this point repeatedly, both to comfort and to exhort those whose consciences were troubled by their lack of feeling. 'In case of affliction', he insisted, 'we must not liue by feeling, but by faith.' We must believe God's promises and act on them, rather than waiting like waverers for our emotions to confirm our actions. Indeed, for Perkins, one mark of true faith is that we trust God's promises over our own feelings, so that even 'when we feele our wretchednesse and miserie, [faith] makes vs beleeue our happinesse'.[88]

Cowper took this to the next logical step. If Christians' faith was 'neuer greater then when their feeling is weakest', then such weakness of feeling should be seen as a gift from God, to bring us to greater maturity. 'If I close the doore of my chamber vpon thee', he imagined God saying, 'it is not to hold thee out, but to learne thee to knocke.'[89] Indeed, the desire for assurance could actually be distorting. We are saved, Henry Scudder pointed out, not by assurance, but by faith. To demand that God give us continual assurance is in fact faithless, like a servant demanding his wages be paid in advance.[90] The truly faithful Christian may feel nothing, but still obeys.

However, this implied, alarmingly, that feelings were a prop which mature Christians might outgrow. It was more common to follow Greenham's analogy of bodily illness. This suggested that feelings of assurance were healthy, but their absence was not fatal.[91] This was how William Walker comforted a dying parishioner troubled by his lack of feeling: his faith was weak, Walker told him, but weak faith was still faith and could still save him. John Hayward used a slightly different image, in which cold-hearted Christians were like chilled, road-weary travellers. They may not feel hungry; they may have to force themselves to swallow the unappetizing fare an innkeeper sets before them; but they know that it will give them strength for the next day's labours.[92]

So if you were bereft of feeling, your ministers and your devotional books had some comfort for you; cold comfort, but comfort nonetheless. The message was—as always—one of perseverance. There was a hope—not a promise—that God would eventually grant you the feelings you sought. But as Foxe's martyr-stories indicated, it might take a long time. God gives his gifts when he chooses. In the

---

[86] Bayly, *Practise of pietie*, 697–8; cf. Cowper, *Most Comfortable Dialogue*, 50–1; Parker and Carlson, 'Practical Divinity', 162.

[87] Rous, *Mysticall Marriage*, 324.

[88] Perkins, *First part of The cases of conscience*, 104–5; William Perkins, *The whole treatise of the cases of conscience* (Cambridge, 1606: RSTC 19669), 347–8; Perkins, *How to live*, 37, 57–8.

[89] Cowper, *Most Comfortable Dialogue*, 32, 50.

[90] Scudder, *Christians daily walke* (1628), 507–18.

[91] For example, Richard Rogers et al., *A garden of spirituall flowers* (1616: RSTC 21207), sig. D2v; Scudder, *Christians daily walke* (1628), 680.

[92] William Walker, *A sermon preached at the funerals of the Right Honourable, William, Lord Russell* (1614: RSTC 24964), 55–6; Hayward, *Sanctuarie of a troubled soule* (1602), sig. ∴1v.

meantime, all you could do was wait and pray.[93] The only consolation was that this persistence in prayer was itself pleasing to God. If you find no comfort in your prayers, Ezekiel Culverwell argued, then you may be troubled; but if you persist nevertheless, God will take particular delight in your faithfulness.[94] And as Scudder pointed out, if you longed for godly feelings, even if you did not attain them, that longing itself was a sign of grace.[95]

[93] Rous, *Mysticall Marriage*, 328–9; Dering, *Godly priuate praiers*, sigs I2v-I3v.
[94] Culverwell, *Treatise of faith*, 326–7; cf. Preston, *Three Sermons*, 75, Goodwin, *Returne of Prayers*, 225.
[95] Scudder, *Christians daily walke* (1628), 585.

3

The Meaning of Mourning

'O wretched man that I am, who shal deliuer me from the bodie of this death!'
Romans 7:24.

TRUE REPENTANCE

Dullness and despair on one side, sweetness and assurance on the other: these are the key coordinates for an emotional map of early modern Protestantism. These emotions mattered not only because of the power of the experiences themselves, but because they were seen to be—to some extent—an index to God's will and thus to your own condition. This produced a paradox. Emotion mattered because—and to the extent that—it was a gift from God, but emotion mattered too much for the believer to remain passive, curiously observing to see what feelings God might send next.

Thus, we come to the emotions and experiences which Protestants actively sought. That internal struggle, to pursue and retain the right emotions, determined what it was to be Protestant, and for most of the rest of this book we will be examining that struggle and the means by which it was fought. Before we turn to those particular battlefields, however, we must sketch out the contested emotional terrain, and first of all, that means repentance.

To modern sensibilities, early Protestantism's culture of repentance is not attractive. If Jean Delumeau was right that early modern Christianity was defined by its 'guilt culture', then early British Protestantism had a particularly pure form of that culture. Other scholars have claimed that this culture was obsessive in the clinical sense, or that puritans 'covertly hated God but found it was safer and theologically more sensible to hate themselves'.[1] The same puritans would, of course, have been equally horrified by 21st-century values such as self-esteem, self-worth, and self-realization. So once we have finished name-calling, it is worth trying to understand what this 'guilt culture' meant to those who lived in it.

Underpinning it was the Protestant doctrine of total depravity. This does not assert that everything human beings did was purely evil—evil, in Augustinian terms, is by definition impure. Rather, it asserts that all human deeds and thoughts

---

[1] Jean Delumeau, *Sin and Fear: The Emergence of a Western Guilt Culture, 13th–18th Centuries* (Basingstoke, 1990); Leverenz, *Language of Puritan Feeling*, 3–7; Kaufman, *Prayer, Despair and Drama*, 22. Cf. the useful discussion in Karant-Nunn, *Reformation of Feeling*, 9.

are to some degree corrupted. Original sin is a 'lurkyng infection', a universal taint of which we cannot purge ourselves.[2] Protestants also insisted that unless you accept this description of yourself, you cannot be saved. Almost the first subject which the English church's official homilies discussed—after the merits of the Bible itself—was total depravity, in a gruelling list of Biblical proofs which finally gave way to an exhortation to repentance.[3]

Was ever a command so obeyed? It is hard to credit the energy which early Protestants put into examining, and condemning, themselves for their innumerable sins. It changed the language: the word 'mourning' came to apply primarily to bewailing your own sins, and only secondarily to lamenting the dead. It shaped prayer books: one influential—and theologically conservative—Elizabethan collection of prayers included seventeen consecutive prayers for repentance and forgiveness of sins.[4] But this was outdone by Nicholas Themylthorpe's *Posie of Godly Praiers*, a best-selling handbook of mainstream Protestant prayers whose owners seem to have used it to destruction—only nine copies survive from at least twenty-nine editions. It professes to be a general book of prayer and thanksgiving, but in fact, of the seventy-one prayers in the collection, forty-five—almost two-thirds—focus on a single subject: repentance. The other third are formal and dignified in feel, but in the prayers of penitence Themylthorpe's text comes alive with dramatic self-abasement. A 'very earnest' prayer for forgiveness is typical:

> Strik Lord my hard hart with the strong poynt of thy deare loue, pierce it with thy mighty power vnto the very bottome, that my head may bring forth water, and my eyes a fountaine of teares, to mourne and lament my manifold sinnes and offences.[5]

For Themylthorpe, and for many of his contemporaries, repentance almost constituted the Christian life. Stephen Denison was explicit on this point in his 1619 funeral sermon for Elizabeth Juxon, which became a best-selling pamphlet. He claimed that, while Juxon had had joy in her faith, joy was merely a stepping-stone to the higher grace of repentance. 'Repentance and selfe-deniall, and base esteeme of her selfe [was] a better grace then ioy.'[6]

This repentance was neither moderate nor proportionate. Lewis Bayly wanted his readers to reach a state at which, if they were asked, 'What is the vilest Creature vpon earth? thy Conscience may answere, Mine owne selfe.' Richard Kilby claimed in the very title of his book that he was 'the worst sinner of all the world'. The young Samuel Ward wrote almost enviously of a woman who believed herself so sinful 'that she was not worthy to enioy the ayre.'[7] Others denied that they deserved to walk on the ground, or claimed they were filthier than pigs and more corrupt

[2] John Foxe, *A sermon of Christ crucified, preached at Paules Crosse* (1570: RSTC 11242), fo. 8r.
[3] *Certain Sermons or Homilies Appointed to be Read in Churches in the time of the late Queen Elizabeth* (Oxford, 1844), 9–13.
[4] Richard Day, *A Booke of Christian Prayers* (1578: RSTC 6429), fos 56v–71r.
[5] Nicholas Themylthorpe, *The Posie of Godly Praiers* (1618: RSTC 23934.5), esp. 2, 157.
[6] Stephen Denison, *The Monument or Tombe-Stone* (1620: RSTC 6603.7), 117–18 (five editions 1619–31).
[7] Bayly, *Practise of pietie*, 280–1; Kilby, *Hallelujah*, title page; Knappen, *Two Diaries*, 107.

than rotting corpses.[8] It was hard to believe, Richard Rogers admitted, 'that so much poyson could be inclosed in so narrow a roome, as within the compasse of one silly man': one reader approvingly underlined the phrase.[9] Nor was there much by way of countervailing virtues. One popular collection of prayers had families confess every Sunday morning that 'we haue done more against thee this weeke past then wee haue done for thee all the dayes of our life'. Indeed, William Crashaw argued that by spurning the chances to do good which God had offered, Christians have turned 'our owne helpes into hinderances, our Comforts into Crosses'.[10] If God gives us rope, all we do is hang ourselves.

Some of the features of the Protestant emotional landscape were only sharply defined relatively late in our period, but this one was present from the beginning. The earliest Protestant texts are filled with exaggerated repentance. One of English Protestantism's first genuine best-sellers, Thomas Becon's *The gouernans of vertue*, opens with a typically extreme confession of sins which 'are so great and so exceadyngly encreased, that they are no lesse innumerable then the sandes of the sea, and thrust me downe, euen as an intollerable weyghte or burden'.[11] In 1548, Miles Coverdale had his readers pray: 'I geue sentence of myne owne extreme madnes, & dooe vtterly altogether myslyke myself, neither is there any thyng present before myne iyes but helle fyer & desperacion.'[12]

Although hyperbolic, these confessions are usually coyly general. Some penitents had genuinely crunchy sins to bite into—for example, Richard Norwood's youthful adultery, fornication, and conjuring. But Protestant consciences were more usually seared by inattention during worship, wandering thoughts, or forgetting God when in company.[13] The spectacle of believers racking themselves over these trivia was easy to mock. Bishop Earle's caricatured 'she-puritan' had a conscience which 'is like others lust, neuer satisfyed'. From within, matters looked a little different. Thomas Goodwin recalled how, before his conversion, he could only perceive his 'grosser acts . . . as in the dark a man more readily sees chairs and tables in a room, than flies and motes'. However, in the illumination which Christ brought, he 'searched the lower rooms of my heart, as it were with candles'. The search unearthed some horrors:

---

[8] Oliver Pigg, *Meditations concerning praiers to almighty God, for the safety of England* (1589: RSTC 19916.3), 3; John Hooper, *The Later Writings of Bishop Hooper*, ed. Charles Nevinson (Cambridge, 1852), 206; Wallington, *Notebooks*, 203.

[9] Rogers, *Seven treatises*, 238; underlining in FSL STC 21215.

[10] Thomas Tuke, *The Practise of the faithfull* (1613: RSTC 24314), 128; William Crashaw, *Londons Lamentation for her Sinnes* (1625: RSTC 6017.5), sig. B1v.

[11] [Thomas Becon], *The Gouernans of vertue, teaching a christen man, howe he oughte dayly to lede his lyfe* (1549?: RSTC 1725.3), fos 2r–4v. This book ran through ten editions, c.1544–1611, but with much variation. The first edition, RSTC 1724.5, survives only in a single, mutilated copy—the passage quoted would be on one of the missing pages—and should be dated to 1544–5, not 1538 as in RSTC (see the English Short Title Catalogue, <http://estc.bl.uk>).

[12] Miles Coverdale, *Devout meditacions, psalmes and praiers* (1548: RSTC 2998.5), sigs D1v–2r.

[13] Norwood, *Journal*, 60; and see, for example, Knappen, *Two Diaries*, 103; Kilby, *Hallelujah*, esp. 90–6.

as if I had in the heat of summer looked down into the filth of a dungeon, where by a clear light and piercing eye I discerned millions of crawling living things in the midst of that sink and liquid corruption.

By which he meant nothing more serious than ambition and vanity.[14]

Before we conclude that early modern Protestant culture was caught up in a frenzy of self-hatred, it is worth noting that this extreme scrupulousness was very far from universal. It was a preachers' commonplace that the common people scarcely knew what penitence was. Of course, they would say that, but it explains their rhetorical strategy. They deliberately intensified their language so as to crack their audiences' thick shell of indifference. 'This iron-flinty age standeth more in need of an Hammer to breake, then of Oyle to supple broken hearts', Robert Linaker believed.[15] Arthur Dent, facing the complaint that he preached 'nothyng but the Lawe, the Lawe, damnation damnation', argued that it was what his godless hearers needed: 'would you haue Plaisters before you haue woundes? Would you haue Phisicke, before you bee sicke?'[16] This frank admission that his role was to wound and sicken his flock's consciences may not be very attractive, and in practice this strategy may have alienated as many people as it converted, but it should also warn us not to confuse pulpit hyperbole against sin with sober assessments of its extent.

Likewise, it is only fair to point out that many preachers and writers were themselves wary of going too far. Linaker, as well as hammering his readers' hearts, also insisted that Christians should neither slander themselves by overstating their sins, nor tempt God by doubting that he can forgive them. He compared the lamenting sinner to a victim of toothache, 'who . . . cries out, that there was neuer any creature in the world so cruellie tormented': an error, but an understandable one.[17] These warnings became a staple of conscience-literature. Perkins was blunt about any claim that a sinner's case was uniquely desperate: 'it is false'. The Ipswich preacher Samuel Ward chided those 'who haue not learned that God will haue them mercifull to themselues'.[18] Richard Sibbes warned, 'We must see that wee doe not make sinnes where God makes none.' But some, he worried, traduce themselves 'as if they had been hyred by Satan the Accuser of the Brethren, to plead for him',[19] and again, this point had been argued since the beginning. Becon denounced sin in blood-curdling terms, but also repeatedly allowed for the possibility that you might examine yourself in the evening, find that you had committed no notable sins that day, and so go to your rest rejoicing.[20]

[14] John Earle, *The Autograph Manuscript of Microcosmographie* (Leeds, 1966), 121; Goodwin, *Works*, II. pp. lv–lxiv.

[15] Linaker, *Comfortable treatise*, sig. A5r.

[16] Dent, *Sermon of Repentance*, sigs C1v, C3v.

[17] Robert Linaker, *A comfortable treatise for such as are afflicted in conscience* (1595: RSTC 15638), 22–5, 36.

[18] Perkins, *First part of The cases of conscience*, 105–6; Samuel Ward, *A Coal from the Altar, to Kindle the holy fire of Zeale* (1615: RSTC 25039), 58. Cf. the easily misinterpreted self-accusation of Ward's namesake, the Cambridge diarist Samuel Ward: see Margo Todd, 'Puritan Self-Fashioning: The Diary of Samuel Ward', *Journal of British Studies* 31/2 (1992), 236–64.

[19] Capel, *Tentations*, 225–6, 255–7; Sibbes, *Bruised reede*, 106–7; cf. Revelation 12:10.

[20] Thomas Becon, *The gouernans of vertue, teachyng a Christen man, howe he oughte dayely to lede his life* (1544?: RSTC 1724.5), fo. 9r.

However, the very tone of these warnings shows us the strength of the penitential tide. If self-accusation sometimes went beyond what was theologically wise, it was not purely theology which drove it.

When Sibbes used the book of Revelation's description of Satan, 'the Accuser of the Brethren', he meant what he said. It was normal to describe the process of self-examination and self-condemnation in judicial terms. When you knelt before your God in penitence, it was a preliminary hearing for the Day of Judgement. And so, we might think, you as the accused sinner would be inclined to defend yourself. However, this judge—Jesus Christ himself—already knows the facts and cannot be deceived. Moreover, you are asking not for acquittal, but for forgiveness. Is your role, therefore, to plead guilty and to appeal to the judge's mercy? Or simply to make the soberest, most objective presentation of your sins that you can, with 'scientific detachment'?[21]

It was neither. Your role in the great courtroom was to act as your own accuser. As a widely-circulated text for family prayer insisted, 'wee come not now to excuse our selues, but to accuse our selues'.[22] This accusation was to be made in the most merciless, even malicious manner which the facts could bear. Seventeenth-century Protestants called this *aggravation*. Sinners were called to 'accusation of your selfe, with a due aggravation of your sinne ... judging and passing sentence against your selfe for sinne'.[23] In other words, when you confess your sins in prayer you should 'make them as great and foule in their natures and circumstances as thou canst'. There was no place for what Daniel Dyke called the 'tricke of extenuation', or playing down your sins. Extenuation might imply that you doubted how sinful your sins really were. Aggravation, by contrast, forced you to confront them in their full horror, and it was far safer to exaggerate than to understate them—even if it strained the truth.[24]

Importantly, aggravation was a matter not of self-loathing, but of enlightened self-interest. The theory underpinning any adversarial legal system—including early modern England's—is that if all the participants fight their own corners to the utmost, within the rules, and trust each other to do the same, then the magistrate will be able to hear every side of a case and arrive at the truth. So earthly prosecutors can—in principle—prosecute those whom they suspect are innocent, safe in the knowledge that the court as a whole will reach a just verdict. This applies *a fortiori* to God's judgement. Therefore, when we lay out an aggressive prosecutor's case against our own sins, it is not an earnest attempt to have ourselves damned. We are simply playing the part allotted to us, and trusting that if we

---

[21] Tom Webster, 'Writing to Redundancy: Approaches to Spiritual Journals and Early Modern Spirituality', *Historical Journal* 39 (1996), 50.

[22] Samuel Smith, *Dauids blessed man. Or, A short exposition vpon the first Psalme* (1617: RSTC 22840), 309 (ten editions 1614–38, and seven more by 1682).

[23] Henry Scudder, *The Christians daily walke in holy securitie and peace* (1631: RSTC 22117), 88; cf. Sibbes, *Bruised reede*, 34; cf. Hildersam, *Doctrine of Fasting*, 123.

[24] Dyke, *Worthy communicant*, 450; Dyke, *Two Treatises*, 67; Edwin Sandys, *The Sermons of Edwin Sandys*, ed. John Ayre (Cambridge, 1841), 104.

play it well, God too will play his. 'If we would iudge our selues', explained 'silver-tongued' Henry Smith, 'wee should not be iudged.'[25]

This could be understood simply as a paradoxical condition for mercy. As John Dod put it:

> With earthly Iudges, the more is confessed by a malefactour, the worse it is likely to goe with him: but it is otherwise with the great Iudge of heauen: the larger and freer our confession is, the easier, the surer, and speedier, shall our remission be.[26]

John Norden admitted that for 'pleading not guiltie' before God, he would be condemned, but to 'crie out against my selfe, guiltie Lord guiltie' was the way to mercy.[27] In particular, it would pre-empt that other, more malicious and relentless accuser:

> When we haue accused our selves what can Sathan that accuser of the brethren say, which wee haue not sayd before, so his mouth is stopt: Hee come too late: wee being Accusers, God is our Discharger.[28]

It is a universal Christian principle. Confession is the route to forgiveness, and the more abject the confession, the freer the forgiveness.

For most early modern British Protestants, however, repentance was more than just accusing yourself. It was also judging and even punishing yourself. Self-punishment, it should be said, is not a metaphor. Early modern Protestants were wary of ascetic penitential practices which they associated with popery and hypocrisy, but by the later Elizabethan period, that wariness was being counterbalanced by a conviction that these practices could be genuinely useful. An influential treatise on fasting from 1580, apparently written by the puritan provocateur Thomas Cartwright, argued that practices such as fasting, austere living, or clothing yourself with dust and ashes had two linked purposes. One was instructive: to remind yourself that you did not deserve food, possessions, or indeed life itself. The other was pre-emptive: to punish yourself and so ensure that God would not need to do so.[29] This sits a little uncomfortably with Protestant orthodoxy, but only a little. Those who cited it were careful not to claim that ascetic practices could atone or satisfy for sin. Instead, their function was to deter and reform the sinner, 'beating downe my bodie that I sin not againe'. Or it was to avert the finite, temporal judgements which sinners endure in this life.[30] The hint that these practices had some redemptive power, however, remained. It was best silenced in an argument which Arthur Hildersam put forward, reuniting the two halves of Cartwright's

[25] Smith, *Sermons*, 900.

[26] John Dod and Robert Cleaver, *Ten sermons tending chiefely to the fitting of men for the worthy receiuing of the Lords Supper* (1611: RSTC 6945.4), 31.

[27] Norden, *Pensiue mans practise*, 43; cf. Rogers, *Seven treatises*, 286.

[28] Dyke, *Two Treatises*, 72.

[29] Thomas Cartwright? and Thomas Wilcox, *Two treatises. The holy exercise of a true fast, described out of Gods word. . . . The substance of the Lordes supper* (1610: RSTC 4314), 28–30. On this book's attribution and publication history, see Albert Peel and Leland H. Carlson (eds), *Cartwrightiana* (Elizabethan Nonconformist Texts, vol. 1: 1951), 118–27.

[30] Rogers, *Garden* (1615), II, sig. B4v; Bayly, *Practise of pietie*, 502.

claim. 'The chief use of a religious fast', he claimed, 'is to humble and afflict the soule with sorrow', and the purpose of sorrow was to avert a worse judgement.[31]

Especially earlier in the period, there was still some unease about asceticism. The Elizabethan Homily 'of repentance' warned that self-chastisement might be hypocritical, citing the Biblical warning to rend your heart rather than your garments.[32] When Persons' *Book of resolution* listed an enthusiastically Catholic set of penitential practices—'fasting, praier, weeping, wearing of sak, eating of ashes'—his Protestant editor felt compelled to point out that ash-eating was purely metaphorical and that readers should not try it at home.[33] But amongst Protestants, at least, there is not much of a division here. For those who supported ascetic practices, their purpose was 'the abasing of our selues, to make our soules low'. Others disliked them because 'euen the most exquisite punishment which I can deuise to my selfe . . . is not sufficient for one of my least sinnes'. This was, in other words, a disagreement about means. What all Protestants shared was the purpose: awakening the conscience.[34] Mere self-accusation was not enough: you must recognize and condemn the full horror of your sins, by cultivating your own inner Hell. John Hooper argued that the true penitent would actively seek 'the same discomfort in his soul that the law of God doth open and proclaim against him for his sins'. You should not expect, Robert Bolton warned, 'to goe to heaven in a bed of downe'. If you do not experience an inner Hell of godly sorrow in this life, an eternal one will await you in the next.[35]

HOW TO REPENT

To mourn rightly for your sins; to reach that pitch of appalled grief which sees them for the horrors they are, and which fully agrees that God must abhor them; and not merely to attain this state once, but to return to it regularly and in perfect earnest throughout your Christian life—this is not easy.

It was a truism that repentance did not come naturally. John Brinsley's popular spiritual handbook, *The True Watch, and Rule of Life,* called it the 'work which is of all other the hardest to flesh and blood'.[36] Sin naturally wishes to conceal and extenuate itself. Sinners are as loath to think of sin as thieves are of the hangman, and the Devil is loath to let them. If we attempt 'to winde up our soules' to self-examination, 'we shall finde our minds like the pegs of an instrument, slip between our fingers, as we are a winding them up'.[37] The only remedy, then, was constant,

---

[31] Hildersam, *Doctrine of Fasting*, 70–2; and see below, pp. 195–9.

[32] Certain *Sermons or Homilies*, 472; cf. Joel 2:13.

[33] Persons, *Booke of Christian exercise*, ed. Bunny, 339; cf. Persons, *Christian Directory*, ed. Houliston, 268.

[34] Torshell, *Saints Humiliation*, 6; Dyke, *Two Treatises*, 67; Dering, *Godly priuate praiers*, A2v; Dod and Cleaver, *Foure Sermons*, 5.

[35] Hooper, *Later Writings*, 320; Bolton, *Three-fold treatise*, III.162.

[36] Brinsley, True Watch (1608), 7 (approx. twelve editions, 1606–37).

[37] Capel, *Tentations*, sig. ¶8r; Goodwin, *Vanity of Thoughts*, 15; William Pemble, *An introduction to the worthy receiving the sacrament of the Lords Supper* (1628: RSTC 19579), 47.

intense, and renewed effort. Like a recalcitrant dog, the soul has to be dragged to and confronted with its sins—by main force if necessary.

Readiness to do this was perhaps the single clearest distinction between the saved and the damned in this life. We are all sinners, but the difference, as Arthur Dent's influential dialogue *The plaine mans path-way to heauen* put it, is between 'the penitent, and the vnpenitent sinner; the carefull, and the carelesse sinner'. The godless sinner 'hath a merry heart', while the godly sinner 'is greeued & confounded in himselfe'.[38] Thus, as John Foxe explained, the elect still sin, but do so 'with a repugnance of will goyng before, and with a repentance of hart folowyng after'. To Dorothy Leigh, author of the most popular devotional work from a woman writer in this period, the elect are those 'that plucke vp their sinnes, as a Gardiner pulleth vp his weedes'; the reprobate, by contrast, quickly abandon themselves to wildness.[39] So while the elect may sin, they do so 'not willingly, nor of set purpose', and grace never allows them 'to lie still in . . . sinne'.[40]

What did this mean in practice? It meant earnestness: confessing 'with feeling, and not formally'. It meant regularity: self-examination and confession should be a daily task, as necessary for the soul as food is for the body. 'Grant mee', the Devon preacher Samuel Hieron prayed, 'to keep daily (as it were) a priuy sessions in the closet of mine owne heart, arraigning my selfe before thy iudgement seat'.[41] Some recommended first thing in the morning, before fresh sins had a chance to encroach on the day; some preferred last thing at night, to have a full overview of the day's sins. Or you could do both. One even suggested that you try both and see which works best.[42]

And it meant thoroughness. As Daniel Dyke firmly put it: 'Generall Confessions, and in grosse, are too too grosse. No, [sins] must be particularly remembred, and ranked, and sorted together in order'. Just as you should tell a doctor all your symptoms, so you should not omit any sins in confession. Sins were like thorns thrust into your flesh: simply removing a few is no use, but you must pull out each one, 'with many a sigh, and many a sorrowfull oh, oh'. This is startlingly similar to the Catholic ambition to list sins exhaustively in confession, and certainly its precise scrupulosity would have surprised first-generation evangelicals. But it had its own, distinctively Protestant logic. Dyke was clear that total recall of sins was neither possible nor necessary. His concern was that vague generalities in confession were too easy on the conscience, and allowed sinners to avoid dealing with specific sins. If

[38] Arthur Dent, *The plaine mans path-way to heauen: Wherein euery man may cleerely see, whether he shall be saued or damned* (1607: RSTC 6629), 268 (25 editions 1601–40); Perkins, *Exposition of the Lords prayer*, 81.
[39] Foxe, *Sermon of Christ crucified*, 20r; Dorothy Leigh, *The mothers blessing* (1616: RSTC 15402), 188 (at least 19 editions, 1616–40). On garden imagery, see below, pp. 166–7.
[40] Linaker, *Comfortable treatise* (1620), 144; Cowper, *Most Comfortable Dialogue*, 22.
[41] Hildersam, *Doctrine of Fasting*, 113; Dyke, *Two Treatises*, sig. A3v; Samuel Hieron, *A Helpe vnto Deuotion* (1608: RSTC 13406.3), 197.
[42] Scudder, *Christians daily walke* (1628), 30; John Clarke, *Holy Incense for the Censers of the Saints* (1635: RSTC 5358), 147; Christopher Sutton, *Godly meditations upon the most holy sacrament of the Lordes supper* (1613: RSTC 23492), 418; BL Egerton MS 2877 fo. 86r; Isham, 'Confessions', fo. 28v; Charles Rogers (ed.), *Three Scottish Reformers* (1874), 121; Hildersam, *Doctrine of Fasting*, 111.

patients do conceal their symptoms from a doctor, Dod warned, what they hide are usually the most dangerous and painful matters, where they fear medical attention.[43]

Hence one of the priorities of self-examination: to detect your 'darling sinne', the one peccadillo which Satan would have you cling to as you reform the rest of your life. This sin might seem inconsequential but is in fact a stumbling-block in the way of your salvation. Ezekiel Culverwell warned that the half-convert and the hypocrite—and who could be sure that they were neither?—'will ever haue some sin so sweete, that he hides it like Sugar-candy vnder his tongue, and cannot forgoe it'.[44] One preacher—expounding Christ's command to pluck out your eye if it offends you—laid out rules by which 'to know our darling sin which is as our eye to vs', rules carefully transcribed by a conscientious hearer.[45]

Since this sin might hide anywhere, the only safe course was a systematic search. Although there were a range of individual schemes for doing this, by far the most widespread method was to use the Ten Commandments, generally—and slightly oddly—assumed to be a comprehensive index of sin.[46] Innumerable catechisms and devotional treatises expounded them in this way. Lewis Bayly was one of many to suggest using the Commandments as a check-list for your own sins; he even provided a full form of confession which took that structure. Some constructed personalized checklists based on the Commandments for their own private use.[47]

But this was not enough for everyone. Nicholas Byfield's popular compendium, *The marrow of the oracles of God,* began with a supposedly exhaustive check-list of all the sins condemned in the entire Bible—including several 'which I could not obserue to be mentioned in any exposition of the commandements'. To measure yourself against this daunting yardstick would, he recognized, take more than one sitting.[48] Even this, however, pales beside the gruelling regime recommended by James Melville to his Fife parishioners, in which the Commandments were only the beginning. They were also to consider the sins committed by each part of their bodies, through each of their senses, in the course of their daily work, and throughout their entire lives from infancy to the present. All this would, he promised, give them 'an ouglie and terrible sight of thy miserie', a promise which may explain why the book did not sell as well as he hoped.[49]

If exhaustive searches did not move you, there were other techniques. Grace Mildmay apparently confessed her sins daily in song, using the metrical psalms.[50]

[43] Dyke, *Two Treatises*, 72, 74; Dent, *Plaine mans path-way*, 344; Dod and Cleaver, *Ten sermons*, 34.

[44] Henry Burton, *Israels Fast. Or a Meditation vpon the Seuenth Chapter of Joshuah* (1628: RSTC 4147), 22; Walker, *Sermon at the funerals . . .* , 54; Culverwell, *Treatise of faith*, 61–2.

[45] FSL MS V.a.280 part II fo. 15r; cf. Matthew 5:29.

[46] On the Commandments in English Protestant culture, see Dr Jonathan Willis' forthcoming work. For alternatives, see James Perrott, *Certaine Short Prayers and Meditations vpon the Lords Prayer and the Ten Commandements* (1630: RSTC 19772), 112–15; BL Egerton MS 2877 fo. 86r.

[47] Bayly, *Practise of pietie*, 564–76; cf. Scudder, *Christians daily walke* (1628), 32–3; Clarke, *Holy Incense*, 14–17; BL Harleian MS 1026 fos 16r-20v.

[48] Byfield, *Marrow of the Oracles* (1619), 4, 31.

[49] Melville, *Spiritual Propine*, 39–40; Melville, *Autobiography*, 12.

[50] Grace Mildmay, *With Faith and Physic: The Life of a Tudor Gentlewoman, Lady Grace Mildmay 1552–1620*, ed. Linda Pollock (1993), 35.

Some recommended keeping a running record of your sins—sometimes 'in thy heart', but sometimes an actual notebook. Others recommended—in another echo of Catholic practice—that, if simple confession to God did not move you to sorrow, you should confess your offences to a minister or a trusted friend, a practice which 'many times hath melting of heart ioyned with it'. Even if that act of confessing did not produce godly sorrow in itself, a trusty friend might respond with 'wholesome, and sound, and wise reproofe', which might do the trick. If friends' rebukes did not move you, considering their virtues—which threw your own sins into sharp relief—might.[51] And if you were deaf to friends, you might at least listen to God's reproaches. Since it was widely assumed that illness or worldly misfortune were punishments for sin, they could also be spurs to repentance, sometimes pointedly so. For example, an eye infection might lead you to ponder 'if thine eye haue not glanced on women, whereby lust hath bene bred'.[52]

But although mourning for sins was essential, it was not sufficient. Arthur Dent was scathing on the point. If good intentions were repentance, 'so should euery sicke man repent'; if calling on God's mercy were repentance, 'so should euery foole repent'.[53] True godly sorrow was enduring, not a passing mood. Some who thought they were penitent were merely 'sermon-sick', an affliction as temporary as seasickness. True repentance was distinguished by its earnestness for reformation of life.[54] Henry Mason was perhaps already showing signs of his trajectory towards Laudianism when he argued that your penitential acts should match your sins: 'the plaister should be as large as the sore'.[55] But we should not look for too much of a division here. No Protestants believed that moral reformation could in any sense atone for sin, and all believed that repentance meant actions, not words—or, to be precise, that true repentance was marked by a sincere and earnest intent to moral reform, whether or not that intention was fully carried out.

All of which meant that it was easier to recommend true repentance than to attain it. There was a steady drumbeat of concern about false or hypocritical repentance. 'O might those sighes and teares returne againe/Into my breast and eyes', wrote John Donne, fearing that he had 'mourn'd in vaine' for his sins and that his attempted repentance was itself sinful.[56] An anonymous Elizabethan devotion echoes St Paul:

---

[51] John Brinsley, *The True Watch, and Rule of Life* (1611: RSTC 3777), II.53; Byfield, *Marrow of the Oracles* (1622), 242; Dod and Cleaver, *Ten sermons*, 34; Dyke, *Two Treatises*, 41. On written sin-records, see, for example, Dyke, *Two Treatises*, 41; Byfield, *Marrow of the Oracles* (1619), 28–35; and below, pp. 395–7.

[52] BL Egerton MS 2877 fo. 86r.

[53] Dent, *Sermon of Repentance*, sig. A6v (at least 39 English editions 1582–1642, plus one in Welsh).

[54] Sibbes, *Bruised reede*, 36; cf. Dyke, *Worthy communicant*, 158; Daniel Dyke, *The mystery of selfe-deceiuing. Or A discourse and discouery of the deceitfullnesse of mans heart* (1614: RSTC 7398), 92; Byfield, *The Signes*, 37.

[55] Henry Mason, *Christian Humiliation, Or, A Treatise of Fasting* (1625: RSTC 17602), 37.

[56] John Donne, *The Poems of John Donne*, ed. Herbert J. C. Grierson (Oxford, 1912), 323.

Why doo I not mourne and bewaile before thee, after such a sort, that teares might spring out of mine eies? I would faine, but I am not able, bicause I cannot doo that which I desire to doo.[57]

The obvious recourse was to pray to be granted true repentance. When the earl of Bothwell was brought to public repentance in 1589, this was his theme: his statement—in its entirety!—was, 'I wald wish to God, that I might mak sik a Repentance as mine heart craueth: and I desire You all to pray for it.' Elizabeth Hastings, the countess of Huntingdon, prayed similarly in private, at more length and perhaps in more earnest. 'I cannot offer up to thee o Lord a broken & a contrite heart, nor shedd a teare, myne eyes are drie, my heart at ease'; and she prayed at least for the grace 'to greive that I cannot greive'.[58]

Others could at least clear that hurdle. One 17th-century Englishwoman claimed that sometimes, 'through griefe that I could not sorrow enough, I have fallen into a great measure of weeping'. She was not the only penitent to weep for her inability to weep.[59] Ministers had words of consolation for such people. Daniel Dyke assured them that 'to grieue because wee cannot bee grieued, goes currant for godly sorrow'. And Wallington took it as a good sign that, although 'I cannot vpon Fastdays geet my heart in that humbling meltting frame which many others haue', he was nevertheless 'much troubled' by this failure.[60] Which serves as a reminder that all the paraphernalia of repentance—prayers, checklists, even amendment of life—are, in the end, so much surface froth. What you do matters only insofar as it heightens, or testifies to, your affections. True repentance is what you feel.

THE END OF REPENTANCE

What was the point of all this self-flagellation? In theory, to attain assurance in this life and Heaven in the next. This was the housework of the soul: a regular chore amply justified by the benefits of living in peace and order rather than amidst moral squalor, and by the hope of being fit to receive a divine guest. How far we believe that claim is another matter. Sensible spring-cleaning could blur all too easily into an obsessive spiritual hygiene which was never satisfied. In such cases, the promised peace was a will-o'-the-wisp, and its impossible pursuit a peculiarly bleak form of self-enslavement. It is time to hear how Protestants described the rewards they found from their regimes of repentance.

Sometimes these rewards do not really convince. John Bruen's explanation for spiritual agonies—that 'if we did not stay some while vnder gods hand, wee should

[57] Bentley, *Monument of Matrons*, 441.

[58] Bruce, *Sermons Preached*, Aa3v; Huntington Library, San Marino, CA, MS 15369 fos 4v–5r; cf. John Bradford, *Godlie meditations vpon the Lordes prayer, the beleefe, and ten commaundementes* (1562: RSTC 3484), sig. O1v; John Brinsley, *The True Watch, and Rule of Life* (1622: RSTC 3782.5), II.184*, 187.

[59] Powell, *Spirituall Experiences*, 78; cf. Thomas Tymme, *A silver watch-bell* (1640: RSTC 24434), 290; Themylthorpe, *Posie of Praiers*, 197.

[60] Dyke, *Two Treatises*, 6; FSL MS V.a.436, p. 43.

not know how sweet his mercy is'—is a pretty poor attempt to justify the ways of God. Likewise, the radical Elizabethan lawyer Andrew Kingsmill described the love of God as cooling drops of mercy which 'refresh the hote hart of man, flaming and boyling with the smoking fire of Gods furie'.[61] Consolation arising from an interruption to sufferings is real enough, but we would normally regard someone who voluntarily embraces pain, so as to find pleasure in the few moments when it ceases, as disturbed.

Much more common was a functional view of repentance: it was a means to an end, a sharp breakfast before a merry supper. The great Scottish preacher, Robert Bruce, shed some important light on this in a sermon on King Hezekiah's illness. God had declared unambiguously that Hezekiah would die, but when the king repented, God instead promised him fifteen more years of life. God was not, Bruce insisted, therefore inconstant or deceitful. Rather, all God's threats are conditional, whether or not a condition is openly stated. In this life, even the most final and unambiguous condemnation has 'a conditioun annexed . . . to wit, except he repent, except he seeke me, and make his recourse to me be prayer'.[62] The point has a wider importance: this is how to read the bloodcurdling threats which rumble through so much early modern preaching. If the promise of grace and mercy was not explicit, it was always implicit. The constant purpose of repentance was renewed grace.

When the promise was made explicit, it was sometimes described again as a mere contrast: retreating into repentance the better to advance into grace, a kind of spiritual run-up. Daniel Dyke wrote:

> The lower ebbe, the higher tide. The deeper our descent in Humiliation, the higher our ascent in Consolation. . . . Surely after the most toylesome labour is the sweetest sleepe.[63]

And the Somerset cleric John Andrewes, in one of his populist devotional chapbooks, promised that

> They that haue mourned & sorrowed, and truly lamented for their sinne, shall receiue Crownes of glory for euer: they that haue watched and praied in the night, & fasted in the Bridegroomes absence, shall now rest in the day that hath no night.[64]

This reasoning, in which repentance is an inverted image of grace, is scarcely Protestant; but it was nevertheless widespread.[65]

Others spelt this out more carefully. The preface to the popular anthology, *A garden of spirituall flowers*, laid out a spiritual road-map from repentance through grace and peace to amendment of life. It warned that the first stage was essential

---

[61] BL Harleian MS 6607 fo. 39v; Andrew Kingsmill, *A Viewe of mans estate, wherein the great mercie of God in mans free iustification by Christ, is very comfortably declared* (1574: RSTC 15003), sig. H1r–v.

[62] Bruce, *Sermons Preached*, sig. B8v; cf. Isaiah 38.

[63] Dyke, *Two Treatises*, 30–1.

[64] John Andrewes, *A celestiall looking-glasse: to behold the beauty of heaven* (1621: RSTC 592), '31', recte 33.

[65] Cowper, *Triumph*, 330; Hildersam, *Doctrine of Fasting*, 100.

(apparently fearing that some readers might skip straight to the happier material), but added that it was not a matter of appeasing God's wrath. Rather, the purpose of repentance was preparatory, to break unbelievers' hearts and 'to make them fit to receiue the Gospell, and prepare them to his voyce'.[66] It did so, Scudder argued, by softening penitents' flinty hearts so that they may pray 'more deuoutly, more feelingly, more feruently, and with more assurance of a gracious hearing'. Moreover, in Henry Bull's view, it sharpened desire: 'earnest sorow and vexation of minde' for sin engendered 'a feruent desire to obtayne comforte, helpe and succour at Gods hande'.[67] Crucially, it certified that desire's sincerity. Expounding Psalm 51, where the penitent psalmist speaks of his bones being broken, John Dod claimed that this pain was the basis of the psalmist's confidence before God: 'for then hee might bee assured, that hee came not to God as an hypocrite with a double heart, but as a true penitent person with a troubled hear.' Weeping in sorrow, William Pemble wrote, testifies to the penitent that 'God is at peace with him'.[68]

One recurring image described repentance as medicinal.[69] Michael Sparke's *Crumms of comfort* opened with a fanciful 'recipe' for repentance, in which various virtues are simmered over the fire of love until 'the black foam of worldliness' is boiled off, and the resulting mixture is drunk down 'burning hot next to thy heart'. A little too cute to be taken seriously, perhaps, but one pious layman liked it enough to transcribe it in his commonplace book.[70] Daniel Dyke's variant struck a particularly important nerve. Repentance, he wrote, 'is not so sowre and crabbed a thing as most thinke. . . . The sheepe of Christ know that to feed vpon this salt marsh is the onely preseruatiue against the rot'. *Salt* was an allusion to tears of repentance, which 'haue a purging and a raising vertue'.[71] Thomas Playfere, a Cambridge theologian with a reputation for flowery rhetoric, took the same metaphor in another direction:

> Christ suppes with vs, when we entertaine him, as Marie did, with the salt teares of repentance & griefe. . . . For the salt teares of our repentance, are the onely drinke, which Christ will drinke with vs.[72]

We shall be seeing a good deal more of pious tears and the value which Protestants placed on them, but for now it is enough to notice their cathartic, healing presence at the heart of this process.

If repentance allowed sinners to see themselves clearly, it also, crucially, allowed them to see God clearly. As Catherine Brekus puts it, the point was 'not to wallow in the ugliness of sin but to heighten their awareness of God's "astonishing"

[66] Rogers, *Garden* (1616), sigs A2r–4v.

[67] Scudder, *Christians daily walke* (1628), 34; Bull, *Christian praiers*, 7.

[68] Dod and Cleaver, *Ten sermons*, 53; Pemble, *Introduction to worthy receiving*, 46.

[69] Valentine, *Private Devotions*, I.6 (eleven editions 1631–40, of which a total of five copies survive).

[70] Sparke, *Crumms of comfort*, sigs A11r–12r; Saxby, 'Miscellany', fo. 53v (the transcription omits one phrase, presumably in error).

[71] Dyke, *Two Treatises*, 5, 17; cf. Gee, *Steps of Ascension*, 225.

[72] Thomas Playfere, *Hearts delight. A sermon* (Cambridge, 1603: RSTC 20010), 26.

grace'.[73] To feel the reality of your own sins was to gain a clearer view of God's majesty. Perkins argued that true adoration of God depended on the Christian having 'a vile and base estimation of himselfe, as beeing but dust and ashes'.[74] Bolton had a more positive reading of what is essentially the same argument: 'By bringing true contrition and brokennesse into thy heart, thou shalt bring downe the great majesty of heaven to dwell in it, as in a royall throne.'[75] Either way, the net effect was to raise the penitent's heart to a lustre besides which the scouring of repentance scarcely deserved to be noticed.

This is, of course, preachers' rhetoric, but not always merely so. Archibald Johnston of Wariston described how one day he had woken alarmed to find his heart hardening into security, but that after reflecting on his sins he came 'to youle [bewail], mourne, and lament with many tears to my great contentment'. Another Scot, William Struther, observed that 'to feele our hearts melting in a godlie sorrow, is matter of vnspeakable joy'.[76] One Englishwoman claimed that:

> The most comfort to my spirit is, when I am weeping for my infirmities ... Me thinks I find such joy ... that I could dwel there, having no comfort in the world like that.[77]

It was in true mourning that you could feel the power of assurance, know that your election was secure since it depended not at all on you, and be overwhelmed by the majestic generosity of God.

It seems only fair to give the last word on this subject to Nehemiah Wallington. 9 February 1643 was a fast day, and began badly for Wallington: he rose soon after 2:00 a.m. to go to the fast, but went 'as a dogge to hanging: much drawing and hanging backe'. Chatting to a neighbour in church before the ordinance began, he was suddenly overwhelmed with a sense of sin, such that 'I could not speake without weepeinge ... the woman looked on me wondering what ailed'. That set the mood for the rest of the day. At the end he commented, 'this day was one of the best heart breking day and in keeping close to God then I have done a long time'.[78] 'The best heart breking day': that is a glimpse of the liberation which earnest Protestants could find in abject repentance.

---

[73] Catherine A. Brekus, 'Writing as a Protestant Practice: Devotional Diaries in Early New England' in Laurie P. Maffly-Kipp et al. (eds), *Practicing Protestants: Histories of Christian Life in America* (Baltimore, 2006), 24.

[74] Perkins, *Whole treatise*, 257; cf. Nicholas Bownde, *Medicines for the plague that is, godly and fruitfull sermons* (1604: RSTC 3439), 143; Wallington, *Notebooks*, 49–50.

[75] Bolton, *Three-fold treatise*, III.162; cf. Rous, *Mysticall Marriage*, 83–4, 86.

[76] Wariston, *Diary*, 69–70; William Struther, *Scotlands Warning, or a Treatise of Fasting* (Edinburgh, 1628: RSTC 23370), 75.

[77] Powell, *Spirituall Experiences*, 75–6.

[78] Wallington, *Notebooks*, 181–2.

4

Desire

'We knowe not what to praie as we oght, but the Spirit it self maketh request for vs with sighs, which can not be expressed.' *Romans 8:26*

THE NEED FOR DESIRE

True repentance was necessary for the earnest Protestant, but not sufficient. You also had to yearn: for holiness, and for God himself. Such desire, when it came, swept all before it. It was not necessarily pleasant. Here is how George Herbert described it in a poem titled *Longing*:

> With sick and famisht eyes,
> With doubling knees and weary bones,
>   To thee my cries,
>   To thee my grones,
> To thee my sighs, my tears ascend:
>   No end?
> My throat, my soul is hoarse;
> My heart is wither'd like a ground
>   Which thou dost curse.
>   My thoughts turn round,
> And make me giddie; Lord, I fall,
>   Yet call.[1]

But bitter as such desire might be, it was at least real. An honest emptiness that desired fulfilment was more nourishing than the false satisfaction of 'security'. True holiness is beyond reach in this world, and so an earnest desire for it is next best. This priority is there in British Protestantism from the beginning. William Tyndale wrote that the Christian longs for God as the sick long for health, and that prayer is 'a desire of the spirit to God-ward'. The Henrician Primer of 1545 concludes with a prayer for 'the desires of the life to come'. In the following century, Richard Rogers argued that Christians must hunger after redemption,

---

[1] Herbert, *Works*, 148.

'and desire it aboue all things . . . feruently & constantly, so as nothing can satisfie them without it'.[2]

The precise object of this desire mattered less than its intensity. It might be desire for preaching: Robert Bolton described Christians 'gasping for it, as the dry and thirstie ground for drops of raine'. It might be a 'breathing after' the sacraments and prayer. William Cowper said that true Christians have 'such an insatiable desire, that in this life they can neuer be satisfied with hearing, reading, praying, and communicating'.[3] But godly desire extended beyond such mundane matters. It might be the believer's 'desire to be a sound Christian with all his heart';[4] or desire for a particular prayer to be answered;[5] or the desire to glorify God, a desire which William Perkins described vividly as a burden on the soul to be cast off through praise.[6] John Bradford's perennially popular *Meditations* spoke simply of desire 'that thy kingedome mighte come euery where' and 'for the encrease of thy spirit'.[7]

At root, all these desires with which the Christian might be 'rauished' are one: the desire for God.[8] The longing which earnest Protestants described and to which they aspired was a love affair, frequently expressed—as was traditional—in the sexually intense language of the Song of Songs. John Hayward's *Sanctuarie of a troubled soule*, for example, prayed: 'Set me wholy on fire with thy loue, thy sweete loue, thy longing loue, thy chaste loue; with desire of thee, with contentment, with ioy, with sacietie in thee.'[9] His insistence that this desire is chaste is of course both correct and conventional—Donne's confession that he would never be chaste 'except thou ravish me' being the best-known example. But it is also a licence. If this desire is chaste, it is safe to give free rein to overwhelming passions within it. And truly, it is a lover's experience which these Protestants describe. It is an all-pervading desire, which may be as painful as it is joyful—but it is a pain that you seek and treasure. It is a desire that longs and joys in the desire itself, as well as in the God whom it desires. It is a desire which burns to describe itself, to spill out its vision to an uncaring world, but it is also, in the end, speechless.

This desire can be contrasted instructively with the desire of hypocrites and idolaters. We might expect that Protestants would see this as misdirected desire, but they commonly denied that it was desire at all: rather, a passing feeling which 'comes to nothing after', mere 'flashes', or 'idle, lazie, and lusking wishes, such as

[2] William Tyndale, *Doctrinal Treatises and Introductions to Different Portions of the Holy Scriptures*, ed. Henry Walter (Cambridge, 1848), 93; *The Primer, in Englishe and Latyn, set foorth by the Kynges maiestie* (1545: RSTC 16040), sig. V6r; Rogers, *Garden* (1616), sig. A6r.

[3] Bolton, *Discourse about happinesse*, 71; Wodenoth, 'Expressions', 123; Cowper, *Triumph*, 347; cf. Dent, *Sermon of Repentance*, sig. B7r-v.

[4] Richard Sibbes, *The Complete Works of Richard Sibbes*, ed. Alexander B. Grosart (Edinburgh, 1862–4), VI.98.

[5] Gouge, *Whole-Armor of God*, 343; Tuke, *Practise of the faithfull*, 50.

[6] Perkins, *Exposition of the Lords prayer*, 71–2.

[7] Bradford, *Godlie meditations*, sigs I3v-4r (eight editions 1562–1633); this meditation was also reprinted in Bull, *Christian praiers*, 28–9, (nine editions 1568–1614).

[8] Dent, *Sermon of Repentance*, sig. B7r.

[9] Hayward, *Sanctuarie of a troubled soule* (1602), 35–6; cf. Rous, *Mysticall marriage*.

the sluggards', never enough actually to rouse you.[10] Nicholas Byfield used this as a touchstone: 'the desires of the wicked' are 'dull and cold', whereas holy desires 'are fierie, that is, such as cause the heart of the man, to burne within him'. This was how Hayward could reproach himself for being 'rather willing then desirous, with my soule to loue thee', and pray,

> that the coales were throughly kindled with desire, and blowne with delight into a full flame. O sacred fire, how comfortably doest thou burne?...How desirous are they more and more to burne, whome thou doest enflame?[11]

Only true desire can burn with that intensity, and that burning is itself earnestly to be desired.

In other words, this is a desire that brings its own fulfilment. 'Bring longing, hungry, enlarged desires', Jeremiah Dyke declared, 'and fat and marrow shall be our portion.... A mouth wide opened, shall be a mouth full filled.' How could it not, if indeed 'desire...before God is praier it selfe'?[12] The Lancashire gentlewoman Katherine Brettergh was assured by one of her counsellors that if 'she had a desire to pray and beleeue, shee did pray and beleeue, and that so effectually, that hell gates should not ouercome her'. Richard Rogers argued that to 'seeke feruently to be setled in beleeuing' is, in fact, to believe; a colleague of his claimed, more dubiously, that if 'you desire with all your heart' to feel assurance of salvation, 'then doubt not, you shall feele it'.[13] The theological basis for this kind of argument was plain: godly desires were themselves a gift from God. It is impossible to long for grace unless you already have it.[14]

This was a wonderful means of negotiating predestination's pitfalls. Crudely, the argument was that the more you wanted salvation, the more likely you were to be saved. But it also raises a host of problems, the most obvious being infinite regression. If desire is equivalent to what is desired, what about desire for desire? And so forth? This was an urgently practical problem, not merely a logical hall of mirrors. The desire for desire was just as real as sorrow for lack of sorrow.[15] But was the desire for desire evidence of grace? Scudder apparently thought it was, urging those who felt themselves bereft by God to 'set about Prayer for it as well as you can, then God will enable you to pray for the spirit, and you shall haue it'. William Gouge was more austere, arguing that the unregenerate 'may earnestly wish for Faith, & desire God to giue it him', but cannot actually pray for it, since faith is a precondition for prayer.[16] This may seem like hair-splitting, but the logic is

---

[10] Sibbes, *Works*, VI.98–9; Dyke, *Mystery of selfe-deceiuing*, 97–8; cf. Dyke, *Worthy communicant*, 474.

[11] Byfield, *The Signes*, 85–6; Hayward, *Sanctuarie of a troubled soule* (1602), 145, 195–6.

[12] Dyke, *Worthy communicant*, 461–3; Tuke, *Practise of the faithfull*, 51.

[13] William Harrison, *Deaths aduantage little regarded, and The soules solace against sorrow Preached in two funerall sermons* (1602: RSTC 12866), III.15; Rogers, *Garden* (1616), sigs A6v, C5r.

[14] Sibbes, *Bruised reede*, 146.

[15] See above, p. 59.

[16] Scudder, *Christians daily walke* (1628), 687; Gouge, *Whole-Armor of God*, 260.

watertight, as is the barrier between human impotence and divine sovereignty which Gouge was determined to preserve.

In short, the problem of desire faced Protestants—again!—with a theological conundrum. In Reformed Protestantism, true desires, like other holy affections, are gifts which God gives from mere grace to his elect. As such, exhorting Christians to cultivate true desires is as futile as exhorting them to grow taller. And yet, Protestants consistently exhorted one another to do exactly that, just as they urged congregations full of predestined souls to repentance. There are explanations for this apparent contradiction, explanations which are viable if not entirely satisfactory. There is always obedience and honouring of God. According to this view, ministers preach, not because they expect anyone to listen to them, but because they are commanded to do so and because in doing so they justify the condemnation of those who are predestined not to listen to them. Or they are providing God's providence with the means to be fulfilled: he may grant holy desires to someone, but do so through the medium of your preaching. More controversially, there is the doctrine that R. T. Kendall dubbed 'preparationism', which teaches that unregenerate souls can, by effort, make themselves ready for grace—a doctrine which some (like Gouge) regarded as a fatal unravelling of predestination.[17]

Happily, we do not need to untangle this theological skein. Our concern is with how believers navigated this problem on the ground, and they did so by embracing both sides of the paradox. They used the presence—or absence—of desire as a sign of election. But they also used a range of means to stir up such desires within themselves.

KINDLING DESIRE

To prove that holy desires could only be gifts from God, it was common to cite Romans 8:26, the epigraph to this chapter and perhaps the single most cited verse in all Reformed Protestant devotion. The verse taught that prayer itself was God's work in the believer; and also that it was a matter, not of words, but of inexpressible sighs, or—as the King James translation had it—of 'groanings'. It was obvious, to early modern readers, that this referred to the desires we have been considering, desires which went beyond that which human speech could express. Without such desire, William Perkins insisted, there can be no true prayer, but that, Henry Bull's best-selling Elizabethan prayer book taught, is the natural human condition: to be 'dull and without all lust to pray'. Citing this verse, he described the only alterna- tive: the Holy Spirit 'stirreth vp our harts, giueth vs a desire and a boldnes to pray', a 'feruent desire and longing' which 'commeth not of our selues'. Gervase Babington was even blunter on this point. True desire 'is not at our commaundement, we

[17] Kendall, *Calvin and English Calvinism*. The state of the debate on this issue is well summarized in—and moved on by—Dixon, 'Calvinist Theology', esp. 177–80.

cannot haue it when wee will, the Lord hath reserued it to himselfe to giue, when, and where, and to whome, and in what measure it pleaseth him'.[18]

How should you respond to this doctrine? One route was to revel in it, in classic predestinarian fashion: to celebrate God's sovereignty, finding peace in the knowledge that you need not—and cannot—manufacture such feelings for yourself. Desires, Richard Sibbes argued, are 'the breathings of the Spirit', and as such they are 'trials of the truth of grace' which 'shew the temper and frame of the soul'. Robert Bruce promised his Edinburgh congregation that, if they had even the slenderest desire to pray, it was the work of the Spirit and so a sign of their regeneration. As Henry Greenwood put it, 'holinesse of desire doth seale Gods fauour to me'. If you found yourself spiritually hungry and thirsty, God be praised.[19]

However, the fact that true desires were from God did not absolve Christians from responsibility. Bull's affirmation of God-given desire quoted above was immediately followed by a warning that 'we may not be negligent and slouthfull to dispose and stirre vp our selues therto', but must instead pray at once for due fervour. Others agreed that Christians must actively seek God's gifts.[20] This was not, quite, a contradiction, not if you can accept that God can make a prayer its own answer. But it is, at the least, a little slippery. Henry Scudder tackled the problem using the Biblical image of the pool of Bethsaida, whose waters were periodically stirred by an angel; when this happened, the first invalid to reach the pool was healed. The invalids, Scudder argued, could not stir the waters by their own power; but they could wait for the angel's action with hair-trigger alertness. Just so, Christians must wait for the Spirit to stir up their own too-still waters: *waiting* here meaning something active, a constant readiness to leap on the slightest sign of God's action.[21] It is an appealing analogy, although not really compatible with the hard-boiled Calvinist doctrine of irresistible grace. It is less evidence of Calvinist doctrine unravelling under pressure, however, than a sign of how most believers managed to deal with its supposed contradictions from day to day.

Scudder's image of the angel was a play on what was by far the most common Biblical trope used in this connection: 'stirring up' of the Spirit within you.[22] In an age of central heating, 'stirring up' has become a half-dead metaphor, but in pre-modern Britain it referred to something which everybody saw, or did, almost every day. If a fire 'lyes raked up in the ashes, here and there a coale', it may seem dead, but a little stirring, a little blowing, and it may burst into fresh flame—fire, as

---

[18] Perkins, *Exposition of the Lords prayer*, 41; Bull, *Christian praiers*, 7–8; Gervase Babington, *A profitable Exposition of the Lords Prayer* (1588: RSTC 1090), 21.

[19] Sibbes, *Works*, VI.98, 100; Robert Bruce, *Sermons vpon the Sacrament of the Lords Supper* (Edinburgh, 1591?: RSTC 3924), sig. S8v; Greenwood, *Treatise of . . . Iudgement*, sig. F1v; Linaker, *Comfortable treatise* (1620), sig. A6v.

[20] Bull, *Christian praiers*, 8; Babington, *Profitable Exposition*, 22–6; Bruce, *Sermons Preached*, sig. Z1r.

[21] Scudder, *Christians daily walke* (1628), 683–7; cf. John 5:4.

[22] II Timothy 1:6, where the Greek makes the image of fire explicit.

always, being an image of God's presence.[23] It is a metaphor which provides a neat resolution to the problem of grace and works: our efforts—the stirring—are no more than the trigger for renewed grace, while both the fire itself and the fuel which it burns are already provided. In fact, the key human action it requires is a simple acknowledgement of need—a recognition that a fire is slowly dying away. As Robert Harris put it in his popular treatise on prayer, you must 'confesse thy coldnesse and present deadnesse, and so by stirring thou shalt gather some warmth'.[24]

As even this usage suggests, however, *stirring* had further meanings. It could mean bodily exercise: rather than lapse into cold, dull idleness, you must stir yourself. Hence Michael Sparke's exhortation 'to stirre vp our dull and heauy hearts to Prayer': out of your chair and onto your knees! John Preston compared forcing yourself to pray to using exercise to warm limbs which are numb from cold: the very effort brings its own reward.[25] Or again, as in Scudder's use, stirring might refer to waters. Nicholas Bownde preached that

> our hearts in prayer must bee working, like the great Ocean Sea, that sometimes commeth with great billowes, so that it bringeth vp things that are at the bottome of it. So we . . . must stirre vp the least desire that we haue, euen from the bottome of our hearts: and though our hearts were moued before, yet when wee come to such a thing, they must bee mooued a great deale more.[26]

But whether *stirring* is taken to mean fire, muscles, or waves, the implication is the same. This is a call to action: to movement, disturbance, shaking, and unsettling. This restless, unquiet dynamism is one of the hallmarks of early modern Protestant piety.

How do you actually go about stirring up desire? Chiefly, through the everyday staples of piety: reading, prayer and meditation, hearing sermons, and receiving the Lord's Supper. Scudder thought the Christian at the metaphorical poolside should wait for 'the motions and stirring of Gods word in you by Gods meanes', that is, 'reading, hearing, and meditating of the Word'.[27] If that seems general, it is because almost any meditation might do the trick. Considering and 'aggravating' your sins might, for example, lead to your being 'kindled with continuall prayer and desire', as you realize how desperate your need for God is.[28] Alternatively, you could meditate on God's love, which was, William Cowper reckoned, 'of all other meanes, the most forcible to rauish our hearts after the Lord'.[29] Or you could recall your own former experiences. Samuel Ward tried to stir up his desires by recalling his 'sweet experience and sense of the favor of God . . . on Sunday before

---

[23] Dyke, *Worthy communicant*, 425–6 (where the image is used in a slightly different context); Scudder, *Christians daily walke* (1628), 52–3.

[24] Harris, *Peters enlargement* (1627), 35 (nine editions 1624–40; this passage only appears from this, fifth edition onwards).

[25] Sparke, *Crumms of comfort*, sig. A4r; Preston, *Saints Daily Exercise*, 75.

[26] Bownde, *Medicines for the plague*, 130–1.

[27] Scudder, *Christians daily walke* (1631), 775.

[28] Bull, *Christian praiers*, 29; Sibbes, *Bruised reede*, 34.

[29] Cowper, *Triumph*, 338; cf. Rous, *Mysticall Marriage*, 287–8.

Sturbridge fayre'. George Herbert found that the recollection of past joys could kindle longing for more, observing how the memory of 'but one half houre of comfort . . . feeds not, but adds to the desire'.[30] Looking forward to joys to come could be equally potent. God's promises were a favourite theme of meditation throughout the period. Jeremiah Dyke, who compared stirring up grace to warming up for a race, advised his readers to 'take some of the promises and set thy faith to worke upon them'.[31] Other portions of Scripture could also serve the turn. Perkins even hoped that his readers' hearts might, like King Josiah's, 'melt at the reading of the law'.[32]

Alternatively, there was the direct approach. Prayers for holy desires are a staple of Protestant devotion, whether in a conservatively-flavoured Elizabethan best-seller asking to 'powre into our hartes a desire' for eternal life; the 'short Praier for zeale to pray' which opened John Norden's *A pensiue mans practise*; or Michael Sparke's prayer 'to couet with an ardent desire, those things which may please thee'.[33] This might be theologically ticklish—if you truly lack the grace of desire, you cannot pray for it—but in practice, brute force could sometimes work. Lewis Bayly advised those disinclined to pray to 'bend . . . thy Affections—will they, nill they—to so Holy an exercise'. As we shall see, dogged persistence was something which Protestants valued. Sibbes gave this a theological gloss: 'grace is strengthened by the exercise of it', he argued, and added that that fact itself is a work of grace and not the mundane consequence of forming habits.[34] Perhaps: but in practice the result looked much the same. In October 1587, Richard Rogers worried that he could not find a desire to godly study in himself, and resolved to 'labour to maintaine a delight in me that way'. Otherwise, he told himself, he risked 'many grevous calamities', calamities which 'I desire to feare'. Writing his encyclopaedic *Seven Treatises* a decade and a half later, he advised his readers to 'nourish and hold fast a loue and liking' of their godly duties.[35] We can see a glimpse of what this self-training might mean in the life of a less resourceful and more desperate cleric, Richard Kilby. In the midst of a drawn-out crisis in 1614, Kilby reproached himself bitterly: he had been praying for the grace to repent, but without 'enforc[ing] my selfe to practice the means', which was, he felt, mere mockery of God. 'Neglect of practice sheweth cold devotion. Therefore I purpose to force my selfe unto this businesse.'[36] This was a kind of spiritual mouth-to-mouth resuscitation:

---

[30] Knappen, *Two Diaries*, 121; Herbert, *Works*, 154.

[31] Dyke, *Worthy communicant*, 429; cf. *The Fountayne or well of lyfe, out of whiche doth springe most swete consolations* (1534?: RSTC 11211), reprinted in 1548–9 and 1626; Fawkener, *Collection of Promises* (six editions 1629–40, and a further seven by 1688).

[32] Perkins, *Whole treatise*, 296.

[33] *A godly garden out of the which most comfortable herbs may be gathered* (1574: RSTC 11555), fo. 141r (thirteen editions, 1569–1640); Norden, *Pensiue mans practise*, 9 (42 editions, 1584–1640); Sparke, *Crumms of comfort*, sig. E11r.

[34] Bayly, *Practise of pietie*, 264; Sibbes, *Bruised reede*, 208.

[35] Knappen, *Two Diaries*, 62; Rogers, *Seven treatises*, 246.

[36] Kilby, *Hallelujah*, 91. On Kilby and his struggles, see Peter Lake, 'Richard Kilby: A Study in Personal and Professional Failure' in W. J. Shiels and Diana Wood (eds), *The Ministry: Clerical and Lay* (Studies in Church History 26, 1989), 221–35.

desperately pressing the rhythms of life onto an apparently dead soul, and persisting grimly until something stirred. The persistence might reflect faith—itself a spark of life—or it might be because to accept defeat would be to succumb entirely to despair.

Wiser heads steered clear of such bludgeoning.[37] Daniel Dyke, a young minister of puritan leanings, wrote a hefty and best-selling book on the subject: *The mystery of selfe-deceiuing: or A discourse and discouery of the deceitfullnesse of mans heart*. His advice on cultivating desires was subtler than Rogers'. Rather than blowing yourself hoarse trying to revive cold ashes, he argued, you should watch for some hint of grace first—and then strike.

> Doest thou feele at any time, that thy heart is warmed with good motions...doest thou feele any sparkled of the heauenly fire; take thou the bellowes presently, blowe till they flame, cherish, and make much euen of the smoaking flaxe.

If the opportunity was neglected, he warned, the flowing tide would soon ebb. 'Within an houre, or lesse, all our heat is gone, our affections are growne chil.... And why? because we stroke not the iron whiles it was hot.'[38] Like Scudder waiting by the pool, Dyke both knew that grace must come first, and also believed that when it came, it could and must be seized.

ZEAL

Once desire was fully awakened, it led Protestants to a coveted, transported state, a state which they described most commonly as *fervour* and as *zeal*. The religious life of the earnest Protestant was, in large part, a quest to be fervent and zealous.

Fervour, universally taken to be an essential feature of Christian piety, is linked etymologically to fire, heat, and warmth, and in early modern usage the word was constantly linked with those images. Metaphors of vigour, water, and life also recur. Fervour was the polar opposite of coldness, dryness, and dullness. It was the quality which distinguished the sincere Christian from the hypocrite. Like all sincerity, it was easy to mock. Its defenders felt that they were swimming against the tide, in an age of sardonic, sceptical irony and sloth, which called lukewarmness discretion and true zeal fanaticism.[39] This was, of course, not a Protestant innovation. Zeal as an ideal of behaviour pervades the Old Testament; in classical times, it was a quality to which many Jews aspired and for which many Romans—especially Stoics—despised them. In this, at least, Latin Christianity firmly followed its Jewish heritage. The *Imitation of Christ* prayed for fervour: 'we grow chill, but are set on fire by you'. Persons' *Book of Resolution* requires meditation with 'fervour and vehemency'.[40]

---

[37] Rowan Williams, 'Religious experience in the era of reform' in Peter Byrne and Leslie Houlden, *Companion Encyclopaedia of Theology* (1995), 583.

[38] Dyke, *Mystery of selfe-deceiuing*, 352–3.

[39] Ward, *Coal from the Altar*, 5.

[40] Thomas á Kempis, *The Imitation of Christ*, ed. and tr. E. M. Blaiklock (1979), 112; Persons, *Booke of Christian exercise*, ed. Bunny, 7.

Protestants of all shades echoed these sentiments. A conservatively tinged English primer of Henry VIII's reign had its users repent that they love God 'not feruently as I oughte to do'. What Christian could possibly disagree?[41]

Protestant fervour, however, was focused particularly on prayer. Occasionally we find the word applied to other Christian exercises. Richard Greenham's disciples commented on 'his great zeal and fervency of speaking' when talking of God, and Richard Kilby even prayed to be able to read Scripture fervently.[42] *Zeal* has a slightly broader range of uses. But prayer was where Protestants expected to find fervour's fast-beating heart. Indeed, without fervour, there *was* no prayer. Prayer was defined as 'the feruent desire of the mind to God', 'the vigor & feruent intention of a mans Heart'.[43] Certainly it was only fervent prayers that could expect an answer. Even those who did not define prayer by its fervour did believe that prayers must be fervent to be answered. Thomas Goodwin claimed 'that the Scripture sayes, that the fervent prayer onely prevailes'—and if Scripture did not in fact exactly say that, everyone knew that was what it meant.[44]

But what, exactly, are fervour or zeal in this context? Even to ask is to miss the point. Defining fervour is like pinning a butterfly to a card: fervour is the very opposite of dispassionate scholarly objectivity. The only way truly to understand it is to experience it, or something analagous to it. But Protestants' descriptions of it do at least allow us to make such analogies.

To pray, speak, or act fervently is, simply, to do those things as if you mean them, without hypocrisy. Fervour is ardour, vehemence, hunger, or 'the stretching out of the affections'. Nicholas Bownde compared the fervent Christian to a man who has fallen down a well: 'hee would not onely call and crie for helpe, but he would straine his voyce, as much as hee could'.[45] This nicely captures the sense of earnest urgency, but fervour was marked less by fear than by hope. In John Preston's popular treatise on prayer

> A man is said . . . to bee fervent, when he puts all his strength to prayer, when he is very earnest, and importunate with the *Lord,* when he strives, and contends with him, though hee finde many difficulties, and impediments, yet he breakes through all.[46]

Fervour, then, is what the term 'God-bothering' might have been coined to describe.

[41] *A spirituall Counsayle, very necessarye for euery persone to haue* (1540?: RSTC 5871.9), sig. B1r.

[42] Parker and Carlson, *'Practical Divinity'*, 143; Kilby, *Hallelujah*, 10.

[43] Thomas Knell, *A godlie and necessarie Treatise, touching the vse and abuse of praier* (1581: RSTC 15033.33), sig. B2r; Bod. MS Rawl. C.473 fo. 4r. Cf. Bradford, *Godlie meditations*, sig. A4r; Perkins, *Whole treatise*, 266; Gerhard, *Meditations*, 236; and see below, pp. 99–102.

[44] Goodwin, *Returne of Prayers*, 233. The reference is apparently to James 5:16 ('The prayer of a righteous man auaileth muche, if it be feruent'). Cf. Edward Dering, *Mr. Edward Dering, his godly priuate prayers for Christian families* (1624: RSTC 6690), sig. A8r; Brinsley, *True Watch* (1611), II.53–4.

[45] Byfield, *Marrow of the Oracles* (1622), 548, apparently quoted by Nehemiah Wallington in LMA Guildhall MS 204, p. 305; Bownde, *Medicines for the plague*, 131, 133.

[46] Preston, *Saints Daily Exercise*, 117–18.

The word *zeal* was used slightly differently. Byfield described fervour as one of the components of zeal, along with willingness, so the zealous person is one who acts both with fervour and resolution.[47] There was some disagreement over quite what zeal was, however. Daniel Dyke saw it as 'a compounded affection of Loue and Anger', a compound which he compared to the way light and heat are joined together in fire.[48] But the Ipswich preacher Samuel Ward, in a best-selling pamphlet, disagreed. Zeal was not a single emotion, he argued, but 'an hot temper, higher degree or intension of them all'; its opposite was coldness or lukewarmness. 'In plaine English, zeale is nothing but heate'—hence his use of *zealous* and *fervent* almost interchangeably. All emotions can be zealous; all good emotions should be. This was the line which William Fenner followed in his *Treatise of the Affections;* his final chapter described zeal as 'a high strain of all the affections'.[49] If every emotion exists to glorify God, then zeal is the state in which every emotion is rightly directed and expressed to the uttermost. This, not Stoicism, is Reformed Protestantism's emotional aspiration: to blaze with every human passion, and to do so more purely and brightly than human flesh can bear.

As with desire, so with zeal: this was indeed something which Protestants earnestly sought even as they recognized that it was in God's sole gift. Prayer books are filled with petitions to 'graunt mee a pure intention, a feruent deuotion . . . wholly rauished and possessed with zeale'; and even 'that my prayers may bee so feruent, so zealous, so affectionate toward thee, that they may draw downe thy mercies vpon me'.[50] They knew, of course, that prayer could be a means to kindle zeal as well as a request for God to do so. Richard Kilby deliberately punctuated his prayers with frequent 'Amens', 'because I would be very earnest, and effectually fervent in my desire'.[51] But none of this could change the fact that—as Gervase Babington put it—'wee are not able of our selues to pray with that feruentnesse of spirite'.[52] Zeal and fervour were graces: which meant, of course, that they were doubly comforting to those who experienced them. A widely circulated treatise on self-examination insisted that 'feruent praying, can the Diuell giue to no hypocrite, for it is the speciall worke of the Spirit of God'. Bolton argued that 'if a man feele this fervent . . . hee may undoubtedly assure himselfe that he is sanctified by faith'.[53] So it is no surprise to find Nehemiah Wallington asking himself 'how shall I know I haue Feruency', and listing various symptoms of it.[54]

We might wonder why Protestants should have wished to be continuously in such an exhausting and unbalanced state. The Elizabethan cleric Thomas Knell warned against the danger of being 'quiet and settled' in mind, which might

---

[47] Byfield, *Marrow of the Oracles* (1622), 476.
[48] Dyke, *Two Treatises*, 134–5.
[49] Ward, *Coal from the Altar*, 3–5 (five editions, 1615–27); Fenner, *Treatise of the Affections*, 142.
[50] Themylthorpe, *Posie of Praiers*, 26; Sparke, *Crumms of comfort*, E8r; cf. Dering, *Godly priuate praiers*, sig. E1r.
[51] Knell, *Godlie and necessarie Treatise*, sig. A4r; Kilby, *Hallelujah*, 166.
[52] Babington, *Profitable Exposition*, 21.
[53] Rogers, *Garden* (1615), II.E5v; Bolton, *Three-fold treatise*, II.167; cf. Byfield, *The Signes*, 70.
[54] FSL MS V.a.436 pp. 112–13.

'quench the feruencie of praier', but it is not obvious that inner quietness is a bad thing.[55] John Preston's best-selling treatise on prayer suggested one answer. God values fervour in prayer, he argued, not for its own sake but because he uses it to reshape us even as we pray:

> When a man is fervent in prayer, it sets all the wheeles of the soule the right way, it puts the heart into a holy, and spirituall disposition, and temper. . . . Hee will haue prayer fervent . . . because, by vertue of that fervencie, the heart is made better.[56]

Fervour thus becomes a means to moral renewal. But it was more normal to treat fervour, not as a means, but as a self-authenticating end in itself. John Ball's catechism taught its thousands of readers that 'hunger after Christ must be feruent, as a thirstie man longeth for drink'.[57] Protestants long to be fervent as lovers long to be in love, and there is no arguing with them.

But by the end of our period there was an undercurrent of unease about zeal emerging. For not all zeal is godly zeal, and even godly zeal may need careful handling. Robert Bolton carefully distinguished between 'naturall fervencie' (an innate tendency towards heat and passion), 'artificall fervencie' (the deliberate attempt to cultivate fervour 'by art and industry') and true, spiritual fervour, which arises neither from natural humours nor human effort but from God. In practice, the three were not easy to tell apart. Hypocrites' prayers might appear fervent; they might even come to be lulled into 'security' by the apparent zeal of their own prayers.[58] And even true zeal needed to be tempered. Daniel Dyke worried that 'when we see a Christian, at the very first dash breake foorth into zeale, aboue the age of his Christianity, it is but an ill signe'.[59] When John Winthrop looked back on his teenage self, he—like so many of us in the same position—saw just such an unbalanced youth, 'full of zeal . . . which outranne my knowledge'. And he noted with pleasure how, aged twenty-nine, he navigated a spiritual crisis without any such error, 'prayeing fervently yet without any distemper of affection'.[60] The suspended Scottish minister Archibald Simson compared true ministers to candles, which combine light and heat; similarly, ministers must combine knowledge and zeal. Knowledge without zeal is like moonlight, bringing no warmth, but 'zeal without knowledge is furie'.[61] This sort of argument led to zeal being redefined, sometimes almost out of existence. Ezekiel Culverwell claimed that sometimes 'the sleepy prayer wherin truth through weaknes, offered vp in faith, is accepted', while the outwardly fervent but inwardly faithless prayer is not. Preston took this a step further. It was not merely that 'a cold prayer . . . will prevaile

---

[55] Knell, *Godlie and necessarie Treatise*, sig. A8v.

[56] Preston, *Saints Daily Exercise*, 116.

[57] John Ball, *A short treatise contayning all the principall grounds of Christian religion* (1631: RSTC 1316), 98 (eleven editions 1628–37, and a further 45 by the end of the century).

[58] Bolton, *Three-fold treatise*, II.174; Dyke, *Mystery of selfe-deceiuing*, 105; Culverwell, *Treatise of faith*, 327.

[59] Dyke, *Mystery of selfe-deceiuing*, 87.

[60] Winthrop, *Papers*, 156, 211.

[61] Tweedie, *Select Biographies*, 122.

sometimes as well, as a fervent prayer', since all true prayer is a gift of the Spirit. Rather, for Preston, persisting in prayer despite feeling dull and discouraged *was* fervour.[62]

If this reduces zeal to an abstraction, we can, however, also see something of what zeal and fervour meant in practice. Zeal did not follow a script, for it was by definition heartfelt and spontaneous. However, certain patterns do recur, which can be seen both from the outside—how fervour expressed itself in words and actions—and from within—when the zealous describe the experience of zeal.

Naturally, we see fervour most clearly in prayer. William Hacket, the deranged visionary and agitator executed in 1591, had a politically useful afterlife as a symbol of puritan fanaticism. Job Throckmorton described Hacket at prayer:

> Many strange pawses hee had in his prayer, and that a pretie while together, saying nothing, but onely groned and murmured to himselfe, and then hee would suddenly burst out into some passionate outcrie and exclamation . . . speaking sometimes in a kinde of lowe and base voyce, and sometimes againe in so high a voyce, that I thinke he might easily haue bene heard into the streetes: yet were most of his wordes vttered with much earnestnesse and feruencie, with puffings and beatings in a kind of snatching maner, as if he had bene halfe windlesse, and out of breath.

The Elizabethan regime's apologists claimed that a visit to any puritan prayer meeting would reveal 'the like disorder, like outcries, zeale without reason, like humming, like sighing and groaning'. *Humming* is not widely attested, but—as we shall see—all of the rest were indeed part of the standard repertoire.[63] Robert Bolton described 'the Spirit of prayer' as 'fervent and stirring . . . with groanes and sighs, and strong cries'.[64] For some—especially women, who were not supposed to be so vocal—exhibiting fervour was harder. It was said of the godly matriarch Elizabeth Juxon that 'the more holily that any one conferred, or prayed, or gaue thankes, the more heartily she shewed her zeale in saying Amen'; but there is only so much zeal that can be packed into a single word.[65] There was no barrier, however, to persistence and regularity in prayer. A treatise appended to the first post-Reformation English edition of the *Imitation of Christ* claimed that the godly, 'being as it were rauished beside themselues . . . pray the whole daye togither, without hauing anye minde of their meate'.[66] Such demonstrative symptoms are, perhaps, what led Bolton to warn that some hypocrites 'may seeme outwardly more fervent in prayer than some of Gods faithfull servants'.[67]

If Hacket was a flawed image of fervent prayer, the perfect one was of course Jesus Christ himself. In particular, his miraculous feat of sweating blood while he prayed became an unattainable benchmark for true zeal. In 1610 the royal chaplain

---

[62] Culverwell, *Treatise of faith*, 327; Preston, *Three Sermons*, 75; Preston, *Saints Daily Exercise*, 117.
[63] Matthew Sutcliffe, *An Answere Vnto a Certaine Calumnious letter published by M. Iob Throkmorton* (1595: RSTC 23451), fos 60v, 61v; and see below, pp. 208–14.
[64] Bolton, *Three-fold treatise*, II.167.
[65] Denison, *Monument or Tombe-Stone*, 104–5.
[66] *A short and pretie Treatise touching the perpetuall Reioyce of the godly, euen in this lyfe* (1568: RSTC 24230), sig. C7r; cf. Bradford, *Godlie meditations*, sig. I4r.
[67] Bolton, *Three-fold treatise*, II.174.

Anthony Maxey preached a sermon on the subject, which was swiftly published and ran through seven editions. This claimed that in Christ's prayer 'euerie word affoorded a droppe of blood', and described his state almost more as fever than fervour:

> His heart trembled, his ioynts shooke, his pores opened, and all in a sweate, he fell groueling and prayed. . . . So earnestly did he pray and sweate, that in the flame of this passionate feruor . . . thorow and thorow his garments it trickled to the ground.[68]

Bownde likewise believed that in the Passion, Christ 'strained himself to the vttermost not onely in bodie but in minde, and so earnestly prayed . . . that with it hee spent all his strength in soule and bodie', almost killing himself with prayer.[69] This is all very well as an impossible exemplar—and it was certainly used as such[70]—but some drew more practical lessons. As we shall see, weeping was strongly associated with true piety, but Thomas Playfere's sermon on the subject warned that tears must be sincere: 'drops of blood issuing from the heart, such as Christ did sweate in the garden'.[71] That was usually as far as the image was taken. John Clarke did ask, 'is the true Christian sometimes hot in prayer? hee will sweat'.[72] But in chilly Britain at least, most Protestants preferred to keep perspiration as a metaphor.

If these comments give us some idea of what fervour looked like, some witnesses also described what it felt like. The eighteen-year-old Elizabeth Isham was 'full of that joy which Religion kindeled in mee', one result of which was that 'through the vehemency of my zeale I offered my affections to thee my God'.[73] But zeal and fervour could be sorrowful as well as joyful, and indeed swing from one to the other and back again within the same prayer. Archibald Johnston of Wariston described how in a single day he 'was transported out of thy body by love, by hope, by joy, and above al by admiration', and then 'heavily cast doune and melted befor God'; what united both experiences was their fervour.[74] The elect Christian, Nicholas Byfield claimed, 'doth feele his heart oftentimes on a sudden surprised with strange impressions, sometimes of sorrow, sometimes of feare and awfull dread of God; sometimes of feruent desires after God'.[75]

At times, zeal seems to have transcended joy and sorrow altogether. Francis Rous prayed that 'these kisses of Christ Iesus kindle in thee such a fervent love of Christ, that thy soule may pant to bee united to him in a perfect and consummate marriage', a love expressed in 'groaning complaints'.[76] The finest example of this that I know of is a letter from the Scottish revivalist preacher John Welsh to his

[68] Anthony Maxey, *The golden chaine of mans saluation . . . 4. seuerall sermons before the King* (1610: RSTC 17687), sigs B3r, B5v; cf. Luke 22:44.
[69] Bownde, *Medicines for the plague*, 132.
[70] e.g. Sandys, *Sermons*, 38; Hooper, *Later Writings*, 314.
[71] Thomas Playfere, *The Meane in Mourning. A Sermon* (1596: RSTC 20015), 97–8; cf. Thomas Sorocold, *Supplications of Saints. A Booke of Prayers* (1612: RSTC 22932), 106.
[72] Clarke, *Holy Incense*, 50.
[73] Isham, 'Confessions', 20v.
[74] Wariston, *Diary*, 24–5.
[75] Byfield, *Marrow of the Oracles* (1622), 172–3.
[76] Rous, *Mysticall Marriage*, 224–5.

patroness, the Countess of Wigton. In Pauline mode, Welsh begins by expressing his desire for death, and then launches into an extended, astonishing ecstatic address to Christ:

> My soul panteth to be with thee.... I desire to be with thee, and do long for the fruition of thy blessed presence.... Thou who knowest the meaning of the spirit, give answer to the speaking, sighing, and groaning of the spirit. Thou who hast inflamed my heart to speak to thee in this silent, yet lovely language of ardent and fervent desires, speak again unto my heart, and answer my desires.

There is much, much more in this vein. Throughout, ecstasy is paralleled by a keen sense of absence, with groaning and sighing. Finally, after nearly two thousand words of these raptures, he tears himself away, with the telling comment 'I must remember myself'. If this has been bliss, it is the bliss of self-forgetfulness. Only then, for the first time in the letter aside from the opening pleasantries, does he actually turn to address the lady to whom he is writing.[77]

In other words, the recurrent use of *fire* as an image for fervour and zeal was neither etymological accident nor idle analogizing. 'Fire' was the single word which Blaise Pascal used to describe his indescribable experience of God on 23 November 1654. British Protestants a couple of generations earlier would have known what he meant.[78] As a house-fire warms chilled limbs, so Christopher Sutton could say of Christian zeal that 'if I am cold in deuotion, here I may warm me'. As fire melts sealing-wax, so Jeremiah Dyke described the fervour of repentance as 'a melting, a warming, and a softning of the heart, and a fitting it for the seale'. Gilbert Primrose spoke of 'the heat of the spirit that melteth the yce of our frozen eyes, & maketh the waters flow'.[79] As fire gives light, so a pseudo-Augustinian meditation on 'the feruentnesse of loue' could describe it as 'brighter then all light', and ask of God's majesty, 'What fire is it that warmeth my hart? What light is it that spreaddeth his beames into my hart?'[80] As fire warms food and makes it palatable, so 'no sacrifice is welcome to God without some fire, some warmth'. As fire purges and consumes, so an early Elizabethan Protestant could pray, 'kendle in vs the Fire of thi loue, to the pourginge, wastinge, & consuming in vs, al filthines and abhomination in vnright-eousnes'.[81] Above all, fire is alive, never still, always spreading, consuming itself heedlessly as it reaches upwards in self-offering. 'Kindle, o kindle my desires... with the fire of zealous loue to burne alwayes, and flame vpon the Alter of my hart', prayed Thomas Sorocold. 'How desirous are they more and more to burne, whome thou doest enflame?', asked John Hayward's ever-popular *Sanctuarie of a troubled soule*.[82] As a symbol of Protestantism's yearning restlessness, we could do worse than that paradoxical desire to burn forever.

---

[77] Tweedie, *Select Biographies*, 18–22.

[78] On Pascal, see Campbell, *Religion of the Heart*, 23–4.

[79] Christopher Sutton, *Godly meditations vpon the most holy sacrament of the Lordes Supper* (1601: RSTC 23491), 49; Dyke, *Worthy communicant*, 448; Primrose, *Christian Mans Teares*, 250.

[80] 'Augustine', *Certaine select prayers*, sigs G4r, L4v (five editions, 1574–86).

[81] Harris, *Peters enlargement* (1627), 30; FSL MS V.a.482 fo. 9r; cf. Dyke, *Two Treatises*, 135.

[82] Sorocold, *Supplications of Saints* (1612), 121; Hayward, *Sanctuarie of a troubled soule* (1602), 196.

5
Joy

'I knowe a man in Christ...which was taken vp into the thirde heauen....
He was taken vp into Paradise, & heard wordes which can not be spoken.'
II Corinthians 12:2, 4.

PROTESTANTS AND HAPPINESS

Even if we accept that early modern Protestantism embraced the emotions, to suggest that it was joyful may stretch credibility. Yet it was a truism of Protestant pastoral theology that true Christians can and ought to be happy. The best-selling Protestant devotional books of the period include titles like *The iewell of ioye*, *The perpetuall Reioyce of the godly*, *Hearts delight*, *A discourse about the state of true happinesse*, *A Helpe to true Happinesse* or *The way to true happines*. But the recurrence of the phrase *'true* happiness' is a clue that 'happiness' and 'joy' had, in this context, changed their meaning from the normal vernacular usage.

The paradox is obvious. On the one hand, as Jean Williams points out, many puritan texts 'express immense enjoyment...sometimes even ecstatic in nature'. Scholars now regularly point out that even for the precise, piety did not equal misery. Yet these comments sometimes still have a grudging or surprised air to them,[1] and puritanism's reputation for maudlin gloom is not merely posterity's slander. Richard Hooker had this to say about his puritan enemies:

> Every worde otherwise then severely and sadly uttered, seemed to pearce like a sword thorow them. If any man were pleasant, their maner was presently with deepe sighes to repeate those words of our Saviour Christ, Wo be to you which now laugh, for ye shal lament.[2]

Such views were a staple of anti-puritan writing. The moderate royalist Thomas Fuller spoke against the 'affected gravity' of those who 'antedate their age to seem

---

[1] Jean Williams, 'Puritanism: a piety of joy', *Kategoria* 10 (1998), 12; Bruce C. Daniels, *Puritans at Play: Leisure and Recreation in Colonial New England* (New York, 1995). Bozeman, *Precisianist Strain*, 170, suggests that puritans found 'a cheering sense of achievement' in their own self-perceived elite status.

[2] Richard Hooker, *Of the Laws of Ecclesiastical Polity: Preface, Books I to IV*, ed. Georges Edelen (Cambridge, MA, 1977), 43. The description purported to be of Anabaptists but was transparently intended to apply to English Puritans.

farre older then they are, and plait and set their brows in an affected sadnesse'.[3]
Some in the broad puritan coalition clearly agreed. Richard Greenham felt the need
to deny that 'wee should keep a continual sorrowing', and believed 'that sathan
under the colour of repentance did bring many into an extream sadnes and
stricknes'. The court preacher Thomas Playfere opposed those who taught that
Christians 'shouldst abandon all delight'. Joseph Hall's influential *Meditations*
worried that 'many Christians doe greatly wrong themselues with a dull and
heauy kind of sullennesse', and Robert Bolton tried to refute the claim that the
godly lead 'a life full of vncomfortablenesse, melancholy, austeritie and sadnesse'.[4]

The impetus behind these puritan denials—which become less convincing the
more they are repeated—was openly a polemical and apologetic one. The belief that
earnest piety meant unhappiness hardly attracted converts. Richard Rogers was well
aware of the charge that some of those 'who are more religious than the most part of
others' were 'euer sad and sorrowfull', a perception which 'causeth many to shun
religion'. He urged believers to 'moderate their heauines, that they may offend as
few as they may'.[5] Lewis Bayly's *The practise of pietie*, the best-selling Protestant
devotional work of the period, also tackled the evidently widespread belief
that earnest piety makes Christians—especially the young—'to waxe too sad and
pensiue'. He again denied that this was so, arguing that Christian joy in fact
transcended worldly joy, but he was then driven to defend 'the godly sorrow of
the godly' as quite different from worldly sorrow, which hardly helped his case. And
by the next page he was declaring: 'Better it is to goe sickly (with Lazarus) to
Heauen, than full of mirth and pleasure, with Diues, to Hell.' When he turned to
the subject of mirth later in the book, he handled it with fastidious distaste,
deploring 'the frothie wit of a filthy nature'. 'If', he added, 'thou be disposed to
be merrie . . . be as merrie as thou canst, onely in the Lord.' Clearly merriment was,
at best, unbecoming a Christian.[6]

For while Protestants of all stripes wanted to insist that they could be joyful, they
also wanted to make it very clear that they did not mean worldly joy. The early
Elizabethan treatise *The perpetuall Reioyce of the godly*, which was the first systematic
attempt in English to deny that Protestants are miserable, argued that Christians are
'rauished as it were besides themselues', and therefore 'they refraine from wine, doe
fast, sigh, are sorye, weepe, continue all night in prayer . . . and by other meanes doe
tame their fleshe'. The worldly, observing this, conclude that they are 'pieuish or
melancholike'; in fact they merely suffer from 'ouermuch ioye'.[7] Behind the sheer
brass neck of this claim lies a wider willingness to redefine 'joy' almost out of
recognition. In particular, Bayly's coolness towards mirth was widely shared.
Nicholas Bownde noted with disdain that the godless, when they are merry, 'fall

   [3] Thomas Fuller, *Thomas Fuller's The Holy State and the Profane State*, ed. Maximilian Graff Walten
(New York, 1938), II. 81.
   [4] Parker and Carlson, 'Practical Divinity', 136, 178; Playfere, *Hearts delight*, 8; Joseph Hall,
Meditations and Vowes, Diuine and Morall: A third Century (1606: RSTC 12680.5), III.13; Bolton,
Discourse about happinesse, 46.
   [5] Rogers, *Seven treatises*, 55–6.   [6] Bayly, *Practise of pietie*, 211–14, 294.
   [7] *Short and pretie Treatise*, sigs B3v–4r.

into an immoderate profusion and laughter', while the godly sing psalms.[8] If Protestants commended laughter at all, it was only in the Biblical sense of laughing opponents to scorn and triumphing in victory, which was hardly going to help their reputation for good fellowship. William Whateley acknowledged, grudgingly, that since God created laughter it must have a legitimate purpose, but added that 'one must not giue himselfe to it'. He would have understood the 18th-century American aspiration to 'sober mirth'.[9] In a 1647 tract, the Presbyterian minister John Angier argued that to laugh or even to smile in church betrayed 'fleighty thoughts of Gods worship'. He admitted that God could place such 'sudden, full and forcible joy' into believers that, in extremis, they could not help but smile, but to laugh was wholly unacceptable, because 'the ordinance gives no such occasion'. Since ministers do not crack jokes, to laugh in church proved that you were not paying attention.[10] Whatever else Protestantism was, it was not *fun*.

Early modern Catholics would not, of course, have conceded an inch to their Protestant opponents on solemnity. But some Protestants did worry that their reputation for austere melancholy had a confessional edge. According to the Laudian John Duncon, English converts to Catholicism claimed that they found the emotional experience of their new religion more satisfying than the old. They would say:

> Though we employed our selves in *holy and religious duties*, with diligence and earnestnesse; yet we wanted those *comforts & delights* in them which we now find: there are no *joys* like those *joys* we now *tast*, since we were *reconciled to the Church of Rome*.[11]

Naturally this supported Duncon's advocacy of more structured piety in the Church of England. But he was not alone in the fear that Protestantism's strict sorrowfulness was costing converts.

One obvious response was to make joy a duty. As Greenham pointed out, the Bible's repeated injunction, 'Rejoice!', is not an encouragement but a 'flat precept'.[12] Sometimes this was explicitly about public relations: being visibly joyful might win converts. This applied particularly to mourning for the dead, where Protestants were concerned not to grieve as those who have no hope. 'At the burials of the faithfull', Thomas Becon's hugely popular *The sycke mans salue* taught, 'there shuld rather be ioy & gladnes, then mourning & sadnes.'[13] However, the duty to be joyful was more an obligation to God and to yourself than to your neighbour. Sometimes it was phrased softly, in terms of a permission: as in Thomas Ford's insistence that 'God loves not to see us lumpish and melancholy, but chearfull and

[8] Nicholas Bownde, *The Doctrine of the Sabbath, Plainely layde forth, and soundly proued* (1595: RSTC 3436), 237–8.
[9] William Whately, *The Redemption of time* (1606: RSTC 25318), 23; Daniels, *Puritans at Play*, 17–19; cf. Pigg, *Meditations concerning praiers*, 30.
[10] John Angier, *An Helpe to Better Hearts, for Better Times* (1647: Wing A3164), 84–6.
[11] Duncon, *Returnes*, 98.
[12] Parker and Carlson, 'Practical Divinity', 178.
[13] Thomas Becon, *The sycke mans salue* (1561: RSTC 1757), 151–2 (25 editions 1560–1632).

joyfull in his service',[14] but the positive requirement remains unmistakable. As a preacher in Oxford in 1605 put it, 'we ought to be delighted in [God], and in none other delites',[15] and since spiritual joy was fitting for the Christian, to offer anything less was 'to prouoke the Lord'. Playfere warned that 'no man may come into the court of our king, which . . . hath not on the wedding garment of ioy and *delight* in the Lord'.[16] 'Those that have no joy in their religion', Archibald Simson declared, 'are atheists.'[17] The precept applied especially to hard times. As worries crowded around the Northamptonshire lawyer Robert Woodford, he reminded himself sternly that 'a Christian is called to reioysinge'. John Brinsley taught a duty to 'patience with cheerefulnesse in the middest of all our Trials', and Hugh Latimer claimed that 'where God requireth a thing to be done, he will have it done with a good-will, with a merry heart'.[18] It is reminiscent of Ming the Merciless: all creatures shall make merry under pain of death!

But it will not do to be too cynical about this, because the joy which Protestants spoke about was neither theoretical nor vanishingly rare. Their testimonies make clear that this was a vivid and life-changing experience, and while it is impossible to quantify it, it was plainly not altogether unusual. Rather than hearing exhortations to be joyful, it is time to hear those who actually were.

ENDURING JOY

We might divide the joy which early modern British Protestants felt in their faith into two forms: the enduring and the occasional.

Enduring joy—a settled inner peace in God—was more aspired to than enjoyed, but the aspiration is worth noticing because its mood is so strikingly different from everyday Protestant piety. This is a religion of striving, yearning, sorrowing, intense self-observation, and self-reproach, which aspires to burning desire and zeal, and which fears stagnation, 'security' and back-sliding. So perhaps—or perhaps not—it is surprising to find at its heart a longing for spiritual peace, a steady, and enduring joy in which the believer can rest.

The most popular and sustained exposition of this is a treatise by George Webbe, a distinguished preacher who could be found in puritan company but who was also made a bishop during the Laudian supremacy. Webbe's *The practice of quietnes* promised its readers that they might attain

> a peaceable disposicion of the whole man . . . a meeke heart, a contented minde, a
> charitable eye. . . . Our mindes should bee like vnto the Adamant, which no knife can

---

[14] Thomas Ford, *Singing of Psalmes the Duty of Christians* (1653: Wing F1516), '153', *recte* 137; cf. Playfere, *Hearts delight*, 8–9.

[15] FSL MS V.a.23 fo. 40v.

[16] Bownde, *Doctrine of the Sabbath*, 240; Playfere, *Hearts delight*, 9. Cf. Bradshaw and Hildersam, *Direction*, 129–30; Bayly, *Practise of pietie*, 608.

[17] Tweedie, *Select Biographies*, 124; cf. Rogers, *Seven treatises*, 55.

[18] Woodford, 'Diary' 23.xi.37 recto; Brinsley, *True Watch* (1608), 44; Latimer, *Sermons and Remains*, 112.

cut; like the Salamander, whom no fire can burne; like the Rocke, which no waues can shake.

The world, the flesh, and the Devil, Webbe warned, would conspire to disturb and unsettle Christians: but they should find their perfect rest in Christ.[19]

This quietness could be understood on a worldly or a spiritual level. The former—which is not quite so common—stresses how true faith can foster an almost Stoic indifference to worldly misfortune. In this way, William Perkins described how common humanity frets over the cares of life and strives vainly for riches, while faithful Christians commend such matters to God, sleep soundly, and can accept either triumph or disaster with equanimity. Christians, Henry Scudder promised, 'may liue without taking thought, or care in any thing'.[20] But this was easier in theory than in practice. When our sources give us real glimpses of earnest Protestants wrestling with adversity, they seem as likely as anyone to have their attention consumed by it. Robert Woodford knew he should rejoice in his troubles, but his diary is punctuated by his money worries, and by the sequence of near catastrophes and minor triumphs which navigating them involved. Woodford did not want for faith, but peace was a luxury he could not afford.[21]

More commonly, however, quietness was described in spiritual terms, as peace of conscience. This may seem strangely grudging, no more than the absence of inner war. If Protestant piety consisted largely of training the conscience in self-accusation, the peace to which these same Protestants aspired sometimes seems to be little more than the silencing of that same inner voice, the absence of 'heart-eating, and heart-vexing griefe, feare, distrust and despaire'.[22] Their more easygoing neighbours might find the whole enterprise a little quixotic, but notice the exalted terms used to describe this peace of conscience. For Thomas Becon, peace brings 'quiet minds & contented consciences' and 'is the greatest treasure vnder the sun'.[23] In her ever-popular *The mothers blessing*, Dorothy Leigh promised that nightly confession of sins to God 'brings so sweete contentment to the soule, minde, and conscience of man, that nothing can offend it', and that none of this world's tawdry pleasures can compare.[24]

This is partly about assurance. The assured Christian, Bolton wrote, 'lies downe in peace that passeth all vnderstanding: He is filled with ioy, that no man can take from him'.[25] As that suggests, a quiet conscience was more often a consequence of assurance than grounds for it. George Herbert's poem *Conscience* wonderfully describes its subject as a nuisance, to be beaten away with the cross of Christ like

[19] Webbe, *Practise of qui[e]tnes*, esp. 6, 10, 17, 28 (seven editions, 1615–38).
[20] Perkins, *How to live*, sig. A2r–v; Scudder, *Christians daily walke* (1628), 326; cf. John Norden, *A pensiue mans practise. Or the pensiue mans complaint and comfort. The second part* (1609: RSTC 18626a.5), 83.
[21] Woodford, 'Diary'.
[22] Scudder, *Christians daily walke* (1628), 337, 355.
[23] Thomas Becon, *The pomaunder of prayer* (1565: RSTC 1747), fos 27v–28r.
[24] Leigh, *Mothers blessing*, 87–9.
[25] Bolton, *Discourse about happinesse*, 71.

a malcontented dog. Addressing it, he says, 'Peace pratler, do not lowre:/Not a fair look, but thou dost call it foul.'[26] Again, faith trumps feeling.

But in practice, this link between peace and assurance was problematic. Robert Persons' *Book of Resolution* promised that the resolved Christian would enjoy 'heavenly peace, and tranquillitie of mind', a promise which his Protestant editor felt the need to weaken considerably, despite the fact that he believed in assurance of salvation and Persons did not.[27] Indeed, tying peace to assurance immediately, and self-defeatingly, invites you anxiously to measure your own inner peace. Daniel Dyke's best-selling posthumous treatise on self-deception included a lengthy section analysing inner joy, in which the durability of the experience was the key criterion. He compared true joy to a spring of fresh water, 'orderly, and leysurely', renewing itself even in the burning drought of persecution, whereas false joy was 'a standing poole, which is dried vp in the heate of the summer', and which brings forth no fruit.[28] Theologically sound, perhaps, but it is hard to believe that these strictures brought much comfort to those in distress of conscience, since they imply that distress of conscience is itself a worrying sign. Inner peace would find earnest Protestants' intense self-consciousness to be a restless bedfellow.

Unsurprisingly, then, enduring peace was longed and prayed for more than it was enjoyed. From the beginning, Protestants prayed for peace, but they did so as lovers pledge faithfulness, as much in stubborn, self-fulfilling hope as in expectation. Miles Coverdale's collection of psalms and hymns half-echoed Augustine by praying, 'My herte is never set at rest,/Tyll thy swete worde have conforted me.' An unpublished early Elizabethan prayer book begged, 'that I maie rest in thee, and that mi harte maie fullie bee pacified and quieted in thee'. The most popular of the Elizabethan collections declared that in prayer we can find 'most ioyful & perfect quietnes', and some editions incorporated a set of prayers asking, 'Graunt mee aboue all things I may . . . fully quiet & pacifie my heart in thee'.[29]

It is hard to know how far such prayers were answered. The best evidence we have for inner experience—journals and autobiographical accounts—naturally pay more attention to change and variation than they do to constant states. The diarist who enjoys a settled inner peace for a decade will not note the fact every day. Even so, there is a striking paucity of references to enduring joy in these sources, especially compared to the frequency with which the prescriptive literature recommends it. There are some exceptions, such as intervals of peace and joy following conversion. Arthur Wodenoth described an extended period of 'soule ravishing delight and contentment' after his conversion, during which he was indifferent to worldly poverty.[30] Richard Norwood claimed that the seven months following his

[26] Herbert, *Works*, 105–6.
[27] Persons, *Booke of Christian exercise*, ed. Bunny, 198–9; cf. Persons, *Christian Directory*, ed. Houliston, 167.
[28] Dyke, *Mystery of selfe-deceiuing*, 79–87; cf. Bolton, *Discourse about happinesse*, 71.
[29] Coverdale, *Remains*, 560; FSL MS V.a.482 fo. 17v; Bull, *Christian praiers*, 2; Henry Bull, *Christian praiers and holie meditations* (1596: RSTC 4032), 364. Cf. William Hunnis, *Seuen Sobs of a Sorrowfull Soule for Sinne* (1583: RSTC 13975), 3.
[30] Wodenoth, 'Expressions', 123–4.

conversion were a time of 'wonderful solace and delight'.[31] But such interludes were often followed by further crises. Others attained a more settled spiritual peace in middle age, although—as in Nehemiah Wallington's case—this may simply reflect the impossibility of maintaining a pitch of spiritual crisis for decades on end. John Winthrop is the exception. Looking back on his life in his mid-fifties, he saw spiritual turmoil and crises until he was thirty, but recalled that at that age, 'the good spirit of the Lord breathed upon my soule', and he was never the same again. 'Now could my soule close with Christ, and rest there with sweet content, so ravished with his love, as I desired nothing nor feared anything, but was filled with joy unspeakable.' This state lasted 'divers months', and if it slackened thereafter, 'I was now growne familiar with the Lord Jesus Christ, hee would oft tell mee he loved mee, I did not doubt to believe him'. He would still regularly fall into 'dead heartedness, and presumptuousnesse', but never for long.[32]

Most, however, found that such ebbs and flows overwrote any deeper peace. Margaret Hoby occasionally noted in her diary that on a particular day she had experienced 'good quiatt of Conscience and rest', 'much Comfort by his spiritt', but while she would pray for this state to continue it seems to have been fleeting.[33] The question, then, is how this experience of occasional and intermittent peace can have been held together with an expectation of enduring and constant peace. We have a hint of the answer from James Melville, who said of his younger self that, 'onlie now and then I fand sum sweit and constant motions of the feir and love of God within me'.[34] That bracketing of constancy and inconstancy sums up the paradoxes here. These experiences were, as a matter of chronological fact, occasional and passing. But the experience itself contained a sense of timeless constancy. For as long as it lasted, it seemed to be enduring; or, to put it less cynically, these are temporary glimpses of something which appeared eternal, and that perception could become truer than the immediate experience. Thomas Goodwin described how a Christian might endure twenty years in which 'thy soule is battered, broken, hardened', but how a single word of peace from God brings such satisfaction 'that he would bee content to bee as many yeers more, in his spirituall conflicts, to enjoy but the like light, one halfe houre'.[35] This is a joy and peace which can flourish in the midst of suffering and strife, and we have no reason to doubt that it was real. But it is also fair to note that it is some way from the ordinary meaning of those words.

FLEETING JOY

Occasional joy is more widely and vividly documented: sudden, transporting ecstasy, the stab of delight which lifted believers, as it seemed, into the very presence of God. Archibald Johnston of Wariston described an event which is again reminiscent of Pascal:

---

[31] Norwood, *Journal*, 84. [32] Winthrop, *Papers*, 158–60.
[33] Hoby, *Diary*, 103, 140. [34] Melville, *Autobiography*, 37.
[35] Goodwin, *Returne of Prayers*, 274–5.

O saule, remember to Gods glory and thy comfort on Sunday, 28 day of Julie, 1633, in thine auine chalmer, betuixt 4 and 6 heurs, wonderfully God poured out thy heart lyk walter befor him, evin mor extraordinarily nor ever he had doone in al thy lyftyme befor.[36]

His precision was not unusual. Richard Norwood, at his conversion, suddenly experienced 'a clear and heavenly apprehension of my Savior Jesus Christ with comfort and joy unspeakable'. This lasted, he guessed, nearly an hour, until 'Christ seemed as it were to be about to withdraw himself gently and lovingly'; but he added that 'one hour of these joys did far surpass all the joy and pleasure that I had had all my life long if it were put together'.[37] Others did better than an hour or two. Isaac Ambrose recalled that on 20 May 1641

the Lord in his mercy poured into my soul the ravishing joy of his blessed Spirit. O how sweet was that Lord unto me? I never felt such a lovely taste of Heaven before. . . . It continued with me about two days.[38]

Did he sleep and eat during this transport? Perhaps. John Downame claimed that some believers became so enrapt that they spent a 'great part of their time' soaring in heavenly contemplation, 'not stooping towards the earth, but when they are forced by naturall necessity; which being satisfied, and their bodies and mindes somewhat refreshed, they doe, as weary of the earth, raise vp their soules, and renew their wonted flight'.[39] *Forced* is perhaps the word, however. John Winthrop recalled one occasion on which he was brought 'to suche a heavenly meditation of the love betweene Christ and me, as ravished my heart with unspeakable ioye'—a state in which he entirely forgot a series of practical matters, including his own supper.[40]

These experiences were often associated with illness or with the deathbed, a pattern which makes sense equally in medical, psychological, or theological terms. Robert Bolton argued that experiencing 'the ioies of heauen' while dying was proof of 'a sympathy . . . betwixt the life of grace and endles glory'—a foretaste of the bliss the elect were about to enter.[41] Katherine Stubbes, according to her husband's highly stylised account, repeatedly burst out laughing on her deathbed—laughter here garnering a rare positive mention. 'If you sawe such glorious visions, and heauenly sightes as I see', she explained, 'you would reioyce and laugh with me.' A decade later another dying godly gentlewoman, Katherine Brettergh, interrupted those praying for her, crying 'Oh the ioyes! the ioyes! the ioyes! that I feele in my soule! oh they be wonderfull! they be wonderfull! they be wonderfull!'[42] For a first-hand account of a comparable experience, we can turn to the future minister Robert Blair, who, one July night in the early 1620s,

---

[36] Wariston, *Diary*, 75.   [37] Norwood, *Journal*, 81–3.
[38] Isaac Ambrose, *Media: The Middle Things* (1650: Wing A2958), 71.
[39] John Downame, *A guide to Godlynesse or a Treatise of a Christian Life* (1622: RSTC 7143), 535.
[40] Winthrop, *Papers*, 202.
[41] Bolton, *Discourse about happinesse*, 140; cf. Becon, *Sycke mans salue*, 477–8.
[42] Philip Stubbes, *A christal glasse for christian women* (1592: RSTC 23382), sig. A4v; Harrison, *Deaths aduantage*, III.31.

contracted a violent fever and decided that he was dying. But far from being frightened, he longed to enter God's presence:

> Though that scorching fever was burning my body, yet the love of God burning more fervently in my soul made me to feel no pain at all. It was not possible for my tongue then, nor my pen now, to express the great gladness and exulting of my spirit. I extolled my Lord and Saviour, yea, I sang to him.

After 'some hours' of this, the fever broke, he realized he would live, 'and the vehemence of my rejoicing also abated'. However, a further period of fever the following morning did bring 'a renewed rejoicing in God, though not so high as the former'.[43] Clearly this joy was delirious, but perhaps not merely so.

When he had recovered, Blair asked a minister what he should make of the experience. He was told to treasure the memory, but 'that I should not frequently expect the like'.[44] It was sage advice. For a few blessed individuals, 'flashes of joy' did become almost routine. The diary of John Forbes of Corse is full of claims that, in a particular day's prayers, he 'received . . . a sweet & lucid influence of spirituall & heavenlie consolation, love, joy, peace, & assurance forever', or something of that sort.[45] For most, however, these experiences were a good deal rarer. Some earlier writers express a blithe confidence that joy is a universal Christian inheritance,[46] but—presumably in the face of bitter pastoral experience—this gives way to warnings that some believers would rarely or never encounter it, perhaps not even at the point of death.[47] In August 1638, Samuel Rogers wrote in his diary, 'The Lord shimmeres through the clouds, and I am glad; oh it is uncomfortable to live a day without a sun.'[48] But others endured months or years in darkness. Divines tended to explain this both as a trial of faith, and also by insisting that the fleeting, elusive quality of these experiences was part of their nature. Francis Rous argued that God rarely gives us such joys for the same reason that we rarely give wine to children: 'it is too high for them'. George Herbert wrote about the stab of emptiness left by joy's sudden passing. 'It cannot be. Where is that mightie joy,/Which just now took up all my heart?'[49]

Indeed, these 'flashes' were often associated with moments of darkness. The young Nehemiah Wallington, looking at the stars one night, was 'ravished with the favour of God'; the next moment the Devil was tempting him to throw himself out of the window. William Cowper saw this as providential: glimpses of grace are given to arm us before trouble, or to relieve us afterward. Rous made the same point in more positive terms:

> Let us think that the parcels of glory, joy and strength which we now receive in the visitations of Christ Iesus, are a kind of wages paid aforehand to encourage us more cheerfully & confidently to the worke of doing and suffering.[50]

---

[43] Blair, *Life*, 17–18.   [44] Blair, *Life*, 18.

[45] Goodwin, *Works*, II. lii; Forbes, 'Diary', 45.

[46] For example, *Short and pretie Treatise*, sigs B7v–8r; Rogers, *Seven treatises*, 54–5.

[47] Culverwell, *Treatise of faith*, 50–4, 313; Denison, *Monument or Tombe-Stone*, 64–9.

[48] Rogers, *Diary*, 158.   [49] Rous, *Mysticall Marriage*, 330; Herbert, *Works*, 56.

[50] Wallington, *Notebooks*, 33; Cowper, *Triumph*, 71–4; Rous, *Mysticall Marriage*, 71; cf. Day, *Booke of Christian Prayers*, fos 105v–106r.

Still more strenuously, Robert Bolton argued that, occasionally, the Spirit inspires 'thoughts of spiritull rauishment, and vnutterable rapture, flashes of eternall light ... such an vncouth extasie and excesse, as is farre aboue ... the tongue of Angels, or heart of man'. The Christian who enjoys such a visitation feels 'as if he had the one foot in heauen alreadie'.[51]

This claim—that moments of joy now are glimpses of Heaven to come—was pastorally very powerful. There was straightforward encouragement to be had from it: Rous urged his readers to let 'the peeces and earnests of heavenly joyes' redouble their longing.[52] But it could also be used to flesh out the rather abstract Protestant doctrine of Heaven. There was an *a fortiori* argument: if 'the little sponkes of that joy' are so overwhelming, how much more joyful must Heaven itself be? There were entrancing word-pictures to be painted. This was a theme of John Andrewes' popular chapbook *A celestiall looking-glasse*, in which he argued—amongst other things—for Heaven's sheer size: 'all that euer God made besides heauen it selfe, is but as a prick or small point'.[53] There was reproach, too, suggesting that Christians have not taken the hope of Heaven to heart as they ought. Bolton urged Christians to meditate on Heaven daily, so that the 'beames of that incomparable ioy, should be able to dispell those mists of fading vanities', the so-called worldly pleasures.[54]

That suggestion of Bolton's brings us back, once again, to the paradox of grace and agency. These glimpses of Heaven were entirely God's work, an act of sheer grace, but believers nevertheless hoped that they could encourage them. Joy could, of course, strike at any moment, for the wind blows where it wills; but even so, there were patterns, visible to us as they were to contemporaries.

One important absence is worth observing. We might expect that joy would be tied to worldly events, either personal good fortune such as recoveries from illness, births, marriages, victories at law and so forth, or fortunate providences for the wider Church such as Protestant armies' victories, the accession of godly monarchs, or deliverance from terrors like the Spanish Armada and the Gunpowder Plot. But while events of that kind were certainly celebrated, those celebrations have a completely different emotional register from the transporting ecstasy of God's presence. Joy at worldly good fortune of any kind was qualitatively different from enjoying God for himself. The occasional Protestant voice points out that the two are not incompatible. Richard Norwood eventually came to believe that God 'doth not forbid us taking delight in that wherein there is indeed true delight, but is the author and giver of it'. Rous described worldly pleasures as a down-payment of greater to come. But it is more common to emphasize that spiritual joy is 'even a ioy of a different kind and character from other ioyes'. 'Hee that is full of this sweet spiritual ioy', Daniel Dyke claimed, 'loatheth the sweetest and most delicious honycombes of the flesh, or the world.' This was apparently what Elizabeth

[51] Bolton, *Discourse about happinesse*, 139.
[52] Rous, *Mysticall Marriage*, 224–5.
[53] Andrewes, *Celestiall looking-glasse*, 16; Bruce, *Sermons Preached*, sig. X2v; Foxe, *Sermon of Christ crucified*, fo. 28v.
[54] Robert Bolton, *Some generall directions for a comfortable walking with God* (1626: RSTC 3251), 65; Persons, *Booke of Christian exercise*, ed. Bunny, 155.

Isham meant when, aged eighteen and 'full of that joy which Religion kindeled in mee', she decided, in 'the vehemency of my zeale', to forgo marriage. She kept to the resolution despite her suitors, to at least one of whom she was clearly drawn.[55] Nothing compared to her first love.

Naturally, then, this love's joys came most of all when believers were consciously in God's presence. Joseph Hall, whose work was read across the Protestant spectrum in the 17th century, wrote that through meditation 'we are rauished with blessed Paul into Paradise; and see that heauen which we are loath to leaue, which we cannot vtter'. It is worth noticing how cognitive and consciously intellectual this is.[56] The 1568 tract *The perpetuall Reioyce of the godly* claimed that, while the common herd are tormented with worldly cares, the faithful 'doe sweetely solace themselues with most pleasant thoughtes, and thinke themselues present among the companies of angels'. Listing the doctrines to be meditated on, it advises Christians to fix their minds 'vpon these and such other cogitations', promising that they will lead directly to outbursts of uncontrollable joy.[57] Thomas Tymme claimed that 'if there be a Paradise in this life, it is in one of these two, either in religious Meditation, or else in holy Studies, and godly Speculation'.[58] The implication was that a serious effort at meditation could generate joy. This indeed was John Winthrop's experience. On a journey to London in February 1617, he worked hard to concentrate on his meditations rather than looking around him as he travelled. 'I founde it verye hard to bringe my heart heerunto, my eyes were so eager of wanderinge.' But it was worth it:

> After I gatt into it, I found great sweetnesse therein. . . . I am not able to expresse the understandinge which God gave me in this heavenly matter, neither the ioye that I had in the apprehension thereof.[59]

In this case, at least, grace and effort complemented one another smoothly.

Testimonies from across our period describe the joy to be found in straightforward prayer. It could bring 'sweet & strong consolation'; 'it taketh away the bitterness of all afflictions'; 'it is a sweet thing to open our harts to our God, as to a frinde'.[60] In particular, prayer could bring moments of relief to those in spiritual turmoil. Winthrop, passing through such a period in his youth, recalled that 'sometimes I should find refreshing in prayer'; for James Melville, on his deathbed, 'his only refreschment and releiff . . . wes prayer'.[61] John Norden implied that this ought to work almost automatically. In his hugely popular dialogue

---

[55] Norwood, *Journal*, 75; Rous, *Mysticall Marriage*, 93–5, 256; Dyke, *Mystery of selfe-deceiuing*, 78; Isham, 'Confessions', fo. 20v.

[56] Joseph Hall, *The Arte of Divine Meditation* (1606: RSTC 12642), 3–4; see below, pp. 262–70.

[57] *Short and pretie Treatise*, sigs B4v–B6r.

[58] Thomas Tymme, *A siluer watch-bell* (1610: RSTC 24424), sig. A3r.

[59] Winthrop, *Papers*, 196–7.

[60] Forbes, 'Diary', 8; Hugh Latimer, *Sermons by Hugh Latimer*, ed. George Elwes Corrie (Cambridge, 1844), 444; Brilliana Harley, *Letters of the Lady Brilliana Harley*, ed. Thomas Taylor Lewis (Camden Society old series 58: 1854), 15.

[61] Winthrop, *Papers*, 157; Melville, *Autobiography*, lviii; cf. Rogers, *Diary*, 94, 131.

between Hope and the pensive man, the pensive man is persuaded to pray. No sooner has he said 'Amen' than Hope eagerly enquires how he feels now, seeing that 'thou hast had a good scope to conferre with God: and no doubt but thou hast receiued by it no small consolation'. Indeed, the pensive man replies that he already finds his burdens lifted and strength renewed.[62]

Other religious exercises could have the same effect. We shall return to the joys associated with receiving the Lord's Supper. Preaching was less reliably cheerful, but the Exeter merchant, Ignatius Jurdain, was said once to have experienced 'such inward joyes, and ravishings of spirit as were unexpressible' during a sermon.[63] Bible-reading brought Nicholas Byfield such 'sensible comfort and rauishing of heart' that he described particular texts as 'wells of ioy'.[64] In particular, there was psalm-singing, which left the Cheshire gentleman John Bruen 'ravished in his spirit, with holy and heavenly joy'. To Francis Rous, psalm-singing's power to comfort and refresh the sorrowful and weary was proverbial. 'How often doe wee see a sicke Soule, to begin a Psalme, even in the belly of Hell, and yet end it in Heaven', with 'high Iubilations and Extasies[?]'[65] But plenty of singers began in Heaven: psalm-singing was often described as almost involuntary, songs of praise bursting out from the believer. This was Robert Blair's experience during his feverish ecstasy, when he sang Psalm 16 and others. Cowper imagined God reminding the believer that he 'hath filled thy heart with ioy, and thy mouth with songs of praise'. According to *The perpetuall Reioyce of the godly*, to meditate on God's benefits will lead believers 'to brast out into the praises of God, into Psalmes and Hymnes, into spirituall songs, singing and making melodie in their heartes vnto the Lord'.[66]

This image of joy spontaneously bursting into well-known song is an important clue to the nature of the experience. When Protestants who had experienced joy of this kind attempted to describe it, they regularly found that language failed them, and were reduced to stating that it was inexpressible, 'ioy vnspeakeable'.[67] But when human language fails, the words of Scripture remain. This is frustrating for historians: we would prefer to hear believers using their own words, and tend to discount the use of Scripture as mere quoting. We are forced, however, to accept using Biblical words, 'the language of God', could be more heartfelt than any vernacular.[68] If we want to taste the quality of this joy, we must follow the Biblical tropes which are used.

---

[62] Norden, *Pensive mans practise . . . The second part*, 53–4; cf. Psalm 1:3.

[63] Clarke, *Collection*, 457; and see below, pp. 346–51, 354–61.

[64] Nicholas Byfield, *Directions for the private readeing of the Scriptures* (1618: RSTC 4214), sig. A7r; cf. George Wither, *A Preparation to the Psalter* (1619: RSTC 25914), 3.

[65] William Hinde, *A Faithfull Remonstrance of the Holy Life and Happy Death, of Iohn Bruen* (1641: Wing H2063), 71; Francis Rous, *The Booke of Psalmes, in English meeter* (Rotterdam, 1638: RSTC 2737), sig. A2r–v. Cf. Parker and Carlson, *'Practical Divinity'*, 193; Winthrop, *Papers*, 197; Alec Ryrie, 'The Psalms and Confrontation in English and Scottish Protestantism', *Archiv für Reformationsgeschichte* 101 (2010), 124–7.

[66] Blair, *Life*, 17; Cowper, *Most Comfortable Dialogue*, 20; *Short and pretie Treatise*, sig. B6r; cf. Ephesians 5:19.

[67] Byfield, *The Signes*, 65.

[68] Narveson, *Bible Readers*, 55; and see below, pp. 224–32.

There were plenty to choose from. There is ascension, rising 'vpon the wings of faith, vnto the glory of the Empyrean Heauen', as in St Paul's visionary experience.[69] Or there is longing to die, again following St Paul's pattern.[70] The very act of bursting out into involuntary praise was itself a Biblical trope. Cowper had God ask the believer, 'Canst thou deny that I haue . . . made thy tongue burst out in glorying speeches?'[71]

But the most recurring Biblical image used for these ecstasies is, again, *sweetness*.[72] 'Sweet' had a superlative quality to it which can be lost on our own cloyed, overweight age. The reason why Calvin—for example—returned repeatedly to God's sweetness is that this was amongst the highest praise he could find. Its appeal was philosophical as well as visceral. In its medieval use—which was very widespread—sweetness had intellectual overtones, partly for etymological reasons: *suavitas* can refer both to sweetness and to persuasion, and *sapio* means both to taste and to know. It was only natural to describe knowledge and inner experiences as sweet.[73] This extended effortlessly to meditation on and contemplation of God. Bolton claimed that for the true Christian, knowledge of God

> is entertained and enioyed with a peculiar kind of sweetnes; with an impression of incomparable ioy and pleasure: It is far sweeter vnto him than hony, and the hony combe.[74]

Others saw sweetness more explicitly as an emotional accompaniment to true knowledge. A prayer of John Brinsley's asked that a true understanding of God's mercies might give rise to 'a sweete feeling of thy loue and fauour'. Richard Rogers put the causation the other way, arguing that 'without that sweete smell of his loue, wee should be vtterly lumpish, and farre from all cogitation' on God.[75] There is, of course, no contradiction. Sweetness is truth, and truth sweetness.

Even more significantly, for a tradition which abhorred dryness, sweetness was linked to water: taste, in the Aristotelian view, depended on moisture. When the psalms urged you to taste and see that the Lord is sweet—as some translated or paraphrased the text—and when they described the believer panting with thirst for God, they appeared as the same urgent, intoxicating need.[76] And the language of sweetness was often paired with the language of water, sometimes merging to speak of wine. Persons' *Book of Resolution* promised the Christian a 'sweet stream of pleasure' which would make believers 'droonken with the unspeakable joy'. John Hayward may have been deliberately echoing this when he described holy joy as

---

[69] Bolton, *Some generall directions*, 64; 2 Cor 12:1–4.

[70] Philippians 1:21–23. See above, 84–5, and below, 463–4; Rogers, *Seven treatises*, 59–61; Norwood, *Journal*, 82.

[71] Cowper, *Most Comfortable Dialogue*, 7; see, for example, Isaiah 44:23, 49:13.

[72] Amongst well over a hundred Biblical uses of the word, many associated with the odour of sacrifices, see, for example, Psalms 19:10, 119:103; Song of Songs 2:14, 5:13, 5:16; Revelation 10:9–10.

[73] I. John Hesselink, 'Calvin: Theologian of Sweetness', *Calvin Theological Journal* 37/2 (2002), 329; Mary Carruthers, 'Sweetness', *Speculum* 81/4 (2006), esp. 1000, 1008.

[74] Bolton, *Some generall directions*, 64; Bolton, *Discourse about happinesse*, 103.

[75] Rogers, *Seven treatises*, 59; Brinsley, *True Watch* (1622), II.199.

[76] Carruthers, *Sweetness*, 1001; Psalms 34:8, 42:1; cf. Rogers, *Seven treatises*, 64.

'a floud of pleasure . . . wherewith the hearts of the godly being watered, and (in a manner) Made drunken, they loose all sence of earthly things'.[77] A popular Elizabethan set of pseudo-Augustinian meditations included this meditation on joy: 'O sweete loue, O louyng sweetnes, let my belly eate thee, and let my bowels be filled with the pleasant wyne of thy loue.'[78] Richard Day's *Booke of Christian Prayers* injected a note of caution. He prayed: 'fill my minde with the streames of thy pleasures, & make my hart louesick with the sober drunkennes of thy loue'.[79]

The unmistakable word of warning in that aspiration to *sober* drunkenness raises an important question: to what extent was this kind of ecstasy a puritan preserve? Day's more conformist readership tended to distrust spontaneous exhibitions of religious emotion. Fear of enthusiasm was not yet central to conformist English religion—that would follow from the shock of Civil War-era sectarianism—but as we have already seen, it was certainly present, stirred by various indecorous puritan activities.[80] It is worth emphasizing, however, that this was a second-order disagreement. Everyone agreed that Protestants ought to rejoice in their faith: the difference was about how that joy was expressed. A prayer like this might easily have come from a puritan pen:

> Possesse my mind continually with thy presence, and rauish it with thy loue, that my onely delight may be, to bee embraced in the armes of thy Protection. . . . Be thou a Light vnto mine eyes, musick to mine eares, sweetenesse to my taste, and a full contentment to my heart.

But this is the Laudian point-man, John Cosin.[81] Certainly Cosin, like other conformists and Laudians who spoke similarly of transporting joy, took a dim view of certain expressions of that emotion, including psalm-singing. But an inner ectasy, perhaps accompanied with silent tears, fitted entirely with his vision of the Christian life; and is not very different from puritan aspirations.

Indeed, Cosin's prayer introduces our final Biblical image, not so ubiquitous as sweetness, but with comparably deep medieval roots and packing even more punch: *ravishing*.[82] This conveys a sense of lifting and of self-forgetfulness: so, for example, Michael Sparke wrote of how the believer wakes at midnight and is 'rauished in spirit, or . . . rapt vp to heauen with good and godly desires'.[83] Rous, who used the image extensively, linked it to wine, using the Biblical wedding of Cana. If Christ provides wine for our spiritual marriage to him, he asks, 'how doth that ravish the spirits that drinke it?'[84] It is also the very opposite of enduring peace or joy. Being ravished is a dynamic experience, and while it may have enduring consequences, it

---

[77] Persons, *Booke of Christian exercise*, ed. Bunny, 183; Hayward, *Sanctuarie of a troubled soule* (1602), sig. A3r–v.

[78] 'Augustine', *Certaine select prayers*, sig. P1r–v.

[79] Day, *Booke of Christian Prayers*, fo. 86r.

[80] See above, p. 74.

[81] John Cosin, *A Collection of Priuate Devotions: in the Practice of the Ancient Church* (1627: RSTC 5816.4), 77–8.

[82] Song of Songs 4:9 (King James Bible), and especially Revelation 1:10, 4:2.

[83] Sparke, *Crumms of comfort*, sig. A6r.

[84] Rous, *Mysticall Marriage*, 51.

is in itself brief. Above all, it is an experience in which the subject is passive. Indeed, it has more than a whiff of violence about it, as John Donne's use of it made plain. Even when human agency is mentioned, there is that undercurrent of force: Cowper described meditation as a 'meanes . . . most forcible to rauish our hearts'.[85] That fits nicely with a predestinarian theology which preaches irresistible grace, and with the experience of being overwhelmed with unexpected, unlooked-for joy; it also fits with the keen sense that this is an experience from outside the self. It is also, as with every use of the Song of Songs to describe God's relationship with the believer, strongly gendered. Almost every use of this metaphor that I have found comes from a male pen.[86] Perhaps it was inappropriate for pious women to express the desire to be ravished, even spiritually, or perhaps the prospect simply did not seem very appealing.

THE PARADOXES OF JOY

Throughout this exploration of Protestants' emotional world we have met paradoxes. This is not an accident. Paradox has been in Protestantism's genome ever since Martin Luther, who revelled in it with reckless abandon. This fondness for paradox is not simply a theological quirk, but a consequence of the Protestant reading of the doctrine of Christ. The ultimate paradox is God's self-abasement in Christ, and the death of the innocent to redeem the guilty. The reason Luther's vision was so intoxicating was that, for him, this paradox turned the world upside down.[87] Glory and the cross, guilt and innocence, sin and grace, youth and age, despair and assurance, joy and sorrow: in Protestant theology, these apparent opposites were the warp and weft of faith, woven together to the glory of God.

This was at least as true of Protestants' emotional experience as it was of their doctrines. For here there was an important underlying principle at work. As Cowper put it, 'the working of the Lord oftentimes is by contraries'. With God, nothing is as it seems. Luther would say that God's 'strange' work conceals his 'proper' work. Just as the gospel of grace was for so long hidden by the stern mask of the law, and just as persecution is a sign of God's favour, so apparent opposition from God and denials of grace are in fact his encouragement of his elect to greater faith and zeal.[88] As Perkins put it: 'God is a most louing father to them that haue care to serue him euen at that instant when he shewes himselfe a most fierce and terrible enemie.'[89] We have already seen that emotion could, in some sense, act as a source of revelation for Protestants, but that many Protestants were wary of this line of

---

[85] Cowper, *Triumph*, 338.

[86] For one revealing exception, see below, p. 94.

[87] On Luther's continued theological influence in England, see Alec Ryrie, 'The Afterlife of Lutheran England' in Dorothea Wendebourg (ed.), *Sister Reformations: The Reformation in Germany and England* (Tübingen, 2011).

[88] Cowper, *Triumph*, 16; and see below, pp. 247–56.

[89] William Perkins, *A Declaration of the true manner of knowing Christ Crucified* (Cambridge, 1596: RSTC 19685), 7.

argument.[90] This was not because they doubted that God could and did speak to believers through their emotions. It was because they knew that, sometimes, what he said was the opposite of what he meant.

This principle of 'contrary grace'—that feelings and perceptions are likely to be the exact opposite of reality—was very widespread.[91] It was a mainstay of conscience-literature, a genre whose argument can be summed up as follows: if you fear that you are not saved, that suggests that you are, whereas if you are blithely secure about your salvation then you are probably in trouble. The fearful should take comfort, and the confident should be afraid. But the principle pre-dates conscience-literature as such. Hugh Latimer preached that if you 'feel your own wretchedness and filthiness', but have faith nevertheless, 'you may be sure . . . that you are elect and predestinate to everlasting life'. John Hooper argued that weakness of faith was a gift, whose purpose was to teach us the virtue of humility. In a famous sermon preached in 1570, John Foxe spoke of the need simultaneously to daunt the bold with threats of judgement, and to lift up those who 'lye gronyng vnder the feere of Gods heauy indignation'. The path through despair to hope was a well-trodden one.[92]

By the early 17th century, this truism had become universal to the point of banality. In part this was simple pastoral practicality. As the literary scholar Charlotte Clutterbuck shrewdly observes, the consciousness of sin drew early modern Christians to God as much as it separated them from him. 'Sin . . . forces the soul to approach God as a lover, a "Thou", in the intimacy of dialogue'.[93] It is bad to know yourself to be a sinner, but it is worse not to know it. Hence a vein of bluntly reasoned reassurance. If you fretted that you could derive no profit from sermons, Robert Linaker asked you, 'How comes it to passe that you haue found out this fault?' The very fact of fretting proved that you had some measure of grace.[94] Robert Cleaver expounded the principle that 'they are likely to fall into least euil, who are most fearefull of falling into the same'. By this logic, even apparent lack of faith could be a good sign. Richard Rogers argued that if you lack faith, but 'complaine bitterly of the want of it' and 'striue against doubting', that shows a true faith that runs deeper than feeling.[95] Others picked up on a medieval theme which Latimer, amongst others, had echoed: those who are struggling with doubts and temptations have proof of God's favour in that very fact, 'for, if they

---

[90] See above, pp. 39–48.

[91] Kaufman, *Prayer, Despair and Drama*, 8.

[92] Latimer, *Sermons and Remains*, 175–6; Hooper, *Later Writings*, 222; Foxe, *Sermon of Christ crucified*, fo. 6r–v. Cf. Joseph Ketley (ed.), *The Two Liturgies, A.D. 1549, and A.D. 1552: With Other Documents Set Forth by Authority in the Reign of King Edward VI* (Cambridge, 1844), 378; Gervase Babington, *A briefe conference betwixt mans frailtie and faith* (1584: RSTC 1082), 31; Parker and Carlson, 'Practical Divinity', 193.

[93] Charlotte Clutterbuck, *Encounters with God in Medieval and Early Modern English Poetry* (Aldershot, 2005), 8.

[94] Linaker, *Comfortable treatise* (1595), 60. Cf. Bownde, *Medicines for the plague*, 139; Perkins, *Whole treatise*, 348.

[95] Dod and Cleaver, *Ten sermons*, 228; Rogers, *Garden* (1616), sig. A6v; cf. Ezekiel Culverwell, *The way to a blessed estate in this life* (1623: RSTC 6118.3), 14; and see above, pp. 46–7.

were not of God, the diuell would neuer be so busie with them'. Satan does not disturb those who are already sleeping securely in his domain.[96]

This kind of argument was no doubt reassuring, but it gives rise to troubling paradoxes of its own. If you seek encouragement in your own discouragement, success will undo itself. This was most obviously problematic when pride and humility were at issue. As Bolton observed, 'a godly man . . . may be proud that he is not proud, euen of his humilitie . . . . So endlesse are the mazes of Satans circular temptations.' Thomas Tuke's popular collection of prayers observed that some professed believers

> are *humble-proud*, proud of humblenesse: but indeed he, that is proud of humilitie, doth want humilitie, and swels with insolencie. . . . Let no man thinke he deserues to bee heard for his humilitie.[97]

But it was easier to diagnose than cure this problem. Nehemiah Wallington was appalled by his own 'pride in Humiliti . . . the more humble I am, the more proud I am'. He was at a loss to know how to escape this cycle.[98] Perhaps the only way out of it would have been a lively sense of the ridiculous, but that was not early modern Protestantism's strong point.

These paradoxes, however, were not simply pastoral. Beneath them lay a deeper theological paradox: that believers find strength in dependence and weakness. This was a principle of which all attentive Christians were aware, but—as Robert Blair put it, reflecting on a moment of revelation in his own life—'it is one thing to know a truth naturally', and another to attain to the 'true and spiritual knowledge [which] is affectionate and practical'. So, as Richard Sibbes argued, God brings us to spiritual desolation in order to foster exactly that kind of heartfelt dependence.[99] George Herbert described it from within. When he reached the point at which 'none of my books will show' what is to be done, at which head-learning is useless, only one course remained: 'though thou troublest me, I must be meek;/In weaknesse must be stout'.[100] But it is important to notice that this was not simply a pleasing paradox; rather, a sober description of reality. The experience of being broken, Protestants insisted, produces true strength. 'Onely a rent and broken heart, is a whole and sound heart.' Sibbes argued that 'wee learne to stand by falls, and get strength by weaknes discovered, we take deeper root by shaking'. Daniel Featley even applied this principle to that ultimate moment of human helplessness, childbirth, exhorting women to find strength in their 'greatest weakness': whether we read that as compassionate or as crass, it was in earnest. We may perhaps take John Donne's witness a little more seriously: lamenting that 'my devoutt fitts come

[96] Dent, *Plaine mans path-way*, 244; cf. Latimer, *Sermons by Hugh Latimer*, 441, Hieron, *Helpe vnto Deuotion* (1608), 111; Cowper, *Triumph*, 43.

[97] Bolton, *Discourse about happinesse*, 27; Tuke, *Practise of the faithfull*, 16–17 (nine editions 1613–36, of which a total of two copies survive).

[98] LMA Guildhall MS 204, p. 24.

[99] Blair, *Life*, 22–4; Sibbes, *Bruised reede*, 342–3.

[100] Herbert, *Works*, 48.

and go away/Like a fantastique Ague', he added that 'Those are my best dayes, when I shake with feare.'[101]

A more vivid and unusual example comes from the famous, notorious revivalist meeting at Kirk o'Shotts in Lanarkshire in June 1630.[102] The minister John Livingstone spent the entire Sunday night in prayer. On the Monday morning, contemplating the sermon he was about to preach, 'there came such a misgiving of spirit upon me, considering my unworthiness and weakness, and the multitude and expectation of the people', that he was sorely tempted to creep away somewhere to hide—and presumably to sleep. Instead, he steeled himself to preach, and did so for an hour and a half, on God's promise to replace hearts of stone with hearts of flesh. At the end, exhausted, he intended to close with a few words of exhortation. Instead, 'I was led on about ane hour's time in ane strain of exhortation and warning, with such liberty and melting of heart as I never had the like in publick all my life.'[103]

Here, perhaps, we can see how this pursuit of paradox connects to the question of joy. As with the ambiguous image of ravishment, the language here is not straightforwardly happy. The desire for God, and the sense of a consummation which is transporting but—in this life—only ever provisional, is a matter both of pleasure and of pain. Yet the more this kind of pain burns you, the more keenly you cherish it. Sweetness is all very well, but as Featley observed, 'in our spirituall oblations nothing pleaseth GOD that is onely sweete, and hath not some smacke in it of biting truth'.[104]

We are dealing here with emotions that have reached such a pitch that it is unclear whether they are sweet, bitter, or passions so hot that their taste can no longer be discerned. As the language of burning suggests, there is sometimes a sense of danger about it. This is also the case with the single example of a woman using the language of ravishment which I know. The Arminian matriarch Lettice Cary prayed, 'Come not so near, O Lord, with these heavenly ravishments', fearing lest her flesh 'break asunder'.[105] Yet even mortal danger was sought and embraced. Believers longed to die in their ecstasies. Joy and sorrow became interchangeable and indistinguishable. 'I could not tell', Winthrop wrote, 'whither were greater my sorrowe, ioye, desire or feare.'[106] William Pinke's popular handbook for self-examination described the Biblical prodigal son in terms which sound as if he knew what he was talking about:

> O what a swelling, a thronging, a wrastling did he now feele in his bowels of tendrest passions, impatient for want of expression! O how did he now lay about him with teares of sorrow and teares of joy, being much pusled, whether it would best become to prosecute his joy most or his sorrow.[107]

---

[101] Dyke, *Two Treatises*, 53; Sibbes, *Bruised reede*, 282–3; Featley, *Ancilla Pietatis*, 614; Donne, *Poems*, 331.

[102] On these meetings, see Leigh Eric Schmidt, *Holy Fairs: Scottish Communions and American Revivals in the Early Modern Period* (Princeton, 1989).

[103] Tweedie, *Select Biographies*, 138–9.

[104] Featley, *Ancilla Pietatis*, sig. A9r.

[105] Duncon, *Returnes*, 90–1.

[106] Winthrop, *Papers*, 192.

[107] Pinke, *Tryall of a Christians loue*, III.12–13 (six editions, 1630–59: this section only added in the second edition).

The perpetuall Reioyce of the godly described how the saved 'reioyce in the Lord . . . with feare and trembling'. And Samuel Rogers, who wrestled so often with dullness and dryness, could sometimes report, as he did at the end of a spiritually tumultuous month in which his beloved sister had died, that he was 'broken to peices with joy; drunk with comfort'.[108]

Were early modern Protestants happy? In the normal sense of the word, perhaps not, but they scorned that sense. It is either their glory or their tragedy that they saw the sharp pangs of what they called joy, the long droughts of its absence, and the elusive promise of its durability as their birthright. They would not have traded it for the mess of what the world around them called happiness.

---

[108] *Short and pretie Treatise*, sigs B2v–3r; Rogers, *Diary*, 154.

PART II

THE PROTESTANT AT PRAYER

In Part I, we surveyed the emotional landscape within which early modern Protestants lived and moved: the dullness which they feared, the repentance whose necessity they recognized, the desire and zeal which they tried to kindle, and the joy and the states beyond it for which they hoped. Much of this emotional landscape was common to western Christians, and indeed much of it simply to human beings, although under the stark light of Reformed Protestant theology it took on a distinct appearance, and cast some unfamiliar shadows. Confessional differences became sharper, however, when early modern Protestants tried to find paths through that landscape from day to day. The rest of this book asks: how did early modern British Protestants go about being Protestant? We must begin with the heart of the matter: private prayer.[1]

The distinction between private and public prayer was widely made by early modern commentators. John Bradford, for example, breezily divided public prayer, 'that is called comon praier', from private, 'as when men praye alone'. Unfortunately, this is not as simple as it looks.[2] The boundary was a blurry and moveable one. Margaret Hoby regularly distinguished between public prayers, which involved the household, and private prayers, said alone, yet she also recorded having 'praied priuat with Mr Rhodes', her household chaplain.[3] Elnathan Parr divided private prayer into 'less priuate with the familie' and 'more priuate, by one alone'. A few others were explicit in using three categories, with 'private' meaning household, family, or conjugal prayer, while 'personall' or 'secret' meant solitary. But this kind of clarity was fairly rare, especially in

---

[1] Prayer as a subject is only now beginning to attract early modern scholars' attention. Much of what work there is has been done by literary scholars, such as Kaufman, *Prayer, Despair and Drama* (Urbana and Chicago, IL, 1996); Richard Rambuss, *Closet Devotions* (Durham, NC, and London, 1998); Kate Narveson, 'Publishing the Sole-talk of the Soule: Genre in Early Stuart Piety' in Daniel W. Doersken and Christopher Hodgkins (eds), *Centered on the Word* (Newark, NJ, 2004); and *Elizabeth Tyrwhit's Morning and Evening Prayers*, ed. Susan M. Felch (Aldershot, 2008). For historians' contributions, see Virginia Reinburg, 'Hearing Lay People's Prayer' in Barbara Diefendorf and Carla Hesse, eds, *Culture and Identity in Early Modern Europe (1500–1800)* (Ann Arbor, MI, 1993); and Martin and Ryrie, *Private and Domestic Devotion*.

[2] Bradford, *Godlie meditations*, sig. A2v; Erica Longfellow, '"my now solitary prayers": *Eikon basilike* and changing attitudes toward religious solitude', in Martin and Ryrie, *Private and Domestic Devotion*.

[3] Hoby, *Diary*, eg. 65, 68, 73, 82. On household prayer, see pp. 363–81.

devotional literature.[4] This is more than a semantic problem. It was all very well to argue that 'if priuate Deuotion cometh once to be knowne, it ceaseth to be priuate', or to claim optimistically that anyone could pray in secret, regardless of their circumstances.[5] In practice, however, privacy and solitude in prayer were often very difficult for early modern people to achieve, nor were they always desired. The blurry conceptual division reflects the conditions of early modern life. Nevertheless, contemporary usage did recognize a division, and so must we. The focus of this part of the book, then, is prayer and other devotional practices undertaken by a single individual, either in genuine solitude or with others' involvement being only incidental, although many of the points raised apply to household and public devotion as well.

---

[4] Gouge, *Whole-Armor of God*, 428–9; Parr, *Abba Father*, 2; William Crashaw, *Milke for Babes. Or, a North-Countrie Catechisme* (1618: RSTC 6020), 7; Woodford, 'Diary', e.g. 27.xii.1637 verso; Duncon, *Returnes*, 2.

[5] Featley, *Ancilla Pietatis*, 3; Gouge, *Whole-Armor of God*, 429.

6

The Meaning of Prayer

'I haue had more vnderstanding then all my teachers: for thy testimonies are my meditacion.' *Psalm 119:99.*

THE WORTH OF PRAYER

We have to begin by asking what early modern Protestants thought prayer was, but we also have to notice that this is not how they themselves approached it. Prayer was experienced before it was defined. The theory was deduced from the practice, although practice was then reshaped by theory. This is not a reason to neglect the definitions offered, however. If theory is abstracted from experience, so much the better; for it is the experience which we are trying to reach.

The definitions do not change in their essentials across our period. William Tyndale defined prayer as 'a mourning, a longing, and a desire of the spirit to God-ward, for that which she lacketh'. Thomas Becon, in the first English Protestant treatise devoted specifically to prayer, used Augustine's definition: 'a lyftinge vp of a pure mynde to God, wherein we aske somewhat of hym'. The same Augustinian definition was echoed in the official Elizabethan homily on prayer, and continued to be used throughout the period.[1] Becon gave a fuller definition in his catechism: 'Prayer is an earnest talk with God, proceeding from a very inward, deep, and brenning or fervent affection of the heart, craving somewhat at the hand of God'— and he also borrowed Tyndale's definition (unattributed).[2] John Bradford described prayer as 'a simple, vnfained, humble and ardent openinge of the heart before God'; the Elizabethan cleric Thomas Knell called it 'the humble and ardent exposition or laieng open of the mind before God . . . the feruent desire of the mind to God, proceeding of a certaine necessitie'.[3] So prayer is about longing, lifting, earnestness, and desire, and it is a matter of the spirit and the heart. In other words, it is the active expression of the Protestant emotional life, and it has no necessary connection to the use of words, or with outward activity of any kind. In practice, this would turn out to be more complicated.

---

[1] Tyndale, *Doctrinal Treatises*, 93; Thomas Becon, *A newe pathwaye unto praier* (1542: RSTC 1734), sig. B5r; *Certain Sermons or Homilies*, 289; e.g. Sandys, *Sermons*, 76; Clarke, *Holy Incense*, 13.
[2] Thomas Becon, *The Catechism of Thomas Becon: with other pieces*, ed. John Ayre (Cambridge, 1844), 125.
[3] Bradford, *Godlie meditations*, sig. A2r; Knell, *Godlie and necessarie Treatise*, sigs B1v–B2r.

By the turn of the 17th century, a little more precision was creeping in. Good Calvinists, with their emphasis on divine sovereignty, stressed that prayer must be in accordance with God's will.[4] William Perkins wrote that to pray is 'to put vppe request to GOD according to his worde from a contrite hearte in the name of Christ with assurance to be heard'[5]—a definition so packed with theological detail that you could preach a series of sermons expounding it, which is more or less what some divines did. In the 1630s, the printed version of John Preston's sermon-series on 'the whole dutie of prayer' would become a best-seller.[6] However, the main theme continued to be that prayer must be heartfelt, 'the opening and making known of a mans inward desire'.[7]

Some immediate features of these definitions are worth noticing. First is the priority which Protestants of every shade placed on prayer. This should not be surprising, but some conformists and Laudians argued, tendentiously, that puritans valued preaching over prayer, and the calumny has stuck.[8] In fact, prayer was rhapsodized across the spectrum. We find the Laudian John Browning describing it as,

> the just mans Safegard: the Divels scourge: the Spirits earnest: this is the Nurse of love: the Friend of peace: the Soules solace: our Accesse to God: the Meanes of salvation.[9]

That echoes, perhaps deliberately, George Herbert, a conformist Calvinist, whose poem *Prayer (I)* famously defines prayer with a string of images: 'the Christian plummet sounding heav'n and earth', 'Christ-side-piercing spear', 'Heaven in ordinarie', 'the souls bloud'.[10] Perkins was less of a poet, but the subject could stir him too. To pray, he wrote, was to speak 'the most heauenly tong that euer was':

> By praier you may . . . put your hand into the cofers of Gods treasures and inrich your selfe . . . come in presence, and haue speech with *Iehoua* the king of heauen and earth.[11]

For the Edinburgh preacher Robert Bruce, it was 'the life of the saull . . . the best gift that ever God gaue man'. The Elizabeth homily asserted that 'there is nothing in all man's life . . . so needful to be spoken of, and daily to be called upon, as hearty, zealous, and devout prayer'.[12] Such claims were entirely uncontroversial.

Why was prayer so valuable? Its spiritual and material benefits were important, naturally, but at heart to pray is, in a Biblical image beloved of early modern writers,

---

[4] See, for example, Rogers, *Seven treatises*, 282.

[5] Perkins, *Exposition of the Lords prayer*, 3.

[6] Preston, *Saints Daily Exercise* (at least nine editions, 1629–34).

[7] Gouge, *Whole-Armor of God*, 335–6; cf. Ball, *Short treatise*, 108.

[8] The issue is usefully discussed in Lori Anne Ferrell, 'Kneeling and the Body Politic' in Donna B. Hamilton and Richard Streier (eds), *Religion, Literature and Politics in Post-Reformation England, 1540–1688* (Cambridge, 1996); and Arnold Hunt, *The Art of Hearing: English Preachers and their Audiences, 1590–1640* (Cambridge, 2010), 52–3.

[9] John Browning, *Concerning publike-prayer, and the fasts of the Church* (1636: RSTC 3919), 68.

[10] Herbert, *Works*, 51.

[11] Perkins, *Exposition of the Lords prayer*, sig. A2r–v.

[12] Bruce, *Sermons vpon the Sacrament*, sig. S8v; *Certain Sermons or Homilies*, 284.

to pour out your heart before God.[13] Pouring yourself out is a fertile metaphor. It implies weeping, on which more later, and it can only be done if the heart is not in the state of dryness which early modern Protestants particularly abhorred.[14] More profoundly, it implies utter self-emptying. The bottom of your heart is laid bare. William Cowper criticized those whose prayers are 'petitions lawfull enough, and agreeable to Gods word, but not poured out in feruency'.[15] This sense of self-abandonment made pouring a metaphor for prayer which appealed especially to puritans and radicals,[16] but it was used across the Protestant spectrum as a symbol of religious earnestness.

Such earnest self-emptying was beyond what mere willpower could achieve. True prayer, it was generally acknowledged, was neither a human 'work' nor a human response to God's work. Rather, it was itself God's work, drawing devotees into intimacy with himself. It was a truism that, as John Dod put it, 'God is delighted with the faithfull supplications of his deare children',[17] but within a Reformed Protestant theological framework, God was delighted with prayers because those prayers were themselves entirely his own work, in the person of the Holy Spirit. It was a commonplace that prayer lifted believers to God's presence, but this should not be taken to mean that the believers actually do the climbing:

> Prayer is a golden chaine, which God lets downe from heauen; when we lay hold of it, we thinke we draw God to vs; but indeed, wee are by it drawne vp to him.[18]

Thomas Goodwin emphasized that God was the first, the effective, and the final cause of all true prayer. In creation he said, Let there be light. Similarly, in the life of the Christian, he says, 'Let there be a prayer, and there is a prayer'. Otherwise it was merely words. The radical Henoch Clapham spelt the matter out in categorical terms:

> Prayer, is nothing else but a powring foorth of the soules-sense according to the instinct and motion of GOD his holy Spirit. . . . No vtteraunce *mentall* or *vocall* is true Prayer, otherwise then it is vttered by the Holy Ghostes direction.

Clapham and George Herbert would perhaps not have agreed about many things, but on this, there is not much to choose between Clapham's view and Herbert's description of prayer as 'Gods breath in man returning to his birth'.[19]

---

[13] See, for example, I Samuel 1:15; Psalms 62:8, 142:2. Amongst many early modern uses of this image, see Latimer, *Sermons by Hugh Latimer*, 312; *Certain Sermons or Homilies*, 284, 289; Sandys, *Sermons*, 76, 275, 398; Bull, *Christian praiers*, 4; Rogers, *Garden* (1616), sig. C4r; Wariston, *Diary*, 42, 91.

[14] See above, pp. 20–6, and below, pp. 187–95.

[15] Cowper, *Triumph*, 91.

[16] See, for example, Henoch Clapham, *A Tract of Prayer* (1602: RSTC 5346.5), sig. A3r; George Gifford, *A Short Treatise against the Donatists of England* (1590: RSTC 11869), 20.

[17] Dod and Cleaver, *Ten sermons*, 130.

[18] Parr, *Abba Father*, 29. Cf. Thomas Tymme, *The Chariot of Devotion* (1618: RSTC 24415a), sigs A2v–3r.

[19] Goodwin, *Returne of Prayers*, 87; Clapham, *Tract of Prayer*, sig. A3r–v; Herbert, *Works*, 51.

This doctrine of prayer was present in 16th-century sources—unsurprisingly, given its Biblical and medieval roots.[20] However, in the 17th century, it moved to the devotional foreground. Nicholas Byfield made it a ground for praise, urging his readers to give thanks whenever they felt any inclination to pray or enjoyed any good emotions during prayer. Thomas Tuke used it to warn those who 'imagine that they can make *Powerfull* prayers' that it is the Spirit's intercession, and not eloquence, that makes prayer prevail. William Gouge faced head-on the knotty problem of how those who lack faith can pray for it, and answered it bluntly: they can't. Such a person 'may earnestly wish for Faith, & desire God to giue it him', but such wishes and desires are not true prayer. This was austere, but the only way around it was Clapham's highly idiosyncratic view that unholy people can, 'according to the motion of the Holy spirit', pray truly and effectively, even though they lack saving faith.[21]

As we shall see, this concern had a series of knock-on effects on how Protestants went about the business of prayer, but first, it brings us up against a persistent, revealing, and—at first sight—odd phenomenon: inability to pray.

INABILITY TO PRAY

Early 17th-century devotional literature regularly notices the plight of 'them that cannot pray'. The condition was taken seriously. 'No man is the child of God, nor hath the spirit of Christ in him', Arthur Hildersam warned, 'that is not able feelingly and fervently to call God Father, and to pray unto Him', and that perhaps was to be expected.[22] But the problem was also widespread amongst the most earnest believers. Ezekiel Culverwell, next to a marginal note stating 'Many troubled that they cannot pray', claimed: 'What more ordinary complaint doe wee heare made by many worthy Christians in their extremities, then this to their friends, O helpe mee, I cannot pray?'[23] Quite what was preventing these worthy Christians from praying is not entirely clear.

Sometimes the problem was a limited one. Many of these complaints referred to extempore prayer; in other words, some people found it hard to string words together to make a coherent prayer, a peculiarly puritan concern. When Robert Harris addressed this problem, he did so under the question, 'What if a man be so dumb and barren, that hee can say nothing when hee should pray?' He reassured readers that if they could do no more than repeat a simple prayer, babble incoherently, or indeed if they were dumbstruck, God would accept what they had to offer. Some claims to be 'vnapt to praye' seem to be expressing no more than ordinary

[20] See, for example, 'Augustine', *Certaine select prayers*, sigs C7v–8r.
[21] Byfield, *Marrow of the Oracles* (1622), 241; Tuke, *Practise of the faithfull*, 13–14; Gouge, *Whole-Armor of God*, 260; Clapham, *Tract of Prayer*, sig. A5v.
[22] Hildersam, *Doctrine of Fasting*, 35–6.
[23] Culverwell, *Treatise of faith*, 331–2. Nehemiah Wallington copied this passage out into his book *A record of Gods Marcys*, under the heading 'Comfort to ye troubled that cannot praye'. LMA Guildhall MS 204, p. 307.

humility. Others complained of inability to pray because of distractions or forget-fulness, which we should understand as inability to pray *adequately*. Richard Sibbes consoled these sufferers: 'GOD can picke sense out of a confused prayer.'[24]

One of the fullest accounts of this problem comes from the nonconformist minister Robert Linaker. His *Treatise, for the reliefe of such as are afflicted in conscience* details his own spiritual struggles, so as to persuade his afflicted readers that they are not alone. He not only laments praying coldly and 'vnsauourly', but adds that 'sometimes I cannot pray at all'. As a result, in his daily prayers 'I am constrained for the most part to plod on in an ordinarie course of words and matter, without change or varietie', and if he is called on in company to pray, 'a sudden feare doth so surprize mee that my breath is stopt vp, that I am not able to speake a word'. But still, he adds, he sometimes feels the stirrings of grace in him.[25] This was clearly distressing, but is perhaps not very important. In itself, it may only tell us that those who valorized extempore prayer, but were not articulate enough to carry it off, had made a rod for their own backs.

Such straightforward explanations do not always work, however. Linaker also admitted that 'sometimes though you do what you can, you cannot pray, for your life', which sounds like more than inarticulacy. When a writer exhorts us to pray now, on the grounds that 'the time may com when wee cannot pray', what does it mean?[26] Perhaps some possible future incapacity during illness, although it was more common to emphasize that no-one is ever too far gone to pray. But illness might be linked to spiritual incapacity. We are told that the young Katherine Brettergh, reciting the Lord's Prayer on her deathbed, broke off half-way through, saying, 'I may not pray; I may not pray (being interrupted, as she said, by Satan)'. Later, when a counsellor asked her 'whether she could pray, she answered: O that I could. I would willingly, but he will not let me'.[27] More intriguingly, some devotees claimed to have been prevented from praying, not by the Devil, but by God—which makes sense, if prayer is understood as God's action within the believer. When one of John Knox's correspondents asked him to pray for her husband in 1557, Knox replied that he would like to, but that 'prayer is not alwayis in the power of man. . . . The Prophetis of God are oft impeidit to pray for sic as carnallie thay lufe unfeanedlie'. Knox was unusually ready to claim to be a prophet, but Robert Bruce, preaching in Edinburgh in 1590, provided a more respectable version of the same argument. If we persist in prayer for something, he told his congregation, that fact itself proves that we are praying in accordance with God's will, for if 'the lord had rejected our prayer altogether, it is not possible to continue in prayer'.[28] In England, Thomas Goodwin raised the same issue in 1641, asking what happens when we pray for those whom God has rejected. He was clear that

---

[24] Harris, *Peters enlargement* (1627), 34–5; Clement Cotton, *The mirror of martyrs* (1613: RSTC 5848), 139; Scudder, *Christians daily walke* (1628), 582; Sibbes, *Bruised reede*, 146–7.

[25] Linaker, *Comfortable treatise* (1620), 125–8.

[26] Linaker, *Comfortable treatise* (1620), 115; Bod. MS Rawl. D.384 fo. 1r.

[27] Harrison, *Deaths aduantage*, III.13–14.

[28] John Knox, *The Works of John Knox*, ed. David Laing (Edinburgh, 1846–64), IV.245; Bruce, *Sermons Preached*, sig. V7r–v.

such prayers do at least do us credit, but added that God 'will in the end cast them out of our prayers and hearts, and take our hearts off from praying for them . . . by withdrawing the spirit of supplication'. Even though a Christian may still wish to pray for these reprobates, he will find that God 'makes his tongue cleave to the roof of his mouth'.[29] All these examples suggest that inability to pray could be more than simply a matter of inarticulacy.

Yet this was an age when almost all Protestants, puritan and conformist alike, accepted the legitimacy of the use of set prayers in both private and public devotions.[30] So total inability to pray is, on one level, nonsense. Those who could not read prayers could certainly remember some, even if it was only the Lord's Prayer. But this phenomenon will actually reveal something of the Protestant understanding of prayer to us.

Those who complained of inability to pray were sometimes advised, in effect, to stop fussing and get on with it. 'If thou canst not pray', Dorothy Leigh advised, 'fall downe on thy face . . . and say, God be mercifull to mee a sinner', or confess your inability to pray to God, and do so at least twice daily until you receive the necessary grace: a solution which might reassure some and miss the point entirely for others. A popular collection of scriptural promises urged the reader who 'findest thy selfe vnable to pray' to use Christ's own prayers from John's Gospel. As we have seen, John Preston argued that, just as you can only prepare for a race by running, so you can only ready yourself for prayer by praying. This was John Winthrop's experience: 'when I sett myselfe seariously to prayer etc: thoughe I be very unfitt when I beginne, yet God dothe assist me and bowes his eare to me'.[31] Sheer effort had its place.

A more comforting—and less common—variant held that people can sometimes pray without knowing it. Culverwell spoke of those who 'can doe nothing but sigh and groane, not able to set aright their hearts to pray to God'; a glance at one of the most familiar verses in the Bible, Romans 8:26, suggested that in fact, such sighs and groans *were* prayer. John Ball's catechism took that verse to mean that 'sometimes the childe of God prayeth best when hee knoweth not that he prayeth at all'.[32] After all, if it is the Spirit who prays in us, and not we ourselves, he does not need our help.

For most Protestants, however, these approaches missed the point. Inability to pray was a very real problem. Anyone could 'babble and speake many words', but prayer is a matter of the heart and of the Spirit, who cannot be summoned by mere effort.[33] 'The noyse of our lips, without the voice of the heart', warned Elnathan Parr, 'is no more a true prayer, then ringing of belles, or babling of a Parrot'. At its simplest level, this is merely the perennial Protestant fear of

[29] Goodwin, *Returne of Prayers*, 61–8.
[30] See below, pp. 214–24.
[31] Leigh, *Mothers blessing*, 69–70, 72–3; Fawkener, *Collection of Promises*, 44, 56; Preston, *Saints Daily Exercise*, 34–5, 74–6; Winthrop, *Papers*, 167.
[32] Culverwell, *Treatise of faith*, 331–2; see below, pp. 212–14; Ball, *Short treatise*, 133; cf. Cowper, *Most Comfortable Dialogue*, 40.
[33] Perkins, *Exposition of the Lords prayer*, 128; cf. Parr, *Abba Father*, 43–4.

hypocrisy, the 'white Devil' which might lurk beneath any outwardly pious act. It is no surprise to hear warnings of the false prayers of those who 'vse onlie the outward exercise and ceremonie of confession & praier', of time-serving ministers who 'cunningly furnish themselves, with a formall method, and outwarde forme of sincere and sanctified prayer', and of the hypocrite who is 'more zealous and feruent with others, then alone by himselfe'.[34]

The out-and-out hypocrite, however, is only the tip of this iceberg of frozen devotion. In a treatise published in 1611, Robert Bolton distinguished between what he called 'gross' and 'formal' hypocrites. Gross hypocrisy is self-conscious and deliberate; formal hypocrisy is that 'by which a man doth not onely deceiue others with a shew of piety . . . but also his owne heart'.[35] This is, of course, a fearsome state. If there are some who pray without knowing, others believe themselves to be praying but in fact are not. This is a logical consequence of the doctrine that true prayer is the work of the Spirit, and as the emphasis on that doctrine increased in the 17th century, so did this corollary. So Preston argued that God hears the Spirit's prayers made through us, but that if our prayers are merely 'the expression of our owne spirits . . . these the *Lord* regards not, hee knowes not the meaning of them'. 'A wicked man can not pray', Linaker said bluntly, 'because he can not beleeue.' It was axiomatic that 'the prayer of vnbeleefe is abominable'; it was, as Richard Capel put it, 'to say, rather than to pray a prayer'.[36]

Capel's comment, however, was addressed at a more specific problem: prayer contaminated by sin or by sinful desires—such as Augustine's famous prayer to be chaste, but not yet. In Protestant hands, the old principle that God does not hear a sinner's prayer was given a new twist. The Protestant doctrine of total depravity held that all human beings are steeped in sin, which on the face of it makes all prayer impossible. One way out of this paradox was to use intentions as a test. Hugh Latimer explained that as long as a devotee 'is in purpose of sin, he cannot pray . . . but he that hath a penitent heart, to leave his sins and wickedness, that same is he whose prayers shall be heard'. So the prayers of conscious and deliberate sinners cannot be heard, but those of penitent or negligent sinners can. The distinction became a truism. This was, in effect if not in intention, to restore the reviled Catholic distinction between venial and mortal sin.[37]

This could, in practice, be what inability to pray meant. The theologians warned that God would not hear sinners' prayers, and those who were conscious of their sins often found it impossible to pray. In *Hamlet*, Claudius' attempt to pray was stymied by his own blood-guilt: 'Pray can I not,/Though inclination be as sharp as will./My stronger guilt defeats my strong intent.' The sonnet in which John Donne

[34] Parr, *Abba Father*, 44; Knell, *Godlie and necessarie Treatise*, sig. B7r; Thomas Adams, *The white deuil, or The hypocrite vncased* (1613: RSTC 131), 33; Bolton, *Three-fold treatise*, II.173–4; Dyke, *Mystery of selfe-deceiuing*, 105; and cf. Dixon, 'Predestination and pastoral theology', 258–75.

[35] Bolton, *Discourse about happinesse*, 34.

[36] Preston, *Saints Daily Exercise*, 3; Linaker, *Comfortable treatise* (1595), 43; Harris, *Peters enlargement* (1627), 33; Capel, *Tentations*, 159.

[37] Latimer, *Sermons by Hugh Latimer*, 507; cf. Perkins, *Godly and learned exposition*, 236; Sibbes, *Works*, VI.98; and see below, pp. 413–14.

admitted 'I durst not view heaven yesterday' confronted essentially the same difficulty.[38] The Scottish minister Robert Blair recorded a night in 1616 when he had set about his devotions after 'a dangerous visit to ensnaring company': he found that 'the Lord did let out so much displeasure and wrath, that I was driven from prayer'. Two years earlier, a more troubled English minister, Richard Kilby, had similarly 'so merily delighted my self with prophane talk, that . . . I was forced to goe praierlesse to bed, because my soule was confunded and ashamed to look up towards God'.[39] Explaining this kind of thing in theological terms was simple enough. John Brinsley argued that sin drives the Holy Spirit away, so that, amongst other things, 'wee shall bee made vnable to pray as wee ought'.[40] But the increasingly popular conscience-literature took another tack, emphasizing that this felt inability to pray was itself one of the fetters of sin, which Christians ought to strive to break. Culverwell encouraged those who were kept from prayer only 'by the sense of their owne vnworthinesse'. John Clarke understood that if a Christian is conscious of sin, it 'may tongue-tie him a while . . . yet when his lips move not, nor his voyce is heard, his desires will beate strongly upward', and this is true prayer. Sibbes was similarly encouraging, but would not bend too far on the point. A sinner can pray, but an unrepentant sinner who maintains an intention to sin 'sealeth up the lips, so that the soule cannot call God Father'.[41] Comfort could only take you so far.

Indeed, the warning that God would be deaf to the prayers of hypocrites or unrepentant sinners merely softened a longer-established theme: that he would hear, and be angry. A Dutch Protestant handbook to Christian living that was one of the first best-sellers of the English Reformation warned that to pray without feeling, earnestness, and penitence is 'to scorne, & mocke wyth God'. Thomas Knell worried that too many prayers treated God 'as a scarecrow in a garden, which can do neither good nor harme'. Those who pray such mocking prayers, warned John Dod, will find that 'their praiers tumble downe againe vpon their heads, and bring them iudgements in steed of mercies'.[42] Theologically this made sense, but it was not much help pastorally. If you are a sinner, conscious of your guilt, and you are told that sinful prayers only provoke God, then you might well conclude it is safer not to pray at all.

Whether believers were really deterred from prayer is unclear. In John Norden's best-selling handbook, the 'pensive man' laments, 'Yet alas, how dare I cast vp my heart to the heauens, in hope of comfort? for hee hath shut vp the passage thereof from mee'—meaning that, since all his afflictions are a well-deserved judgement, he

---

[38] *Hamlet* III.iii.41–3; Donne, *Poems*, 331.

[39] Blair, *Life*, 12; Kilby, *Hallelujah*, 88–9, 104.

[40] Brinsley, *True Watch* (1608), 28; cf. Rogers, *Garden* (1615), II sig. E3v.

[41] Culverwell, *Way to a blessed estate*, 9–10; Clarke, *Holy Incense*, sig. A5v; Sibbes, *Bruised reede*, 148–50, 170.

[42] Cornelius van der Heyden, *A Bryefe Summe of the whole Byble*, tr. Antony Scoloker (1550?: RSTC 3018), sig. E6v (four editions 1549–53, with a further edition in 1568); Knell, *Godlie and necessarie Treatise*, sig. B5r (cf. Galatians 6:7); Dod and Cleaver, *Ten sermons*, 63; cf. Latimer, *Sermons by Hugh Latimer*, 388; Sparke, *Crumms of comfort*, sig. A7v.

can hardly ask God to spare him. Norden disagreed with this scruple, but the fact that he spent most of the first part of the book addressing it suggests that it was not imaginary.[43] We can see something like it, perhaps, in a minister of Isaac Ambrose's acquaintance, who found when he attempted a day of prayer that 'the terror of Conscience had so worn out his Spirit, and wasted his body, that he was not able (as he said) to perform'.[44] But as with Norden's pensive man, this difficulty was swiftly overcome. The real problem seems to have been a subtler one.

Even the most austere Protestants knew that there was one prayer a sinner could and must make which would certainly be heard: a prayer of heartfelt repentance. Yet, such a prayer cannot be summoned up at the snap of the fingers. True repentance requires you to face your own sins squarely; you may be as reluctant to do that as to lift the bandage on a wound which you fear is infected, but until the truth is confronted, there is no chance of achieving the tearing honesty necessary for true prayer. Indeed, sinners may, rather than face God and their own guilt, choose to avoid prayer, or reduce it to formality, and since that is in itself sinful, the problem is a self-reinforcing one. This was the case that John Winthrop found himself in in 1607. His spiritual duties had lapsed into formality; and his wife then fell ill with an ague, which he interpreted as punishment from God for his laxity. 'Beinge in this trobble I was wholy unable to raise up my selfe, neither could I pray a great while.'[45]

Steeling yourself to prayer was, proverbially, 'a most hard, and difficult thing'. Bringing your heart to repentance is like wringing water from a rock, and wresting the mind away from its earthbound preoccupations to focus steadily on God is scarcely easier.[46] After all, as Preston argued, we are earthly creatures for whom prayer is essentially alien. There is no state naturally inclined to prayer. Distress torments us; happiness lulls us; business distracts us; idleness fills us with vain thoughts. Richard Rogers, reviewing his spiritual progress one New Year's Eve, admitted that he was unable to bring himself to a habit of regular prayer more than once a day, and that for reluctance, not for lack of time.[47]

The phenomenon of inability to pray, then, shows us two faces of Protestant prayer: alternately, childishly easy, and impossibly difficult. Easy, in that the mechanical business of saying prayers could scarcely be more so; difficult, in that it was the heart, not the mouth, which mattered. Difficult—indeed, impossible— in that true prayer came from the Spirit, not from yourself, but easy for the same reason, for all you needed to do was allow the Spirit to speak through your own sighs and groans. Difficult because nature revolted against it, and easy because grace made it possible. At the core of both ease and difficulty was an alarming simplicity: to pray meant merely to strip your heart bare before God and to hear his voice speaking through you. No wonder some people found themselves unable to do it.

[43] Norden, *Pensive mans practise ... The second part*, 14 (seven editions, 1594–1633).
[44] Ambrose, *Media*, 75.
[45] Winthrop, *Papers*, 162.
[46] Narne, *Pearle of prayer*, 306–8, 347.
[47] Preston, *Saints Daily Exercise*, 37–8; Knappen, *Two Diaries*, 73; cf. Goodwin, *Vanity of Thoughts*, 15.

PRAYER AND MEDITATION

That daunting, bare simplicity—meeting God, unmediated—was the ideal. In practice, of course, complexity crept in. Habits had to be formed and errors regulated, the inexperienced needed guiding and the weak encouraging. The mere encounter with God on the mountaintop is all very well, but the urge to make tabernacles, to build structures, to subdivide, and organize, is an inveterate and a necessary one.

It was common for early modern Protestants to divide prayer into several 'parts'. There was, however, no simple agreement about what those 'parts' might be. Augustine Bernher, at the beginning of Elizabeth's reign, had a tripartite division: prayer begins with confession of sins, proceeds to praise of God, and concludes with intercession; that is, requests for 'such things as be needful . . . in this world'. A much-reprinted translation of a collection of prayers by the Bohemian Lutheran, Johann Habermann, suggested four parts to prayer: 'deprecation' (that, is confession), supplication (requests for yourself), intercession (requests for others), and thanksgiving. Archbishop Sandys divided prayer primarily into petition and thanksgiving, and subdivided petition into requests (prayer for bodily or spiritual gifts for ourselves), supplications (prayer for mercy and remission of sins for ourselves), and intercessions (prayer for others). His primary division, at least, was widely shared. Henry Bull's best-selling Elizabethan prayer book said simply, 'Of prayer there be two parts: peticion and thankesgeuing'.[48] In the 17th century, it became more common to separate out confession as a distinct third part of prayer. Richard Rogers also wanted to put thanksgiving first, one sign of a common concern that this was the Cinderella of Christian prayer. 'Forget not this', John Brinsley said of thanksgiving: 'wee all faile in it'.[49]

These varied schemes may be evidence principally of the era's zeal for classification, but they contain some important hints. Take, for example, William Perkins' characteristically subtle classification. He extracts a fourfold distinction from I Timothy 2:1, which urges 'supplications, praiers, intercessions & giuing of thankes'. Intercession and thanksgiving are straightforward; he takes supplication to mean requests to God 'to remooue some euill from vs', while prayer means the positive request for good things for ourselves. Where or whether confession fits into this scheme is not entirely clear, but the ambiguity about the word *prayer* itself is more interesting. Although Perkins accepts that all four of his categories could be called prayer, he wants to argue that 'to pray, properly is to intreate of God the gift of some good thing concerning our selues: and in this sense, it is onely one part of that holy worship of God, which is called Invocation'.[50]

[48] Latimer, *Sermons by Hugh Latimer*, 311–12; Habermann, *Enimie of securitie*, sig. b9v (fifteen editions, 1579–1620); Sandys, *Sermons*, 76–7; Bull, *Christian praiers*, 22; cf. Bradford, *Godlie meditations*, sig. A2r.

[49] Rogers, *Seven treatises*, 282; Brinsley, *True Watch* (1608), 37. Cf. Ball, *Short treatise*, 110–11; Scudder, *Christians daily walke* (1628), 169.

[50] Perkins, *Godly and learned exposition*, 230.

That particular classification was Perkins' idiosyncrasy, but others agreed that not all heartfelt communication with God should be described as prayer. Thomas Becon, in the 1540s, had separated prayer and thanksgiving, since his Augustinian definition of prayer—'a lyftinge vp of a pure mynde to God, wherein we aske somewhat of hym'—made request an essential part of it. In the 1620s, Robert Harris similarly but more explicitly argued that since thanksgiving does not involve a request, it is not prayer. Praise could be excluded on the same basis. Archibald Johnston of Wariston described prayers and praises as distinct categories, and also recorded being so overwhelmed with God's love that he did not know 'quhither to praise or to pray'.[51]

This is more than a semantic distinction. It has long been apparent that Reformed Protestantism had a more circumscribed concept of prayer than did contemporary Catholicism. It is not merely that Protestants had reservations about set prayers, and entirely rejected praying in a language unknown to the devotee. The more adventurous reaches of contemporary Catholic prayer featured imaginative, contemplative, and mystical practices which Protestantism viewed with suspicion. This helped to feed the view, widespread then and now, that Protestantism's devotional life was impoverished by comparison to Catholicism's. The pioneering historian of English Protestant prayer, the brilliant Catholic literary scholar, novelist, and polymath, Helen C. White, was characteristically crisp on the point. Puritan prayer, she wrote, was a 'desert of seventeenth century orderliness which only escapes formalism by virtue of its unfailing earnestness and sincerity'. At best it had a 'homely vitality'.[52] Whether or not this is quite fair, it is true that the Protestant view of prayer was resolutely *verbal*. Whether aloud or silent, it was understood that words were the normal medium—normal, not invariable.[53] Michael Sparke's commonsense definition of prayer as 'a familier speech with God' captures the mood.[54] This was a high intimacy with God, but of a prosaic, everyday kind, which mistrusted and could not attain to the more rarefied spiritual disciplines of the Catholic world.

Yet, while early modern British Protestants had a tightly circumscribed understanding of prayer, they also engaged in devotional practices which they did not always describe as prayer, but which make their devotional lives look a little less impoverished; and this brings us to the subject of meditation.

'Meditation' is a word with a long and distinct history in Christian piety. The English word 'meditation'—from which the verb 'meditate' was later deduced—dates back to the 13th century at least. It is derived, perhaps via French, from the Latin *meditatio*, which can mean either thinking over or contemplating something, or a practice or exercise. More specifically, 'meditation' referred to a well-established but ill-defined genre of pious writing. The most famous meditations

---

[51] Becon, *Newe pathwaye unto praier*, sigs B5r, P8v; Harris, *Peters enlargement* (1627), 26; Wariston, *Diary*, 96, 104.

[52] Helen C. White, *English Devotional Literature (Prose) 1600–1640* (Madison, WI, 1931), 152.

[53] See below, pp. 208–14.

[54] Sparke, *Crumms of comfort*, sig. A3v.

were those of St Bernard of Clairvaux; an English translation was published under the title *Medytacions of saynt Bernarde* in 1496. Another well-known set of meditations was ascribed to Augustine of Hippo. You could not ask for medieval or patristic exemplars whom Protestants would have respected more, and they happily embraced the word and the genre.[55] We find English Protestants using the word regularly from the 1530s onwards, in books like *An Epitome of the Psalmes, or briefe meditacions vpon the same* (translated by Richard Taverner from a Lutheran original, and published in two editions in 1539), or Queen Katherine Parr's *Prayers or meditacions* (twelve editions from 1545–61). The word was also applied, from the early 1530s onwards, to English translations of the primer, in which the miscellaneous pious texts at the end of the primer's traditional core were described as 'certeyn prayers & godly meditations'.[56] If that suggests a latent association with traditional and conservative religion, John Bradford's embrace of the genre in his *Godlie meditations*—a posthumous best-seller—should disabuse us. English Protestant Bibles used 'meditation' more or less where the Vulgate had used 'meditatio'. The word's distribution across the Bible is worth noting. Seventeen of the word's twenty uses in the Geneva Bible fall in the psalms, and fully eight of them in Psalm 119, the longest psalm, whose theme is the law of God. All eight of those are essentially the same: 'I wil meditate in thy precepts'; 'I wil meditate in thy statutes'; 'Oh how loue I thy Law! it is my meditacion continually'.[57]

In other words, 'meditation' did not have a precise meaning for 16th-century English Protestants (there is much less evidence of its usage by Scots).[58] At one end, meditation blurs into prayer: the frequency with which the two words are coupled together as near-synonyms is no accident. Some cited the aphorism—ascribed to Bernard—that prayer is the speech of the soul to God, and meditation that of God to the soul.[59] At the other end of the range, it can seem, as White put it, that 'sometimes [meditation] connotes very little more than "thoughts about"'. This is the implication of William Prid's pseudo-Augustinian best-seller, *The glasse of vaine-glorie*, in which he claimed that those who do not meditate are by definition thoughtless and bestial. Words like 'musing' or 'cogitation' are regularly used as near-synonyms for meditation.[60] (The word 'contemplation', however, was more rarely used in this context by English Protestants in this period.[61]) Less

---

[55] Green, *Print and Protestantism*, 277–88.

[56] *A prymer in Englyshe with certeyn prayers & godly meditations* (RSTC 15986. London: John Byddell for William Marshall, 1534).

[57] Psalm 119:15, 48, 97.

[58] Green, *Print and Protestantism*, 279; Louis L. Martz, *The Poetry of Meditation: A Study in English Religious Literature* (New Haven and London, 1962), 13–14.

[59] Hall, *Arte of Divine Meditation*, 78; John Hayward, *The sanctvarie of a troubled soule* (1618: RSTC 13006.5), II sig. R7v.

[60] White, *English Devotional Literature*, 154; William Prid, *The glasse of vaine-glorie* (1585: RSTC 929), sig. A5v. See, for example, *Christian Prayers and Meditations in English French, Italian, Spanish, Greeke, and Latine* (1569: RSTC 6428), sigs a4r, b2r; 'Augustine', *Certaine select prayers*, sig. P3v; Sutton, *Disce viuere*, 1; Rogers, *Seven treatises*, 235.

[61] For two examples, see Tyrwhit, *Elizabeth Tyrwhit's Morning and Evening Prayers*, 94–5; Featley, *Ancilla Pietatis*, sig. A5v. In neither case is the word used with precision, unlike in contemporary Catholic devotion. To my knowledge, the earliest English-speaking Protestant to distinguish clearly

common but perhaps more revealing is the term 'soliloquy', which was applied to texts which were more affective and passionate, and less informative and didactic. That mood is important; more so, perhaps, than the strict definition of soliloquy as speech addressed to the self. Written meditations throughout our period are indeed commonly addressed to the self—in exhortation or in reproach—but they are equally often addressed to God, or not obviously addressed to anyone, and some are addressed to the Devil, to abstractions such as the Church or Faith, or to historical figures from Adam onwards. Many move seamlessly from one mode of address to another.[62] This blending is frustrating for those of us who like categories, but it is hardly surprising that thoughts about spiritual matters should blend so easily into prayer proper.

Within that loose range of meaning, however, we can pick out some constant themes in the 16th-century Protestant use of the word. One is a close association of meditation with reading and—less frequently—writing. It was something you did while reading, or indeed it was itself a form of reading: echoing medieval *lectio divina* and the psalms' talk of meditating on God's law. George Gifford cited Psalm 1 to argue that 'God requireth euen of the poore labouring man that he should (if he will be blessed) meditate in his Lawe'. A decade later, he defined meditation as 'all that is done in studying and musing when one readeth'.[63] Richard Greenham, who warmly recommended the practice, defined it as making 'that which wee have read to bee our owne', or as 'when reason discourseth of things read'. He explicitly saw meditation as forming a devotional triangle with reading and prayer: 'To read and not to meditate is unfruitful, to meditate and not to read is dangerous for errours, to meditate or to read without praier is hurtful.' He also reckoned you ought to meditate on what you heard, a process which Samuel Hieron compared to digestion. Hieron applied it to sermons; Margaret Hoby applied it to hearing books read aloud to her, and reproached herself when she failed to do it. Her practise was to write such meditations down for later reading, closing the circle. The book of meditions to which her diary refers does not survive, but we do have Grace Mildmay's equivalent, containing written meditations which she described as 'the exersise of my mynde from my youth vntill this date'.[64]

between contemplation and meditation was John Downame, who described meditation as 'lower and meaner' than contemplation. For Downame, contemplation was 'fit only for such as by long exercise haue attained to much perfection', and consisted in dwelling on 'intellectual, sublime and heauenly' subjects both in understanding and in imagination, so that the practitioners might 'soare (with the Eagle) an high pitch in their heauenly thoughts, and . . . spend heerein great part of their time'. Downame, *Guide to Godlynesse*, 534–5. After our period certain English Protestants did come to speak of contemplation much more precisely and distinctively: see Tom Schwanda, *Soul Recreation: The Contemplative-Mystical Piety of Puritanism* (Eugene, OR, 2012); Thomas White, *A method and instructions for the art of divine meditation* (1655: Wing W1847B).

[62] Narveson, 'Publishing the Sole-talk'. For a particularly wide variety of modes of address, see the meditations in Sutton, *Godly meditations* (1601).

[63] Gifford, *Briefe discourse*, fo. 73v; Gifford, *Short Treatise against the Donatists*, 25.

[64] Parker and Carlson, 'Practical Divinity', 243, 342; Samuel Hieron, *The Preachers Plea* (1604: RSTC 13419), 256–7; Hoby, *Diary*, 71, 95; Mildmay, 'Meditations', I, p. 5.

If meditation was linked to the written word, however, it was not tied to it. Bradford's meditation on the Lord's Prayer consists of a series of lengthy prayers, one expounding each clause of the prayer. At the end of each section, there is an instruction such as 'Heare think vpon the state of religion, and the life of the professours of the gospell, that you may lament some, pray for some, and giue thankes for some'.[65] Reading a meditation, in other words, is not meditating—any more than reciting a prayer is praying. A written text was merely one of many possible starting points for meditation. Erasmus had urged his readers to base spiritual meditations, through allegory and metaphor, on the most everyday of sights.[66] The theme was taken up in Juan Luis Vives' instructions for daily meditation, which were introduced to a mass English audience by John Bradford, and very widely copied and imitated thereafter. Vives suggested meditations—some authors called them prayers—to be used at every point of the day, extracting spiritual significance from the most commonplace actions. Rising from bed in the morning is an occasion for meditating on the Resurrection; seeing the daylight, for meditating on the light of God; dressing, for meditating on the Fall and human shame—and so on.[67] With practice, almost anything could be made an occasion for meditation, and indeed, the mere remembrance of God and of his actions and attributes, without outward prompting, was occasion enough. The ceremonialist Christopher Sutton, who was an enthusiast for meditation, urged the recollection of Christ's life and 'the reuoluing of his benefites' in the mind, a practice which he promised would 'mooue man to loue God'. As well as 'meditation of the under-standing', Greenham also recommended 'meditation of the affections', meaning a concentrated effort to recall some matter of spiritual significance 'and make it worke upon our affections'. This could be done at any time. Greenham's own practice was to do it when lying awake in bed.[68]

The fullest early exposition of the practice of meditation comes from the Essex puritan Richard Rogers. The surviving portion of his diary, from the late 1580s and early 1590s, is full of references to meditation: whether on Scripture, on his own previously written meditations, on his diaries, or simply on his thoughts.[69] In his back-breaking *Seven Treatises* (1603), he tackled the subject comprehensively. Meditation, for Rogers, began with, but was more than, careful thought. We must 'set our minds on worke', but the point is 'that our affections may thereby be moued . . . so that we may make some good vse of it to our selues'. If there is any boundary between meditation and prayer, however, it is simply that he expects the former to lead to the latter. He defines meditation as a 'sweete and heauenly

[65] Bradford, *Godlie meditations*, sig. B6v.
[66] Desiderius Erasmus, *Enchiridion Militis Christiani: an English version*, ed. Anne M. O'Donnell (Early English Text Society 282: 1981), 103–6.
[67] Helen C. White, *The Tudor Books of Private Devotion* (Madison, WI, 1951), 163, 189, 193. Versions of Vives' meditations are found, amongst many others, in *Christian Prayers and Meditations in English*; Bull, *Christian praiers*; John Bradford, *Godly meditations vpon the Lords prayer* (1597: RSTC 3487).
[68] Sutton, *Disce viuere*, 2; Parker and Carlson, 'Practical Divinity', 203, 212, 343.
[69] Knappen, *Two Diaries*, e.g. 66, 70, 81, 100.

communing with the Lord and themselues', thoughts that inevitably become prayers. In addition, he adds that if 'we sign, moane, complaine to God, or reioyce . . . that also is meditation, and most commonly ioyned by prayer'.[70]

So we should be wary of dismissing 16th-century Protestants' spirituality as arid or word-bound. Certainly, both their prayers and their meditations were wordy, but while their practice of meditation may have been a matter of cognition and intellectual rigour, it was also, in a broad sense, contemplative, and clearly affective. Ill-defined theory does not point to impoverished practice. But for all that, there is no hiding the gulf that had opened up, by about 1600, between Catholic and Protestant meditative practice. Catholics could draw unproblematically on medieval meditative traditions, both in their traditional monastic forms and in the adventurous alternatives for the uncloistered which began to emerge in the 14th century. During the 16th century, Catholic practices of meditative and contemplative prayer became immeasurably more sophisticated and subtle. The Jesuit spiritual traditions are the best-known aspect of this, but Luis de Granada's *Book of Prayer and Meditation* and the *Spiritual Combat* ascribed to the Theatine Lorenzo Scupoli testify to the breadth of this renewal. English Catholics were quick to take up this tradition, producing translations and reworkings of these and other books, as well as their own original variations.[71] Some of these works quickly found a Protestant readership—needless to say, there was no traffic the other way.[72] At least one Protestant divine began to produce meditative works which owed a debt to this Catholic tradition. Christopher Sutton drew on the Jesuit Luca Pinelli for his meditations which suggested, for example, that readers place themselves imaginatively at the Last Supper or at Calvary.[73]

It was against this background that the most significant British Protestant treatment of meditation emerged. Joseph Hall was a young minister and poet with puritan roots but audacious tastes. During a visit to the Netherlands in 1605, he saw contemporary Jesuit spirituality at first hand. It was presumably during the same visit that he came across a 1494 meditative treatise, the *Rosetum exercitiorum spiritualium et sacrarum meditationum*, by Jean Mombaer, of the Brethren of the Common Life in Brussels. Hall knew the work's date but not the author's name, which frustrated him, because he felt this 'obscure nameless Monke' deserved greater honour. On his return to England he published two books drawing on what he had found. The first, better-selling, and less remarkable is his *Meditations and Vowes*, a set of two hundred short 'meditations'—soon augmented by another hundred—which are perhaps better described as aphorisms. It went through at least ten editions by 1621. His follow-up, *The Arte of Divine Meditation*, was less

[70] Rogers, *Seven treatises*, 235–56, esp. 235–6.

[71] Martz, *Poetry of Meditation*, esp. 5–9; Andrew Taylor, 'Into his secret chamber: reading and privacy in late medieval England' in James Raven et al. (eds), *The Practice and Representation of Reading* (Cambridge, 1996), 43–6.

[72] See below, pp. 284–92.

[73] Sutton, *Godly meditations* (1601), 172–3, 214–23; Sutton, *Godly meditations* (1613), 377–8; Kenneth Fincham and Nicholas Tyacke, *Altars Restored: The Changing Face of English Religious Worship, 1547–c.1700* (Oxford, 2007), 67–8.

commercially successful—four editions in four years, but none thereafter—but far more influential. It laid out for the first time a comprehensive theory of meditation for an English-speaking Protestant audience, drawing heavily on Mombaer and other late medieval sources—notably the early Hebraist Wessel Gansfort—but firmly adapted for Protestant use. It is the watershed of the English Protestant meditative tradition.[74]

The debt to the Brethren of the Common Life is significant. The increasing sophistication and self-confidence of English Protestant meditation after Hall, and its increasing readiness to dally with imaginative, contemplative, and even mystical approaches to prayer, can look like the prodigal's return: impoverished Protestant spirituality recognizing the greater riches of contemporary Catholicism, but if there are parallels between the Protestant and Catholic traditions, a strong case can be made that they reflect a shared spiritual ancestry rather than direct influence. Ignatius Loyola, too, had read Mombaer.[75] Hall's achievement was to adapt that medieval tradition so as to do justice both to it and to the emergent Protestant practice.

Hall did not see meditation as something esoteric, a practice only for 'hidden Cloysterers'. For him, meditation, like speaking in prose, was universal. 'We all meditate; one how to do ill to others; another how to doe some earthly good to himselfe.' In other words, meditation is thought: focused, purposeful thought. It is not, therefore, an end in itself. We do not meditate for the sake of meditating; it aims at a particular outcome. 'Divine meditation', therefore, is 'a bending of the mind vpon some spirituall obiect, through diuers formes of discourse, vntill our thoughts come to an issue'. The recognition of 'diuers formes' is important. Meditation can be expressed through a soliloquy, through prayer proper, or other means. It is defined not by the process but by the 'issue' at which it aims. So while meditation may develop into prayer, or even take the form of prayer, it is distinct from it. It 'begins in the vnderstanding, ends in the affections; It begins in the braine, descends to the heart'. It is therefore a purgative and preparatory discipline. By it 'we descrie our weakeness, . . . get more light to our knowledge, more heate to our affections, more life to our deuotion'. Its benefits are clear: 'Hee shall neuer find ioy, neither in God nor in himselfe, which doeth not both knowe and practise it', but that joy is the issue of meditation, the end at which it aims, not the meditation itself. Citing the psalmic injunction to 'taste and see' that God is good, Hall argues that in fact we must always see before we taste, since 'sight is of the vnderstanding; taste, of the affection'.[76]

This is a meaningful definition, but a very open-ended one, and part of Hall would clearly have liked to leave it there. However, he knew that if he was going to recommend this for everyone, he needed to provide a little more guidance. So first he subdivided meditation into two basic varieties, extemporal and deliberate.

[74] Hall, *Arte of Divine Meditation*, sig. A4r-v; Martz, *Poetry of Meditation*, 332–3; White, *English Devotional Literature*, 160–1.
[75] Schwanda, *Soul Recreation*, 129–33.
[76] Hall, *Arte of Divine Meditation*, 2–7, 65, 85, 151.

Extemporal (or 'occasional') meditation is that triggered by daily sights and sounds, allegorizing and spiritualizing them much as Vives had done. Hall's own *Meditations and vows* consists largely of meditations of this kind.[77] Deliberate meditation, when we self-consciously set ourselves to meditate without an external prompt, is his main focus in *The Arte of Divine Meditation*. Here, through Mombaer, Hall had a splendid structure to draw on, in the shape of Wessel Gansfort's *Scala meditationis*, which provided an eleven-step structure for meditation. Hall reproduced it, but with some misgivings. He feared that it smacked of 'obscurity', and so stopped short of recommending it. Good Calvinist that he was, he would not be too prescriptive or too exclusive in matters of devotion. Yet the *Scala*'s scheme consumes nearly a third of his book. What strikes the modern reader is that the first ten of its eleven steps are to do with logical analysis. The subject meditated upon is systematically examined from a series of different angles before what Hall calls the 'difficult and knotty part of Meditation' is finished. Only then, in the final step, do we allow the findings of our analysis to bleed through to the affections. But this, Hall insists, is 'the very soule of Meditation. . . . All our former labour of the braine, is only to affect the heart'.[78]

This masterful work of synthesis, which reunited the emergent Protestant practice of meditation with the traditions of late-medieval humanism, defined the subject across the Protestant spectrum for the rest of our period. Elizabeth Isham, John Bruen, and Elizabeth Hastings, the countess of Huntingdon, all included Hall's meditative writing among their favourite spiritual texts. In a sermon published in 1615, Samuel Ward praised meditation, but refrained from any lengthy comment, for it was 'an Art lately so taught, as I shall neede onely, to point at the choise theames'; a marginal note referred to Hall. In his vast *Guide to Godlynesse*, John Downame declared that Hall 'leaueth all others farre behind him', adding that for anyone else to write on the subject would be like writing another *Iliad* after Homer (before, naturally, proceeding to do just that).[79] Those who did not cite Hall echoed him. Samuel Smith's popular exposition of Psalm 1 described meditation as applying the thoughts of the brain to work on the affections, borrowed Hall's metaphor of chewing the cud, and also compared divine to worldly meditation.[80] While the generic breadth of what could be described as a 'meditation' persisted, Hall's *Meditations and vows* also had its imitators. Arthur Warwick's popular *Spare-Minutes; or, resolved meditations and premeditated resolutions* is merely witty moralizing, although he does, again, define meditation as 'the wombe of our actions'.[81] Donald Lupton's *Obiectorum Reductio* follows Hall's definition of extemporal meditation more closely. Lupton finds spiritual meanings in such

[77] See below, p. 417, on the effort to keep thoughts focused on God.
[78] Hall, *Arte of Divine Meditation*, pp. 7, 86–150, esp. 86–8, 149–50.
[79] Isham, 'Diary', 1634; Hinde, *Faithfull Remonstrance . . . of Iohn Bruen*, 142; Huntington Library, San Marino, CA, MS 15369 fo. 26r; Ward, *Coal from the Altar*, 52; Downame, *Guide to Godlynesse*, 533.
[80] Smith, *Dauids blessed man*, 135–40.
[81] Arthur Warwick, *Spare-Minutes; or, resolved meditations and premeditated resolutions* (1634: RSTC 25097), 32 (seven editions, 1634–9).

unlikely sights as a toad (he and it are both loathsome), a chained dog (who, like
Satan, is restrained from his full malice), and even his own shadow (which only
attends him in the light, just as flatterers only attend the prosperous). Some of these
would have fallen foul of Hall's warning that extemporal meditations should not be
'too farre-fetcht'.[82]

Hall's most pervasive influence—and the point where his definition fit best with
Protestant theological preoccupations—was his dynamic view of meditation. For
him, it was neither a state nor a goal, but a purposeful intellectual process. This
emphasis set him apart from Jesuit-inspired meditations like Sutton's, which simply
had the devotee imaginatively recreate the events of, for example, the Passion. As
Helen White put it, the difference is between 'contemplation as an approach to
communion' and 'resolution, as a prelude to action'—where *action* is sometimes
inner and spiritual. Hall's instrumental view of meditation as a gateway to prayer
and a means of purging the self was echoed by figures as various as the puritan
Henry Scudder, the moderate Daniel Featley, and the Laudian John Browning.
Elnathan Parr compared meditation to tuning an instrument before playing it;
Thomas White, after our period, to the kindling of a fire.[83] A preacher's anecdote
from the 1660s neatly captures this sense of meditation's dynamism. A dying father
solemnly charges his loose-living son to spend fifteen minutes each day in solitary
thought, on any subject he wishes. The practice, inevitably, brings the young
wastrel to self-awareness and repentance.[84] This was how meditation was supposed
to work.

How far this reflects real experience is another matter. There is no mistaking the
widespread interest in the subject. No spiritual practice which lacked an explicit
New Testament basis was more widely recommended.[85] But it is hard to say
whether Hall's recommendations were followed in practice, partly because Hall
and his successors so scrupulously avoided being prescriptive. Although he believed
that you should approach prayer through meditation, he also urged that meditation
should begin with prayer, and compared the two to inseparable twins. John
Hayward, who picked up on that image, explained that his practice was 'oftentimes
in the middest of Meditation to break into prayer: sometimes in the middest of
Prayer to pause vpon Meditation'—and those contrasting verbs, *break* and *pause*,
give us as clear a sense of the difference between the two as we are going to get.[86]

In practice, the relationship between meditation and prayer was less one of logic
than of mood. While texts described as 'meditations' may be framed as prayers,
they are often reflective in feel. For meditation was not aimed at stirring up the
affections in general, but at a specific emotional register. Grace Mildmay called her

[82] Donald Lupton, *Obiectorum Reductio: Or, Daily Imployment for the Soule* (1634: RSTC 16945),
6–7, 24–6, 33–4; Hall, *Arte of Divine Meditation*, 17.
[83] White, *English Devotional Literature*, 179; Scudder, *Christians daily walke* (1628), 110–12;
Featley, *Ancilla Pietatis*, 1; Browning, *Concerning publike-prayer*, 86–7; Parr, *Abba Father*, 9;
Thomas White, *A method and instructions for the art of divine meditation* (1655: Wing W1847B), 4–5.
[84] Oliver Heywood, *Heart-Treasure* (1667: Wing H1767), 94.
[85] An exception might be the linked discipline of spiritual writing, on which see below, pp. 298–
314.
[86] Hall, *Arte of Divine Meditation*, 78; Hayward, *Sanctvarie of a troubled soule* (1618), II sig. R7v.

meditations 'the consolation of my soule, the joye of my hart & the stabilitte of my mynde'. Daniel Featley claimed that meditation would 'settle my thoughts and affections, and compose my soule to rest'. 'Let thy soule swim in heavenly meditations', Thomas Tymme urged. John Winthrop believed that good meditative habits 'keepe the heart well ordered' and felt that his own lack of such habits 'is an occasion that I am ofte unsettled'.[87] Meditation was often described as digesting or ruminating. Our discussion of Protestant emotions suggested that calm and peace were more aspired to than enjoyed in this period.[88] Perhaps meditation gives us a more optimistic view of that subject.

Or perhaps not; for just as meditation and prayer in practice blurred into one another, so did consolation and zeal. Sutton, for example, believed that meditation on God would lead Christians 'feruently to desire him, to loue him, & to sigh after him with mourning'. Robert Bolton described being 'possest with meditation', giving rise to a 'feruencie of the heart, [which] cannot possiblie be enclosed within the compasse of the breast'. Cowper would have us 'earnestlie and feruently meditate', so that 'our Soule shall be inflamed with his loue'. Another Scot, Archibald Johnston of Wariston, described receiving sudden, overwhelming experiences of assurance while meditating, so much so that he could not but cry aloud.[89] Meditation, in other words, was associated with the full range of good Protestant affections. It is idle to label one or other end of this range as more authentic. The mood is indeed less ardent and more ruminative than with other prayers. But the emphasis that meditation is not a state but a process does also make it difficult simply to rest in it.

If indeed you managed to do it at all. For all Hall's reassurances, meditation was widely experienced as dauntingly difficult. There are endless exhortations to meditate; warnings to those who 'vse it sleightly' or who 'meditate by snatches, neuer chewing the cud'; laments as to the 'rarenes' of the practice. 'Many of Gods people omit it, because they know not how to doe it', Scudder claimed: at best they manage 'transient thoughts'.[90] This, at least, was a theme which the Catholic literature shared.[91] Nor was this difficulty restricted to the godless masses beloved of preachers' rhetoric. Richard Greenham commented on the intense difficulty of meditating, as distractions and interruptions crowded in on the mind. John Winthrop found it 'a most difficult thinge'.[92] That is, attempts at meditation often failed cleanly to strike the emotional notes that its advocates described. The result must have been that meditation was often a matter of self-conscious fret

[87] Mildmay, 'Meditations', I.30; Featley, *Ancilla Pietatis*, sig. A5v; Tymme, *Watch-bell* (1640), 294; Winthrop, *Papers*, 209.

[88] See above, pp. 80–3.

[89] Sutton, *Godly meditations* (1613), 389; Bolton, *Discourse about happinesse*, 4–5; Cowper, *Triumph*, 339–40; Cowper, *Most Comfortable Dialogue*, sig. A4v, pp. 64–5; Wariston, *Diary*, 21–2, 26.

[90] Paul Baynes, *Briefe Directions vnto a godly Life* (1618: RSTC 1626), 246; Ward, *Coal from the Altar*, 57; Leigh, *Mothers blessing*, 23; Scudder, *Christians daily walke* (1628), 123.

[91] Persons, *Booke of Christian exercise*, ed. Bunny, 8–9.

[92] Parker and Carlson, 'Practical Divinity', 209; Winthrop, *Papers*, 209.

and effort, very different from the self-forgetful bliss of which Mildmay and others spoke.

Wariston can have the last word on this subject. Describing a night of spiritual turmoil, he wrote that 'my saule was confounded and reeled to and fra lyk ane drunken man . . . fra meditation to prayer, fra prayer to meditation, 3 on my knees, 3 of againe'.[93] So it seems that Wariston knelt to pray, but not to meditate. Again, this suggests that he at least intended meditation to have a contemplative quality, which might or might not be addressed directly to God, but the image of the distraught young man bouncing up from his knees and falling to them time and time again suggests something different. Meditation certainly enlarges the area of early modern Protestant spiritual experience from the narrower confines of what they chose to call prayer. And while it is clearly important that the two cannot be separated, it is also clearly important that contemporaries chose to use distinct words. Meditation did have its own methods, moods, and taste; but that taste was as much aspired to as experienced. At best, meditation might help you to see more clearly, but what you saw was Reformed Protestantism, with its tight logic and its well-marked emotional and spiritual paths. There was nothing novel or subversive about meditation. What it could do was to teach you how to be a better Protestant.

[93] Wariston, *Diary*, 43–4.

7

Answering Prayer

'When ye pray, vse no vaine repetitions as the heathen . . . for your Father
knoweth whereof ye haue nede, before ye aske of him.' *Matthew 6:8.*

WHY PRAY?

Reformed Protestants' commonsense, everyday definition of prayer—asking God
for things—immediately raises a problem. What is the point of asking God for
anything? An omniscient God knows our needs better than we do ourselves, and is
hardly likely to change his mind on a point because we badger him. This is a
perennial problem of Christian prayer, but the daunting Protestant emphasis on
God's sovereignty only sharpened it. An almost nonsensical prayer of Thomas
Becon's encapsulates the paradox: 'Make me . . . O lord of that number, whom
thou from euerlasting haste predestinate to be saued.'[1] Behind that problem crowds
a series of others. What, if anything, does prayer do? If believers can ask things of
God in prayer, what can they ask, and what answers can they hope for? How does
prayer relate to action in the world?

These were live pastoral issues in the early modern period, to which divines paid
considerable attention. The Elizabethan homily on prayer set the tone with this
robust condemnation:

> Most fond and foolish is the opinion and reason of those men, which therefore think
> all prayer to be superfluous and vain, because God searcheth the heart and the reins,
> and knoweth the meaning of the spirit before we ask.

But the homily did not actually provide much of an argument to defend this
assertion. Nor did William Perkins, when he described such questions as 'flat
Atheism'. Shouting down doubts in this way is not particularly impressive, and
may, as Peter Iver Kaufman has suggested, betray a real contradiction between
Protestants' professed beliefs and their real convictions.[2] There is, however, another
reading of it. In his *Booke of Christian Prayers*, Richard Day urged his readers to
'thinke it not superfluous to pray, because God already knoweth what we neede',

---

[1] Becon, *Pomaunder of prayer*, fo. 44r.
[2] *Certain Sermons or Homilies*, 285; Perkins, *Godly and learned exposition*, 232; Peter Iver Kaufman,
'"Much In Prayer": The Inward Researches of Elizabethan Protestants', *Journal of Religion* 73/2
(1993), 164.

and laid out several arguments on the subject. His final point is the most telling: the Christian should pray 'because thou doest hourely want that grace, which [God] will assuredly geue'.[3] The experience of petitionary prayer is that it precedes logic. In need, the Christian cries out to God simply because it seems natural to do so. In this sense, Perkins' claim that questioning prayer is atheism is not name-calling, but a simple description. Prayer is just something that Christians do, whether it makes sense or not. The subsequent quarrels, doctrines, and rationalizations are all under the shadow of that primary fact.

That said, doubts about the efficacy of prayer were perfectly real, and the rebuttals came thick and fast. One important strand—significant, but on its own insufficient—had been laid out by Augustine and by Aquinas, and was much reiterated in our period. This argues that a key purpose of prayer is not to change God's mind—which is of course impossible—but to change yourself; that it is, as Vincent Brümmer puts it, a form of self-therapy.[4] Here, again, prayer blurs into meditation. In our period, John Preston made the point most bluntly:

> When you goe about to striue with God in prayer . . . you alter not him, but your selues: for those arguments that you vse, are not so much to perswade him to helpe you, as to perswade your hearts to more faith, to more loue, to more obedience.[5]

This could work in several ways. Inevitably, one of the most important was repentance. Conscientious petitionary prayer involves humbling yourself before God, admitting your dependence, and bowing your will, and a series of commentators recognized that all of these things ease the process of repentance.[6] The purpose of prayer, Robert Harris claimed, is 'principally to acknowledge our dependancie and his soueraigntie'. John Hooper argued that we persist in prayer so as to repent the more earnestly; or, as Dorothy Leigh put it, Christ says to us in prayer, 'I know thy sinnes alreadie, but I would know whether thou knowest them or no'.[7]

However, if prayer humbles, it can also comfort and exalt. John Norden's *Pensive mans practise* included 'a comfortable Praier, whereby the distressed man may comfort himselfe in his miseries'. That explicit admission that prayer is directed to the self rather than to God may simply be careless phrasing, although, as we have seen with meditation, early modern Protestants did not worry very much about the difference between talking to God and talking to yourself.[8] Perkins, too, believed that we pray in order 'to ease our woeful hearts, by powring them out vnto the Lord'.[9] Nor did it stop there. Thomas Knell claimed that we pray 'that thereby our

[3] Day, *Booke of Christian Prayers*, sig. ☞2v.

[4] Vincent Brümmer, *What Are We Doing When We Pray? A Philosophical Inquiry* (1984), 23–6; cf. David Keck, 'Sorrow and Worship in Calvin's Geneva' in Marc R. Forster and Benjamin J. Kaplan (eds), *Piety and Family in Early Modern Europe* (Aldershot, 2005), 212; Thomas, *Religion and the Decline of Magic*, 175.

[5] Preston, *Saints Daily Exercise*, 44–5.

[6] *Certain Sermons or Homilies*, 284; Day, *Booke of Christian Prayers*, sig. ☞2v; Bradford, *Godlie meditations*, sigs K1v–2r.

[7] Harris, *Peters enlargement* (1627), 31; Hooper, *Later Writings*, 317; Leigh, *Mothers blessing*, 80–1, 137.

[8] Norden, *Pensive mans practise . . . The second part*, 49; see above, p. 111.

[9] Perkins, *Godly and learned exposition*, 247.

heart and desire may be inflamed feruentlie to seeke him, to loue and to worship him'.[10] It is as when we declare our love for another person: it is done both to express love and in order to love all the more. Richard Rogers compared prayer to a bellows, which 'giueth life to Gods graces in vs, which before lay in vs halfe dead; as faith, hope, care of dutie . . . euen as the fire is quickned by blowing'. He cited what he claimed was a proverb: 'pray well, and liue well'. One reader found the idea striking enough to underline it.[11]

This whole approach to prayer was clearly important, but equally clearly it was not enough. Consciously attempting to 'pray' in order to change yourself, rather than to talk to God, is unlikely to succeed. Self-therapy is a proper by-product of prayer, but not its proper purpose. Of course, the intense self-awareness which Protestant prayer cultivated is profoundly important. But the people we are studying insist on bringing God into picture, and therefore so must we.

There was one straightforward, unanswerable, unsatisfying riposte to the question 'why pray': because God says so. The numerous Biblical injunctions to pray make it a mere matter of obedience, not for believers to reason why.[12] Hugh Latimer warned those who felt they could choose whether or not to pray, 'remember that it is the commandment of God'. The argument could work several ways. It was 'a great sinne . . . not to render this seruice to God', since it implied that a lack of true faith. By contrast, the act of prayer was 'a sacrifice well pleasing to God', and was indeed what human beings were created to do. An anonymous 17th-century writer stressed that it was 'a priviledg for dust and ashes to make addresses to the eternall God of heaven, (afore whom the cherubims cover their faces)'.[13] But this only sharpened the obligation: who would dare spurn such a privilege?

Bare obedience might seem an unsatisfyingly blunt answer to the question of why we should ask God for things; however, it contains a more fruitful line of argument. God commands not merely that we should pray, but specifically that we should petition him. So God does know our needs whether or not we pray, but he wants us to pray before meeting those needs. The Edinburgh preacher Robert Bruce spelled this out. Prayer cannot compel God to act, but since it is a part of honouring God, and since God wishes us to know our dependence on him, he withholds blessings until we have prayed for them. Richard Sibbes put it thus: 'God will be sued unto for all the favours he bestows. . . . Ordinarily, what we have if we be his children, we have it as a fruit of prayer.' Dorothy Leigh used an analogy. A servant has been promised a gift by his master, only on the condition that he asks for it. If he then neglects to ask, will the master not be rightly angered by the contempt shown to him?[14]

---

[10] Knell, *Godlie and necessarie Treatise*, sig. A4r.

[11] Rogers, *Seven treatises*, 287, 352; underlining in FSL STC 21215.

[12] See, for example, Bradford, *Godlie meditations*, sig. I8v; Day, *Booke of Christian Prayers*, sig. 2v; Leigh, *Mothers blessing*, 79–80.

[13] Latimer, *Sermons by Hugh Latimer*, 508; Bull, *Christian praiers*, 14–15; Perkins, *Godly and learned exposition*, 231–2; Gouge, *Whole-Armor of God*, 412; Bod. MS Rawl. D.384 fo. 1r.

[14] Bruce, *Sermons Preached*, sigs F4v–5r; Sibbes, *Works*, VI.96; Leigh, *Mothers blessing*, 133–5. Cf. Perkins, *Exposition of the Lords prayer*, 15.

This is a neat argument: a little too neat. It does not fit with routine claims that prayer was 'omnipotent'. The Elizabethan Homily cited a string of patristic authorities on the point: for example, St John Chrysostom, arguing 'that there is nothing in all the world more strong than a man that giveth himself to fervent prayer'. Cowper called prayer 'the hand of a Christian, which is able to reach from earth to heauen, and take forth euery manner of good gift out of the Lords treasurie'. Thomas Goodwin called prayer a 'transcendant priviledge of power', and claimed that devotees 'have the honour to be accounted Co-workers together with God'.[15] Naturally, this sort of thing is hyperbole, intended chiefly to stir Christians to devotion, but—since we are dealing with Reformed Protestants—it also has a theological underpinning. If, as we have seen, true prayer was not a human action at all, but the work of God, then a true prayer is by definition in keeping with God's will—which, as we shall see, does not mean that all requests will be granted. Therefore, as Perkins pointed out, to ask how prayer can change God's mind makes no sense:

> As God hath decreed the euent of all things, so likewise he hath appointed the meanes whereby his decree shall be effected: and prayer many times, is a principall meanes to bring Gods will to passe. . . . Praier is not contrarie to Gods decree, but a subordinate meanes to bring the same to passe.[16]

This brings formidable problems of its own, because it re-emphasizes that people can only pray if given the grace to do so, but that is at least a familiar problem for Reformed Protestants. And that, it seems, is all that they felt they needed to say on the general problem of prayer.

WORLDLY AND OTHERWORLDLY PRAYER

Most Protestant attention focused instead on more practical problems: what should we pray for, and what answers should we expect? Here there was a very clear consensus from a very early date, based on the Gospel principle that we should pray in faith. As Thomas Cartwright put it, 'praier . . . can neuer be truly made, without hope of obtaining the grace, that is praied for'.[17] Without confidence that a prayer will be granted, it certainly will not be. The question, of course, is whether such confidence can be justified. The answer was to divide the benefits for which Christians could pray into the spiritual and temporal, which were to be sought in different ways.

Spiritual benefits such as salvation, repentance, faith, and all virtues or fruits of the Spirit should be prayed for *unconditionally*. In other words, Christians could simply ask God for these gifts, and expect to receive them. It was true that the gift could be delayed, sometimes for a very long time, but, so the argument ran, these

---

[15] Robert Harris, *Peters enlargement upon the prayers of the Church* (1624: RSTC 12839.7), 8; *Certain Sermons or Homilies*, 286; Cowper, *Triumph*, 90; Goodwin, *Returne of Prayers*, sig. A4v, A8r.
[16] Perkins, *Godly and learned exposition*, 232.
[17] Cartwright and Wilcox, *Two treatises*, 34.

spiritual benefits were promised unconditionally by God to his faithful people, and believers could therefore claim those promises with certainty. Temporal benefits, however—meaning any worldly event whatsoever, whether recovery from illness or victory in war—must only be prayed for *conditionally*. Christians who asked for such benefits could not know whether—in the particular instance—their request was in accordance with God's will. They might, for example, want good health when God knew that in fact a period of illness would teach them patience and humility, or spare them some temptation or misfortune. Therefore, like Christ in Gethsemane, they had to ask to receive their benefit *if* it were God's will. That escape clause was essential. It was absolutely routine for it to be used explicitly, and as Archbishop Whitgift argued, 'although it be not expressed, yet it is always understood'.[18]

One of the features of this system, as perhaps of all Christian systems of prayer, is that it is logically closed and therefore impossible to disprove.[19] If requests for temporal goods are not answered, that merely proves that it is not God's will to answer them. Requests for spiritual goods are trickier, and indeed if they are repeatedly fruitless the devotee's faith might begin to waver. But it is equally likely that, for example, a repeated and earnest prayer for patience might be self-fulfilling. You might well make an extra effort to be patient, in order to show sincerity in your prayer and also so as to bolster your own faith by demonstrating that the prayer had worked. If a longed-for spiritual benefit nevertheless failed to materialize, there were still good explanations on tap. Perhaps your prayers were inadequately faithful— perhaps, indeed, they were not true prayers at all. Perhaps God was delaying granting them in order to strengthen your faith. Or perhaps God had already granted them, but the fact was hidden from you: real faith and felt faith were not the same thing. In other words, this doctrine of prayer could accommodate every possible outcome.

Inevitably this can seem like a sinister system of social control. It is, however, worth the effort of seeing it from the other side. Assertions that prayer is powerless are equally impossible to disprove. This is not logical trickery but simply the nature of the question.[20] More importantly, whatever the logic might say, the efficacy of prayer *was* widely doubted in early modern Protestant cultures, amongst nominal and earnest believers alike. The real value of this view of prayer was not to box doubters in but to teach them the Reformed Protestant doctrine of God. We can see this most clearly in the critique of inappropriate forms of prayer: forms that tried to tie God's hands, to specify how he ought to answer prayers, or which were not

---

[18] John Whitgift, *The Works of John Whitgift*, ed. John Ayre (Cambridge, 1851–3), II.473–4. There are too many complete or partial expositions of this system to list, but see Becon, *Newe pathwaye unto praier*, sigs H6v–I5r; Latimer, *Sermons and Remains*, 172–4; *A prymmer or boke of priuate prayer . . . auctorysed and set fourth by the kinges maiestie* (1553: RSTC 20373), sigs b4r-6r; Perkins, *Whole treatise*, 267–8. Archbishop Sandys assumed to his congregation in York that it was a question 'wherewith ye are throughly acquainted': Sandys, *Sermons*, 77. Cf. also Bull, *Christian praiers*, 19–20; Sparke, *Crumms of comfort*, sigs A6v-7r; Clarke, *Holy Incense*, 10.

[19] As Keith Thomas has pointed out: *Religion and the Decline of Magic*, 136–7.

[20] Brümmer, *What Are We Doing When We Pray?*, 1–5.

based on sufficient faith. All of these, critics held, were based on inadequate understandings of God. Hugh Latimer, for example, argued that those who promised that God would act in a particular way—healing an illness, for example—might seem to be showing great faith. In fact, it was the opposite. They were saying, in effect, 'He shall be no more my God, except he come.' They ought to have prayed conditionally and submitted to God's will. Thomas Knell was scathing of those who came to God with 'foolish demandes . . . what-soeuer it liketh them to dreame', or who tried to wheedle, flatter, or manipulate him.[21] Richard Norwood, looking back on his twelve-year-old self from middle age, read his former prayer habits in this way. He had prayed frequently and earnestly, but did so 'thinking: it may be God doth hear men's prayers and will grant me what I now crave'.[22]

The most important spiritual lesson of the distinction between conditional and unconditional prayer, however, was one of priority. As the young Norwood knew, the commonsense view of petitionary prayer focuses on worldly benefits. But those who were theologically serious about prayer understood that temporal, conditional prayers were a sideshow. This is of course not a distinctively Protestant point,[23] but the Reformed focus on God's sovereignty allowed it to be made with particular force. The Homily on Prayer made the hierarchy clear. 'When we have sufficiently prayed for things belonging to the soul, then'—and only then—'may we lawfully, and with safe conscience, pray also for our bodily necessities'.[24] It was a common-place to point out that the Lord's Prayer begins, not with daily bread, but with God's name, will, and kingdom: we do not 'ask forthwith at the first chop our necessaries'. Cartwright even suggested, mischievously, that since prayer for bodily needs forms only one of seven clauses in the Lord's Prayer, Christians should only devote one seventh of their prayers to such needs.[25]

This priority was, naturally, because spiritual goods were far more desirable than worldly ones. The prayers of the godly, Bishop Cowper claimed, are always for blessings, a subject on which they are 'insatiable', whereas the worldly foolishly seek lesser things. Thomas Goodwin made a stirring appeal to Christians not to devote their prayers to trifles, but to 'this thriving trade of entercourse with God; the returns whereof are better than the merchandise of silver, and the gain ther of, than fine gold'.[26] The use of the financial image, however, tells us that this argument was swimming against a worldly tide. Henry Scudder vividly compared the devotee choosing topics for prayer to a judge beset by clamouring plaintiffs. Rather than listening to the noisiest first (worldly concerns) a wise judge will 'consider whose

---

[21] Latimer, *Sermons by Hugh Latimer*, 348; Knell, *Godlie and necessarie Treatise*, sig. A3v. This was not as simple as it might seem, however, since persuading and even arguing with God *were* accepted parts of Protestant prayer: see below, pp. 247–56.

[22] Norwood, *Journal*, 10.

[23] See, for example, Erasmus, *Enchiridion*, 100–2.

[24] *Certain Sermons or Homilies*, 296.

[25] Latimer, *Sermons by Hugh Latimer*, 302; Whitgift, *Works*, II.478; cf. Bownde, *Medicines for the plague*, 130.

[26] Cowper, *Triumph*, 98–101; Goodwin, *Returne of Prayers*, sig. A11r.

turne it is, and what is the most important sute; and dispatch them first'. Worldly petitions should be kept waiting at the door while more important matters are dealt with. If they burst in nevertheless, he advised, 'giue them no hearing, but dishearten them, and rebuke the porter and keeper of the doore of your heart'.[27] Yet it took more than exhortations to silence worldly needs' clamour. Printed prayers and liturgical prayers did usually follow the prescribed order, beginning with spiritual concerns, with worldly matters being given secondary and sometimes cursory treatment. But talk *about* prayer did tend to focus on worldly requests. While good Protestants certainly used the spiritual sections of their set prayers, it is fair to suspect that they found it easier to pray the latter, worldly parts with fervour.

The theory of conditional prayer for worldly goods was clear enough. John Norden's austere view was that your submission to God's will must be so complete that you must not state even a *preferred* outcome: 'thou maiest not ioyne thine owne fantasies to the will of God'. Lord, either save my child's life or not, as you see fit.[28] It is no surprise to find that devotees struggled to abrogate their own wills in this way. The diary of Robert Woodford, an impecunious Northamptonshire lawyer, gives us some glimpses of this. When Woodford was faced with a decision about which he was genuinely uncertain, such as a choice about the direction of his career, he could easily enough pray, 'Lord direct & order every thinge for the best for the Lords sake I desire to wayt vppon thee'. But when his newborn son John fell dangerously ill in December 1637, his prayers were much more straightforward: 'I and my deare wife have besought the Lord for him with earnestnes.' While acknowledging that God might take him, they made their own preference clear. This time, it was a happy outcome, and when giving thanks for John's recovery, Woodford added a prayer, 'that we may not sett our affections too much vppon him or any worldly thinge but graunt that we may love the creatures in thee & for thee'.[29]

What was asked of believers under such circumstances was, as they frankly admitted, superhuman; that is, it could only be attained by the work of the Spirit. No-one recommended Stoic indifference to loved ones' illnesses and deaths—or, indeed, to your own. That pain, however, should be translated not into simple prayer for the desired outcome, but into earnest submission to God's will and into searching out your sins. Sometimes the results seem shockingly callous and self-centred to modern eyes. It was almost routine to interpret others' sufferings as punishment from God for your own sins. As we have seen, this was how John Winthrop viewed the ague from which his first wife suffered in 1607.[30] When Thomas Shepard was in anguish over his second wife's death, he looked back on his many earlier bereavements—his first wife and three of his six children—and commented, 'I saw that if I had profited by former afflictions of this nature I should not have had this scourge.'[31] We may suspect that the struggle to pray correctly—that is, conditionally—was partly informed by fear that doing it

[27] Scudder, *Christians daily walke* (1628), 44–5.
[28] Norden, *Pensive mans practise . . . The second part*, 43.
[29] Woodford, 'Diary', 22.viii.1637 recto, 17.xii.1637 recto, 20.xii.1637 verso–recto.
[30] Winthrop, *Papers*, 162.   [31] Shepard, *God's Plot*, 70.

incorrectly would invite the feared punishment. Also, as well as manipulating God, devotees may have been manipulating themselves. Conditional prayer prepared you for the possibility that the worst might happen, and might also help to avert a crisis of faith. While Winthrop and Shepard's attitude may seem distasteful, we see a different side of this kind of piety in Nehemiah Wallington, who saw all five of his children die, four of them in infancy. Two of these deaths in particular shook Wallington to the core, so much so that 'I brooke all my . . . promises and cove-nantes with my God'. It was his wife Grace who consoled him, reminding him of the comfort which they could both find in submission to God's will. 'It is your daughters weading day', she reasoned, 'and will you grive to see your daughter goe home to her Husband Christ Jesus?' Eventually, Wallington could draw comfort in believing that he was blessed through the loss of his children, for they were his treasure, and if his treasure was in Heaven, his heart would be there also.[32]

Such perfect submission was the ideal, but in practice, attempts to manipulate events through prayer were inevitable. One technique was to pray 'conditionally' by presenting God with fixed alternatives and asking him to choose between them; which may have felt like submission to his will, but also curtailed his options. Hugh Latimer, for example, advised those whose clergy opposed the Gospel to 'pray unto God, and he will either turn his [the curate's] heart, and make him better; or remove him from thee'. The evangelical gentlewoman Rose Throckmorton, fulminating against Mary I's oppression, 'often prayed earnestlye to god to take either her or me forth of the world'. The young Archibald Johnston of Wariston, struggling with his own lust, repeatedly prayed, 'Lord, eyther keape me from being tempted; or, in the tentation, let me find thy reneuing grace'—and by 'grace', he meant not chastity but a 'laufil remedie': that is, a wife.[33] The alternative which none of these devotees were willing to contemplate was that their situation would remain unchanged.

Another possibility was to look for exceptions to the general rule of conditional prayer. This helped to drive the burgeoning interest in God's promises in Scripture, for if God had unambiguously promised a particular outcome, then his will was already clear and conditionality was unnecessary. The most popular compendium of this kind, *A Collection of certaine Promises out of the Word of GOD*, at times has a whiff of magic about it. It advises the reader, for example, that,

> if thou wantest children, apply, Deut 7.14. . . . There shall neither be male nor female barren among you. . . . If thou hast conceiued, apply this promise for keeping of it, Exod. 23.26. There shall none cast their young, nor bee barren in thy land.

There is no hedging of this with conditionality—although there is also a further promise which is taken as a word of comfort for those who, despite Deuteronomy, remain childless.[34] We find a similar sense of desperation crowding out theological caution in the Scottish minister John Scrimger. Scrimger had lost 'some children' already when his daughter fell gravely ill. In his prayer for her, 'I . . . began to

[32] Wallington, *Notebooks*, 59, 64; cf. Matthew 6:21.
[33] Latimer, *Sermons by Hugh Latimer*, 304; BL Additional MS 43827A fo. 18r; Wariston, *Diary*, 2.
[34] Fawkener, *Collection of Promises*, 149–51 (six editions 1629–40, and seven more by 1688).

expostulat with God, in a fitt of great displeasure', demanding that God heal her. Happily, as we shall see, God often favoured the importunate. 'At last it was said to me, "I have heard thee at this time, but use not such boldness in time coming, for such particulars".' He returned to find the girl recovering.[35]

Under such intense stress, it is understandable that strict propriety in prayer should come under some pressure, but by the end of our period, cases like Scrimger's were beginning to undermine the po-faced orthodoxy of conditionality. The most common exception was on the deathbed. As we shall see, some gravely ill Protestants would refuse to pray for recovery, believing that it was God's will that they should die. This was usually taken as a sign of piety, not of presumption.[36] In a treatise published in 1641, Thomas Goodwin generalized the point. He claimed that 'God sometimes gives a speciall faith' concerning a particular temporal event, which makes conditional prayer unnecessary. 'There may be a particular strengthening and assuring of the heart, that God will doe such a thing for a man.' He added that this was unusual, and also that even these assurances did not guarantee that the promised event would take place—the prophet Jonah, after all, had been assured by God that Nineveh would be overthrown. But the permission thus granted to pray unconditionally was all too tempting.[37]

PRAYER AND ACTION

A different problem turned on the relationship between prayer and action, where there was another clear but finely balanced orthodoxy. This permitted—or, indeed, obliged—believers to use worldly 'means' as well as prayer to achieve a desired outcome. The 'means', however, must be subordinate to prayer. The question was most often discussed in relation to medicine. Every respectable Protestant accepted that the sick should make due use of physicians. Medicine was God's provision for the sick, just as food was his provision for the healthy. However, medical treatment of illness must always be contained *within* spiritual treatment. Hence, for example, William Perkins' insistence that, when ill, you should always send for the minister before you send for the physician, and that you should sanctify medicine with prayer just as you would say grace before eating. Lewis Bayly's *Practise of pietie* included a text for just such a prayer before taking medicine, and Bayly, similarly, held that the first recourse for the sick Christian was prayer and self-examination, before medical advice is sought.[38]

However, this neat sequence—in which prayer, spiritual counsel, and self-examination deal with an illness's root causes, and a physician then tidies up the leftover symptoms—worked better in theory than in practice. For one thing, not all physicians were willing to play the subordinate role that divines scripted for them,

---

[35] Tweedie, *Select Biographies*, 308.   [36] See below, pp. 462–4.
[37] Goodwin, *Returne of Prayers*, 58–60, 110–13.
[38] William Perkins, *A salve for a sicke man* (Cambridge, 1595: RSTC 19742), 61, 70–7; Bayly, *Practise of pietie*, 626, 634, 644–8; and see below, pp. 381–9.

and patients cannot afford to be too choosy. Richard Greenham tackled one knotty question: was it legitimate to use a popish physician's services? The answer was a grudging yes, but he hedged it with no less than ten caveats, including a warning that we should use 'spiritual means of praier, fasting, searching the inward causes of our visitation' before resorting to a Catholic medic.[39] The question of responding to epidemics, where prevention was sought just as earnestly as cure, made the matter look different again. John Hooper boldly argued in the 1540s that plague was caused by sin, not by putrefaction or poison, and so you could only save yourself by fleeing moral, rather than material, corruption.[40] This, however, is more attractive as a preacher's pose than as sober counsel. The consensus was shifting steadily towards pragmatic, medical methods of dealing with infection across our period, and this shift affected divines too. The prayer in time of plague in Thomas Sorocold's *Supplications of Saints* emphasizes sin as the root cause of disease, asks not to trust too much to 'means', but also prays for 'strength to our medicines', and asks blessings on 'our shifting places for more security'.[41] Or consider William Crashaw, a moderate puritan minister in Whitechapel who saw the plague of 1625 at first hand, 'walking hourely through the valley of the shadow of Death', and burying more than two thousand of the victims. His book of devotions for use during the epidemic was itself a sign of pragmatic compromise: it was in place of daily prayers in church, which had been banned for fear of further contagion. Some diehards opposed that decision, but Crashaw supported it. His text focused on spiritual matters, but he was also forthright with his medical advice. He recommended using 'all helpes of Nature and Art' against the plague, and warned against those who claimed that neighbourly charity should trump quarantines. The godly died alongside sinners, he pointed out—all too prophetically, for he himself was apparently one of the epidemic's last victims. That was perhaps because of his one concession to idealism: his insistence that ministers, physicians, and all others with public roles had a duty to 'stand in thy Station [and] make Conscience to doe thy duty', rather than fleeing the city.[42]

As these strictures make clear, the broad 'orthodox' position—which advocated prayer supported by appropriate effort—saw itself as the mean between two opposed errors. One is the error of those who doubted prayer's power, who—as Thomas Tuke put it—'worke and pray not' and are 'set wholly on the earth'. We can well believe that this was common enough, but Tuke also claimed that there was an opposite party, those who 'pray and worke not', and 'would seeme to be all for heauen'. (Tuke's own view was that 'I will both worke and pray: for God hath made Munday as wel, as Sunday'.)[43] We struggle to find many cases of such hyperspirituality in earnest: there was, for example, a man who, during the Ulster revivals of the early 1630s, 'took up an erroneous opinion, that there was need of no other

[39] Parker and Carlson, '*Practical Divinity*', 135.

[40] John Hooper, *Early Writings of John Hooper*, ed. Samuel Carr (Cambridge, 1843), 333.

[41] Sorocold, *Supplications of Saints* (1612), 256–7; Patrick Wallis, 'Plagues, Morality and the Place of Medicine in Early Modern England', *English Historical Review* 121/490 (2006), 1–24.

[42] Crashaw, *London's Lamentation*, sigs A2v–3v, D3v–6r; *ODNB*.

[43] Tuke, *Practise of the faithfull*, 35; the same contrast is found in Brinsley, *True Watch* (1608), 37–8.

mean to be used but prayer, whatever ailed soul or body, young or old, corn or cattle'. He refused to give medicine to his horse, only being persuaded back to common sense with 'some difficulty'.[44] More significant than such quixotic individuals is what Daniel Dyke's best-selling *The mystery of selfe-deceiuing* had to say on the subject. In Dyke's view, the sinner who has a false, temporary, and ineffectual faith, 'praies idlie, and lazily, and doth not together with his lippes in praying, moue his hands, in indeuouring for that he praies'. What looks like faith is in fact sloth. Michael Sparke, similarly, argued that it was hypocritical 'not to seeke that by diligence, which we make shew to seeke by Prayer'. Tuke even anticipated a favourite slogan of the modern age: 'God helpes the helpefull, such as are ready to helpe themselues.'[45] We do not need to accept such polemic wholesale to believe that a strong doctrine of prayer could be a convenient cloak for lassitude or fatalism. But we should also recognize that the 'orthodox' view of this matter was in tension with the overwhelming emphasis on God's sovereignty, and that it was tied up with the wider Protestant horror of idleness.[46]

This worry—crudely, that some people preferred prayer to action because prayer is easier—touched on a weak point in Reformed Protestantism's theological armour. That emphasis on divine sovereignty, the matching emphasis on human corruption and the doctrine of grace which bridged that gap—all of this led to accusations of antinomianism. Antinomianism is the ancient Christian heresy (or straw man) which argues that, if God forgives sin freely, then sin does not actually matter very much. While respectable Protestant theology never taught this doctrine, it did leave each individual's spiritual state and pious practices in his or her own hands, and plenty of them did not use that liberty as they were supposed to. By the early 17th century, puritan divines were increasingly concerned that Christian liberty might be a licence for hypocrisy—not least because genuine antinomian ideas were bubbling up.[47] Those concerns fed the rising insistence that true prayer must be matched by effort, just as true faith must express itself in works.

This applied above all to prayers of self-examination and repentance. If these were not accompanied by real efforts at self-renewal, they were clearly hypocritical. As Richard Kilby put it, 'to pray unto thee for the grace of repentance, and not to enforce my selfe to practice the means, is a kinde of mockery'.[48] It was easy to parrot a prayer of penitence, even to do it and to mean it, but as Sibbes put it, 'it is not sleepy habits but Grace in exercise that preserveth us'. That phrase—'Grace in exercise'—could stand as a summary of the tensions between human and divine action here. Perkins explained it slightly differently. He used a favourite Gospel proof-text for the doctrine of grace—'a good tre can not bring forthe euil frute'—to

---

[44] Blair, *Life*, 63

[45] Dyke, *Mystery of selfe-deceiuing*, 105; Sparke, *Crumms of comfort*, sigs H7v–8r; Tuke, *Practise of the faithfull*, 29; cf. Sibbes, *Works*, VI.103.

[46] See below, pp. 442–4.

[47] Alec Ryrie, 'Counting sheep, counting shepherds: the problem of allegiance in the English Reformation' in Peter Marshall and Alec Ryrie (eds), *The Beginnings of English Protestantism* (Cambridge, 2002), 99–105; Como, *Blown by the Spirit*; Bozeman, *Precisianist Strain*.

[48] Kilby, *Hallelujah*, 91.

argue that true faith must, of its nature, eventually produce grounds for assurance. But he advised those waiting anxiously for their own tree of faith to crop that they should work for it, watering the tree with rigorous pious effort. 'Men must not dispaire, but vse good meanes, and in time they shall be assured.'[49] 'Good means' were all the stocks-in-trade of Protestant piety: prayer, meditation, reading, sermon-attendance, and reformation of life. If by now it is no longer clear where effort ends and grace begins—if, indeed, it is no longer clear whether the two can be distinguished, owing to the Spirit's work in the believer—that is perhaps the point.

VOWS AND COVENANTS

The problematic relationship between prayer and action came to a sharp point in the question of vows and covenants.

We might not expect this to be an issue for Reformed Protestants. Vows were a routine part of Catholic pious practice, and Protestants rejected them in general as supernumerary works, and in particular for their association with vows of clerical and monastic celibacy. Many of the first generation of evangelical reformers had themselves broken such vows, which led them to develop a multi-stranded critique of the practice. They argued that vows breached Christ's warnings against illegitimate oaths. They pointed out Scriptural examples of vows which should never have been made, and having been made should never have been kept. They argued that vows to avoid sin were superfluous, since Christians should avoid sin anyway; that vows which restricted Christian liberty in some lawful matter were wrong; and that vows were a form of idolatry, since they involved placing your faith in your own willpower or in the vow itself, rather than in God.[50]

But the practice refused to die. Some vows continued to be used liturgically, in baptism, in marriage, and in ordination, which presumably helped to make the practice seem normative.[51] The Biblical material cuts both ways: while some Biblical vows were clearly ill-advised, other texts emphasized the solemnity of vows, and the promise to 'paie my vowes vnto the Lord' runs through the psalms.[52] Even in the first generation, Thomas Becon, expounding one such text, was forced to admit that as well as 'popysh, monkysh, supersticious & pharisaicall vowes, inuented of the ydle braynes of men', there were also 'pure godly, wholesome & christen vowes'.[53] If the Bible is ambiguous about vows, it unequivocally approves of covenants—a theological theme which was of particular importance to Reformed Protestantism. Nor was the habit of pious vow-making easily broken. Early modern society as a whole was structured by oaths, covenants, and mutual obligations—

---

[49] Sibbes, *Bruised reede*, 32–3; Perkins, *First part of The cases of conscience*, 66.

[50] Alec Ryrie, *The Gospel and Henry VIII* (Cambridge, 2003), 74–84.

[51] On the impact of baptismal vows, see below, pp. 332–3.

[52] Psalm 116:14; cf. Psalms 22:25, 50:14, 61:8, 66:13, 116:18; Numbers 30; Deuteronomy 12; Ecclesiastes 5:5.

[53] Thomas Becon, *Dauids harpe ful of moste delectable armony* (1542: RSTC 1717), sig. G8v.

especially in Scotland, where the Reformed emphasis on covenant echoed the long-standing Scottish practice of bond-making.

Whatever the reason, early scepticism towards pious vows did not last. References to voluntary vows and covenants gather pace from the later 16th century onward. Two of the pioneers were the Essex puritan ministers and neighbours Richard Rogers and Ezekiel Culverwell. Rogers and Culverwell prayed together regularly, and in November 1587 they decided to

> renue our covenaunt more firmly with the lorde . . . to geve to our selves lesse liberty in the secretest and smallest provocations to evel . . . that as much as might be we might walk with the lord for the time of our abideinge here below.

This may sound vague, but it evidently felt like a spiritual breakthrough. At the end of the month they renewed the covenant. Meeting with other local ministers, who were fretting about cooling zeal and decaying ardour, Rogers 'urged them to see the necessitie of this covenaunt makeinge, which I lately entred into'.[54] Some twenty of them joined in the 1588 'Covenant', which Rogers proudly reproduced in his compendious *Seven Treatises* (1603). The covenant's text runs to a little over eleven thousand words. The first half is a heartfelt but generic bewailing of the covenanters' sins; only then does it begin to make promises, most of which are unremarkable pledges to adhere to a fairly standard model of pious Protestant behaviour (prayer, reading, participation in public worship, and so forth). Only the emphasis on fasting is at all unusual, and even that is left studiedly vague.[55] What is remarkable about this covenant is not what they did, but that they did it at all.

By the time Rogers went public with his covenant, other voices were cautiously discussing the adoption of voluntary disciplines. William Perkins wrote on the subject in the late 1590s, although the book in question was published posthumously, in 1606. Perkins defined a vow as 'a promise made to God of things lawfull and possible'. Based on baptismal vows, he admitted that vowing could be 'a stay and proppe to further and helpe vs' in our faith. But he hedged this permission about with warnings and exceptions, and the discussion leaves the strong impression that the safest course is simply not to do it.[56] A slightly warmer treatment came from the royal chaplain and future bishop Henry Parry, preaching in 1603. Parry agreed that vowing smacked both of popery and of Judaism, but insisted that if done right it could be 'reasonable and commendable'. Where Perkins had listed the different kinds of unacceptable vows, Parry offered a typology of acceptable ones. Another royal chaplain, George Hakewill, warned the future Charles I against 'wicked', 'rash' or 'shameful' vows, but this was a brief aside in a long sermon series whose title—*King Dauids vow for reformation*—inescapably implies that there was another side to the question.[57]

From then on, the note of caution diminishes. Some divines remained ambiguous. Richard Capel, in the 1630s, recognized the value of vows, but worried that they were

[54] Knappen, *Two Diaries*, 64, 66–8.
[55] Rogers, *Seven treatises*, 477–92.   [56] Perkins, *Whole treatise*, 400–7.
[57] Manningham, *Diary*, 205–6; George Hakewill, *King Dauids vow for reformation* (1621: RSTC 12616), esp. 4–6.

being overused.[58] One sceptic, in particular, is worth noting: Richard Rogers' former covenant-partner, Ezekiel Culverwell. Thirty-five years on from that covenant, in his *Treatise of faith*, he was distinctly cool about vows. Resolutions to avoid a particular sin rarely succeed, he warned, and worse, they mark a lack of faith. 'Some . . . promise to themselues more strength of faith, patience, loue, and other like graces, then indeed they haue, which when they come to triall, find it farre otherwise.' He recalled a famous episode from the Marian persecution, in which one Protestant loudly proclaimed that he would be faithful unto death, only to give way when the crisis came, while a colleague who doubted his own resolve was given the grace to stand firm. In other words, this is again a matter of grace and effort. Culverwell feared that vows, covenants, and resolutions might crowd out grace. By this time, however, he was swimming against the tide. But as we shall see, he was not the only one whose youthful enthusiasm for covenants turned sour.[59]

The situation in Scotland was somewhat different, since the making of bands and covenants had long been an everyday part of Scottish culture, and one which the Protestant reformers took up enthusiastically. There was still room for scepticism. Bands were different from vows in that they were collective, not individual, and in that God was not a party to the agreement, but a witness to and guarantor of it. So when Robert Bruce was forced by the text he was expounding to tackle vowing in 1591, he gave a vanishingly narrow definition in which a true vow was merely a promise to give thanks to God in the event that a prayer is answered. Any other 'foolish vowes' were no better than 'those vnlawfull vowes of the Papists'.[60] But the distinction between covenants and vows was a fine one, and Scots' enthusiasm for the former made it natural to experiment with the latter. At the 1596 General Assembly, for example, John Davidson presided over a meeting for collective repentance. Apparently unexpectedly, at the end of the proceedings, Davidson called on those present 'to hold up their hands to testify their entereing in a new league with God', and almost all did so. The point is not simply that this was a covenant with God, rather than a band between believers. There was apparently also no text for it, and perhaps not even any spoken terms. All the formal record states is that those present covenanted 'to walke more warilie in their wayes and more diligently in their charges'. Even if the covenant was collective, the unspoken vows which constituted it will have varied from individual to individual present.[61]

In the 17th century, vows and covenants became almost commonplace, in both countries. William Gouge—Culverwell's nephew and Rogers' protégé—was an enthusiast. Although he laid down rules for right vowing, and also admitted that there was an awkward shortage of New Testament references to the practice, he claimed that 'to vow in praying doth much sharpen our prayers, and make vs more eagerly call vpon God', and that it also helps to distinguish hypocritical lip service

---

[58] Capel, *Tentations*, 287–97.
[59] Culverwell, *Treatise of faith*, 124, 415–16.   [60] Bruce, *Sermons Preached*, sigs T6v–7r.
[61] W. J. Couper, *Scottish Revivals* (Dundee, 1918), 19–22; cf. John Spottiswoode, *History of the Church of Scotland*, ed. M. Russell (Edinburgh, 1848–51), III.6

from real and costly devotion.[62] Other references over the years that followed suggest how conventions were developing. For example, everyone agreed that you must not vow to do evil, or make a vow without the right to do so—for example, a wife had limited scope to make vows without her husband's permission—and that such vows, if made, ought not to be kept. However, we begin to find warnings that vows which were legitimate, but foolish, were nevertheless binding. 'When you have made such a vow rather lose your life than breake it.'[63] Or again, William Crashaw insisted that—unlike the Scots covenant of 1596—vows should not be inward, unspoken matters of the heart. Rather, the heart should 'vtter and publish the same promise, the better to bind it selfe to obedience'.[64] Vows were no longer to be vague intentions or wordy platitudes, but precise contracts with clear and binding terms. Naturally, this applied particularly to collective covenants, where the participants implicitly or explicitly undertook to hold one another to their promises. In Dorchester, the minister John White attempted to use adherence to a covenant knows as the 'ten vows' to police admission to communion—until the court of High Commission stopped him.[65]

Not all of these covenants conformed to the theorists' scruples. Capel, in 1633, defined a vow as 'a promise . . . made to GOD . . . with condition of obtaining somewhat at Gods hands', and it seems that this kind of nakedly conditional vowing was indeed widespread.[66] This is, to put it mildly, in some tension with the standard Protestant emphasis on the worthlessness of human works, but some such vows are unabashed attempts to bargain with or manipulate God. Children, in particular, seem to have done this. They had perhaps not yet learned better theological behaviour, or were simply more used to a functioning moral system of reward and punishment. Thomas Shepard recalled how his father fell ill when he himself was ten years old. He not only prayed 'very strongly and heartily' for his father to live, but also 'made some covenant, if God would do it, to serve him the better'. The bargain failed: his father died, and as an adult he recognized that the covenant was inappropriate. Similarly, Richard Norwood, aged twelve, also 'sometimes made vows to God which I was careful to observe', but which 'proceeded of a very wavering heart without any true faith that I can discern', and were aimed at securing some worldly benefit or other.[67] Two Scottish examples show a more ambiguous face. Aged about six, Robert Blair was profoundly affected by a visiting preacher's sermon, and vowed that if he became a preacher himself, he would preach his first sermon on the same text, a vow whose eventual fulfilment he recorded with satisfaction. In 1571, the fourteen-year-old James Melville made a 'promise and vow' to pursue a ministerial vocation; clearly a solemn event for him, as he claimed that his vow determined his decisions at key moments over the next

[62] Gouge, *Whole-Armor of God*, 437–9.

[63] Kilby, *Burthen*, 36; cf. Byfield, *Marrow of the Oracles* (1622), 555–6; Ball, *Short treatise*, 170–1.

[64] Crashaw, *London's Lamentation*, sig. C8r.

[65] David Underdown, *Fire from Heaven: Life in an English Town in the Seventeenth Century* (New Haven and London, 1992), 91–2.

[66] Capel, *Tentations*, 287–8.

[67] Shepard, *God's Plot*, 39; Norwood, *Journal*, 10.

five years.[68] Shepard, Norwood, and Melville were all able to view their childhood vows through more theologically sophisticated adult eyes, but not everyone could do the same. Capel claimed that 'Satan doth push on every boy and girle on any occasion, to runne into a corner and there to make vowes'. He may have been right.[69]

Not that mature Protestants outgrew vow-making. In particular, they returned to it in moments of desperation, especially when life was in danger. When Robert Woodford's newborn son was dangerously ill, he prayed that if the boy recovered, 'I have promised that by the Lordes helpe it shall be a further ingagement to me to walke with the Lord; I shall receave him againe as given a new.'[70] If you were sick yourself, making vows seems to have been almost routine. The Devon puritan minister Samuel Hieron provided a prayer of thanksgiving for recovery from illness, in which the convalescing patient prays, 'Make me euer mindfull of the vowes & promises which I made in my sicknesse, to serue thee more faithfully then heretofore.' He, and others, assumed that such vows were a routine part of sickness, and wanted to jog their readers' consciences with the memory of them. William Crashaw not only assumed the practice, but encouraged it, telling his readers that in time of plague, they should 'promise and vow, that if thou . . . bee preserued, thou wilt performe some speciall seruice to him, his Church or Children, more then before'.[71]

Vows were not, however, always the product of a crisis. If Robert Blair is any guide, some Protestants—perhaps particularly Scots?—could make them for almost trivial reasons. On 19 February 1626, Blair lost his Bible. After fruitlessly searching, 'it was casten in my mind to crave it from God, and an engagement if he would. As I was speaking this, it was brought to me.'[72] Not many others were quite so cavalier with their bargains, but it is a matter of degree. Rogers was doing it in the 1580s, recording in his diary, 'An other covenant I made if I might be free from Bishops as I have these 4 years.' The interest in God's promises could also be given this twist. As the author of *A Collection of certaine Promises* put it, 'when thou applyest any promise, seeke out the condition, and labour to keepe it, and doubt not of the performance of what is promised'.[73] Or it could simply become routine. In his preface to Edward Dering's collection of family prayers, Bishop Cooper advised that prayer should always be accompanied by 'renewing our Vowes and Couenants with the Lord, when soeuer wee looke to speede well from him'.[74]

In other words, there was a spectrum. At one end was outright bargaining with God, which might be at its crudest in childhood or on the sickbed. But even here there is sometimes more than meets the eye. The story of Blair's lost Bible might

---

[68] Blair, *Life*, 5; Melville, *Autobiography*, 24, 37, 55.

[69] Capel, *Tentations*, 290.

[70] Woodford, 'Diary', 29–30.viii.1637 verso.

[71] Hieron, *Helpe vnto Deuotion* (1608), 159; Crashaw, *London's Lamentation*, sig. C8r; cf. Tuke, *Practise of the faithfull*, 175.

[72] Blair, *Life*, 119–20. As Woodford's use of the word shows, *engagement* was a near-synonym for *covenant* in this period.

[73] Knappen, *Two Diaries*, 80; Fawkener, *Collection of Promises*, 206–7; cf. Brinsley, *True Watch* (1608), 64.

[74] Dering, *Mr. Dering, his godly priuate prayers*, sig. A9r.

seem almost magical, but he recorded it both to praise divine providence, and also to emphasize how, through this trivial incident, God had brought him to a renewed commitment. At the other end, Cooper's exhortation can make these vows sound like little more than an earnest intention of good behaviour. Since—as we have seen—right intention was an essential element of true prayer, the vow as such almost disappears from sight.

Almost: but not quite. We see a sign of this in the way some Protestants made use of vows, even vows couched in the vaguest terms. Archibald Johnston of Wariston described what he called a vow, which was simply that, if God might give him consolation in his distress, 'that thy saule, thy heart, and thy body sould blisse and praise him extraordinarily for it'.[75] This was hardly manipulating God, but—like so many devotees—he may have been manipulating himself. At the time, Wariston was in the grip of a drawn-out spiritual crisis, sparked by the sudden death of his young wife, in which he repeatedly expressed a longing to die. The several vows he made during this episode all shared the same desperate desire for a turning-point. In the providential narrative of his suffering, the story which God was writing on his life, this vow might—he evidently hoped—mark the beginning of a new chapter.

He was not alone in using a vow to try to force a turning-point onto his life. During his own torment in 1614, suffering from an agonizing case of the stone, Richard Kilby repeatedly made vows and covenants in an attempt to reset the clock and restart his relationship with God. It did not work very well; indeed, each vow had to contend with the failure of its predecessors, driving him to ever more extreme statements. Finally he promised to resign from the ministry if he did not adhere to his rule, and asked that if he broke *that* promise, 'let mee everlastingly bee forsaken of Jesus Christ'. But if he did succeed, he begged that 'thou wilt be mercifull unto me touching this horrible disease', and he underlined this as forcefully as he could. 'I offer up this vowe unto thee for an everlasting deede, and thereunto unchangeably say, Amen. Be it never changed.'[76] Kilby's narrative finishes soon after, and he clearly wished us to think this last gasp had worked, but we may have our doubts.

One difference between Wariston and Kilby's desperate vows was their content. Against Wariston's vagueness, Kilby vowed something very like a rule of life. His 'rules', which cover twenty-eight duodecimo pages, include a detailed daily regime of pious activity, alongside more abstract aspirations to be mindful of God and to avoid sin.[77] John Winthrop twice made similar 'covenants', in 1607 and 1613. The first was apparently quite vague—he promised to reform some rather generic sins in return for 'a new heart, [and] joy in his spirit'. But the second was more exacting, its numbered points covering matters such as how to spend his money. That covenant was, again, clearly meant to signify a fresh start in life; his father-in-law had just died, leaving him a substantial inheritance, and he himself had recently recovered from a serious illness. Winthrop was familiar with Rogers' earlier covenant and may

---

[75] Wariston, *Diary*, 64.   [76] Kilby, *Hallelujah*, 58–60, 87, 92, 133–4.
[77] Kilby, *Hallelujah*, 59–87.

have been directly inspired by it.[78] Rogers' nephew John Rogers, too, followed the family tradition in his 'Sixty Memorials for a Godly Life', a set of directions which look more like a model to be imitated than a personal pious exercise. No. 48 is the recommendation that the believer should 'take him to a Daily Direction, and some set Rules, thereby looking constantly to his Heart all the Day.... If a Man tie not himself thus to Rules, his Heart will break from him.'[79]

We know of no-one who took this advice more to heart than Nehemiah Wallington. Again, it began as an attempt to turn over a new leaf, after the desperate temptations of his late teens. In 1619, the twenty-one-year-old Wallington felt led 'to draw out some Artickles for the reforming of my life'. He began with forty, but added to them regularly until by 1631 he had 77 articles. These mix abstract and precise rules—he vowed to bear no malice to anyone and to trust in God; also, never to conceal any faults in his wares from customers, and to give half of any money he should find to the poor. Notably, one of the first rules was 'when I am in trouble that I make vowes and pray vn to God'; the next, 'that when I am deliuered out of trouble I striu to keepe my voues'. He later added a pledge to 'read these my Artickels once in a weeke'. What was truly distinctive about Wallington's articles, however, was the financial penalties which he imposed on himself for breaching them, with the money to go to the poor box: a farthing for being idle, tuppence for failing to teach those under his care, much like the 'swear boxes' occasionally used in our own age. This has a superficial reasonableness: while Kilby's broken vows landed him in agonies of conscience, Wallington was realistic enough to recognize that he would sometimes fall short, and to put in place a genuine but proportionate deterrent. The problem remained, of course, that some of his articles were too vague to enforce clearly. How was he to know if, for example, he had grieved sufficiently for others' breaches of God's law, and so whether he ought to pay a farthing? Reviewing his discipline in 1637, he admitted that 'I am runn so farre on the score with my God and in deate to the poore that I am never able to pay itt'. He begged forgiveness and began again with a clean slate.[80] Andrew Willet, a conformist Calvinist cleric with more poise than Wallington, supposedly found an easier way through this dilemma. He had 'lawes and ordinances set up in tables, directing his family in their severall offices and duties', with 'penall comminations for offenders'—but these were 'very rarely put in execution'.[81]

For those who did not adopt such full-scale covenants—and even for those who did—there was the more everyday alternative of piecemeal vows aimed at reformation of life. The target was usually a particularly troublesome sin, and the reasoning was that a vow concentrated the mind. If you firmly and self-consciously committed yourself to avoid a particular sin, you might succeed, by using fear of your own future guilt to motivate yourself. As John Dod put it, 'if we should fall' into sin

[78] Winthrop, *Papers*, 162–3, 168, 199.
[79] Cotton Mather, *Magnalia Christi Americana* (1702), III.109–113.
[80] LMA Guildhall MS 204, pp. 35–6, 42; Wallington, *Notebooks*, 38, 47–9; Seaver, *Wallington's World*, 32.
[81] Andrew Willet, *Synopsis Papismi, That is, a generall view of Papistrie* (1634: RSTC 25700a.5), sig. b2v.

having vowed not to, 'the breach of our vow would so pierse and wound our harts, that it would make vs much stronger against new assaults'.[82] Daniel Dyke spoke of the deceitfulness and inconstancy of our hearts and wills, and urged us therefore 'by solemne vowes, and protestations of our repentance, as it were with strong ropes, to binde, and hold fast these fugitiues'. He suggested that vows, and especially written vows, could be used to reproach a straying heart and to recall it to obedience. This, as one anonymous writer explained, is why vows should be spoken or written: 'becaus its harder to break promises then purposes, what hath gonne from mee then what is onely within mee'.[83]

We can see this at work in the case of Richard Norwood, who, in the midst of the crisis of his conversion, decided to vow one week's abstinence from his 'master sin'—which he did not name. The limited time span was not because he positively intended to return to it, but because he knew his weakness and dared only take a week at a time. Even that would be tough: he knew that 'without a vow I could not stand so long'. But it worked, for a time at least, and he was able to renew the vow for several weeks. Or again, in 1634 Samuel Rogers—Richard's grandson—committed an obscure sin involving his attraction to a woman. Nothing very much happened, apparently, but he was profoundly ashamed and conscious of being sorely tempted. As a result, he made a vow, whose terms he did not describe but which he called '(as it were) a second conversion', and of which he continued to be conscious for years to come.[84]

What made these vows powerful was that breaking a solemn promise before God was felt to be a desperate matter. Capel wrote that 'a vow broken doth punish the heart of a Godly man extreamly; no man can say how much, but they who have felt the smart of it'. Plenty of witnesses agree with him. Both Richard and Samuel Rogers were appalled when they realized that they been breaking, or even 'nibling at', their vows. Winthrop, reviewing his covenant, found that his breaches of it 'brake my heart, and forced me to an humble and searious submission, in abundance of teares'.[85] Kilby found his own covenant-breaking agonizing:

> Is it possible that thou canst forbeare the powring of thy just and wrathfull vengeance upon me? . . . Woe is mee! there is no possibility of repentance. I cannot stedfastly continue in the purpose of resisting my sins. . . . O I have no faith.[86]

Wallington gives us a more prosaic, but perhaps more telling example. He had made a vow never to eat without giving thanks first, but one day in December 1642, he absentmindedly bit into a pear. 'My heart smote me . . . for breaking promise', and he wondered, fearfully, if God might make him choke.[87]

Vows to abstain from sin were probably the commonest kind in the early 17th century, but there were other variants. Some people forswore practices which were

---

[82] Dod and Cleaver, *Ten sermons*, 40.
[83] Dyke, *Mystery of selfe-deceiuing*, 349–51; Bod. MS Rawl. D.384 fo. 1r.
[84] Norwood, *Journal*, 70; Rogers, *Diary*, xxiv–xxviii, 3.
[85] Capel, *Tentations*, 290; Knappen, *Two Diaries*, 81; Rogers, *Diary*, 26; Winthrop, *Papers*, 211.
[86] Kilby, *Hallelujah*, 89.
[87] Wallington, *Notebooks*, 178.

not actually sinful. So, for example, John Winthrop vowed not to use a gun for hunting game-birds, both because it was dangerous and because he was a bad shot—he commented 'God (if he please) can giue me fowle by some other meanes'.[88] More striking, however, is the practice of vowing to perform a particular pious action. Sometimes it is not clear whether this is a vow as such—a solemn and binding promise—or merely a personal resolution which could be changed when it suited. Richard Greenham, for example, 'compounded with himself three times a day to pray... using also daily 3 portions of 119 Psalm'.[89] The word *compounded* suggests something stronger than a mere intention, but that he compounded with *himself*, rather than with God, suggests something less than an actual vow. A generation later he might have been less fastidious. In 1622 the fourteen-year-old Elizabeth Isham had 'a great fit of the wind collick... the worst fit that ever I remember I had', frightening and very painful. 'Evere since I have dayly said the 103 psalm'—she did not explicitly call it a vow, but it seems likely that this was based on a desperate pledge made in her sickness. Similarly, in 1638–9, the moderate conformist James Howell observed that he fasted every Saturday night in preparation for the Sabbath, and had done so 'ever since I was a youth in Venice, for being delivered from a very great danger'. Wariston, too, vowed that if God would deliver him from all his troubles, he would 'turne al the Psalmes in prayses as I haive turned them unto prayers during my affliction'; that is, he would write a series of paraphrases. He also vowed to take notes at every sermon he attended, and to keep every Wednesday as a fast day 'until my delyvrie from my troubles'.[90]

That last vow was at least time-limited—albeit imprecisely. This was in keeping with Greenham's cautious advice, which Capel cited approvingly, 'to vow, but for a time'. For example, someone tempted to excessive drinking might forswear it for a month, 'and then see what he can doe, whether he can forbeare without a vow'. If not, then another time-limited vow might be in order. Vows, on this view, were a crutch to be dispensed with as soon as possible. Capel disapproved of 'perpetuall vowes', which seemed altogether too popish.[91] Norwood would have agreed. We have seen how he initially vowed to avoid his 'master sin' for a week at a time. Success, however, led him rashly to vow perpetual abstinence, which proved too much: he promptly fell back into the—still unnamed—sin.[92] But relatively few of those who made vows at all heeded these warnings. Wariston, for example, vowed to give all his earnings from his first year of legal practice, and then a tenth of his takings in perpetuity, to 'pious uses and goodlie persones', and at a later date noted with satisfaction that, so far, he had stuck to it. Isham, at the age of eighteen, 'offered my affections to thee my God... desiring that it might be more acceptable to thee... that I might not marry'. This was not precisely a vow of celibacy, but for the pious Protestants of her grandparents' generation, it would have seemed

---

[88] Winthrop, *Papers*, 165.   [89] Parker and Carlson, *'Practical Divinity'*, 158.
[90] Isham, 'Diary', 1622; Isham, 'Confessions', fo. 17r; James Howell, *Epistolæ Ho-Elianæ. Familiar Letters Domestic and Forren* (1645: Wing H3071), VI.47; Wariston, *Diary*, 104, 132, 137.
[91] Capel, *Tentations*, 291–2.   [92] Norwood, *Journal*, 71.

shockingly Romish.[93] We need not ask what they would have made of Isham's near-contemporaries, two young women in Nicholas Ferrar's community at Little Gidding, who took private vows to remain unmarried and to devote themselves to fasting and prayer.[94] But by then it was becoming possible for Protestants such as George Herbert or even Richard Baxter to value the single life again. Vows which would have seemed like outrageous popery a few decades earlier were, by the 1630s, almost within the pale of Protestant acceptability.

An important final perspective on this subject comes, once again, from Wallington. Having tested the use of covenant-making almost to destruction, he eventually concluded that the whole thing was a mistake. Looking back from the 1640s, he wrote that although it had its uses, 'yett will I never perswade any Christian to follow my example in this'. The problem was the one which early evangelicals had identified, to which the sceptical tradition running through Perkins, Culverwell, and Capel had returned, and which stymied Norwood's attempt to forswear his 'master sin'. Wallington wrote:

> I would of myselfe (by these Articles) runne in all hast apace even at a gallope to Heaven. But now I find it by wofull experiance that I am intangled and have laid to heavie a burden on myselfe . . . so that now att the last I must lay downe all and say (with the poore publiken) The good Lord be martifull to mee a sinner.

The fundamental problem was that—as all Reformed Protestants knew—'in ons owne strength shall no man stand'.[95] Yet covenant-making could easily become an attempt to do just that. Vows could be merely a means of self-control, which for sinners, even elect sinners, is liable to be both futile and damaging. The more theologically astute vows invoked divine grace, but by tying that grace to a voluntarily adopted discipline they could be seen as presumptuously conscripting God to fight a human cause. Winthrop eventually concluded that vows were 'snares to my Conscience': either they were ill-advised abstentions from 'lawfull comforts', or they compounded his sin when he failed to keep them.[96]

But the cause was lost. Once the earliest reformers' instinctive suspicion of vows had faded, the practice steadily seeped back, gaining theological respectability despite itself as it burgeoned in the early 17th century. Scriptural witness, deep patterns of Christian piety, the nature of childhood religion, the vacuum left—in England at least—by the absence of external disciplinary structures, and the desperate need for weapons in the unending battle against sin—all these things ensured that Protestants simply *were* going to make vows. Those who had learned the hard way might warn that this was a blind alley. But many—most?—Protestants were nevertheless at least going to take a few steps along it. Vows were simply too useful and powerful a religious practice to be stamped out by a mere Reformation.

[93] Wariston, *Diary*, 122; Isham, 'Confessions', fo. 20v.

[94] Trevor Cooper, ' "As wise as serpents": the form and setting of public worship at Little Gidding in the 1630s' in Natalie Mears and Alec Ryrie (eds), *Worship and the Parish Church in Early Modern Britain* (Aldershot, 2012).

[95] Wallington, *Notebooks*, 49, 270.   [96] Winthrop, *Papers*, 157, 163–4.

EXPERIENCING ANSWERS

So far we have been skirting around what might seem like the main issue: did Protestants expect their prayers actually to be answered?

It is a crass but necessary question. Crass because, as divines emphasized, the real purpose of prayer was union of the heart and will with God. Even when you ask for something specific in a prayer, it was conventionally argued that such a prayer is always *answered*: for 'no' and 'not yet' are answers. Indeed, if you had prayed conditionally, as you should have, they were answers which you had already anticipated. But given all that, some were still lumpishly wanting to ask: does prayer actually change things? And the answer was yes: but not straightforwardly so.

Stories of answered prayers were as popular with early modern Protestants as with any other Christians. Perhaps they described those stories as providential rather than miraculous, but the boundary between the two is notoriously blurry.[97] The mysterious territory of human illness and health was particularly debatable land. So, for example, John Winthrop noted that during his wife's agonizingly extended labour in 1620, he prayed in the adjoining room, and that at the very moment he rose from his knees he heard the baby cry; all was well. Thomas Shepard recalled how, during his son Thomas' dangerous illness, 'the Lord awakened me in the night and stirred me up to pray for him', and in the morning 'I found him suddenly and strangely amended'.[98] A tale of the Suffolk noncon-formist Samuel Fairclough had him praying for his two-year-old son one Saturday afternoon and only discovering later that, at that precise moment, the boy had been providentially spared from mortal danger.[99]

Another natural arena for discerning answers to prayer was public affairs. During epidemics, for example, earnest devotees begged—conditionally, of course—for deliverance, often using officially authorized forms. When the plague eventually abated, it was natural to see this as an answer to prayer. When plague hit Ayr in 1606, the minister John Welsh organized collective prayer, 'and accordingly after that the plague decreased'. Deliverances from national dangers—supremely, the defeat of the Spanish Armada—were interpreted in the same way.[100] Robert Harris blamed the disasters suffered by the Protestant cause early in the Thirty Years' War on English Protestants' failure to pray, arguing, 'when was it otherwise, when did the Church of God euer ioyne in a common petition to God but they sped? no instance to the contrary'. The Church's collective prayer, he claimed, can achieve anything. 'If men be sicke, pray them whole; if poore, pray them rich; if sad, pray them merry.' A lifetime earlier, Hugh Latimer had argued that even the prayer of a few could have this effect, as Moses' prayers turned aside God's wrath from Israel. After his death some claimed that he himself had been one such, recalling his

---

[97] Alexandra Walsham, *Providence in Early Modern England* (Oxford, 1999).
[98] Winthrop, *Papers*, 237; Shepard, *God's Plot*, 35.
[99] Samuel Clarke et al., *The Lives of sundry Eminent Persons in this Later Age* (1683: Wing C4538), 167.
[100] Tweedie, *Select Biographies*, 30; Pigg, *Meditations concerning praiers*, sig. A7r. Protestant England's other great deliverance, the Gunpowder Plot, could not be read in the quite same way, since in that case the specific danger had not been the subject of prayer beforehand.

persistent prayers during Mary I's reign for the Gospel to be restored to England and for Princess Elizabeth to be preserved.[101]

A more telling example is the godly Cheshire patriarch John Bruen, who, we are told, used to lead his family and neighbours in prayers, and 'seldome did they meet againe to pray, but they had some new and fresh cause of praise and thanksgiving'.[102] That is, they not only found such happy providences, but they specifically sought them out, and expected to discover them according to the rhythm of regular prayer. What they found might not be exactly what they had asked for, but that is the nature of providence. To find signs of this kind would of course have bolstered your faith, but searching for signs is itself evidence of faith, the faith which is ready to see God's hand at work in the world. Similarly, to tell others about such an incident will bolster *their* faith, as long as they have enough faith to believe you. It will also bolster your reputation for godliness, both because you were able to discern God's hand at work and because your prayers were answered in the first place. In other words, the lively trade in anecdotes about answered prayer tells us that a great many early modern Protestants had a degree of faith in the power of prayer, but also wished to have more, wished others to have more, and wished others to think that they had more. By the same token, it suggests that a great many early modern Protestants—often, perhaps, the same people— sometimes found it hard to believe that prayers really were answered.

The careful recording of these extraordinary and providential answers to prayer does, however, tell us that they were seen as remarkable: unusual graces rather than everyday experiences. The more routine way that answers to prayer were experienced was less tangible and more inward. This did not make it any less God's action. Indeed, in one case there was a frankly miraculous, or at least revelatory, air to this: the use of prayer to aid decision-making, in the belief that God would guide you in the right path. Pious Protestants understood that the making of substantial decisions, like every other significant action, ought to be undergirded by prayer. When Richard Greenham was asked by a visitor to judge on a weighty matter, he was said to have replied, 'Sir neither am I able to speak nor you to hear beecaus wee have not praied.'[103] This could sometimes mean a full day—or much more—laying a problem before God.

Such prayer could simply be for the wisdom to choose aright, but sometimes there was more to it than that, as two young Scotsmen wrestling with decisions about marriage show us. Archibald Johnston of Wariston, having decided that he ought to marry, agonized over his choice of bride. Eventually he asked God to guide him through his friends' counsel. When a match was proposed, however, he was taken aback. He wanted a wife who was 'meak and faire', but he was told that Jean Stewart, aged thirteen, was 'hastie and kankard, and that hir faice was al spoiled by the poks'. The disfigurement in particular shocked him when he met her. He consented to the match 'having no hope of it nor great lyking to it'. But after lengthy prayer, Wariston received assurance that God would bless him, not punish

[101] Harris, *Peters enlargement* (1624), 5–7; Latimer, *Sermons by Hugh Latimer*, 322–3, 509.
[102] Hinde, *Faithfull Remonstrance . . . of Iohn Bruen*, 73.
[103] Parker and Carlson, 'Practical Divinity', 150.

him, by the marriage. The care with which Stewart herself prayed before accepting his proposal was an encouraging sign. And he was indeed blissfully happy during their all-too-brief marriage; he believed that she had been too.[104] John Livingstone's decision was more drawn out. After Janet Fleming was recommended to him as a bride, he spent nine months 'seeking as I could direction from God anent that business', and did not actually speak to her. But finding himself travelling with her and some others one day, he discussed a text of Scripture with her, 'wherein I found her conference so judicious and spiritual that I took that for some answer of my prayer to have my mind cleared'. After further prayer, 'I got abundant clearness that it was the Lord's mind I should marry her.' However, he also noted that it was a further month or more 'before I got marriage affection to her . . . and I got it not till I obtained it by prayer'. They went on to have fifteen children.[105]

Wariston and Livingstone, then, expected God to guide their decisions in two ways. One was through tangible outward signs, which the faithful Christian waiting expectantly on a providential God might read. The expectation that God gives providential guidance through outward signs in answer to prayer was pervasive, if not entirely respectable. The simplest form of this was the practice of opening a Bible at random and taking the first verse which your eyes lit upon as a word from God aimed directly at your current need. That might seem like sorcery, but it had its more decorous variants. After all, if you did happen to stumble across a verse which brought you particular comfort, it was only natural to thank God for laying that text before you.[106] But why stop at the Bible? Robert Blair once prayed in the midst of his spiritual anguish for a sign: he asked that 'the reeds growing near by, which were so moved by the wind as he was tossed in his spirit', should cease to shake, and accordingly they did.[107] Others might balk at putting God to the test in that way, but it was easier to disapprove of it than to stamp it out. The Essex puritan minister, John Beadle, worried that 'we talk much of Providence, and indeed we are apt to make Providences to serve our turns'. He cited the prophet Jonah, who fled rather than obey God, and then chanced to find a ship ready to lead him away. Beadle feared that his own contemporaries would have read the appearance of such a ship as providential approval from God.

> This is a great part of the Religion of our time, here was a providence, and there was a providence; yea, a continued series of providential actings: but no man asks, Where is the Precept requiring, or the Promise encouraging?

Gadding after signs, he warned, was a snare into which too many Protestants had fallen.[108]

The other, the more respectable, and more important means by which God guided Wariston and Livingstone, and by which he might answer all prayers, was

---

[104] Wariston, *Diary*, 2–8.   [105] Tweedie, *Select Biographies*, 151–2.
[106] Thomas, *Religion and the Decline of Magic*, 139–41; Wariston, *Diary*, 22. See below, pp. 292–5.
[107] Tweedie, *Select Biographies*, 324.
[108] John Beadle, *The journal or diary of a thankful Christian* (1656: Wing B1557), 80. Although not published until 1656, this book appears to be based on sermons delivered in the 1630s and early 1640s.

within. As we have already seen, God was expected to speak through the emotions.[109] As a younger man, Livingstone had prayed over the choice between an early marriage and the life of a laird, or pursuing his studies in medicine. 'After many to's and fro's, and much confusion and fear, anent the state of my soul, I thought it was made out to me that I behoved to preach Jesus Christ'—and so that, third path was the one he took.[110] Direct intervention within the self might itself be an answer to prayer. The fifteen-year-old Thomas Shepard found it difficult to take coherent notes at sermons, prayed about the matter and 'I presently the next Sabbath was able to take notes who the precedent Sabbath could do nothing at all that way'. Henry Burton, in prison in 1637, prayed for resolve, 'and immediately upon my prayer I was filled with a mighty spirit of courage and resolution, wherewith I was carried up farre above my selfe, even as it were upon Eagles wings'. He then prayed that he would remain at this pitch throughout his sufferings, and he claimed that that request, too, was granted.[111]

These accounts still have a whiff of the miraculous about them, but when we are thinking of emotion as an answer to prayer, the boundary between the mundane and the miraculous quickly dissolves. These are subjective, unverifiable experiences, but they could feel like being touched by the finger of God. This is why the distinction between prayer as appeal to God, and prayer as self-therapy, ultimately breaks down. For one of the chief purposes of Protestant prayer—as of any Christian prayer—was explicitly to change yourself, by asking God to work that change. Elizabethan guides to prayer emphasized that the chief benefits of prayer were that it brings 'singular rest and quietnes to our conscience', that in it 'we finde most ioyful & perfect quietnes', that 'by it is wrought in vs, the hate of sinne'.[112] It is hardly a distinctively Protestant claim, but it is all the more powerful for that. We may leave the subject with the words of Johann Gerhard, a German whose work—most unusually for a Lutheran—became a best-seller in English, and who here was drawing on Bernard of Clairvaux:

> In the time of Prayer there are many changes wrought in the soule: For Prayer is the light of the soule, and oftentimes leaves Him in joy, whome shee found in despaire.

When Christ prayed, he was transfigured.[113] That, ultimately is what early modern British Protestants—like all Christians—meant when they said that prayer was powerful, and that is what they hoped to achieve when they prayed.

---

[109] See above, pp. 40–8.   [110] Tweedie, *Select Biographies*, 133.

[111] Shepard, *God's Plot*, 39; Burton, *Narration*, 12.

[112] Bull, *Christian praiers*, 2; James Cancellar, *The alphabet of prayers, verye fruitfull to be exercised and vsed of euerye Christian man* (1573?: RSTC 4560), sig. A4r.

[113] Gerhard, *Meditations*, 232 (nine editions 1627–40, three printed in Scotland; cf. the earlier and aggressively edited translation of the same book, *A christian mans weekes worke*, trans. R. Bruch (1611: RSTC 11764) which went through four editions 1611–32); Luke 9:29.

8

The Practice of Prayer

'When thou prayest, enter into thy chamber: & when thou hast shut thy dore,
pray vnto thy Father which is in secret.' *Matthew 6:6.*

So much for the theory. It is time to ask how, in practice, early modern British
Protestants actually went about the business of prayer. Where, when, how often,
with what posture and words (if any): these questions matter because, at least as
much as the theological framework, they capture the experience of prayer.

They are also questions which Reformed Protestants were very reluctant to
answer. The theologians and preachers who considered how to pray routinely
opened their discussion by insisting that Christians might pray however the Spirit
led them.[1] This scrupulous permissiveness is fundamental to the rest of this
discussion. It is frustrating, since we want to know what these people actually
did. Yet the insistence that, in the end, prayer is an intensely individual matter,
simply for the believer and God, is itself an important historical fact. Beyond that, it
tells us to expect considerable variety in the practice of prayer. Not endless variety,
since the principle of liberty existed within a culture of conformity and alongside an
ethic of humility, both of which encouraged Protestants to pray as their neighbours,
ministers, and teachers did. Yet they were also positively encouraged to explore
alternatives. Indeed, having an idiosyncratic pattern of prayer could be a sign of
peculiar piety, guided by the Spirit rather than by convention. Moreover, the
emphasis on liberty gave ordinary Protestants choices; and even the choice to
conform to convention was a choice. Many of them may not have wanted this
freedom—indeed, the preachers' repeated emphasis on it suggests some reluctance
to embrace it—but it was thrust upon them regardless.

CONTINUOUS PRAYER

The fundamental models of how to pray were Biblical. Here immediately there was
a problem, for a series of New Testament texts demanded that Christians should
'pray continually'.[2] This is a daunting requirement, and doubly so for Reformed
Protestants, who had no place for monasticism or the vowed religious life. William
Crashaw's popular 'North-Countrie' catechism posed the obvious question: 'How

---

[1] See, for example, Rogers, *Seven treatises*, 326.
[2] Most explicitly, Luke 21:36, I Thess. 5:17.

can wee alwayes pray, seeing wee must worke in our callings?'.[3] To say nothing of eating and sleeping. We can usefully begin by noticing how early modern Protestants dealt with this apparently impossible requirement.

The question matters because they really did want to do it. Continual prayer might be impossible, but it was a magnificent aspiration. Divines were ready to claim that Christians ought to pray or meditate 'night and day', or to echo the Old Testament precept to speak of the Law continually.[4] Richard Rogers was withering on the subject: how else could Christians think of passing

> the long sommers day, and the wearisome winter nights? Doe men . . . thinke, that there is no other, nor better way to take vp their mindes . . . but like brute beasts, and wilde Irish, to passe their time?[5]

Rather, Daniel Dyke said, we should 'wish with the Prophet, that our heads were continuall, vnemptiable fountaines of teares'.[6] More common than such sombre, dutiful talk, however, was an emphasis on the joy of continual prayer. Nehemiah Wallington wrote in his commonplaces that 'if thou haue skill to pray continuallie, it will make thee reioyce continually'. This, as Rogers explained, was because continual prayer would calm 'the froth of our owne braines, as endlesse and needlesse wandrings, vaine cogitations, and foolish and noisome desires'. Such a blissful inner state would, John Norden pointed out, only stir you the more to 'be a continuall Petitioner'. Richard Sibbes was more direct. For him, prayer was simply 'the life and breath of the soul. Take away breath and the man dies; as soon as the soul of a Christian begins to live he prays.'[7] This is all very splendid, but what did it mean in practice, other than steady guilt for those who failed to achieve it?

Occasionally we find Protestants attempting to take this literally. During the reign of Mary I, Thomas Hudson spent six months in hiding, in a tiny den carefully concealed by a stack of firewood, and passed the time, we are told, 'reading and praying continually'. That is both an unusual situation and a questionable account, but more convincing and intriguing testimony comes from the Northamptonshire gentlewoman, Elizabeth Isham. In her late twenties, she embarked on a new spiritual regime, modelled on the example of her grandmother, who used to 'spend her time wholly in devotion doing nothing else besides'. In her youth, Isham had marvelled at this regime, but having tasted it herself she no longer did so. 'For many whole dayes I have don nothing but this.' But while less exceptional than Hudson's situation, Isham's was still very singular. Unmarried but financially

---

[3] Crashaw, *Milke for Babes*, 40.

[4] For example, Bull, *Christian praiers*, 31; Gifford, *Briefe discourse*, fo. 73v; John Calvin, *The Psalmes of David and others. With M. John Calvins Commentaries*, tr. Arthur Golding (1571: RSTC 4395), sig. *2v; FSL MS V.a.519, fo. 3r–v. Cf. Deuteronomy 6:6–9; Joshua 1:8.

[5] Rogers, *Seven treatises*, 116.

[6] Dyke, *Two Treatises*, 48; cf. Jeremiah 9:1.

[7] LMA Guildhall MS 204, p. 304; cf. John Trundle?, *Keepe within Compasse* (1619: RSTC 14898.5), sig. A5r; Rogers, *Seven treatises*, 328; Norden, *Pensive mans practise . . . The second part*, 49–50; Sibbes, *Works*, VI.96.

comfortable gentlewomen might have few obligations, and indeed relatively few opportunities, to pass their time with worldly concerns.[8]

If anything, Protestant divines warned against such heroic piety. Rogers saw it as a mark of an infant faith: new converts might be tempted to neglect their worldly duties in order to pray, which was no more than idleness in pious clothes. Less sternly, Samuel Ward warned that 'ouermuch prayer, reading, and study, may be a wearinesse both to flesh and spirit'. He compared this to smothering a fire with too much wood. Not, he added, that it was a common problem. 'It so rarely happeneth that I neede not mention it.'[9]

But in that case, what did it mean to pray continually? Some of the explanations seem in fact to be explaining it away. So 'pray continually' might be glossed as meaning that you should pray twice or thrice daily. Richard Waste compared the Christian to a perfumier, who might only handle his product three times a day but who, as a result, 'maketh him selfe, & all things hee handleth to smell there of all the daye longe'.[10] A more convincing alternative took 'continually' to mean 'persistently' or 'unremittingly' rather than literally 'without stopping'. Latimer declared, with preacherly hyperbole, that we should pray 'without intermission: when we go to our bed, when we rise in the morning, when we go about our business, or when we are on horseback, ever pray; for a short prayer is able to bring a great thing to pass'. John Preston argued that, just as you keep a horse trained for the day you need it, so you keep your prayer muscles trim by constant exercise. Dorothy Leigh's image was a garden: even if weeded and watered assiduously for years on end, it will still speedily turn into a jungle if neglected.[11]

The deeper answer which was becoming commonplace in the early 17th century was that continual prayer was not something you did, but something that inhabited you. Crashaw's answer to his conundrum—how is continual prayer possible?—was that 'wee may alwayes lift vp our hearts to God'. Whatever we are doing outwardly, our spirits may bask in God's presence. Rogers would not have us spend every waking hour in formal devotions, but argued that we should cultivate pious habits of mind so that they 'cloath and beautifie our soules throughout the day, and haue their setled abode in vs'. Robert Saxby's treatise on prayer argued that whenever a true Christian acts, 'a thought prayeth in his heart' for the action. 'Thus we may pray and heare, pray and speake, pray & eat, pray and studie, pray and work together.' Richard Baker's popular meditations on the Lord's Prayer put it felicitously. In the old law, he recalled, sacrifices were not offered continuously, but the fire on the altar was never extinguished. 'So, though we doe not continually offer to God the calves of our lips; yet the Fire of devotion, and spirituall fervency must continually be burning in our hearts.'[12]

---

[8] Foxe, *Actes and monuments* (1570), 2232; Isham, 'Confessions', fo. 34r–v.

[9] Rogers, *Seven treatises*, 120–1, 323–4; Ward, *Coal from the Altar*, 58.

[10] Preston, *Saints Daily Exercise*, 15–16; Bod. MS Rawl. C.473 fos 5v–6r; cf. Byfield, *The Signes*, '71' (*recte* 95).

[11] Latimer, *Sermons by Hugh Latimer*, 509; Preston, *Saints Daily Exercise*, 74; Leigh, *Mothers blessing*, 82–3.

[12] Crashaw, *Milke for Babes*, 40; Rogers, *Seven treatises*, 328; Saxby, 'Miscellany', fo. 152r; Richard Baker, *Meditations and Disquisitions upon the Lords prayer* (1636: RSTC 1223), 5–6.

This might sound as if continual prayer is being redefined out of existence, but it had its consequences. It was a commonplace that, as well as regular, scheduled, and deliberate prayer, Christians should also make use of spontaneous, occasional, and extempore prayer, which William Perkins called 'the secret and sudden lifting vp of the heart to God, vpon the present occasion'.[13] It was a subject to be handled with caution. On the one hand, everyone approved of sudden and unpremeditated prayers, or 'spirituall eiaculations'. Perkins and Leigh urged that those who felt any stirrings of a desire to pray in themselves should seize the moment; Wallington vowed to do just that.[14] Michael Sparke urged his readers to 'short and pithy prayers, as the lifting vp of the heart into heauen, secretly and sodainly: & this short kinde of Prayer, ought to be vsed, as any occasion offers it selfe, euery hour in the day'. Readiness to pray in this fashion testified to a heart which was alive to God.[15] And yet spontaneous prayer had its dangers. It could be a sign of disorderly enthusiasm—although even John Cosin conceded that 'all kind of eiaculatory or sudden, deuoute, and holy Praiers are not to be condemned'. Or it could distract you from other holy duties. Thomas Goodwin warned against being distracted by prayer 'at unseasonable houres and times'; God only truly calls you to occasional prayer when you have time for it.[16]

Worse, if you grew too accustomed to praying whenever you felt the urge, you might cease praying when your feelings were dull. 'Some thinke', Elnathan Parr noted disapprovingly, 'that we must neuer pray, but vpon the sudden & extraordinary instinct and motion of the Spirit.'[17] The young Richard Norwood was one such, for he 'did not set myself constantly to prayer . . . but only as I was excited by some good motion or fit opportunity, esteeming that to be sufficient'. This obviously made sense at the time—why force yourself to pray, when you were so often ready to pray in any case?—but looking back, Norwood recognized it as a grave error. Occasional, spontaneous prayer certainly had its place, but William Gouge argued that it should 'be vsed as salt with meat'. Seasoning is all very well, but it is no substitute for a regular, balanced diet.[18]

TIMES OF PRAYER

So, beneath the aspiration to continual prayer, and the scattering of occasional prayer, lay—in theory at least—the bedrock of regular prayer. What did *regular* mean?

[13] Perkins, *Whole treatise*, 282; and cf. the distinction between deliberate and occasional meditation, pp. 114–15 above.
[14] Richard Bernard, *A Weekes Worke. And a Worke for every weeke* (1616: RSTC 1964.3), 21; Leigh, *Mothers blessing*, 73; Rogers, *Garden* (1616), sig. B4v; LMA Guildhall MS 204, p. 35. Cf. Howell, *Epistolæ Ho-Elianæ*, VI.48; Bod. MS Rawl. C.473 fo. 2v.
[15] Sparke, *Crumms of comfort*, sig. A6v; Bolton, *Three-fold treatise*, II.175–6.
[16] Cosin, *Collection of Priuate Devotions*, sig. A6v; Goodwin, *Returne of Prayers*, 90, 93.
[17] Parr, *Abba Father*, 31.
[18] Norwood, *Journal*, 72, 77; Gouge, *Whole-Armor of God*, 412–13.

The normal answer from Protestant divines was that set personal prayer should take place daily, and at the same times each day, but that the precise pattern was up to the individual. For those who wanted them, there were Biblical precedents. Psalm 119, supposedly King David's composition, declared 'seuen times a daie do I praise thee': it was this text which justified the traditional seven monastic hours of prayer. Translating this into Protestant laypeople's lives was rarely practical, but at least one pious gentleman conscientiously followed a sevenfold structure,[19] and one anti-puritan satire imagined a 'distracted puritan' who enthused, 'Come heare mee pray nine times a day'—although that is hardly to be taken seriously.[20] In reality, the echo of monastic practices was a positive deterrent. When John Cosin's radically ceremonial book of devotions toyed with a sevenfold structure, Henry Burton dismissed it as fit only for 'Abbey Lubbers', who have nothing else with which to fill their idleness. Burton reckoned that David's 'seuen times' was mere hyperbole, which 'signifieth onely his frequent praying'—a point on which the Geneva Bible's annotations supported him.[21] Lewis Bayly drew on a different verse from the same psalm to make a less ambitious suggestion: that David, as well as praying three times daily, had also risen at midnight to pray. But he did this in order to make a general exhortation to faithfulness, and stopped short of specifically recommending that practice.[22] Similarly, while George Herbert recognized that 'the Godly have ever added some houres of prayer' to the basic twice-a-day model, he insisted that 'these prayers are not necessary, but additionary', and could be omitted without troubling the conscience.[23]

The strictest model of private prayer to be widely recommended was thrice daily. Again there were Biblical precedents. Psalm 55's model, of prayer at evening, morning, and noon, was observed by Richard Greenham, by James Howell, and by several members of the Isham household.[24] Richard Kilby's vows in 1614 committed him to prayer 'at least three times everie day'—a phrase which Michael Sparke's devotional best-seller echoed. Some linked thrice-daily prayer to meals, observing that if we feed the body three times, the soul deserves no less.[25] However, it was also widely recognized or conceded that this set a high bar. Sparke provided noon-time devotions for each day of the week, but they were considerably shorter than his morning and evening prayers. The sentiment that prayer should be *at least*

[19] Psalm 119:164; Hinde, *Faithfull Remonstrance . . . of Iohn Bruen*, 156; cf. Day, *Booke of Christian Prayers*, sig. ☞3r; Sparke, *Crumms of comfort*, sig. A4r; Sandys, *Sermons*, 263.

[20] Corbett, *Poems*, 243; cf. FSL MS V.a.399 fo. 64v.

[21] Henry Burton, *A Tryall of Private Devotions* (1628: RSTC 4157), sig. D3v–4r, E3r; cf. Cosin, *Collection of Priuate Devotions*, 5.

[22] Bayly, *Practise of pietie*, 266; cf. Psalm 119:62. On midnight prayer, see Ryrie, 'Sleeping, waking and dreaming'.

[23] Herbert, *Works*, 272. Herbert's twofold structure may have referred to the Prayer Book offices of morning and evening prayer, which clergy were obliged to say daily: but those were usually seen as 'public' prayer, on the rare occasions when clergy commented on them at all. See below, pp. 317–29.

[24] Parker and Carlson, 'Practical Divinity', 158; Howell, *Epistolæ Ho-Elianæ*, VI.48; Isham, 'Confessions', fos 8r, 18v; Psalm 55:17. Cf. Daniel 6:10; Bull, *Christian praiers*, title page; Day, *Booke of Christian Prayers*, sig. ☞3r; Sandys, *Sermons*, 263.

[25] Kilby, *Hallelujah*, 62; Sparke, *Crumms of comfort*, sig. A3v; Bod. MS Rawl. C.473 fos 5v–6r; Denison, *Monument or Tombe-Stone*, 92.

twice a day recurs in the literature: a third episode was ideal but often impractical, given the commitments of working life.[26] For example, in Dorothy Leigh's advice—'pray when the world is asleepe, for assoone as it is awake, it will cry and call on thee'—we can hear something of the tension between piety and caring for children. In the 1660s, Edward Wetenhall recommended twice-daily prayer as the acceptable minimum, and added, 'Oftener I may, as at noon, seldomer I well cannot.'[27]

By 1600 this was the standard compromise between pious ideal and quotidian reality: regular prayer twice a day, morning and evening.[28] Morning prayer was normally to be made immediately after rising, before breakfast; evening prayer sometimes preceded, sometimes followed a meal. It was a discipline shared by English and Scottish Protestants, and by puritans, conformists, and Laudians. When Richard Norwood did eventually adopt a regular pattern, this was it. Thrice-daily prayer was presumably impractical for Nehemiah Wallington, who had to keep shop hours, but he took his twice-daily commitment seriously. He insisted that we should omit sleep rather than omit prayer, and that we should not dare to eat in the morning, nor to sleep at night, without having prayed first.[29]

That note of self-reproach, however, tells us that even this discipline was more aspired to than observed. And, especially earlier in our period, there were plenty of devotees willing—in practice or even in theory—to fall back on a once-a-day pattern, as an acceptable bare minimum. Some accounts suggest devoting yourself to meditation, self-examination, or pious study at one end of the day, with the implication that briefer and less introspective prayers could be squeezed in at the other.[30] When the young convert Thomas Shepard first set himself to regular meditation, he did it 'sometimes every morning but constantly every evening'. Some divines implicitly endorsed this minimum.[31] Others did so openly. James Cancellar's popular *Alphabet of prayers* urged, 'let no day passe thee, but that thou once at the least doe present thy selfe to GOD in prayer'. Robert Bolton allowed that 'if a man doe but once a day seriously and solemnly thus cast vp the eye of his Faith', that would be sufficient. The rule recommended by the Durham layman, Gilbert Frevile, in the 1580s was, 'once in the daie at the least priuate prayer,

---

[26] See, for example, Gouge, *Whole-Armor of God*, 444; Smith, *Dauids blessed man*, 141 (although by the next page this has gone up to 'at the least, three times a day'); Narne, *Pearle of prayer*, 446; Willis, *Mount Tabor*, 2.

[27] Leigh, *Mothers blessing*, 75 (cf. Walker, *Sermon at the funerals . . .*, 46); Edward Wetenhall, *Enter into thy Closet, or a Method and Order for private Devotion* (1666: Wing W1495B), 14.

[28] Amongst many examples, see Dent, *Plaine mans path-way*, 321; Ward, *Coal from the Altar*, 50–1; Thomas Taylor, *Christ Revealed: or The Old Testament explained* (1635: RSTC 23821), 149; *Two treaties the first concerning the Holy Scriptures in generall* (Hamburg, 1640: RSTC 24260), 26–7.

[29] Mather, *Magnalia*, III.109–10; Clarke, *Collection*, 9; Rogers, *Three Scottish Reformers*, 121; FSL MS V.a.459, *passim*; Duncon, *Returnes*, 4; Norwood, *Journal*, 83–4; LMA Guildhall MS 204, p. 305.

[30] See, for example, Winthrop, *Papers*, 168; Byfield, *Marrow of the Oracles* (1619), 39; 'Anne Phoenix' [ps. for Anthony Fawkener?], *The Saints Legacies: Or, A Collection of certaine PROMISES out of the word of God* (1633: RSTC 10635.3), sig. *7v; Clarke, *Holy Incense*, 140, 147–8.

[31] Shepard, *God's Plot*, 42; see, for example, Culverwell, *Way to a blessed estate*, 5; Harris, *Peters enlargement* (1624), sig. A3v.

& meditation to be made'.[32] It was an uncomfortable and obvious truth: many even of the spiritually earnest did not pray nearly as much as their ministers would have liked. It was all very well to insist on thrice- or twice-daily prayer, but how many even seriously attempted it, let alone kept to it for any length of time?

Yet, what little evidence we have does suggest that a great many early modern British people did actually have some regular habits of prayer. Even ministers who were working themselves into a froth of indignation about their people's godlessness rarely claimed that their flocks did not pray at all. It was much more common to complain that their prayers consisted of parroting the Lord's Prayer, the Creed, and the Ten Commandments, the three texts which—in England—had to be learned for admission to communion, and which were used liturgically every Sunday.[33] The latter two are not, strictly speaking, prayers, but were used as such as regularly as they had been before the Reformation. (In 1630 Ambrose Fisher claimed, of the Creed, that 'commonly Children take it for a Prayer by tradition from their ignorant Elders'.)[34] Asunetus, the 'ignorant man' in Arthur Dent's *Plaine mans path-way to heauen*, believed that 'if a man say his Lords praier, his Ten Commande-ments, and his Beliefe, and keepe them . . . no doubt he shall be saued'; that is, Dent evidently believed that the Asunetuses of the world did indeed pray after some fashion. A generation later, James Perrott lamented the habits of the 'multitudes of people, who vsing only the Lords Prayer, or reading the Tenne Commandements, with out premeditation or knowledge what either of them contains, do yet think that they haue sufficiently serued God'. Jeremiah Dyke, likewise, believed that too many of his countrymen 'know not what praying meanes', by which he meant that they mistook 'mens customary formalities' for real prayer. John Brinsley believed that 'the greatest part . . . doe seldome or neuer pray priuately, vnlesse perhaps they vse the Lords prayer without vnderstanding'.[35] The testimony to widespread habits of prayer here is to be taken seriously; the disdain for meaningless formality, less so.

Indeed, that disdain had its consequences. Especially early in our period, there was a worry that fixed habits of prayer were popish or monastic. Thomas Becon, in the first English Protestant treatise on prayer, devoted considerable space to rebut-ting this argument. Part of the difficulty was the need to affirm Christian liberty, and 'the conscience of ony christen man, which oughte to be free to serue God at all houres'.[36] That permissiveness would seem alarming to a later generation. Samuel Smith's popular treatise on Psalm 1 rebuked those 'who can be content now and then to heare, reade, pray, and meditate, &c. But this must be at their leisure, when they haue nothing else to doe.'[37] Such people were not necessarily the 'carnal

[32] Cancellar, *Alphabet of prayers*, A5v (eight editions, 1564–c.1610); Bolton, *Some generall directions*, 65; BL Egerton MS 2877 fo. 83v.

[33] See below, pp. 230–2.

[34] Ambrose Fisher, *A defence of the liturgie of the Church of England* (1630: RSTC 10885), 103; cf. Perkins, *Godly and learned exposition*, 233.

[35] Dent, *Plaine mans path-way*, 25; Perrott, *Certaine Short Prayers*, sig. A10v; Dyke, *Worthy communicant*, 492–3; Brinsley, *True Watch* (1611), II.2.

[36] Becon, *Newe pathwaye unto praier*, sigs O3v–6r, P8r.

[37] Smith, *Dauids blessed man*, 147 (ten editions, 1614–38).

Protestants' of preachers' fears. Richard Rogers lamented that there were 'too many (and yet the people of God)', who make no conscience of daily prayer 'but thinke it enough at sometimes to haue this care'.[38] And yet Rogers himself readily changed his own pious routine. In February 1590 he noted in his diary that he had adopted a new regime three weeks earlier, and that he was very pleased with it. However, his pledge—'I endeavour to see one year thus passed, that it may be a glass to me hereafter'—suggests that he knew it was easier to embark on such a pattern than to stick to it.[39] There is no doubt that Rogers and many other earnest Protestants intended to pray regularly, but the only resources which could compel them to do so were habit and their own consciences. Such resolutions were easier made than kept.

When they did pray, how long did they spend doing so? Here again, ministers' aspirations and pastoral realities were painfully separated. Heroically long prayers were sometimes recommended, but inevitably they were very much the exception. Sometimes this is mere hyperbole, as in the Elizabethan claim that the godly 'pray the whole daye togither, without hauing anye minde of their meate, yea, and continue al night in prayer also'.[40] A handful of individuals are described, in awed tones, as being 'unwearied in religious exercises', and able to persist for hours on end, although there is usually a certain vagueness about quite how many hours are meant.[41] John Welsh supposedly 'reckoned the day ill spent if he staid not seven or eight hours in prayer', but it is clear both that this was very singular and that Welsh must have had many ill-spent days. For ministers, this kind of regime was at least conceivable. For others it was impossible, and the only way of managing a really substantial period of regular prayer was to rise very early.[42] At best, extended prayer would be an occasional achievement. Richard Waste recommended spending 'twoo houres of euery daye vppon Gods sole seruice'—if and only if you have the leisure to do so. Similarly, John Rogers recommended spending 'an Hour or two alone' when particularly unsettled or troubled. William Pemble, who reproached his readers for giving too little time to pious exercises, recommended spending 'an houre or twain in a week, a day in a moneth' on self-examination.[43] Indeed, some of the period's best-selling meditations would have taken a good two hours to work through in full. But that would hardly have been a daily discipline.

All things being equal, longer prayers were assumed to be better prayers, but it was widely recognized that all things were rarely equal. Hugh Latimer praised lengthy prayer 'when the spirit and the affections serve; for our Saviour himself spent a whole night in prayer'.[44] For those of us on a lower spiritual plane, however,

---

[38] Rogers, *Seven treatises*, sig. B3v.
[39] Knappen, *Two Diaries*, 96.
[40] *Short and pretie Treatise*, C7r.
[41] Tweedie, *Select Biographies*, 346, and cf. 307; Knappen, *Two Diaries*, 95; Clarke, *Collection*, 38–9.
[42] Tweedie, *Select Biographies*, 3; Ryrie, 'Sleeping, waking and dreaming'.
[43] Bod MS Rawl. C.473 fo. 3r; Mather, *Magnalia*, III.112; Pemble, *Introduction to worthy receiving*, 49–50.
[44] Latimer, *Sermons by Hugh Latimer*, 353.

brevity had its place. Sometimes it is an acceptable second best: 'if we cannot make a long prayer, let vs make a short'.[45] But others argued—paradoxically, they felt—that 'though prayers bee but short, yet may they pierce the heauens'. John Winthrop's experience is revealing. Sometimes, he reflected, he had 'bestowed a great deale of tyme in prayer', but to no avail, since his heart was not in it; whereas at other times 'a short meditation, or prayer, a secreat grone, or desire sent up into heauen' would bring him 'unspeakable peace and comforte'. The point, as John Preston put it, was that 'the *Lord* takes not our prayers by number, but by waight'.[46] There was a surprisingly broad consensus that 'Prayer must be SHORT' and 'thy words must be few', from Laudians through centrists to puritans. Robert Bruce, who was certainly capable of extended prayer, was said sometimes to be 'very short in prayer . . . but then every sentence was like a strong bolt shott up to heauen'.[47] Brevity, that is, had a rhetorical effect. A few pithy words can strike home where a rambling monologue does not—and since devotees can be moved by their own prayers, this applies as much to private as to public prayer. It was both an encouragement and a challenge to those who felt themselves inadequate to pray. They did not need to craft long orations, but they did need to make every word count.

This emphasis on quality rather than on quantity made excellent theological and pastoral sense, but it also meant that the pass had already been sold. John Redman recognized this as early as 1551. 'Wee haue learned', he wrote, 'that God careth not for long prayers, but for a good heart': and so prayer is abandoned and faith withers in its absence. 'The deuotion is so dull, that with the short prayer it is nothing stirred, and the prayers is so short, that the deuotion, vnlesse it were more quicke, cannot arise.' With blunt common sense he added, 'if prayer be the eleuation of the minde toward God . . . then the longer it is, the better it must bee'.[48] Paid-up Protestants, hamstrung by scruples and allergic to prescriptive formalities, would not lay down the law so starkly. As a result, they struggled to hold any kind of line.

Yet they did, sometimes, try. There were those who recommended an hour. 'Colde ye not watche with me one houre?', Christ had reproached his disciples, and his early modern English disciples still felt the sting. Samuel Smith deplored those who 'in twenty four houres hardly can spare one to serue God'. John Brinsley's popular *True Watch, and Rule of Life* began with a lament that 'I find my selfe . . . so weake, that I am not able to spende one houre thus with thee'.[49] Some of these 'hours' seem to be symbolic, but sometimes at least an interval of sixty minutes is plainly meant. Grace Mildmay recalled that her mother used to spend an hour alone in prayer every morning. Nehemiah Wallington vowed in 1629 'to double

---

[45] Dod and Cleaver, *Ten sermons*, 125.

[46] Bernard, *A Weekes Worke* (1616), 21; Winthrop, *Papers*, 191; Preston, *Saints Daily Exercise*, 29; cf. Tuke, *Practise of the faithfull*, 6–7.

[47] Featley, *Ancilla Pietatis*, 29; Byfield, *Marrow of the Oracles* (1622), 546; Clarke, *Holy Incense*, 48; Parker and Carlson, 'Practical Divinity', 179; Tweedie, *Select Biographies*, 307.

[48] John Redman, *The complaint of grace, continued through all ages of the world*, ed. William Crashaw (1609: RSTC 20826.5), 75–6.

[49] Matthew 26:40; Smith, *Dauids blessed man*, 145; Brinsley, *True Watch* (1608), 8.

my Saruice vnto thee and to spend one hower in reading and prayr in the morning and on houer in the euening except some grate thing hinders mee'.[50]

Great things did have a way of hindering, however, and most divines were realistic enough to recognize the fact. William Whateley's popular sermon *The Redemption of time* recommended that when 'thou hast more leasure then ordinarie', you should spend at least 'one tenth part of the foure & twentie houres' on your devotions—but recognized that this was exceptional, and we may guess he scarcely expected to be taken at his word. His more quotidian advice was not 'to spend more time in any pastime vpon any day, then in religious exercises'.[51] All too often, however, prayer bit into hours of work rather than of leisure. John Preston recommended that it be observed nevertheless, promising that 'the time that is spent in calling vpon *God* hinders you not in your businesse'. Prayer was, he argued, akin to oiling a wheel or sharpening a scythe, a preparation that would in fact speed your work. This works better as preacher's rhetoric than as practical time management. Henry Scudder, more pragmatically, warned devotees to 'lay not too great a taske vpon your selfe': meaning 'so much, as will take vp more time then the workes of your calling, and other needful affaires will permit'. Otherwise your prayers would simply become 'tedious and burthensome', tempting you to abandon them altogether.[52]

One hint of actual practice comes from the lengths of the prayers printed for devotional use. These rarely run to more than a couple of thousand words and could therefore be read aloud in less than twenty minutes—often much less. They might also be extended by meditation, reading, extempore prayer, or being joined with other printed prayers, but they imply a certain minimum for the tolerably conscientious Protestant. (That is also roughly the time that most people can manage to kneel without intense discomfort.) We have some textual support for this guess. A few held out for half an hour, like Wallington before his 1629 'doubling',[53] but we also find Lewis Bayly lamenting that the modern Christian 'thinkest it too long to continue in Prayer but one quarter of an houre', and several others named the same period of time in their reproaches.[54] Those who were stung by these rebukes might well have responded that plenty of their compatriots measured their daily prayers in seconds rather than minutes—a muttered Lord's Prayer at bed time, a swift table-grace. Fifteen minutes daily was a reasonable compromise, enough for some real earnestness, but not so long as to be impractical or daunting. It was not, perhaps, enough, but it was as much as many earnest lay Protestants could manage, and as little as their ministers were willing to allow.

[50] Mildmay, *With Faith and Physic*, 29; LMA Guildhall MS 204, p. 43.
[51] Whately, *Redemption of time*, 17, 19, 71.
[52] Preston, *Saints Daily Exercise*, 32; Scudder, *Christians daily walke* (1628), 40–1.
[53] Mather, *Magnalia*, III, 110; Clarke, *Holy Incense*, 140.
[54] Bayly, *Practise of pietie*, 266; Bolton, *Three-fold treatise*, II.168; Smith, *Dauids blessed man*, 146; Saxby, 'Miscellany' fo. 69v.

PLACES OF PRAYER

Christians can in theory, and early modern Protestants did in practice, pray anywhere and everywhere. There was only one overriding condition for private prayer: solitude. Devotees should 'retire to some secret place', 'where wee may be most secret, and freest from distractions'.[55] Christians, not least medieval Christians, had long sought solitude to pray. But the practicalities of seeking solitude, and the reasons why—and extent to which—Protestants sought it, shaped their experience of prayer enough for us to pause on the subject.

The Protestant urge to seek solitude to pray seems to have been almost instinctive. Archibald Johnston of Wariston's diary repeatedly describes how he was 'forced' to retire to his room to pray. One day, he thought he had finished, and went downstairs to rejoin the rest of the household, but then the Scripture on which he had been meditating came to his mind again, and 'not being aible to containe myselth I was forced to runne up the stair, and thair I poured out my heart to God'. Similarly, the young Nehemiah Wallington was one day so overcome in church that he ran home and shut himself in his chamber. Elizabeth Melville's poem, *A Godlie Dreame*, began by describing her reaction to a wave of mourning and self-loathing: 'In companie I could no wise remaine,/But fled resort, and so alone did goe.' Richard Rogers blamed his spiritual backsliding in 1588 on his inability to find space and time to be alone.[56] Henry Burton, imprisoned in Lancaster Castle in 1637, had a different problem. He was alone in his cell, but the cell below him contained

> five witches, with one of their children, which made such a hellish noise night and day, that I seemed then to be in hell. . . . I was deprived of the sweetnesse of my privacy, and of the only solace of my solitary prison, when I could not either pray, or meditate, or yet sleep quietly.

He fought back by singing psalms loudly enough—he hoped—to disturb them.[57] We might have hoped that he would show a little sympathy for the wretched women and the child, but while his comments testify to his callousness, they also show how earnestly he sought peace and solitude.

The reasons were plain enough. There were Biblical precedents: Christ, in particular, regularly withdrew to pray alone.[58] There was Burton's problem, of distraction; both overt disturbance, and sights or sounds which would stir 'cogitations of worldly busines'. Robert Bruce warned that if we pray in public, 'there is no

[55] Bayly, *Practise of pietie*, 564–5; Brinsley, *True Watch* (1608), 24. Cf. Elizabeth Jocelin, *The Mothers Legacie, To her vnborne Child* (1624: RSTC 14624), 26; Clarke, *Holy Incense*, 145; Rogers, *Garden* (1616), sig. C3v.

[56] Wariston, *Diary*, 42, 50–1, 91; Wallington, *Notebooks*, 38; Elizabeth Melville, *A Godlie Dreame* (Edinburgh, 1620: RSTC 17814), sig. A2r; Knappen, *Two Diaries*, 77.

[57] Burton, *Narration*, 16.

[58] Cited in, amongst others, Latimer, *Sermons by Hugh Latimer*, 218; Bradford, *Godlie meditations*, sig. I4v; FSL MS V.a.394 fo. 6r; Izaak Walton, *The Complete Angler and The Lives of Donne, Wotton, Hooker, Herbert and Sanderson*, ed. A. W. Pollard (1906), 26.

incident that falleth in our senses, but it wil draw vs from that commoning quhilk we haue with God'.[59] 'The noise of Cains hammers in building Cities', Oliver Heywood cautioned after our period, 'drowns the voice of conscience.' As their Bibles told them, God speaks in 'a stil and soft voyce'.[60]

Two more substantial reasons were added. First, solitary prayer was a touchstone of faith. It was a truism that the hypocrite 'prayes more often, more zealously with others, than alone by himselfe', whereas the true Christian is 'more deuout in priuate then in publike'. As such, readiness to pray in private 'affordeth the truest triall of the vprightnesse of a mans heart'.[61] The title page of the popular, unsophisticated moralizing tract *Keepe within Compasse* presented solitary prayer as a guard against atheism (see Figure 1). As well as reassuring you of your sincerity, solitary prayer also spared you the temptation to 'ostentation and hypocrisie' or to 'inward pride' which was inevitable when others saw you pray. This, after all, was why Christ had urged devotees to 'enter into thy chamber: & ... shut thy dore.' As Daniel Featley irrefutably pointed out, 'if priuate Deuotion cometh once to be knowne, it ceaseth to be priuate'.[62] Light should not be let in on the magic.

Fig. 1. John Trundle?, *Keepe within Compasse* (1619, RSTC 14898.5), title page. The title-page illustration of this moralising tract sums up early modern social ethics ranging from the need for private prayer to the obligation to remain within your 'calling'.
Bodleian Library, Oxford.

[59] Gerhard, *Meditations*, 236; Bruce, *Sermons Preached*, sig. C2v; cf. Parr, *Abba Father*, 5–6.

[60] Oliver Heywood, *Heart-Treasure* (1667: Wing H1767), 93; I Kings 19:12.

[61] Clarke, *Holy Incense*, 51; Featley, *Ancilla Pietatis*, 4; Gouge, *Whole-Armor of God*, 428. Cf. Struther, *Scotlands Warning*, 72; Hunnis, *Seuen Sobs*, 7–8; Brinsley, *True Watch* (1608), 24–5.

[62] Matthew 6:6; Parr, *Abba Father*, 6; Gouge, *Whole-Armor of God*, 429; Featley, *Ancilla Pietatis*, 3. Cf. Perkins, *Godly and learned exposition*, 339.

The second, linked reason, was pragmatic: only in solitude can you be truly open in prayer. As William Cowper put it:

> The presence of man is oftentimes a great impediment of the free communing of our soules with God, and that the children of God will boldly communicate those secrets to the Lord, which they will not vtter to their dearest friends.[63]

Listening ears hobble prayers. Richard Kilby warned that if you knew your prayers were overheard, 'then is it a hundred to one, that the divells, and the private pride of your owne heart, will marre all, and make your devotions loathsome in the sight of God', for you would start praying eloquently, hoping to impress your hearers.[64] Moreover, some secrets should not be overheard. 'It is not fit nor safe', Featley warned, 'that any should heare vs ripping vp our whole life, and ransacking our heart, and laying open all our most secret corruptions.'[65] Listeners might be shocked. Worse, they might laugh. Not everyone in early modern Britain accepted that ardour in prayer was appropriate behaviour, and it was taken for granted that you would wish to conceal, for example, pious tears.[66] Paul Baynes believed that a believer's tears would be no more pitied 'than the sight of a Goose going barefoote', and the melodramatic self-abasement of Protestant penitence, regretted William Struther, 'would finde an vncheritable censure' from many observers.[67] A century earlier, the Catholic devotional writer Richard Whitford had commented more bluntly on exactly the same problem: when he recommended regular prayers, lay people would reply, 'yf we shuld use these thynges in presence of our felowes, some wold laugh us to scorne and mocke us'.[68] It was a perennial problem—and Whitford's concern is a reminder that while private prayer might distinguish the sincere from the hypocritical believer, it was of no value for distinguishing Protestants from Catholics.

What makes these truisms more complicated is that early modern Protestants desired solitude while at the same time fearing and distrusting it. In part this was a reaction against Catholic devotional patterns which valued withdrawal and the eremetical life. Richard Baxter believed this deterred many Protestants from solitary prayer.[69] In part, it was a simple affirmation of the value of good company. Christians were, it was said, like sticks, stronger in a bundle than alone; or like coals, which burn more brightly if kept together.[70] But underlying this was a deeper, more atavistic suspicion of solitude, which was often linked with melancholy and suicide.[71] Nehemiah Wallington's youthful temptations began when the

[63] Cowper, *Triumph*, 21–2. Cf. Sandys, *Sermons*, 275.
[64] Kilby, *Hallelujah*, 170.
[65] Featley, *Ancilla Pietatis*, 724–5.
[66] Bruce, *Sermons Preached*, sig. C2v; Hildersam, *Doctrine of Fasting*, 119; and see below, pp. 187–95.
[67] Paul Baynes, *A Helpe to true Happinesse* (1635: RSTC 1643.5), 82; Struther, *Scotlands Warning*, 72.
[68] White, *Tudor Books of Private Devotion*, 157.
[69] FSL MS V.a.394 fo. 7r; Longfellow, '"my now solitary prayers"', 55.
[70] Hall, *Meditations and Vowes*, I.105; Lupton, *Obiectorum Reductio*, 65–7; and see below, pp. 390–7.
[71] Perkins, *First part of The cases of conscience*, 92–3; Byfield, *Marrow of the Oracles* (1622), 348; Scudder, *Christians daily walke* (1628), 408–9; Houston, *Punishing the Dead?*, 306.

Devil urged him 'to runn awaie and to goe into some sollitarie place'. He later reproached himself: 'O thou troubled soule take heed of solittarinesse and of parrleing with the Divell.' The Devil does not miss such opportunities, Richard Capel warned: 'we are alone thinking on heaven by some Well-side, he seeing us alone . . . thrusts at us with a tentation to cast our selves into the water'.[72]

Solitude was also linked to idleness. Lonely hours would be filled with 'ranging or wandring' thoughts, with 'wicked thoughts . . . in your minde and Phantasie', or indeed with active plotting of evil. In this sense, too, 'Solitarines is Satans opportunitie.'[73] William Fulwood's popular *The Enimie of Idlenesse* was, its preface made plain, also the enemy of solitude.[74] The obvious answer to this problem was to fill solitary hours with godliness. 'If thou bee alone', Michael Sparke recommended, 'take one of these companions with thee; eyther thy Prayer-Booke, or thy Bible, good thoughts, or charity.' Such solitude is not truly solitary, for you are in God's presence. With the Word of God, 'thou shalt not need a better companion'. But this could not quite lift the suspicion from solitude, for who could guarantee the orthodoxy of solitary religion? Henry Scudder feared that too much reading and meditation alone would lead to conceit, heresy, and apostasy.[75] Richard Hooker was more scathing. Ostensibly describing Anabaptists, but plainly also meaning puritans, he warned that 'when they and their Bibles were alone together, what strange phantasticall opinion soever at any time entred into their heads, their use was to thinke the Spirit taught it to them'. Being alone with the Bible, then, was positively dangerous. Hooker would have sympathized with the good people of Ayr, alarmed by the piety of their radical minister John Welsh. Welsh spent whole nights praying alone in the parish church; it gave him a local reputation not as a holy man, but as a witch.[76]

It is no surprise, then, that 'private' prayer was often less than entirely solitary. The concept of 'privacy' was only weakly formed in our period, and certainly lacked its modern categorical clarity and ethical value.[77] We might imagine that the condition of solitary prayer is that the devotee can neither be watched nor overheard, but that is anachronistic. In the 1660s, Edward Wettenhall described his practice of keeping two shut doors between himself and the rest of the house while praying, 'to the end that my voice . . . might not be heard without'.[78] Leave aside for the moment the sheer impossibility of this advice for almost everyone. Before the Civil Wars, even the aspiration would have seemed fastidious. Solitude was not a matter of invisibility or inaudibility, but a state of mind. 'It is

---

[72] Wallington, *Notebooks*, 32, 34, 35, 38; Capel, *Tentations*, 335–6.

[73] Rogers, *Garden* (1616), sig. F4v; Scudder, *Christians daily walke* (1628), 97–8; cf. Rogers, *Seven treatises*, 334; Whately, *Redemption of time*, 36–7; and see below, pp. 441–6.

[74] William Fulwood, *The Enimie of Idlenesse* (1568: RSTC 11476), esp. sig. A6r (at least ten editions, 1568–1621).

[75] Sparke, *Crumms of comfort*, sig. L2v; Goodwin, *Vanity of Thoughts*, 44–5; Scudder, *Christians daily walke* (1628), 109.

[76] Hooker, *Laws . . . Books I–IV*, 44; Tweedie, *Select Biographies*, 8.

[77] Longfellow, '"my now solitary prayers"'; Lena Cowen Orlin, *Locating Privacy in Tudor London* (Oxford, 2007).

[78] Wetenhall, *Enter into thy Closet*, 6.

more possible', Joseph Hall taught, 'for some thoughtfull men to haue a solitary mind in the midst of a market, than for [others] to be alone in a wilderness.' The pious believer may be alone in a crowd, but will be joined in the prayer-closet by a choir of angels.[79]

Wettenhall's soundproofing advice also indicates that while devotees might seek to avoid being distracted, they were happy enough to provide distractions for others. The Suffolk cleric John Carter used to pray daily 'in his Closet . . . very loud, and mostly very long', deliberately keeping the volume high to 'give a good example for secret prayer to his children, and servants'. His biographer saw no incongruity in using the word 'secret' in this context.[80] The godly Cheshire matriarch, Jane Ratcliffe, 'used as much privacy as might be' in her prayers, but her biographer John Ley claimed that 'such a singular gift (as shee had) could not bee hid but servants and some secret female friends must know it'. She was particularly concerned that men, especially ministers, should not overhear her, but Ley, despite being a minister, managed to eavesdrop on her devotions three times. He apparently had no sense that this might be unethical.[81] Perhaps Ratcliffe half-intended to be overheard? This certainly seems to have been the case for Elizabeth Melville, who in June 1630, after an all-night prayer meeting in her chamber, retired to bed for 'privat devotion . . . and drew the curtains, that she might set herself to prayer'. But from behind the bed-curtains her 'great motion' in prayer could clearly be heard, and the room quickly filled again with those who were keen to hear her.[82] For women, especially, the porous boundary between company and solitude could provide opportunities.

Of course, real solitude, in the modern sense, was sometimes sought and sometimes found. And it is likely under-represented in our sources, since Christ's injunction to pray secretly was sometimes taken seriously, and truly secret prayer does not leave much mark on the historical record. But for almost everyone in early modern Britain, privacy of the modern kind—quiet rooms, large houses, tight-fitting doors—simply did not exist. Nor was it necessarily what those who claimed to seek 'solitude' wanted.[83]

Where, then, did early modern Protestants seek such solitude as they wanted?[84] Here, Biblical and patristic examples were not much help, since precedents could be cited for prayer at home, abroad, inside, outside, in every room, in bed, or even in a bath.[85] Especially at the beginning of our period, Protestant writers positively celebrated the liberty to pray anywhere, and in particular opposed the notion that

[79] Hall, *Arte of Divine Meditation*, 53; Nuttall, *Holy Spirit*, 137–8.

[80] Clarke, *Collection*, 9.

[81] John Ley, *A patterne of Pietie. Or The Religious life and death of that Grave and gracious Matron, Mrs. Jane Ratcliffe* (1640: RSTC 15567), 61, 63.

[82] Tweedie, *Select Biographies*, 346–7.

[83] Orlin, *Locating Privacy*, esp. 152–92.

[84] The study of early modern 'sacred space' has begun to illuminate this subject: see Will Coster and Andrew Spicer (eds), *Sacred Space in Early Modern Europe* (Cambridge, 2005). Physical space is the organizing principle of Cambers, *Godly Reading*, to which I am indebted.

[85] Hall, *Meditations and Vowes . . . A third Century*, III.49; cf. similar lists in Cowper, *Triumph*, 24; Gouge, *Whole-Armor of God*, 428.

prayer in a church building had any special value. They merged the Old Testament's emphasis on the temple as the site for prayer with the New Testament principle that the Christian is a temple of the Holy Spirit, so that 'mine house, the field, the high-waies shall bee my Temple, and my chiefest care shall be to cary a Temple alwaies with me, in me'.[86] It could be liberating. Elizabeth Juxon claimed on her deathbed that 'her chamber, and closet, and orchard, and garden, and watergate, and turret, and euery corner could testifie that she had dearely and earnestly sought after God'. For John Bruen, it was a matter of principle: 'hee would not bee too much observed to frequent one place [for prayer], lest he should draw himselfe into some suspition of vanity or hypocrisie'.[87] But the young Wallington's case suggests that restless, continuous motion could also be a sign of despair or disturbance. He travelled from London to York and back, believing that, like Cain, he was cursed to wander the earth: 'I could not abide in no place nor no place could abide mee.' Joseph Hall advised that, while prayer was permissible anywhere, it was best to stick to a single place, for 'we find God neerer vs in the place where wee haue been accustomed familiarlie to meete him'.[88] Without such habits, it was all too easy to fall away from regular prayer altogether. In 1551, during the first flush of Protestant liberty, John Redman worried that those who claim they can pray anywhere in fact hardly pray at all.[89]

Later generations would perfect one solution: the prayer-closet, a room set aside wholly for private prayer. Wettenhall provided the classic description in the 1660s.[90] Such dedicated spaces seem to have been rarer before the Civil War, even amongst those who could afford them: but the word 'closet' was very widely used to describe a private or semi-private indoor space for prayer. The 1611 King James Bible put the word in Christ's mouth, urging devotees to 'enter into thy closet' (Tyndale, and the Geneva Bible, used the word 'chamber'); this both reflected and hastened the word's hardening into a piece of specialist jargon. Thomas Bentley assumed his reader would pray in 'thy closet' when at home, and Perkins advised that private prayer should be 'in priuate houses and clozets'.[91] At the turn of the century, Lady Margaret Hoby prayed in a room she called a closet; as we have seen, Elizabeth Juxon's ubiquitous prayers sometimes took place in hers; and Lettice Cary referred to praying habitually 'in my private closet'.[92]

It seems unlikely, however, that any of these 'closets' were purpose-built or wholly dedicated prayer rooms. Any secluded space or storage room could be made to serve as a 'closet', and some 'closets' of which ministers spoke were metaphorical,

[86] Becon, *Newe pathwaye unto praier*, sigs K3r–5v; Bradford, *Godlie meditations*, sig. A3v; Tuke, *Practise of the faithfull*, 32; cf. Babington, *Profitable Exposition*, 69–8*; Bentley, *Monument of Matrones*, 413.

[87] Denison, *Monument or Tombe-Stone*, 122; Hinde, *Faithfull Remonstrance . . . of Iohn Bruen*, 156.

[88] Wallington, *Notebooks*, 50–1; Hall, *Arte of Divine Meditation*, 53–4.

[89] Redman, *Complaint of grace*, 76–7.

[90] Wetenhall, *Enter into thy Closet*, 5–9; cf. Richard Rambuss, *Closet Devotions* (Durham, NC, and London, 1998).

[91] Bentley, *Monument of Matrons*, 413; Perkins, *Whole treatise*, 280. On closets and their fluid meanings, see Orlin, *Locating Privacy*, 296–326.

[92] Hoby, *Diary*, e.g. 106; Denison, *Monument or Tombe-Stone*, 122; Duncon, *Returnes*, 2, 39.

closets of the heart.[93] As Andrew Cambers has observed, in this period the physical prayer-closet seems to have been predominantly a woman's space.[94] In these wealthy households, men had other private spaces, notably the study. The closet emerged, initially, as a practical, but gendered and highly class-specific, solution to a wider problem.

For the closet-less classes, what were the alternatives? The chamber, or bedchamber, was the most obvious room to adapt as a prayer room, eased again by the pre-1611 translations of Matthew 6:6. This was what Richard Rogers and Dorothy Leigh expected their readers to do, and it was what earnest Protestants such as Archibald Johnston of Wariston, Katherine Brettergh, and William Proud appear to have done.[95] Or there were studies: predominantly masculine rooms, but women sometimes used them too—Jean Stewart spent two hours praying alone in her father's study before agreeing to marry Wariston.[96] But since most people in this period lived in houses where there were more people than rooms, finding solitude indoors was not a simple matter. It was a problem from which spiritual writers tended to shy away, and again it was one which particularly afflicted women. John Rogers did consider how sailors or those in large families could pray alone, but simply warned such people to make more of an effort. William Gouge refused even to acknowledge the problem, recommending private prayer for servants and children on the grounds that 'none can hinder secret praier'.[97] Perhaps some anticipated Susanna Wesley's practice, and simply put a cloth over their heads in the midst of domestic chaos to create a tiny, symbolically private space. But only a matriarch could get away even with that trick. No servant would dare.

One obvious domestic space for prayer remained: the bed, where most people could reasonably hope to spend some time undisturbed. Helpfully, there was Biblical support. Protestants who reeled off lists of places for prayer commonly included the bed amongst others, and midnight prayer was seen as having a particularly intimate quality to it.[98] We have already met Richard Greenham and Elizabeth Melville praying or meditating in bed. John Forbes of Corse filled his diary with references to having 'prayed in my bed vnto the Lord', to 'meditating in my bed in the morning', and spiritual struggles 'in the night in my bed'.[99]

However, prayer in bed was no panacea. For one thing, the bedchamber was no more private than anywhere else. Beds were commonly shared with spouses, siblings, or fellow-servants (to say nothing of the bedbugs). One objection that Richard Whitford imagined to his prescribed regime of prayer was that 'we done lye .ii. or .iii. somtyme togyder': solitude in bed was a luxury mostly confined to the

---

[93] For example, Gerhard, *Meditations*, 236; Hieron, *Helpe vnto Deuotion* (1608), 197.

[94] Cambers, *Godly Reading*, 47.

[95] Rogers, *Seven treatises*, 235; Leigh, *Mothers blessing*, 136; Wariston, *Diary*, 42, 50–1, 91; Harrison, *Deaths aduantage*, III.8; Francis Rogers, *A sermon preached . . . at the funerall of William Proud* (1633: RSTC 21175), sig. D2v.

[96] Wariston, *Diary*, 12.

[97] Rogers, *Seven treatises*, 242; Gouge, *Whole-Armor of God*, 429.

[98] Psalm 4:4; Babington, *Profitable Exposition*, 68*; Duncon, *Returnes*, 40; Ryrie, 'Sleeping, waking and dreaming'.

[99] See above, pp. 112, 158; Forbes, 'Diary', 7, 16, 62.

wealthy.[100] That did not necessarily preclude prayer. The prophet Isaiah wrote of how King Hezekiah, on his sickbed, 'turned his face to the wall, and praied', which Robert Bruce interpreted as an attempt to find 'ane secret place' without distractions in the very public space of a royal bedchamber.[101] But this would only work if prayers were silent, which was often not the case. A popular set of Lutheran-derived meditations declared, 'The Saints wil be ioiful with glorie, and sing loude vpon their beds', which cannot have endeared the saints to their bedfellows.[102] Two Scots give us glimpses of what this may have meant. As a boy, James Melville boarded with his schoolmaster, and shared a room with the man's sickly wife, who habitually prayed in her bed. The example, he recalled, 'did mikle [much] profit me; for I ley in hir chamber and heard hir exerceises'. Similarly, as a young minister in the 1590s, John Welsh boarded with a parishioner and shared a bed with his host's young son. The boy later recalled how Welsh, when he went to bed, would 'lay a Scottish plaid above his bed-clothes, and when he went to his night prayers... sit up and cover himself negligently therewith, and so to continue'.[103] These two boys were impressed by their elders' earnest nocturnal piety; others would have begrudged the disturbance. In any case this was hardly solitude.

Prayer in bed faced another, more fundamental problem: it was too comfortable. The example of the disciples at Gethsemane warned that sleep and prayer should not mix. 'Some neuer pray till they goe to bed, and so sleepe preuenteth them', William Gouge harrumphed.[104] Even if you managed not to stay awake, lying in comfort was not conducive to true prayer. Thomas Playfere cited the Song of Songs ('In my bed by night... I soght him, but I founde him not') to argue that the bed was the wrong place from which to seek Christ, who had nowhere to lay his own head. 'Goe into the garden among the bramble bushes, and there you shall find him, not sleeping, but sweating dropps of blood for your redemption.'[105] Lying back did not seem to suit the occasion.

An alternative to the bedchamber was to take yourself to an attic, tower, or rooftop. The pull of high places was widely felt. The classic location for a minister's study was the attic, the highest room in the house. Long galleries, meditative spaces for the wealthy, were also normally on a house's top floor.[106] This was a matter of preference as well as of architectural pragmatism. There were Biblical precedents. St Peter prayed on a rooftop; Moses, Elijah, and Christ each prayed on mountains, and were reunited on one. Wetenhall cited Christ's example when advising that prayer-closets should be in an elevated location. This was partly so that they might be 'most remote from the noise, company, and disturbance of the people', but also because

---

[100] White, *Tudor Books of Private Devotion*, 157.
[101] Bruce, *Sermons Preached*, sig. C2v; Isaiah 38:2. The idiom is used in the same sense in Babington, *Profitable Exposition*, 28.
[102] Habermann, *Enimie of securitie*, 45 (fifteen editions, 1597–1620).
[103] Melville, *Autobiography*, 17; Tweedie, *Select Biographies*, 3.
[104] Gouge, *Whole-Armor of God*, 456.
[105] Playfere, *Power of praier*, 29; Song of Songs 3:1.
[106] Cambers, *Godly Reading*, 73–4; Orlin, *Locating Privacy*, 227–9.

some secret property there is in such high and eminent places, whence we may behold the heavens and overlook the earth, which to me raiseth the soul and elevates the affections, as if we derived or partaked more from heaven, by how much neerer we come to it.[107]

In 1634 Lucy Robartes wrote a meditation 'composed by walking on the top of a house', describing 'what a contented solitude doth this place afford mee where I am neerer in place to heaven and in affection. I overlooke the world and seem to be scarce now a partie in it.' Anne Clifford and Elizabeth Juxon both periodically prayed in turrets and towers. Those who did not have access to literal towers might yearn for metaphorical ones. Paraphrasing the Song of Songs, Francis Rous described the rapt soul as 'treading on the top of the earth with the bottome of her feet. . . . Let her stand in this watch-tower, and looke out for her lover, as the watch-man looks out for the morning.' To be lifted up was to rise above earthly corruption and be closer to God. It was the same urge as led some in 1630s England to dream spiritual-philosophical dreams of travel to the Moon.[108]

As well as closeness to God, high places promised a perspective on his creation. Clifford prayed in her tower at dawn, so as to see the sunrise. The young Nehemiah Wallington habitually prayed in 'the hie garret' at his father's house, and even in the midst of his temptations described 'seeing the starres Gods glorious creaters and meditating what a glorious place heaven is, and . . . finding peace in my conscience, and being ravished with the favour of God'. Strikingly, however, this swiftly gave way to a strong temptation to throw himself to his death. Perhaps the vertiginous danger of high places was part of their appeal.[109] We can see the same interplay between elevation, despair, and the hand of God in a 17th-century Englishwoman who, struggling with doubt, 'went up into the highest roome that was in the house, and looked forth at the window to see if I could see God'. She could not, but:

> I beheld the Trees to grow, the Birds to flie, the Heavens how they were hanged, and all things that were before me, then I thought *they could not make themselves, no more then I could make my selfe, and that we must needs have a Maker.*[110]

Above the bustle, God and his world could be seen for what they were.

This brings us to the obvious alternative to finding an enclosed private space for prayer: the great outdoors. As scholars have begun to notice, pious Protestants, like their medieval forebears, regularly went outside to pray, read, and meditate.[111]

---

[107] Wetenhall, *Enter into thy Closet*, 5–6.

[108] Gwyn Howells, 'Cobwebs in the Temple of God: the Brief Life of Lady Lucy Robartes 1615/6 to 1645/6?', *Lanhydrock House Journal* 1 (2001), 16 (I am grateful to Tara Hamling for providing me with a copy of this article); Denison, *Monument or Tombe-Stone*, 122; Anne Clifford, *The Diaries of Lady Anne Clifford*, ed. David J. H. Clifford (Stroud, 1990), 41; Rous, *Mysticall Marriage*, 282–3; David Cressy, 'Early Modern Space Travel and the English Man in the Moon', *American Historical Review* 111/4 (2006), 961–82.

[109] Clifford, *Diaries*, 41; Wallington, *Notebooks*, 33–4.

[110] Powell, *Spirituall Experiences*, 176.

[111] Cambers, *Godly Reading*, 110–16; Jane Dawson, ' "Hamely with God": a Scottish view on domestic devotion' in Martin and Ryrie, *Private and Domestic Devotion*, 35–7; Alexandra Walsham, *The Reformation of the Landscape: Religion, Identity, and Memory in Early Modern Britain and Ireland* (Oxford, 2011).

Separatists and dissidents gathered to pray in the open air, as Lollards had before them.[112] But our sources are also full of individual prayer while walking in fields, woods, or moors. Some devotees went outside specifically in order to pray.[113] It was a habit especially of students—young, earnest, and poor. Farmers near Cambridge must have grown used to pious young men wandering through their crops—or, in one case, lying down amongst them to pray his way sorrowfully out of a terrible hangover.[114] There were practical reasons for taking your devotions into the fields. As some writers observed, they provided the privacy which few indoor spaces could. Some sought out particularly secluded spots—from John Livingstone, who spent a day praying in a 'secret cave' in Lanarkshire, to Richard Norwood, who, arriving early for a duel and thoroughly frightened, 'withdrew myself into a thicket and went to prayer'. Providentially, his opponent never came.[115]

The great practical advantage of prayer outdoors was that, in early modern Britain, almost everyone lived within walking distance of rural isolation. Even Londoners could reach wild places on foot. The field was the pauper's closet. The disadvantage was exposure. Britain's unpredictable weather would play havoc with any attempt to pray outdoors with strict regularity. Its rather more predictable seasons had their own effects. James Howell rose early to pray all year round, but 'in the Summer time, I am oft-times abroad in som privat field, to attend the Sun rising'; such seasonal distinctions must have been very widely observed. In early 17th-century Scotland and Ulster, summer was the season for open-air communions.[116] Winter did offer its opportunities. In December 1625, John Forbes of Corse enjoyed morning meditative walks in which 'I beheld the moon & the starrs shyning clearlie above in the heaven round about': in Aberdeen at that time of year, he would not have needed to rise very early for that.[117] Still, if prayer outdoors was as significant a part of pious practice as our sources suggest, we may guess that British (and especially Scottish) Protestants prayed significantly more in the summer than in the winter. The fact that so many were willing to invest in that extravagant novelty, a long gallery—an indoor space created for walking in private—implies that when outdoor meditation could not be had, it was sorely missed.[118]

As Forbes' stargazing suggests, the open air offered devotees more than seclusion. Like rooftops, towers and garrets, it also offered inspiring sights. We

[112] Henry Martyn Dexter, *The Congregationalism of the Last Three Hundred Years as Seen in its Literature* (New York, 1970: facsimile of 1880 original), 257; John Foxe, *Actes and monuments of matters most speciall in the church* (1583: RSTC 11225), 818; Walsham, *Reformation of the Landscape*, 234–52.
[113] See, for example, Rogers, *Three Scottish Reformers*, 121; Hoby, *Diary, passim*; Tweedie, *Select Biographies*, 138, 308; Hinde, *Faithfull Remonstrance... of Iohn Bruen*, 142, 156; Clarke, *Lives of sundry Eminent Persons*, 167; Duncon, *Returnes*, 40; Foxe, *Actes and monuments* (1570), 1731.
[114] Shepard, *God's Plot*, 41, also 42–5; cf. Knappen, *Two Diaries*, 115.
[115] Rogers, *Seven treatises*, 235; Harrison, *Deaths aduantage*, III.8; Tweedie, *Select Biographies*, 133; Norwood, *Journal*, 32–3.
[116] Howell, *Epistolæ Ho-Elianæ*, VI.48–9; Schmidt, *Holy Fairs*.
[117] Forbes, *Diary*, 48.
[118] Orlin, *Locating Privacy*, 226–61.

are accustomed to thinking of nature-piety as a modern innovation, a child of Romanticism, but it was—in a distinctive way—alive and flourishing in the Reformation era.[119] In Dent's *Plaine mans path-way to heauen* we first meet the hero, the minister Theologus, walking in a meadow, declaring that it is his 'pleasure at this time of the yeere . . . to take the fresh aire, and to heare the sweet singing of birds'.[120] The Elizabethan *Treatise touching the perpetuall Reioyce of the godly* was fulsome on the matter:

> Christians doe take incredible delectation especially among other men, at this wonderful ornature and beautie of the worlde. . . . How reioice they, euen from the very bottome of their harts as oft as they doe remember Gods goodnesse, which woulde haue all the other Creatures to serue for mans necessities: Woods, Groues, Hils, Large meadowes & Pastures, Fields, Gardens of pleasure, fountains and springs of water.[121]

This was not an exclusively Protestant phenomenon, but it was a strikingly discriminating one. 'Woods, Groues, Hils': but I have found no trace of any pious meditation on the built environment. The implicit vision of Heaven is not that of the New Testament—the City of God, the new Jerusalem—but that of Genesis: the garden of Eden. They are interested in the natural creation, albeit creation as cultivated and managed by human hand.

Two broad aspects of that creation in particular stand out. First, the skies. As we will see, prayer very often had an upward aspect. But it also helped that, in the age before light pollution, virtually all Christians could have access to the heavens. Weather permitting, Wallington could stargaze from his father's house in the centre of London. The *Perpetuall Reioyce* believed that Christians rejoiced 'at the most pleasant sight of the sunne, at the starres shining by night', and it seems to have been right. Richard Bernard's populist dialogue, *A Weekes Worke,* urged its readers to 'behold and looke vp often to the heauens, as thy eternall mansion'.[122] John Hayward's *Sanctuarie of a troubled soule* depicted just such a scene: Jonah seated beneath a tree gazing up at the sun (Figure 2). Forbes of Corse, as well as admiring the winter stars, also recorded how 'beholding the Sun in his rysing I praised God for yt outward light, & prayed for the spirituall light of Gods loving Countenance'. Such spiritual readings of the heavens could be life-changing. In her early forties, the Yorkshire gentlewoman Alice Thornton vividly recalled how, aged four, the words of Psalm 147:4—'he counteth the starres and calleth them all by theire names'—had sparked 'the first dawning of God's Spirit in my heart'.[123]

When you lowered your eyes from the heavens, the most inspiring natural sights were living things, whether animal or vegetable. This included thanksgiving for

---

[119] Walsham, *Reformation of the Landscape,* 89, 328–40.

[120] Dent, *Plaine mans path-way,* 1.

[121] *Short and pretie Treatise,* sigs C8r–D2r.

[122] *Short and pretie Treatise,* sig. C8r; Bernard, *A Weekes Worke* (1616), 94 (at least five editions 1614–33, of which only four copies in total survive).

[123] Forbes, 'Diary', 45; Alice Thornton, *The Autobiography of Mrs Alice Thornton,* ed. Charles Jackson (Surtees Society 62, 1873), 6–7.

Fig. 2. John Hayward, *The sanctuarie of a troubled soule* (1602: RSTC 13003.7), sig. 2r. A rare visual depiction of the common practice of outdoor prayer, apparently intended to be the prophet Jonah. We may assume that British outdoor devotees were usually more warmly dressed.

By permission of the Folger Shakespeare Library.

crops and other practical benefits of the natural world,[124] but it soon moved beyond it to a more selfless awe at the wonder of creation itself. Lewis Bayly urged his many readers to

> walke into the fields, and meditate vpon the Workes of God: for in euery Creature thou maist read, as in an open Booke, the Wisedome, Power, Prouidence, and goodnesse of Almighty God.[125]

Elizabeth Isham, who passed some of her long hours in drawing and embroidering flowers, 'learned in them all to Glorifie thee my God, and maker, whose workes all praise'. Richard Waste's private devotions recall how the 'sight of Hills &

---

[124] Knappen, *Two Diaries*, 115; *Short and pretie Treatise*, sig. C8v.
[125] Bayly, *Practise of pietie*, 477–8.

Dales ... & the grasse, hearbs, & flowers' reminded him of God's power and providence. From 1641 onward, the Lancashire minister Isaac Ambrose took month-long spiritual retreats every May and June into the 'sweet silent Woods' near Weddicar, in Cumberland. It was a 'solitary and silent place to practise especially the secret Duties of a Christian'. Returning after eleven months' absence in May 1648, he noted in his diary: 'No sooner stepped in, but the green Trees, and Herbs, and the sweet singing of Birds, stirred up my soul to praise God.'[126] We may doubt whether Ambrose's wife, left to care for three small children, found his retreats quite so peaceful.

For some of those who could not vanish to the woods for weeks on end, there was an alternative: the garden.[127] Gardens were the outdoor equivalent of prayer-closets. For the few who could afford them, they were an ideal place of prayer: solitary, convenient, and filled with tamed and beautified nature. There might even be shelter. Anne Clifford had a 'standing' in her garden, to which she retired to pray. For pious gentlewomen, particularly, prayer in gardens or orchards seems to have been routine, but they were not an exclusively female space.[128] John Welsh made a practice of praying in his garden in the middle of the night, perhaps preferring stars to flowers. Nehemiah Wallington recalled that 'the first time that ever I prayed in privat myselfe' was when, aged ten, an outbreak of illness killed his brother and sent him to live with his grandmother for some weeks. 'I there went into the garden [and] under the Arber kneelling down against the Banke I prayed.... I thought I did see the heavens opened.'[129]

Those who did not have gardens of their own were not necessarily excluded from garden-spirituality. This is partly because the division between private gardens and open fields was blurry: Robert Blair, visiting London in 1633, prayed in Greenwich Park.[130] It is more, however, that the 'garden', like the 'closet', was both a literal and a symbolic place. The Biblical witness was as important as always: as well as Eden, there is the garden paradise of the Song of Songs.[131] There was also a deep association between gardens and monastic piety, popularized by the pre-Reformation primers' routine claim to be gardens of the soul. That image, with its implication of rarefied withdrawal, made some early Protestants uneasy (notably Luther). Some preferred a very different Biblical garden, Gethsemane. Hugh

[126] Isham, 'Confessions', fo. 24r; Bod. MS Rawl. C.473 fo. 2r; Ambrose, *Media*, 74, 76, 79; Isaac Ambrose, *Looking unto Jesus* (1658: Wing A2956), 256; Schwanda, *Soul Recreation*, 83, and esp. n. 35 for other contemporary examples of nature-piety. I am grateful to Dr Schwanda for drawing my attention to Ambrose, for discussions on this topic, and in particular for allowing me to consult pre-publication proofs of his book.

[127] On early modern British gardens, see Charles Quest-Riston, *The English Garden: A Social History* (Harmondsworth, 2001); Roy Strong, *The Renaissance Garden in England* (1979); Walsham, *Reformation of the Landscape*, 311–25; Jane Dawson, '"Hamely with God": a Scottish view on domestic devotion' in Martin and Ryrie, *Private and Domestic Devotion*, 35–7.

[128] Clifford, *Diaries*, 32, 50; Hoby, *Diary*, 66; Harrison, *Deaths aduantage*, III.8; Denison, *Monument or Tombe-Stone*, 122. For examples of men praying in gardens, see Tweedie, *Select Biographies*, 108; Hinde, *Faithfull Remonstrance ... of Iohn Bruen*, 156.

[129] Tweedie, *Select Biographies*, 15; Wallington, *Notebooks*, 266–7.

[130] Blair, *Life*, 94.

[131] Song of Songs 4:12, 16; 5:1; 6:2, 11.

Latimer denounced the wealthy for the vanity of their 'goodly gardens', urging them to recall Christ's agonies—'a goodly meditation to have in your gardens!'[132] But the association was too strong to be broken. From the first English primer, titled *Ortulus anime: the garden of the soule* (1530), horticultural metaphors infested English Protestant writing like perennial weeds. *The garden of wysdom* (1539), *The poore mans garden* (1571), *A godly garden* (1574), and *A garden of spirituall flowers* and its sequel (1609 and thereafter), were all best-sellers—and that is before we come to the allusions to flowers, fruit, nosegays, pomanders, and so forth. These bouquets were often anthologies, gathered, as Abraham Fleming's popular *Diamond of deuotion* put it, 'out of the sweete and odiferous Garden of Gods Word'.[133] Private compilers imitated the style in their own titles.[134] If you could not gain entry to a real garden, you could at least lose yourself in a paper one.

One outdoor site of prayer remains: the open road. Travel in early modern Britain was an uncomfortable and dangerous business, but also a tedious and time-consuming one. It therefore provided a splendid opportunity for prayer. If you happened to be travelling for religious reasons—'gadding' to a sermon, for example—then that might be only natural. However, as John Donne discovered when riding westward on Good Friday 1613, all travel had a seam of spiritual symbolism running through it. Protestants roundly rejected pilgrimage in the medieval sense, but the term itself was taken into their vocabulary even before Bunyan reclaimed it fully.[135] Literal journeys could be freighted with spiritual meaning—whether it is exiles crossing to Ireland or New England, or the young Richard Norwood, yearning to sail to the Indies and wondering 'whether the heavens did not touch the earth in some places, as at the horizon? . . . Why might not . . . Gardens of Paradise be found?'[136] The same was true of the most everyday journeys. The puritan tutor Richard Blackerby was 'much in walking Prayer', and,

> like the old Peripateticks . . . would oft call forth his Scholars abroad, and teach them both Natural and Divine knowledge. . . . He walked continually before them, as the Picture of Jesus among his Disciples.[137]

Which suggests that those who walked while praying out of doors were not simply trying to keep warm, and that those who prayed while travelling were not simply filling time piously. Walking and praying had a deeper congruence.

Travelling prayer was not, then, simply a matter of filling 'spare time' with prayer, or using devotion 'to shorten the tediousnesse of the iournie'.[138] Reformed

[132] Tyrwhit, *Elizabeth Tyrwhit's Morning and Evening Prayers*, 25; see above, p. 161; Latimer, *Sermons by Hugh Latimer*, 225.

[133] Fleming, *Diamond of deuotion*, 209.

[134] For example, Bod. MS Eng. c.2693.

[135] Heyden, *Bryefe Summe*, sigs N4v–6r; Bull, *Christian praiers*, 114–16; Sparke, *Crumms of comfort*, sig. M8r. Cf. Collinson, *Religion of Protestants*, 247.

[136] Norwood, *Journal*, 38–9.

[137] Clarke, *Lives of sundry Eminent Persons*, 58–9.

[138] Amongst many examples, see Goodwin, *Returne of Prayers*, 93; FSL MS V.a.519 fo. 3r; Latimer, *Sermons by Hugh Latimer*, 509; Winthrop, *Papers*, 209; Wariston, *Diary*, 52; Sibbes, *Works*, I.cxxxv; Hinde, *Faithfull Remonstrance . . . of Iohn Bruen*, 142; Mildmay, 'Meditations', 66.

Protestantism was a dynamic faith, always in motion, yearning for progress, fearing backsliding. Perhaps this is why travelling prayer could provoke such raptures. Norwood, making a three-mile journey on foot soon after his conversion, found that 'my heart was so abundantly replenished with heavenly joys . . . that I did not so much walk but rather went leaping all the way'. John Winthrop and Robert Woodford were similarly 'graciously affected in prayer' while journeying. Richard Rogers, travelling home one evening in 1587, 'was taken upp in a veary heavenly sorte, reioiceing'; when he reached his destination 'I began to waxe colde'. Not that travelling prayer was always joyful. In 1571, the young James Melville, running an errand for his father, was suddenly overcome with grief over his thwarted education and fell to his knees. Eventually he received consolation and continued on his way, singing psalms as he went.[139]

There were difficulties, however. Travel was distracting: John Winthrop found that 'I was wont to lose all my tyme in my iournies, my eyes runninge upon everye obiect, and my thoughts varieing with everye occasion'.[140] The greatest potential distractions, but also the greatest potential helpers, were travelling companions. The image of travellers who fall into conversation was a hackneyed literary cliché of the period, a too-easy means of setting up a dialogue between stock characters.[141] But clichés usually have some basis in reality, and it seems reasonable enough that strangers travelling in the same direction, on a quiet road, might seek to stick together, for good fellowship, for mutual advantage, and for safety. Michael Sparke provided a prayer for travellers which asked, amongst other things, for 'honest, ciuill, & good company for my Companions'. Travellers prearranged that good company when they could. When Richard Rogers spent two days in February 1587 travelling with his friend Ezekiel Culverwell, he felt it had been the highlight of his month, with 'much time bestowed in the way about our christian estat'. Prearrangement most likely lay behind Robert Blair's finding a fellow minister as his travelling companion on a ten-mile journey in 1623: they sang psalms all the way.[142] But providential encounters happened too. Robert Woodford one day fell happily into conversation with a like-minded fellow-traveller: 'we spoke about Comunion tables & bowing'. Richard Norwood recalled that, in his godless teenage years, he once spent a three-mile journey in the company of one Goodman Stranks, a travelling pedlar, who 'by his pious and Christian conference—which he used frequently—inflamed my heart with sundry good motions and purposes'.[143] We may doubt whether all of Stranks' travelling-companions enjoyed his company so much.

---

[139] Norwood, *Journal*, 84; Woodford, 'Diary', 24.x.1637 recto; Winthrop, *Papers*, 159, 195–7; Knappen, *Two Diaries*, 67; Melville, *Autobiography*, 24.

[140] Winthrop, *Papers*, 196. Cf. Knappen, *Two Diaries*, 58–9; Hoby, *Diary*, 109.

[141] See, amongst many other examples, Robert Copland, *The Highway to the Spital-House* (1535–6), in A. V. Judges (ed.), *The Elizabethan Underworld* (1930), 4; Dent, *Plaine mans path-way*, 3–4; Walton, *Complete Angler*, 9.

[142] Sparke, *Crumms of comfort*, sig. M9r; Knappen, *Two Diaries*, 53; Blair, *Life*, 50.

[143] Woodford, 'Diary', 20.i.1637–8 recto; Norwood, *Journal*, 12.

But if the peaceful, sheltered solitude necessary for sustained prayer could be found neither in private houses nor in the open air, that left one, tempting, alarming possibility. What about church buildings? Here pragmatic concerns struggled with confessional fears and temptations. Robert Harris had two criteria for choosing places of prayer: choose 'that which is 1. freest from distraction, 2. farthest from suspition and appearance of hypocrisie'.[144] Churches, then, would not do, and indeed our sources refer to private prayer in churches relatively rarely. But they were alluring too, even for unimpeachable Calvinists. It is perhaps not entirely surprising that ministers should have sometimes chosen to go and pray in their own, empty churches, which were in a sense their space. Some of the clearest references to this practice describe ministers praying in church with loud voices and being overheard, which is again a strangely performative privacy.[145] But it was not only ministers. When John Bruen was six or seven years old, a stern telling-off from his father drove him to pray in the family chapel, where he found such comfort that he went back the next day, trying in vain to recapture the experience—much to his biographer's discomfort.[146] Private chapels were, again, an ambiguous space, but there is no ambiguity to Archbishop Sandys' advice that Christians should pray 'in all places, especially that place which, being sanctified to this use, is therefore called the house of prayer'.[147] In its own terms, this was hard to argue with, and as we shall see, plenty of Protestants entirely untouched by Laudianism were happy to accord a special status to church buildings.[148] But it also opened some alarming possibilities. Thomas Browne, in the 1630s, echoed Sandys by arguing that 'a resolved conscience may...adore her Creator any where, especially in places devoted to his service', but then used this argument to justify praying in Catholic churches and even showing outward devotion to crucifixes.[149]

Protestant prayer, then, was supposed to be all but continuous, but there was often no good place in which to do it. Closets and gardens were expensive rarities. Houses thronged with people; so did roads. Fields were all very well in good weather, but this was the so-called 'Little Ice Age'. Churches were fraught with ideological dangers. Solitude was longed for, feared, and scarcely to be had. Perhaps this is part of what gives Protestant piety its restless nature; Protestant devotees were literally on the move. Habits of prayer which might aspire to be unchanging would often have to negotiate places for themselves almost daily. In any case, we should bear in mind that wherever you went in early modern Britain, you were liable to stumble across muttering figures communing with their God, and trying to carve out a private space in a public world while always being conscious of that world's eyes.

---

[144] Harris, *Peters enlargement* (1627), 32.
[145] Tweedie, *Select Biographies*, 8; Clarke, *Collection*, 16.
[146] Hinde, *Faithfull Remonstrance...of Iohn Bruen*, 7.
[147] Sandys, *Sermons*, 77.
[148] See below, pp. 324–5.
[149] Thomas Browne, *Sir Thomas Browne: Selected Writings*, ed. Geoffrey Keynes (Chicago, 1968), 8–9.

POSTURE AND GESTURE

Closely linked to the question of where people prayed is the question of the postures and gestures they used. This is of more than antiquarian interest. It is not merely that religious gesture was often politically sensitive. Bodily experience matters to human beings. Praying standing, with arms upraised and palms upturned, of necessity feels very different from praying prostrate and face down, and the learned symbols associated with different postures deepen those differences.[150] This was understood and explicitly articulated in our period. Henry Mason justified his comment on the matter thus:

> The outward acts and behauiour of the body, as they come first from the heart, so they reflect vpon the heart againe, and there they doe increase and confirme that affection, from which they sprang.[151]

To understand how Protestants prayed, we need to know what they did with their bodies.

Again, however, research is complicated by professed indifference. Gestures in prayer were universally agreed to be 'meane & indifferent thynges'. Indeed, in reaction to Catholic practices, Protestants felt that too much attention to this matter looked like hypocrisy and lumpish materialism.[152] However, by the 17th century the tone of these permissions was shifting. Lewis Bayly's *Practise of pietie* affirmed Christian liberty, but also worried about giving carnal Christians an excuse for laxity and profanity. William Perkins wrote that 'we may vse any gesture, so it be comely, and decent, and serue to express the inward humility of our hearts'. Phrases like 'any decent gesture' or 'some reverend gesture' became the norm. Robert Harris accepted that all gestures were legitimate, but 'thats the fittest that best 1. stirres affection, 2. expresses reuerence'. 'The gestures of body', Gervase Babington pointed out, 'are helpes also of affection.'[153] What you do with your body does not affect God, but it does affect you.

This may seem like mere coyness. Those who say that your gesture should be 'humble, deuout, & full of decent Reuerence', but do not specify any further, often do seem, as we shall see, to have a pretty sharp idea of what that gesture should be.[154] But the vagueness is important in itself. Joseph Hall urged his readers to 'vse that frame of body that may both testifie reuerence, and in some cases help to stirre vp further deuotion', and gave a very wide range of suggestions, but he also suggested that postures should vary from occasion to occasion, a point which we

---

[150] Paul Connerton, *How Societies Remember* (Cambridge, 1989), 73–4.

[151] Mason, *Christian Humiliation*, 41.

[152] Becon, *Newe pathwaye unto praier*, sig. C1r–2r; Ramie Targoff, *Common Prayer: the language of public devotion in early modern England* (Chicago and London, 2001), 9–10; Nuttall, *Holy Spirit*, 70.

[153] Bayly, *Practise of pietie*, 193–5; Perkins, *Whole treatise*, 279; Sparke, *Crumms of comfort*, sig. A5r; Preston, *Saints Daily Exercise*, 85; Harris, *Peters enlargement* (1627), 32; Perkins, *Exposition of the Lords prayer*, 167; Babington, *Profitable Exposition*, 28.

[154] Bod. MS Rawl. C.473 fo. 4r; cf. Crashaw, *Milke for Babes*, 42.

should take seriously.[155] Habit and conformity no doubt ensured that most people who prayed regularly did so in the same way, or small range of ways. But divines explicitly presented them with an expansive menu of gesture and posture, and encouraged them to sample it at will. There is every reason to think that, in gesture as in the time and place of prayer, individual Protestants' experience of prayer was more diverse than we might think.

That said, once we come down to brass tacks, the advice and practice on posture seem to have been pretty conservative. Relaxed postures were generally frowned on. To sit or to recline for prayer was widely condemned as 'vnmannerly', showing 'little reuerence and humility'. To pray 'lazily upon thy bed' was worse, unless you woke in the night, or were too ill to be anywhere else.[156] But as these condemnations themselves show, those practices were in fact widespread. Perkins explicitly permitted prayer sitting down.[157] Here the boundary between prayer and meditation becomes important. Meditation was by nature more relaxed. Richard Bernard recommended sitting as a posture for meditation.[158] Sir Richard Rich's funeral monument, which shows him reclining meditatively with a book (see Figure 3), idealizes this kind of studious piety. In the 1660s Wetenhall was even recommending that a prayer-closet be furnished with 'a hard *couch* or great chair on which I might some times lean my weary and aching head'.[159] We may guess that a great many devotees listened to their aching bones rather than to their ministers' strictures in this matter.

What they should have been doing instead is equally clear. Thomas Tymme's *Chariot of Devotion*, after carefully explaining that any posture was permissible, added plainly, 'God will haue vs to kneele before him'.[160] Kneeling to pray, both publicly and privately, was supported by ample Biblical witness and invariable Christian practice, and it remained the norm throughout our period and beyond. As Leonard Wright's best-selling *A Summons for Sleepers* put it, 'the meetest gesture and seemliest behauior at praier and thanksgiuing, is kneeling'. Gouge agreed that since we must be reverent and humble in prayer, 'kneeling is the fittest gesture to express both these, and most proper to prayer'. From the other end of England's Protestant spectrum, Ambrose Fisher agreed: 'to kneele in Prayer is, though not always necessarie, yet for the most part expedient: as being the most significant symbole of . . . reuerence'. Claiming to have 'kneeled to God' was a simple metonym for prayer.[161]

---

[155] Hall, *Arte of Divine Meditation*, 60–4; and see below, p. 177.
[156] Gouge, *Whole-Armor of God*, 341; Parr, *Abba Father*, 24; Tymme, *Watch-bell* (1640), 295; Rogers, *Garden* (1616), sig. F3r.
[157] Perkins, *Whole treatise*, 279.
[158] Richard Bernard, *The Faithfull Shepherd* (1621: RSTC 1941), 28.
[159] Wetenhall, *Enter into thy Closet*, 7.
[160] Tymme, *Chariot of Devotion*, 17–18.
[161] Leonard Wright, *A Summons for Sleepers* (1589: RSTC 26034.3), 30 (seven editions 1589–1637, four of them in 1589); Gouge, *Whole-Armor of God*, 341; Fisher, *Defence of the liturgie*, 160; Jocelin, *Mothers Legacie*, 3.

Fig. 3. Monument to Richard, Lord Rich, Felsted, Essex. Rich, in life a notoriously unscrupulous politician, is here recast as a model of piety, pausing to meditate on what he has read.

Scholarship on this subject has sometimes been confused by the controveries over kneeling to receive communion in both England and Scotland.[162] It is worth emphasizing that kneeling was controversial *only* in that very specific context. Admittedly, after the 1618 Perth Articles imposed kneeling at communion on a reluctant Scotland, some Scots developed scruples about kneeling under other circumstances, but even radical ministers gave this 'foolish opinion' short shrift.[163] It was precisely *because* kneeling was such a universal symbol of worship that kneeling before a communion table was felt to be idolatrous. Outside that setting, kneeling to pray was an expected and entirely uncontroversial norm.

Kneeling was absolutely standard for individual prayer and for family devotions, as numerous personal testimonies and ministerial instructions testify.[164] The few

[162] For an example of careless comment on this, see Horton Davies, *The Worship of the American Puritans, 1629–1730* (New York, 1990), 150; for a more considered treatment, see Ferrell, 'Kneeling and the Body Politic'.

[163] Narne, *Pearle of prayer*, 448–9; cf. William McMillan, *The Worship of the Scottish Reformed Church, 1550–1638* (Dunfermline, 1931), 151–2, 161–2.

[164] Amongst many examples, see Bayly, *Practise of pietie*, 244, 251, 316; P. R. Seddon (ed.), *Letters of John Holles 1587–1637: Volume I* (Thoroton Society Record Series 31, 1975), 55; Anthony Walker (ed.), *The Holy Life of Mrs Elizabeth Walker* (1690: Wing W305), 18; Duncon, *Returnes*, 8; Kilby, *Hallelujah*, 10, 63; Wariston, *Diary*, 21–2, 47–8, 54; Rogers, *Seven treatises*, 349, 396; Rogers, *Garden* (1616), sig. F6r.

even faintly plausible visual representations of family prayer, such as that of Bishop Pilkington's family (Figure 16, Chapter 14, p. 367), reinforce the image. The most popular printed forms of prayer continually refer to praying 'vpon the bended knees of our bodie' or the like.[165] When pious friends met to pray—at their friends' sickbeds, to consult about business, in clandestine conventicles, even en route to their own executions—they fell to their knees.[166] Preachers expected all their people, not only the earnestly godly, to kneel in prayer, and Samuel Hieron's worry—that 'albeit there be many kneelers and speakers . . . yet there are fewe true petitioners vnto God'—suggests that this was a motion which most Protestants were willing to go through.[167]

Why, aside from the mighty force of custom? Spiritually speaking, kneeling had two virtues. First, it was a universally accepted symbol of submission and humility. 'Bow thy knees', Bayly urged, 'in witnesse of thy humiliation.' Occasionally this was spelt out—John Browning saw kneeling on the earth as an acknowledgement that we are mere earth ourselves—but it was normally seen simply as obvious. Indeed, kneeling was not merely a sign of inward humiliation, but a help to it. You bent the knee to God so that you might more easily bend the heart to him. John Bruen's family prayed together 'bowing the knees of their hearts, as well as the knees of their bodies'.[168] Like most other devotional tricks, this did not always work. Grace Mildmay once lamented that 'my feeble knees bowed themselves unto God and my heart's desire was to bend itself likewise unto him, but it had no power to perform the same'. Since the inner attitude matters more than the outward posture, sometimes kneeling can become entirely metaphorical: we find devotees praying 'vpon the knees of mine heart', 'vpon the bended knees of our hearts', or 'with bended heart'.[169] These prayers could in theory be said in the comfort of an armchair, although those with enough bodily agility were probably on the floor with everyone else.

This raises the other great spiritual advantage of kneeling: sheer physical awkwardness. Kneeling for prayer normally meant what William Gouge called kneeling upright: the knees on the floor and the thighs, torso, neck, and head all vertical. This, as Gouge observed, 'will keep thee from drousinesse'.[170] Funeral monuments normally depict devotees in this posture (Figure 4). The alternative to kneeling upright—which is agonizingly difficult to maintain for more than a few minutes, if you are not made of stone—was to lean your elbows on a table or a prayer-desk, a

[165] Sparke, *Crumms of comfort*, sig. B12r; Richard Bernard, *A Weekes Worke. And a Worke for every weeke* (1628: RSTC 1964.7), 211; Thomas Scorocold, *Supplications of Saints. A Booke of Prayers and Prayses* (1616: RSTC 22933), 153; Hinde, *Faithfull Remonstrance . . . of Iohn Bruen*, 71–2.

[166] Foxe, *Actes and monuments* (1570), 1700, 1731–2; Becon, *Sycke mans salue*, 357, 518; Hooper, *Later Writings*, 612.

[167] Hieron, *Helpe vnto Deuotion* (1608), sig. A4r–v; cf. Brinsley, *True Watch* (1608), 37; Dent, *Plaine mans path-way*, 321.

[168] Bayly, *Practise of pietie*, 195; Browning, *Concerning publike-prayer*, 70; Parr, *Abba Father*, 24; Hinde, *Faithfull Remonstrance . . . of Iohn Bruen*, 72.

[169] Mildmay, *With Faith and Physic*, 74; Norden, *Pensiue mans practise*, 69–70, 182; Gee, *Steps of Ascension*, 185; Sutton, *Godly meditations* (1601), 151.

[170] Gouge, *Whole-Armor of God*, 456–7.

Fig. 4. Monument to Sir Alexander Culpepper, Goudhurst, Kent. The typical, unforgivingly upright posture of prayer is only partly ameliorated by a plump kneeler.
Permission granted by the photographer, Peter Jewitt.

posture which again is widely depicted in funeral monuments (Figure 5). Some devotees probably eased the discomfort by crouching down, maintaining a kneeling posture while bowing the body and sitting back on the haunches. The devotee depicted in Hayward's *Sanctuarie of a troubled soule* appears to be moving in this direction (Figure 6). But this, too, can still become awkward or painful before very long, especially for those whose joints are no longer in the first flush of youth. The funeral monuments do at least suggest, mercifully, that it was normal to kneel on a cushion. We are told of one gentleman who anxiously asked his minister 'whether it were lawfull in his priuate prayers ... to kneele vpon a Cushion?', but he was understood to be being over-scrupulous.[171]

---

[171] John Chadwich, *A sermon preached at Snarford in Lincolnshire* (1614: RSTC 4930), 24–5.

Fig. 5. Monument to Thomas Wylmer, Staverton, Northamptonshire. Kneeling at a prayer-desk was a common trope in funeral monuments, and perhaps also in life.
Permission granted by the photographer, Lloyd Patton.

Kneeling, in other words, can be an active, painful struggle. For those seeking to emulate Christ's bloody sweat in Gethsemane, this was meat and drink. Protestants celebrated the patristic precedents for endurance kneeling. They were edified, and daunted, by preachers' tales of St James, whose knees grew 'as hard as the hoof with continual praying'; of St Gregory of Nazianzen's sister, whose 'knees seemed to cleaue to the earth, & to growe to the very ground, by reason of continuance in praier'; or of St Gregory's aunt, who had 'elbowes as hard as horne . . . by leaning to a deske, at which she vsed to pray'.[172] Protestantism's own heroes were not to be outdone. Hugh Latimer 'so long . . . continued kneeling, that he was not able for to rise without help', and it was said both of John Bradford and of Richard Capel that 'he had been almost ever upon his knees'.[173]

Ordinary believers were never going to manage such heroism, but the physical challenge of kneeling was universal, especially as joints stiffened with age, and it was part of the spiritual experience. Lettice Cary recalled that her spiritual comforts had 'strengthned my feeble knees'. Grace Mildmay reproached herself—'you feeble knees, bowe your selues vnto him'—in the expectation of divine assistance.

[172] Playfere, *Power of praier*, 42–3; Sandys, *Sermons*, 38.
[173] Latimer, *Sermons by Hugh Latimer*, 322; Richard Capel, *Capel's Remains*, ed. Valentine Marshall (1658: Wing C471), sig. A7v.

Call vpon me in the day of tribulation I will deliuer thee ,and thou
shalt praise me .Psal. 50.

Fig. 6. John Hayward, *The sanctuarie of a troubled soule* (1602: RSTC 13003.7), sig. H9v.
Some devotees might crouch down at their desks rather than kneel upright, a less painful but
also more dynamic posture. The devotee here looks up to the Tetragrammaton.
By permission of the Folger Shakespeare Library.

William Narne warned his readers that 'thou will sometimes find . . . thy knees
wearie', but that they should nevertheless persist. Richard Kilby, more humbly,
vowed to kneel 'so long as I am able', but then, some pernickity souls would not
kneel at all for fear of 'wresting their ioynts'.[174] The spiritual humbling and the
physical struggle of kneeling come together in George Herbert's claim that 'my

[174] Mildmay, 'Meditations', II.53; Duncon, *Returnes*, 39; Narne, *Pearle of Prayer*, 297–8; Kilby,
Hallelujah, 62; Wright, *Summons for Sleepers*, 30.

knees pierce th'earth'. A few lines later he is 'deep drawn in pain', a pain that is perhaps not exclusively spiritual.[175]

For those who really could not kneel, standing up was an acceptable alternative.[176] Standing had its own spiritual meanings. It suggested defiance: the Biblical image of the believer who will 'stand in the gap', that is, save the nation from judgement by earnest prayer, was cited in the wake of the Armada.[177] During one spiritual crisis, John Winthrop 'knelt downe to praye . . . but could not'; so he 'endeavoured to pray standinge . . . strivinge with the Lord for helpe against my weaknesse'. Thus he was able to overcome his sins and find relief.[178] Standing in someone's presence was also a sign of reverence, or of supplication. Robert Harris used a vivid image: 'the child that stands before his father and appears in his place at supper time with his trencher in his hand, speakes with his countenance'. This was presumably what John Bruen intended when he had his household 'stand in Gods presence' for family prayers.[179] Since we are also told they knelt, perhaps this was simply another metaphor, or perhaps his prayers were sometimes so lengthy that his family's knees could not last out to the end.

For kneeling and standing were not strictly alternatives. Some devotees, by the end of our period at least, found particular value in the action of *falling* to their knees, a dynamic movement which suggests a sudden crumpling of the soul's sinful defiance in total submission to God. We find instructions not simply to kneel, but to fall to your knees, linked to pivotal devotional moments such as Sabbath preparation, or having completed a catalogue of your sins.[180] In 1643, Nehemiah Wallington visited a disturbed woman consumed with fear of her own sins. One sign of that was that she would periodically 'burst out a weeping and crying out . . . falling upon her knees' and begging God's forgiveness—much to her children's distress. Archibald Johnston of Wariston had a more ordered but more rigorous practice. Using a commentary on the Ten Commandments as a framework for confessing his sins, he fell to his knees afresh after considering each commandment and 'particularly humbled' himself.[181] This was perhaps strictly for the young and agile.

Falling in self-abasement could go further than merely kneeling. Sometimes at least, earnest Protestants prayed fully prostrate, grovelling before God. This could, again, be merely metaphorical. As Susan Karant-Nunn has pointed out, the cry 'Let us prostrate ourselves', was an almost invariable refrain to John Calvin's sermons, but we should not envisage the people of Geneva falling on their faces in church. Norden's engagingly inconsistent claim to be 'prostrate vpon the knees of my heart'

[175] Herbert, *Works*, 162.
[176] Perkins, *Godly and learned exposition*, 230; Gouge, *Whole-Armor of God*, 341, 457; Hildersam, *Doctrine of Fasting*, 52.
[177] Ezekiel 22:30; Pigg, *Meditations concerning praiers*, sig. A7r.
[178] Winthrop, *Papers*, 200.
[179] Harris, *Peters enlargement* (1624), sig. A3v; Hinde, *Faithfull Remonstrance . . . of Iohn Bruen*, 68. Cf. Hildersam, *Doctrine of Fasting*, 52.
[180] Clarke, *Holy Incense*, 148; Kilby, *Burthen*, 39–40; Scudder, *Christians daily walke* (1628), 37.
[181] Wallington, *Notebooks*, 211; Wariston, *Diary*, 94; cf. 118.

shows how metaphors could become separated from actual practice.[182] It was common for prayers intended for family use to include phrases such as 'we doo here present our selues ... humbly prostrating our selues before the throne of mercie', or for individual devotees to be told to be 'prostrate before thy Throne of grace' or 'falling low at his footestoole'.[183] Did those who used these prayers remain on their knees, or did they take the instruction literally? If so, was it only for that moment, or did they remain on their faces? Some references to 'prostrating the body' were clearly meant literally. Dorothy Leigh urged her readers to 'fall downe on thy face, as the Publican did', if they were in private.[184] For more concrete examples, we have to look to the Scots, who were more enthusiastic about prostration than the English. One of William Struther's reasons for recommending solitary prayer was that it allowed for melodramatic piety, including 'prostrating of our bodie'. John Forbes of Corse described praying 'in my studie being prostrat before God vpon my bellie, & having before me vpon the floor the psalmes in Hebrewe', which sounds awkward as well as uncomfortable. The disciples of James Glendinning, a maverick Scots preacher in Ulster, prayed 'laying their faces on the earth'.[185] Prostration, even amongst radicals, was in this period usually done discreetly. But it happened.

It is the same with other forms of theatrical piety, such as tearing your clothes, plucking out your hair or beard, wearing sackcloth, or beating your breast. These practices had strong Biblical backing, but were also strongly associated with Catholicism. Breast-beating in particular was linked to the Mass, and for most of our period Protestants were wary of it. The only positive reference to it I have found in the 16th century is lifted directly from old primer texts.[186] By the turn of the 17th century cautious citations of the Biblical precedents are creeping in.[187] Bayly's *Practise of pietie* twice recommends 'smiting thy breast with thy fists' as part of penitence. A few more allusions to the practice begin to appear thereafter.[188] It was, at least, a part of Protestantism's pious vocabulary. But I know of only one direct testimony to its use, and again it is a disapproving one: William Hacket, the deranged pseudo-prophet executed in 1591, was said to have used 'beatings' in his frenzied prayers.[189] If other Protestants did this, they did it behind closed doors.

The norm, then, was kneeling, with certain permissible or questionable variations. But this is only the beginning. If there was a classic Protestant posture of

---

[182] Karant-Nunn, *Reformation of Feeling*, 113–14; Norden, *Pensiue mans practise*, 40.

[183] Dering, *Godly priuate praiers*, sig. C4v; Tuke, *Practise of the faithfull*, 127; Brinsley, *True Watch* (1622), II.208; Sparke, *Crumms of comfort*, sig. H11v; Scudder, *Christians daily walke* (1628), 37.

[184] Gouge, *Whole-Armor of God*, 336; Bentley, *Monument of Matrons*, 413; Leigh, *Mothers blessing*, 70.

[185] Struther, *Scotlands Warning*, 72; Forbes, 'Diary', 72; Blair, *Life*, 72.

[186] *Godly garden*, fo. 81v; White, *Tudor Books of Private Devotion*, 186–7.

[187] Perkins, *Godly and learned exposition*, 234; Gouge, *Whole-Armor of God*, 431; cf. Tymme, *Chariot of Devotion*, 17 on wearing sackcloth.

[188] Bayly, *Practise of pietie*, 195, 565; Jocelin, *Mothers Legacie*, 26; Primrose, *Christian Mans Teares*, 63–4; Bolton, *Three-fold treatise*, III.163.

[189] Sutcliffe, *An Answere*, fo. 60v.

Fig. 7. William Hunnis, *Seuen Sobs of a Sorrowfull Soule for Sinne* (1583: RSTC 13975), sig. a4v. King David is depicted at prayer with his eyes and hands lifted to the Tetragrammaton.

Bodleian Library, Oxford.

prayer in this period, it had three elements: kneeling, lifting up hands, and lifting up eyes. This trio had also been absolutely standard pre-Reformation practice.[190] It is depicted very widely in funeral monuments and other portrayals of Protestants at prayer (Figures 5, 6, 7), and it would be tedious to recount all the references to it in

---

[190] John Craig, 'Bodies at prayer in early modern England' in Mears and Ryrie, *Worship and the Parish Church*, 184.

our textual sources.[191] Most of the explicit references to it are 17th-century, but it can be found in a best-selling text as early as 1550.[192] We must consider both hands and eyes in turn.

Lifting the hands was based on long-established Christian practice and on St Paul's much-cited injunction to pray 'lifting vp pure hands'.[193] There is some ambiguity, however, about the gesture. It is often described as lifting hands up to Heaven, or to God, which suggests something slightly different from the dignified folded hands at chest level depicted on so many funeral monuments.[194] Does this mean that early modern Protestants prayed in the manner of some modern Charismatics or evangelicals, with hand raised above the shoulder, apart and palms upturned? It is not a trivial question—the emotional flavour of the experience turns on it—but it is difficult to answer clearly.

Prayer with hands apart was certainly sometimes used, but if it had confessional associations, they were not with radical puritanism but rather with ceremonialism. This was, amongst other things, the posture of a priest saying Mass. A French woodcut from the 1530s which showed King David praying over a sacrificial lamb with his hands apart (see Figure 8) clearly evoked that kind of imagery, while also suggesting that the gesture need not be restricted to priests standing before the altar. The same suggestion resurfaces amongst 17th-century Laudians, who would happily approve of the Christian who 'spreadeth his hands towards heauen'.[195]

But the gesture was not exclusive to ceremonialists. William Gouge cited the precedent of King Solomon, who had 'stretched out his hands towarde heauen' when he prayed—in the King James Bible, less ambiguously, he 'spread forth' his hands—although Gouge did class 'lifting vp the hands' and 'stretching abroad the armes' as alternatives. The Marian martyr John Denley, at the stake, 'put his hands abrode & sang' a psalm. When the wife of the Scots minister Patrick Simson died, she 'in the moment of her departure spread forth her hands, and cryed loud, "Come, Lord Jesus"'.[196] However, these are all references to unusual or exceptional circumstances, and while we often find Protestants lifting up their hands on the deathbed, we are not told whether the hands are together or apart.[197] Presumably those weakened by illness could hold such a posture for longer if their hands were supporting one another.

---

[191] For some examples among many, see Parr, *Abba Father*, 24–5; Bayly, *Practise of pietie*, 195; Mason, *Christian Humiliation*, 41–2; Sparke, *Crumms of comfort*, sig. A5r; Wallington, *Notebooks*, 211; Mildmay, 'Meditations', II.53.

[192] Cornelius van der Heyden, *A Bryefe Summe of the whole Byble*, trs. Anthony Scoloker (RSTC 3018: London, 1550?), sig. M7r.

[193] I Timothy 2:8. Amongst many references to this text, see Sandys, *Sermons*, 77, 398; Habermann, *Enimie of securitie*, 6; Dod and Cleaver, *Ten sermons*, 63; Cosin, *Collection of Priuate Devotions*, 19.

[194] Craig, 'Bodies at prayer'. For the trope of raising hands to heaven, see, for example, Erasmus, *Enchiridion*, 44; Melville, *Autobiography*, 252; Wallington, *Notebooks*, 211; Featley, *Ancilla Pietatis*, 2; Mildmay, 'Meditations', II.53.

[195] Mason, *Christian Humiliation*, 42; cf. Browning, *Concerning publike-prayer*, 71.

[196] Gouge, *Whole-Armor of God*, 336, 431 (cf. I Kings 8:22); John Foxe, *Actes and monuments of these latter and perillous dayes* (1563: RSTC 11222), 1249; Tweedie, *Select Biographies*, 109.

[197] Hinde, *Faithfull Remonstrance . . . of Iohn Bruen*, 226; FSL MS V.a.248 fo. 7v.

Fig. 8. *This prymer of Salysbery vse* (Rouen, 1538: RSTC 16001), sig. L2r. Here David is shown praying with his hands apart, in a traditional Eucharistic gesture.
© The British Library.

A further, much-cited Biblical reference complicates matters: Moses watching the battle between the Israelites and the Amalekites. 'When Moses held vp his hand, Israel preuailed', but when he lowered it, the battle turned in the Amalekites' favour. So when Moses grew weary of standing with hands upraised, his two companions helped him, each holding up one of his arms. Thus the battle was won. This weird story had long been seen as a parable of prayer, urging the importance of persistence. The Geneva Bible's notes gave it this gloss: 'we se how dangerous a thing it is to fainte in prayer'. Lettice Cary evoked the story when she recalled how God's '*Comforts* have held up my weary hands, in prayer'.[198] This

---

[198] Exodus 17:11–12; Duncon, *Returnes*, 39. See, for example, Erasmus, *Enchiridion*, 43; Pigg, *Meditations concerning praiers*, sig. A7r; Goodwin, *Returne of Prayers*, 161.

interpretation was made canonical by Bayly's *Practise of pietie*. On the title-page of its earlier editions (Figure 9), Moses becomes an allegory of prayer, aiding the spirit in its battle with the flesh, with faith and fasting holding his tired arms. His hands are clearly apart. Was that simply because the wording of the text makes it inevitable? Even so, we can hardly ignore a model of prayer on the title-page of the century's best-selling devotional book.

Yet it was very unusual. Another praying figure at the top of the same title page is more typical, with his arms crossed on his breast. Later editions of the Bayly's book featured a slightly redesigned title-page in which Moses' hands appear to be together. The witness of funeral monuments is virtually uniform: at least in those decorous circumstances, devotees' hands were pressed together, with the fingers pointing diagonally up and away from the body (not straight up). There may be practical sculptors' considerations at play here—separated hands would be far more vulnerable to damage—but two-dimensional images broadly agree (Figure 5). So too do a few fragments of explicit textual evidence. The earliest Protestant primer tells us that table-graces were said with 'handes eleuated and ioyned togither', and the best contemporary image we have supports this (see Figure 18, Chapter 14, p. 384).[199] Elizabeth Jocelin tells her reader to 'weare thy knees, wring thy hands' in prayer, although that suggests a motion distinct from the funeral monuments' ordered calm.[200] We may leave this problem with a woodcut from Foxe's *Actes and Monuments* (Figure 10). The man on the left is praying with his hands in front of him but not quite touching one another, and the fingers slightly apart, a posture which can hardly have been sustained motionlessly for more than a few minutes. This may suggest, if nothing else, that while earnest Protestants probably habitually prayed with their hands together, they would also change posture during prayer, and might sometimes adopt alternatives, depending on personal habit, time, and place, physical comfort, or the mood of the prayer.

It is because of the connection to mood that this matters. We can imagine the different emotional resonances that different ways of holding the hands and arms might have, but it is hard to go beyond imagination. We do, however, know something of the meaning which they linked to these gestures. In the 15th century, Denis the Carthusian believed that praying with hands clasped stimulated and internalized devotion, although whether that persisted into our period, across the ocean and through the confessional boundary is unclear.[201] Closer to home, we find Edmund Bicknoll in 1579 describing a man meeting someone he had wronged as 'holdyng vp his handes (after the manner of our asking of forgeuenesse)'. The lifting up of hands in prayer was regularly linked to supplication, and specifically to begging for mercy. James Melville, praying desperately for mercy when horribly

---

[199] George Joye, *Ortulus anime. The garden of the soule* (Antwerp, 1530: RSTC 13828.4), sig. H2v; on table-graces, see below, pp. 381–8.

[200] Jocelin, *Mothers Legacie*, 26.

[201] Paul Saenger, 'Books of Hours and Reading Habits of the Later Middle Ages' in Roger Chartier (ed.), *The Culture of Print* (Cambridge, 1989), 152–3.

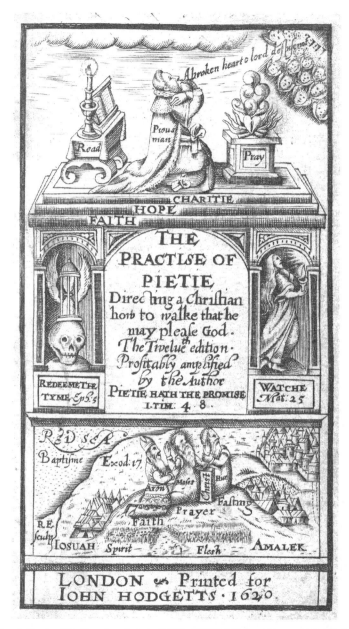

Fig. 9. Lewis Bayly, *The Practise of pietie* (1620: RSTC 1604), title page. Bayly's book, the most popular devotional work of the age, shows a devotee in typical posture at the top, flanked by images of reading and prayer; commands to 'watch' and to 'redeem the time' in the centre; and a remarkable image of Moses praying against the Amalekites, hands apart.
Bodleian Library, Oxford.

Fig. 10. John Foxe, *Actes and monuments of these latter and perillous dayes* (1563: RSTC 11222), p. 1260. Note the posture of the prisoner on the left.
By permission of the Folger Shakespeare Library.

sick on the North Sea, 'lift[ed] upe pitifull hands'.[202] Perhaps that is what the imprisoned figure in Foxe's picture was doing.

However, the gesture was also about lifting *up*—that is, towards God. Early modern Christians knew, of course, that God is omnipresent. But the strong sense that Heaven did indeed have a physical location meant that lifting or raising yourself to God was more than a metaphor. Just as devotees sought out high places to pray, their hands and eyes were drawn upward in prayer. It seemed too natural to need explaining. Devotion, Daniel Featley wrote, was 'a spiritual muskle mouing only vpward, & lifting vp the hearts, eyes, and hands continually vnto heauen'. It was merely an outward action, 'that we should remember our selues to be farre of from God, vnlesse we lifte vp our harts and mindes also on high', and yet it did

[202] Edmund Bicknoll, *A swoord agaynst swearyng* (1579: RSTC 3049), fo. 37v; Habermann, *Enimie of securitie*, 6; Sutton, *Godly meditations* (1601), 151; Melville, *Autobiography*, 252.

indeed remind people. Elnathan Parr called lifting the hands 'a signe and a helpe of our confidence and feruency'—a sign, but also a help.[203] Indeed, a help so reliable that it was surprising when it did not work. 'I have lifted up my hands unto God', wrote Grace Mildmay, evidently taken aback, 'with an earnest motion of my heart likewise to be lifted up unto God, but it had no power to effect the same!'[204] Lifting the hands was associated throughout our period with the morning's first prayer, whose purpose is to lift the newly wakened heart to Heaven for the day.[205] When Thomasine Winthrop was dying, she would not let her hands be tucked into her bedclothes, 'desiringe that she might have hir hands and all at libertie to glorifie God'. Bayly urged his readers to 'lift vp thine eyes, and thy hands, in testimony of thy confidence'.[206] Here perhaps the classic palms-together posture was particularly appropriate, offering yourself up rather than opening the hands in the hope of receiving.

There is a further hint contained in this gesture of lifting up arising from a different issue: that of hats. In an age when most people kept their heads covered most of the time, removing the hat was a potent symbol of respect. John Craig and Arnold Hunt have tracked the controversies in England over the use of hats in public worship, in which the old practice of men doffing their caps at the mention of Jesus' name gave way, from 1604, to an order for men's heads to remain bare throughout the service. The order was widely resisted, for the pious bristled at what looked like creeping popery and the impious wanted to keep their heads warm.[207] Yet, in private prayer, uncovering the head seems to have been an accepted norm.[208] It could be a risky one. When Richard Norwood was a new convert

> a superstitious conceit prevailed with me, namely that it was necessary or at least fitting to have the head uncovered, not only in solemn prayer but even almost in all religious duties as reading, meditation, examination, etc. Whereby I got a very dangerous cold in my head.[209]

So part of the answer of what devotees did with their hands while they prayed was that they held their hats. It should be emphasized, however, that this was very strongly gendered. Women were expected to keep their heads covered while they prayed, as St Paul had taught.[210]

When we come to eyes, the evidence is much plainer. Modern western Christian practice associates prayer with closed eyes, but it was absolutely standard in our

---

[203] Featley, *Ancilla Pietatis*, 2; Bull, *Christian praiers*, 4; Parr, *Abba Father*, 25.

[204] Mildmay, *With Faith and Physic*, 74.

[205] FSL MS V.a.482 fo. 0r; Bentley, *Monument of Matrons*, 364; Hinde, *Faithfull Remonstrance . . . of Iohn Bruen*, 68.

[206] Winthrop, *Papers*, 186; Bayly, *Practise of pietie*, 195.

[207] Craig, 'Bodies at prayer'; Arnold Hunt, 'The Choreography of Common Prayer in Early Modern England', paper delivered to the Society for Reformation Studies conference, Cambridge, April 2009.

[208] Wright, *Summons for Sleepers*, 30; Gouge, *Whole-Armor of God*, 341; Bayly, *Practise of pietie*, 365; Burton, *Narration*, 17; Tweedie, *Select Biographies*, 12, 108–9.

[209] Norwood, *Journal*, 91.

[210] I Corinthians 11:5.

period for devotees across the confessional spectrum to pray as their medieval forebears had done, with the eyes open and gazing upwards, the head often being slightly elevated (see Figures 2, 6).[211] Like both kneeling and hand-raising, this was said to be a means of ordering your affections Godward,[212] but there was a deeper reason. Again, to look upwards was actually to look in God's direction—as the frequent depiction of devotees looking up to the Hebrew Tetragrammaton, the name of God, makes clear (see Figures 7, 9). It was more than a metaphor. Tara Hamling has drawn out attention to the edifying plasterwork images which which wealthy Protestants decorated their ceilings. This was what they saw when they lifted their eyes in prayer.[213]

'Eyes... frequently lifted up towards heaven' was an accepted sign of and metonym for piety. 'If I but lift mine eyes, my suit is made', Herbert wrote.[214] Indeed, eye-lifting was if anything even more widespread than kneeling, since its great advantage was that it could be done at any time, discreetly, swiftly, and regardless of bodily infirmity—whether distraught in a wood, in the midst of a fight, or on the deathbed.[215]

But by the turn of the 17th century, some disquiet was brewing over the use of the eyes in prayer. As John Craig has pointed out, we begin to hear anti-puritans such as Leonard Wright mocking 'turning vp the white of the eye' as 'an hipocritical shew of holinesse'.[216] Wright, however, equally deplored churchgoers who would not 'looke vp to heauen when they pray, for wrinkling theyr ruffes'. His and others criticisms do not seem to be directed at merely looking upwards, but literally at those who 'turned up the white of eye'; that is, rolled the eyes back in the head. Or, as one versifier put it: 'A puritane is he that when he prayes/His cowled eyes doth vpp to heavene raise.'[217] Turning up the white of the eye and raising *cowled* eyes both imply that, while the devotees' eyes are open, they cannot actually see, and here, perhaps, we can see the beginnings of prayer with eyes closed, which, by mid-century, some were positively recommending. Those who could not quite bring themselves to do that might put their piously removed hats over their faces. Craig convincingly connects this shift to worries about distraction. The eyes were a potent source of temptation when praying, and disciplining the eyes both in prayer and in everyday life was a standard concern for the zealous. If hats, cowls, or eyelids were necessary to keep temptation away, so be it. To the less scrupulous, however,

---

[211] Craig, 'Bodies at prayer'. For conformist and Laudian examples, see Bentley, *Monument of Matrons*, 364; Browning, *Concerning publike-prayer*, 70–1.

[212] Babington, *Profitable Exposition*, 28; Parr, *Abba Father*, 25; Mildmay, 'Meditations', II.53.

[213] Tara Hamling, 'To See Or Not To See? The Presence Of Religious Imagery In The Protestant Household', *Art History* 30/2 (2007), 170–97.

[214] Clarke, *Collection*, 9; Fleming, *Diamond of deuotion*, 139; Herbert, *Works*, 103. Herbert alludes to Psalm 121:1; cf. the Geneva Bible's marginal notes on that verse; Browning, *Concerning publike-prayer*, 70.

[215] Wallington, *Notebooks*, 33; Tweedie, *Select Biographies*, 12; FSL MS V.a.248 fo. 7v.

[216] Craig, 'Bodies at prayer'; Leonard Wright, *A display of dutie dect vvith sage sayings* (1589: RSTC 26025), 13.

[217] Wright, *Summons for Sleepers*, 30; Thomas Heywood, *A pleasant conceited comedie, wherein is shewed, how a man may chuse a good wife from a bad* (1602: RSTC 5594), sig. G3r; Earle, *Microcosmographie*, 117; FSL MS X.d.475 fo. 3r.

it looked offensively like an assertion of difference—either that, or a preparation for falling asleep.[218]

Distraction, however, was not the only problem about gazing upwards. If casting the eyes upwards was a mark of spiritual confidence and elevation, what if you did not feel that confidence? When John Donne 'durst not view heaven', when Nicholas Themylthorpe was 'ashamed O Iesu, to lift vp my eyes vnto thee', and when John Norden was 'not worthy to lift vp mine eies vnto thy throne', we must assume they meant what they said.[219] Perkins cited the Biblical seraphs covering their faces before God, and Gouge saw 'casting down the eies' as a gesture of prayer.[220] In other words, the shift to closed eyes and lowered heads may have been driven, not only by pragmatic concerns about concentration, but by the long-standing Protestant aspiration to self-abasement.

TEARS

A further bodily manifestation of prayer is important enough to deserve a section to itself. Pious weeping, like most of the rest of Protestant pious practice, had a long medieval history and was thriving amongst contemporary Catholics. As Alison Shell has pointed out, modern scholarship has, tendentiously, associated weeping strongly with Catholicism.[221] Protestants, however, also took it up with enthusiasm. Part of its appeal was that, unlike posture, weeping is not quite voluntary. Tears can sometimes be summoned, encouraged, or choked back by deliberate effort, but not always. This made them all the more powerful.

The association between tears and prayer was, as always, bolstered by Biblical example. In prayer, Archbishop Sandys believed, the true Christian 'weepeth bitterly with Peter, or nightly watereth his couch with tears, as David'. Tears were, he suggested, 'the fountain of prayer'. 'Prepare therfore thy selfe, and *soul to pray with teares*', urged an influential Elizabethan prayer book.[222] By the 17th century, weeping at prayer had become a positive duty. Nehemiah Wallington's worked-out method for battling his sins began, 'First offen prayer with teares to God'. Roger Bolton argued that, since Christ has given us 'a fountaine of his owne deare, warme hearts-blood', we must in return give him 'a counter-well, as it were, of weeping'. To repent, Lewis Bayly wrote, you should 'pricke thy heart with sorrow, that melting for remorse within thee, it may be dissolued into a fountaine of teares'. This is presumably what Elizabeth Isham meant by 'forcing my selfe to weepe'.[223]

---

[218] Craig, 'Bodies at prayer'; Wallington, *Notebooks*, 42; Parker and Carlson, 'Practical Divinity', 182–3; Mildmay, 'Meditations', 7.

[219] Donne, *Poems*, 331; Themylthorpe, *Posie of Praiers*, 206; Norden, *Pensiue mans practise*, 40.

[220] Perkins, *Godly and learned exposition*, 234; Gouge, *Whole-Armor of God*, 336.

[221] Christian, 'Provoked Religious Weeping'; Alison Shell, *Catholicism, Controversy and the English Literary Imagination* (Cambridge, 1999), 57, 87–8; Karant-Nunn, *Reformation of Feeling*, 23–6.

[222] Sandys, *Sermons*, 157; Matthew 26:75; Psalm 6:6; Day, *Booke of Christian Prayers*, sig. ☞3r.

[223] Wallington, *Notebooks*, 41; Bolton, *Three-fold treatise*, III.160; Bayly, *Practise of pietie*, 502, 565; Isham, 'Diary', 1635.

Pious weeping happened both in public and in private, but the public devotional weeping which had enlivened medieval piety became rarer in our period.[224] The processions and sacraments which had once triggered it had disappeared or changed profoundly. The most common site of public weeping was the sermon, but even this was an oddly private form of public weeping. All eyes were (supposedly) on the preacher and therefore only he should see the silent tears trickling down the audience's faces—unless, of course, his vision was blurred by his own tears. There might be weeping at other parts of public worship, such as fasts or when receiving the Lord's Supper.[225] More private meetings sometimes occasioned tears. In 1587, when Richard Rogers urged the Essex ministers to adopt a covenant, the need for it 'was acknowledged amongst us with teares'. Isaac Ambrose described how, in a prayer meeting, one man's fervent prayers 'opened the fountains of all eyes about him, and caused a flood of tears in my Chamber'. The testimonies and prayers of the dying were particularly likely to provoke tears in those who heard them, although deathbeds could perhaps be expected to be a little lachrymose.[226] In general, however, there was some reticence about public weeping. In his paraphrase of the seven penitential psalms—titled, significantly, *Seuen Sobs of a Sorrowfull Soule*—William Hunnis argued that weeping in 'the sight of men' was an open invitation to hypocrisy. Repentance should be made 'in my chamber secretlie', and made

> Not onelie with the teares of eies,
> but teares set from alow,
> That is, from bottome of my hart.[227]

It was a common scruple. When, for example, Katherine Brettergh's hagiographer described her as weeping 'most bitterly' during her pious reading, it was a rare glimpse of an essentially private event. Similarly, although Jane Ratcliffe's prayers were 'no dry Devotion, but steeped, and drenched in showres of tears', she did her best to conceal this. Some individuals wept in private, only to betray themselves by emerging with a 'face all blubbered with tears'. Daniel Featley argued that true Christians could be distinguished from hypocrites by virtue of their being 'more deuout in priuate then in publike'. Amongst other things, this meant that 'the penitent, or compassionate eye, which droppeth in publike should runne and gush our with riuers of water in priuate'.[228] Only behind closed doors can you really let yourself go.

And they did. The examples pile up: John Bruen, Lettice Cary, Anne Clifford, John Forbes of Corse, Elizabeth Isham, Richard Kilby, Richard Norwood, Richard Rogers, John Winthrop—all of these testify to having wept in their private prayers

---

[224] Christian, 'Provoked Religious Weeping', 35–8, 46.

[225] See, for example, Wallington, *Notebooks*, 150; Mildmay, *With Faith and Physic*, 29.

[226] Knappen, *Two Diaries*, 68; Ambrose, *Media*, 75; Melville, *Autobiography*, lvii; Denison, *Monument or Tombe-Stone*, 100.

[227] Hunnis, *Seuen Sobs*, 7–8.

[228] Harrison, *Deaths aduantage*, III. 9; Clarke, *Collection*, 426; Mildmay, *With Faith and Physic*, 29; Wariston, *Diary*, 12; Featley, *Ancilla Pietatis*, 4–5.

more or less routinely.[229] Archibald Johnston of Wariston, who developed an idiosyncratic distinction between 'deprecatorie' and 'impretatorie' tears, recalled that as a child there were certain Biblical passages which he 'could not weal read . . . without som tears of bairnly compassion'. He wept over whether to marry; he wept 'tears in abundance' when he first prayed with his fiancée; and on the morning of their wedding he gave thanks 'with tears running over thy scheaks lyk walter'. As a much reprinted sermon by Thomas Playfere put it, Christians weep in fervent prayer 'as a seething pot runneth ouer'. Tears sometimes simply could not be contained.[230]

But Protestant tears did not just happen. They were longed for, striven for, treasured, and, if absent, worried about. It was, in fact, precisely their semi-involuntary nature which made them precious. This went to the heart of the problem of Protestant emotion. True penitence was, for Reformed Protestants, a gift of grace which only the Holy Spirit could give, and which was given only to the elect. But distinguishing true penitence from false was tricky, and tears were the single most important clue—not an infallible one, but they sometimes came pretty close. William Narne spelt the matter out. 'It is very difficile to lament for thy sinne and iniquitie', and just as difficult 'to weepe bitterly, with repenting Peter, and to powre out thy teares' for sin. Both require a miracle akin to God's bringing water from a rock in the wilderness—in this case, the water of tears from a stony heart.[231] The particular appeal of tears as a sign of election, however, was that the miracle was not quite so stark. It was not as if you had to wait for God to change the colour of your eyes. Most people cannot and could not weep at will, but they can and did foster and encourage tears, and learn to do so ever more effectively. So this was both a sign of God's utterly sovereign choices, and a sign which could be influenced by individual believers.

This argument was sometimes made with surprising simplicity. In a best-selling tract, Henry Greenwood imagined a Christian accused by Satan of hypocrisy. 'Shewe me Gods seale', demands Satan: prove that you are saved! The Christian's knock-down reply is: 'I can weepe for sinne, and I hate sinne in my selfe and others . . . which are the Armes of Christe in his seale.' William Cowper similarly imagined God reassuringly citing a believer's 'inward contrition for thy sinnes, which hath broken out into teares' as proof of election. Nicholas Byfield's best-selling tract on how to discern whether or not you are among the elect, *The Signes*, notes that the regenerate Christian 'is oftentimes dissolued into much sorrow for his sinnes, while he stands before the face of God'.[232] Gilbert Primrose's *The Christian Mans Teares* took a slightly different tack. Primrose was clear that 'weeping is a gift of God', and he placed it—together with tearing clothes, plucking out hair, and

[229] Hinde, *Faithfull Remonstrance . . . of Iohn Bruen*, 72; Duncon, *Returnes*, 8; Clifford, *Diaries*, 70; Forbes, 'Diary', 8; Isham, 'Diary', 1635; Kilby, *Hallelujah*, 106; Norwood, *Journal*, 81; Knappen, *Two Diaries*, 56; Winthrop, *Papers*, 160, 166, 199, 211.
[230] Wariston, *Diary*, 6, 9–11, 45–6, 143; Playfere, *Meane in Mourning*, 17.
[231] Narne, *Pearle of prayer*, 347; cf. Clarke, *Holy Incense*, 50.
[232] Greenwood, *Treatise of . . . Iudgement*, sig. F2r; Cowper, *Most Comfortable Dialogue*, 20–1; Byfield, *The Signes*, 97–8.

other signs of anguish—amongst the 'Symptomes' of true mourning. He asked: 'Can a man have a true feeling of his evils, and not weep? . . . The heart wounded to the quicke, sendeth up to the eyes rivers of teares'. And so, naturally, we find earnest believers taking careful note of their own tears, or lack of them, as evidence of the Spirit's presence, or absence.[233] As Byfield said, a Christian 'must obserue how the Lord deales with him in prayer, and . . . be wonderfull thankful, if he can get but one teare'.[234] That single tear could mean the difference between Heaven and Hell. Even if it was not necessary for salvation, it might be for assurance. John Andrewes' best-selling chapbook *The Conuerted Mans New Birth* warned:

> It is not euery little sob, or sigh, that brings Repentance sufficient to please God. . . . It will cost him many a prayer, and many a teare, before he can be certayne or sure to haue pardon for his sinnes.[235]

The incentive to set yourself to weeping was obvious.

The pitfalls were equally clear, and were addressed most succinctly in a posthumously published treatise by the Essex minister John Smith. Smith asked 'whether euery man or woman who truely repent them of their sinnes, must and doe necessarily shed teares for them?' Put that way, there is only one answer: neither tears nor their absence prove anything about salvation. But Smith was aware that this was a pastoral minefield. 'The most part of all the Religion of the world', he commented, 'is this, that if a man can bring himselfe to shed a few teares, by and by they thinke themselues to bee safe', and he imagined that his opinion would provoke a storm of protest. 'How can a poore Christian take any comfort in his Teares', readers would ask, 'if teares bee not alwayes a true signe of Repentance?' In other words, Smith believed that pious tears were not a preserve of the godly elite, but a rough-and-ready index of salvation which formed a part of England's popular Calvinism. If he worried that such tears were sometimes hypocritical, he was even more concerned about the opposite problem, of those who could not weep and so doubted their salvation. 'The want of teares doth . . . perplexe many.' He had a degree of comfort to offer them, insisting that no-one could weep for *all* their sins, and that sometimes grief for sins is so extreme that even tears are impossible. Yet he continued to see tears as immensely important. They are powerful in themselves: 'the teares of the godly . . . are mightie and quickning (like *Aqua fortis*) which make strong and lasting impressions of vertue and of grace'. Although in theory it was possible for Christians to repent without weeping,

> There was none of the holy men of God but they haue wept for sinne. . . . All that are truely converted shall shedde teares at one time or other, though not in a like measure.

---

[233] Primrose, *Christian Mans Teares*, sig. A8v, 63–4, 249. See, for example, Bradford, *Godlie meditations*, sig. C2r; Bruce, *Sermons . . . with Collections*, 135; Knappen, *Two Diaries*, e.g. 56, 75.

[234] Byfield, *Marrow of the Oracles* (1622), 241.

[235] John Andrewes, *The Conuerted Mans New Birth* (1629: RSTC 595), 27.

Tears were not an infallible guide to salvation. But they were about as close as you could get.[236]

Others who questioned the link between tears and salvation tended to focus on one side of the question or the other. So it was common enough to make the obvious point that moistened eyes were not, in themselves, signs of a regenerate soul. As Primrose pointed out, tears are a medical phenomenon—caused by 'vapours condensed in the brain'—and in themselves they are as natural, and therefore as valueless, as 'the howling and yelling of beasts'. True tears are 'not droppes of water, running from the eyes which may be soone forced with onions or such like, but drops of blood issuing from the heart'.[237] Weeping for pain or worldly loss has no spiritual value. Indeed, as several divines pointed out, hypocrites can be moved to tears by an eloquent sermon, or even, for a passing moment, be truly sorry for their sins. But 'though they shed riuers of teares, though they water their couches, and euen bathe, and soake themselues in this salt brine', if the tears do not presage amendment of life, they are mere water.[238] Tears might still be a sign of election, but only if they were the right kind of tears. Distinguishing the kinds was as difficult as ever.

The other side of the problem was inability to weep. In the 16th century, this seems to have been dismissed simply as a symptom of insufficient repentance,[239] but pastoral reality eventually made itself felt. William Perkins, subtle and humane as always, was one of the first to argue that in some cases, overwhelming sorrow can cause 'a nummednesse of the heart' rather than weeping, and moreover that 'sometimes the complexion will not affoard teares': that is, some people are physiologically more predisposed to weep than others. 'In such there may be true humiliation, though with drie cheekes'. Both lines of argument were picked up and echoed by a number of other divines. The physiological argument in particular was appealing, because it provided a test: if you could never weep for any cause, then failing to weep for sin was acceptable, but if worldly grief could provoke tears, sin should do the same.[240]

This problem was a strongly gendered one. Women and children in early modern Britain wept relatively readily. As a rule, adult men did not. Primrose dwelt on this issue. 'Men when they are exhorted to weep', he wrote, 'are accustomed to say, that weeping is more womanish than manly.' His reply was bluntly to denounce masculine culture as brutish, arguing that 'the most part of the evill that is done in the world, is done by men', and trying to shame men with women's greater piety and virtues. All true enough, no doubt, but not much of a

[236] John Smith, *Essex Dove, Presenting the World with a few of her Oliue Branches* (1633: RSTC 22799), 331–41.
[237] Primrose, *Christian Mans Teares*, 58–9, 98, 172.
[238] Dyke, *Mystery of selfe-deceiuing*, 95–6; Byfield, *The Signes*, 37; Dyke, *Worthy communicant*, 161; Rogers, *Seven treatises*, 51; Bolton, *Discourse about happinesse*, 36; Pinke, *Tryall of a Christians loue*, III.27–8.
[239] See, for example, Bentley, *Monument of Matrons*, 441.
[240] Perkins, *First part of The cases of conscience*, 55. Cf. Dyke, *Two Treatises*, 45; Primrose, *Christian Mans Teares*, 237–41; John Mayer, *Praxis Theologica* (1629: RSTC 17743), sig. Ddd2r; Smith, *Essex Dove*, 338.

solution. But while other divines noticed that it was thought 'vnbeseeming the grauitie and courage of men, thus to weepe as children or babes, and to shed teares as women of weake spirit', no-one had any better ideas for tackling the problem.[241] This was a real point of tension between Protestantism and masculine culture in early modern Britain. To weep as an adult male was, in one sense, to preserve a childhood habit: although childhood religion is very largely a mystery to us, a series of sources refer to boys weeping for sin, including the young Wariston, Wallington, and Thomas Goodwin.[242] For grown men who had lost the knack, this was a real obstacle. Richard Baxter's inability to weep for his sins gravely troubled him, until he was persuaded that he had a 'Nature not apt to weep'.[243] How many other potential converts fell at that hurdle? This may explain the emphasis on keeping weeping private: tears were not so much hypocritically holy as shamefully woman-ish. When Robert Bruce preached on King Hezekiah's tears, he took it for granted that he would want to hide them by turning his face to the wall.[244] To modern eyes, Protestant culture's celebration of weeping seems impressively emotionally literate, but it may have been unwise to make so much of a practice which was despised by, and indeed largely inaccessible to, a large part of the adult population.

One partial solution was, again, to turn weeping into a metaphor. That way your eyes could stay dry but you could still weep inwardly. As Christopher Sutton put it, 'the teares of the heart may suffice'; or, in the less grudging words of Thomas Tuke's popular prayer book, 'the best teares are the throbs of a broken and bleeding heart'.[245] Oddly, this kind of approach may have been helped by Biblical hyper-bole. The prophet Jeremiah had prayed, 'Oh, that my head were ful of water and mine eyes a fountaine of teares'; the psalmist spoke of eyes which 'gush out with riuers of water'. It was easy to treat these much-cited images as flights of rhetorical fancy which were no more to be attempted in earnest than wearing sackcloth and ashes.[246] The Catholic poet Robert Southwell even extended these images: where others spoke of tears washing away sin, he wrote 'Huge horrors in/high tides must drowned be'. Protestant readers devoured this enthusiastically.[247] But it is easy to imagine embracing this sort of language while remaining dry-eyed.

The most-cited Biblical image of all is particularly telling. Psalm 56:8 claims that God has 'put my teares into thy bottel'. There is no evidence at all that actual tear-bottles or lachrymatories were used in this period, and it seems unlikely that the

---

[241] Primrose, *Christian Mans Teares*, sigs A2r–8r; William Narne, *Christs Starre* (1625: RSTC 18359), 240.

[242] Wariston, *Diary*, 45–6; Wallington, *Notebooks*, 266; Goodwin, *Works*, II.lii; cf. Philip C. Almond (ed.), *Demonic Possession and Exorcism in Early Modern England: Contemporary Texts and their Cultural Contexts* (Cambridge, 2004), 179.

[243] Baxter, *Reliquiae Baxterianae*, 7.

[244] Bruce, *Sermons Preached*, sig. C2v; Isaiah 38:2–3.

[245] Sutton, *Godly meditations* (1601), 280; Tuke, *Practise of the faithfull*, 13.

[246] Jeremiah 9:1; Psalm 119:136; cf. Lamentations 3:48. See, for example, Norden, *Pensive mans practise . . . The second part*, 6; Tuke, *Practise of the faithfull*, 162; Crashaw, *London's Lamentation*, sig. A6r; Gee, *Steps of Ascension*, 225–6; Featley, *Ancilla Pietatis*, 125; Andrewes, *Conuerted Mans New Birth*, 6–7.

[247] Robert Southwell, *St Peters complainte Mary Magdal. teares. Wth other workes*, ed. W. Barrett (1620: RSTC 22965), sig. A9r (eleven editions, 1595–1636).

ancient world ever really used them either; they were a passing Victorian fad. But early modern Protestants were enthralled by the idea that their tears did not merely evaporate but were kept and treasured by God. The Geneva Bible's marginal comment on the verse emphasized that God remembers and will avenge his people's suffering. This meaning persisted—Thomas Goodwin linked the psalm to the Apocalypse when he wrote of 'bottles of teares a filling, Vialls a filling to be powred out for the destruction of Gods enemies'[248]—but 17th-century uses of the verse tended to be more individual. It could mean that your struggles were not in vain: 'the teares you shed are not spilt, for the Lord hath put them all into his Bottell'.[249] It could be self-reproach for weeping the wrong kind of tears: John Smith doubted that one tear in a thousand was worthy to be collected, and Lettice Cary imagined seeing 'the small bottle of my penitential tears . . . brought forth, and set by the bottle of my tears for worldly crosses'.[250] Above all, it could be used to emphasize the worth of tearful prayer, for God would not so carefully harvest something unless it were precious.[251] Primrose had a more fanciful image for the same thing. He described a tree whose sap, when it falls into a river, congeals into amber. 'So when our teares fall into the riuer of the mercies of God, they become there a most preciouss iewell.'[252]

The appeal of these images was that they resonated with the Protestant experience of pious weeping. If tears could not actually guarantee election—and clearly, plenty of people thought that they almost did—they did have other benefits to offer, benefits which we might group under three headings. First of all, they made prayer powerful, simply by being the plainest outward sign of zeal and ardour. 'The cloud-cleauing thunder of th'almightie', Thomas Playfere claimed, 'can not make such a ratling sound, and such a roaring noyse in the eares of man, as our teares do in the eares of God.'[253] Aemilia Lanyer believed that tears 'enforced' pity from Christ; Wariston described them as 'conjuring' assurance; Gouge wrote that tears were 'powerfull with God', a passage which Wallington copied into one of his notebooks.[254] Some played on the contrast between eloquent words and inarticulate weeping. Weeping 'smothereth the words', but before God, tears are 'the fluent and most current Rhetoricke', 'a speaking voice in Gods eare'. As Primrose put it: 'No prayers . . . come back so swiftly from the Throne of grace with grace & grants, as prayers of teares'.[255]

The second benefit which tears offered flows from the first. As well as forcibly bending God's ear, tears were seen to have an almost automatic redemptive power.

[248] Goodwin, *Returne of Prayers*, 37; cf. Revelation 16.

[249] Linaker, *Comfortable treatise* (1620), 59.

[250] Smith, *Essex Dove*, 295; Duncon, *Returnes*, 48; cf. Narne, *Pearle of prayer*, 347.

[251] Gouge, *Whole-Armor of God*, 431; Ley, *Patterne of Pietie*, 61.

[252] Primrose, *Christian Mans Teares*, II.13.

[253] Playfere, *Meane in Mourning*, 18–19; cf. Herbert, *Works*, 66.

[254] Aemilia Lanyer, *The Poetry of Aemilia Lanyer: Salve Deus Rex Judaeorum*, ed. Susanne Woods (Oxford, 1993), 93; Wariston, *Diary*, 143; Gouge, *Whole-Armor of God*, 431; LMA Guildhall MS 204, p. 306.

[255] Primrose, *Christian Mans Teares*, 56; Featley, *Ancilla Pietatis*, 112; Tymme, *Chariot of Devotion*, 23.

Sometimes this is a matter of God's being compelled by them. William Narne would have Christians 'striue and wrestle with the Almightie by prayer and supplication, by strong crying and teares'; John Mayer, less violently, argued that tears 'breake the Lords heart that he cannot but be moued with compassion towards vs'.[256] But tears' intrinsic power could sometimes bypass God altogether. 'Very strong and vile sinnes', Thomas Playfere argued, 'are weakened and washt away with teares.' Imagining our sins being recorded on a charge-sheet, he suggested that 'if we blur it dayly with weeping vpon it, our teares wil be like *aqua fortis*, to take out the hand-writing quite and cleane, that God shall neither reade nor see our sins'.[257] The implication that tears were powerful in themselves was no accident. Daniel Dyke described weeping as 'scouring away the filthinesse of our sinnes. . . . This salt brine takes away all our raw humours, and . . . dissolues the clowds of our iniquities'. John Gee's popular *Steps of Ascension vnto God* described tears as medicinal, praying, 'Let then mine heart like a Limbeck distill the soueraigne water of repentance into mine eyes.'[258] Of course, these are all merely metaphors. None of these authors would seriously have suggested that human tears have any real power. But metaphors have a way of taking on a life of their own, particularly if they offer earnest Protestants the prospect of a handhold on the sheer, insurmountable wall of God's sovereignty. Mayer felt the need to point out that it is actually Christ's blood, not our own weeping, which redeems us.[259] Part of the appeal of tears was the chance, for a few moments, to forget that stark fact.

If this was theologically perilous, the third, and perhaps the greatest, benefit which tears offers takes us to much safer ground: the immediate relief and even joy which weeping could bring. Even if they were not actually tears of joy, the very fact of them was a sign of grace, from which the weeper could draw comfort. 'I got abundance of tears' from a particular meditation, Wariston recorded triumphantly. Richard Rogers described the 'delight exceedinge' with which he held tightly to the 'savour' of his tears while preaching and meditating one Sunday.[260] But that struggle points us to an important feature of weeping: it is not a state but a process, and while it may sometimes be miserable to endure, its outcome is another matter altogether. Nowadays we might say that weeping can be a cathartic experience which can expel toxins or rebalance hormones. That is not quite how William Narne put it, but he did cite Ovid to the effect that 'there is a certaine pleasure to weepe, that sorrow by teares is fulfilled, and also expelled'. Or, as he put it in an earlier treatise, 'as after great showres, the aire is made clean and pure, so after the raine of teares, followeth serenitie and tranquillitie of mind'.[261]

It was rarely spelt out so clearly, but the effect Narne described was widespread. Elizabeth Melville described how 'mine heart was eas'd when I had mourn'd my fill'. The Somerset gentleman Edward Rodney prayed, 'Graunt me thos teares

---

[256] Narne, *Pearle of prayer*, 342; Mayer, *Praxis Theologica*, sig. Ddd2r.
[257] Playfere, *Meane in Mourning*, 10–11; cf. FSL MS V.b.198 fo. 66v.
[258] Dyke, *Two Treatises*, 17–18; Gee, *Steps of Ascension*, 225.
[259] Mayer, *Praxis Theologica*, sig. Ddd2r–v.
[260] Wariston, *Diary*, 157; Knappen, *Two Diaries*, 66.
[261] Narne, *Pearle of prayer*, 38; William Narne, *Christs Starre* (1625: RSTC 18359), 243.

which thou hast promised shall end in Ioye, that mourning which thou hast blessed.'[262] Robert Blair, ministering in Ulster, gives us a glimpse of this at work. He was due to preach a pair of sermons on Heaven and Hell, but 'could not fix either upon matter or method', and spent the day before they were due 'in great sorrow and perplexity'. Finally he lay down on his bed to meditate, and fell asleep. But then:

> Suddenly waking, my eyes gushed out with tears, and presently both matter and order broke out with clearness, so that I fell a discoursing, first upon the one subject, then the other, and retained the same till publicly I delivered what I then discoursed.[263]

The tears were a moment of release. This experience meshed with the more theological claims that tears were signs of grace, wings of prayer, and a means to compel God. Weeping was both understood, and felt, to be transformative. It was a lived sacrament which poured out sorrow so that—sometimes, at least—joy or peace could take its place. It was a point which Gilbert Primrose made with the help of another Biblical image. He exhorted his readers to weep for their sins, tears which would, of course, be collected in God's bottle, but which then 'the Lamb of God [would] turne into the wine of heavenly comforts, when they shall be called unto his marriage-Supper'.[264] As earnest for tears as early modern Protestants might be, they were always a means to an end. They wept so that their tears might be wiped away.

'HUMILIATION'

One final element of the Protestant practice of prayer deserves brief attention: bodily abstinence. Protestants rejected the theology of merit associated with ascetic practices in the Catholic tradition, but they did not reject the practices themselves. Fasting, and other forms of asceticism such as 'watching'—that is, drastically curtailing sleep—were grounded in Scripture and in long Christian usage, and were accepted signs of holiness. They were simply too valuable for Protestants to relinquish them.

That said, fasting was certainly used much less than in the Catholic world. At the Reformation, set calendrical fasts were abolished or made secular in both England and Scotland. The liberty which Protestantism offered from irksome regulations such as fasts was one of its chief attractions, especially in the early years. By the mid-16th century, some reformers were worrying that fasting had fallen into almost total disuse, and there is no doubt that some Protestants continued to see it as worryingly popish. The result was a deliberate attempt to revive fasting in the second half of the century, in two distinct forms. First, both north and south of the border, the

---

[262] Melville, *Godlie Dreame*, sig. A2v; FSL MS V.a.520 fo. 26v; cf. Duncon, *Returnes*, 8; Sutton, *Godly meditations* (1601), 66, 152–3.
[263] Blair, *Life*, 60.
[264] Primrose, *Christian Mans Teares*, sig. A1v.

established Churches created public fasts, irregular events occasioned by particular public crises, through which a whole parish, a whole city, or the whole nation might appeal to God with one, hunger-sharpened voice. That lies beyond our scope here.[265] Second, individual believers were encouraged to fast as a private, voluntary pious discipline.

As with any private pious practice, quite how you did this was a matter of Christian liberty: but this time there were very clear models. William Perkins, Henry Mason, Samuel Torshell, John Browning, Thomas Cartwright, Henry Scudder, Henry Burton, and others from across England's Protestant spectrum agreed that a private fast ought ideally to be a twenty-four hour affair, consisting of total abstinence from food and perhaps even from water, from dusk to dusk. It should not be longer, since that would presume on God's assistance; it might be shorter if your health made that prudent. As well as abstaining from food and drink, you should rise early on a fast day—meaning perhaps two in the morning—and also abstain from worldly work, fine clothing, music, recreation, and the marriage-bed. You might sleep on the floor, or on sackcloth. If you left your house at all, it would be to distribute alms and to visit the poor. In other words, a fast day should be a kind of mid-week Sabbath, given over to prayer, study, and self-examination. Indeed, English commentators insisted that fasts should not be celebrated on a Sunday. Since Sunday was already dedicated to God, squeezing a fast into the same day was slightly sharp practice. By contrast, Sunday fasting was the norm in Scotland, but since the standard Scottish fast, public or private, was an eight-day affair, consisting of full fasts on two consecutive Sundays with a week of severe abstinence between them, it was hard to accuse the Scots of cutting corners.[266]

How widely this or anything like it was truly practised, we cannot know.[267] As an arduous and inherently unpleasant discipline, we might guess that it was restricted to a small number of enthusiasts. We do at least have some examples to cite, who collectively give an impression of a gathering confidence in the practice from shaky Elizabethan beginnings. Richard Rogers derived considerable strength from fasting: lamenting his habitual sinfulness one day in September 1589, he wrote,

> Yet I see sometimes when I have fasted, or throughly seasoned my hart with good medit[ation] and praier, . . . that I have felt and found my hart as well contented in such a sober course and in subduinge all inordinate affec[tions] every way as I can wish . . . This day fasting I can say the same.

When it failed to work, he could be frantic. Eighteen months earlier, he wrote, 'I had no smalle hope that I should have been much the better my our late fast', being

[265] On the Protestant attack on fasting, and the creation of public fasts, see Alec Ryrie, 'The fall and rise of fasting in the British Reformations' in Mears and Ryrie, *Worship and the Parish Church*.
[266] Scudder, *Christians daily walke* (1631), 79–87; Torshell, *Saints Humiliation*, 6–8; Mason, *Christian Humiliation*, 9; Burton, *Israels Fast*, 15; Perkins, *Godly and learned exposition*, 328–9; Browning, *Concerning publike-prayer*, 167, 210–12; Cartwright and Wilcox, *Two treatises*, 28; Ryrie, 'Fall and rise of fasting'.
[267] On the special case of communion fasting, see below, pp. 342–4.

in particular grieved that he had been denied the 'grace of weepinge'. And so, paradoxically, 'grief hath taken hold of me in exceeding maner', and he could not be settled until he had resolved to fast again at the next opportunity. John Rogers' rule of life included the resolution that 'there must be now and then the use of Fasting, to purge out Weariness and Commonness'. Richard Greenham was encouraging his disciples to fast in the 1570s. Samuel Ward was doing it, and rebuking himself for not doing it as a student in Cambridge in the 1590s. Richard Kilby, drawing up his spiritual discipline in 1614, resolved that 'I must often times, so far as my weake body will endure, pray fasting'.[268] For the Scottish revivalist John Livingstone, his new converts' readiness to adopt this new discipline was a mark of their sincerity.[269] And naturally, there is Nehemiah Wallington. When battling lustful temptations in 1624, he resolved that he and his wife should spend a Sunday in fasting and prayer, with the result that, after a fifteen-year battle with this particular sin, 'dare say I was never so chast to my remembrance as I am now the Lords Name bee praised for it'.[270]

These testimonies collectively help to explain what early modern Protestants thought fasting was for. It was an outward sign of inner repentance. The word *humiliation* was regularly used as a near synonym for fasting—with humiliation the purpose of the exercise, and fasting the means by which it was achieved. Fasting was a means of testifying to God and to yourself that your repentance was not merely lip service, but rather a reflection of true sorrow for sin. A fast was meant to signify that you were unworthy even of eating; by abstention from the marital bed, you acknowledged that you were 'unworthy of any posteritie, or remembrance on the earth'.[271] Fasting might, as Thomas Becon suggested in the first full-length English-language treatment of the subject, be a natural, almost involuntary response to sin, as inevitable as a sick person's loss of appetite. A true fast takes place when the Christian is so overcome with sorrow for his own sins that 'the verye trouble of hys heart wyl not suffer him to eat or drynke'.[272] But rather than simply waiting for such unintended fasts to take shape in them, Becon's successors discovered that fasting could provoke as well as express inner sorrow. The Laudian John Browning gave this advice to those who could not mourn sincerely for their sins:

> Let him but fast; and I dare warrant him to mourne. Hunger will bring the stoutest stomackes under: it will make them bend. . . . If thou canst not mourne, betake thee to

[268] Knappen, *Two Diaries*, 75–6, 89; Mather, *Magnalia*, III.111; Parker and Carlson, 'Practical Divinity', 135; Knappen, *Two Diaries*, 110; Kilby, *Hallelujah*, 62.

[269] This appears to be the meaning of Elizabeth Melville's claim to Livingstone that 'God hes begunne to work a happy change in Jhon Graye;—he hes assayed your viii. dayis, and weireis not yet. . . . Some othir also hes gottin gude'. The reference is to the eight-day fasts normal in Scottish usage. Tweedie, *Select Biographies*, 356–7.

[270] Wallington, *Notebooks*, 56. See also, amongst many examples, D'Ewes, *Autobiography*, 9, 353, 428–9; Ley, *Patterne of Pietie*, 74–5; Wariston, *Diary*, 54–5, 137; Winthrop, *Papers*, 235; Rogers, *Diary*, 106; Shepard, *God's Plot*, 53.

[271] Bolton, *Three-fold treatise*, III.58.

[272] Thomas Becon, *A fruitful treatise of fasting* (1551: RSTC 1722), esp. sigs C5v–6r.

fasting, & that will make thee mourne. If thou canst mourne, yet notwithstanding fast, and that will make thee mourne yet more.[273]

'The chief use of a religious fast is to humble and afflict the soule with sorrow, and grief . . . to make us the better to feele what sinne is, and what it hath deserved at Gods hands', as Arthur Hildersham put it in the 1620s.[274]

Fasting, then, was not a meritorious work, but a prudent one. It was a whetstone which sharpened prayer, much as kneeling or casting up the eyes did. This was partly for simply physiological reasons. William Perkins argued that fasting 'causeth watchfulnesse, & cuts off drowsinesse, and so makes a man the more liuely and fresh in prayer'.[275] The point was not only that a full stomach makes you drowsy, but also that it leads to 'vnchaste and fleshly lusts', and to pride and self-will. 'On the contrary side, fasting, and pinching of the body, and putting it to hardnesse, they are meanes to coole the bloud, and tame the spirits, and pull downe the pride of the flesh.'[276] The experience was widely shared. George Herbert revelled in,

> . . . The cleannesse of sweet abstinence,
> Quick thoughts and motions at a small expense,
> A face not fearing light:
> Whereas in fulnesse there are sluttish fumes,
> Sowre exhalations, and dishonest rheumes,
> Revenging the delight.[277]

This had its practical side: advising Christians to have a small lunch on Sundays if they wished to stay awake through catechism class.[278] Yet fasting's power to liberate the soul from the flesh was as much ideal as practical. When Samuel Torshell preached that 'the will is Bird-limed with the earth, and fasting doth untangle it', and that fasting turns our affections from 'sawcy servants' to obedient ones, his point was not simply medical.[279]

Whatever the explanation, the experience and conviction of early modern Protestants of all stripes was that prayer was made more powerful when joined with fasting. The Biblical evidence helped. When Christ rebuked his disciples for their failure to cast out a particularly stubborn demon, he added: 'This kinde can by no other meanes come forth, but by prayer, and fasting.'[280] But that implication that fasting gave extra force to prayer fitted well with Protestant devotees' experience. When Henry Mason had exhausted all his arguments for the use of fasting, he was left with one final appeal to his readers:

If any man will please to make tryall in himselfe, his owne experience will be a better proofe than all sayings of other men. . . . If after tryall made in religious manner, they find not their attention more quicke, their deuotion more fiery, their prayers more

---

[273] Browning, *Concerning publike-prayer*, 168.   [274] Hildersam, *Doctrine of Fasting*, 62, 72.
[275] Perkins, *Godly and learned exposition*, 330.
[276] Mason, *Christian Humiliation*, 24, 26–7, 29–30, 156–62.   [277] Herbert, *Works*, 86.
[278] Kilby, *Burthen*, 43.   [279] Torshell, *Saints Humiliation*, 5, 11–12.
[280] Mark 9:29. Cf. Hildersam, *Doctrine of Fasting*, 62; Scudder, *Christians daily walke* (1631), 72–3; Knappen, *Two Diaries*, 84.

feruent, their meditations more spirituall, and themselues, as it were, turned into other
men: then they may suspect that the ancient Fathers of the Church . . . haue with faire
words perswaded men to vnnecessary paines.[281]

Never mind the theory; fasting *worked.*

Fasting's role in prayer, then, was both simple and invaluable. It was an
intensifier, in a religious culture which valued intensity above all. If your knees
had already cleaved to the earth and you had sweated blood in prayer, here was a
final and deceptively simple means of giving your prayers force. Fasting's particular
power was as a weapon in the endless battle with formality, hypocrisy, security, and
dryness. Almost any other pious activity can be dulled into routine by repetition,
but the human body never truly gets used to being hungry. A twenty-four hour fast
can be virtually guaranteed to produce an urgent, gnawing, awareness of your own
need and emptiness, and to dispel complacency and self-satisfaction. It was no
accident that Bayly's *Practise of pietie* depicted fasting, with faith, as one of the two
supports of prayer (see Figure 9). Those who were willing to embrace it discovered
that it was not, primarily, a matter of theology or of obeying a Biblical pattern. It
was a practical, and intensely effective, means of bringing a jaded devotee's prayers
to a bitingly sharp point.

---

[281] Mason, *Christian Humiliation*, 36.

9

Speaking to God

'One of his disciples said vnto him, Master, teache vs to praye, as Iohn also taught his disciples. And he said vnto them, When ye pray, say, Our Father . . .'
Luke 11:1–2

PREPARATION AND FORMALITY

The central Protestant understanding of prayer was, simply, speaking to God. Prayer was a matter of the heart, but almost always it was also a matter of words, which had to be chosen for the purpose. Immediately this brings us up against a perennial tension of Christian prayer. Believers should speak to God intimately, unreservedly, pouring out their soul. And yet they should also speak reverently, mindful of their unworthiness. For early modern British Protestants, these two principles were unusually finely balanced.

The issue arises most sharply at the moment of starting to pray. Protestants were supposed to pray as much and as often as practically possible, but they also preserved the medieval concern about praying without adequate preparation. In the first generation, Hugh Latimer insisted that 'when you will talk with God, and pray to him, you must be prepared', and Thomas Becon warned that neglecting preparation was 'a very derision and mocking of God'. Under Elizabeth, William Perkins condemned 'rash praying, without due preparation . . . when men pray onely on the suddaine, by the motion of the spirit, as they vse to speake'. In the 1620s, Henry Scudder argued that preparation was necessary to 'keepe your selfe from that rude and rash thrusting your selfe into Gods holy presence'.[1] But there was carrot as well as stick. When we prepare rightly, Perkins promised, 'our harts are thereby warmed with the comfortable heat of Gods holy spirit'—implying, once again, that the link between human and divine action was a complex one. With right preparation, Scudder claimed, you will pray 'more vnderstandingly, more distinctly, more humbly, more deuoutly, more feelingly, more feruently, and with more assurance of a gracious hearing'.[2] Nor were these exclusively puritan preoccupations. James Howell claimed that 'I use not to rush rashly into prayer without a trembling

---

[1] Latimer, *Sermons by Hugh Latimer*, 344; Becon, *Catechism*, 128; Perkins, *Godly and learned exposition*, 243; Scudder, *Christians daily walke* (1628), 33–4; cf. Bayly, *Practise of pietie*, 249.
[2] Perkins, *Exposition of the Lords prayer*, 26; Scudder, *Christians daily walke* (1628), 34; cf. Melville, *Spiritual Propine*, 6; Dyke, *Worthy communicant*, 45.

precedent Meditation'. John Browning worried that 'the heart is too hasty', and that if left to itself it will lurch from irreverence to irrelevance, 'not minding the Majesty to whom it prayeth'. The solution: conscientious preparation.[3]

When we ask *how* to prepare, however, the consensus dissolves. What was clear was that preparation was a matter of achieving the right state of mind: reverent, humble, and attentive to the business at hand. This might mean no more than a moment of gathering your thoughts. The official Elizabethan homily on public prayer argued that congregations should do this simply in the time it took for a minister to say 'Let us pray', and for them to kneel. Other Elizabethan texts were almost as minimalist, and terse instructions simply to 'frame thy selfe to all dutifull reuerence & seemlines', or to 'consider his almighty Majesty, and your owne vile basenesse', persist into the 17th century.[4] The point of this kind of thing is obvious enough: to inoculate yourself against slipping into merely habitual, formal, or distracted prayer, and instead actually to pay some focused attention to what you are doing.

However, a moment's pause before prayer might well not be enough, and could all too easily become mere habit itself. More elaborate instructions were there from the beginning. Thomas Becon devoted eight chapters of his *A newe pathwaye unto praier* (1542) to eight topics which should be considered before prayer. The official primer issued in Edward VI's reign urged a regime of self-examination before prayer, and the suggestion that preparation meant repentance was taken up with enthusiasm by later puritans. Lewis Bayly neatly summarized the principle: 'Before thou prayest, let God see that thy heart is sorrowfull for thy sinne: and that thy minde is resolued . . . to amend thy faults.'[5]

By contrast, those Protestants for whom repentance was not quite so pivotal might, like Howell, talk instead about meditation. This was John Clarke's advice, although he slipped some repentance in too: 'Meditate before you pray, of Gods greatnesse, of his judgements, of our sinnes, &c.' But meditation itself needed preparation, and indeed Joseph Hall, its most influential exponent, urged that we should pray before meditating rather than the opposite.[6] One common solution to this problem was to use the Bible. Reading before prayer meant that you could use God's Word, rather than your own willpower, to still and focus yourself. This habit was there from the very beginning. In 1528 the evangelical student Anthony Dalaber, having helped a wanted agitator escape from Oxford, promptly retired to his rooms to pray. But first, he 'tooke the new Testament in my hands . . . and with many a deepe sigh and salt teare, I did wyth much deliberation read ouer the 10. chapter of S. Mathew his Gospell', in which Christ sends his disciples out as sheep in the midst of wolves. Only when he had finished the chapter did he fall to 'feruent prayer'. Later writers would regularly advise the use of selected Bible

[3] Howell, *Epistolæ Ho-Elianæ*, VI.49; Browning, *Concerning publike-prayer*, 81.
[4] *Certain Sermons or Homilies*, 323–4; Cancellar, *Alphabet of prayers*, sig. A7r; *Godly garden*, fo. 1r–v; Sparke, *Crumms of comfort*, sig. A4v; Kilby, *Burthen*, 21.
[5] *Prymmer . . . set fourth by the kinges maiestie* (1553), sig. b2v; Bayly, *Practise of pietie*, 251. Cf. Perkins, *Godly and learned exposition*, 236; Norden, *Pensive mans practise . . . The second part*, 42.
[6] Clarke, *Holy Incense*, 48; Hall, *Arte of Divine Meditation*, 78–80.

passages as a preparation for prayer,[7] but we can still feel something of Dalaber's urgency in the case of Robert Blair, who, when travelling in 1633, dreamed one night that his wife, back at home, had died. He awoke distraught, and his first thought was prayer; but he did not pray lying in his bed. Rather, he leapt up, 'putting on my clothes quickly, that I might pour out my heart in prayer'. Even then, before he actually knelt to pray, he 'laid hold upon my bible', and read from the prophet Ezekiel. He needed to speak, but he needed to listen more.[8]

For those who lacked the Biblical self-confidence necessary to make this work, however, published devotional guides had another, paradoxical alternative to offer. We see this in, for example, the influential *Booke of Christian Prayers* assembled by Richard Day in 1578. For all its daunting lists of means to prepare for prayer—weeping, 'watching',[9] almsgiving, fasting—the text actually begins with a short prayer titled 'The Preface, or preparation to prayer'. This asks God to 'dispose my hart, open my lips, and guide me by thy holy spirite, to a true acknowledgement of all my sinnes, that my prayer may be heard of thee'. Prayers to be able to pray might be logically nonsensical, but they were also a staple of the genre.[10]

The contradiction is not quite so stark as it appears, since the point was often to use a scripted prayer in preparation for extempore prayer—a problem to which we will return shortly. Clarke's description of preparatory prayer as 'a description, or compellation of God'—what we might call an invocation—also suggests a qualitative difference with 'normal' prayer,[11] but this does not solve the problem. How should you prepare to pray the preparatory prayer? The only certain way out of this infinite regression was not to pray at all, which was hardly the outcome that divines were seeking. Although some earlier writers had simply dismissed such concerns out of hand,[12] in the 17th century it became clear that the difficulties were real. John Preston's highly popular *The Saints Daily Exercise* tackled it head-on:

> Many times when we are not fit [to pray], we thinke to make our selues fitter, by spending time in thoughts, and meditations before, which I denie not but they may be profitable, but . . . the best way to fit our selues to this duty . . . is, not to stay till we haue prepared our selues by meditation, but to fall presently vpon the dutie.

If you want to pray, then pray. Attempting preparation before turning to God was like trying to fight Satan without divine support. Richard Sibbes, similarly, worried that some people felt themselves unworthy to pray, and urged that 'as every Grace increaseth by exercise of it selfe, so doth the grace of prayer; by prayer wee learne to pray'.[13] This is both theologically and pastorally appealing, but it means that the notion of preparing to pray, and of approaching God with appropriate reverence,

---

[7] Foxe, *Actes and monuments* (1583), 1195. Cf. Perkins, *Exposition of the Lords prayer*, 25; Parr, *Abba Father*, 8–9.
[8] Blair, *Life*, 96–7.
[9] On 'watching', that is, forgoing sleep, see Ryrie, 'Sleeping, waking and dreaming'.
[10] Day, *Booke of Christian Prayers*, sig. ☞3r, fo. 1r. Cf. Hayward, *Sanctuarie of a troubled soule* (1602), 199–205; Themylthorpe, *Posie of Praiers*, 25–7; Sparke, *Crumms of comfort*, sig. A10r–v.
[11] Clarke, *Holy Incense*, 13.
[12] Bull, *Christian praiers*, 14–15.
[13] Preston, *Saints Daily Exercise*, 34–6; Sibbes, *Bruised reede*, 148–50.

almost disappears. In that respect, Preston and Sibbes were swimming against a strong tide.

For the question of preparation was only a curtain-raiser for the whole, bitter dispute about formality and informality in prayer. This dispute might seem to fit the classic division between puritans and conformists.[14] Take, for example, the *Admonition* controversy between John Whitgift and Thomas Cartwright. In his systematic assault on the Book of Common Prayer, Cartwright eventually reached the collect for the twelfth Sunday after Trinity, which prays for 'those things which we in our unworthiness dare not ask'. To his ears, this 'carrieth with it still the note of the popish servile fear, and savoureth not of the confidence and reverent familiarity that the children of God have through Christ'. But Whitgift did not see Cartwright's confidence as reverent at all. The collect, he argued, was a

> token not of servile fear, but of true humility . . . God forbid that we should so presume of ourselves, that we should shut humility, and the acknowledging of our own unworthiness, from faithful and hearty prayer.[15]

Puritan zeal confronts Anglican humility: is there anything more to say?

A little. It is certainly true that most of those who argued for informality and immediacy in prayer were of a puritan stamp, such as Sibbes ('Goe boldly to God . . . neuer feare to go to God'), and Preston ('If thou come in [Christ's] name . . . it will breede boldnesse in thee').[16] There is John Dod, urging Christians to imitate the woman with haemorrhages, who boldly touched Christ's garment in the crowd without his permission; or John Winthrop, arguing that 'we should have religion in as familiar practice as our eatinge and drinkinge', since the alternative is to confine God to the church building and exclude him from everyday life.[17] But we can find some similar views from sources which are not quite so predictable. William Cowper, for example, urged

> Goe on with boldnesse to the throne of grace. . . . Praier . . . is the hand of a Christian, which is able to reach from earth to heauen, and take forth euery manner of good gift out of the Lords treasurie.[18]

Or consider the best-selling and controversy-shy Elizabethan collection of meditations ascribed—falsely—to St Augustine. One of these texts, 'Of the boldnesse of the soule that loueth God', declared that 'loue procureth familiaritie with God, familiaritie procureth boldnesse, boldnesse tast, and tast continuall hungering'.[19] No puritan could have put it better.

It is when we look at the other side of the debate, however, that partisan divisions really break down. Again, there are predictable voices. John Cosin would have us 'call vpon the awfull Maiesty of Almighty God . . . in the graue & pious language of Christs CHVRCH', and Lancelot Andrewes disparaged those who pray 'in familiar or

---

[14] See, for example, Nuttall, *Holy Spirit*, 58, 64–5.   [15] Whitgift, *Works*, II.475–6.

[16] Preston, *Saints Daily Exercise*, 140–3; Sibbes, *Bruised reede*, 26.

[17] Dod and Cleaver, *Ten sermons*, 65; Winthrop, *Papers*, 236.

[18] Cowper, *Triumph*, 88–90.   [19] 'Augustine', *Certaine select prayers*, sigs Q2r–4r.

homely manner' and 'make but a shallow of this great deep'. The Elizabethan homilies taught that 'the person, that so babbleth his words without sense in the presence of God' is 'a contemner of his almighty majesty'. 'Better it were not to pray', wrote Matthew Sutcliffe, 'then as some do without signe of humilitie, deuotion, or religious reuerence.'[20] But these views were not confined to the conformist establishment. A bridging figure like Daniel Featley was swift to condemn those who 'suddenly and rudely rush vpon Almighty God, neuer thinking that he is a consuming fire'. Standard moderate puritan texts from Henry Bull's prayers through to John Ball's catechism emphasized the need for 'reuerent feare' in prayer and urged that 'we may not rashly conceiue or vtter any thing before him'. No less a puritan luminary than Richard Rogers, while urging his readers to frequent prayer, went out of his way to add 'a speciall caution herein, that we do not for all our oft recourse to this duty, goe about them with the lesse reuerence'.[21]

The point is that most early modern Protestants would have applauded both sentiments. They aimed, like Jane Ratcliffe, to be 'neither over strange with God, like the ignorant that praieth nothing but out of bookes, nor over homely with him, like the vaine *Pharisaicall Puritans*'. No less a puritan than William Gouge had argued that words in prayer 'must be ... neither ouer-curious, nor ouer carelesse and loose'. The former error was a self-conscious affectation; the latter 'argueth too light esteeme, and too great neglect of him to whom wee make our prayer'. This middling position rejected formality because it used 'elegant & obscure' language, was led by custom, and tended to superstition, but it absolutely insisted that prayer must be 'full of decent Reuerence'.[22] Whitgift himself would have agreed. Like many others, he used the image of the patriarchal family to describe prayer. The Christian's model for prayer, he argued, is the 'due reverence that a good child oweth to a most natural and loving father'. Nicholas Byfield used the same image to convey the right blend of confidence and humility in prayer. A best-selling Elizabethan treatise took a slightly different tack, comparing the Christian to a wife faithfully and submissively petitioning her loving husband.[23] Prayer could be intimate, loving, and familiar, but never chatty, casual, or presumptuous.

Those patriarchal analogies are more than throwaway illustrations. The spectrum from formality to informality in prayer does not, in fact, map neatly onto the spectrum from conformist to puritan. Instead, it maps on to how socially determined particular approaches to piety were. It is no coincidence that John Preston's chief witness in his defence of informality was Martin Luther, a man whose reputation as a pastoral theologian rode very high amongst his British readers.[24] Luther's fiercely individualistic theology generally paid very little attention to

[20] Cosin, *Collection of Priuate Devotions*, A7r; Lancelot Andrewes, *Ninety-Six Sermons* (Oxford, 1870), III.33; *Certain Sermons or Homilies*, 324; Sutcliffe, *An Answere*, fos 60v–61r.
[21] Featley, *Ancilla Pietatis*, 14–17; Bull, *Christian praiers*, 3–4; Ball, *Short treatise*, 113; Rogers, *Seven treatises*, 380.
[22] Ley, *Patterne of Pietie*, 59–60; Gouge, *Whole-Armor of God*, 340–1; Bod MS Rawl C.473 fo. 4r; Scudder, *Christians daily walke* (1628), 50; Sandys, *Sermons*, 104; Cowper, *Triumph*, 87; Gouge, *Whole-Armor of God*, 413.
[23] Whitgift, *Works*, II.476; Byfield, *Marrow of the Oracles* (1622), 254; Hutchins, *Davids Sling*, fos 5v–6r.
[24] Ryrie, 'Afterlife of Lutheran England'.

human society, emphasizing an intimate, immanent relationship with God. As such he exemplified a passionately informal, even abandoned model of prayer. Reformed theology, by contrast, emphasized both the Christian community and God's transcendance. The result was that, as Susan Karant-Nunn has pointed out, where Luther sought intimacy, Calvin valued dignity and submission.[25] The struggle for informality can be seen, not simply as puritans against conformists, but as a Lutheran insurgency against a Calvinist establishment; and within our period, at least, the insurgency was contained.

One factor above all kept the conformist-Calvinist view in the ascendant. Of all the social analogies used for prayer, the most powerful was not familial but royal. To pray was to approach God as a petitioner approaches a king. 'Let vs ... go boldely vnto the throne of grace', urged the epistle to the Hebrews, and as this image of prayer became a firm favourite amongst Protestant devotional writers, throne-talk frequently eclipsed the command to boldness.[26] As Virginia Reinburg has pointed out, the steady Protestant comparison between prayer and petitioning a king was a deliberate ploy. As well as underlining Protestants' political conformity—no small concern, for a movement frequently accused of sedition—it was a stark contrast with medieval piety's complex, mediated systems of patronage-prayer. Catholic devotees commonly approached God through his saints, just as petitioners approached their sovereigns via nobles and courtiers. Protestants had direct access to the king's person.[27] The price was that the kingly metaphor for prayer became all-pervasive.

Sometimes this was mere analogy. A fanciful evangelical pamphlet first published in 1547, *An heauenly acte concernynge how man shal lyue*, presented the Ten Commandments in the genre of an act of Parliament, complete with lawyerly jargon: St Paul became God's Lord Chancellor, Moses the Speaker, Christ the vice-gerent. It struck a chord: it went through three editions in a single year and was reprinted as late as 1604. It may have given Hugh Latimer the idea of comparing the coming heavenly kingdom to a great parliament.[28] The same blurring of the line between secular and divine authority can be seen in the 17th-century proverb that spending the Sabbath idly was like clipping the queen's coins, or in Arthur Hildersam's analogy between receiving the sacrament unworthily and vandalizing the royal arms.[29] Innocent enough, perhaps, but it all tied heavenly and earthly hierarchies together.

When these images were applied to prayer, however, they emphasized the peril of speaking improperly to a king whose wrath is death. This was an argument for

[25] Karant-Nunn, *Reformation of Feeling*, 130.
[26] Hebrews 4:16. The image dominates Richard Sibbes' *The spirituall favorite at the throne of grace* (1640: RSTC 22512). Amongst many, many other uses of it, see Norden, *Pensiue mans practise*, 7; Cowper, *Triumph*, 84; Primrose, *Christian Mans Teares*, 56; Sparke, *Crumms of comfort*, sig. H11v; Hinde, *Faithfull Remonstrance ... of Iohn Bruen*, 72; Capel, *Capel's Remains*, sig. A7v. Preston worried about the Christian who 'dares not come to the throne of grace': Preston, *Saints Daily Exercise*, 143.
[27] Reinburg, 'Hearing Lay People's Prayer', 22–33.
[28] *An heauenly acte concernynge how man shal lyue* (1547?: RSTC 95), esp. sigs A5v, b1r; Latimer, *Sermons by Hugh Latimer*, 362–3.
[29] Manningham, *Diary*, 45; Bradshaw and Hildersam, *Direction*, 7–8.

preparing before prayer: Perkins argued that you should no more 'boldlye without consideration . . . rushe into the presence of GOD' than you would burst into a prince's chamber. William Narne cited the Biblical story of Esther, who risked forfeiting her life by coming to the king uninvited: we too, he argued, take our lives in our hands whenever we come into God's presence.[30] To minimize this risk in an earthly court, petitioners make themselves presentable, and devotees were urged to do the same. 'What Courtier presumeth to come into the Kings presence in stinking and nastie cloathes?', Daniel Featley asked.[31] Those who used this analogy were of course clear that it referred to inner, moral cleanliness rather than dressing smartly, but you would not need too many scruples to fear that praying while unkempt was disrespectful. No wonder Blair, even in great urgency, stopped to dress before praying.

The same logic applied to the conduct of the royal audience. 'As mortall men endure not the sawcie and vnrespectfull carriage of suiters', Elnathan Parr warned, 'so GOD much more requires, that wee should serue him in feare.'[32] Instead, as Robert Harris put it,

> pause before thou speak. . . . If a man would not deliuer an Oration to a Prince ex tempore and sodainely, it will not become vs to open our mouths rashly before our maker.[33]

Narne recalled how the boldest commoner can become tongue-tied when actually faced with a king, and urged the same respect. 'As it is an easie thing to speake of a King, but not so easie to speake to him: so is it easie to speake of GOD, but not to GOD.' A prayer, Thomas Tymme argued, must be made in all humility and discretion 'that it may be fit for Gods court of Requests'.[34] The obvious conclusion was that whatever was said should be concise and to the point. Kings are busy people. Speak before God, Michael Sparke urged, as before 'a King or great person', meaning, 'be not rash with thy mouth . . . for God is in the heauens, & thou art on the earth; therefore let thy words be few'.[35] Say what you have to, and then stop bothering him.

That may seem an odd lesson to draw for prayer, but there is more. The royal analogy taught Christians not only how to approach God, but how to manage him. Thomas Becon argued that, just as petitioners tidy themselves up before approaching a king, so a devotee should 'vse some menes wherby, he maye excyte & stoore vp the beneuolence and good wyll of God towarde hym'—losing sight, for a moment, of the evangelical doctrines of grace and total depravity. A lifetime later, Nicholas Bownde urged his hearers to pledge their faithfulness to God in

[30] Perkins, *Exposition of the Lords prayer*, 24; Narne, *Pearle of prayer*, 318.

[31] Featley, *Ancilla Pietatis*, 11; cf. Henry Tozer, *Directions for a Godly Life: Especially for Communicating at the Lord's Table* (1628: RSTC 24161), 56.

[32] Parr, *Abba Father*, 11; cf. Hildersam, *Doctrine of Fasting*, 83.

[33] Harris, *Peters enlargement* (1624), sig. A3r–v.

[34] Narne, *Pearle of prayer*, 326; Tymme, *Chariot of Devotion*, 18.

[35] Sparke, *Crumms of comfort*, sig. A4v, quoting (and taking out of context) George Webbe's words in Rogers, *Garden* (1616), sig. F8v.

prayer, arguing that when you vow faithful service to a king, that 'will greatly mooue him'.[36] Thomas Goodwin took this even further. It was one thing to explain the need to persist in prayer by analogy with petitioners' patience in waiting for an audience with a king, a loose but serviceable analogy. It was another to point out that 'suitors at Court observe . . . their times of begging, when they have Kings in a good mood, which they will be sure to take the advantage of', and to suggest that Christians, too, should choose their moment to pray, and 'strike, whilest the iron is hot'. His professed meaning—that if we feel the urge to pray, we should seize the moment—is unexceptionable, but the metaphor almost overwhelms it.[37]

The royal image did not quite sweep all before it. It could be used, not to daunt the believer with God's unapproachability, but to fashion an alluring—and very Lutheran—paradox. Yes, God is more majestic than any earthly king, but this makes his invitation to intimate familiarity all the more astonishing. 'Whom would it not delight to talke with the Kinges grace, if he were amytted therto?', asked Becon. 'What a treasure than it is to talke with the King of Kynges & Lorde of Lordes.'[38] John Brinsley described his book, *The True Watch*, as 'your key into . . . the presence chamber of his glorious Maiesty: whereby you may bee admitted at all times, to most familiar conference'.[39] This kind of argument naturally shifted in the 1640s, when royal imagery became rather more problematic. Even some royalists were wary of identifying God too closely with Charles I. John Milton's solution was to see worldly monarchy and divine kingship as opposites, not analogies. He contrasted 'those cautious words to be us'd before Gentiles and Tyrants' to 'those filial words, of which we have so frequent use in our access with freedom of speech to the Throne of Grace'.[40] God is king of kings, but that does not mean the earthly variety can tell us anything about him.

Another undercurrent questioned whether the royal analogy was valid at all. There is a little of this in the Elizabethan homily on prayer, which amongst other things attacked prayer to saints. It recognized that 'in king's houses, and courts of princes, men cannot be admitted, unless they first use the help and means of some special nobleman'. But God, the homilist pointed out, is not limited like a human king, an obvious point which collapses this and many other royal analogies. A posthumous treatise by the moderate cleric Thomas Knell worried that devotees were allowing the royal analogy to distort their prayers, leading them to imagine that God 'is but a man, to whom they speake faire, and flatter, to receiue some thing of him thereby'.[41] A more sustained questioning of the image came from the stout anti-puritan Ambrose Fisher. Some puritans, he claimed, disliked the collective recitation of the general confession, on the grounds that petitioners before a prince do not speak in unison but choose one person to act 'as a common mouth'.

---

[36] Becon, *Newe pathwaye unto praier*, sig. L4v; Bownde, *Medicines for the plague*, 143.

[37] Goodwin, *Returne of Prayers*, 14–15, 88–9.

[38] Becon, *Newe pathwaye unto praier*, sig. B1v.

[39] Brinsley, *True Watch* (1611), II. sig. N2v.

[40] John Milton, *Complete Prose Works*, ed. Merritt Y. Hughes (New Haven and London, 1962), III.506.

[41] *Certain Sermons or Homilies*, 291; Knell, *Godlie and necessarie Treatise*, sig. A3v.

Fisher had fun with this. The same logic, he pointed out, would prohibit psalm-singing, 'for it will hardly be decent before a Prince to declare a suite singing'. And, he added mischievously, this threatened to restore prayer to saints, 'seeing we hardly approch to Princes, but by manifold mediators'.[42] The point was clear: God is not a human king, and metaphors of kingship should be kept on a short leash.

In our period at least, this was so much shouting into the wind. In the 1640s, these images would change very rapidly, and habits of prayer with them, but for the time being, prostrating yourself fearfully before the throne of grace was what most Protestants thought prayer was, and their image of what a throne might be was formed from the only comparison they had to hand. It was natural; for the regimes in power and those who wanted to be their friends, it was also politic; and it gives a consistent undertow of formality and dignity to what follows.

WORDS, SILENCE, AND GROANS

If, as William Narne pointed out, Christians could become tongue-tied with awe when before God; and if, as Protestant theologians all affirmed, what mattered was the prayer of the heart uttered by the indwelling Spirit, not the words spoken by the lips; then did prayer need to be spoken at all?

The simple answer was no. The official homilies taught that 'there needeth no speech when we pray'. As the best-selling advice book *Keepe within Compasse* put it, 'A religious man may pray and neuer open his lips'. It was an oft-repeated truism.[43] As Robert Bruce put it, 'sighing, mourning, and lifting vp of the eies, is als good language to God, as any language spoken be the toong'.[44] The point was and is almost too obvious to need making.

Yet if silent prayer was permissible, it was not recommended. Perkins' conclusion—that 'the voice then in priuat praier . . . may be omitted, for it is not absolutely necessary'—conveys the grudging sense of this approval. The dumb-struck and the inarticulate could take comfort in the fact that they could still pray truly, but this was definitely not ideal. God, promised Robert Harris, 'will pitie speechlesse prayers, as wee doe maimed men, whose tongues are cut out'.[45] Perkins, discussing deathbed prayer, pointed out that the dying may reach a point at which they are incapable of speech: at that point, he reassured his readers, silent prayer is

---

[42] Fisher, *Defence of the liturgie*, 45–6.

[43] *Certain Sermons or Homilies*, 322; Trundle, *Keepe within Compasse*, sig. A4v. The Biblical passages used to justify this were Hannah praying silently (I Samuel 1:13–15), and—more tendentiously, but more frequently—Moses at the Red Sea, who is not recorded as praying in words but to whom God said, 'Wherefore cryest thou vnto me?' (Exodus 14:15). See Becon, *Newe pathwaye unto praier*, sigs C2v–3r, C4r; *Deuout psalmes and colletes* (1547: RSTC 2999), sig. A2r–v; Latimer, *Sermons by Hugh Latimer*, 143–4; Coverdale, *Devout meditacions*, 1v; *Certain Sermons or Homilies*, 314; Knell, *Godlie and necessarie Treatise*, sig. C1v; Perkins, *Exposition of the Lords prayer*, 4–5; Ball, *Short treatise*, 108; Warwick, *Spare-Minutes*, 30–1.

[44] Bruce, *Sermons Preached*, sig. K2r.

[45] Perkins, *Exposition of the Lords prayer*, 166–7; Harris, *Peters enlargement* (1627), 34–5. Cf. Linaker, *Comfortable treatise* (1595), 47; Perkins, *Whole treatise*, 285.

entirely appropriate. Lewis Bayly, similarly, provided a prayer to be said while dying, 'with thy tongue if thou canst, else pray in thy heart and minde'. There is no doubting which is the preferred option.[46]

Similarly, when we find active approval of silent prayer, it is usually qualified, a special case or being used to make some other polemical point. Sometimes it is an echo of medieval or contemporary Catholic piety, in which silent prayer was much more highly valued, and which persisted in the post-Reformation primer tradition.[47] John Bradford's injunction to say the psalms 'in the hart', and his contrasting comment that 'children . . . vse their tonges & words in praying to thee', betray his dependence on the meditations of Juan Luis Vives. John Foxe approvingly quoted from the Inquisition's account of the piety of the Waldensians, who would daily 'continue in their prayers with silence, so long as a man may say 30. or 40. times pater noster',[48] but this would remain a historical curiosity until the advent of the Quakers.

Alternatively, silent prayer might be praised in order to disparage thoughtless recitation. Heart without tongue was better than tongue without heart. Thomas Tuke compared the voiceless and the heartless prayer—'one praies and speakes not, another speakes and praies not'—not to praise the former but to condemn the latter. Prayers such as Edward Dering's—'Graunt good Father, that I may not praye in words or in sound of speach, but in spirite and faith'—do not advocate silent prayer, they damn mere lip-labour. Or again, silent prayer was recommended for use 'in company, in the midst of businesses, when we are ouerwhelmed with temptations'— that is, when there is no alternative.[49] But for real advocacy of silent prayer, we are driven to one argument, which surfaces relatively late in our period and would remain marginal until the Civil War era. This was the claim that, as Daniel Dyke put it, 'sometimes affection . . . is so strong that wordes faile'. Even Dyke, however, expected that such devotees would 'haue more matter then wordes' and be 'short' in their prayers; that is, they would use few, heartfelt words, not lapse into silence. Robert Harris took this a step further, arguing that silent prayer could be 'the strongest voyce of all' when speech fails. But for the time being, this remained an unusual view.[50]

Why this dislike of silent prayer? Extremists like William Hacket, who prayed with 'strange pawses . . . saying nothing', but 'onely groned and murmured to himselfe', discredited silence.[51] Much more damaging was the association with Catholic piety, which even made whispering or murmuring suspect. Becon insisted that in prayer, God wants 'the pure affeccion of the herte, & not the whysperynge noyse of the lyppes', and later generations did not forget the stereotype of papists who 'mutter ouer vpon there beades'.[52] Throughout our period, the words *murmur* and *mutter* were strongly linked to sedition, carping and cowardice. Silent or

---

[46] Perkins, *Salve for a sicke man*, 89–90; Bayly, *Practise of pietie*, sig. Ll2r.

[47] See, for example, *Godly garden*, fo. 115v.

[48] Bradford, *Godlie meditations*, sig. I5v; Foxe, *Actes and monuments* (1583), 236 (recte 232).

[49] Tuke, *Practise of the faithfull*, 2; Dering, *Godly priuate praiers*, sig. F4v; Gouge, *Whole-Armor of God*, 411.

[50] Dyke, *Two Treatises*, 80–1; Harris, *Peters enlargement* (1627), 26; cf. Nuttall, *Holy Spirit*, 65–6.

[51] Sutcliffe, *An Answere*, fo. 60v.

[52] Becon, *Newe pathwaye unto praier*, sig. C4r; Saxby, 'Miscellany', fo. 69v.

inaudible prayer had a whiff of danger about it; it might cloak heresy or treason. Thomas Playfere argued, with a hint of menace, that 'as our dealing with men must be as in the sight of God: so our prayer to God, must be as in the hearing of men'. His phrasing—*as* in the hearing of men—implies that we should still pray aloud even if alone; we should make no prayer unless we would be willing for it to be overheard. Walls have ears. Interestingly, Playfere insisted absolutely categorically on vocal prayer. 'It is euident', he preached in the turbulent 1590s, 'that as meate and drink . . . must go in at the mouth: so on the other side, prayer, the spirituall food of the soule, must go out of the mouth.'[53] What made it evident? Perhaps it would have been indelicate to explain.

But there were also positive reasons to favour vocal prayer. There were numerous Biblical precedents.[54] There was a perceived obligation to God, who 'gaue vs the voice, as well as the hart to blesse him withall'. The whole body should glorify God, but the tongue above all, which was 'of all other parts of a mans body the most proper and excellent instrument of Gods glory'.[55] There were, in addition, practical points: praying aloud can be used to 'keepe the wandering minde in compasse'. 'Our minds begin to stray from our Prayer conceiued in silence', Gervase Babington pointed out—although, oddly enough, this obvious and practical point was made relatively rarely.[56] Another, slightly commoner practical argument held that praying aloud will 'edifie the brethren' who hear you. As such, Gouge pointed out, it helps brethren to be unified, and so to 'pertake of the mutuall prayers one of another'. John Browning's slightly different view was that 'charitie, in the good of others requires it; for by our voices cheerefulnesse, we cheere, encourage, and edifie one another'.[57]

The people who were really edified by vocal prayer, however, were the devotees themselves. The most cited reason for praying aloud is that it 'stirreth vp the affections of the heart', and the 'inward desire and feruencie of the mind'.[58] This could, ideally, become self-reinforcing. 'The voice often stirs vp the hart', Perkins said, '& againe, the vehemency of affection doth often draw out a voice.' Speech was compared to bellows, which inflame the heart, or a chimney, which by containing the fire of devotion intensifies it. But it was only the heat of devotion bursting into words which produced speech in the first place.[59] In other words, silent prayer implied both that your devotion was no more than smouldering, and that you were willing to allow it to sputter out. Browning, lamenting the religious failings of his age in time-honoured preacherly fashion, cited the use of silent prayer as evidence: 'Surely, that the mouth should be wanting, never was heard til our

---

[53] Playfere, *Power of praier*, 7.
[54] Coverdale, *Devout meditacions*, fo. 2r.
[55] Perkins, *Exposition of the Lords prayer*, 166; Parr, *Abba Father*, 27; Gouge, *Whole-Armor of God*, 412; Becon, *Newe pathwaye unto praier*, sig. M4r–v.
[56] Perkins, *Whole treatise*, 276; Babington, *Profitable Exposition*, 27. Cf. Parr, *Abba Father*, 27; Preston, *Saints Daily Exercise*, 86–7; Clarke, *Holy Incense*, 48.
[57] Ball, *Short treatise*, 109; Gouge, *Whole-Armor of God*, 411; Browning, *Concerning publike-prayer*, 76.
[58] Perkins, *Whole treatise*, 276; Bull, *Christian praiers*, 33. Cf. Preston, *Saints Daily Exercise*, 86; Ball, *Short treatise*, 109; and see above, p. 133.
[59] Perkins, *Exposition of the Lords prayer*, 166; Gouge, *Whole-Armor of God*, 412; Parr, *Abba Father*, 27.

frozen age.'[60] Indeed, the voice may even have given prayer power. Richard Baker's popular *Meditations and Disquisitions* argued that we should pray aloud so as

> to fright the devill. For, he sees not our hearts, but hee heares our tongues: and when he heares our words . . . he feares they come from our hearts, in that feare he trembles.[61]

This was a little idiosyncratic, but it only reinforces the underlying point. In almost all circumstances, prayer aloud was seen as the ideal. Silent prayer, while legitimate, was a poor relation. The range of arguments advanced to explain this tells its own story: before Protestants had logically justified this prejudice, it was something they knew in their bones, and it made sense. After all, for Protestants, prayer was not a matter of contemplation, ecstasy, or spiritual communion, but of 'familiar communicacion with God', speaking as a child to a father, a wife to a husband, or a subject to a king.[62] With one significant exception which we shall come to shortly, that communication was therefore verbal. While words could indeed remain unspoken, that must surely always be second best.

Indeed, Protestant prayer was not only normally spoken: it was often noisy. A few commentators did advise praying quietly, on the grounds that loud prayer 'wearieth the spirits', is 'clamorous' and may even attract mockery,[63] but such soft voices seem to have been shouted down. John Welsh's prayers at night were said to make 'a silent but constant whispering noise', and his wife was able to sleep through them, but they were loud enough to wake visitors.[64] Under other circumstances Welsh himself, like many others, especially puritans and particularly Scots, made a virtue of volume. We have already met his and John Carter's noisy prayers in their respective parish churches, and Carter's deliberately 'very loud' prayers at home.[65] Archibald Johnston of Wariston's diary repeatedly mentions shouting during his prayers. An early Elizabethan private prayer book reads, 'Heere mee O mi god: beholde how lowde I crie vnto thee', words which could scarcely have been whispered. 'Religion they bawl out', John Phillips said in his vicious satire of puritan piety,[66] and certainly overhearing vocal prayer could be a memorable experience. John Livingstone told a tale of Robert Bruce's being late for the pulpit. A bellman was sent to fetch him, but returned, perplexed, to say that he did not think Bruce would come. He had listened at Bruce's door, and 'I hear him always saying to another that he will not nor cannot goe except the other goe with him, and I do not hear the other answer him a word at all'. Livingstone made fun of the bellman's foolishness, in not realizing that Bruce was speaking to God,[67] but whether the bellman really was a simpleton, or whether this mode of prayer was

[60] Browning, *Concerning publike-prayer*, 76.
[61] Richard Baker, *Meditations and Disquisitions upon the Lords prayer* (1636: RSTC 1223), 6.
[62] Becon, *Newe pathwaye unto praier*, sig. B1r.
[63] Bod MS Rawl C.473 fo. 4r; Bernard, *Faithfull Shepherd*, 28–9.
[64] Tweedie, *Select Biographies*, 37.
[65] See above, pp. 157, 158.
[66] Wariston, *Diary*, 81–2, 91; and cf. 26; FSL MS V.a.482 fo. 12v; John Phillips, *A Satyr against Hypocrites* (1655: Wing P2101), 24.
[67] Tweedie, *Select Biographies*, 307.

genuinely unusual, is harder to say. Bayly's dictum—'prayer in priuate deuotion should be one continued speech, rather than many broken fragments'—seems to suggest the former, but perhaps this kind of advanced prayer was not what Bayly had in mind.[68]

There are two significant exceptions to the rule that prayer was normally spoken aloud. One—the use of writing instead of speaking—we will return to in Chapter 12. The other was groaning and sighing. These practices had a much-cited proof-text in Romans 8:26, which describes the Spirit praying within the believer in sighs or groans, and implies that these are the noises Christians make when the ardour or urgency of prayer becomes inexpressible. John Craig has drawn our attention to groaning's place in the soundscape of early modern English worship.[69] The qualms about silent prayer which we have already discussed perhaps go some way to explain it: this was a compromise between speech and silence, in which the believers did not have to form words but could still audibly demonstrate a conformable piety, encourage others, and stir up their own affections.

The words *sigh* and *groan* were used almost interchangeably. George Herbert was one of a very few to distinguish them, writing that he 'sent a sigh to seek thee out' and then 'tun'd another (having store)/Into a grone'.[70] It is clear that a very wide range of sounds were meant. Sometimes we hear of inward sighing and 'the grones of our hearts which passeth in silence', a 'silent, yet lovely language of ardent and fervent desires'. It is common enough to find preachers, such as Bishop Earle's 'grave Divine', 'making his hearers . . . grone', but whether such groans were audible or not is another matter, as we shall see.[71] Daniel Featley suggests the aural range at play when he claims that 'the afflicted soule, which sometimes stealeth a groane, and fetcheth a sigh in the Church, offers vp often prayers with strong cries at home'. Certainly, we find references to 'hearty groans', 'groning and cryings out', even—in the case of one dying man unable to speak—'deep-diving and great groans'. Richard Greenham 'sent forth many sighes and grones' in prayer, 'so as sometime his wyfe hath thought him to bee very sick'.[72] These cases imply what decorum suggests: that the loudest groans tended to be reserved for private settings.

Groans were not necessarily wordless. Bayly offered a set of short prayers to be used in time of illness, which he described as 'sighes'.[73] But it was normal to see groaning as what you did when words failed you. Elizabeth Melville's *Godlie Dreame* described how she set herself to pray, 'but sighes our set me so,/I could doe nought, but groane, and say no more'. James Melville promised that the Spirit will 'steir thee vp with sighes and sobbes, and zealous motions in the minde that

---

[68] Bayly, *Practise of pietie*, 268.

[69] See above, p. 66; John Craig, 'Psalms, groans and dogwhippers: the soundscape of worship in the English parish church, 1547–1642' in Will Coster and Andrew Spicer (eds), *Sacred Space in Early Modern Europe* (Cambridge, 2005).

[70] Herbert, *Works*, 162.

[71] Norden, *Pensiue mans practise*, sig. A10r; Tweedie, *Select Biographies*, 21; Clarke, *Holy Incense*, sig. A5v; Earle, *Microcosmographie*, 9–10.

[72] Featley, *Ancilla Pietatis*, 4–5; Sandys, *Sermons*, 398; Wallington, *Notebooks*, 50; D'Ewes, *Autobiography*, 9; Parker and Carlson, *'Practical Divinity'*, 203.

[73] Bayly, *Practise of pietie*, 744.

cannot bee expressed be the mouth'.[74] Often, however, Protestants groaned not because they were too overwhelmed to speak, but rather because they were too inarticulate or stony-hearted to speak rightly. Robert Linaker encouraged his tongue-tied readers: 'if you cannot pray in set wordes, and in fine order ... can you not sigh and groane inwardly?' 'If words will not come, sigh', Robert Harris advised. In his first conversion, Richard Norwood prayed 'not so much in words (which I was unapt at) as in sighs and groans'.[75] Since these groans were the work of the Spirit, they were more eloquent than any words. Linaker said that we groan like a child who is too ill to speak, and that, like that child's, our groans speak volumes to our Father, 'piercing deeply into his eares'. Or, as George Herbert wrote,

> ... Grones are quick, and full of wings,
> And all their motions upward be;
> And ever as they mount, like larks they sing;
> The note is sad, yet musick for a King.

He also, in one of his rare poetic mis-hits, declared that all the worship of Solomon's temple 'is not so deare to thee as one good grone'.[76]

But as Craig has observed, this also gave groans another meaning; they could join the list of signs of election.[77] John Bradford described 'sighing vnspeakably' as a distinguishing characteristic of the godly. The proliferating 17th-century treatises on the signs of election habitually mentioned prayer with 'many earnest and hearty groanings'.[78] So, as night follows day, we find devotees praying to be able to groan. 'Graunt we pray not with lyppes alone,/But wyth the heart depe sighe and grone', begged an anonymous tract produced by the Marian exiles.[79] In other words, Protestants took comfort in and longed for groans very much as they did with tears. And indeed, groaning and weeping were very commonly bracketed together.[80]

The great difference between groaning and weeping, of course, is that weeping is at least partly involuntary, whereas anyone can groan. Hypocritical groaning was therefore an obvious concern. Richard Hooker mocked puritans for their lugubrious 'deepe sighes', but they shared his worry. A preacher in Oxford in 1605 warned his congregation that 'we canne not purge our selves or our soules with sighinge': real repentance cut deeper, a point which struck one young hearer enough that he wrote it down. The famed preacher Samuel Hieron penned a prayer doubting 'that

---

[74] Melville, *Spiritual Propine*, 6; Melville, *Godlie Dreame*, sig. A2v.

[75] Linaker, *Comfortable treatise* (1620), 130; Harris, *Peters enlargement* (1624), sig. A3v (this section was lifted wholesale in Clarke, *Holy Incense*, 145); Norwood, *Journal*, 81.

[76] Linaker, *Comfortable treatise* (1620), 130, 132; Herbert, *Works*, 106.

[77] Craig, 'Psalms, groans', 109–10; Wariston, *Diary*, 20.

[78] Bradford, *Godlie meditations*, sig. I4r; Bolton, *Three-fold treatise*, II.167, 175; Brinsley, *True Watch* (1611), II.32; Brinsley, *True Watch* (1608), 144–5; Byfield, *The Signes*, 96; Gouge, *Whole-Armor of God*, 336; and cf. Sutton, *Godly meditations* (1613), 389.

[79] *A trewe mirrour or glase wherin we maye beholde the wofull state of thys our realme of Englande* (Wesel?, 1556: RSTC 21777), sig. C3v. Cf. Dering, *Godly priuate praiers*, sig. D5v; Habermann, *Enimie of securitie*, 3; Sandys, *Sermons*, 398; Prid, *Glasse of Vaine-glorie* (1600), sig. F10v.

[80] See, amongst many examples, Bradford, *Godlie meditations*, sig. C2r; Maxey, *Golden chaine*, sig. B2r; Parr, *Abba Father*, 25; Andrewes, *Celestiall looking-glasse*, 17; Wariston, *Diary*, 165.

I groane vnder my sinnes with such an effectuall and pearcing feeling as is fit'.[81] However, there is surprisingly little in this vein, perhaps because groaning was so obviously volitional that there was limited scope for fooling others with it, and much less for fooling yourself.

Indeed, groaning's voluntary nature offered an opportunity. As well as being a sign of God's presence, it could be a means of stirring up the Spirit within yourself. Groaning, Elnathan Parr advised, will 'worke thee to more liuelinesse and feruency'. It was not unusual for printed prayers to put words like 'with sighes and grones vnfeined (for sinne) my humbled soule doth call vnto thee' into devotees' mouths. Such prayers invited unfeigned, but deliberate and self-conscious, effort.[82] As Henry Bull put it, if we find prayer difficult, we must 'labour with inward gronings vnto the Lorde'. Herbert described how, when his heart had no more praise to give God, 'Then will I wring it with a sigh or grone,/That thou mayst yet have more'. The image of groaning as *wringing* water from a stony heart is a compelling one, and one which a hostile witness of separatist worship had used half a century before. The conventiclers' practice was to 'sob, or sigh, as if they woulde wringe out teares'.[83] The groan or sigh, then, was an all-purpose devotional bridge. It could span the gap between speech and silence, between devotion and the inadequacy of words to express it, between the voluntary and the involuntary, between hearts of stone and hearts of flesh, and between the devotee's own actions and the work of the Holy Spirit. No wonder that early modern Protestants were so ready to be encouraged by their own, and by others', sighs and groans. Their hope, and experience, was that, when they tuned a sigh into a groan, the Spirit within them might take up the melody.

SET AND EXTEMPORE PRAYER

And so to the most controversial question about early modern prayer. Assuming that your prayer consisted of words, what should those words be?

In the 1640s, this dispute formed into hard and enduring battle-lines, drawing on disputes that had been flaring up regularly since the 1570s. By then, the two most clearly staked-out positions were those of the royalist establishment and the puritan radicals. The former held that public prayer must always, and private prayer should usually, follow set forms which provided full, authorized texts—in particular, the Book of Common Prayer. The latter rejected the use of any set forms at all, arguing that all prayers should be conceived by the person speaking them. But even after 1640, this division was less stark than it appears, and especially in our period. What if a set form was memorized and repeated as if it was the speaker's own words?[84] What if a devotee used a set form as the basis for a prayer, but did not

[81] Hooker, *Laws . . . Books I–IV*, 43; FSL MS V.a.23 fo. 18r; Hieron, *Helpe vnto Deuotion* (1608), 108.
[82] Parr, *Abba Father*, 45–6; Sparke, *Crumms of comfort*, sig. H11v.
[83] Bull, *Christian praiers*, 5; Herbert, *Works*, 157; Dexter, *Congregationalism*, 257.
[84] For an example of this, see Judith Maltby, *Prayer Book and People in Elizabethan and early Stuart England* (Cambridge, 1998), 7.

recite it verbatim? Was a set form which consisted wholly, or largely, of Biblical quotations (or paraphrases) equally offensive? Were set forms as offensive in private use as in public? What if extempore prayer fell into a linguistic rut (as it tends to), repeating the same phrases, or echoing phrases heard from others' prayers? Anyone who permitted ministers, or heads of household, to lead prayers saw those prayers as, in part, models to be imitated: what made imitation different from the use of a set form? Must prayer always be strictly extempore, or could it be written in advance by the person using it? Was using a detailed list of topics for prayer—as, for example, Sir Robert Harley did—tantamount to using a set prayer, or was it merely a memento? Could prayer even be considered and planned mentally in advance? Even John Milton had no time for 'unpremeditated babling'.[85] The point is twofold. First, the polar extremes of this debate were so rarefied as to be uninhabitable. Second, within our period, very few Protestants had even struck out purposefully toward those extremes. The liveliness of the disputes should not blind us to the broad, temperate consensus where most resided.[86]

In England, before 1640, flat opposition to the use of any set forms of prayer was a fringe view, the province of a few separatists. The establishment feared and roundly denounced such separatism, but within our period the threat remained more potential than real. The more serious critique was not of set forms in general, but of the Book of Common Prayer in particular. The classic Elizabethan puritans of the 1570s and 1580s did not seek to abolish all liturgy, nor to replace the Prayer Book with a 'rubric book' such as the 1644 Directory of Worship, which scarcely ever prescribed specific words to be said. Some of them wished to purge the Prayer Book of particular errors; others to replace it with something like the Scottish Book of Common Order, which still included copious prayers which the minister was encouraged to say verbatim. In other words, the serious debate about set prayers in public worship before 1640 was not about whether they were legitimate, but about the specific text of the Prayer Book, and whether and when ministers could legitimately pray extempore alongside their use of set forms.[87]

When we come to private prayer, the ideological lines were even blurrier. (We will return to the intermediate case of family prayer.) Certainly, Protestants' views on the relative merits of set and extempore prayer in private varied, but virtually everyone accepted that both were legitimate and would continue to exist side by side. The Laudian stormy petrel, John Cosin, came as close as anyone did to warning his readers against praying extempore in private, urging them to 'auoid, as neer as might be, all extemporall effusions of irkesome & indigested Prayers'— but even this was preference, not prohibition. Other conformists shared some of his

---

[85] BL Additional MS 70089 fo. 1r–v (I owe this reference to Fiona Counsell); John Milton, *Complete Prose Works*, ed. Merritt Y. Hughes (New Haven and London, 1962), III.507.

[86] On the dramatic hardening of these debates after 1640, see Christopher Durston, 'By the book or with the spirit: the debate over liturgical prayer during the English Revolution', *Historical Research* 79/203 (2006), 50–73; on the continued fluidity of the debate in the 1640s and 1650s, see Judith Maltby, '"Extravagencies and Impertinencies": Set Forms, Conceived and Extempore Prayer in Revolutionary England' in Mears and Ryrie, *Worship and the Parish Church*.

[87] Targoff, *Common Prayer*, 45–6; Durston, 'By the book', esp. 52–3.

qualms about 'Babbling', 'tedious repetitions and stammeringes', 'sencelesse Tau-
tologies', and 'idle words, irreverent, unmannerly, ridiculous . . . in their suddenly
conceived prayers'.[88] But these are criticisms not of extempore prayer as such,
merely of bad extempore prayer. Puritan divines, too, agreed that extempore prayer
could be 'confused, and either very defectiue or very tedious'. Christ's warning
against imitating the prayers of the 'heathen', who 'thinke to be heard for their
muche babling', was much cited. Robert Linaker, remarkably, admitted that these
problems beset his own prayers. In a published letter of pastoral counsel, he claimed
that his prayers were

> such poore, drie, naked, and sillie stuffe, both for words and matter, that . . . I should
> be vtterly ashamed, that you or any other should come within the hearing of my
> babling praiers.[89]

Hyperbole, perhaps, but if a published minister could make such claims, what hope
could there be for everyone else?

If you were naturally eloquent in your prayers, that was no better. Puritan
hagiographers sometimes lauded their heroes' prayers as 'filled with . . . savoury
arguments' or 'eloquent in her entercourse with God', but there was a profound
suspicion of 'painted eloquence or court-like complement' in prayer.[90] The 'ambition of eloquence & selfe complacencye', as Richard Waste called it, should have no
place in prayer. It was a form of 'effectation', Gouge argued, which 'sheweth that men
in praying seeke their owne praise rather then Gods'. Even in private, there was
danger in crafting elegant supplications rather than laying bare your heart. Joseph
Hall warned that 'God . . . will not be mocked by any fashionable forme of sute, but
requires holy and feeling intreatie'.[91] Perkins' disciple Thomas Tuke imagined two
devotees. One prays with 'sweetnesse of words' and 'keepes time and measure', but is
not heard; the other 'keepes no good order, yet gets his suit. . . . This had the arte, but
the other had the hart'. The proof of this is that such eloquence dries up in a real
spiritual crisis. Protestants were taught, in other words, to measure their own and
each others' prayer not by their 'gifts in performing them', but by 'the faith, the
sincerity, the obedience, the desires exprest in it'.[92] This helped, among other things,
to fuel Reformed Protestantism's stubborn anti-aesthetic: as Richard Kilby put it,
'God loveth plain speech'. 'Pack-staffe plainnes' came, for some, to represent 'the
simplicity of the Gospell'.[93] Such simplicity reached its apogee in the so-called Bay
Psalm Book of 1640, the first book printed in North America, which rejected 'the

[88] Cosin, *Collection of Priuate Devotions*, sigs A5r–v, A7r; FSL MS V.a.1 fo. 64r; Richard Bancroft,
Tracts Ascribed to Richard Bancroft, ed. Albert Peel (Cambridge, 1953), 72; Sutton, *Disce viuere*, 296;
Browning, *Concerning publike-prayer*, 85.
[89] Gouge, *Whole-Armor of God*, 416; Linaker, *Comfortable treatise* (1595), 46. Cf. Matthew 6:7.
[90] Capel, *Capel's Remains*, sig. A7v; Ley, *Patterne of Pietie*, 40.
[91] Bod. MS Rawl C.473 fo. 4v; Gouge, *Whole-Armor of God*, 340; Hall, *Arte of Divine Meditation*,
169; cf. Dod and Cleaver, *Ten sermons*, 187.
[92] Tuke, *Practise of the faithfull*, 2–3, 13; Dyke, *Mystery of selfe-deceiuing*, 104; Goodwin, *Returne of
Prayers*, 225.
[93] Kilby, *Burthen*, 22 (the phrase is emphasised with a manicule); Featley, *Ancilla Pietatis*, 22; cf.
Calvin, *Psalmes of David*, sig. *4v.

sweetnes of any paraphrase' on the grounds that 'Gods Altar needs not our pollish-ings', a claim amply justified by its garbled, sometimes almost incomprehensible verses.[94] That was extreme, but the central dilemma here was well summed up by Elnathan Parr. We should 'striue more to pray with feeling, then to bee eloquent'. But nor should we 'goe forward and backward . . . vnseasonably repeating ouer the same things. . . . God . . . likes not negligence or vnaduisedness in his seruice'.[95] So we should pray advisedly, but without eloquence; feelingly, but with good order. It would be enough to drive anyone to set forms.

Some separatists aside, virtually all British Protestants accepted set forms' legit-imacy. The radical Henoch Clapham, who had disavowed his former separatism but retained a great many idiosyncrasies, explicitly denounced the view that 'no wordes borrowed from else where . . . can be deliuered for Prayer'. After all, the heart, not the words, determine the value of a prayer. Even the straw man whom Ambrose Fisher created for his anti-puritan dialogue accepted that 'set prayer to priuate men may be granted'.[96] It is true that, as Peter Iver Kaufman has empha-sized, most puritans—and a great many others who would stretch that word to meaninglessness—believed that extempore prayer in private was ideal,[97] but they did not therefore reject set forms. James Melville put the standard argument nicely. All Christians ought to be able to 'speake vnto your God, and tell him your awin tale without . . . words put in your mouth be others'. And perhaps, when 'al had attained to that perfection, quhilk euery one should preasse vnto', that could be done, but for the time being some still needed 'grounds and formes, whereby to frame and direct their prayers'. So set forms had their place, and indeed Melville offered some of his own, but he begged his readers

> onely to vse these, till it shall please the holy Ghaist, b[y] the exercise of the word of God to instruct and plennish your hearts, so that out of the aboundance thereof your mouths may alwaies speake to the praise of God, edification of others, and your owne perpetuall joy.

The extemporal paradise was postponed.[98]

Set forms, then, were understood to be the prayers of the simple, which—as Miles Coverdale put it—'maie reduce them from grosse carnalitee and imperfec-cion to a more godly trade'. By the turn of the century, it was a cliché to describe them as 'a crutch to leane vpon': necessary for 'weak ones who haue good affections, but want inuention, vtterance, and such like parts'. Lurking in that conception is a worry about dependency, a fear that the invalids will become too accustomed to their crutches ever to walk unaided.[99] Before the Reformation, images had

---

[94] *The Whole Booke of Psalmes, Faithfully Translated into English Metre* (Cambridge, MA, 1640: RSTC 2378), sig. **3v.

[95] Parr, *Abba Father*, 28–32.

[96] Clapham, *Tract of Prayer*, sig. A4v; Fisher, *Defence of the liturgie*, 11.

[97] Kaufman, *Prayer, Despair and Drama*, 16–17.

[98] Melville, *Spiritual Propine*, 6–8.

[99] Coverdale, *Devout meditacions*, fo. 2r; Perkins, *Whole treatise*, 277; Tymme, *Chariot of Devotion*, 37; Preston, *Saints Daily Exercise*, 83; 'Dwalphintramis' [i.e. John/Richard Bernard?], *The Anatomy of the Service-Book* (1641?: Wing B1998), 101; Hinde, *Faithfull Remonstrance . . . of Iohn Bruen*, 69–70.

sometimes been described as lay people's books, necessary for 'yonglynges' in the
faith, but in fact they had formed a part of everyone's piety, clergy and laity, young
and old alike.[100] Did set forms, similarly, masquerade as temporary supports for the
weak but instead form pillars of almost everyone's practice? Did anyone, in fact,
outgrow them?

Some, clearly, did. When Richard Norwood first set himself to regular prayer,
'being altogether unapt to conceive of myself fit words of prayer, I used some of those
prayers at the end of the Bible', presumably meaning those in the metrical psalter.
A year or more later he first 'practiced to pray without a set form of prayer'.[101] Aged
twenty-six, Elizabeth Isham detected 'dullnes and a decay' in her devotions, and
resolved that 'insted of often saying my catichisme . . . [and] my prayres often with
the commandments and the Creed', she would devote herself every evening to self-
examination, to thanksgiving, and to 'making known my wants'. But this did not
mean she was abandoning set forms. We find her, five years later, reading 'prayres in
divers Bookes, that I might the better learn to pray my selfe'.[102] She might totter a few
steps unaided, but the crutches were never cast away.

It was a standard puritan view that 'they are very weake Christians that cannot
pray without a prescribed forme'. We do not need set forms to speak to other
people, divines reasoned, so why should we need one to speak to God? The simplest
peasant, Robert Bolton argued, can plead for what he needs before his betters: what
more is prayer?[103] Perhaps they even meant it. But pleading your case before your
betters is never very easy, less so if it cannot be done face to face, and less so still if
you are reared on fearsome warnings about approaching your betters inappropri-
ately. If set forms of words for doing so are all but universally known, most people
would find it merely sensible to stick to them.

In practice, extempore prayer was and was seen to be an exceptional gift, above
most people's ambitions. Lewis Bayly's suggestion to pray extempore 'if thou haue
the gift of Prayer' may seem oddly passive, but was realistic.[104] Most people
assumed that they did not have it and were not about to get it. Richard Baxter
recalled that, in his Shropshire childhood in the 1620s, his pious father—reviled by
his neighbours as a puritan—never prayed 'but by a Book or Form, being not ever
acquainted then with any that did otherwise'. Until he left home he had never
heard anyone pray extempore. Elizabeth Isham did not have quite such a sheltered
childhood. When their minister visited during her mother's illness, she was moved
by 'those effectuall prayiers which he powred out for her, having a good gift in
praying extempory', but the implication was that this was a special, and specifically
ministerial gift.[105] When Samuel Hieron took up his Devon cure of Modbury in

[100] Ann Eljenholm Nichols, 'Books-for-laymen: the demise of a commonplace', *Church History* 56
(1987), 457–73; Erasmus, *Enchiridion*, 178.
[101] Norwood, *Journal*, 83, 91.
[102] Isham, 'Confessions', fo. 28r–v; Isham, 'Diary', 1635, 1640.
[103] Gouge, *Whole-Armor of God*, 418; Preston, *Saints Daily Exercise*, 83; Bolton, *Three-fold treatise*,
II 168–9.
[104] Bayly, *Practise of pietie*, 317.
[105] Baxter, *Reliquiae Baxterianae*, 3–4; Isham, 'Confessions', fo. 11r.

1599, he found that his parishioners were willing to pray in private, but could only do so with 'stammering and lisping tongues'. It led Hieron to recognize that 'there is a great deale more arte in the cariage of a sute to be put vppe vnto God . . . then euery one . . . can at the first attaine vnto'. Hence his best-selling book *A Helpe Vnto Deuotion*. In the second edition, Hieron added prayers for use by people in various walks of life, from magistrates to students. Strikingly, his prayer for ministers, and *only* that one, was glossed with an apology for implying that other ministers could not form their own prayers. Clearly he assumed that, when dealing with lay people, that implication was usually correct, and he also reckoned that some ministers, at least, needed the help.[106] George Herbert's country parson faced a similar problem, but was untroubled by it. He simply taught his people their private prayers 'till they have learned them'.[107]

Of course, the best evidence that most British Protestants saw no need to discard their 'crutches' is the torrent of set forms which flowed off the printing presses.[108] The existence of hundreds of different books of prayers, many of them best-sellers, and many of them written by the best-known divines of the day, puritans and conformists alike, tells its own story. That is, it tells us that there was a broad, deep, and persistent market for pre-written prayers which all parts of the religious establishment were keen to encourage, or at least willing to exploit. It does not tell us anything about the large majority of the population who did not use these books, whether because they could not read them, could not afford them, did not want them, or did not need them. Nor, in itself, does it tell us anything about how those who owned books of prayers used them. But it does give us some important clues.

The sheer scale and variety of printed prayers is the first of these. As Virginia Reinburg has pointed out, the Book of Hours tradition had long accustomed pious and literate western Christians to collecting prayers 'the way twentieth-century cooks collect recipes'. The result was a habit of pious 'rummaging' through your collection to find a prayer to fit the occasion.[109] In the Reformation period, the range of choices expanded exponentially. Even in 1542 Thomas Becon was impressed by the 'plentie of prayers prepared for vs in the Englysshe tonge . . . [and] publyshed vniuersally', but the deluge had scarcely begun. Authors themselves regularly acknowledged the fact. Nicholas Themylthorpe hoped that if readers used his new prayer book, it would 'auoyde the trouble of reading many, the number of keeping many and most of all the burthen of bearing many. . . . My selfe and some of my friends are desirous to haue one onely Booke to beare about vs'. In the same year, Elnathan Parr agreed that there were 'many good Prayer-bookes in euery mans hand'.[110] But the hope that any one book could satisfy any one devotee

---

[106] Hieron, *Helpe vnto Deuotion* (1608), sigs A7r–8v (at least 22 editions 1608–40); Samuel Hieron, *A Helpe Vnto Deuotion* (1610: RSTC 13406.5), 389. Cf. Clarke, *Collection*, 38–9.

[107] Herbert, *Works*, 241.

[108] Tyrwhit, *Elizabeth Tyrwhit's Morning and Evening Prayers*, 30.

[109] Virginia Reinburg, 'Prayer and the Book of Hours' in Roger S. Wieck (ed.), *Time Sanctified: The Book of Hours in Medieval Art and Life* (New York, 1988), 40.

[110] Becon, *Newe pathwaye vnto praier*, sig. B1v; Themylthorpe, *Posie of Praiers*, sigs A3v, A5r; Parr, *Abba Father*, sig. A6r.

was increasingly forlorn. Prayer-books themselves sometimes assume that their readers are using other prayer-books in tandem.[111]

Indeed, divines positively recommended variety. Those who always stick to one form, William Gouge argued, 'little obserue Gods different manner of dealing with them at seuerall times'.[112] James Perrott compared his readers not to recipe-collectors but to herb-gatherers, who 'goe not onely to one garden, medow, or fielde to gather them, but vnto many'. This is what Elizabeth Isham did aged twelve: gathered her daily devotions from a wide range of sources, 'not tieing my selfe alwaies to one Praire Booke for I found that viriaty quickened my Spirites'.[113] Variety was a long-term as well as a daily business. New prayers or collections would be found, used assiduously for a while, and then displaced by others. Archibald Johnston of Wariston, for example, spent a couple of weeks working his way systematically through Byfield's *Marrow of the oracles of God*, using its prayers as he went, before moving on to prayers by Lewis Bayly, Daniel Featley, and Henry Scudder.[114] Early modern Protestants, in other words, used set prayers like modern listeners use recorded music. Individuals would have favourite items and genres, but novelties were always being sampled, could take up places alongside reliable classics for a while, and might even join their ranks. Diverse materials were jumbled together according to individual taste and without regard for publishers' intentions. There were set forms, but there was not common prayer.[115]

Once chosen, how were set prayers used? Earlier in our period, most authors seemed to expect users to read them verbatim from the page. Becon promised that, if you wished to pray but did not know how, his *Flour of godly praiers* would 'minister to thee godly, conuenyente and mete prayers'. He gives us a glimpse of what he meant, along with an outrageous piece of product-placement, in his best-selling dialogue, *The sycke mans salue*. In this, one of the characters asks for a copy of the *Flour of godly praiers* and reads a prayer for the dying aloud from it. And there is at least some evidence that printed prayers were indeed used this way. In the 1574 edition of *The sycke mans salue*, one prayer uttered by another of the characters begins on the last line of a page, with the rest of the text overleaf. In one copy, a contemporary reader has written the opening words of the prayer into the space at the top of the second page, so that the whole text could be read without having to turn the page. It looks as if the prayer was being used wholesale.[116] Others at least expected their prayers to be used verbatim. Richard Day instructed readers of his prayers to 'use them as I haue taught thee'. Richard Kilby's best-selling *Hallelujah* includes a prayer for King James I, but in the post-1625 editions the king's name was changed to Charles. Given that the prayer was explicitly set within Kilby's

---

[111] See, for example, Hutchins, *Davids Sling*, 335.

[112] Gouge, *Whole-Armor of God*, 419; cf. Rogers, *Seven treatises*, 410; Bownde, *Medicines for the plague*, 133.

[113] Perrott, *Certaine Short Prayers*, sig. A9r–v; Isham, 'Confessions', fo. 16v.

[114] Wariston, *Diary*, 104, 114–15, 118–19, 126–9, 144, 157, 160–1.

[115] Tyrwhit, *Elizabeth Tyrwhit's Morning and Evening Prayers*, 32.

[116] Thomas Becon, *The Flour of godly praiers* (c.1550: RSTC 1719.5), sig. A6v; Becon, *Sycke mans salue*, 518; FSL STC 1761, 121–2; White, *English Devotional Literature*, 176.

personal crisis in 1614, this was odd, but it implies that readers were expected to use it and that the publisher wished to spare them from having to make even that obvious adjustment.[117]

But not all readers were glued to the page. One obvious alternative—an appealing one, in an age of expensive books and low literacy—was memorization. Children first learned to pray this way, and the habit stuck. Books of prayers instructed readers that specific texts should be 'learned by hart, and said without booke'.[118] There is a confessional tinge to this—Cosin, for example, was a particular advocate of prayer's being 'committed vnto perfect memorie', and the length and variety of some puritan prayers made memorization impractical.[119] But from John Brinsley's provision of a prayer to be 'practise[d] . . . vntill wee haue learned it', through James Perrott's claim to be writing for 'the vsers and learners of Prayers', to Anne Clifford's mention of how she 'spoke a prayer of Owens' during a moment's pause in a stressful day, it seems that memorizing prayers was an almost universal Protestant practice.[120]

Recitation from memory—or half-memorization, glancing at a familiar text—points us towards a distinct experience of following a printed form. This is a way of making a prayer your own, which was something all advocates of set forms encouraged. Set forms were to be used 'with integritie & vprightnes of iudgement, with deuotion void of hypocrisie, with faithful inuocation'.[121] Richard Waste, dedicating his written prayers to his children, urged:

> Read them not for custom sake, nor to remoue idlenes . . . but only to serue & prayse God in them when you feele the spiritt of God to kindle your mindes with heauenly motions: Keep them in your memories, & vse them in your daily practices.[122]

As we move into the 17th century we find verbatim use being increasingly discouraged. Richard Rogers defended the use of set prayers but also claimed that we are 'tied . . . not to the words themselues'.[123] Thomas Rogers warned that 'to tie thyselfe alwaies' to a strictly verbatim use was 'foolish, superstitious, and wicked', which was further than most others would go. But even those like Elizabeth Jocelin, who recommended using specific set forms, also recommended personalizing them, adding breezily that they are 'easily reduced' to fit the user's circumstances.[124] What was written was not necessarily what was said.

---

[117] Day, *Booke of Christian Prayers*, sig. ☞6v; Kilby, *Hallelujah*, 68.

[118] Bentley, *Monument of Matrons*, 403.

[119] Cosin, *Collection of Priuate Devotions*, 13, 175.

[120] Brinsley, *True Watch* (1611), II. 56; Perrott, *Certaine Short Prayers*, sig. A9r; Clifford, *Diaries*, 29. 'Owen' was John Owen, epigrammist and bishop of St. Asaph. Cf. Clapham, *Tract of Prayer*, sig. A5r.

[121] Hutchins, *Davids Sling*, 335; Kilby, *Hallelujah*, 63.

[122] Bod. MS Rawl C.473 fo. 1r.

[123] Rogers, *Seven treatises*, 224, 402–3; cf. Bradford, *Godlie meditations*, sig. B6v; John Davidson, *Some helpes for young Schollers in Christianity* (Edinburgh, 1602: RSTC 6324.5), sig. F2r; Hieron, *Helpe vnto Deuotion* (1608), sigs A7v–8r.

[124] Habermann, *Enimie of securitie*, sig. r9r; Jocelin, *Mothers Legacie*, 77.

Increasingly, printed prayers themselves took account of this in two ways. First, devotees could be provided less with finished prayers than with building-blocks and blueprints. Some prayer-books had indexes enabling readers to find short sections from within lengthy prayers to tackle specific problems.[125] In the 17th century, we start to find detailed frameworks for prayer being spelled out, so that users might stick to the structure where they must but extemporize where they could. The most obvious place for this was in prayers of confession, which quite often included a gap where 'thy secret sins, which doth most burthen thy conscience' could be inserted: few things are more obviously individual.[126] This is one of the roots of the distinctively prosaic, restrained, and austere prose style of the printed Protestant prayer, which contrasts so strongly with the heightened rhetoric of Baroque Catholicism. Kate Narveson attributes this to 'the writer's conception of his proper realm of control over the reader'. Authors wrote prayers in order to present readers, not with a finished picture, but with an outline which they could complete themselves. (This, too, helped to foster a devotional anti-aesthetic.)[127]

Some approaches were more systematic. Later editions of John Brinsley's *True Watch, and Rule of Life* included four consecutive and lengthy paraphrases of the Lord's Prayer, explicitly intended as a progressive training in prayer. Users are told first to read each section, then to cover the actual prayers with their hands so that they cannot be read, looking instead at the short summary of what was asked: then, they should 'trie how wee could ask it our selues'. Eventually, by memorizing the series of subheadings, it ought to be possible to pray a prayer which, while it would clearly bear Brinsley's imprint, would equally clearly be the devotee's own.[128] Lewis Bayly, Elnathan Parr, and Daniel Featley similarly provided their readers with skeleton prayers, to be fleshed out with the individual's sins, requests, and thanksgivings. Bayly also provided fuller texts for those who needed more support, but was careful to add that they should use 'these or like words'.[129] John Clarke's *Holy Incense for the Censers of the Saints* was the most systematic of all, providing a detailed diagrammatic representation of the topics to be covered in prayer, and eighty pages of Scriptural quotations organized by topic so that your prayers might be formed from appropriate 'Scripture-Phrases'. To pray from Clarke's book would have been like trying to speak a foreign language by flicking the pages of a phrasebook, and it is no surprise that there was no second edition,[130] but it represents a wider ambition. Rather than a passive crutch, set forms could—it was hoped—provide a training regime for their readers' under-developed devotional muscles.

[125] Habermann, *Enimie of securitie*, sigs r9v–11r; Fleming, *Diamond of deuotion*, 83–180; Johann Gerhard, *Gerards meditations written originally in the Latine tongue* (Cambridge, 1631: RSTC 11773).
[126] Bayly, *Practise of pietie*, 253; cf. Sparke, *Crumms of comfort*, sig. D4r–v; Leigh, *Mothers blessing*, 153.
[127] Narveson, 'Publishing the Sole-talk', 118; and see above, pp. 216–17. Cf. White, *English Devotional Literature*, 238–9.
[128] Brinsley, *True Watch* (1611), II.56–7.
[129] Bayly, *Practise of pietie*, 316–34; Parr, *Abba Father*, 38–41, 58–79; Featley, *Ancilla Pietatis*, 27–8.
[130] Clarke, *Holy Incense*, esp. 9–11.

The other way for set forms to span the gap from scripted to extempore prayer was to provide models to be imitated, not texts to be recited. Readers, after all, are accustomed to reading books, and we might expect them to read prayers, and perhaps meditate on them, before or instead of actually praying them. Some authors openly expected this. John Rogers, providing a very lengthy prayer on a Christian's daily duty, cautioned that he did not 'vrge anie to vse it daily', but intended it rather 'sometimes to stirre vp those that feele themselues dead and vnfit to pray, by reading it ouer'.[131] The preface to Thomas Sorocold's collection made the distinction explicit. 'If ye find them worthy the name of prayers, vse them', he wrote. 'If otherwise, yet take them as meane grounds of Prayer and meditation, to set your deuout thoughts a worke.' Even the separatists conceded that 'read prayers . . . serue for meditation'.[132]

Set forms could be a means of teaching a skill, not of putting words into devotees' mouths. Oliver Pigg hoped his prayers of thanksgiving after the defeat of the Spanish Armada would help his readers' prayers, 'though thou do it more shortly and in other words'. The purpose of the prayers in Samuel Hieron's *Helpe vnto Deuotion* was that readers

> seeing the order and course of Prayer, and by acqainting themselues with words and formes of speach agreeing to the nature of such an exercise . . . may at last, like little children . . . be able to performe this holy duety.[133]

These were not texts. They were teaching tools.

Indeed, the didactic aspect of printed prayer—and, indeed, of public prayer—became one of its dominant functions in this period, a dramatic reversal of the pre-Reformation pattern.[134] As scholars of the subject have often noticed—usually with distaste—Protestant prayers are commonly 'couched in a language of instruction'. At best such prayers are 'miniature homilies', at worst, caught in a 'half-controversial vise'.[135] This was evident from the very beginning. Early evangelicals were bursting with urgent and transformative doctrines which the wider population needed to hear whether they knew it or not. What better way than to spread them than in printed prayers, so that devotees might preach the Protestant gospel to themselves unawares? Miles Coverdale frankly acknowledged that the purpose of his 1548 *Devout meditacions, psalmes and praiers* was that 'we maie bee the more prouoked & stirred to know our sinfull state . . . & to seke vnto God': this was a teaching, not a devotional tool. Indeed, it was full of teaching-prayers, explaining doctrine to God and providing Scriptural citations as proof. Edward VI's official primer also contained such lightly disguised sermons.[136] Thomas Becon was the

---

[131] Rogers, *Seven treatises*, 410.

[132] Sorocold, *Supplications of Saints* (1612), sig. A8r; Gifford, *Short Treatise against the Donatists*, 20.

[133] Pigg, *Meditations concerning praiers*, sig. A6r; Hieron, *Helpe vnto Deuotion* (1608), sig. A5r–v.

[134] See below, pp. 322–3.

[135] Leverenz, *Language of Puritan Feeling*, 5; Narveson, *Bible Readers*, 3; White, *English Devotional Literature*, 94; cf. White, *Tudor Books of Private Devotion*, 169–70, 179; C. J. Stranks, *Anglican Devotion* (London, 1961), 20.

[136] Coverdale, *Devout meditacions*, esp. fo. 2v, sigs D1v–5r; *Prymmer . . . set fourth by the kinges maiestie* (1553), esp. sigs R6v–8r.

early master of this genre. *The Flour of godly praiers* had its readers expound the Gospel to God, and deliver miniature diatribes against idolatry, swearing, drunkenness, and idleness in the guise of prayers against those sins.[137] The technique was routine throughout our period. Perhaps the most egregious example is William Hunnis' ten-page prayer to the Trinity which painstakingly informs God of his true nature. One of the plainest is Edward Hutchins' evening prayer which dwells on nightfall as a symbol of mortality, adding, 'O sweet Iesus of thy mercie beat this lesson into my head, and roote it in my hart'.[138]

This pattern became a little less prevalent in the early 17th century: perhaps the need for doctrinal instruction by any means necessary was less urgent. It did survive, especially in catechisms, which might well conclude with a 'prayer containing the effect of this Catechisme', summarizing the doctrine taught.[139] But we also find prayer books like Thomas Sorocold's hugely popular *Supplications of Saints*, which, citing Augustine, declared that its prayers 'are not mingled with discourse, for God desireth not to take admonition or information from our reports'. And indeed, the book avoids didacticism and is written with a terse elegance throughout. Daniel Featley mocked those who 'discourse profoundly in their prayer, as if they meant in good earnest to teach Almighty God'—although he then went on to provide a lecture on sabbath observance in the guise of a prayer for Sunday mornings.[140]

Crass as this may seem, it had a purpose and even a market. If some Protestants preferred to imbibe their doctrine in prayer rather than in sermon form, who can blame them? How else should they have praised God, if not by celebrating wonderful truths about him? And why should they not pray for knowledge and understanding of those truths, given how important that knowledge was? These would not be the only prayers which served in part as their own fulfillment, and given the risk—especially early in the period—that those who read prayers might not properly understand the doctrines they celebrated, it was an author's duty to spell them out. It could even make theological sense. True prayer was the work of the Spirit, so hearing and learning from another voice praying through you was integral to the experience, whether the other voice was the Spirit directly, or the Spirit as mediated through a human minister. When Protestants read and used set forms of prayer, they expected that learning would be a part of their worship.

PRAYING IN SCRIPTURE PHRASE

So far we have considered set forms specifically composed for use in private prayer, which claimed little or no official status, but there were two other sources of set

---

[137] Becon, *Flour of godly praiers*, fos 3r–7v, 114r–129v; cf. Thomas Becon, *The Gouernaunce of Vertue, teching al faithful Christians, howe they oughte dayly to leade their lyfe* (1560?: RSTC 1726), e.g. sigs Gg5r–8r; Becon, *Pomaunder of prayer*, e.g. fos 16r–17r, 26v–27v, 45r–54r.

[138] Hunnis, *Seuen Sobs*, 68–79; Hutchins, *Davids Sling*, 16.

[139] Dering, *Mr Dering, his godly priuate prayers*, 53–5; cf. William Gouge, *A short Catechisme* (1627: RSTC 12128), sigs C7r–D2r; Sparke, *Crumms of comfort*, e.g. sigs I5v, L6v–8v.

[140] Sorocold, *Supplications of Saints* (1612), sig. A7r (26 editions, c.1612–40, and 22 more by 1723); Featley, *Ancilla Pietatis*, 20, 151–5.

forms which did make such claims: the Bible and (in England) the Book of Common Prayer.

The Bible is the more important but the less controversial. Later opponents of set prayer sometimes extended their prohibition to the use of the prayers in the Bible itself, but before the Civil War this argument was scarcely considered. Using Biblical words was in many ways the perfect solution to the problem of what to say in prayer. Human words were by definition inadequate and indeed corrupt, but if true prayer was supposed to be the work of the Spirit within, what better words to use than those which the Spirit himself had inspired? George Wither argued that if 'in your prayers, you vse the words which the holy Ghost himselfe hath taught, there can be no petitions more powerfull to preuaile with him'. To pray in Scriptural words was already to speak the language of Heaven.[141] Hardly anyone in this un-Pentecostal age expected or experienced the New Testament miracle of speaking in tongues; there was no need for it when you could speak in scripture-phrase, and no other words were adequate to the experience of fellowship with God. If God speaks to us through Scripture, then it is only natural to reply in kind, and the Bible's distinctive timbres become a shared lovers' language. Or as Leigh Eric Schmidt puts it, 'the divine intimacy of evangelical piety was formed in a scriptural echo chamber'.[142]

Surviving written prayers are soaked in Scriptural quotation, half-quotation, paraphrase, and allusion: Biblical 'patchworks', 'mosaics', or 'collages' assembled into distinctive creations. Presumably those who were experienced at extempore prayer attempted the same thing.[143] Bishop Earle mocked the 'she-puritan' who 'ouerflowes so with the Bible that she spills it upon euery occasion, and will not cudgell her maydes without Scripture': an indictment of hypocrisy, but also a testimony to the aspiration to be soaked in the Bible's language. Indeed, Henry Burton worried that the self-conscious pursuit of 'a neate concatenation of Scripture phrases' could distract devotees from truly heartfelt prayer.[144] But it was only natural for Protestants to want their prayers to be—as was said of John Bunyan— 'Bibline'. Thomas Becon—an assiduous Scriptural patchworker—wrote of one of his prayer-books that,

> I haue trauayled to the vttermooste of my power too vse in theese prayers as fewe woordes of my owne as I coulde, and to glene oute of the fruiteful fyelde of the sacred scryptures, what so euer I founde meete for euery prayer that I made, that when it is prayed, not manne but the holy Ghost may seme to speake.[145]

For most, this aspiration was too obvious to state.

[141] Wither, *Preparation to the Psalter*, 130; Narveson, *Bible Readers*, 52–5.
[142] Richard C. Lovelace, 'The Anatomy of Puritan Piety: English Puritan Devotional Literature' in Louis Dupré and Don E. Saliers (eds), *Christian Spirituality: Post-Reformation and Modern* (1989), 318; Schmidt, *Hearing Things*, 48.
[143] Narveson, 'Publishing the Sole-talk', 113; White, *Tudor Books of Private Devotion*, 142; Tyrwhit, *Elizabeth Tyrwhit's Morning and Evening Prayers*, 41.
[144] Earle, *Microcosmographie*, 119; Burton, *Israels Fast*, 22.
[145] Becon, *Flour of godly praiers*, sig. A6v.

Not everyone needed their Biblical prayers predigested like this. Some authors provided not the finished product but collections of scriptural sentences which could be used as a resource for prayer. John Clarke claimed that 'even any meane Christian, of ordinary parts, and invention' who used his topically indexed set of Scriptural excerpts 'may be able soone to spinne . . . much heauenly matter and words . . . on any Subject whatsoever'.[146] On the other hand, of course, devotees could simply use the Bible's own prayers wholesale. A crude but revealing early example of this is a 1544 volume produced by the evangelical printer Richard Grafton, based on the work of the idiosyncratic Lutheran reformer Otto Brunfels. *Praiers of holi fathers, Patryarches, Prophetes, Iudges, Kynges, and renowmed men and women of eyther testamente* delivered exactly what it promised. Almost every prayer in the Bible is there, including some prayers—such as Nehemiah's repentance for the Jews' miscegenation, or Christ's lengthy prayer for his disciples in John 17— that would make no sense in any Christian's mouth. There is almost no indication what readers were supposed to do with these texts.[147] Later collections of Biblical prayers were a little more carefully selected: we find a set of Old Testament prayers in Edward VI's Primer, for example, and one of Perkins' works ends with a series of St Paul's prayers, given 'that thou mightest knowe them, and in thy praiers follow them'.[148] The essential rationale, however, is unchanged.

Some Biblical prayers were particular favourites, such as the blessing from Numbers 6:24–6 ('The Lord blesse thee, and kepe thee, The Lord make his face shine vpon thee . . . '); it was often paired with Paul's Trinitarian blessing in II Corinthians 13:14 ('the Grace').[149] The most fertile source of Biblical prayers, naturally, was the Book of Psalms: 'the Bible of the Bible', generally believed to reflect every facet of human life and seen as unique. 'Whereas al other scriptures do teach vs what God saith vnto vs, these praiers of the saints do teach vs, what we shal saie vnto God': they were 'excellent plat-formes of true, harty, and earnest prayers', and were widely used as such.[150] The psalms were collaged, paraphrased, and pastiched. Even Sternhold and Hopkins' metrical psalms were apparently said as prayers,[151] and the psalm texts themselves were ubiquitous. The traditional seven penitential psalms were particular favourites, not only for traditionalists but for as

[146] Clarke, *Holy Incense*, 267–8; cf. *Christian Prayers and Meditations in English*, sigs Aa1r–Gg4V; Fawkener, *Collection of Promises*; see above, p. 222.

[147] Otto von Brunfels, *Praiers of holi fathers*, ed. Richard Grafton (1544?: RSTC 20200); cf. the shorter 1535 edition. As White points out, this collection also stands in the primer tradition: White, *Tudor Books of Private Devotion*, 136–7.

[148] *Prymmer . . . set fourth by the kinges maiestie* (1553); Perkins, *Exposition of the Lords prayer*, 172.

[149] See, for example, Bull, *Christian praiers*, 141; Dering, *Godly priuate praiers*, sigs C7r, C8v; Babington, *Briefe conference*, 139; Sutton, *Disce mori*, 268; Tymme, *Siluer watch-bell* (1606), 290; Cowper, *Triumph*, 368; Crashaw, *Milke for Babes*, 59, 63; Featley, *Ancilla Pietatis*, 131; Valentine, *Private Devotions*, 98.

[150] Ryrie, 'Psalms and Confrontation', 114–16; Theodore Beza, *The Psalmes of David, truly opened and explaned by Paraphrasis* (1581: RSTC 2034), sig. a3v; Smith, *Dauids blessed man*, 1–2.

[151] Clarke, *Holy Incense*, final section. See, for example, Becon, *Sycke mans salue*, 358–9, 373–4, 375–6; Thomas Becon, *The pomaunder of prayer* (c.1567: RSTC 1747.5), fos 29v–32r; BL Royal MS 17.A.xvii fos 19r–23r; and cf. Ryrie, 'Psalms and confrontation', 116–18. On 'collage psalms', see below, pp. 304–5.

hardline a Calvinist as Archibald Johnston of Wariston.[152] But while penitence echoed a perennial theme of Protestant prayer, the psalms also had a more distinctive voice to add. Finding words with which to praise God in prayer is, generally, difficult. As Charlotte Clutterbuck has pointed out, it can easily drift into vague abstraction which is very difficult to sustain.[153] Since Protestants keenly felt their duty to praise God, and—sometimes—the urge to do so, this was a problem, and it was one to which the psalms provided the purest solution. For those who were dumbstruck before the throne of God, a well-chosen psalm could extol him like nothing else that could issue from human tongue.

One Biblical prayer above all was used: the prayer taught by Christ, known to Catholics as the Paternoster. Some early English Protestants—Hugh Latimer, for example—retained that name, but this was awkward, since they were insistent that their people learn it in English rather than Latin. So in the 1540s we find it described as 'the prayer of our Lord Iesus which he taughte his discyples', as 'the praier which our Lorde and Maister Christe taught', and eventually as 'the Lordes prayer called the pater noster'. Within a generation, the term 'the Lords prayer' had become universal, so much so that Richard Kilby needed to remind his readers that 'the Lords Praier [is] so called, because our Lord Jesus Christ made it'.[154]

Early modern Protestants used it constantly: puritans and conformists, English and Scots alike. It appears very regularly in printed prayers as a conclusion. Regularly, not invariably: sometimes it was used, and sometimes not, and I have been at a loss to discern any pattern. It is common to find in a single set of prayers that the concluding Lord's Prayer is sometimes used, sometimes omitted, for no very obvious reason.[155] When it is used as a conclusion in this way, the whole text is occasionally printed, but it is much more normal to see 'Our Father &c'. Everyone who could read, and virtually everyone who could not, could fill in the rest. In family prayer, the whole household normally joined their voices. Some preachers led their congregations in reciting the prayer, and early in the period this was explicitly in order to help them to learn it.[156] The plural form of the prayer—*our* Father—obviously lent itself to collective use, but it is also found attached to prayers which have been in the singular up to that moment. We have ample testimony of private devotees using it in solitary prayer, and it appears in private, manuscript devotional works as well as in print.[157] John Bradford argued that the

---

[152] Wariston, *Diary*, 169; Hannibal Hamlin, 'Sobs for Sorrowful Souls: Versions of the Penitential Psalms for Domestic Devotion' in Martin and Ryrie, *Private and Domestic Devotion*.

[153] Clutterbuck, *Encounters with God*, 11–15.

[154] Latimer, *Sermons by Hugh Latimer*, 326; Otto von Brunfels, *Praiers of holi fathers*, ed. Richard Grafton (1544?: RSTC 20200), fo. 49v; Coverdale, *Devout meditacions*, fos 1v–2r; Becon, *Gouernans* (1549), fo. 6r, copied in Heyden, *Bryefe Summe*, sig. N2v; Foxe, *Actes and monuments* (1570), 1700; Day, *Booke of Christian Prayers*, 11v; Clarke, *Collection*, 4; Kilby, *Burthen*, 28.

[155] For example, Sorocold, *Supplications of Saints* (1612); Tuke, *Practise of the faithfull*; Sparke, *Crumms of comfort*. One prayer in the latter work does not explicitly call for it but ends by referring to 'that prayer which thou hast taught me', suggesting that it was regularly used even when not specifically called for: sig. C11r.

[156] Latimer, *Sermons by Hugh Latimer*, 307–8; Foxe, *Sermon of Christ crucified*, fo. 29r, sig. T3v.

[157] For example, see Day, *Booke of Christian Prayers*, fo. 7r–v; Prid, *Glasse of Vaine-glorie* (1600), sigs F10r–v; Harrison, *Deaths aduantage*, III.15–16; Tuke, *Practise of the faithfull*, 117, 127; Bernard,

use of a plural prayer when alone was appropriate to put Christians in mind of the communion of believers.[158]

No mainstream figure opposed its use before 1640. Ambrose Fisher's caricatured puritan went out of his way to disapprove of the 'Zeale' of those who rejected it.[159] The reverse argument was far commoner: not, we should reject the Lord's Prayer because we reject set prayers, but, the use of set prayers is legitimated by the Lord's Prayer, 'a set forme of prayer prescribed by our Sauiour himselfe'. 'Auncient and worthy diuines haue reuerenced it as a praier', William Perkins insisted. Even the 1644 *Directory for the Publique Worship of God* agreed that it 'is not only a Pattern of Prayer, but it selfe a most comprehensive Prayer' to be used verbatim.[160] Richard Kilby urged his readers, 'use often to say the Lords Praier'; the popular Jacobean writer Henry Greenwood argued that Christ made the prayer short 'that it might bee often repeated'.[161] The directness and simplicity of Christ's command—'when ye pray, say, Our Father . . .'—was difficult to contest. Richard Day's *Booke of Christian Prayers* argued that Christ 'commaunded all men to pray, & . . . pre-scribed vs a forme of Prayer in expresse wordes'.[162] The implication that its verbatim use was actually compulsory might have been a little strong for some Protestants' sense of Christian liberty, but everyone could have agreed with the countess of Huntingdon's sentiments. In her commonplace book, she concluded her morning prayer with the Lord's Prayer—written out in full—and added, 'in that most perfect forme of prayer that hee hath taught mee I conclude this my weake & imperfect prayer'.[163] It was, simply, the perfect prayer.

Which of course was the problem: it was almost too good to be true. Whenever a pious action could be performed by mere effort, Protestants worried about hypoc-risy. Praying the Lord's Prayer was good. Merely reciting it was emphatically not. 'There cannot be deuised any praier more absolute, more perfeicte or more piththie', Miles Coverdale wrote, but 'the labour of pronouncyng holy wordes' is futile. George Gifford's imagined carnal Protestant, Atheos, defied calls to serious prayer by asking, 'Can yee haue any better prayer then the Lordes prayer, when they praye that, can yee requier more?' Gifford replied that 'there can bee no better prayer then the Lordes Prayer, and he which prayeth that right must needes be saued'. But of course praying it right was the issue. As Latimer argued, 'a man may serve the Devil with saying the *Pater-noster*, when he saith it with a defiled mind.'

A *Weekes Worke* (1616), 92; Bayly, *Practise of pietie*, 263, 278, 329, 334; Clarke, *Collection*, 4, 9; Mildmay, 'Meditations', II.75.

[158] Bradford, *Godlie meditations*, sig. B2r.

[159] Fisher, *Defence of the liturgie*, 48.

[160] Rogers, *Seven treatises*, 224; Perkins, *Exposition of the Lords prayer*, 22; *A Directory for the Publique Worship of GOD* (1644: Wing D1544), 38. However, the Directory opposed congregational repetition of this or indeed any other prayer.

[161] Kilby, *Burthen*, 28; Henry Greenwood, *[Greenwoods workes]* (1616: RSTC 12327), II.81.

[162] Luke 11:2, cited in e.g. Crashaw, *Milke for Babes*, 45; Day, *Booke of Christian Prayers*, fo. 11v.

[163] Huntington Library, San Marino, CA, MS 15369 fo. 4r.

He and many others emphasized that the prayer must not only be used, but used 'understandingly'.[164]

But what did that mean in practice? Increasingly, it was taken to mean liberty—even obligation—to depart from the actual text. John Norden, who called the prayer 'the first plot of perfect praier, pure precious and profound', added, 'yet are we not so strictlie tied to the wordes therof onely, but that we may . . . dilate vpon the same'.[165] It was a prayer in its own right, but also an outline or pattern for more extensive prayer. Again, this is wholly uncontroversial. Catechetical works across the spectrum used the clauses of the Lord's Prayer as a teaching framework; preachers expounded it; Bradford's meditations on it were much-reprinted and much-imitated. The paraphrases available ranged from those which simply expanded each clause with two or three sentences to book-length texts,[166] and some devotees did it for themselves. Robert Woodford, writing a prayer for his family in 1637, slipped effortlessly in and out of the text:

> Oh my god stretch the winge of thy sure proteccion over me and my family this day, give vs this day our daily bread & forgive vs our trespasses that are past & lead vs not into temptacion for time to come. . . . I have but 2 groats left, Lord supply me I pray.[167]

The very artlessness of this was a Protestant ideal.

Two surviving broadsheets from the 1620s give us a rare glimpse lower down the social scale. Both provide lightly expanded texts of the Lord's Prayer. One (Figure 11) claims to be 'necessary for all Housholders to learne, and to teach their Children and Seruants', and schematically extracts eight points from each clause of the prayer. The final 'Amen', it tells us, is to be said with 'Attentiue Cogitation, Sincere Speech, Daily Exercise, Continuall Desire'. How widely such sheets were dispersed we cannot say, although their survival rate is very poor. Both of these, like most other such imprints, survive only in single copies, although one claims to be the third impression. Nor do we know how those who owned them used them, although one of these sheets, *A divine descant*, was written to be sung. However, they certainly testify to an anxiety that the words of the Lord's Prayer were merely being parroted, and they suggest that enough of the simpler sort shared those anxieties that the printers could shift a few hundred, or a few thousand, copies.[168]

---

[164] Coverdale, *Devout meditacions*, fo. 1v; Gifford, *Briefe discourse*, fo. 71r; Latimer, *Sermons by Hugh Latimer*, 328–9, 377; Perkins, *Exposition of the Lords prayer*, 62; Greenwood, *Workes*, II.80; Parr, *Abba Father*, 87; Tozer, *Directions for a Godly Life*, 169–70; Kilby, *Burthen*, 28–9.

[165] Norden, *Pensiue mans practise*, sig. A9v; cf. Rogers, *Seven treatises*, 224.

[166] For example, see Christopher Sutton, *Godly meditations vpon the most holy sacrament of the Lords Supper* (1630: RSTC 23494), 338–40; Kilby, *Burthen*, 29–31; Parr, *Abba Father*, 89–105; Greenwood, *Workes*, II.79–117; Richard Baker, *Meditations and Disquisitions upon the Lords prayer* (RSTC 1223. London: Anne Griffin, 1636).

[167] Woodford, 'Diary', 25.xi.1637 recto.

[168] *A Short Interpretation of the Lords Praier* (1627: RSTC 16823); cf. *A diuine descant full of consolation, Fitting a soule plung'd in desolation* (c.1620?: RSTC 6766.5); Tessa Watt, *Cheap Print and Popular Piety* (Cambridge, 1991).

Such expositions hardly solved the problem, however. Even if widely used, they could simply lead to their users parroting a longer, non-Biblical text. In practice, they could do no more than bail out a few bucketfuls from the vast swamp of formality and ignorance in which—so earnest, learned Protestants feared—most of the people were sodden. This was the fundamental problem with the Lord's Prayer, as Gifford had indicated: not that it was wrong to use it, but that so many people were content to use no other. As we have already seen, the simple recitation of the Lord's Prayer, often with the Creed and even the Ten Commandments—the three texts most generally displayed in most post-Reformation parish churches—was central to most British people's practice of prayer in the post-Reformation period, and was the full extent of it for many of them.[169] If puritan divines worried about the use of the Lord's Prayer, this was why: not that it was bad, but that its recitation could lull the common people into thinking that they were actually praying. As Perkins put it, 'their repetition of the Lords praier without vnderstanding or deuotion, is no praier with God, when they doe it onely of custome, and rest in the worke done'.[170] The difference between the godly and the godless, to Robert Harris, was that the former 'varies his petitions according to his needs and occasions', while the latter 'hath but one salue for euery sore, a Pater noster, a Credo, &c'.[171] Using the Lord's Prayer was not exactly *wrong*. But—this line of argument held—its actual words should only be a small part of your devotion. There is a strong whiff of spiritual elitism here. To pray the Lord's Prayer verbatim is to pray like the common people, or like children. The godly ought not to be so limited. If open opposition to the prayer had not yet germinated, we can perhaps see its seed here.

On the other hand, the picture that Perkins, Bolton, and Harris paint—of a country filled with muttered English prayers—represents a real success for Protestantism, and one which did not come easily. From the 1530s, the campaign to persuade English lay people to learn these newly translated texts was in the vanguard of the evangelical project. The first wave had met with significant resistance from both clergy and people. 'They jest at it', the veteran evangelical George Constantine complained in 1539, 'calling it the new Paternoster and new learning'. But a decade into Elizabeth's reign it was possible for mass-market prayer books to instruct their readers to use the Apostles' Creed, as well as the Lord's Prayer, without feeling the need to give the whole text.[172]

The learning of these texts remained the starting-point of Christian education throughout our period. When Archibald Johnston of Wariston was trying to educate his new, barely-teenage wife in godliness, he quizzed her 'in the principals of religion, making hir repeat the Lords Prayer, the Comands, and the Belief'. Elizabeth Isham tell us that when she was only a little younger, 'being zelus to doe

---

[169] See above, p. 160.
[170] Perkins, *Godly and learned exposition*, 233; cf. Bolton, *Three-fold treatise*, II.170–1.
[171] Harris, *Peters enlargement* (1627), 37.
[172] 'A Memorial from George Constantine to Thomas Lord Cromwell', *Archaeologia* 23 (1831), 59; *Godly garden*, fo. 55r; *This booke is called the Treasure of gladnesse* (1574: RSTC 24193.5), fo. 4v.

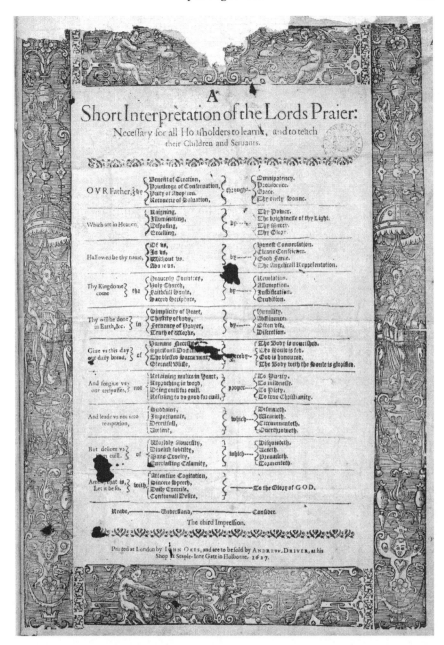

Fig. 11. *A Short Interpretation of the Lords Praier* (1627: RSTC 16823). This gives one hint as to how the Lord's Prayer may have been used as the basis for longer devotions.

well I affton repeted my prayes ... together with the ten commandements and Belliefe'—a practice that she later rejected as 'vaine repetition and much babbeling'. Others, including Katherine Brettergh and indeed Wariston himself, continued to recite these texts devotionally into adulthood.[173] So we should not be so quick as learned contemporaries were to dismiss this as mere lip-labour. In the 1620s Henry Tozer alleged that the Lord's Prayer, Creed, and Commandments 'are dayly repeated of those of the meaner and more simple sort', but the only criticism he offered was the claim that the texts were 'not so well vnderstood, as they should be': which suggests that, even from this zealous graduate's perspective, this repetition was not mere parrotting. We have something similar from George Gifford: that rare thing, a minister who actually attempted to understand his unlearned flock. His view, as early as 1581, was that five-sixths of the people of England

> doe vnderstand so much in the commandements, Lords prayer, & Articles of the faith, that it were a greate shame for a godly man to haue a childe of x. yeeres old for to know no more.[174]

He meant that as an indictment, but it was also an achievement. If most of the population understood these core texts as well a well-drilled ten-year-old, then the Reformation was not doing too badly.

COMMON PRAYER AND PRIVATE DEVOTION

If English ploughboys and milkmaids learned their new paternoster, Commandments, and Creed, they did so above all through the Book of Common Prayer. Those texts' regular recitation, Sunday by Sunday, drummed them into memory. According to one over-clever puritan calculation, the Prayer Book service made it theoretically possible for the Lord's Prayer to be used eight times in a single Sunday meeting.[175] Repetitions of this kind were amongst the features which persuaded some puritans that the Prayer Book was an 'vnperfect boke, culled & picked out of that popishe dunghil, the Portuise and Masse boke ful of all abhominations'.[176] The fiercest controversies, however, centred on its use in public worship, and in particular on whether ministers might alter or omit sections which troubled their consciences. Our concern here is different: the use of texts from the Prayer Book in private devotions. Since no-one was obliged to use it, and since those who did were free to adapt it as they saw fit, this was not nearly so controversial. It turns out that the Prayer Book was used in private prayer much like the Bible itself. The Prayer Book model in general, and some aspects of it in particular, were very influential on

---

[173] Wariston, *Diary*, 11; Isham, 'Confessions', fos 4r, 6v–7r; Harrison, *Deaths aduantage*, III.16; Wariston, *Diary*, 54–5.

[174] Tozer, *Directions for a Godly Life*, 169–70; Gifford, *Briefe discourse*, fo. 43r.

[175] Fisher, *Defence of the liturgie*, 48, 51–2. This was only possible if morning prayer, the ante-communion, baptism, marriage, churching and burial were all celebrated consecutively.

[176] John Field and Thomas Wilcox, *An Admonition to the Parliament* (Hemel Hempstead?, 1572: RSTC 10848), sig. A8v.

models of private prayer throughout our period, and not only amongst conformists and conservatives.

The Prayer Book's cultural importance now hardly needs to be emphasized. Its language was pervasive, in everyday and literary use as well as in devotion. Quotations and echoes of its phrases crop up constantly in devotional materials; it is often unclear whether or not the allusion is deliberate.[177] As a boy, Richard Baxter's parish church was served by an elderly reader with poor eyesight, who recited the service 'without Book'. By then, most adults in England could probably have done the same.[178] The book was ubiquitous. It was England's third most widely circulated volume, after the Bible and the metrical psalms. All three were commonly bound together. Whereas in the 1580s, the queen's printer was complaining that the psalm book far outsold the Prayer Book, a generation later the liturgy was becoming a staple of lay as well as of ministerial ownership.[179] People began to carry it with them. 'Wheresoeuer thou goest', Michael Sparke advised in 1627, 'take one of these companions with thee; eyther thy Prayer-Booke, or thy Bible'. Or both: William Proud, an English soldier killed at Maastricht in 1632, was said routinely to carry the weapons that were the tools of his trade, but also 'for his Christian warfare . . . his Bible, his Prayer booke, and other Authors'. It is 'in every Mans hand amongst us', claimed John Browning. The pretext for Ambrose Fisher's 1630 anti-puritan dialogue was that a caricatured puritan spotted Fisher's conformist alter ego carrying 'in your hand an English Masse-booke'. But it was not only the shock troops of the Laudian revival who went so armed. Edward Wetenhall's later manifesto for Protestant prayer suggested that any good prayer-closet should be furnished with a copy of the Prayer Book.[180]

How was it used in private devotion? Sometimes, wholesale. The official primer of Edward VI's reign included 'an order of priuate prayer for Morning and Euening euery daye in the weeke', which was the 1552 Prayer Book service almost unchanged.[181] Some of the Marian martyrs used or adapted the Prayer Book services privately or in small groups during their imprisonment. The first Elizabethan edition of Thomas Becon's *Gouernaunce of Vertue* included a cut-down version of the Prayer Book service of morning prayer. Another variant was published in the 1569 best-seller *A godly garden*. A suspected radical conventicle in Essex in 1584 were found to be praying according to the form 'establisshed by publick authority'.[182] Robert Openshaw's catechism recalls a godly Elizabethan household whose

[177] Maltby, *Prayer Book and People*; Targoff, *Common Prayer*. See, amongst many examples, Sorocold, *Supplications of Saints* (1612), *passim*; Bayly, *Practise of pietie*, 770; Isham, 'Confessions', fo. 20r; FSL MS Add. 1266 fo. 2v.

[178] Baxter, *Reliquiae Baxterianae*, 1.

[179] Green, *Print and Protestantism*, 516–17; Maltby, *Prayer Book and People*, 26–7; Beth Quitslund, *The Reformation in Rhyme: Sternhold, Hopkins and the English Metrical Psalter, 1547–1603* (Aldershot, 2008), 243.

[180] Sparke, *Crumms of comfort*, sig. L2v; Rogers, *Sermon preached . . . . at the funerall*, sig. D2v; Browning, *Concerning publike-prayer*, 74; Fisher, *Defence of the liturgie*, 3; Wetenhall, *Enter into thy Closet*, 7.

[181] *Prymmer . . . set fourth by the kinges maiestie* (1553), esp. sig. c4r. Most (not all) of the service was shifted from the plural to the singular, and the absolution was simply used as a prayer.

[182] Foxe, *Actes and monuments* (1570), 1700, 1735; Becon, *Gouernaunce* (1560), sigs Hh2r–5v; *Godly garden*, fo. 9r–v; BL Lansdowne MS 157 fo. 186r.

pious routine was disrupted when their parish minister was deprived, presumably for nonconformity. Thereafter they took to daily prayer in the household, using exclusively Prayer Book material. Richard Baxter was raised on just such a diet a generation later, his father praying at home 'by a Form out of the end of the Common-Prayer Book'.[183]

But Prayer Book materials were mixed promiscuously with other prayers. Specific Prayer Book texts repeatedly surface in other contexts: the prayer for the monarch, the pre-communion exhortation, the Gloria in Excelsis, specific versicles and responses, specific collects.[184] The young Baxter's normal menu of prayers drew on Bradford, another unnamed book of prayers and the Prayer Book general confession. As a child, Elizabeth Isham was given a copy of *A godly garden*, which spurred her to a discipline of daily prayer—but as well as the *Garden*, she drew on '2 or 3 prayers which are in the servis booke'. No less a puritan than John Bruen had a page in his commonplace-book headed 'Out of the booke of common prayer', where he transcribed some of its most edifying prayers. And these are only the explicitly acknowledged uses. Unacknowledged quotation and half-quotation of Prayer Book material was everywhere. *A godly garden* itself lifted phrases from the Prayer Book canticles, and paraphrased the general confession.[185] A series of Elizabethan collections, published and unpublished, scattered Prayer Book texts freely in with those culled from other sources.[186] Early modern Protestants gathered prayers wherever they could find them, and what more obvious source than the best-known book of prayers in England?

A few texts surfaced especially frequently, of which much the most striking is the Prayer Book Litany. The Litany is a rhythmic, repetitive order for intercessory prayer, associated with processional use and closely following medieval patterns. It was the first portion of the Prayer Book service to be published, in 1544, under Henry VIII's capricious eye. Unsurprisingly, some puritans found it especially odious. A 1641 anti-Prayer Book diatribe singled it out as 'the most offensive' part of the book, 'no better than . . . conjuring or juggling of the Magitians'. It was a well-established view—in Elizabeth's reign, Raphael Holinshed recorded that some likened the Litany to 'coniuration and sorcerie'. But Holinshed himself believed that it was 'an inuocation in mine opinion not deuised without the great assistance of the spirit of God', and a great many evidently agreed with him.[187] The Marian martyr George Marsh claimed that his custom was to say the Litany daily; after he was arrested, this became twice daily. Another martyr, John Alcock, was arrested for

[183] Robert Openshaw, *Short questions, and answeares, contayning the Summe of Christian Religion* (1633: RSTC 18828.5), sig. A5v; Baxter, *Reliquiae Baxterianae*, 3.
[184] See, for example, Sandys, *Sermons*, 444; Tyrwhit, *Elizabeth Tyrwhit's Morning and Evening Prayers*, 76; Norden, *Pensiue mans practise*, 236; Sorocold, *Supplications of Saints* (1616), 395–7; Valentine, *Private Devotions*, 343; Isham, 'Confessions', fo. 1r.
[185] Baxter, *Reliquiae Baxterianae*, 4; Isham, 'Confessions', fo. 8r; BL Harleian MS 6607 fo. 17r; *Godly garden*, fos 7v–8r, 11r–21r.
[186] See, for example, Thomas Sternhold, John Hopkins et al., *The Whole Booke of Psalmes, collected into Englysh metre* (1562: RSTC 2430), 395–6; Becon, *Pomaunder of prayer*, sigs H5v–L3v; Cancellar, *Alphabet of prayers*, sig. E4r; FSL MS V.a.482 fos 44v–47r.
[187] 'Dwalphintramis', *Anatomy of the Service-Book*, 39–40; Raphael Holinshed, *Holinshed's Chronicles of England, Scotland and Ireland* (1807), I.232.

his ostentatious use of the text. The Litany's association with Henry VIII, and especially its petition for deliverance from the bishop of Rome's detestable enormities, gave it a particular potency in Mary's reign.[188] That particular clause was removed under Elizabeth, but the Litany's popularity only grew. Eight of the best-selling and most influential books of prayers published in her reign included it in full.[189] Printers would not so regularly have spent so much precious paper on such a lengthy text, pushing up their books' prices, unless their readers wanted it. Thereafter the text itself was not so frequently included in prayer books—perhaps because of spreading private ownership of the Prayer Book itself—but the Litany style continued to be imitated.[190] Puritans as well as conformists did this. William Gouge criticized those who recited the text 'for forme and custome sake', but only to stress that its petitions should be said 'from the heart'. And Nehemiah Wallington concluded his account of a fire on London Bridge in 1633 with the words, 'From Fire and watter Sudden death, Sinne and Gods wrath good Lord deliuer vs'.[191] For a wide spectrum of English Protestants, the Litany's conjuring and juggling had become an ingrained part of their language of prayer.

Another influence was subtler but even more pervasive, and this relates to the British Reformation's most resolutely non-barking doctrinal dog: the doctrine of the Trinity. Although there were occasional panics about anti-Trinitarian radicalism, the doctrine was in fact almost untouched throughout Britain's Reformation controversies. Most Protestants affirmed the Trinity and then left it alone. The first British Protestant theologian to build anything substantial on the doctrine was John Owen, after the Restoration. In our period, there are at best glimpses of real engagement with the triune nature of God, usually connected to the doctrine of prayer: Christian prayer can be described as the Spirit within the believer praying to the Father through the Son. William Perkins suggested that those who did not understand this 'make but a colde and slender kinde of praying'.[192] In which case, there was a good deal of cold and slender prayer around, because there are few signs of this advice being followed. A few full-scale prayers to the Trinity were published in the Elizabethan period; but these were usually thinly disguised treatises on Athanasian orthodoxy, which in any case soon petered out.[193] Published prayers

---

[188] Alec Ryrie, 'The slow death of a tyrant: learning to live without Henry VIII, 1547–63' in Mark Rankin et al. (eds), *Henry VIII and his Afterlives* (Cambridge, 2009), 84–5; Foxe, *Actes and monuments* (1570), 1694, 1732, 1735.

[189] [*The primer set furth at large, with many godly and deuoute prayers*] (1559: RSTC 16087); Becon, *Gouernaunce* (1560), 434–45; Becon, *Pomaunder of prayer*, sigs H5v–I8r; *Christian Prayers and Meditations in English*, sigs G1r–12v; Bull, *Christian praiers*, 303–23; Cancellar, *Alphabet of prayers*, sigs D1v–5r; *Godly garden*, fos 31v–45v; Prid, *Glasse of Vaine-glorie* (1600), sigs I9v–12v. Cf. Tyrwhit, *Elizabeth Tyrwhit's Morning and Evening Prayers*, 50; *Deuout psalmes and colletes* (1547: RSTC 2999); Becon, *Flour of godly praiers*, fos 156v–163v.

[190] See, for example, *This booke is called the Treasure of gladnesse*, fos 53r–55r; Sutton, *Disce mori*, 261–7; Valentine, *Private Devotions*, 8–26 *et seq.*

[191] Gouge, *Whole-Armor of God*, 378; FSL MS V.a.436 p. 29. Wallington's phrase is an echo of the Litany's language, not a direct quotation.

[192] Perkins, *Exposition of the Lords prayer*, 32.

[193] For example, Becon, *Pomaunder of prayer*, fos 3v–8r; *Godly garden*, fos 62r–66v; Day, *Booke of Christian Prayers*, fos 12r–21v.

mostly ignored the triune nature of God, sometimes even confusing the Persons. William Hunnis, for example, penned a prayer which gives thanks for 'the death and passion of thy sonne' before seamlessly referring to 'thy deth and passion'. We can imagine that this kind of elision was routine in private prayers.[194]

There are exceptions. Grace Mildmay had a vision in which she 'was most assuredly persuaded in my heart that Jesus Christ together with God his heavenly father and the Holy Ghost three persons and one eternal God, did vouchsafe to visit me'. Elizabeth Isham described coming to a more fully Trinitarian understanding of God in her mid-twenties, which had a considerable effect on her devotions, and she repented of her former clumsiness on this point. Archibald Johnston of Wariston, too, was explicitly Trinitarian in his prayers, repeatedly describing how in prayer he found 'the Fayther reconciled, Chryst interceding, and the Sprit sighing and sobing'. On one occasion he

> conjured the Holy Sprite . . . to joine his sighs and sobs unto Chryst intercession for me . . . [and] cryed unto the Lord God the Fayther . . . that nou he wald hear thir three supplicants, his Sone interceading, his Spirit groaning, and my saule praying evin for to glorifie himselth.[195]

But if this kind of substantive, poised Trinitarianism was not unique to Wariston, it was certainly very rare. All affirmed the doctrine: few fed from it.

If not for edification, how did early modern Protestants use the doctrine of the Trinity? For self-definition, naturally: it asserted their continuity with the early Church and their separation from unsavoury radicals. But the Prayer Book connection points us in another direction. Of all the Prayer Book's words to be echoed in private devotion, the most common are its recurring Trinitarian doxology: 'Glory be to the Father, and to the Son, and to the Holy Ghost . . .'[196] This was a fine way of giving makeshift private devotion a more elevated, 'churchy' polish, but Trinitarian doxologies of all kinds appear throughout this period, as regular as punctuation. Some allude to the Pauline distinction between the Father's love, the Son's grace, and the Spirit's fellowship.[197] But simple invocations of all three Persons— 'O God the father blesse vs, O God the sonne blesse vs, O God the holy Ghost blesse vs'—are more common. Some paraphrase the Prayer Book doxology.[198] These formulae could be used as invocations at the beginnings of prayers, or as recurrent refrains in longer or more poetic prayers;[199] but most commonly they

---

[194] Hunnis, *Seuen Sobs*, 86.

[195] Mildmay, *With Faith and Physic*, 88; Isham, 'Confessions', fos 28v, 35r; Wariston, *Diary*, 21, 48, 51–2, 66.

[196] Targoff, *Common Prayer*; see, for example, Bull, *Christian praiers*, 291; *This booke is called the Treasure of gladnesse*, fos 40r, 60r–v; Bentley, *Monument of Matrons*, 403; Valentine, *Private Devotions*, 74–5; Tyrwhit, *Elizabeth Tyrwhit's Morning and Evening Prayers*, 76.

[197] II Corinthians 13:14; see, for example, BL Egerton MS 2877 fo. 82v.

[198] *Godly garden*, fo. 47v; see also, for example, Fleming, *Diamond of deuotion*, 137; Leigh, *Mothers blessing*, 270; Kilby, *Burthen*, 23; Kilby, *Hallelujah*, 12.

[199] Hunnis, *Seuen Sobs*, 24–5; Coverdale, *Remains*, 543–4, 564–5; Tyrwhit, *Elizabeth Tyrwhit's Morning and Evening Prayers*, 80–2, 86; as Susan Felch points out, Tyrwhit's Trinitarian refrain 'runs through the entire prayer book'.

appear at the end, in the fashion of the Prayer Book's collects. They might be brief: several divines, following the Edwardian primer, recommended that when you rise in the morning, and lay down at night, you should acknowledge that you did so 'in the name of the father, and of the Son, and of the holy gost'.[200] Or they might be expansive, especially from the pulpit.[201] When you heard a preacher mention the three Persons of the Trinity in one breath, it was a good bet that he was almost done.

So the Trinity's devotional use was a matter not of theology, but of ornament, emphasis, and punctuation. The threefold structure of a Trinitarian invocation provided a rhythm to a prayer, especially to its peroration, bringing it to a crescendo. Where a mere *Amen* might seem abrupt, a Trinitarian doxology rounded off a prayer with appropriate solemnity. It was used to provide something like a gilded edge to particularly important prayers. Johann Habermann's *The enimie of securitie* provided morning prayers for every day of the week: only Sunday's opens with a Trinitarian invocation. Or again, such invocations crop up particularly frequently in prayers for the dying.[202] John Bradford began a prayer with the words: 'Oh almightie and euerlasting lord god which hast made heauen earth &c, oh incomphrensible vnitie, oh alwaies to be worshipped most blessed Trinitie . . . ': it is clear that the Trinity's function here is purely rhetorical, a means of providing extra spiritual oomph.[203]

Perhaps this was simply a harmless quirk of devotional language. Composing coherent prayers is harder than it looks, and prefabricated phrases which can be dropped in without a great deal of thought are invaluable. Praising the Trinity provided a pause for devotional breath. However, formulaic prayers of this kind were strongly associated with Catholic piety. This formulaic Trinitarianism, interestingly, was very much an English phenomenon. It did not find a welcome in Scotland's more precise atmosphere.[204] Some in England were uneasy too. A puritan polemicist in 1641 derided the 'tautologicall summing up, and repetition of the titles and Elogies of the Trinity' as mere popery and superstition.[205] The first edition of Foxe's *Actes and monuments* reproduced Thomas Cromwell's supposed prayer on the scaffold: 'O father forgeue me. O sonne forgeue me, O holy ghoste forgeue me: O thre persones in one God forgeue me'. We can well imagine Cromwell saying this, but in subsequent editions, Foxe silently took these embarrassingly popish words out of his Protestant hero's mouth. Similarly formulaic appeals to the Trinity for mercy appeared in the order for public fasting during the

---

[200] *Prymmer . . . set fourth by the kinges maiestie* (1553), sigs b8r, c1v; Themylthorpe, *Posie of Praiers*, 1, 24; Trundle, *Keepe within Compasse*, sig. A6r; Kilby, *Hallelujah*, 82–3.

[201] For example, Crashaw, *London's Lamentation*, sig. C6r.

[202] Habermann, *Enimie of securitie*, 12; and see e.g. Becon, *Sycke mans salue*, 529; Sutton, *Disce mori*, 261; Featley, *Ancilla Pietatis*, 707–10.

[203] Bradford, *Godlie meditations*, sig. N8r.

[204] At least not in lowland Scotland. The blessing of a ship added to the Gaelic translation of the Book of Common Order twice invokes the threefold name with threefold responses. John Carswell, *The Book of Common Order, Commonly Called John Knox's Liturgy. Translated into Gaelic Anno Domini 1567*, ed. Thomas M'Lauchlan (Edinburgh, 1873), 240–1.

[205] 'Dwalphintramis', *Anatomy of the Service-Book*, 40.

plague of 1563, and again in *A godly garden,* but that book stood unapologetically in the medieval primer tradition.[206]

Once again, however, the puritan/conformist division is not clear cut here, even later in the period. We repeatedly find this kind of deliberately formulaic language in the mouths of moderate puritans. Grace Mildmay, for example, prayed:

> Oh Christ, Oh Immanuell, Oh holy one, O sonne of God, O lambe of God which takest away the sinnes of the world: Oh Rock of our strength, oh horne of our saluation, Oh our good shepheard, oh true vyne, oh bread of lyfe, oh fountayne of euerliuing waters: Oh word, Oh true light, oh, waye, oh truth oh, lyfe.

Something only a little more restrained is found in Michael Sparke's *Crumms of comfort.*[207] Lewis Bayly's *Practise of pietie* provided Trinitarian blessings to be recited twice daily. John Bruen did not, so far as we know, invoke the Trinity in this way, but he did write the word 'Hallelujah' in the first leaf of every book he owned, a ritualized practice which might have looked superstitious from a less fastidious Protestant. Others wrote 'Ihus', an echo of the medieval cult of the Holy Name.[208] Perkins' disciple Thomas Tuke applauded the repetition of prayers, as long as it was a matter of the heart as well as of the lips. 'We can double our sinnes . . . why should wee not double our suites for the pardon of them?' Something like this lay behind Richard Kilby's personal verbal ritual: his very frequent, and sometimes doubled, use of the word *Amen.* He did this, he explained, 'because I would be very earnest, and effectually fervent in my desire'.[209]

Set prayers, repeated formulae, and echoes of Bible and Prayer Book could, then, be mere lip-labour, coldly formulaic recitations uttered from habit or for form's sake, with little understanding or attention. But this jaded, Miltonian view does not do justice to the depth of the experience of using such texts. Such words allowed sinners to speak to God, not in their own halting syllables, but with the voice of the Church or indeed of the Spirit. This way fervour could find fluent expression, rather than being choked by inarticulacy or emotion. And it was a way for weak prayer to take wing. To appeal to the Holy Trinity, to recite the Lord's Prayer, to use a psalm, or even to double an Amen was to pray, no longer alone, but with the whole company of Heaven. The very fact that you were not praying in your own words made your prayer invincible.

---

[206] Foxe, *Actes and monuments* (1563), '598', recte 602; Edmund Grindal, *The Remains of Archbishop Grindal,* ed. William Nicholson (Cambridge, 1843), 481; *Godly garden,* fo. 81v; the same prayer was reproduced in Themylthorpe, *Posie of Praiers,* 134.

[207] Mildmay, 'Meditations', II.58; Sparke, *Crumms of comfort,* sigs E4r–5r.

[208] Bayly, *Practise of pietie,* 334, 376–7; Hinde, *Faithfull Remonstrance . . . of Iohn Bruen,* 71; Susan Wabuda, *Preaching during the English Reformation* (Cambridge, 2002), 169.

[209] Tuke, *Practise of the faithfull,* 12; Kilby, *Hallelujah,* 166.

10

Prayer as Struggle

'When Iaakob was left him selfe alone, there wrestled a man with him vnto the breaking of the day.' *Genesis 32:24.*

We have dwelt at some length on the practicalities of prayer: time, place, posture, words, and we have done so in the teeth of Protestant divines' insistence that these were matters of indifference. As Richard Waste put it, 'the soule of prayer . . . is the vigor & feruent intention of a mans Heart'.[1] The outward aspects matter because they reflected, and affected, what happened within. But it is now, at last, time to consider the inner experiences of prayer which early modern Protestants sought, and found.

PERSISTENCE AND SUFFERING

The most urgent and heartfelt prayer—especially within the early modern Protestant concept of prayer—arises out of need. Suffering, fear, struggle, or failure, in one form or another, are more or less constant features of human life, and they were features to which early modern Protestants paid close attention. And they taught and learned one thing above all about how they should pray under such circumstances: *persistently.*

There are obvious reasons why Protestants should have made so much of this perennial Christian theme. Persistence in the face of suffering allows you to exercise virtues such as patience, obedience, and faith. John Hooper counselled that God makes us wait for answers to prayer, not because he is callous or negligent, but because we need to be reminded of our utter dependence on him and of how little we deserve mercy. In that way we learn to accept what God gives us, rather than demanding what we want from him. Edward Dering saw it as a means by which we can learn our own weakness, and, consequently, discern the Spirit at work within us.[2] These simple themes persist through the period. Persistence is a sign of grace. The godless 'are feruent in prayer at the first, luke-warme in the middest, and keycold in the end'. The elect, by contrast, when their prayers do not meet with an immediate answer, may be 'as one that goeth down to the pit, it troubleth him as a

---

[1] Bod MS Rawl C.473 fo. 4r.
[2] Hooper, *Later Writings*, 247–9, 317; cf. Latimer, *Sermons by Hugh Latimer*, 165–7, 346–7; Dering, *Godly priuate praiers*, sigs I2v–3v.

sore crosse'. Yet 'though thine heart remaine barren in thine owne feeling', you still persevere, and will pray for the grace to do so all the more.[3]

Perseverance in prayer was not only Protestants' response to affliction; it was also the primary lens through which they understood God's purposes in permitting it. We suffer so that we might pray. 'When do I remember thee, but when affliction enforceth me?', asked Elizabeth Tyrwhit.[4] That was said with a note of self-reproach, but most Protestants recognized that it was both natural and right that affliction should spur prayer. God permits suffering partly in order to show us our need for him. Gabriel Powel used the image of nursing mothers weaning their children, who 'annoynt their breasts with bitter mustard'; similarly, God uses bitterness to wean us from worldliness. The future Bishop King preached that, like St Thomas, 'we are so obstinat wee will hardly beeleve, except Gods judgmentes thrust fingeres and nayles into our sydes'. The claim that affliction is 'euer adding life to our prayers' was a commonplace.[5]

Therefore, 'the problem of suffering is, paradoxically, not how to avoid suffering but how to suffer'.[6] Affliction is a gift. What matters is to use it wisely. 'Make vse of euery stroke of God', John Dod counselled.[7] Quite what that might mean is another matter. Samuel Hieron offered a prayer for use in response to worldly losses: 'Let this abridgement be a schoolemaster vnto mee, that I mai learne by it to draw mine affections from these fading and transitorie commodities.' Typically, however, the benefits of affliction are couched in more general and more passive terms. To John Bradford, suffering was a medicine: the worse it tastes, the better it is for you. 'Lustily, therefore, drink the cup; Christ giveth it.' A preacher in Oxford in 1605 used a still more passive image: 'the good stone is squared of, and knocked with the hammer to make it good and fitt for the building'.[8] Another recurrent metaphor was cooking:

> Raw flesh is noysome to the stomacke . . . and vnmortified men and women be no creatures fit for God; and therefore they are to be soaked and boyled in afflictions, . . . that they haue in them some rellish acceptable vnto God.[9]

It is a vivid image, but what do such passive conceptions of suffering mean in practice? How can you best assist the boiling process?

Fundamentally, by patient submission. Without patience, Henry Scudder argued, 'you are but halfe a Christian. . . . It is more rare, and more difficult to

---

[3] Tymme, *Chariot of Devotion*, 24; Byfield, *The Signes*, 98; Fawkener, *Collection of Promises*, 42; Capel, *Tentations*, 166–7.

[4] Tyrwhit, *Elizabeth Tyrwhit's Morning and Evening Prayers*, 82.

[5] Powel, *Resolued Christian*, 17; Manningham, *Diary*, 101; Mason, *Christian Humiliation*, 32, 35; cf., amongst many others, Pigg, *Meditations concerning praiers*, sig. A3v; Hayward, *Sanctuarie of a troubled soule* (1602), sigs 3r–4r; Warwick, *Spare-Minutes*, 36–8.

[6] Clifford Geertz, 'Religion as a Cultural System' in Michael Banton (ed.), *Anthropological Approaches to the Study of Religion* (1968), 19.

[7] Dod and Cleaver, *Ten sermons*, 10; cf. Dering, *Godly priuate praiers*, sig. H7r; Sparke, *Crumms of comfort*, sigs H12v–I4r.

[8] Hieron, *Helpe vnto Deuotion* (1608), 90; Bradford, 'An exhortacion', 247; FSL MS V.a.23 26r.

[9] Rogers, *Garden* (1616), sig. D3r; cf. George Abbot, *Brief Notes upon the whole Book of Psalms* (1651: Wing A65), sig. A7v.

obey in suffering, then to obey in doing'.[10] This call to patience was directed particularly at the sick. In an age without effective painkillers, the pressure on the gravely ill to curse or to despair must sometimes have been overwhelming. Hugh Latimer described accepting sickness patiently as 'the best service that thou canst do'. William Perkins argued that accepting afflictions 'with patience, meeknes, and lowlinesse' would train us in the virtues we will need when we come to our last illnesses.[11] But of course, this patience was not purely passive. As a prayer of Edward Dering's emphasizes, true patience is when we 'continually call vpon thee by hartie prayers, although we feele no release at all'. To wait for God is not to be silent.[12]

Similarly, Perkins' notion of using affliction to train your virtues suggests more than mere patience. He approvingly cited the example of the martyr Thomas Bilney:

> who oftentimes before he was burned, put his finger into the flame of the candle, not onely to make triall of his ability in suffering, but also to arme and strengthen himselfe against great torments in death.[13]

Protestantism tended to be wary of self-imposed suffering of this kind, which was too easily associated with Catholic practices and claims of merit. Yet they also embraced the principle which Martin Luther called the theology of the cross, a principle which had a deep influence on British Protestantism.[14] This held that Christ's sufferings were a pattern which his disciples must follow. Edward Hutchins quoted Christ's claim, 'I am the waie', and asked: 'But what was his waie to heauen? a crosse was his waie to the crowne, and thus would he leade thee to immortal glorie.' Powel described suffering as Christ's livery, 'the very principal & roiall garment which himselfe was clad with in this life. . . . Hee is a malapert seruaunt, that refuseth to weare his Maisters liuerie'. Or as Richard Sibbes put it more prosaically, 'No sound whole soule shall ever enter into heauen.' Being broken was essential.[15]

As a living doctrine, this has two opposed effects. If you are suffering, it is an encouragement. Your afflictions are not a sign of God's anger, but an honour and an essential stage in your salvation. The apostles 'reioyced, that they were counted worthy to suffer' for Christ's sake.[16] But if you are enjoying peace, prosperity, and health, the doctrine is more daunting. You should not officiously impose afflictions on yourself, a presumptive, fanatical, and popish practice. God disciplines those whom he loves, a much-cited verse argued, but that does not mean that you can

---

[10] Scudder, *Christians daily walke* (1628), p. 200. Cf. the similar discussion on p. 222, on which Nehemiah Wallington took extensive notes: Folger MS V.a.436 pp. 21–2.

[11] Latimer, *Sermons and Remains*, 185–6; Perkins, *First part of The cases of conscience*, 139–40; Perkins, *Salve for a sicke man*, 46–7; cf. Sparke, *Crumms of comfort*, sig. E1v.

[12] Dering, *Godly priuate praiers*, sig. A5v.

[13] Perkins, *Salve for a sicke man*, 47–8.

[14] Ryrie, 'Afterlife of Lutheran England', 227–34.

[15] Hutchins, *Davids Sling*, 266; Powel, *Resolued Christian*, 214–15; Sibbes, *Bruised reede*, 27–8; cf. Becon, *Sycke mans salue*, 16; Melville, *Godlie Dreame*, sig. A5v.

[16] William Bradshaw and Arthur Hildersam, *A preparation to the receiving of the Sacrament* (1617: RSTC 3511), fos 27v–28r.

make him love you by disciplining yourself. What you could do, however, was pray for appropriate affliction. During the plague of 1625, William Crashaw prayed, 'we begge not the remoouing of thy Iudgement, till it hath wrought thy worke' in purging Christians' hearts. Latimer suggested that the prayer to be delivered from evil might be, for some people, a prayer to be delivered from worldly good fortune. Francis Rous gave this a more mystical twist, arguing that 'Love delights in doing and suffering; yea it is angry when it may not be suffered to suffer'.[17]

This strange dance with suffering is at its most tangled when dealing with the spiritual affliction of temptation. The Lord's Prayer unambiguously asks not to be led into this, but the logic of the Protestant view of afflictions led in the opposite direction. Protestant commentators repeatedly stumbled over this point. Sometimes the petition was simply turned into a prayer for the strength to resist temptation, which is not quite the same thing, or it became a prayer only against *overwhelming* temptation, while still claiming that 'temptations needfull be/thy seruants strength to trie'. Another approach was to use paradox to redefine the problem: 'to bee without temptation is the greatest temptation'. Perkins, at least, explicitly recognized that there was a tension here, although he then simply overruled the words of the prayer with the doctrine. Latimer was even blunter. 'To be tempted of God is a good thing. . . . There is nothing so dangerous in the world as to be without trouble, without temptation.' He added that Christians 'should say, *Proba me*, "Lord, prove me and tempt me"'.[18]

In other words, the theology of the cross was being conscripted into the wider search for signs of grace in the individual's life. You did not search out affliction, but you watched anxiously to see whether affliction had searched you out. An anecdote which Latimer used repeatedly, and which Becon also borrowed, tells of St Ambrose visiting a nobleman who had never known ill fortune of any kind. Ambrose concluded that God could not be present in such a house and swiftly left it—not a moment too soon, because the earth promptly opened and swallowed it up.[19] Powel argued that being 'suffered to enioy continually all sorts of delights' was like being fattened for the slaughter: 'a most ruefull scourge of God, and a token of a reprobate soule'. The first Book of Homilies preached that 'nothing should . . . put us in such horrible fear' as when we know that we have deserved punishment from God, 'yet he striketh not, but quietly suffereth us in the naughtiness that we have delight in'. If God does not discipline you, clearly he does not love you.[20] Whether the contented and prosperous really took this to heart is another matter. Thomas Adams' comment in a best-selling sermon—'I would haue no man make

[17] Crashaw, *London's Lamentation*, sig. B7r; Latimer, *Sermons by Hugh Latimer*, 443; Rous, *Mysticall Marriage*, 81; cf. Hebrews 12:6.
[18] Heyden, *Bryefe Summe*, sigs G6v–7r; *A trewe mirrour or glase wherin we maye beholde the wofull state of thys our realme of Englande* (Wesel?, 1556: RSTC 21777), sig. C4r; Hunnis, *Seuen Sobs*, 45; Harrison, *Deaths aduantage*, III.20; Greenwood, *Workes*, II.111; Perkins, *Exposition of the Lords prayer*, 138–9; Latimer, *Sermons by Hugh Latimer*, 435; cf. Gerhard, *Meditations*, 405.
[19] Latimer, *Sermons by Hugh Latimer*, 435–6, 483; Becon, *Sycke mans salue*, 60–1.
[20] Powel, *Resolued Christian*, 229–30; *Certain Sermons or Homilies*, 77. Cf. Norden, *Pensiue mans practise*, 34–5; Rogers, *Seven treatises*, 118; Brinsley, *True Watch* (1608), 47; Hooker, *Laws . . . Books I–IV*, 43.

his riches an argument of Gods disfauour'—suggests that the idea was at least plausible,[21] but in practice this was probably more a rhetorical effect than a real problem. We do not actually see much sign of health and prosperity being taken as a warning or a judgement. As we shall see, it was just as plausible to interpret it as a sign of God's approval.[22]

When this argument was made, in fact, it was usually simply to reinforce its much more popular mirror image: that suffering is a proof of God's favour. Writing to a group of evangelical conventiclers arrested under Mary I, John Hooper described their imprisonment as 'a singular favour of God, and a special love of him towards you . . . a sign that he trusteth you before others of his people'. The logic extended to more peaceful times and more mundane or inward afflictions. 'Fierce combats', William Gouge insisted, 'doe giue vs more assurance that the Lord is still our God, and wee his souldiers, then light or no assaults.'[23]

This was, in fact, a core Protestant conception of the Christian life. 'It is so ordained of God', Latimer preached, 'that we should have war, yea, and nothing but war, a standing war.' Becon agreed that 'the lyfe of manne vpon earthe is nothinge els then a warrefare and contynuall aflycte wyth her ghostly enemies'.[24] Again the theme echoed on throughout the period, for conformist and puritan alike,[25] and again, those who did not feel that they were engaged in such perpetual combat were warned that this was a dangerous sign. 'The Devil letteth them alone', Latimer declared, 'because they be his already; he hath them in bondage, they be his slaves.'[26]

To persist in prayer under affliction, then, was to persist patiently, but it was also to persist in struggle, and that sense of endless struggle is one of the defining features of Protestant prayer.

THE ARMOUR OF GOD

For early modern Protestants, prayer was a battle. To pray was to embark on spiritual warfare against a daunting array of opponents. Only the most implacable prayer-warrior could emerge victorious.

This notion was of course no novelty. The most influential devotional work in 16th-century Europe, Erasmus' *Handbook of a Christian Soldier*, was built around it. The idea flourished in post-Reformation Catholic piety too, only reinforced by confessional strife, but Protestants, as ever, used it in a distinctive way.

---

[21] Adams, *The white devil*, 57.

[22] See below, pp. 452–6.

[23] Hooper, *Later Writings*, 616; Gouge, *Whole-Armor of God*, 53. Cf. Becon, *Sycke mans salue*, 65; Norden, *Pensiue mans practise*, 34–5; Rogers, *Seven treatises*, 118; Rogers, *Garden* (1616), sig. B8r; Andrewes, *Conuerted Mans New Birth*, 16–18; Dyke, *Worthy communicant*, 314–16.

[24] Latimer, *Sermons by Hugh Latimer*, 493; Becon, *Fruitful treatise of fasting*, sig. G1v.

[25] See, for example, Sutton, *Disce mori*, 63; Cowper, *Most Comfortable Dialogue*, sig. A3r; Narne, *Pearle of prayer*, 336; FSL MS V.b.198 fo. 67r.

[26] Latimer, *Sermons*, 441.

Any Christian who embraces this theme will reach for one Biblical passage above all: the call to don the armour of God in the letter to the Ephesians. Robert Bruce was appointed to his living in Edinburgh on the strength of a sermon on the passage; John Cosin chose it as one of the relatively few fixed Scriptural passages in his *Collection of Priuate Devotions*. One of the daily meditations Richard Rogers suggested was 'on the seuerall parts of the Christian armour, how God hath appointed to strengthen him thereby'.[27] Published and unpublished prayers for the armour of God were commonplace; personal covenants vowed daily 'to put on my Armour'.[28] It was a cliché. A preacher could urge that Scripture 'must be to us as armour not hangd up but putt on', and his audience would understand the reference; Francis Rogers, preaching at a soldier's funeral, found that the comparison almost made itself. John Andrewes even dreamt up the alternative armour of Satan: 'the brest plate of iniury, the girdle of falshood, the shoos of discord, the shield of infidelity, the helmet of mistrust, with the piercing darts of cruelty'.[29]

The image derives its power from its contradictions. The virtues which the text calls armour—verity, righteousness, faith, peace—make it clear that this is a strictly mental fight, but the martial analogy sets the mood. The dissonance between outward perception and spiritual reality was positively celebrated. Take, for example, this exhortation:

> Take a good hert vnto you, shrincke not. Fight a good fight. . . . God is your graund captain. You fighte vnder the banner of that most mighty and victorious Emperour Iesus Christ. Only continue, as you haue begon, and the daye is yours.

These words were spoken, not at Harfleur or Tilbury, but in Thomas Becon's *The sycke mans salue*, addressed to a dying man entering his final spiritual struggles.[30] The technique—a classic preacher's device—was boldly to ascribe a meaning to events which was entirely different from what met the eye, lifting the curtain of the mundane world to provide a glimpse of the spiritual reality underneath. Latimer liked to tell audiences that 'in this hall, amongst this audience, there be many thousand devils. . . . If we could see them, we should perceive them to hop and dance upon our heads for gladness'.[31] It would be enough to make anyone's scalp prickle, and it was a call to arms.

Indeed, the Biblical armour of God was if anything too passive and defensive. As various commentators pointed out, the passage only mentions one actual weapon: 'the sworde of the Spirit, which is the worde of God'. The notion that Scripture was the Christian's essential weapon was taken up with enthusiasm.[32] It was also

---

[27] Ephesians 6:11–17; Bruce, *Sermons . . . with Collections*, 9; Cosin, *Collection of Priuate Devotions*, 101–2; Rogers, *Seven treatises*, 240.

[28] For example, *This booke is called the Treasure of gladnesse*, fos 2v–3r; FSL STC 19358.2, flyleaf, verso; Mather, *Magnalia*, III.109.

[29] FSL MS V.a.394 fo. 18r; Rogers, *Sermon preached . . . . at the funerall*, sigs C1r–2r; Andrewes, *Conuerted Mans New Birth*, 20.

[30] Becon, *Sycke mans salue*, 530–1.

[31] Latimer, *Sermons by Hugh Latimer*, 438–9, 493.

[32] Latimer, *Sermons by Hugh Latimer*, 505; Becon, *Fruitful treatise of fasting*, sig. A6r; Becon, *Sycke mans salue*, 371–2; cf. Rogers, *Sermon preached . . . . at the funerall*, sig. D2v.

elaborated. For George Wither, the Psalter was not only a weapon in its own right, but 'a skilfull Muster-Maister', by which the Christian 'is directed how to manage his Armes'. William Cowper argued that 'euery Booke of sacred Scripture wee may call a seuerall Armour-house, furnished [with] . . . weapons of warre, both invasiue and defensiue'.[33] Another obvious weapon, prayer itself, which was tacked on to the end of the Biblical analogy, was regularly cited as 'a scourge to Satan', 'the christian man's special weapon, wherewith to strike the Devil'.[34] It seemed only natural to complete the Scriptural image by drawing in more modern military technology. 'All the Armories in the world', William Struther declared, 'haue not so terrible *Canouns* to Satan, as faithfull hearts grieued for sinne: Neither so fearefull *Bullets*, as feruent prayer.' John Andrewes' elaborate description of prayer's armoury included 'the Cannon shot of deepe sighes . . . the Arrowes of bitter teares'.[35]

These comments give us some flavour of these spiritual battles. The fight is sometimes described as a battle against your carnal self, or against sin, but even then it is usually personified.[36] So when Joseph Hall promises that in meditation 'we ransacke our deepe & false harts, find out our secret enemies, buckle with them, [and] expell them', the 'enemies' might simply be your own sins, but they might be something more elemental. Michael Sparke wished his readers to 'striue against our rebellious nature', but also, in the same breath, against 'an huge hoast of spirituall enemies'.[37] The martial metaphor of prayer depends on—even conjures up— diabolical opposition. To strap on the armour of God was to grapple with Satan, who until that moment had held you unresistingly in his grasp.

We have not yet paid much attention to the Devil's role in prayer. Protestants were as intensely conscious of him as their medieval predecessors had been, but their Devil was a different beast.[38] Latimer's vision of devils dancing on his people's heads was a hold-over from that old world. His successors had a more insidious but less immediately terrifying vision. Once, Richard Greenham recalled, Satan had been known 'by hornes, by huge collours, by clawes, or by an hollow voice', and was 'woonderfully feared', but now that he was preached as 'a more secret adversary, a spiritual tempter, a privy overthrower of the soule, no man almost regards him'.[39] In fact, earnest Protestants were as liable to terrifyingly vivid encounters with the Devil as anyone else. On various occasions the young Nehemiah Wallington met the Devil 'flying about the chamber like unto a blacke crooe', slept with a sword by his bedside in case the Devil troubled him, and flung his shoes away in case the Devil was in them.[40] Nor did Protestants deal with diabolic assaults very differently from their forebears. The blind and ignorant, Perkins claimed, 'spit at

[33] Wither, *Preparation to the Psalter*, 125; Cowper, *Triumph*, sig. A2r.

[34] Sandys, *Sermons*, 78; Latimer, *Sermons by Hugh Latimer*, 506; cf. Ephesians 6:18.

[35] Struther, *Scotlands Warning*, 46; Andrewes, *Conuerted Mans New Birth*, 22; cf. Gouge, *Whole-Armor of God*, 343.

[36] For an exception, see Rogers, *Seven treatises*, 238.

[37] Hall, *Arte of Divine Meditation*, 2; Sparke, *Crumms of comfort*, sig. G12r.

[38] Nathan Johnstone, *The Devil and Demonism in Early Modern England* (Cambridge, 2006).

[39] Parker and Carlson, *'Practical Divinity'*, 224.

[40] Wallington, *Notebooks*, 36–8.

the naming of him, and say that they defie him with all their hearts', but while he disliked the spitting, defiance was another matter. 'Resist the deuil, and he wil flee from you', they read in their Bibles, and took it to heart.[41] 'I would wee would feare God more and Satan lesse', wrote Richard Capel: the Devil was a broken reed for Protestant theologians, powerless for all his lies and temptations. Yet that theological understanding did not mesh well with most Protestants' experience and practice. Bishop Earle said of his caricatured she-puritan that 'it is a question whether she is more troubled with the Divell, or the Divell with her, she is alwaies challenging and dareing him'.[42] She might have taken that as a compliment, but it also captures an uncomfortable tendency in this kind of Protestantism: to pay attention to Satan rather than to God.

If raw terror was no longer Satan's stock-in-trade, what were Protestants fighting against when they fought him? Two things in particular; despair, which we have already considered at length and will return to below,[43] and distraction. This gave a focus to a perennial and slippery problem: the sheer difficulty which devotees experienced in keeping their minds on what they were doing. 'By-thoughts', as Perkins called them, were a constant problem.[44] Complaints about 'wandring wanton thoughts, vaine, foolish and idle imaginations', 'the importunate flies of worldly cogitations' that buzz around the distracted devotee, are standard fare throughout the period.[45] The problem had its merely natural side: we are, Daniel Dyke argued, like 'musical instruments, that will be put out of tune with the least distemper of the aire'. But Dyke also pointed out that the same person who nods off during a sermon can concentrate all night at the gaming tables.[46] Why should concentrating on spiritual matters be so hard? (The answer which seems obvious from a modern perspective—the unstructured, abstract nature of the endeavour—was not one that they discussed.) There was a theological answer: prayer was simply unnatural for sinners.[47] And there were mundane answers. Richard Greenham, practical as always, saw distraction as a sign of inadequate preparation for prayer, and Robert Harris ascribed it to general mental indiscipline. Joseph Hall recognized that if you were 'loded with housholde-cares', you would be prone to distraction, and he gave shrewd and humane advice on how to lay them down.[48]

But one more explanation remained: distraction was the Devil's work. Indeed, it was exactly the kind of thing which Protestants expected him to do. Dyke observed that Satan had tempted Christ during prayer, and argued that Christians could expect nothing less. Some divines even observed that Satan sometimes suggested

[41] Perkins, *Exposition of the Lords prayer*, 74–5; James 4:7; see, for example, Latimer, *Sermons and Remains*, 11–12; Wallington, *Notebooks*, 38; Winthrop, *Papers*, 198.

[42] Capel, *Tentations*, 34–5; Earle, *Microcosmographie*, 119–20.

[43] See above, pp. 27–34, and below, pp. 464–8.

[44] Perkins, *Exposition of the Lords prayer*, 55; Perkins, *Whole treatise*, 286; Perkins, *Godly and learned exposition*, 237–8; the term is also used in Bull, *Christian praiers*, 5.

[45] Browning, *Concerning publike-prayer*, 80; Tymme, *Chariot of Devotion*, 25.

[46] Dyke, *Mystery of selfe-deceiuing*, 353; Dyke, *Two Treatises*, 237.

[47] See above, p. 104.

[48] Parker and Carlson, *'Practical Divinity'*, 209; Harris, *Peters enlargement* (1627), 33; Hall, *Arte of Divine Meditation*, 30–1; cf. Scudder, *Christians daily walke* (1628), 46.

'good motions and meditations . . . vnseasonably', luring Christians to pray during sermons, or to recall sermons when they should be praying—anything to distract them from the pious task at hand.[49] This was alarming, but also, in its own way, comforting. It meant that the struggle against by-thoughts was neither mundane nor inconsequential. It was a sign that the Devil had been thrown onto the defensive. He strives to distract us in prayer 'because Prayer is the maine ram, that batters downe the wals of his kingdome'.[50] So when Lady Margaret Hoby found her thoughts wandering in church one Sunday, she could write in her diary:

> This day, as euer, the diuell laboreth to hinder my profitable hearinge of the word and callinge vpon god, but the Lord, for his mercis sach strengthen, his children to rissist and ouer Come.[51]

A problem which might feel trivial is re-presented as a matter of life and death. That thought in itself might help you to concentrate. When John Livingstone found himself unable to concentrate in the pulpit, a colleague urged him to persist, 'to get (as he called it) ane mends of the Devil'. With the stakes thus raised, he performed better.[52]

We may conclude this with a tale about the minister David Dickson, who was expelled from his parish for nonconformity and moved to the other end of Scotland so as to be able to preach. In his new home, however, Dickson discovered that sermon preparation, which had once taken him an hour or two per sermon, now consumed two days or more. Instead of blaming the disruption of the move or shaken confidence, he concluded that 'the devils of the North [were] worse than the devills in the West'.[53] Two things are worth noticing about that claim. First, it reminds us that while the Protestant Devil had been defeated by God, he could still be an insidiously real force in believers' lives, and second, it was a practical and useful conclusion. It will have assured Dickson that he was a child of God, worthy of Satan's baleful attention. It will also have provided an obvious plan of action: to pray for divine assistance. And it will have situated his personal difficulties in the cosmic drama of salvation, which amongst other things gave comfort about the eventual outcome. The great attraction of donning the armour of God, and closing for combat with Satan under Christ's captaincy, is that final victory can never be in doubt.

WRESTLING WITH GOD

The battles with sin, self, and Satan were, however, only the warm-up act for Protestantism's pious struggles. For the main event, we return to the question of what it meant to pray persistently.

---

[49] Dyke, *Two Treatises*, 236–7; Denison, *Monument or Tombe-Stone*, 94; cf. Goodwin, *Returne of Prayers*, 90; Goodwin, *Vanity of Thoughts*, 18.
[50] Clarke, *Holy Incense*, 47.   [51] Hoby, *Diary*, 66–7.
[52] Tweedie, *Select Biographies*, 139.   [53] Tweedie, *Select Biographies*, 317.

Our starting-point is the widely cited Biblical example of the Canaanite woman who appealed to Christ to heal her daughter. Christ appeared to reject her, but she renewed her appeal undaunted; he then praised her boldness and granted her request.[54] The point to note is that Christ met her appeal, not with silence, but with an active rebuff, and her response was not to wait patiently and humbly, but to argue with Christ until he conceded the point. That was precisely the lesson which her many Protestant admirers learned. William Cowper wrote:

> Let vs not therefore bee cast downe when the Lord worketh with vs after his own maner of working, by means vnknown to vs: let vs … with that woman of Canaan, cleaue to him the faster, when he seemes to put vs away.[55]

Arthur Hildersam agreed that if God will not answer our prayers, then it may be so that 'he might cause us hereby to cry lowder, and to be more importunate and fervent with Him in our prayers. For, so dealt He with the good woman of Canaan'. Latimer expounded a different Gospel passage, the parable of the importunate widow, to similar effect.[56]

So when early modern Protestants felt their prayers to have been rejected by God, they did not—as we might expect—repent for their ill-advised asking and submit humbly to divine providence. Instead, they saw this situation as the great trial of faith, an arena where all their God-given reserves of fervour and zeal would be needed but where, through grace, they would ultimately prevail. We shall see that early modern Protestants understood their lives as a progressive series of spiritual crises. These moments of unanswered, redoubled prayer fit that narrative beautifully.[57] Faithful persistence in the face of suffering was exactly what early modern Protestants expected to have to do. It gave their suffering meaning, and—potentially—brought them comfort in its midst.

If a single word can describe this mindset, it is *importunate*. There is only one relevant use of the word in the Bible, but it described better than anything else the attitude to which Protestants aspired in prayer, and it entered British Protestantism's jargon.[58] It describes prayer which will not take no for an answer; shameless prayer, which beats on Heaven's door and badgers God, doggedly taking a petition back and back for as long as it takes. Its simplest meaning was mere persistence: 'you must be importune, and not weary, nor cast away prayer'. But inevitably it applied to the mood and manner of prayer too. Hildersam took it to mean praying 'as they that will receive no nay'. Nicholas Byfield's advice ('thou must be instant, and not faint, or be discouraged'), and Ezekiel Culverwell's ('our onlie refuge is to

---

[54] Matthew 15:22–8; see, for example, Dering, *Godly priuate praiers*, sig. I3v; Habermann, *Enimie of securitie*, sig. b12r; Hunnis, *Seuen Sobs*, 5. Cf. Luther's use of this passage to the same effect: David C. Steinmetz, *Luther in Context* (Bloomington, IN, 1986), 30.

[55] Cowper, *Triumph*, 20. On the distinction between God's 'strange' and 'proper' work, alluded to here, see above, p. 91 and below, p. 250.

[56] Hildersam, *Doctrine of Fasting*, 42; Latimer, *Sermons by Hugh Latimer*, 165–7; cf. Luke 18:1–8.

[57] See below, pp. 416–22.

[58] Luke 11:8. In the Geneva Bible—but not the King James version—the word is also used, with negative connotations, in Judges 14:17, 16:16.

flie to God, and to ply him with fervent Prayer'), both capture something of this insistent urgency.[59]

The Canaanite woman, and many other Biblical examples, exemplify one distinctive feature of importunity in prayer: arguing with God. Protestant culture only slowly found the courage to do this, but it then made up for lost time. Initially we find devotees citing Biblical promises, or, as Latimer did, using prayers which 'put [God] in remembrance of his goodness shewed unto our forefathers': laying promises and precedents before God and asking for his mercy on that basis. Latimer believed that 'there is nothing more pleasant to God' than to hear such appeals based on his own words and character.[60] Such arguments became bolder. Richard Capel's prayers, it was said, were 'filled with . . . savoury arguments'. John Hayward sought to persuade God that it is in his nature to receive penitent sinners, almost wheedling him with appeals to Christ's Passion. This was the spirit in which Archibald Johnston of Wariston prayed, distraught, one night in July 1633: 'on my knees half desperat I put God in memorie and read unto him his auine promise'.[61] The implication that God's memory needs jogging may seem ridiculous, but Richard Sibbes explained unapologetically that this kind of lawyering makes for good prayer:

> It is an excellent skill and art in prayer, to have strong arguments. . . . It is a pitiful thing now, for Christians . . . to come to God only with bare, naked petitions . . . and have not reasons to press God out of his own word. They cannot bind God with his promise, nor with arguments that he hath been bound with before.

Infants who want something from their parents need only cry, he added, but when an older child has a request, 'the father looks for arguments that are moving to press him with'.[62]

In part—as so often in prayer—these 'arguments' are actually self-directed. Reciting God's past works and promises, Sibbes pointed out, warms and elevates the heart, and 'when the heart is thus raised and warmed, all the petitions come easily off'. Similarly, Elnathan Parr, urging his readers to imitate the psalmists' insistent questioning of God's apparent faithlessness, praised 'the power of these Interrogations. . . . Whose heart akes not in the very reading of them? How doe they increase our feeling, and raise our desires?'[63] But prayer was never merely self-directed rhetoric, and Sibbes' repeated talk of arguments *binding* God is no accident. If we warm our hearts, we do it to be able to bind God the better. This was put most forcefully by a Huguenot immigrant minister, who called his readers to 'vanquish & subdue' God. Citing Biblical examples of patriarchs who had turned God's hand aside through prayer, he argued that 'when with a zealous and feruent

[59] Latimer, *Sermons by Hugh Latimer*, 144–5; Hall, *Arte of Divine Meditation*, 40; Hildersam, *Doctrine of Fasting*, 41–2; Byfield, *Marrow of the Oracles* (1622), 549; Culverwell, *Treatise of faith*, 83.
[60] Latimer, *Sermons by Hugh Latimer*, 144.
[61] Capel, *Capel's Remains*, sig. A7v; Hayward, *Sanctuarie of a troubled soule* (1602), 71–2; Wariston, *Diary*, 43.
[62] Sibbes, *Works*, VI. 95–6.
[63] Ibid. VI. 95; Parr, *Abba Father*, 51–2.

spirit we doe encounter him in prayer, then doe we bind him (as it were) hand and foote, that hee cannot stirre'.[64] The image of binding was widely used: prayer, for Thomas Playfere, was 'a cord, wherewith we binde Gods hands, when he is readie to smite vs for our sinnes'.[65] Another trope emphasized how, through prayer, the earnest believer can 'stand in the breach' against God, and 'hinder him from executing his iudgements'.[66] Arguing with God, then, gives way to constraining or even commanding him. Thomas Knell claimed that in prayer 'we do call foorth God . . . to come and shew himselfe'. Thomas Goodwin took this furthest. Quoting God's words to the prophet Isaiah—'commande you me'—he described this as a 'transcendant priviledge of power . . . universally extended' to all God's people.[67]

On the face of it, this is simply silly, and it could certainly go wrong. Thomas Tuke feared that 'some imagine that they can make Powerfull prayers, thinking with their words and arguments to preuaile with God Almightie'; prayers are heard through Christ's intercession, not for 'multiplicity of reasons'.[68] Some people, Daniel Featley tutted,

> cast vp Prayers with strong lines to heauen, as it were (by force) to pul down a blessing from thence; somtimes they expostulate with God in a sawcie, and sometimes pose him in a ridiculous manner.[69]

Richard Norwood, as a young convert, decided to use brute force in prayer. 'I thought I would be so importunate that I would have no denial. . . . I thought I might obtain anything with importunity.' Eventually, however, he found himself 'stricken with some fear, and was sensible as it were of a check from God'. He concluded that graces are given when God chooses, not when we demand them, and approached prayer with a little more awe thereafter.[70]

Persuading, commanding and compelling God were, however, paradoxical rather than merely nonsensical. What made them so was the insistence that God wills us to do so. This can—again—be traced back to Luther, whom Perkins cited approvingly in this connection.[71] Luther's distinction between God's 'strange' work and his 'proper' work explains that God's denials of us are mere feints or bluffs, made specifically to build our faith and to redouble our prayers. God loses arguments with us because he intends to, and is bound because he wants to be— like a parent who lets a child win a game, but not without giving some semblance of a match. As Sibbes put it, 'CHRIST may act the part of an enemy, a little while', but all the time he 'supplyes us with hidden strength' to oppose him. So when he appears as an enemy, 'let us oppose his nature and office against it, he cannot deny

---

[64] Daniel Tuvill, *Christian Purposes and Resolutions* (1611: RSTC 24393.3), '234', '239' (*recte* 260–1). The author may in fact have been another naturalized Huguenot, Jean de Turval.

[65] Playfere, *Power of praier*, 2.

[66] Perkins, *Exposition of the Lords prayer*, 15, 18–19; Hildersam, *Doctrine of Fasting*, 34; and see above, p. 177.

[67] Knell, *Godlie and necessarie Treatise*, sig. A2v; Goodwin, *Returne of Prayers*, sig. A4v.

[68] Tuke, *Practise of the faithfull*, 13–14; cf. Denison, *Monument or Tombe-Stone*, 9.

[69] Featley, *Ancilla Pietatis*, 20.

[70] Norwood, *Journal*, 86–7.

[71] Perkins, *First part of The cases of conscience*, 96.

himselfe, hee cannot but discharge the office his Father hath layd upon him'.[72] Thomas Shepard shows us what this meant in practice. When his newborn son was taken dangerously ill in 1635, God 'stirred me up to pray for him, . . . and many arguments to press the Lord for his life came in'. So both the urge to pray, and the arguments, were provided directly by God, and the boy recovered.[73] This doctrine may seem either queasily self-centred or openly callous, but it has this advantage: it licences stubborn, insistent, and impertinent prayer, the prayer which will not give up because it knows that 'no' means 'yes'. It also fuelled a habit of combat and compulsion in prayer which goes well beyond what we have so far considered.

Tuke can introduce this to us, in a kind of reworking of the Gospel parable of the pharisee and publican:

> Two men pray for the kingdome of God, one importunatly, the other remisly: the violent caries it away: the cold suiter goes away empty. For God loues the laborious, and contemnes the lazie. . . . Pray feelingly if thou wouldest be heard fauourably: & if thou woullest taste of Gods beneuo[l]ence, be thou sure to presse him with all violence.

Nehemiah Wallington made a similar contrast in one of his notebooks: ordinary prayer knocks at Heaven's door, 'but an importunate prayre perceth it'.[74] The violence of the language here is particularly striking. God's weaponry is turned against its maker. Prayer could be a full-scale military assault. By it, Thomas Knell wrote, 'we enter into the verie sanctuarie of heauen, and there euen presentlie or openlie chalenge at Gods hand his promises'. George Herbert defined prayer as an 'Engine against th'Almightie'.[75] John Ley described Jane Ratcliffe's prayers in terms so vivid that they seem to echo the contemporary butchery of the Thirty Years' War:

> Such was her holy violence . . . as that she seemed not to knocke at heaven gate for another to open it, but to make a batterie upon it her selfe, and to breake in by the powerfull importunity of her owne supplications. Prayers and teares have beene accounted by the best Christians in former times their best weapons, and doubtlesse still are the most potent artillerie of the Church.[76]

If an artillery bombardment seemed inappropriate, there was the older, equally vivid, and perhaps more attainable vision of prayer as an arrow, able to 'pierce the heauens', penetrating God's defences and compelling his surrender.[77] Samuel Torshell, in a plague-time fast sermon, described the pestilence as God shooting his arrows at England, and so he rallied his hearers:

> Now this Countie intends it selfe for the Skirmish; and to fight with Gods weapons, against Gods judgements. Fasting dayes are dayes of pitcht Battell; God fights, and the Supplicants fight; prayers are the shafts, which are delivered flying to heaven.[78]

[72] Sibbes, *Bruised reede*, 185–7; cf. Narne, *Pearle of prayer*, 360, 421–2.
[73] Shepard, *God's Plot*, 34–5.
[74] Tuke, *Practise of the faithfull*, 7–8; LMA Guildhall MS 204, p. 303.
[75] Knell, *Godlie and necessarie Treatise*, sig. A5v; Herbert, *Works*, 51.
[76] Ley, *Patterne of Pietie*, 60–1.
[77] For example, Brinsley, *True Watch* (1611), II.54; Gouge, *Whole-Armor of God*, 343.
[78] Torshell, *Saints Humiliation*, 1.

God was being fought with his own weapons, in accordance with his will, but the battle was in deadly earnest.

By the 17th century, this kind of spiritual combat was described using one Biblical image above all. The book of Genesis describes how, one night, the patriarch Jacob wrestled with a stranger, whom the Geneva Bible's marginal note describes as 'God in forme of man'. Although the stranger lamed Jacob, Jacob refused to release him until he blessed him, which he duly did. Jacob then commented that he had 'sene God face to face'.[79] This mysterious story became a key reference point for Protestant piety, and wrestling with God a key metaphor for prayer. In Scotland, in particular, it seems to have become everyday spiritual jargon, with sometimes comical results: in the 17th century, it seemed natural to talk of 'meetings for wrestling and prayer'.[80] Scottish sources will routinely describe a pious individual as 'a mighty wrestler with God', 'a great wrestler', or as spending 'days and nights wrestling', 'much time in prayer and wrestling'. Wariston had 'strong wrestling with God in unutterable groans and unnumbrable tears'; John Forbes of Corse had 'fearefull wrestlings & comfortable victories'; the young William Cowper 'was trained vp with the wrestlings of God'.[81] Cowper even published a book on the subject: *Jacobs wrestling with God: or, the triumph of a christian* appeared in at least twelve editions from 1606–39. Wrestling was not quite so fundamental for English Protestants. Its puritan connections are made plain by the Brewster family, who were to sail to New England on the *Mayflower*, and who named one of their sons Wrestling. English usage often linked wrestling particularly with the practice of fasting.[82] But the image was still used across the confessional spectrum, and even appeared in English domestic decoration (Figure 12). We should persevere in prayer 'as Jacob ceased not to wrastle', advised Richard Greenham; 'learne of Iacob to wrastle with God', urged Elizabeth Jocelin. The proto-ceremonialist Christopher Sutton declared that 'all our watching, and fasting, and praying, is like Iacobs striuing with the Angell, O blesse me Lord'.[83]

More than any other Biblical passage, this strange story legitimized the notion of struggling with God. Almost the only other use of the word 'wrestle' in contemporary English Bibles was in the discussion of the armour of God in the letter to the Ephesians, a connection which helped to make combat with God in prayer seem like the highest form of spiritual warfare.[84] William Narne was amongst those who explicitly linked wrestling with God to fighting with the Devil, arguing that in

---

[79] Genesis 32:24–30.

[80] Bruce, *Sermons...with Collections*, 140.

[81] Tweedie, *Select Biographies*, 30, 307; Bruce, *Sermons...with Collections*, 144; Wariston, *Diary*, 165; Cowper, *Life and Death*, sig. A3r; Forbes, 'Diary', 16. Cf. Struther, *Scotlands Warning*, 54; Narne, *Pearle of prayer*, 341–2; Blair, *Life*, 85.

[82] For example, Cartwright and Wilcox, *Two treatises*, 15; Fisher, *Defence of the liturgie*, 31; Scudder, *Christians daily walke* (1631), 137. In Bolton, *Three-fold treatise*, the title of vol. 3 is 'The Saints Soule-exalting Humiliation; or Soule-fatting fasting: Which (Iacob-like) prevailes with God'.

[83] Parker and Carlson, *'Practical Divinity'*, 230; Jocelin, *Mothers Legacie*, 26; Sutton, *Disce mori*, 83. Cf. Brinsley, *True Watch* (1622), II.201; Preston, *Saints Daily Exercise*, 117; Clarke, *Holy Incense*, sig. A4r; Valentine, *Private Devotions*, 132–3.

[84] Dyke, *Worthy communicant*, 404–5.

Fig. 12. Overmantle, Bradninch Manor, Devon. A rare visual depiction of the recurring wrestling-Jacob trope, which evades the problem of how to depict God by having Jacob wrestle with an angel.

Permission granted by the photographer, Dr Tara Hamling; and by the owner, John Timperley.

prayer we must 'fight and wrestle against all opponents' in 'continuall warrefare', progressing from the world, sin, and Satan to God. Protestants were taught that the entire created and uncreated order, the heavens and the earth, stood against them, and that, in this impossible struggle, still 'in all these things thou will be more than a conquerour through him who loveth thee'.[85] Bishop Forbes, preaching on wrestling Jacob in Aberdeen in 1626, warned that 'the Lord sometymes doth ... present his own terror to his own dear children', but that he does this,

> to exercise them, to comfort them & to confirm them against all feares & assaults ... by giving them the victorie in this so great a conflict with God himselff, & consequentlie assuring them of certain victorie over all things.[86]

If we have wrestled with God and prevailed, who can stand against us?

Naturally, this is given its fullest expression in Cowper's treatise, which revels in the paradoxes of the subject. Just as God saves us from our sins by confronting us with them, and delivers us from evil 'by letting Sathan loose for a while vpon vs', so God did not bring Jacob the sleep of 'carelesse securitie, but hee tosses and shakes him to and fro, and exercises him with fighting and struggling all the night long'. Of course, neither he nor we could stand against God on our own, but 'by his secret grace he vnderprops vs. . . . It is God in vs who ouercommeth himselfe opponing vnto vs'. If we are rebuffed, we should renew our efforts, because we know God's rejection of us does not show his true nature, and if we act on that knowledge we show our faith. Jacob struggled with a 'holy wilfulnesse', desiring a blessing above all. 'This is a strife, which pleaseth the Lord, for in effect it is no other thing but a constant affirmation that his truth is inviolable.'[87] Once again, then, this opposes perception and reality as sharply as possible. When all is lost, when the world and God stand firm against you, that is the moment to dig in your heels and tighten your grip in faith that the dawn must be near. No wonder early modern Protestants could be such stubborn enemies.

The specifics of the story of wrestling Jacob also had something to offer. More than mere battle with God, wrestling involves unyielding effort and persistence. Perkins' disciple Robert Hill, urging persistence in prayer, cited Jacob as a model: 'let not vs let him go till wee be heard'.[88] Robert Harris imagined a Christian whose prayers are rejected: 'this is (saith hee) but to try me, therefore he spits vpon his hands, and takes better hold ... and poures so many petitions, and arguments vpon God, that there is no resistance'. In his family prayers, John Bruen 'would so wrestle with God by prayers and teares, like *Jacob*, that hee would not let him go, untill like an *Israel*, he had by praying and weeping prevailed with him'.[89] (Presumably he would not let the family go either.) This is still patience, of a sort, but an even more active patience than that of the importunate suitor. It is the patience which knows

---

[85] Narne, *Pearle of prayer*, 336, 342; cf. Romans 8:37.
[86] Forbes, 'Diary', 60.
[87] Cowper, *Triumph*, esp. 15–18, 34–7, 44–5, 82, 91.
[88] Robert Hill, *Christs prayer expounded, A Christian Directed, and a Communicant prepared* (1606: RSTC 13472), sig. A7r; cf. Brinsley, *True Watch* (1608), 169.
[89] Harris, *Peters enlargement* (1624), 16; Hinde, *Faithfull Remonstrance . . . of Iohn Bruen*, 72.

that, if it presses hard enough, relentlessly enough, and for long enough, it will eventually be able to squeeze out a few drops of mercy. If the physical struggle of kneeling was part of the Protestant experience of prayer, the conviction that you were wrestling with God gave meaning to it.[90] Aching knees, cramped muscles, and gritted teeth might feel like victory.

Another element of the story—Jacob's injury—also proved fruitful. It could be used simply to mean that even apparent defeat was a sign of imminent victory, and was therefore a further call to persist.[91] But this detail was obscure enough that it could be made to mean almost anything. In particular, it could be applied to the ongoing struggle with sin. Some might feel, for example, that after a bout of prayer-wrestling, their sins were worse than ever. Harris argued that this was Jacob's wound: your sins were clearly in their death-throes, 'as the fowle struggles, and sprunts most when the head is off'. Some might rise from their knees with their sense of sin unchanged. Henry Scudder comforted them:

> If when you haue wrastled and contended with God in praier, you are forced to goe halting and limping away in the sense of your infirmities, as Iacob did; bee not dismayed, for it is a good signe that you haue preuailed with God as Iacob did.

Some might feel that they had triumphed over their sins. William Struther explained that 'this is the fruite of our wrestling with God . . . . Though we haue preuailed, our corruption will bee so disjoynted, as it be not so strong thereafter'.[92] The image could be made to fit any set of facts.

Another reading of wrestling Jacob takes us in a different direction. Wrestling is a peculiarly intimate form of violence, not very different from embracing. We hold onto God in prayer-wrestling because we are trying to overpower him, but also because we wish to cling to him. One late Elizabethan preacher blended the language of wrestling with the imagery of the Song of Songs, urging his hearers to 'seek vnto him, whom thy soule loveth . . . run after him, and take hold of him by the armes of faith'.[93] Another, more common and more revealing motif linked the language of wrestling and of tears. This was suggested by the only explicit Biblical cross-reference to the wrestling Jacob story, in which the prophet Hosea wrote that Jacob 'had power ouer the Angel, & preuailed: he wept and prayed vnto him'. In a culture which already associated tears with powerful prayer, this was heady stuff. Nehemiah Wallington, arguing for the power of tears in one of his notebooks, transcribed the verse from Hosea, amending it to assert that Jacob prevailed *by* weeping. Thomas Playfere argued that 'weeping is more pearching, and more forcible to perswade God, and euen to wound his heart, then all the eloquence, then all the rhetorick in the world'—and cited Hosea's account of Jacob.[94]

---

[90] See above, p. 173–7.   [91] Sibbes, *Bruised reede*, 284.
[92] Harris, *Peters enlargement* (1624), 18; Scudder, *Christians daily walke* (1628), 53; Struther, *Scotlands Warning*, 54.
[93] FSL MS V.b.214 fo. 91v; Song of Songs 3:1–4.
[94] Hosea 12:4; LMA Guildhall MS 204, p. 306; Playfere, *Meane in Mourning*, 17–18.

This linking of violence and tears—two of the most potent elements of Protestant prayer—was literally irresistible. God was powerless before it. 'Prayers, and Teares', William Struther observed, 'are the kindlie weapons of Gods Church, which . . . ouercome God, and bow him to mercie.'[95] Weeping, which washes your corruption from you, also brings you into conformity with God's will, and wrestling, like all prayer, is not really the work of the human sinner, but of the Holy Spirit. The combination of the two makes arguments irresistible, and violence overpowering. Describing a day of prayer and fasting, Wallington noted with satisfaction that 'there were many that tuged hard with the Lord that day and weept abundantly'.[96] The tears made the tugging possible. It was when sinners were truly and bitterly brought low that God could fight within them, and that they could stand in the gap, confronting the world, the Devil, and God, confident that none of them could prevail. If they only abandoned themselves, they could bend the universe to their will, or rather, God would use them to bend himself to his own will. This humble defiance and war-like penitence was the heart of Protestant prayer.

[95] Struther, *Scotlands Warning*, 45; cf. Brinsley, *True Watch* (1608), 169; Brinsley, *True Watch* (1611), II.14; Andrewes, *Conuerted Mans New Birth*, 22.
[96] Wallington, *Notebooks*, 151; cf. 180. 'Tugging' was a near-synonym for wrestling in early modern usage.

PART III

THE PROTESTANT AND THE WORD

Private prayer was the lifeblood of Protestant piety, the central love affair between God and the believer, but it did not exhaust the practices of Protestant piety, and the second half of this book considers the other practices which supported or accompanied it. In Parts IV and V we will consider how Protestant piety was enacted in public and in the course of Protestant lives. But first we must look at another kind of private piety: the intense, complex relationship between Protestants and the written word.

11

Reading

'For the worde of God is liuelie, & mightie in operation, and sharper then anie two edged sworde . . . and is a discerner of the thoghtes and the intentes of the heart.' *Hebrews 4:12*

LITERACY AND LEARNING

In Arthur Dent's seminal dialogue, *The plaine mans path-way to heauen*, Asunetus—an ignorant but well-meaning man who will, in the end, be converted—protests at his godly neighbours' insistence that he attend sermons and read the Bible. For people like him, he says, that is simply impractical. 'We cannot liue by the scriptures: they are not for plaine folke, they are too high for vs.' He adds that in any case he cannot read. Remarkably, none of the other characters in the dialogue respond in any way to that final admission. Indeed, some time later, the minister, Theologus, accuses Asunetus of having 'scant a Bible in your house', and adds that even if he has one, 'it is manifest that you seldome read therein, with any care or conscience. . . . You read not two Chapters in a weeke'. Asunetus' reply suggests that even he has forgotten that he is supposed to be illiterate. Theologus goes on to recommend that Asunetus work through three substantial catechisms.[1]

The fact that Dent scarcely notices a complaint which he himself inserted in his text is a sign of one of early modern Protestantism's most important blind spots. This was book-religion, and that in itself could be unattractive. Another *vox populi* in a puritan dialogue, George Gifford's Atheos, rejected his more zealous neighbour's religion by asking, 'What woulde yee haue men doe? . . . Sitte mooping always at their bookes, I like not that.'[2] But for a substantial majority of the population of early modern Britain, it was not a matter of preference. Like Asunetus, they could not read. Did Protestant piety have anything to offer such people, or did it, like Dent, simply ignore the problem?

It was possible to be a zealous but illiterate Protestant. Private prayer and public worship were open to literate and illiterate alike—if not quite equally open. But the illiterate were excluded from what was, to ministers at least, a central part of Protestant experience, and they 'must needs fare the worse'.[3] What the Protestantism of the illiterate felt like is almost impossible to know, since the written sources we turn

---

[1] Dent, *Plaine mans path-way*, 27–8, 134–5, 324b.
[2] Gifford, *Briefe discourse*, fo. 3r.   [3] Rogers, *Seven treatises*, 586.

to can never show it to us directly. All we can do is glimpse them through their educated brethren's condescending eyes, but a few themes do emerge nevertheless.

One particular illiterate Protestant has recently become well known: John Bruen's servant Robert Pasfield, or 'Old Robert', who was 'ripe in understanding, and mighty in the Scriptures' despite being 'utterly unlearned', but Pasfield is a poor exemplar of illiterate Protestantism. For a start, he was not *entirely* illiterate: he could not 'read a sentence, or write a syllable', which implies that he could recognize letters, numbers, and perhaps some words. If he could not, it is hard to see how he managed to act as the family's 'Index' to Scripture, or to use the girdle for which he is famous—this was marked with a series of knots and marked thongs to help him recall the numbers of chapters and verses of each book in the Bible. More importantly, Pasfield is presented not as an exemplar, but as a kind of godly pet or *idiot savant*.[4] Aside from him, examples of godly illiteracy are very rare. There are the blind, some of whom might memorize large chunks of the Bible—even, allegedly, the whole thing.[5] John Foxe told bracing tales of medieval and even contemporary illiterates who had assiduously memorized Scripture.[6] But in the age of the printing press, illiterate Protestants were more often objects of condescension than sympathy. Ben Jonson's pen-portrait of an illiterate gaoler converted by a godly prisoner described how the man could now 'pare his nailes, and say his prayers'. Amongst John Phillips' satirical parade of churchgoing hypocrites is 'old *Robin*',

> Who although write or read he neither do,
> Yet hath his Testament chain'd to his wast,
> And his blind zeal feels out the proofs as fast,
> And makes as greasie Dogs-ears as the best.[7]

A more charitable reading of this would suggest that illiterate Protestants were ashamed to admit their condition.

Illiterate Protestants were usually advised bluntly to adopt one of two paths. First, to seek out someone who could read to them.[8] This was certainly sometimes possible. Elizabeth Isham remembered her pleasure at hearing one of her maids, who was literate, excitedly tell another, who was not, what she had just read in the Bible. Nicholas Bownde, who urged illiterate families to equip themselves with Bibles so that any literate visitors could read to them, also suggested that they could produce their own in-house solution by having their children taught to read, so that they could read aloud to their parents. And this too happened in real life; it was how the Cardiff fisherman Rawlins White learned his Gospel.[9] The prospect of learned

---

[4] Hinde, *Faithfull Remonstrance . . . of Iohn Bruen*, 56–8. See Tara Hamling, 'Old Robert's Girdle: Visual and Material Props for Protestant Piety in Post-Reformation England' in Martin and Ryrie, *Private and Domestic Devotion*; R. C. Richardson, *Household Servants in Early Modern England* (Manchester, 2010), 135–7.

[5] Foxe, *Actes and monuments* (1570), 2137; Melville, *Autobiography*, 22; Hunt, *Art of Hearing*, 103.

[6] Foxe, *Actes and monuments* (1570), 1726; Foxe, *Actes and monuments* (1583), 236, 823.

[7] Ben Jonson et al., *Eastward hoe* (1605: RSTC 4970), sig. H4v; Phillips, *Satyr*, 2.

[8] See, for example, Rogers, *Seven treatises*, 290; Brinsley, *True Watch* (1608), 52. Cf. Thomas Cranmer, *Miscellaneous Writings and Letters of Thomas Cranmer*, ed. John Cox (Cambridge, 1846), 103.

[9] Isham, 'Confessions', fo. 14r; Bownde, *Doctrine of the Sabbath*, 202; Foxe, *Actes and monuments* (1570), 1726.

youths teaching their ignorant elders was almost a cliché of the Reformation, and tickled Protestantism's taste for paradox, but it was also a reality. As a pious schoolboy, Jeremy Whitaker used to read his sermon notes aloud to his Yorkshire neighbours. In June 1611, a huge storm terrified the young Simonds D'Ewes, his schoolmates, and their neighbours. Some feared that the Day of Judgement had come, and as a result 'there came divers poor people to the school to desire some of the scholars to go with them to their houses, and to read prayers there'.[10] Just occasionally, a pious, literate, eight-year-old is exactly what you need.

Much the better solution, however, was actually to learn to read, and the urgings to do this become more categorical through our period. Thomas Becon's early pragmatism on the subject—advising the devout on what to do 'yf thou canst rede'—was soon overtaken by a zeal to spread literacy. Occasionally there is a recognition that some are 'incapable of Instruction to learne to reade', or indeed have to work for a living and are too busy. But Rogers had no patience with such excuses: is God's word not worth a little work? When he visited his parishioners, George Herbert's country parson inquired in the same breath whether they prayed and sang psalms, and whether or not they could read: failure in either department was clearly reprehensible.[11] To modern eyes, this seems like mere elitism, but there is another side to it. The need and opportunity to read God's Word was itself a powerful impetus to learn to read. Isham learned to write so that she could write down her prayers, and when older she spent two or three years teaching one of her mother's maids every day 'till she could read in the bible'. Herbert's parson undertook to teach everyone in his household to read, 'so that his family is a Schoole of Religione, and they all account, that to teach the ignorant is the greatest almes'. Dorothy Leigh's best-selling advice book similarly urged its readers that all of their children, boys and girls, rich and poor, must be taught to read the Bible, and suggested that even labouring families could find time on the Sabbath to do this. Henry Burton was encouraged to read by his mother, who showed him an English New Testament which had belonged to his grandfather in Mary I's reign; when he could read it, she promised, he could have it.[12] The invocation of Mary's reign, when Protestants had risked their lives to read, was no accident. Why, the preachers reasoned, should those who lived in the heedless security of peaceful times show any less commitment?

This bracing approach to illiteracy points us to a wider feature of early modern Protestant piety. One reason that modern instincts tend to have sympathy for the illiterate, while early modern ones simply told them to learn to read, is that our age values learning much less than theirs. The intellectualism of early Protestantism is hard to overestimate. When John Foxe described the wave of Protestant conversions that had supposedly swept through the Suffolk village of Hadleigh, he did not

[10] Clarke, *Collection*, 160; D'Ewes, *Autobiography*, 39.

[11] Becon, *Gouernans* (1549), fo. 10r; *Two treaties the first concerning the Holy Scriptures*, 8; BL Royal MS 18.B.xix fo. 9v; Rogers, *Seven treatises*, 586; Herbert, *Works*, 248.

[12] Isham, 'Confessions', fos 5r, 17r; Herbert, *Works*, 240; Leigh, *Mothers blessing*, 24–5; Burton, *Narration*, 1.

speak of transformed lives or spectacular holiness, but rather of how the people 'became exceeding wel learned in the holye scriptures', so that 'the whole towne seemed rather an Uniuersitie of the learned, then a town of Cloth-making or labouring people'.[13] Protestantism was a movement born and bred in universities, and it aspired to turn Christendom into a giant university, in which Christians would spend their time in private study or in attending the lectures and seminars which they called sermons, prophesyings, and conferences.

The Protestant priority on learning, and the blurring of learning and holiness, shows itself in several ways. Prayers for right knowledge, and for the deeper understanding that followed from it, were part of the Protestant devotional repertoire from the beginning. Thomas Becon had his readers pray 'gyue me vnderstandynge . . . so that I wyth a gladde hart searche thy lawe', and described the Holy Spirit as 'the schole master to lead the faithful into all truth'. Most other Tudor collections of prayers provided prayers for true knowledge of God or undefiled understanding of Scripture.[14] The theme became less pressing in the 17th century but still persisted, especially in children's prayers or in prayers before hearing sermons.[15] There was a constant readiness also to see study as a work of piety. This was natural for ministers, since it was part of their vocation.[16] But in the 17th century, lay people, too, were being exhorted to adopt this pattern. For Lewis Bayly, studying divinity was a normal part of Sabbath observance.[17] Children especially were taught that study was a pious duty, and this is how lasting habits of mind are formed. As a boy Richard Sibbes had to walk three or four miles to school each day, but shunned the company of other boys on the road, since they teased him for his poverty. Instead, his habit was, 'as soon as he could rid himself of their unpleasing company, to take out of his Pocket or Sachel, one Book or other, and so to goe reading and meditating'.[18] Thus a story of bullying and ostracism becomes one of choosing to turn away from the world, and of finding God by walking with your nose in a book.

Protestants stressed learning because they believed that salvation came, not merely through faith, but through well-informed faith. 'They must be first full of knowledge, that will be full of goodnesse', Jeremiah Dyke insisted: 'ignorant persons cannot say that they are in the covenant of grace'. Knowledge, that is, was not faith, but it was a precondition for it. According to John Dod, 'a man may know more then hee beleeueth; but hee can neuer beleeue more then hee knoweth'.

---

[13] Foxe, *Actes and monuments* (1583), 1518. On Hadleigh see John Craig, 'Reformers, conflict and revisionism: the Reformation in sixteenth-century Hadleigh', *Historical Journal* 42 (1999), 1–23; on Protestant intellectualism, John Morgan, *Godly Learning: Puritan Attitudes towards Reason, Learning and Education, 1560–1640* (Cambridge, 1986).

[14] Becon, *Gouernans* (1544?), fos 102r–v; Becon, *Pomaunder of prayer*, fos 35v–36r; Coverdale, *Remains*, 541; Bull, *Christian praiers*, 156; Day, *Booke of Christian Prayers*, fo. 89v; Dering, *Godly priuate praiers*, sigs D1v–2r, F3v, H5v–6r.

[15] For example, Thornton, *Autobiography*, 13; Gee, *Steps of Ascension*, 2–3.

[16] Knappen, *Two Diaries*, 55–7, 60, 62, 65, 76; cf. Sandys, *Sermons*, 333; Latimer, *Sermons by Hugh Latimer*, 320.

[17] Bayly, *Practise of pietie*, 443.

[18] Sibbes, *Works*, I.cxxxv; cf. Cowper, *Life and Death*, sig. A3v; Gee, *Steps of Ascension*, 327–8.

'The Lorde oure God', claimed Anthony Gilby, 'is the God of knowledge.'[19] Quite how much knowledge was enough was a trickier matter. One obvious approach was to list essential doctrines. Lewis Bayly's diagrammatic representation of pious practice begins with, and is dominated by, what the pious must *know* (Figure 13), and accordingly, he spent the first sixty pages of his best-selling book expounding the nature and attributes of God. However, it was more usual to measure knowledge by the individual's opportunity and capacity. Ignorance, like illiteracy, was innocent if you could not help it, but if you had opportunities for learning and spurned them, woe betide you.[20] The Edwardian Book of Homilies echoes Erasmus in claiming that no-one can be called a Christian 'if he will not apply himself . . . to read and hear, and so to know the books of Christ's gospel and doctrine!'[21] In 1549, John Hooper provided a prayer to be said before hearing the Bible read, which asked God 'to illuminate our minds, that we may understand the mysteries contained in thy holy law; and into the same self thing that we godly understand, we may be virtuously transformed'. Understanding became a part of sanctification.[22]

So if learning was not a Christian's highest attainment, it was certainly the first. The process of conversion was often understood as one of enlightenment. 'Education', for Richard Baxter, 'is God's ordinary way for the Conveyance of his Grace'; effectual calling, William Cowper agreed, begins with 'the illumination of the mind'. One Scottish preacher saw it as his role to nurture his people 'in the fear and information of the Lord'.[23] This was underpinned by the conviction that, as Dent put it, 'ignorance is a sinne', and not merely a sin, but a seedbed of sin: 'ignorance of God's word', Hooper warned, 'bringeth with it a murrain and rot of the soul'. Nearly a century later, William Pemble agreed that 'he thats ignorant must needs be wicked, even because he is ignorant'.[24] Thus ignorance was viewed with horror and derision, not indulgence or pity. When Gifford's Atheos praised his time-serving curate, his neighbour Zelotes sneered back, 'I smell how vnmeete he is, and also howe ignorant you are'. William Pinke at least recognized the danger of pride here, reminding his readers that but for the grace of God, 'you might haue groped & stumbled in a thicker mist of stupidity then now befooles your vnnurtured brethren'. Jeremiah Dyke, by contrast, was openly contemptuous of those

[19] Dyke, *Worthy communicant*, 99, 105, 111; Dod and Cleaver, *Ten sermons*, 75. Anthony Gilby, *An answer to the deuillish detection of S. Gardiner* (1548: RSTC 11884), fo. 2r. Cf. Lucien Joseph Richard, *The Spirituality of John Calvin* (Atlanta, 1974), 119; Sandys, *Sermons*, 424.

[20] For example, Perkins, *Whole treatise*, 298–301; Perkins, *How to live*, 53; Dyke, *Worthy communicant*, 112.

[21] *Certain Sermons or Homilies*, 1, 5. Cf. Erasmus, *Christian Humanism*, 99–100; Dod and Cleaver, *Ten sermons*, 73.

[22] Hooper, *Later Writings*, 3; cf. Hooper, *Early Writings*, 33.

[23] Baxter, *Reliquiae Baxterianae*, 7; Cowper, *Triumph*, 223; Margo Todd, *The Culture of Protestantism in Early Modern Scotland* (New Haven and London, 2002), 50–1; Packer, *Quest for Godliness*, 69.

[24] Dent, *Plaine mans path-way*, 328b; Hooper, *Later Writings*, 200; Pemble, *Introduction to worthy receiving*, 22.

            The Protestant and the Word

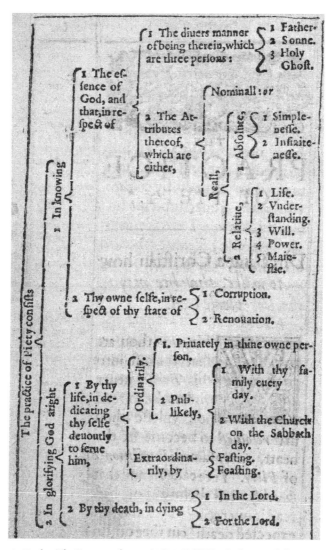

Fig. 13. Lewis Bayly, *The Practise of pietie* (1620: RSTC 1604), p. 2. 'The practice of piety consists of 1. In knowing.' A vivid depiction of the primacy of the intellect in Protestant piety. Bodleian Library, Oxford.

who claimed to be ignorant but well-meaning. 'Thus silly creatures delude they themselves, and their owne soules. . . . Your mindes are naught, starke naught.'[25]

If that seems harsh, it is because ignorance was seen not as a passive emptiness, innocent of knowledge, but rather as an active, malignant force. It was not the

[25] Gifford, *Briefe discourse*, fo. 2v; Pinke, *Tryall of a Christians loue*, II.26; Dyke, *Worthy communicant*, 110–11.

absence of learning, but the wilfull rejection of it. Queen Katherine Parr blamed her former sins on 'a blinde guyde called Ignoraunce, who dimmed so mine eyes, that I could neuer perfectlye get any sighte of the fayre, goodly, streight, and ryght wayes'.[26] This made theological sense. If God is truth, naturally 'all sinne is either from false principles or ignorance, or mindlesnesse, or unbeleefe of true'. John Dod argued at some length that sin is inherently foolish—which, if it leads to Hell, it obviously is. As John Norden pointed out, ignorance is 'the mother of disobedi-ence', since we can hardly obey a commandment we have not heard.[27] But if ignorance begets sin, the reverse is also true. Elizabeth Hastings, the countess of Huntingdon, recognized that 'the thicke cloudes & mists of my sinns . . . corrupt my soule & darken my vnderstanding'. Ignorance, therefore, is culpable. It is content with itself, contemptuous of learning, and thus a form of the deadly affliction which Protestants called 'security'.[28]

If the association between sin and ignorance is strong, so is that between virtue and knowledge. True knowledge fills the heart with good things. Thomas Goodwin's first remedy against inward sin was 'to get the heart furnished and enriched with a good stock of sanctified and heavenly knowledge'. Rogers pointed out that the first component of the armour of God was truth, and so that 'holding and keeping the truth' was essential to all spiritual warfare.[29] Again, this worked both ways. One of the marks of a zealous Christian was that 'he desireth newe knowledge, and newe vnderstanding of heauenly thinges', for 'what the heart liketh best, the minde studieth most'.[30] This was indeed the daily ambition of many early modern Protestants. Those using Abraham Fleming's devotions would pray each morning for their souls to be decked 'with the riches of thy true knowledge', rather than with graces or virtues as such. Those using Edward Dering's would ask that 'as this day addeth somewhat to our age, so let thy holy spirit adde therin somwhat to our knowledge & fayth'.[31] Grace Mildmay saw this at work in herself, and was thankful. 'Good education . . . preser-ueth the tender plants & springs of our generation in Christ Jesus.'[32]

The stress on *good* education is important. Not all education was good. Chris-tianity has always had a love–hate relationship with scholarship and the intellect, and if Protestantism veered more towards love, it did not forget the other side of the tradition altogether. The young Robert Blair read Petronius' *Satyricon* for its proverbially elegant Latin, but he was so shocked by its author's morals that he burned it, 'wishing that there had been no more copies of it in the world'.[33] Even

---

[26] Katherine Parr, *The lamentacion of a sinner* (1547: RSTC 4827), sig. A3v.
[27] Sibbes, *Bruised reede*, 302; Dod and Cleaver, *Foure Sermons*, 16–19; Norden, *Pensiue mans practise*, 122.
[28] Huntington Library, San Marino, CA, MS 15369 fo. 2v; FSL MS V.a.519 fo. 4r; and see above, pp. 23–4.
[29] Goodwin, *Vanity of Thoughts*, 43; Rogers, *Seven treatises*, 260; cf. Norden, *Pensive mans practise . . . The second part*, 62.
[30] Dent, *Sermon of Repentance*, sig. B7r–v; Sibbes, *Bruised reede*, 304.
[31] Fleming, *Diamond of deuotion*, 115; Dering, *Godly priuate praiers*, sig. F3v. Cf. Taylor, *Christ Revealed*, 149.
[32] Mildmay, 'Meditations', 23.
[33] Blair, *Life*, 16.

less obviously corrupt knowledge could become a substitute for faith, a source of pride, or simply a distraction from the pursuit of godliness. Edward Dering prayed for learning so as to relieve his conscience, not 'to satisfie vaine curiositie or bragge of knowledge'.[34] Cowper described Adam's sin as one of reaching for knowledge above his station. Even for ministers, whose pursuit of learning should be zealous, it risked becoming an idol. Joseph Hall warned that 'it is noe shame not to know all things, but a just shame to ouer search in any thynge', a dictum which Elizabeth Hastings copied into her commonplace book.[35]

Hence the need to distinguish between different kinds of knowledge. Abstract belief—mere 'story-knowledge', as it was sometimes called—was not faith. Do not trust to be saved simply for believing, a much-cited Biblical passage warned: 'the deuils also beleue it, & tremble'. 'Knowledge swimming in the braine' or 'knowledge and talk . . . is not sufficient', if it is merely 'vayne, blind knowlege, both cold & dead'. True knowledge, and right understanding, would issue in faith, and 'alter and dispose the affection and the whole man'.[36] It was equally uncontroversial to point out that if faith and reason should clash, faith must win out. 'God must bee trusted', William Perkins insisted, 'though that which hee saith bee against reason and experience.'[37] But this point was rarely made in our period. Divines assumed that the case rarely arose in practice. Apparently God did not say such things very often.

With hindsight, we can see that these arguments would lead to the modern distinction between 'head' and 'heart', which sees the intellect and the affections as opposed parts of the person. The distinction first begins to be used in English during our period. As Ted Campbell's valuable study of early modern 'heart-religion' points out, this meaning of 'heart' was a novelty. In medieval usage, the heart had been the seat of the intellect as well as of the will and the passions, since reason was ultimately a matter of intuitive perception. This meant that, at least at the beginning of our period, believers did not oppose the intellect to the emotions in the way which nowadays seems obvious. Archbishop Sandys could in the same breath declare that the Eucharist 'is to feed our souls' and 'is meat for the mind'; the two ideas were virtually synonymous. Reformed Protestants were cerebral, but were not therefore dispassionate.[38] It may, indeed, have been their intense emotional self-awareness, coupled with a pervasive intellectual tendency to anatomize and subdivide, which helped to separate head and heart during our period. In the later

---

[34] Dering, *Godly priuate praiers*, sig. H5r. Cf. Prid, *Glasse of vaine-glorie* (1585), 29–30; Trundle, *Keepe within Compasse*, sig. A6r; Stephen Egerton, *The Boring of the Eare* (1623: RSTC 7527.5), 14–15; Browning, *Concerning publike-prayer*, 186–7.

[35] Cowper, *Triumph*, 121–2; Bolton, *Discourse about happinesse*, sig. A4r; Mather, *Magnalia*, III.110; Huntington Library, San Marino, CA, MS 15369 fo. 26r.

[36] James 2:19; Perkins, *Declaration of the true manner*, 5; Hooper, *Later Writings*, 219; Parr, *Lamentacion*, sig. A7v. Cf. Dent, *Plaine mans path-way*, 17; Scudder, *Christians daily walke* (1628), 113; Mather, *Magnalia*, III.110; Todd, *Culture of Protestantism*, 51.

[37] Perkins, *How to live*, 10; cf. Hall, *Meditations and Vowes*, 140; Trundle, *Keepe within Compasse*, sig. A4v.

[38] Sandys, *Sermons*, 88; Campbell, *Religion of the Heart*, 53; Nuttall, *Holy Spirit*, 36–40; Kaufman, *Prayer, Despair and Drama*, 1.

16th century, Richard Greenham was already distinguishing between those religious exercises which 'do most cheefly whet up affection' and those that primarily 'strengthen judgement and understanding', although he insisted that both effects are always present to some degree. At the turn of the century, the Jesuit controversialist Thomas Wright was arguing that 'the very seate of all Passions, is the hearte', whereas 'our sensitive apprehension hath her seate in the brayne'—although his title, *The Passions of the Minde*, shows that the distinction was not yet clear. Ten years later, Nicholas Byfield distinguished between real and abstract faith by arguing that true saving knowledge 'is not written in the head, but in the heart and bowels', but he still described it as *knowledge*. Richard Sibbes' argument was similar. 'Whensoever [God] doth savingly shine upon the understanding, hee giveth a soft and plyable heart.' The heart fires the understanding, and the understanding softens the heart; the two are intimately connected, but conceived of as distinct. Those whose puritanism was less pure-bred could go further. Daniel Featley believed that devotion 'consisteth rather in the feruour of the affections, then light of the thoughts'.[39] Heart-religion is still in bud, but with hindsight we can see it taking shape.

Within our period, the effect was limited, but it did provide one obvious way of tackling the problem of excessive or distracting learning. Godly knowledge could be redefined, not as complex and arcane learning—which still had its place—but in line with Erasmus' wish that all Christians should be theologians.[40] The perennial Protestant love of paradox could come into play. Christopher Sutton could contrast 'Docta ignorantia and indocta scientia, a learned ignorance, and an vnlearned science'; Stephen Egerton could note that God's mysteries 'are often reuealed to babes in knowledge & learning, when they are hid from the wise'. Robert Blair made a point of claiming to have learned from the simple people he converted, and gloried in the fact that he prayed regularly with a group of husbandmen.[41] This had the great advantage of empowering those outside the dreaming spires. As a girl, Alice Wandesford read with pleasure the Gospel account of how the child Christ 'was able to confound the learned doctors and confute their wisdome'. The illiterate Robert Pasfield could 'be allowed for a Divine, and a Doctor also'.[42] And yet, there was a limit to how far most Protestants would let this reverence for simplicity go in practice. The Isham family maintained 'a simple fellow' whom they admired for 'his Devotion and understanding... beyond some that were more worldly wise'. He prayed thrice daily and 'hoped to be saved by Jesus Christ for he died for him he would say', but he also had 'many strange and idle fancies'. Judith Isham, who particularly favoured him, 'thought he might have a childs place in heaven because of his good inclinenation and harmlesnesse'. The divines she consulted were less

[39] Parker and Carlson, *'Practical Divinity'*, 139; Thomas Wright, *The Passions of the Minde in generall* (1604: RSTC 26040), 33; Byfield, *The Signes*, 111–12; Sibbes, *Bruised reede*, 262–6; Featley, *Ancilla Pietatis*, 2.
[40] Erasmus, *Christian Humanism*, 100.
[41] Sutton, *Godly meditations* (1601), sig. B4v; Egerton, *Boring of the Eare*, 15; Blair, *Life*, 19, 93.
[42] Thornton, *Autobiography*, 13 (cf. Luke 2:42–7); Hinde, *Faithfull Remonstrance... of Iohn Bruen*, 57.

indulgent, doubting that he could be saved 'because they thought he could not deserne the Trinitie'. In a comparable German case, an elderly man who was unable to memorize the Ten Commandments was barred from communion.[43] The simple unlearned could in theory confound the wise, but in practice, learning still usually held the trump card.

This persistent reverence for the intellect made itself felt in particular in women's learning. Protestants inherited the long-standing prejudice that fruitful knowledge shrivelled into barren curiosity much more readily amongst women than men. Elizabeth Jocelin, leaving instructions for the upbringing of her unborn child, wrote that if it should be a girl, 'I desire her bringing vp may be learning the Bible . . . good houswifery, writing, and good workes: other learning a woman needs not'. But, significantly, she could not bring herself to stop there. For a woman to be learned and wise, she added, was glorious; the only problem was that no-one would marry such a paragon.[44] We can see the same dilemma in the early 1650s, when the royalist Sir Ralph Verney was horrified by his god-daughter's zeal for learning. He advised that 'a Bible (with the Common prayer) and a good plaine cattichisme in your Mother Tongue . . . is well worth all the rest and much more sutable to your sex', but she— with her father's encouragement—was determined to learn Latin, Greek, and Hebrew. Again, he warned that she would be unmarriageable, but this does not seem to have deterred her.[45] A generation earlier, Elizabeth Isham—who chose to forgo marriage— had made a similar stand. Her learning had brought her spiritual trials, she felt:

> yet did I not wish lesse contrary to the minde of those that say it is not good for a woman to be too Bookish for if I had not had knowledge especially of thy word I had perished in my affliction.[46]

The wariness of learning was real, but the hunger for it was strong.

This extraordinary, scarcely bridled valorization of learning certainly had its problems. It neither ameliorated Reformed Protestantism's tendency to elitism and self-satisfaction, nor helped to win over those who thought that simplicity was next to godliness, but in early modern Britain, pandering to that view was neither possible nor, perhaps, necessary. It was impossible because to downplay learning was to stray into the confessional crossfire. Protestantism's priority on learning for all Christians was a self-conscious point of separation with Catholicism. Henry Smith was swift to associated those who claimed to offer simple teaching with

> popish priests, which made ignorance the mother of deuotion. . . . To preach simply, is not to preach vnlearnedly, nor confusedly, but plainely and perspicuously, that the simplest which dooth heare, may vnderstand what is taught.

This was a theme as old as William Tyndale's boast, made to a priest, that 'I wyl cause a boye that dryueth the plough, shall knowe more of the scripture then thou

[43] Isham, 'Confessions', fo. 18v; Susan Karant-Nunn, *The Reformation of Ritual* (1997), 97.

[44] Jocelin, *Mothers Legacie*, sigs B5v–6v; cf. Mildmay, 'Meditations', II.5.

[45] Frances P. and Margaret M. Verney, *Memoirs of the Verney Family during the Seventeenth Century* (1907), I.500–1.

[46] Isham, 'Confessions', fo. 27v.

doest'.[47] To admit that godly learning was out of the common people's reach was to yield a key point to Catholicism. In 1554 John Christopherson, soon to become a bishop in Mary I's restored Catholic Church, approvingly cited a patristic tale of a man who set out to learn the psalms, but having learned one verse refused to learn more until he had put that one into practice, a task which took him nineteen years. That attitude was anathema to Protestants of every shade. John Jewel's programmatic debates with Thomas Harding drew the same line. Harding argued that, at the day of judgement, 'we shall not be required to give an account of our understanding, but (faith presupposed) of our charity'. Not so, Jewel replied:

> At the terrible day of the Lord we shall assuredly render account of our wilful ignorance... Christian simplicity is not wilful ignorance, that is to say, to believe every fable that is told, and to examine and know nothing.

A couple of decades later, Robert Persons' *Christian Directory* argued that the wicked would take comfort 'if all ignorance dyd excuse synne'. His Protestant editor, Edmund Bunny, who generally kept his amendments to the minimum, carefully dropped the word 'all'.[48] For Catholics, ignorance could sometimes be an excuse. For Protestants, ignorance and sin were almost synonymous. If that was offensive to the ignorant, too bad.

This is also why Protestants did not need to moderate their high opinion of learning. They had successfully framed the confessional battle as one against Catholicism's 'defence of ignorance' and 'gross ungentle opinion of the simplicity of the people'.[49] In a profoundly hierarchical society imbued with a Renaissance reverence for education, that was a winning strategy. Early modern society was prone, not to the modern disease of dumbing down, but to scholarly ostentation. Gifford's Atheos did not want a minister who would share his own distaste for bookishness. Rather, in a sour echo of Tyndale, he wanted a preacher

> able to speake much latine, and to alleadge all sorts of writers. . . . I will not geue a button for these English Doctors which can alledge no more but out of Paule and Peter. . . . Euery Plowe man nowe a dayes canne alleadge out of Saint Paule.

Arnold Hunt's careful study of preachers' relationships with their congregations suggests that this was a wider truth.[50] Preachers who could use long words, cite obscure doctors, and slip between languages were respected and treasured by their unlearned congregations. Perhaps they were merely status symbols; perhaps they were totems of a quality which ordinary people valued even if they knew it was beyond their reach, or perhaps they really hoped that such people might have something to teach them. This was what Thomas Tymme evidently thought. He

[47] Smith, *Sermons*, 668; Foxe, *Actes and monuments* (1563), '514', recte 518.
[48] John Christopherson, *An exhortation to all menne to take hede and beware of rebellion* (1554: RSTC 5207), sigs X3v–4v; John Jewel, *The Works of John Jewel, Bishop of Salisbury. The first portion*, ed. John Ayre (Cambridge, 1845), 323–4; Persons, *Christian Directory*, ed. Houliston, 12; Persons, *Booke of Christian exercise*, ed. Bunny, 3.
[49] Jewel, *Works... The first portion*, 325, 332.
[50] Gifford, *Briefe discourse*, fos 50r–v; Hunt, *Art of Hearing*, 229–91, esp. 287.

denounced those with 'itching eares' who sought 'superabundant knowledge of the Gospell', and hoped that 'the vulgar sort would be contented with a reasonable and moderate information'.[51] That hope seemed forlorn, but it does at least suggest that divines had no need to apologize for fusing godliness with good learning. That fusion would underpin a culture of mass reading and writing which became one of the most distinctive features of early modern Protestantism.

PROTESTANTS AND THEIR BIBLES

A pamphlet published in 1591 in praise of the recently deceased Katherine Stubbes claimed that

> her whole delight was to be conversant in the scriptures, & to meditate vpon them day and night: in so much that you could seldome or neuer haue come into her house, and haue found her without a bible, or some other good booke in her hands.[52]

If we know one thing about Protestant piety in general, and puritan piety in particular, it is that it was bookish. Early modern Protestants were, or aspired to be, insatiable readers. Partly because they share that passion with modern scholars, and partly because their books are their heftiest material legacy to the present, there has been a great deal of academic interest in their habits of reading and writing.[53] Two scholars in particular have recently drawn our attention to the distinctive experience of early modern Protestant reading. Andrew Cambers has pointed out that reading was not simply a private activity, but a social one. Even those who read alone thought of themselves as part of a reading community. Kate Narveson has provided a stirring description of how liberating the experience of Bible reading could be for early modern Protestants, and of how it dissolved the normal social barriers between clergy and laity, and even between men and women.[54] This is not the place to retrace the ground they and others have covered, but the pivotal significance of Bible reading in Protestant piety means it is important at least to sketch its outline.

Reading meant, first and last, reading the Bible. It would be hard to exaggerate the weight which Protestants of all stripes put on Bible reading. In the first generation of the Reformation, evangelicals had a naïve faith that the simple promulgation of an English Bible would by itself sweep away corruption and popery.[55] It soon became clear that things would not be quite so easy, but the Reformation continued to be, in large part, a struggle to set the Bible before the people and to persuade them to attend to it. Exhortations to Bible reading were a staple of mid-Tudor visitation

---

[51] Tymme, *Chariot of Devotion*, 55, 57.

[52] Stubbes, *Christal glasse*, sig. A2v.

[53] See, for example, Watt, *Cheap Print*; Green, *Print and Protestantism*; Adam Foxe, *Oral and literate culture in England, 1500–1700* (Oxford, 2000); Julia Crick and Alexandra Walsham (eds), *The Uses of Script and Print, 1300–1700* (Cambridge, 2004); William H. Sherman, *Used Books: Marking Readers in Renaissance England* (Philadelphia, 2008).

[54] Cambers, *Godly Reading*; Narveson, *Bible Readers*.

[55] Ryrie, *Gospel and Henry VIII*, 251.

articles, including the enduring Elizabeth injunctions. The Edwardian Homilies began with 'a fruitful exhortation to the reading and knowledge of Holy Scripture', the reformers' first priority; this extolled the Bible's power to heal and transform its readers, describing it as 'more sweet than honey or honey-comb . . . lively, quick, and mighty in operation'. During the plague of 1563, Bishop Grindal put this exhortation in his people's own mouths: the household prayer for use during the plague asks to 'feed our souls, O Lord, daily with the true manna of thy heavenly word'.[56] The priority given to Scripture reading throughout our period is unmistakable.[57] When John Gee provided a series of vague moral exhortations to godliness, the only specific practice he mentioned was daily Bible reading. In 1553 Christopher Tye described all England, from the king down, as engaged in a joint enterprise of Biblical studying. Obviously false, but the state to which Protestants continued to aspire.[58]

Grindal, and others, compared the Bible to manna, the spiritual food which the Israelites gathered every day. Like praying—and for the same reasons—it was no good only reading the Bible when you felt like it, 'by fits vpon rainy dayes'.[59] Exhortations to read the Bible (at least) daily are routine throughout our period.[60] Set times for reading should be chosen and stuck to scrupulously. First thing in the morning was ideal. George Herbert promised that 'who reade a chapter when they rise,/Shall ne're be troubled with ill eyes'. William Crashaw recommended that you 'take for thy Breakfast, in the Name of the Lord, a Chapter of the blessed Bible'; he would also have you take a similar supper.[61]

Indeed, for earnest Protestants throughout our period, this daily discipline was a constant part of life. Some did indeed simply read a chapter a day.[62] Others went much further. Biblical over-eating was a recurring feature of heroic Protestant piety. Katherine Brettergh was said to have read eight chapters daily; William Gouge, fifteen chapters, in three blocks of five. Jeremy Whitaker read the New Testament epistles every two weeks, in Greek; Samuel Fairclough supposedly read the whole Bible every three months for fifty years—'so that it might be said *of him*, that he was a *walking Bible*'. Besides that, the mere twenty times that Ignatius Jurdaine read his Bible seems modest, but Jurdaine also claimed to have read Foxe's *Actes and Monuments*—which is two and a half times longer—seven times. The newly

[56] Walter Frere and William Kennedy, *Visitation Articles and Injunctions of the period of the Reformation* (Alcuin Club Collections 14–16, 1910), II.17, 20, III.2; *Certain Sermons or Homilies*, 1–3; Grindal, *Remains*, 482.

[57] See, amongst endless examples, Becon, *Gouernans* (1544?), 46r–60v; Becon, *Pomaunder of prayer*, 17r; Dent, *Plaine mans path-way*, 178.

[58] Gee, *Steps of Ascension*, 50; Christopher Tye, *The Actes of the Apostles, translated into Englyshe Metre* (1553?: RSTC 2983.8), sig. A2r–v.

[59] Leigh, *Mothers blessing*, 5; Ward, *Coal from the Altar*, 57.

[60] See, amongst innumerable examples, *[Geneva Bible] The Bible* (1586: RSTC 2145), instructions for use; Rogers, *Garden* (1615), II sig. Ar; FSL MS V.a.519 fo. 2v; BL Egerton MS 2877 fo. 83v; Grindal, *Remains*, 129–30.

[61] Gouge, *Whole-Armor of God*, 313; Herbert, *Works*, 96; Crashaw, *London's Lamentation*, sig. C8v.

[62] See, amongst endless examples, Foxe, *Actes and monuments* (1570), 1694; Wallington, *Notebooks*, 267; Hoby, *Diary, passim*; D'Ewes, *Autobiography*, 120; Mildmay, *With Faith and Physic*, 23; Rogers, *Sermon preached . . . . at the funerall*, sig. D2v.

converted Richard Norwood set himself to read at least twenty pages of his Bible daily—and even allowing for folio pages, he must have exceeded his minimum, for in the seven months he maintained this discipline he reckoned he read the entire Old Testament five times and the New ten. Not even Fairclough claimed that rate.[63]

These voluntary disciplines are only one face of the subject. For one thing, householders had a duty to 'see that al that are vnder your charge' should join them in 'reading something of gods word daily'. Nehemiah Wallington, whose own discipline was to read a chapter every morning and evening, ruled that anyone in his household who did not read a chapter daily had to put a halfpenny in the poorbox—or, which may have been a worse punishment, to catch up on their reading.[64] One simple and pleasing way of achieving this was for servants to read their chapter aloud to others in the household. This was a regular practice in the Isham household, for example, where 'those which could read would for the most part every evening read a chapter before me', and where an older servant, Mrs Alce, was particularly treasured as a reader.[65] What was true of servants was doubly true of children, for whom the discipline of daily Bible reading was an education in literacy as well as in theology. Richard Willis' fond recollection of overhearing when 'my little grandchilde was set by her Grandmother to reade her mornings Chapter' gives us a glimpse of the pious routines both of the little girl and of the older woman. When Henry Burton had been induced to learn to read by the promise of his grandfather's New Testament, 'afterwards I was put to read every night two or three Chapters in it to the Family'. Ezekiel Culverwell recommended that children of ten or older should be set daily, not only to read, but to memorize and to recite a chapter of the Bible.[66] The Isham children did this, and although the young Elizabeth found it hard—memorizing the New Testament Epistles was apparently particularly tricky—she persisted with it into adulthood. The young Herbert Palmer, by contrast, 'took much pleasure in learning Chapters by heart'—perhaps to be expected of a future Cambridge head of house. He proceeded to teach others by the same technique. Whether or not the subjects enjoyed it, such mental hammering could stick. Richard Norwood and Archibald Johnston of Wariston both had vivid memories of reading particular Biblical passages as children.[67]

For adults who could choose whether or not, and how often, to read their Bibles, the picture was naturally messier. If plenty stuck, more or less, to a daily discipline, and if plenty more proverbially never opened the thing, there was a sizeable grey area between the two. Once the Reformation was properly under way, almost

---

[63] Harrison, *Deaths aduantage*, III.8; Clarke, *Collection*, 97, 163, 453; Clarke, *Lives of sundry Eminent Persons*, 164; Norwood, *Journal*, 84.

[64] Tuke, *Practise of the faithfull*, 238; Wallington, *Notebooks*, 267, 272; LMA Guildhall MS 204, p. 38.

[65] Isham, 'Confessions', fo. 25v.

[66] Willis, *Mount Tabor*, 199; Burton, *Narration*, 1; cf. Thornton, *Autobiography*, 13; Ezekiel Culverwell, *A ready way to remember the Scriptures* (1637: RSTC 6111), sig. A2v. Cf. Melville, *Autobiography*, 16; Frere and Kennedy, *Visitation Articles*, III.138.

[67] Isham, 'Confessions', fos 12r, 14v; Clarke, *Lives of thirty-two divines*, 184, 190; Wariston, *Diary*, 45–6; Norwood, *Journal*, 8.

everyone who learned to read learned, at least in part, by reading the Bible.[68] Therefore, to be literate was to be, in some measure, Biblically literate, and it was probably also to own a Bible. Take, for example, the Welshman Robert Bulkeley, 'a jolly hail-fellow-well-met country gentleman' given to excessive drinking and regular church attendance, whose six-year diary shows absolutely no signs of earnest piety—apart from one entry which states that one July evening 'I began to read the holy Bible, (Deo propitio)'.[69] A fit of piety, a fit of boredom, or a little of both? For the more earnest, there were also practices short of a daily chapter. Richard Stonley, one of the tellers of the Exchequer under Elizabeth—and an embezzler on a magnificent scale—noted his daily reading in his diary: sometimes a single verse of a psalm, sometimes a whole Biblical chapter, but he seems to have read the Geneva Bible's chapter-summaries more carefully than the text itself. In later years, he took to heading his diary entries with classical epigrams instead. He did not abandon Bible reading, however. Throughout the extant volumes of the diary we find Sunday entries claiming that 'I kept home all the hole day readinge the Scriptures'.[70] Occasionally he also did this mid-week, on a feast day, when he was confined to bed, or simply as a private celebration.[71] If we believe Thomas More's witness, evangelicals had been in the habit of devoting Sundays and holy days to Bible reading from the beginning.[72] It would hardly be surprising if Sunday reading became an anchor which allowed some hard-pressed believers to abandon from the daily chapter while still maintaining some regular Biblical discipline.

Regularity was a matter not only of time, but of order. The Bible is a big book, and simply beginning at page one is daunting. The most common advice from divines was, however, to do exactly that, 'because', as Greenham put it, 'the holy ghost in wisdom hath set the best order to his own word'. 'The Books be writ in Order, Let them be reade in Order', advised Valentine Marshall: 'he that takes the Bible as it lies, will get most good by it'. This is what Grace Mildmay, in her old age, Elizabeth Juxon, and the entire Isham household did.[73] The Civil War-era *Directory for the Publique Worship of GOD* required Bible readings in public worship to proceed in strict order through the book from one week to the next. However, the *Directory* gave no instructions as to where this progressive reading should begin or how much should be covered each week, an implicit freedom which points to the limits of this austere policy. As Edward Wetenhall said after the Restoration, mere progressive reading 'will detain the observer of it a great while in

---

[68] Sherman, *Used Books*, 72.

[69] Hugh Owen (ed.), 'The Diary of Bulkeley of Dronwy, Anglesey, 1630–1636', *Anglesey Antiquarian Society and Field Club Transactions* (1937), 33, 75.

[70] FSL MS V.a.459 fo. 19r, and see, for example, fos 5r, 10v, 15r, 22v, 25r, 31v, 57r, 60r, 89v; FSL MS V.a.460 fos 5r, 6r, 16v, 18v; FSL MS V.a.461 fo. 2v, 39r, 72v–73r.

[71] FSL MS V.a.459 fos 46r, 54v; FSL MS V.a.460 fos 19r, 28r–v, 48v.

[72] Nicholas Harpsfield, *The life and death of Sr Thomas Moore*, ed. Elsie Vaughan Hitchcock (Early English Text Society o.s. 186, 1932), 87. Cf., for example, Brinsley, *True Watch* (1608), 68; Sparke, *Crumms of comfort*, sig. D10r–v.

[73] Parker and Carlson, *'Practical Divinity'*, 206; Capel, *Capel's Remains*, sig. b5v; Bayly, *Practise of pietie*, 247; Mildmay, *With Faith and Physic*, 23; Denison, *Monument or Tombe-Stone*, 85; Isham, 'Diary', 1618, 1620; Isham, 'Confessions', fo. 25v.

those parts of Scripture, which may not edifie him so much, as would the other'. Plenty of readers find the shine comes off when they reach Leviticus. The injunctions to sequential reading themselves testify to the problem. 'Wee must keepe an order in our readings, and not bee now in this place, now in another', Greenham insisted. Richard Rogers and George Webbe warned against reading 'here and there a chapter'. That is, Bible reading was caught between an ordered ideal and a chaotic reality.[74]

In fact, as Peter Stallybrass has argued, most dedicated Bible-readers ended up somewhere between strict sequential reading and cherry-picking anarchy.[75] Randomness had its place. If your Bible fell open at a verse which seemed of particular significance to you, you might well, like Wariston, Isaac Ambrose, or Elizabeth Isham, ascribe it to 'a special Providence'.[76] You might begin your sequential reading in the middle of the Bible. Richard Stonley apparently started his sequential reading with the psalms; Jean Stewart started hers with John's Gospel.[77] Or you might discern an order other than that of page numbers. Stallybrass points out that the Geneva Bible's copious cross-references, the preachers' habit of leading congregations on a steeplechase through Scripture, and long Christian habit which the codex form makes possible, all made flicking back and forth seem a normal part of Bible reading. Those like John Bruen, who kept 'an orderly and constant course in his reading', were not necessarily working steadily through the book. You might, as one Jacobean preacher recommended for his women readers in particular, begin with the easy books of the Bible and save the rest for later—the Song of Songs, he thought, should come last of all. You might, as John Downame advised, read some parts—genealogies, the Levitical ceremonies, obscure portions of the prophets— less frequently than others.[78] You might separate the reading of Old and New Testaments, reading a portion of each daily: this preserved the order of the books, alleviated some of the dryer passages of the Old Testament, and, since it was shorter and so read much more frequently, gave appropriate precedence to the New. There were more elaborate schemes, such as those providing for the whole Bible to be read in a year.[79] In her younger days, Grace Mildmay read the Pentateuch, the Prophets, the Gospels, and the Epistles on four parallel daily tracks. Edward Vaughan published an elaborate and impractical division of the Bible into seven 'degrees' around which you might plan your reading. A slightly more practical approach which appeared later in the century provided a timeline for the entire Old

[74] *Directory for the Publique Worship*, 13; Wetenhall, *Enter into thy Closet*, 42; Parker and Carlson, 'Practical Divinity', 341; Rogers, *Seven treatises*, 289; Rogers, *Garden* (1616), sig. G3v; Hunt, *Art of Hearing*, 178.
[75] Peter Stallybrass, 'Books and Scrolls: Navigating the Bible' in Jennifer Andersen and Elizabeth Sauer (eds), *Books and Readers in Early Modern England* (Philadelphia, 2002), 42–79.
[76] Ambrose, *Media*, 11-0; Isham, 'Confessions', fo. 22v; Wariston, *Diary*, 22.
[77] FSL MS V.a.459; Wariston, *Diary*, 12.
[78] Hinde, *Faithfull Remonstrance . . . of Iohn Bruen*, 71; BL Egerton MS 2877 fo. 92r; Downame, *Guide to Godlynesse*, 648.
[79] See, for example, Isham, 'Confessions', fo. 12r; Capel, *Capel's Remains*, sig. b5v; Byfield, *Directions for private readeing*, esp. sig. A5v; Bayly, *Practise of pietie*, 247.

Testament, so that readers could slot the prophets into the historical books and read everything in chronological order.[80]

English Protestants looking for an ordered, non-sequential pattern of Bible reading had another obvious resource to hand: the Prayer Book lectionary. This had the advantage—or disadvantage—of leaving out some of the more tedious or repetitive sections of the Old Testament, and also most of the book of Revelation, which was potentially much more disturbing than the Song of Songs. Wetenhall considered following the lectionary as a possibility, and in the 1620s Henry Burton was outraged that John Cosin's devotions dropped the sequential readings from the daily offices.[81] But it does not seem to have been much used by lay people in their private devotions.[82] Its unnecessary complexity, its incompleteness or—for some— its association with the Prayer Book may have damned it. What was very widely used, however, was the Prayer Book's ordering of the psalms, dividing them into sixty portions to be used, morning and evening, on each day of the month. (In months with thirty-one days, Psalms 144–150 are repeated.) No less an enemy of the Prayer Book than John Knox adopted this pattern, and no less influential a writer than Lewis Bayly recommended it.[83] Whether or not readers followed the Prayer Book ordering, it was common practice to use a psalm or psalms before or alongside prose Bible readings, and not as part of the main sequence.[84] The psalms were certainly seen as a book apart, 'an Epitome of the whole Bible', and they had a central role both in expressing and in forming Protestant piety.[85] But the priority given to them also points to a deeper question. What exactly do we mean by *reading* in this context?

It did not mean merely eyes passing over print or lips murmuring words. John Downame worried that the regular discipline, 'so many Chapters euery day', might become routine; that readers would 'rest in the deede done, and haue little care how they doe it'. Correct reading was a spiritual as well as intellectual affair. It was, in fact, almost a form of prayer. Reading and prayer, in the Protestant experience, bled into one another; both were means of interacting with someone who was simultaneously present and absent. We cannot see God himself, merely his works, Michael Sparke pointed out: 'so we must pray to him in his glory, but not in shape'.[86] There is a similar distancing in reading. Writers are with their readers, but only in spirit. If we reply to books they cannot hear us, but when we read further, we may find they have already responded; just as we cannot literally hear God's answers to prayer, but

[80] Mildmay, *With Faith and Physic*, 34; Edward Vaughan, *A Plaine and perfect Method, for the easie vnderstanding of the whole Bible* (1617: RSTC 24600), 259–61; John Lloyd, *A good help for weak Memories* (1671: Wing L2655), 72.

[81] Wetenhall, *Enter into thy Closet*, 40–1; Burton, *Tryall of Private Devotions*, sigs D4v–E1r.

[82] One possible exception is Robert Saxby, whom we find one Good Friday transcribing one of the readings set for the day, Isaiah 53. Saxby, 'Miscellany', fo. 62r.

[83] McMillan, *Worship of the Scottish Reformed Church*, 43–4; Bayly, *Practise of pietie*, 247. Cf. Mildmay, *With Faith and Physic*, 29, 34.

[84] See, for example, Wetenhall, *Enter into thy Closet*, 43; Norwood, *Journal*, 83; Byfield, *Directions for private readeing*, 116–17.

[85] Smith, *Dauids blessed man*, 1–2; Ryrie, 'Psalms and confrontation'.

[86] Downame, *Guide to Godlynesse*, 645; Sparke, *Crumms of comfort*, sig. A6r.

when we pray further we may find them within ourselves. Bible reading, for early modern Protestants, was the point at which the two practices fused. They spoke to God in prayer and he replied from the page. Something weirdly like a true conversation became possible. This was why Protestants read their Bibles devotionally, and it determined how they did it.

It meant, first of all, due preparation. To come to the Bible 'vnreuerentlye . . . as vnto prophane wrightings' was, Thomas Becon warned, to flirt with disaster. He echoed Erasmus' citation of the story of Uzzah, whom God struck dead for a far lesser act of irreverence.[87] Ill-prepared readers might approach the text merely formally or inattentively, 'for taske as it were, and for fashion sake'—or, worse, frivolously. 'Some make jests of Gods Word', cautioned Richard Kilby, 'but . . . it is ill jesting with edge-tooles'.[88] Prayer before reading was one obvious solution, and such prayers were a staple of devotional works.[89] But mere solemnity was not enough. Gervase Babington warned that 'if wee reade it ouer ten thousand times our selues, heare it of others carefully & continually, and yet feele not the sweete spirite of the Lorde by it . . . it remaineth a sealed booke vnto vs'.[90] Whether or not you felt the Spirit, of course, was a matter for him rather than for you, but divines could at least exhort you to feel his absence. This is one reason why the Bible itself, and other devotional works, were so often described as flowers, gardens, banquets, jewels, or treasures; anything to remind you that the inked paper in front of you was not merely a book.

This did not mean disengaging the intellect. The right use of the critical faculties was essential to devotional reading. The earliest English Protestant psalm paraphrases, clearly intended as devotional works, explicitly encouraged their readers to compare them critically with the Biblical text itself, which to modern eyes looks more like an academic than a spiritual exercise.[91] Later works regularly advised Bible readers to consult scholars or to read 'Commentaries & learned expositions' alongside the text.[92] This is what it meant to claim that study was a work of piety. The alternative was the intellectual laziness of those who too easily dismissed 'these Scriptures . . . they doe not sinke into my head'. Study of this kind was not, however, abstract or detached. Its purpose was to internalize the text. Dorothy Leigh warned that 'if yee heare the Word, and read it, without meditating theron, it doth the soule no more good then meate and drink doth the body, being seene and

---

[87] Becon, *Fruitful treatise of fasting*, sig. I6r–v. Cf. Erasmus, *Enchiridion*, 48; II Samuel 6:6–7.

[88] Beza, *Psalmes of David*, sig. A5r; Kilby, *Burthen*, 36.

[89] See, for example, Dering, *Godly priuate praiers*, sigs D1v–2r, H4v–5r; Rogers, *Garden* (1616), sigs G3v–4r; Kilby, *Hallelujah*, 10; *Two treaties the first concerning the Holy Scriptures* 25; and cf. LMA Guildhall MS 204, p. 38.

[90] Babington, *Briefe conference*, sigs A2v–3r.

[91] Anthony Cope, *A godly meditacion vpon.xx. select psalmes of Dauid* (1547: RSTC 5717), sig. *3v; Thomas Sternhold, *Certayne Psalmes chosen out of the Psalter of David, and drawen into Englishe Metre* (1549: RSTC 2419), sig. A3r; Robert Crowley, *The Psalter of Dauid newely translated into Englysh metre* (1549: RSTC 2725), sig. ✠2r; and cf. William Baldwin, *The canticles or balades of Salomon, phraselyke declared in Englysh metres* (1549: RSTC 2768), sig. A1v.

[92] For example, *[Geneva Bible] The Bible* (1586), instructions for use; *Two treaties the first concerning the Holy Scriptures*, 35.

felt, and neuer fed vpon'.[93] The image of *hunger* was much repeated. 'Hungring after the word' was, for John Brinsley, a sign of election. Grace Mildmay felt that her 'feeding' on the word was not satisfied 'with a bare reading thereof, (a touch and away) but I must follow upon it over and over, again and again'. This was the urge which led some to gorge themselves on Scripture.[94]

But how? Here Grub Street came to Protestants' assistance, with a flood of printed Bible-reading aids: commentaries, but also digests and indexes to help novice and even moderately experienced readers to find their way around Scripture.[95] We will return to the urge to write such texts, but for now their popularity with readers is worth noticing. The first steady seller in this genre, *The Treasure of gladnesse*, included a set of chapter summaries covering the whole New Testament aside from the Gospels: it went through twelve editions from 1563–1601.[96] In the 17th century, an avalanche of such texts appeared. *The doctrine of the Bible* ran to more than twenty-five editions from 1604–40 some of them titled *The way to true happines*. This text is an impressively succinct summary of the whole Bible in question-and-answer format. Its focus is on practical applications: some books are dispatched swiftly, others dealt with at much greater length. It is, in effect, a kind of revision aid for the Bible, and it is easy to imagine working through it as a pious project. Eusebius Pagit's even briefer *The historie of the Bible* (twelve editions, 1603–40), also used a question-and-answer format but was aimed more at the schoolroom.[97] There were also more ornate and specialist works: John Speed's *The genealogies recorded in the sacred scriptures* ran through over fifty editions from 1610–40. Prominent divines like Nicholas Byfield and Ezekiel Culverwell wrote for this market. Some individuals, like William Gouge, prepared similar guides for themselves—indeed, this is also what Robert Pasfield was doing.[98] Surviving copies of these texts are often bound with Bibles, unsurprisingly, but also with each other: concordances, psalters, genealogies, catechisms—whole libraries of Biblical cribs sewn together.[99] They were printed in every size and format: whatever size your Bible, you could find reading aids to fit it. Given how daunting the Bible can be, some readers doubtless found the aids an easier read than the text itself.

A more ambitious means of pressing the Word onto yourself was to memorize it, a practice which was not confined to illiterates and children. Bishop Shaxton's injunction in 1538 that his clergy should memorize the majority of the New Testament, at the rate of a chapter per fortnight, was wildly unrealistic, but in later generations a few achieved something of the kind, and many more aspired to it. The young lawyer Andrew Kingsmill supposedly memorized a series of the

---

[93] Dent, *Plaine mans path-way*, 137; Leigh, *Mothers blessing*, 23; cf. Gouge, *Whole-Armor of God*, 313; *Two treaties the first concerning the Holy Scriptures*, 34.
[94] Brinsley, *True Watch* (1608), 146; Mildmay, *With Faith and Physic*, 72.
[95] Green, *Print and Protestantism*, ch. 3.
[96] *This booke is called the Treasure of gladnesse*, fos 22r–31r.
[97] Green, *Print and Protestantism*, 152.
[98] Clarke, *Collection*, 98; on Pasfield, see above, p. 260.
[99] For some examples from one library, see FSL STC 19108 copies 1 and 2, STC 25132, STC 25135, STC 25138 copy 1.

New Testament epistles in Greek.[100] The psalms, inevitably, were the most popular texts for such memorization, from the radical Presbyterians of south-western Scotland to the avant-garde ceremonialists of Little Gidding. Memorizing the metrical psalms hardly needed a positive effort, given the mnemonic effect of music and repetition.[101] Sometimes memorization seems to have been undertaken simply as a study aid, or even a kind of party trick. Elaborate and wildly impractical mnemonic aids, which promised to help their users to be able to locate any passage in the Bible instantly, had an established place in the Protestant book market. Even those who were not trying to sell them sometimes recommended using them.[102] 'Memories that wil keepe holie things' were an accepted minor sign of personal sanctity, which no doubt encouraged believers to cultivate them.[103] Another commonly declared motive—to learn Scripture while you have leisure, so that 'when you shall be shut vp into darke prisons' you will still have it with you—seems more implausible, although as we shall see, Protestants took such doom-mongering seriously.[104]

The underlying purpose of memorization, however, was the hope that, if planted in the heart, Scripture would take root there. The widely-used idiom of learning 'by heart' had a different resonance when head and heart were not yet clearly opposed. Ezekiel Culverwell used the emerging distinction, suggesting that memorization would 'fill the Head, and so the Heart, with much heavenly matter'; but for others there simply was no difference between memorization and internalization. Nicholas Byfield, encouraging his readers to memorize the Biblical promises, urged that it was no use simply putting them in a commonplace book: 'we must get them written in our hearts too'.[105] In practice this meant stocking the memory with texts for use whenever they were needed. It could make extemporizing in prayer easier; it could be a source of comfort when walking or when waking in the night.[106] If it were done assiduously enough, it could shape your very thoughts. 'If . . . there be not mines of precious truths hid in the heart', Thomas Goodwin observed, 'no wonder if our thoughts coine nothing but drosse.'[107]

---

[100] Frere and Kennedy, *Visitation Articles*, II.55; Kingsmill, *Viewe of mans estate*, sig. A2r–v.

[101] Tweedie, *Select Biographies*, 314; Cooper, '"As wise as serpents"'; John Case?, *The Praise of Musicke* (Oxford, 1586: RSTC 20184), 151; Bayly, *Practise of pietie*, 366; Melville, *Autobiography*, 22–3.

[102] John Brinsley, *Ludus Literarius: Or, The Grammar Schoole* (1612: RSTC 3768), 259; *Two treaties the first concerning the Holy Scriptures* 31. For some examples, see William Samuel, *An abridgement of all the canonical books of the olde Testament written in Sternholds meter* (1569: RSTC 21690); Henoch Clapham, *A Briefe of the Bible* (Edinburgh?, 1596: RSTC 5332); James Warre, *The Touchstone of Truth* (1630: RSTC 25091), sigs G7r–v; Culverwell, *A ready way*; John Lloyd, *A good help for weak Memories* (1671: Wing L2655).

[103] Bruce, *Sermons Preached*, sig. Bb2v. Cf. Brinsley, *True Watch* (1608), 21; Jocelin, *Mothers Legacie*, sig. a4r; Clarke, *Collection*, 312; Clarke, *Lives of sundry Eminent Persons*, 163.

[104] Clement Cotton, *The mirrour of martyrs, the first and second part* (1631: RSTC 5850), 522; and see below, pp. 422–7. For such exhortations, see Dyke, *Two Treatises*, 257–8; Parr, *Abba Father*, sig. A6r–v; Wither, *Preparation to the Psalter*, 131. On the use of memorised texts in illness, see Bruce, *Sermons . . . with Collections*, 156; Norden, *Pensive mans practise . . . The second part*, 129.

[105] Culverwell, *A ready way*, sig. A2v; Byfield, *Marrow of the Oracles* (1622), 293–4.

[106] See, for example, Bentley, *Monument of Matrons*, 403–4; Culverwell, *Treatise of faith*, 514–15; Clarke, *Collection*, 98; Mildmay, 'Meditations', 66; D'Ewes, *Autobiography*, 95.

[107] Goodwin, *Vanity of Thoughts*, 44.

But, as always when something could be done by mere effort, Protestants would not take this too far. Although they might use the Biblical injunctions that the Word be memorized and bound to heads, hands, and gateposts, they did so rhetorically rather than precisely—to reproach Christians for their laxity, not to urge their emulation.[108] Mere memorization, after all, was no substitute for godliness. If its Jewish and Muslim practitioners did not prove that, its Catholic ones did. John Hooper was dismissive of those monks who 'for custom or bondage to their profession, do learn without the book a great part of the scripture. . . . This availeth nothing; for they understand it not'.[109] Memorization was a useful enough tool, but by itself it was barren. What mattered was not your command of Scripture, but its command of you.

Henry Scudder's advice takes us in another direction. 'Reade the word', he said, 'with an hunger & thirst after knowledge and growth of grace by it.' The point is not to seek knowledge in the abstract, but useful and applicable knowledge. Richard Capel compared Bible-readers to gold miners, using 'an holy skill to finde out golden places fit for our present purpose'.[110] This is a very active model of reading: to search out what applies directly and immediately to you. For early modern Protestants, this process of finding personal applications of the text was the key to correct Bible reading. What made it possible is that, while the text itself might be fixed, the Word is alive. It is, Henry Smith preached, 'like an Epistle sent from God to man', with the intimacy and immediacy of a letter from 'familiar and deare freindes'. Lewis Bayly made the point canonical. The books of the Bible are not 'matters of Historicall discourse', but 'Letters or Epistles sent downe from God out of heauen vnto thee. . . . Reade them . . . as if God himselfe stood by, & spake these words vnto thee'.[111]

Easier said than done. John Winthrop recalled a time when 'I had neere lost the use of Gods worde. . . . My meditations, readinge, and all grewe tedious and unprofitable'.[112] But when it worked, the effects were dramatic. Readers might be stricken in conscience: when Wariston read Lamentations one morning, 'every lyne strak the at the heart and maid thy eies to runne doune with rivers of walter'. For Winthrop, during the crisis of his conversion, even remembering the dire warning in Hebrews 6:4–6 'was like hell to mee'.[113] But while Scripture could lead believers 'to mourne in mirth', it could equally bring them 'to solace in sorrow'. Meditating on Scripture helped ease William Kiffin's fears for his salvation, and brought Wariston comfort and renewed hope as well as condemnation. Richard Norwood's Bible-reading marathon brought him 'wonderful solace and delight'.[114]

---

[108] Deuteronomy 6:6–9, 11:18–21. See, for example, Heyden, *Bryefe Summe*, sig. A6r; Arthur Golding's preface to Calvin, *Psalmes of David*, sig. *2v; Eusebius Pagit, *The historie of the Bible* (1627: RSTC 19108), sig. A1r; FSL MS V.a.519 fo. 3r–v; Bod. MS Rawl C.113 fo. 1r.

[109] Hooper, *Later Writings*, 356; cf. *Certain Sermons or Homilies*, 4.

[110] Scudder, *Christians daily walke* (1628), 102; Capel, *Tentations*, 175; cf. Wither, *Preparation to the Psalter*, 125.

[111] Smith, *Sermons*, 659; Bayly, *Practise of pietie*, 245–6.

[112] Winthrop, *Papers*, 214.

[113] Wariston, *Diary*, 25; Winthrop, *Papers*, 157. Cf. Hoby, *Diary*, 132–3; Harrison, *Deaths aduantage*, III. 9.

[114] Vaughan, *Plaine and perfect Method*, sig. A6r–v; Kiffin, *Remarkable Passages*, 9; Wariston, *Diary*, e.g. 27, 42; Norwood, *Journal*, 84.

The generalized claims that Bible reading brings 'a pleasure sweet', 'vnspeakable pleasure', or 'vnspeakable ioye, and comfort' could be discounted as conventional; even George Herbert's words on the subject—'Oh Book! infinite sweetnesse! let my heart/Suck ev'ry letter, and a hony gain'—could be dismissed as versifying.[115] However, there is more direct testimony that this was a widespread Protestant experience. Elizabeth Isham repeatedly spoke of how she and her family 'delighted' or were 'much pleased' in their godly reading. Nicholas Byfield advised his readers to make a note of the Biblical verses which they 'finde sensible comfort and rauishing of heart in'. Most, he assumed, would be able to find between twenty and fifty such passages.[116]

These relatively passive experiences—whether mourning or rejoicing—were more than matched by the dynamic ones. Bible reading could set Protestants ablaze. 'Let my heart burne within mee when I heare thee speaking vnto mee', begged Elizabeth Hastings' prayer before reading. 'Good and holy bookes are ... as sparkes to kindle the heate of the spirit', Robert Cleaver taught—one reader underlined the phrase.[117] This was not simply a matter of kindling fervency, but of preparing the Christian for spiritual combat. The Elizabethan Homilies taught that diligently reading Scripture would bring the knowledge of God necessary to fight temptation. For Robert Linaker, 'a fit place of Scripture, remembered or alleged in the heate and height of any vehement temptation, is like cold water cast vpon the flaming fire'—reversing the standard metaphor without diminishing its force.[118] Scripture, after all, was the sword of the Spirit, a Christian's only offensive weapon. Richard Capel drew on Luther's experience that, when facing vehement temptation, 'the only remedy is to take to us the sword of the Spirit, that is, the word of salvation'.[119]

Yet if the spiritual experience of Bible reading could be intense, it was not spontaneous. Like any sword, this one was useless if wielded by untrained hands. It was the cumulative effect of diligent, regular study which allowed readers to hear God speaking, and which readied them for the moment. 'Those that know they haue enemies will neuer goe foorth vnweaponed, and Kings alwayes haue their guards', Daniel Dyke pointed out; so Christians should always be forearmed with Scripture.[120] As well as making sense in its own terms, this call to reading as preparation had two other attractions. First of all, it accounted for the many, many times when reading did not produce a stricken conscience, a delighted heart, or a

---

[115] *Short and pretie Treatise*, sig. C3v; Dering, *Godly priuate praiers*, fo. 17r; Rogers, *Seven treatises*, 601; Herbert, *Works*, 58. On Protestantism's discovery of the rapture of Bible reading, see Nuttall, *Holy Spirit*, 21.

[116] Isham, 'Diary', 1618, 1620; Isham, 'Confessions', fo. 5r; Byfield, *Directions for private readeing*, sig. A7r.

[117] Huntington Library, San Marino, CA, MS 15369 fo. 4r; Robert Cleaver?, *A [g]odly form of householde gouernement* (1598: RSTC 5382), sig. A7r; FSL STC 5388 sig. A6v; cf. Leigh, *Mothers blessing*, 94; Perkins, *Exposition of the Lords prayer*, 25–6.

[118] *Certain Sermons or Homilies*, 326; Linaker, *Comfortable treatise* (1620), 191; cf. Wither, *Preparation to the Psalter*, 128.

[119] Capel, *Tentations*, 173; see above, pp. 244–5.

[120] Dyke, *Two Treatises*, 257–8.

blazing spirit. You might have feared that routine and monotony were reducing your discipline to hypocrisy. Instead, you could reassure yourself that you were training for spiritual battles to come. While the reward of your obedience might be delayed, it would be all the sweeter when it came. Second, it was sometimes true. The cumulative effect of a regular discipline could indeed be that your mind, and heart, were slowly moulded into a Biblical pattern. Wither claimed that he had spent 'a few moneths in the study of the Psalmes' before 'my dull soule began to be somewhat sensible of their vnspeakable excellencie'. Grace Mildmay, during the long, isolated, impoverished, and childless years of her early married life, fought her misery by immersing herself in Scripture. 'Wherein I found that as the water pierceth the hard stone by often dropping thereupon, so the continual exercise of God made a deep impression in my stony heart.'[121] The lesson was that, as dry as it—and you—might seem, persisting with Bible reading was as essential as persisting with prayer. In prayer, sufficient stamina would eventually wrestle God into submission. In reading, that same stamina would at last break your own heart, and for early modern Protestants the two came to much the same thing.

PROTESTANT BOOKS AND CATHOLIC BOOKS

The Bible was of course a book apart. Next to it, all human authors were merely finite and fallible, yet this did not lead early modern Protestants to restrict their reading to Scripture. Nehemiah Wallington's personal discipline bound him, not only to read two chapters of the Bible daily, but also to 'read in some other good booke: euery day or night'.[122] That pattern, of matching Biblical and non-Biblical material, was common enough. To confine yourself exclusively to Scripture was to court contempt and suspicion—contempt for those who disregarded learning, and suspicion because undiluted Bible reading was heady stuff, liable to produce idiosyncrasies at best and rank heresies at worst.[123] Most literate, mainstream Protestants were, or aspired to be, voracious readers, and while other books might be categorically different from Scripture, the ways in which readers approached them and the experiences they found in them were very similar. Most of what we have said about Bible reading can also be applied to reading other devout works, but the scope of non-Biblical reading and the manner in which it was done also deserve some mention.

The normal advice on non-Biblical devotional reading was cautious. 'Rather let one or two be read well and often, then many slightly.' Dipping into book after book 'for nouelties sake' was as inappropriate as cherry-picking favourite sections of the Bible. Most divines recommended choosing a few books, and reading and

---

[121] Wither, *Preparation to the Psalter*, 3; Mildmay, *With Faith and Physic*, 34–5.
[122] LMA Guildhall MS 204, p. 38.
[123] See, for example, Thomas S. Freeman, 'Dissenters from a dissenting church: the challenge of the Freewillers 1550–1558' in Peter Marshall and Alec Ryrie (eds), *The Beginnings of English Protestantism* (Cambridge, 2002).

re-reading them thoroughly and faithfully.[124] Pretty clearly, most readers ignored this advice if they could. The vast and steadily expanding market for such books is proof enough. Dorothy Leigh gives us a glimpse of a different attitude. She lamented that 'there bee so manie godly bookes in the world, that they mould in some mens studies, while their Masters are mard, because they will not meditate vpon them'. She compared this to having a wardrobe full of unused clothes while the poor go in rags.[125] Modern children who fuss at their food are reproached with the starving. In the same way, in our period, devouring a nourishing treatise was your duty to the bookless masses.

When books were hard to come by, the standard advice was heeded *faute de mieux*. In the 1620s, rural Shropshire was still a literary desert: Richard Baxter's father owned a Bible, a Prayer Book, John Bradford's meditations, and one other book of prayers, and apparently nothing more. One day a neighbour lent them 'an old torn Book', which turned out to be Edmund Bunny's Protestantized version of Robert Persons' *Christian Directory*. The fifteen-year-old Baxter, who had previously read 'a good Book or two', had his soul upended by these precious pages. Soon after 'a poor Pedlar came to the Door' selling books and ballads, and the Baxters bought a copy of Richard Sibbes' recently published *The bruised reede, and smoaking flax*. Some time later a servant came to them who owned some of Perkins' works.[126] That was not a bad cross-section of moderate puritan divinity, but what is striking is the essential randomness of this collection, and the way in which the Baxters were compelled to treasure and pore over books until they disintegrated.

Those who could read more widely, however, did so. Margaret Hoby, for example, mentions sixteen religious books which she read, or were read to her, between August 1599 and April 1601. Elizabeth Isham's memoirs recall at least fifteen religious books which she had particularly profited from, some of them her own, some borrowed: no doubt there were many more.[127] Nehemiah Wallington was as copious a reader as he was a writer, with a scarcely affordable tendency to bulk buying. When first trying to itemize his duties, he bought three treatises on the Ten Commandments; when 'desirous to die and yet some tims in feare of death' the following year, 'I was given to bye Books consarning death', such as 'Learne to die and death advantage and funerall sarmons, and many such lik book'. When he married, he bought Gouge's just-published *Of Domesticall Duties*.[128] But when even a preacher urging Scripture reading could reel off a list of six authors whom his audience should read, adding that there were 'many others', we can tell that the temptations of mass publication were likely to overwhelm sage advice to cherish a handful of books.[129] If, as Mary Hampson Patterson has suggested, books

---

[124] Baynes, *Briefe Directions*, 298; Rogers, *Seven treatises*, 289; Rogers, *Garden* (1616), sig. G3v; Downame, *Guide to Godlynesse*, 643–4.
[125] Leigh, *Mothers blessing*, 4.
[126] Baxter, *Reliquiae Baxterianae*, 1–4.
[127] Hoby, *Diary*; Isham, 'Diary'; Isham, 'Confessions'.
[128] Wallington, *Notebooks*, 270. The books referred to are Sutton, *Disce Mori*, and Harrison, *Deaths aduantage*.
[129] BL Egerton MS 2877 fo. 92r.

served as 'paper pastors' to lay Protestants, they would be no more content always reading the same book than they would be always listening to the same sermon.

Not that godly books were used once and shelved. Certain devotional books which ran through a great many editions now only survive in a handful of copies, presumptive evidence that they were used to destruction.[130] These were often small and inexpensive books, which had the fourfold merit of affordability, brevity, portability, and large print runs. We may assume that they had a disproportionate impact. This was Richard Kilby's view: he blamed his youthful, short-lived conversion to Catholicism on Robert Persons' *A brief censure*, 'one of the most dangerous books that ever I read', not least because of its brevity: 'for they bee little ones that either doe good or harme unto the greatest number of people'.[131]

Yet, neither authors nor publishers—nor, presumably, readers—could resist the lure of gigantism. (William Perkins, with his string of best-selling, heavyweight, and impressively succinct treatises, is the shining exception.) Bookstalls groaned under volumes with such unintentionally ironic titles as *Briefe Directions vnto a godly Life* (439 pages), *The doctrine of the Bible . . . briefely gathered* (472 pages) or *A briefe forme of learning to liue* (684 pages). When successful devotional books were reprinted, enlargement was the norm and abridgement the exception. Readers who could afford them evidently liked big books. Of the many religious books mentioned in Protestant diaries and autobiographies, three stand out, all of them monsters. In its 1570 edition, John Foxe's *Actes and monuments*, the famous *Book of Martyrs*, ran to over 2,300 folio pages and some two million words. But Foxe's book had a very particular place in Protestant piety, to which we will return.[132] Next to it, Lewis Bayly's *The practise of pietie* is a mere pamphlet, but it still weighed in at over 800 duodecimo pages; its over fifty editions in 1612–40, plus numerous translations, make it the uncontested champion of early modern British Protestant devotional writing. It was read aloud in Protestant households; readers spoke of how it moved them; others prayed from it. When Bishop Earle's 'she-puritan' defied the Devil, 'her weapon is the Practice of piety'.[133] This stodgy book's success is hard to explain, but also hard to deny. Perhaps sheer, safe comprehensiveness was its secret. The same, only more so, applies to the third book, Richard Rogers' *Seven treatises*, which went through six editions from 1602–30. Its title is fitting: at 600 duo pages, this is less a book than a library. Albeit to modern eyes Rogers seems 'a bore . . . a particularly dire writer', plenty of puritans saw his magnum opus as a touchstone of piety. John Winthrop was reduced to tears by it, and may have learned his own practice of covenant-making from it; Thomas Shepard said it was

[130] Sherman, *Used Books*, 5–6.
[131] Kilby, *Hallelujah*, 38. Persons' book runs to 88 octavo pages.
[132] See below, pp. 422–7.
[133] Green, *Print and Protestantism*, 348–51; Isham, 'Confessions', fo. 25v; Isham, 'Diary', 1621; Clarke, *Collection*, 515–16; Huntington Library, San Marino, CA, MS 15369 7r; Wariston, *Diary*, 144; Earle, *Microcosmographie*, 120; Paula McQuade, 'Maternal Catechesis in the Manuscript Miscellany of Katherine Fitzwilliam (c. 1600)', paper delivered to the Sixteenth Century Conference, Cincinnati, Ohio, 27 October 2012.

'the book which did first work upon my heart'.[134] Some readers were, however, daunted by its size. This may lie behind a comment by Rogers' friend Ezekiel Culverwell's that the book ought to be 'better regarded'. It was, along with Foxe's book, one of the very few devotional works to be published in an abridged form—a mere six hundred duodecimo pages—which itself went through five editions from 1618–35. John Bruen prepared his own epitome of it before he realized that there was already one in print.[135] Another reader condensed Rogers' work into a catechism for her children.

It is striking that Bayly and Rogers' books, which so quickly became staples of British Protestant practical divinity, first appeared a long lifetime after the beginning of the Reformation. Rogers, in particular, was consciously trying to fill a gap in the market. Although Protestant readers had plenty of books of prayers and even more printed sermons, before 1600 there was relatively little in the way of practical spiritual advice and exhortation. Rogers' concern was that readers seeking such advice were being lured towards Catholic works. By this he meant, above all, Persons' *Christian Directory*. The *Book of resolution*, as it was generally known, was the most immediately successful work of practical piety of the entire period, and even as a steady seller it is eclipsed only by *The practise of pietie*. The Protestantized edition of Persons' book ran through over thirty editions in fifty years, of which no less than fifteen appeared in a single year, 1585. For Rogers and his friends, the runaway success of this Catholic book and its 'pretended shew of godlines' was alarming. Its effect, Stephen Egerton wrote, was 'to insnare and intangle the minds of ignorant and simple Christians, in the corrupt and filthie puddle of Popish deuotion'. Culverwell claimed that Rogers' book had 'more sound godlines in one leafe, then all their artificiall composed treatises of Resolution'.[136] The compliments were backhanded but sincere. The titles of other Prominent Protestant devotional works, such as Gabriel Powel's *The Resolued Christian, exhorting to Resolution* (seven editions, 1600–23) and John Denison's *A Three-fold Resolution, verie necessarie to saluation* (five editions, 1603–32), are transparent attempts to cash in on Persons' success.

But Persons was not a one-off. Early modern British Protestants had, for want of a better word, catholic tastes in devotional writing. Contemporary and medieval Catholic writers jostle with British and Continental Reformed Protestants on the lists of commercially successful religious books. (There was also a small but noticeable Lutheran presence, but given Reformed Protestantism's unrequited affection for Lutheranism in general and Luther in particular, that is not particularly surprising.[137]) Robert Southwell's book of Catholic devotional poetry, *St Peters complainte*, went through some fourteen London editions, plus one in Edinburgh, from 1595–1636. A Protestantized version of Luis de Granada's *Of*

[134] Winthrop, *Papers*, 199; Shepard, *God's plot*, 43; BL Egerton MS 2877 fo. 92r; Scudder, *Christians daily walke* (1628), sig. A11r–v; Clarke, *Collection*, 453; Dixon, 'Predestination and pastoral theology', 57.
[135] Culverwell, *Treatise of faith*, 90; Richard Rogers, *The practice of Christianitie. Or, An epitome of seuen treatises* (1618: RSTC 21221), et seq; Hinde, *Faithfull Remonstrance . . . of Iohn Bruen*, 142.
[136] Rogers, *Seven treatises*, sigs A3r–v, A6v–7r.
[137] Ryrie, 'Afterlife of Lutheran England'.

prayer and meditation appeared in nine editions from 1592–1634. There were only three editions of Jeremias Drexel's *Considerations upon Eternitie* in our period— 1632, 1636, and 1639—but eighteen more followed over the next eighty-five years. While there was only one London edition of Gasper Loarte's *Exercise of a Christian Life*, in 1594, Rogers believed that this, too, was seducing Protestants from the truth.[138] These are merely the post-Reformation Catholics. Pre-Reformation devotional works were embraced even more enthusiastically. John Bradford's influential meditations appeared in eight editions from 1562–1633, and formed the largest part of Henry Bull's *Christian praiers and holy meditations*—nine editions from 1568– 1614—yet they were based very closely on Juan Luis Vives' prayers. Indeed, as Helen C. White first documented, if you scratched a great many Elizabethan devotional works you would find Vives and the wider medieval primer tradition. As for the most popular devotional work of the late medieval period, the *Imitation of Christ*, two different Protestant English translations together went through twenty-three editions between 1567–1640.[139]

What are we to make of this phenomenon? One obvious interpretation was the one which Rogers and his friends feared, which plenty of contemporary Catholics triumphantly claimed, and towards which several modern scholars of the subject— primary literary scholars—have leaned. This view reads Protestantism's plundering of Catholic devotion as a tacit admission of failure. As White pointed out, Edwin Sandys not only accepted that Catholics regularly reproached Protestants for 'their povertie, weaknes, & coldnes, in that kind, as being forced to take the catholikes books to supply theirs', but admitted that this 'cannot altogither be denied to be true'. Persons himself levelled a similar charge against his uninvited Protestant editor Edmund Bunny, asking 'where or when, any of his religion did either make or set forthe (of them selues) any one treatise of this kinde or subiect?' The only English works that Bunny could come up in reply with were Becon's *The sycke mans salue* and, embarrassingly, Bradford's meditations: Bunny evidently did not know about Bradford's Catholic source.[140] (Unsurprisingly: from Bradford to Ralph Winterton's edition of Drexel, most Protestant editors avoided mentioning that they were drawing on Catholic sources.) A generation later, another defender of Protestant spirituality was forced into the awkward claim that, when it came to devotional writings, 'the Romanists for the most part exceed in bulke, but our Diuines in weight'. Yet it is not clear that this is so. Powel's *The Resolued Christian*, for example, is a pretty poor imitation of Persons: it has a high-handed and declamatory style more suited to polemic than devotion, and tends to deal with pastoral problems—the fear of death, for example—by dismissing them with trite formulae.[141] We have already noted the tendency for Protestant prayers to turn

---

[138] Rogers, *Seven treatises*, sig. A6v.

[139] White, *Tudor Books of Private Devotion*, 184–212; Maximilian von Habsburg, *Catholic and Protestant Translations of the* Imitatio Christi, *1425–1650* (Aldershot, 2011), 118–20; and above, pp. 113–15 (Hall & Mombaer).

[140] White, *English Devotional Literature*, 64–8, 146; Edwin Sandys, *A relation of the state of religion* (1605: RSTC 21716), sig. H2r.

[141] Featley, *Ancilla Pietatis*, sig. A6r; Powel, *Resolued Christian*, e.g. 58–9.

into sermons delivered by other means.[142] So was Protestantism a polemical religion which simply lacked the spiritual depth to do devotion?

A more nuanced, but equally damning, critique would see Protestantism as a religion of doctrine while Catholicism was one of devotion. We have already observed how the intimate connection between godliness and correct knowledge of doctrine infuses Protestant devotional works. For Louis Martz, this precisely was Protestantism's problem: its emphasis on divine sovereignty and human fallibility made most devotional exercises almost impossible.[143] That now seems a distortion, but the Protestant priority on doctrine is unmistakable. It is striking that, in response to Persons' challenge to find Protestant devotional works, Edmund Bunny listed a string of doctrinal treatises and Biblical commentaries—on the grounds that 'the Scriptures . . . treat of *deuotion, pietie*, &c'. This was not because Bunny had no-where else to turn but because, for Protestants, doctrine *was* devotion. Luther's Galatians commentary, for example, which Bunny cited, had a glowing reputation for spiritual solace.[144] And manifestly, Protestants were more dedicated to bringing Biblical scholarship to the masses than were Catholics. But by the 17th century Protestants regularly acknowledged that, justly or unjustly, Catholics had a reputa-tion for greater devotion; and even that, while Catholics' errors were egregious, they were 'more deuoute in that which they doe lesse vnderstand, and are far more frequent in Praier' than most Protestants.[145] According to Henry Burton, good Protestant ladies at court found themselves shamed by

> the vrgent examples of Romane Catholicke Ladies, among whom we conuerse, who presse vs with their exemplarie practise of pietie and deuotion in their Religion, putting vs and our Religion to shame, if we doe not equalize at least, if not outstrip them in point of deuotion.

Burton of course dismissed such devotion as worthless, but he made no attempt to deny that it was real.[146]

We should not be surprised that Protestant devotional practices—unstructured, individualistic, and laissez-faire as they were—lacked the sophistication and rigour of their Catholic counterparts. But nor will it do to dismiss this as a spiritually starved tradition stealing crumbs from the neighbours. Something more interesting is going on here. Consider the opposite case. There was virtually no Catholic use of Protestant devotional materials in this period, and it is easy to see why not. Catholicism's tighter disciplinary structures would have made it tricky, and in any case, most Protestant devotional materials were so shot through with Protestant doctrine that stripping the heresies out of them would have reduced them to ribbons. It is not that Catholics' devotional self-sufficiency was such that they

---

[142] See above, pp. 223–4.

[143] Martz, *Poetry of Meditation*, 156–7; and see above, pp. 261–70.

[144] Edmund Bunny, *A briefe answer, vnto those idle and friuolous quarrels of R.P.* (1589: RSTC 4088), 38; Ryrie, 'Afterlife of Lutheran England', 216.

[145] Ward, *Coal from the Altar*, 30; Perrott, *Certaine Short Prayers*, 135; Brinsley, *True Watch* (1608), sig. B2v.

[146] Burton, *Tryall of Private Devotions*, sig. B3r–v.

would never feel the need to look beyond their borders; rather, that Protestantism was much better equipped than Catholicism to be devotionally omnivorous, and that Catholic materials were much better suited to cross-confessional adaptation than Protestant ones.

Indeed, while some Protestants were hostile to or embarrassed by their use of Catholic materials, others were unapologetic. Richard Braithwaite, presenting a devotional anthology consisting largely of medieval materials, ridiculed the view that 'flowers of this nature . . . lost much of their native beauty, vigour and verdure, because called from a Roman border'. A rose from any other soil would smell no sweeter. This was the classic conformist-ceremonialist manoeuvre, to deny that Protestantism must be a simple negative image of Catholic piety, and argue rather that it should boldly claim whatever was not corrupt from Rome.[147] But the reason this argument was so much repeated is that it did not appeal only to committed ceremonialists. Something of the kind was Bunny's professed reason for setting forth a version of Persons' work:

> To accept of our aduersaries labors so much as is good, may I trust bring to passe with some few of them, that themselves wil better perceive, that wherin they shal do wel, they may looke to be as readily incouraged by us, as, when they do il, to be admonished.

He further justified himself by citing, as a precedent, the successful Protestant editions of the *Imitation of Christ*.[148] Which provides us with two subtler arguments for Protestant use of Catholic materials: the place of the medieval heritage, and the contentious quest for what Bunny called 'pacification'.

Medieval devotional materials were much less problematic for Protestants than contemporary Catholic ones. This is partly the condescension of posterity: the dead do not need to be held to the same exacting standards as the living. Protestant historians who could be stubbornly precise about perceived error amongst their contemporaries were blithely inclusive when dealing with past generations. John Bale's roll-call of the true church included such unlikely figures as Benedict of Montecassino, the Venerable Bede, and even St Dominic. As John Knox put it, some medieval figures could be admired, not because they were right on every point, but because they showed 'some sponk of [God's] light, evin in the tyme of grettast darkness'. 'The blindnesse of that time', said John Foxe, covered a multitude of sins.[149] The reason for such generosity was that the dead could not resist being co-opted by the Protestant cause, and being used to demonstrate that a golden thread of truth had persisted in some form or other even through the most corrupt centuries of Christendon.

This helped to fuel Protestantism's appetite for medieval devotional materials. The rash of republication of Lollard texts, which lent the infant Reformation age if

---

[147] Richard Braithwaite, *A spiritual spicerie containing sundrie sweet tractates of devotion and piety* (1638: RSTC 3586), 226–7; and see, classically, Hooker, *Laws . . . Books I–IV*, 298.

[148] Persons, *Booke of Christian exercise*, ed. Bunny, sigs *2v, *3v.

[149] John Bale, *The Image of bothe churches* (1546: RSTC 1297), sigs M3r, P4v; Knox, *Works*, I.10; Foxe, *Actes and monuments* (1583), 838.

not respectability, is well known.[150] The tendency of Protestant editors to lay hold of more or less innocuous medieval texts and rebrand them as Lollard is less so.[151] It is a sign that orthodox medieval traditions were used as enthusiastically as heretical ones. Protestants were, if not exactly late medieval Christians, at least the heirs of late medieval Christianity. While they deliberately rejected much of that heritage, they could no more rid themselves of it entirely than they could travel back in time to the 1st century; and some parts of it they treasured.

The *Imitation of Christ* is the best-known sign of this. Its enormous popularity crossed the Reformation barrier as if it did not exist. As well as popular pre- and post-Reformation versions, there was a unacknowledged 'bridge' edition in the shape of Queen Katherine Parr's *Prayers stirryng the mynd vnto heauenly medytacions*, the bulk of which was rendered from Book III of the *Imitation*.[152] As Maximilian von Habsburg has argued, the *Imitation* had a dual appeal to Protestants. Firstly, its intensely Christocentric piety and focus on the inner life meshed beautifully with their doctrinal preoccupations. Secondly, it spoke more specifically to English Protestantism's need, in the Elizabethan period, to shift its attention away from the increasingly forlorn hope of further institutional Reformation and towards the less spectacular but ultimately more important work of inner renewal. As with all Protestant versions of Catholic devotional works, translation was not about textual accuracy. It was an 'exegetical exercise', whose purpose was to sieve the original text through Scripture before it was safe for use. This resulted in a series of changes and omissions, mostly minor, some more substantial. But this filtering process did not involve adding explicitly Protestant doctrines to the text. It reduced the *Imitation* to a state which Catholics would have found inoffensive, if a little denatured. The Protestant editors were trying not to recreate the text in their own image, but to purify it to the point at which they and their readers could learn from it.[153]

Much the same can be said, on a smaller scale, of the use of other medieval sources—and, indeed, of Bunny's careful filtering of Persons' text. We have already seen Joseph Hall's careful redaction of Jean Mombaer's *Rosetum* of 1494, a source whose spiritual authority he respected but which he was entirely willing to reshape for his own purposes.[154] The *Treasure of gladnesse*, a tiny 16mo handbook of prayers which went through a dozen editions fron 1563–1601, claims to have been based on 'a very little manuell, . . . written in velam . . . made aboue .CC. yeares past at the least'. It was given a light Protestant makeover, but its contents remain unmistakably medieval.[155] Prayers in the primer tradition continued to find Protestant users well into the 17th century. Some of these were found in

[150] Margaret Aston, 'Lollardy and the Reformation', *History* 49 (1964), 149–70.
[151] Alexandra Walsham, 'Inventing the Lollard Past: The Afterlife of a Medieval Sermon in Early Modern England', *Journal of Ecclesiastical History* 58/4 (2007), 628–55. For another example of the same phenomenon, see *A generall free pardon or charter of heuyn blys* (1542: RSTC 19187).
[152] Philippa Tudor: 'Changing private belief and practice in English devotional literature, *c.* 1475–1550', University of Oxford D.Phil thesis (1984), 66–7.
[153] Habsburg, *Translations of the* Imitatio Christi, esp. 127, 143–4, 146–8, 159–77.
[154] See above, p. 113–15.
[155] *This booke is called the Treasure of gladnesse*; Green, *Print and Protestantism*, 255; White, *Tudor Books of Private Devotion*, 140.

unashamedly conservative collections like Richard Day's *Booke of Christian Prayers* (four editions, 1578–1608). But Thomas Sorocold's *Supplications of Saints*, a prayer book which was reprinted almost every year from 1612–40 and which was used by such mainstream Protestants as Anne Clifford and Elizabeth Isham, also happily included 'the ancient Prayer, called, O bountifull Iesu'.[156] Where Protestants could use medieval devotional materials without compromising on doctrine, they were and continued to be keen to do so.

The most intriguing medieval theme which Protestants took up is the piety of Christ's Passion. Imaginative and often graphic recreations of Christ's sufferings were a vital part of late medieval piety, and scholars have long pointed out that Protestants distanced themselves from the perceived excesses of this tradition. Susan Karant-Nunn argues that, for Protestants, understanding the doctrine of salvation took the place of feeling Christ's agony.[157] The removal of visual depictions of the Passion made the whole business more intangible. Of course Christ's sufferings remained important to Protestants—Christians can scarcely avoid the subject—but as White has pointed out, influential treatments like John Bradford's meditation on the Passion or John Foxe's Good Friday sermon tended to be restrained and descriptive rather than affective lamentations, focusing on Christ's mental anguish rather than his bodily sufferings, and emphasizing the triumph of the cross as much as its tragedy. Foxe's sermon even gave the dying Christ a lengthy victory oration to death and the Devil. He promised 'to set vp here in Paules Crosse . . . a new Crucifixe, a new roode vnto you', by which he meant expounding the doctrine of justification by faith alone.[158] Like Katherine Parr's famous and ambiguous claim that we should meditate on 'the booke of the crucifixe' while never endorsing the use of tangible images, all this risks becoming a little abstract.[159]

So it is worth noticing that, after the first generation, Protestants returned to Passion-piety with increasing enthusiasm and detail, a return encouraged by their use of medieval sources. Even Foxe's account of the Passion—with 'buffets and blowes, mockes and mowes, rayling and reuiling, hammer & nayles, crosse and gibbet, thirst and vinegar, reed and speare'—was hardly bloodless. Day's *Booke of Christian Prayers* is a much plainer echo of medieval patterns. It includes a group of fifteen vivid, affective prayers on the Passion—an echo of the Fifteen Oes, which were themselves linked to Christ's wounds.[160] The anti-Calvinist Christopher Sutton, who drew openly on contemporary Jesuit writings, was detailed and

---

[156] White, *Tudor Books of Private Devotion*, 191–5; Sorocold, *Supplications of Saints* (1612), 259–64; Isham, 'Confessions', fo. 16v; Isham, 'Diary', 1619, 1624; Clifford, *Diaries*, 70.

[157] Susan C. Karant-Nunn, '"Christians' Mourning and Lament Should Not Be Like the Heathens'": the Suppression of Religious Emotion in the Reformation' in J. M. Headley et al. (eds), *Confessionalization in Europe, 1555–1700* (Aldershot, 2004), 114.

[158] White, *Tudor Books of Private Devotion*, 147; White, *English Devotional Literature*, 195; cf. Elizabeth K. Hudson, 'English Protestants and the imitatio Christi, 1580–1620', *Sixteenth Century Journal* 19/4 (1988), 555–7. See, for example, Bradford, *Godlie meditations*, sigs M6r–8v; *Christian Prayers and Meditations in English*, sigs k4v–m2r; Foxe, *Sermon of Christ crucified*, fos 40r–48r, 53v.

[159] Parr, *Lamentacion*, sig. C2r.

[160] Foxe, *Sermon of Christ crucified*, 49r; Day, *Booke of Christian Prayers*, fos 76r–85v.

graphic in his Passion meditations.[161] But so, increasingly, were puritans. Perkins'
Declaration of the true manner of knowing Christ Crucified includes an eight-page
section working through the Passion narrative, using each incident as a call to
repentance, and urging the Christian to 'labour by faith to see Christ crucified in all
the workes of God'. The opening sentence of John Hayward's *Sanctuarie of a
troubled soule* laments how Christ's 'blessed bodie was buffeted with fists, torn
with whips, stretched vpon the Crosse, pierced with nailes and speare, and bathed
in the sweete streames of thine own blood', and when he added a second part to
the book, 276 of its 395 pages were taken up by an extended meditation on the
Passion. There are similarly vivid, sometimes gruesome, passages in works by
Edward Hutchins, George Webbe, Michael Sparke, Gilbert Primrose, and Jeremiah Dyke, amongst others; also, more briefly, in Bayly's *Practise of pietie*.[162] As we
shall see, it was particularly common to link this to sacramental devotion. It was
also used, explicitly, as a means to encourage the tears which Protestant piety so
coveted. Preachers' ability 'to make a Scenicall representation of the death of
Christ', and audiences' readiness to 'weepe devoutly at a Passion Sermon' were
commonplaces for early 17th century Protestants. But they were also commonplaces which continued, explicitly, to be linked to Catholic practices.[163]

The rich seams of medieval piety which focused on inner renewal and sanctification, and on Christ's person and sufferings, were claimed by Protestants as their
own, with increasing self-confidence. And where their Catholic contemporaries
continued to mine it, they were, by and large, happy to borrow and adapt the
results. This was not without its risks. Rogers was right to fear that even sanitized
versions of Catholic texts might seduce readers to Rome.[164] But nor was it slavish
imitation. The moral themes and emotional cadences of Catholic piety were being
fitted neatly into a Protestant doctrinal framework. No wonder that Robert Persons
himself was if anything angrier about Bunny's Protestant edition of his book than
was Rogers.[165]

Persons' anger, however, was sparked not only by the Protestant sheen which
Bunny had given to his words, but by Bunny's explanation of what he had done,
titled a *Treatise Tending to Pacification*. If Bunny had actively been trying to
infuriate Persons, he could hardly have improved on this treatise, which essentially
tells Catholics, in magisterially condescending tones, to calm down. But we have to
assume that Bunny's call for interconfessional peace was sincere. It was common

[161] Fincham and Tyacke, *Altars Restored*, 67–8; and see, for example, Sutton, *Godly meditations*
(1601), 172–3, 214–23; Sutton, *Godly meditations* (1613), 377–8.
[162] Perkins, *Declaration of the true manner*, 30–8; Hayward, *Sanctuarie of a troubled soule* (1602),
1–2; Hayward, *Sanctvarie of a troubled soule* (1618), II.67–343; Hutchins, *Davids Sling*, 17–18,
69–70; Rogers, *Garden* (1616), sig G3r; Bayly, *Practise of pietie*, 600–3; Primrose, *Christian Mans
Teares*, 118–38; Sparke, *Crumms of comfort*, sigs L10r–M1r; Dyke, *Worthy communicant*, 526–32.
[163] Pemble, *Introduction to worthy receiving*, 16–17; Pinke, *Tryall of a Christians loue*, III. 27.
[164] Victor Houliston, *Catholic Resistance in Elizabethan England: Robert Persons's Jesuit Polemic,
1580–1610* (Aldershot, 2007), 44.
[165] Victor Houliston, 'Why Robert Persons would not be Pacified: Edmund Bunny's Theft of The
Book of Resolution' in Thomas M. McCoog (ed), *The Reckoned Expense: Edmund Campion and the
Early English Jesuits* (Woodbridge, 1996); cf. Gregory, '"True and Zealouse Seruice"'.

enough for Protestant devotional materials to lament the divisions among Christians, but such laments were often pretty empty: attempting to end division by
telling everyone else that they were wrong. There is another theme to some of them,
however. The prayer for Christian unity in Thomas Becon's *The gouernans of
vertue*, for example, asked for the grace to 'laye asyde all dissencion' and even
insisted that 'there is but one euerlastynge god & one heuenly father, which thou
art, & one fayth & one baptisme, whyche we all profes that call on thy name'.[166]
To inveigh, not only against contention, but against contentiousness was implicitly
to shape your own behaviour.

This explicit distaste for polemic and doctrinal disagreement would become a
running theme in Protestant devotional works. We might expect Richard Hooker to
contrast the 'reason' which unites Christians with the 'heat of contention' which divides
them. But the sometimes outspoken preacher Samuel Ward agreed that 'there is too
much of this bitter zeale ... in all our books of controuersies'. 'Future ages', Ward
accurately predicted, would see 17th-century theological disputes as ridiculous, 'strife
about trifles'. Another puritan best-seller, George Webbe's *The practice of quietnes*, was
written specifically to encourage 'a peaceable disposicion ... a milde nature, and true
Christian temper, swift to heare, slow to speake, slow to wrath'. Joseph Hall claimed
that he wrote his *Arte of Divine Meditation*, with its medieval roots, because 'I perceiued the number of Polemicall bookes, rather to breede, than ende strifes'.[167] Ian
Green has pointed out that devotional works regularly outsold polemical ones throughout the period, and while that is not a simple index of their popularity, it seems
clear that—especially outside the cities—readers sought edification before bile.[168]

Disliking controversy did not preclude expressing strong views on controversial
matters. Ward, for example, insisted that lukewarmness was worse than excessive
zeal: 'rather let your milk boyle ouer then be raw'. And pacification could be a
matter of policy as well as of principle, aiming, as Bunny explicitly did, to create
devotional common ground across which Catholics could be lured.[169] But this was
only possible because of the nature of devotional life. Throughout this book we
have seen how, when looked at through a devotional lens, the differences between
conformist and puritan Protestants blur, and indeed Protestant devotional texts
often simply resist categorization in these terms.[170] The same is true, to a lesser
extent, of the gulf separating Protestants from Catholics. For all their disagreements, they continued to speak the same devotional language. It is not simply that
devotional texts do not usually involve much controversial doctrine. The dislike for
polemic, and especially the feeling that it was inimical to devotion, meant that the
authors of devotional books positively avoided controversial issues. This was to
evade rather than to solve the problems of confessional strife, but evasion is
important in itself. The omnivorous devotional habits of early modern Protestants

---

[166] Becon, *Gouernans* (1544?), fos 106v–107r.
[167] Hooker, *Laws ... Books I–IV*, 144; Ward, *Coal from the Altar*, 22–3; Webbe, *Practise of qui[e]tnes*,
10, 14; Hall, *Arte of Divine Meditation*, sig. A3r.
[168] Green, *Print and Protestantism*, 233–4.
[169] Ward, *Coal from the Altar*, 40; Persons, *Booke of Christian exercise*, ed. Bunny, sigs *2v–3r.
[170] Patterson, *Domesticating*, 30.

are one sign that, even in this age of antagonism, being Protestant did not necessarily mean hating Catholics.

THE BOOK AS OBJECT

Historians are nowadays accustomed to encountering early modern texts in scholarly editions or digital facsimiles; so we can occasionally forget that books were not disembodied strings of data, but physical objects of paper, ink, and leather, with a certain smell and a heft in the hand, produced not only by an author's endeavour but by an industrial process. Given the importance which books had for early modern Protestants, it is worth considering the implications of their cherished texts' multiple incarnations into physical print.

This question is easily framed as one of 'superstition'. Did Reformed Protestants, who supposedly tried so hard to disenchant the world, nevertheless treat their Bibles as magical objects? Sometimes, yes. Human nature abhors a vacuum, and the Protestant renunciation of magic left an acute gap. Since the Bible was the closest thing to a sacred object that remained, it is no surprise it was sometimes co-opted. Opening a Bible at random could be used as a form of divination. Bibles were sometimes believed to provide magical protection. A stream of stories from the Civil War era describe soldiers whose lives were saved when Bibles in their breast pockets stopped bullets. Bibles were sometimes used in folk medicine. Above all, they were used against the Devil. At least one cleric taught that 'a Bible in the house would keep the Devil out'. Those possessed by demons provided corroboration by attacking Bibles or having seizures when near to them—even when near concealed copies. It made sense. The word of God was the sword of the Spirit, and no other weapon against Satan could be as effective.[171]

Biblical magic of this kind has a certain freak-show fascination, but we should not mistake it for mainstream Protestant practice. It is not simply that sober divines rejected 'the common opinion of our ignorant people' who 'think that the words of Scripture written or spoken, haue vertue in them to doe strange things', or worse, 'turne the Text of Scripture into a charme'.[172] Such comments simply prove that the phenomenon existed. The real problem with concentrating on the wilder fringes of Bibliolatry is that it distracts us from subtler, more ingrained and far more widespread patterns in the relationship between Protestants and their beloved books.

One obvious sign is the habit of carrying books. A puritan, as the satirists repeatedly tell us, is someone who 'hath his Testament chain'd to his wast', who 'att his belte a buffclad bible weares', who 'carryeth a book under his arm and the

---

[171] David Cressy, 'Books as totems in seventeenth-century England and New England', *Journal of Library History* 21 (1986), esp. 98; Schmidt, *Hearing Things*, 48–9; Thomas, *Religion and the Decline of Magic*, 139–41; Ulinka Rublack, *Reformation Europe* (Cambridge, 2005), 159; Andrew Cambers, 'Demonic Possession, Literacy and "Superstition" in Early Modern England', *Past and Present* 202 (2009), esp. 8–14; Hinde, *Faithfull Remonstrance . . . of Iohn Bruen*, 148–50. On the openness of some Protestants to magic, see Alec Ryrie, *The Sorcerer's Tale* (Oxford, 2008), 157–76.

[172] Perkins, *Godly and learned exposition*, 245; Capel, *Tentations*, 173.

Devil in his bosom'—but who for all that might not be able to read a word.[173] Friendlier witnesses agreed that books were part of the uniform, for good or ill. As early as 1550, Thomas Becon was denouncing 'grosse gospellers' who 'haue the holy scriptures swymmyng in theyr lyppes and Gods booke eyther in theyr handes or hangyng at theyr gyrdles', but whose lives were unreformed. 'A Bible vnder your armes', thundered Thomas Adams in his sermon against hypocrisy, 'will not excuse a false conscience in your bosomes.'[174] But if it was a matter of ostentation for some, it was one of conscience for others. Hugh Latimer, preaching before the young Edward VI, told him that it was a king's duty to have a Bible in his presence at all times, even to the point of having a servant bring one when he went out hunting. A pamphlet published in the same year praised the emperor Constantine for having 'caused the newe Testament to be carryed before him for a wytnes of hys faith'. Three years later, a zealous English merchant named William Gardiner carried out a suicidal public desecration of the Mass in Portugal. While waiting in the church for the moment to make his attack, he had 'a Testament in his hand, the which he diligently read vpon'.[175]

Within a generation, Bible-carrying was merely normal. Booksellers offered 'plenty of manuall Psalters and Testaments . . . easie to carry in mens pockets'.[176] Nor did your pockets have to be particularly capacious. The first edition of Lady Elizabeth Tyrwhit's *Morning and Evening Prayers* was a 32mo, barely three inches high, bound with equally tiny editions of the Litany and of Katherine Parr's *Prayers*.[177] Famously, the smallest of all was *Verbum Sempiternum*, a 64mo 'thumb-Bible' prepared by the water-poet John Taylor, which fitted its verse summary of the whole Bible onto pages just over one and a half inches high. Perhaps Taylor's book was more a novelty than a serious devotional object, but if so it was only a parody of a normal practice. The preface to the pseudonymous collection *The Saints Legacies*—a comparatively chunky duodecimo—urged 'all beleevers to make this their pocket book'.[178] Perhaps they did it simply to have devotional resources always to hand. Nehemiah Wallington wrote a collection of God's promises into 'a littel red cover booke to carry about me or be in readinesse to comfort my fainting spirits'. John Bruen 'did usually carry about him some part of the Bible, or his Sermon Note booke, if he went abroad into the field to meditate . . . or were upon a journey', which hints at a certain pragmatism.[179] Or perhaps the mere act of book-carrying was significant. Anne Clifford described a day's walking with a servant and mulling her troubles, 'carrying my Bible with me'. There is no indication that she opened it, but she wanted to record that it was with her.

[173] Phillips, *Satyr*, 2; FSL MS X.d.475 fo. 3r; Haigh, *Plain Man's Pathways*, 129.

[174] Becon, *Flour of godly praiers*, sig. ✠5v; Adams, *The white devil*, 33; cf. Gouge, *Whole-Armor of God*, 318–19; Pinke, *Tryall of a Christians loue*, IV.24.

[175] Latimer, *Sermons by Hugh Latimer*, 120–1; *The olde fayth of greate Brittaygne, and the newe learnynge of Inglande* (1549?: RSTC 24566), sig. C3r; Foxe, *Actes and monuments* (1570), 1543.

[176] Burton, *Tryall of Private Devotions*, sig. E1r.

[177] Tyrwhit, *Elizabeth Tyrwhit's Morning and Evening Prayers*, 50.

[178] 'Phoenix', *Saints Legacies*, sig. B1v.

[179] Narveson, *Bible Readers*, 117; Hinde, *Faithfull Remonstrance . . . of Iohn Bruen*, 142.

Christopher Sutton praised the example of 'a holy matron' who 'was said alwaies to haue caried it [the Bible] next her heart, whereby she approched vnto Christ and Christ, vnto her'.[180] Closed books were still powerful.

Another sign of the same phenomenon is the respect with which Bibles were treated. The official campaigns against Protestant Bibles in the early years of the Reformation had made this a matter of life and death. Avner Shamir's ground-breaking thesis on Bible-burning has pointed out how many English Protestants were willing to risk their lives to save copies of the Bible from destruction. Memories of the role Bible-burning had played in ancient persecutions made the subject particularly sensitive. There was no English equivalent of the French Huguenot Margaret Pierron, who refused to burn her French Bible and so forfeited her own life, but at least two Marian martyrs did go to the flames clutching Bibles to their breasts. Another, Richard Woodman, was asked during his interrogation whether burning a Bible was the same as burning God's Word. It was, he answered; and added that 'he that wyll burne a testamente willingly, wold burne God him selfe if he were here, if he could'. His interrogators laughed, and indeed more sophisticated Protestants found this approach a little crude: but for Woodman and others like him, it was not funny. They had risked their lives to read God's Word. They could hardly abandon it to the flames.[181]

The same instinct can be seen in more peaceful times. Erasmus had called for Christians to 'covet this literature, let us embrace it . . . let us fondly kiss it, at length let us die in its embrace'. Archbishop Cranmer's preface to the Great Bible called Scripture 'the most precious jewel, and most holy relic that remaineth upon earth'. His Ordinal included, as a climactic moment, the presentation of a Bible or New Testament to the newly ordained minister. The gift was accompanied by the words 'Take thou authority' (to read and preach), not 'Take thou this book'; the book was here a symbol, not a text. The English Homilies denounced the Catholic use of relics and images by arguing, 'Should we not, good brethren, much rather embrace and reverence God's holy books, the sacred Bible, which do represent Christ unto us more truly than can any image?'[182] None of these comments necessarily refer to the physical object, but it was not obtuse to hear them that way. It is no surprise that the eleven-year-old Elizabeth Isham, when she found a loose page from a Bible, 'folded it up and made mee a little booke of it and being very ioyent of it I kept it in my poket reading it often to my selfe'. Nor that the Suffolk nonconformist Richard Blackerby insisted that Bibles should be treated with respect, on the grounds that 'there ought a negative Reverence to be given to the out-sides of such sacred Oracles'.[183] And naturally, Bibles appeared at that most spiritually charged site, the Protestant deathbed. Katherine Brettergh asked to be brought hers when dying, and thanked God for it, 'ioyfully kissing it'. On the morning of his death, Robert Bruce could no longer see, yet he too asked to be brought his Bible

---

[180] Clifford, *Diaries*, 51; Sutton, *Disce viuere*, 12.

[181] Avner Shamir, 'Bible burning and the descration of bibles in early modern England', Roskilde University PhD thesis (2010), 191, 193–5, 200–1.

[182] Erasmus, *Christian Humanism*, 105; Cranmer, *Miscellaneous Writings*,122; *Certain Sermons or Homilies*, 328.

[183] Isham, 'Confessions', fo. 14r; Clarke, *Lives of sundry Eminent Persons*, 64.

and to have his finger placed on a particular passage, which he recited from memory. He then held it, blessed his companions and died 'without one groan or shiver'.[184] Erasmus' words could hardly have been taken more seriously.

Brettergh's deathbed also shows us another aspect of the physical Bible's power. When she was struggling with doubts about her salvation, 'sometime she would cast her Bible from her, and say: It was indeede the booke of life, but she had read the same vnprofitably, and therefore feared it was become to her the booke of death.'[185] Scripture brings condemnation as well as comfort. In the 1640s, the teenage Sarah Wight came within an ace of throwing her Bible in the fire when she was similarly overcome with fear of its judgements. This impulse was not so much blasphemy as despairing defiance of God—and is not entirely different from the urge we have already met, to confront, argue, and wrestle with God. Burning a Bible could be a form of symbolic suicide: scarcely less dramatic, but allowing for repentance.[186]

The deathbed requests for Bibles also remind us that not all Bibles were the same. It was common to cherish your own particular copy. There was a practical side to this. As Valentine Marshall explained, 'men shoot best in their own Bowes: work best with their own Tools'. He meant that if you are trying to find an elusive reference, often 'the side of the leafe is remembred, when the chapter and verse cannot be thought on'. Samuel Fairclough, when tracking down a Biblical quotation, was said to recall not only chapter and verse, but also 'the *place* of the page where it was Printed in the *Bibles* of *Barkers Edition*, (of which only, he made use of near *fifty* years together)'.[187] Your own Bible might also be adorned with layers of marginalia and underlinings—early modern readers did not express their reverence for a book by leaving it unmarked—in which you could track your spiritual progress from childhood onwards. One very obvious sign of this was embroidering a cover for your Bible, or decorating in some other way, which showed pains being taken and a certain reverent decency applied to the volume.[188]

A family history attached to a particular copy could give it particular weight. We have already met the young Henry Burton's fascination with the New Testament which his grandfather had kept hidden during Mary I's reign.[189] One of the very few events which Nehemiah Wallington recorded from his childhood was being given a Bible, which he took as a singular proof of his father's love. Elizabeth Isham, too, remembered that she, her brother, and her sister were given Bibles by their father, 'in which I much delighted counting it my cheifest treasure'. As a girl, she was also agog to read her great-grandfather's copy of Henry Bull's *Christian praiers and holy meditations*, in which he had 'marked in many places that he liked'. She treasured the book into adulthood: 'it doth much rejoyce mee . . . to tred in the selfe same stepes towards heaven wherein my forefathers have walked'.[190]

[184] Harrison, *Deaths aduantage*, III.24; Bruce, *Sermons . . . with Collections*, 156.
[185] Harrison, *Deaths aduantage*, III.12.
[186] Shamir, 'Bible burning', 152; and see above, pp. 247–56.
[187] Capel, *Capel's Remains*, sig. b5v; Clarke, *Lives of sundry Eminent Persons*, 164.
[188] Sherman, *Used Books*, 72.
[189] Burton, *Narration*, 1; see above, p. 261.
[190] Wallington, *Notebooks*, 267; Isham, 'Confessions', fos 13v, 14r, 16v.

As yet, we know frustratingly little about the giving of godly books as gifts.[191] We know that books were sometimes given to the poor out of charity, which may have been welcome, and that unsolicited copies of pamphlets were sometimes scattered for propaganda purposes, which certainly was not. More to the point, we know that in certain particular circumstances, books were widely given as gifts among the social elite. Children might give schoolroom exercises to their elders as New Year presents; hosts might, as Erasmus suggested, give their guests books chosen for their particular stations; above all, hungry authors gave their books to potential patrons.[192] Less formal or more personal gifts are much harder to track, but they certainly took place. Some wills specify who should inherit the testator's books, sometimes sending specific volumes to specific individuals—to assist, to edify, to delight, or even to criticize them.[193] The occasional inscription records the gift of a godly book from master or mistress to a favoured servant. Several of Wallington's books were written for members of his family.[194] Elizabeth Tyrwhit owned a particularly precious book, a manuscript of the Wycliffite Bible. An inscription in it, dated New Year's Day a few years before her death, reads:

> sethen I knowe my lyf is short
> and that my book and I must part
> to you my dere and faythful frende
> my chefest juel I doo comend.

Who the 'frende' was, we do not know.[195] For now we can only guess at the extent of book-giving, but my guess, at least, is that it was considerable. The earliest English Protestant book to meet Ian Green's criteria for best-seller status, Heinrich Bullinger's treatise on Christian marriage, may have derived its otherwise surprising popularity from being given as a wedding present. The subtitle of one edition, promising a book 'wherin housbandes and wyfes maye lerne to kepe house together with loue', positively angles for that market.[196] The same may be true of the dreary manuals of household governance which were a publishers' staple throughout the period. Certainly, they seem to modern eyes to be the kind of book which is given to inferiors who evidently need it, rather than bought and read for your own sake. Or take another best-seller, John Dod and Robert Cleaver's sermons on preparation for communion. Every edition was printed in a hefty quarto format, unusually for a

---

[191] Natalie Zemon Davies, *The Gift in Sixteenth-Century France* (Oxford, 2000) is one of the few extended discussions of the subject.

[192] Philip Benedict, *Christ's Churches Purely Reformed: A Social History of Calvinism* (New Haven and London, 2002), 511; Davies, *The Gift*, 69, 84; Ryrie, *Gospel and Henry VIII*, 108.

[193] For an example of the latter, see Sir Edmund Skory's posthumous gift to his wife after a stormy marriage: 'a praier book called The Practise of pietie, desiring that she better love and affect the same than hitherto she had done.' Hamling, *Decorating the Godly Household*, 97.

[194] Seaver, *Wallington's World*, 200; FSL STC 131a copy 2, rear flyleaf.

[195] Tyrwhit, *Elizabeth Tyrwhit's Morning and Evening Prayers*, 71.

[196] Heinrich Bullinger, *The christen state of Matrimonye, wherin housbandes and wyfes maye lerne to kepe house together with loue*, tr. Miles Coverdale (Antwerp, 1543); Carrie E. Euler, 'Heinrich Bullinger, marriage, and the English Reformation: *The Christen state of matrimonye* in England, 1540–53', *Sixteenth Century Journal* 34/2 (2003), 367–93. I am grateful to Dr Euler for discussions on this point.

popular devotional treatise by the early 17th century. Perhaps the intention was that it would be given, bound, as a first-communion gift.

Pending more focused research, we can take this no further. What we do know is that Bibles, and other early modern religious books, were palimpsests layered with meaning. The printed words were overlaid—sometimes entirely obscured—by the individual book's history both before and since it came into the current owner's hands; by additions, emendations, inscriptions, and other forms of personalization, and above all, by the sheer spiritual—and sometimes magical—power which Bibles and other books represented. The Bible was the Word incarnate, an object to live with and die for, God's eternal truth clothed in pulped rag. The same was true, to a lesser extent, of any wholesome book. It is no wonder that Reformed Protestants, who learned from those very books that no physical object could be reverenced and that they must worship in spirit and in truth, sometimes found dealing with books paradoxical.

12

Writing

'Thus speaketh the Lord God of Israel, saying, Write thee all the wordes, that I haue spoken vnto thee in a boke.' *Jeremiah 30:2*

WRITING THE WORD

It is hardly unexpected that literate Protestants were avid readers. What is, or should be, more surprising is that they were also writers.

It is surprising partly because, unlike most Protestant pious practice, lay people's pious writing had little Scriptural warrant or earlier Christian precedent. Yet they wrote in large numbers, some of them at enormous length. What is more, the practice anticipated the prescription. This is clearest in the matter of the spiritual journal.[1] The first British cleric to advocate such journals at any length was John Beadle, an Essex presbyterian who preached on the subject repeatedly from the 1630s onwards, finally publishing a book on it in 1656. He did manage to find a (deeply obscure) Scriptural precedent, but he also claimed that 'the subject is rarely handled. It is as untrodden a path, as ever I have gone; who have had scarce a little day hole of light to direct me.'[2] This was true in the sense that no-one had laid out the theory of godly diary-keeping in print before. Scholars of the subject have commented on how rarely divines commended the practice during this period.[3] There had been a few earlier, much briefer recommendations to do something along these lines, the earliest of which I know is Alexander Hume's 1594 exhortation to recall God's mercies, mercies which Christians 'should collect and keepe for a memoriall in write'.[4] It is not clear whether instructions to 'keep a Catalogue of all thy grossest knowne sinnes' or to 'make a register and book of remembrance

---

[1] Amongst the most useful works on this large subject are Webster, 'Writing to Redundancy'; Sara Heller Mendelson, 'Stuart Women's Diaries and Occasional Memoirs' in Mary Prior (ed), *Women in English Society 1500–1800* (London and New York, 1985), 181–210; Andrew Cambers, 'Reading, the Godly, and Self-Writing in England, circa 1580–1720', *Journal of British Studies* 46/4 (2007); James S. Amelang, *The Flight of Icarus: Artisan Autobiography in Early Modern Europe* (Stanford, CA, 1998). Brekus, 'Writing as a Protestant Practice', provides a useful comparison. McKay, 'English Diarists', usefully discusses the extent to which surviving diaries can be seen to be representative of any wider group.

[2] Beadle, *Journal or diary*, sig. a2v, p. 9; cf. Numbers 33:2—which Beadle described as 'the Israelitish Journall'.

[3] For example, Watkins, *Puritan Experience*, 22–3; Webster, 'Writing to Redundancy', 38.

[4] Alexander Hume, *Ane Treatise of Conscience* (Edinburgh, 1594: RSTC 13493), 73.

of the auntientie of Gods goodnesse to his Church' refer to literal or metaphorical writing.[5] But 17th-century exhortations to 'keepe iournals or day-bookes . . . both of our speciall sinnes, and Gods speciall mercies', or to 'write downe time and place' of particularly important spiritual breakthroughs, are unambiguous enough.[6] Still, they are not much more than throwaway comments.

Yet large numbers of people were already doing it. The oldest surviving British document which we can properly call a Protestant spiritual diary is Richard Rogers' diary, the extant portion of which begins in February 1587.[7] The earliest surviving portion of Richard Stonley's diary takes us back a little further, to 1581, but it is less a spiritual journal than an account-book containing brief notes of Stonley's actions and devotions.[8] What of the Cornish gentleman William Carnsew, whose diary covering 1576–7 mentions a great deal of Protestant theological reading, but normally only has a single line for each day and is principally a record of the weather?[9] If we must pick a winner, the best candidate is probably John Bradford, who was martyred in 1555: it was said that he 'booked euery notable accident each day that passed; and that so, that in the penning a man might see the signes of his smitten heart'.[10]

This does not survive, however, and there is every reason to believe that the survival rate of spiritual journals and diaries generally will have been very low indeed.[11] We know that a great many diarists were concerned to keep their spiritual journals secret, not least because these documents might attempt searingly honest records of sin. A number of diarists took steps to foil nosy parkers, from the childishly simple numerical codes occasionally employed by Nehemiah Wallington and Samuel Rogers, through the use of Latin or Greek, to full-blown ciphers: Simonds D'Ewes' diary consisted of 'several almanacs in a strange and new-invented character . . . utterly unuseful to any but myself'. John Janeway's code was such that even his brother was unable to break it after his death. He lamented that, the diary 'being written in characters, the world hath lost that jewel'. Presumably most such 'jewels' were used as scrap paper by mystified heirs. Those that could be understood may well have been destroyed all the more assiduously, since some secrets should be kept in the family, and indeed, some diarists doubtless destroyed their own work. Wallington was tempted to do so, 'so loth was I it should bee seene'.[12]

By the turn of the 17th century, the number of surviving or well-attested diaries expands markedly. Grace Mildmay's 'diary' is hard to date precisely, but much of

[5] Archibald Symson, *A Sacred Septenarie* (1623: RSTC 22568), 241–2; Clarke, *Holy Incense*, 147–8.
[6] Dyke, *Two Treatises*, 71; Harris, *Peters enlargement* (1624), sig. A4r. Cf. Byfield, *Marrow of the Oracles* (1622), 507–8; Rous, *Mysticall Marriage*, 214–20.
[7] Knappen, *Two Diaries*.
[8] FSL MS V.a.459.
[9] N. J. G. Pounds (ed.), 'William Carnsew of Bokelly and his Diary, 1576–7', *Journal of the Royal Institution of Cornwall* new series 8/1 (1978), 14–60.
[10] Dyke, *Two Treatises*, 41.
[11] Sara Heller Mendelson, 'Stuart Women's Diaries and Occasional Memoirs' in Mary Prior (ed.), *Women in English Society 1500–1800* (London and New York, 1985), 183–5.
[12] D'Ewes, *Autobiography*, 95–6, 135–6; Clarke, *Lives of thirty-two divines*, 191; Blair, *Life*, 31; Wallington, *Notebooks*, 55; Rogers, *Diary*, lxxxi; Clarke, *Lives of sundry Eminent Persons*, 162–3; James Janeway, *Invisibles, Realities, Demonstrated in the Holy Life and Triumphant Death of Mr John Janeway* (1673: Wing J470), 60; Wallington, *Notebooks*, 31.

the material is clearly 16th-century, and it is usually taken to be the oldest surviving Englishwoman's journal. Hard on her heels comes Margaret Hoby's terse but revealing diary, covering the period 1599–1605. John Manningham's student diary, covering 1602–3, contains more lewd jokes than most spiritual journals, but also plenty of sermon notes. Judith Isham, who died in 1625, kept 'nots of her owne hand-writing . . . as rememberances and instructions . . . to make good use of all the Lords mercies and corrections'. Daniel Dyke kept 'a catalogue or diary of his sinnes against God' as a daily discipline before his untimely death in 1614. The first of John Winthrop's spiritual journals begins in 1607. They come thick and fast.[13]

The diarists were men and women, town and country folk, laity and clergy, young and old, English and Scots, earnest conformists and aggressive puritans. Some of their texts are lengthy and meditative, others terse and factual, sometimes little more than account-books. They are addressed to God, to family members, to the author's soul, or to no clear audience at all. Some have daily or regular entries, some occasional. Some are primarily sin-lists, some record meditations, some record daily events; a few anticipate Beadle's advice to pay attention to public affairs. Some are contemporaneous, some retrospective. There is no clear line between diary and autobiography.[14] Often one gives way to the other: Archibald Johnston of Wariston began his 'diary' as a history of the spiritual crisis of his marriage and bereavement, but once it had come up to date it moved seamlessly into being a contemporaneous account.[15] Some surviving spiritual autobiographies are avowedly written up from contemporaneous notes that no longer survive. (In Elizabeth Isham's case, we have both documents.) What is clear is that there was no generally agreed model of what a spiritual diary should be.

Nor is it clear why individuals embarked on them. Margaret Hoby was apparently prodded to try diary-keeping by her chaplain Richard Rhodes, and was certainly more assiduous when he was in the household. Rose Throckmorton may have written her autobiographical reminiscences at the suggestion of her clergyman grandson.[16] John Beadle's personal influence can be credited certainly with one and very likely with two autobiographical projects, albeit both after our period.[17] Elizabeth Isham was presumably influenced by her mother's example. Robert Blair claimed, in the early 1620s, to have imitated 'the practice of some

[13] McKay, 'English Diarists', 195; Mildmay, 'Meditations'; Hoby, *Diary*; Manningham, *Diary*; Isham, 'Confessions', fo. 11r–v; Dyke, *Mystery of selfe-deceiuing*, sig. A5r; Winthrop, *Papers*. For some other attested diaries which appear to date from before 1640, see Tweedie, *Select Biographies*, 347; FSL MS V.a.248 fo. 2v; Thomas Gataker, *The Decease of Lazarus Christ's Friend* (1640: RSTC 11656), 47; Hinde, *Faithfull Remonstrance . . . of Iohn Bruen*, e.g. 135–6; Clarke, *Collection*, 21, 513; Clarke, *Lives of sundry Eminent Persons*, 163.

[14] Scholars have been driven to coin terms such as 'self-writing' and 'ego documents' to contain this diversity. I prefer the traditional 'diary', but this should not be taken to imply daily, regular or strictly contemporaneous entries. James S. Amelang, *The Flight of Icarus: Artisan Autobiography in Early Modern Europe* (Stanford, CA, 1998), 7–8, 28–39.

[15] Wariston, *Diary*.

[16] Hoby, *Diary*, 216, 280; Laura Branch, 'Practical Piety: The Spiritual Autobiography of Rose Throckmorton (c.1526–1613)', University of St. Andrews M.Litt dissertation (2007), 30.

[17] Arthur Wilson, 'Observations of God's Providence, in the Tract of my Life', in Francis Peck (ed.), *Desiderata Curiosa*, vol. 2 (1735), XII.25; Walker, *Holy Life*, 22.

diligent Christians, who daily took brief notes of the condition of their souls'. Isaac Ambrose explained his decision to start a diary in 1641 by saying that God put it into his heart; he also mentioned the example of 'many Ancients that were accustomed to keep Diaries'.[18] Most diarists say nothing on the subject at all.

That is not to say that diaries sprang unparented into being. Clearly there were genres on which they drew: account-books, travel diaries, almanacs, chronicles, students' notebooks, and commonplace books, but these were divergent, secular models. What is remarkable is that they should have converged and have been overlaid with pious practice in this way. More surprising still, very few of them draw on the most obvious model for Christian spiritual autobiography, Augustine's *Confessions*. The simple explanation for this is that there was no English translation of the *Confessions* until 1620, and that was a Catholic version printed on the Continent; an English Protestant edition did not appear until 1631, and was not reprinted until 1650. The Latin text was widely known amongst scholars, but not widely imitated. John Donne's *Devotions vpon Emergent Occasions* is an unusual exception. More intriguingly, the authors of two of the most detailed and revealing Protestant autobiographies, Elizabeth Isham and Richard Norwood, had read the *Confessions*, and both gave that name to their own books. In this period, however, those two stand alone.[19] But for other diarists, in the absence of obvious models, we are reduced to explanations such as the devotional vacuum left by the disappearance of sacramental confession and spiritual direction.[20]

In other words, we are forced to admit that the spiritual diary or autobiography was conceived nearly or fully independently, in many different forms, by many dozens and probably many thousands of early modern Protestants. If they had heard of the concept, few had seen examples. Each diarist was compelled to invent the genre anew. This was not a coincidence; it was a parallel response to a shared social and theological predicament. Because to ask about the genre of the diary is to overlook a more fundamental question: why did so many Protestants choose to express their faith in writing at all?

To answer this, consider John Merbecke, an organist and lay clerk at the Chapel Royal at Windsor now best known for his musical setting of the 1549 Book of Common Prayer. In the late 1530s, Merbecke borrowed a newly published English Bible from a friend. Claiming that he could not afford to buy one, he set out to transcribe it. As a practical project, this made little sense. Once he had paid for paper and ink, his many months of work would scarcely have saved him any money, but he had reached the book of Joshua when an evangelical clergyman named Richard Turner discovered his project. 'Tush, quoth hee, thou goest about a

---

[18] Blair, *Life*, 31; Ambrose, *Media*, 70.

[19] See below, pp. 429–36. Norwood headed his so-called 'journal' 'Confessions': Norwood, *Journal*, 3, 61. Isham's text is usually referred to as her 'book of rememberance', the words which head the text: however, she described it as her 'confessions', and I have adopted this usage, partly in recognition of her acknowledged debt to Augustine. Isham, 'Diary', 1638, 1639; Isham, 'Confessions', fos 6v, 8r, 16r. Cf. Isaac Stephens, ' "My Cheefest Work": The Making of the Spiritual Autobiography of Elizabeth Isham', *Midland History* 34/2 (2009), 182.

[20] Campbell, *Religion of the Heart*, 49.

vayne and tedious labour'. Turner suggested instead that Merbecke should spend his time compiling an English concordance to the Bible, a project that 'requireth not so muche learning, as diligence. And seing thou art so painfull a man, and one that cannot be vnoccupied, it were a goodly exercise for thee.' Turner realized that what Merbecke wanted was not so much a Bible as a Biblical project: endless hours in the presence of the Word. He had the measure of his man. Merbecke set about the concordance, and had nearly completed it when it was seized and destroyed by the authorities in 1543. He himself only escaped burning for heresy by a whisker.[21] Undeterred, on his release he started again from the beginning: his concordance was published in 1550.

Merbecke was neither the only nor the most Stakhanovite British Protestant to try to fill his life with pious writing. The Colchester evangelical Edward Freese, in prison in the early 1530s, wrote endlessly on the walls of his cell with chalk or charcoal, until 'because he would be writing many thinges, he was manicled by the wrestes'. That may sound like madness, but this was an age when paper was expensive and writing on walls or furniture was routine.[22] Paul Seaver guessed that Nehemiah Wallington's fifty books may have run to some 20,000 pages together, and even if that is a little generous it is no wonder that his day job and his family life both suffered. John Bruen's private project of abridging Richard Rogers' *Seven treatises*, and Grace Mildmay's diary—of which the surviving portion breaks off, unfinished, after 912 pages—imply a similarly spendthrift attitude to ink, paper, and time.[23] But for really heroic volumes of writing, we must look, as Merbecke did, to Scripture. Writing felt like the perfect medium in which to consummate Protestantism's love affair with the Bible, and Protestants did so with dizzying ingenuity and persistence.

One model was provided by Thomas Sternhold's collection of metrical psalms, instantly popular on its publication in 1549. A flood of imitations and continuations followed.[24] As well as other paraphrases of the psalms, metrical editions of the Song of Songs, the book of Proverbs, the Acts of the Apostles, and even of the entire Pentateuch were published during Edward VI's reign.[25] A metrical Genesis, a version of the book of Lamentations, and, of course, more psalms followed under Elizabeth.[26] With a few exceptions, like William Hunnis' *Seuen Sobs of a Sorrowfull Soule*, few of these versifications achieved even a shadow of Sternhold's commercial success.

---

[21] Foxe, *Actes and monuments* (1570), 1393; John Merbecke, *A concordance* (1550: RSTC 17300), sig. A3r.

[22] Foxe, *Actes and monuments* (1583), 1027; Juliet Fleming, *Graffiti and the Writing Arts of Early Modern England* (2001), 9.

[23] Seaver, *Wallington's World*, 2, 10–11; Wallington, *Notebooks*, 265; Hinde, *Faithfull Remonstrance . . . of Iohn Bruen*, 142; Mildmay, 'Meditations'.

[24] Quitslund, *Reformation in Rhyme*, 72–3.

[25] Robert Crowley, *The Psalter of Dauid newely translated into Englysh metre* (1549: RSTC 2725); William Hunnis, *Certayne Psalmes chosen out of the Psalter of Dauid* (1550: RSTC 2727); William Baldwin, *The canticles or balades of Salomon, phraselyke declared in Englysh metres* (1549: RSTC 2768); John Hall, *Certayn chapters taken out of the Prouerbes of Salomon* (1550: RSTC 12631), sig. A2r; William Samuel, *The abridgemente of goddes statutes in myter* (1551: RSTC 21690.2); Tye, *The Actes*.

[26] William Hunnis, *A Hyve Full of Hunnye* (1578: RSTC 13974); Christopher Fetherstone, *The Lamentations of Ieremie in Meeter* (1587: RSTC 2779).

Yet pious pens were not deterred. John Hall claimed that he produced his versified book of Proverbs in order to 'haue occupyed suche tymes as moughte haue bene bestowed in ydlenesse or vanytyes'. Archbishop Parker claimed that he produced his metrical psalms as a private project for his own use, and was only prevailed upon to publish them some time later. These claims may be more than polite conventions. We read repeatedly that paraphrases or versifications were undertaken as a pious sickbed exercise. William Moray explained that he had felt compelled to apply himself to some such project during his illness, 'as water if it stand still long and runne not . . . will rotte and stinke'.[27] And certainly, plenty of such projects never saw publication. In 1553 someone was trying to versify the books of Kings. One 17th-century Protestant produced, apparently for private use, a large book of metrical paraphrases of sections of the Old Testament, including the entire psalter.[28]

For sheer pious effort, the prize must go to William Samuel. His 1551 metrical edition of the Pentateuch turned out to be simply a warm-up. In 1569 he published a metrical version of the entire Old Testament, all built around a complex series of acrostics. This bizarre white elephant of a project concludes with a verse which declares:

> The Prophets thus are finished,
> and books Canonicall:
> Apocripha ye shall haue next,
> if death doo not me call.[29]

Perhaps mercifully, death did call, but at least one purchaser was moved to emulate Samuel's example. A copy of his book in the Huntington Library includes a handwritten continuation which covers the whole of Matthew's gospel.

Those without poetic ambitions could also while away the hours, or years, rewriting Scripture. Simply transcribing it, like Merbecke, was a little quixotic, or monkish, in an age of plentiful printed Bibles, but some still did it, and the piety of those who had done so in former times could be respected.[30] And extracting, commonplacing, and rearranging could fill many a blameless hour. At least two of Wallington's books seem to have been mere collections of Biblical extracts. His intention, one morning in 1624, to rise early and 'wright out of the Bible the troubles of the Children of God', is characteristic.[31] A 17th-century commonplace book owned by one Paul Gosnold gives us a glimpse of this kind of thing. Gosnold had gone through the whole Old Testament in order and written down one or more select verses from every book.[32] Some collections were organized thematically. John

---

[27] Hall, *Certayn chapters*, sig. A2r; Matthew Parker, *The whole Psalter translated into English metre* (1567?: RSTC 2729), sig. B2v; William Moray, *Nyne Songs Collected out of the Holy Scriptures* (Edinburgh, 1634?: RSTC 18166), sig. A3r; cf. below, pp. 409–11.

[28] Tye, *The Actes*, sig. A2v; Bod MS Rawl C.113.

[29] William Samuel, *An abridgement of all the canonical books of the olde Testament written in Sternholds meter* (1569: RSTC 21690), sigs A3r–4v, Z8r.

[30] Saxby, 'Miscellany', fos 90r–93r, 106r–119r; Capel, *Capel's Remains*, sig. b5v.

[31] Seaver, *Wallington's World*, 199, nos. 1 and 4; LMA Guildhall MS 204, p. 405; cf. Wallington, *Notebooks*, 33.

[32] FSL MS V.a.478 fos 35r–41r. Cf. Narveson, *Bible Readers*, 51–77.

Bruen made 'collections of promises, precepts, comforts, prohibitions, mercies, judgements, marks of Gods children, brands of wicked men, and many other good things' from his Bible as he read it. Jane Ratcliffe did something similar 'for her private use'. Isaac Ambrose provided detailed instructions for readers who wanted to attempt this at home.[33] In fact, however, the effort was scarcely necessary, since a series of such thematically organized collections of Scripture were available in print.[34] Readers wanted their Bibles digested for them just as much as writers wanted to do the work.

The same can be said of a more sophisticated variant, the Scriptural collage, in which verses from across the Bible—especially the psalms—are cut, pasted, and reassembled into a 'new' text.[35] This was a practice with medieval precedents and was taken up with enthusiasm by Protestants. Collage psalms became a regular feature of published devotional works and private devotional exercises.[36] They could be assembled for particular occasions, as with the official texts published for use during the plague or to mark Elizabeth I's accession day, or the 'Psalmes . . . fitly and sweetly composed of many parts and parcels of Psalmes' sung by Henry Burton's supporters on his triumphant return to London in 1640.[37] One broadsheet produced for use during an epidemic forged a new text out of all the psalm verses which conclude with the obscure Hebrew word rendered *Selah*, a word which the author understood to mean that 'the Spirit hath set a double mark vpon that [verse]'. The public emergency made such a distillation of the psalms' most powerful verses timely: surely God could not resist it.[38]

But the rest of the Bible could be thrown into the blender too. In part this reflects the wider ambition of Protestant writers to make their books, especially devotional works, mere 'patchworks' or 'mosaics' of Scripture.[39] It is moot, for example, whether we should call John Monipennie the author or the editor of *A Christian Almanacke* (1612): well over a quarter of its text consists of direct Biblical

---

[33] Hinde, *Faithfull Remonstrance . . . of Iohn Bruen*, 142; Ley, *Patterne of Pietie*, 32–3; Ambrose, *Media*, 377.

[34] See, for example, Becon, *Gouernans* (1544?), fos 10v–24v; Heyden, *Bryefe Summe*; Thomas Paynell, *The Piththy and moost notable sayinges of al Scripture* (1550: RSTC 19494); *Christian Prayers and Meditations in English*, sigs Aa1r–Gg4v; Bentley, *Monument of Matrons*, 1–49; Fawkener, *Collection of Promises*; James Warre, *The Touchstone of Truth* (1630: RSTC 25091); Clarke, *Holy Incense*.

[35] On the phenomenon which Susan Felch helpfully calls 'collage Psalms', see Tyrwhit, *Elizabeth Tyrwhit's Morning and Evening Prayers*, 41–5; Ryrie, 'Psalms and confrontation', 116–17.

[36] See, for example, FSL MS. V.a.482 fos 36r–39r; Coverdale, *Devout meditacions*, sigs B3r–C1v; Huntington Library, San Marino, CA, MS 15369 fos 1r–2r, 15v–20r; Featley, *Ancilla Pietatis*, 58–60, 76–8; Bentley, *Monument of Matrons*, 403, 424–30; Thomas Tymme, *The Poore Mans Pater noster, with a preparatiue to praier* (1598: RSTC 24419), sigs N1v–P3v, Q2v–4r; William Perkins, *An exposition of the Lords prayer* (1595: RSTC 19702a), 68; Day, *Booke of Christian Prayers*, fos 99v–101r, 71r–72r.; and cf. FSL MS V.a.436 p.45.

[37] *A fourme of prayer, with thankes geuyng, to be vsed euery yeere, the.17. of Nouember* (1578: RSTC 16480), sig. A8v; Grindal, *Remains*, 85–7; Burton, *Narration*, 41.

[38] *To my Christian friend, I.F. comfort in Christ* (1590?: RSTC 2751); reprinted during another epidemic in Nicholas Balmford, *A short dialogue concerning the plagues infection* (1625: RSTC 1338.5), 75–84. Cf. Bownde, *Medicines for the plague*, 129; Beadle, *Journal or diary*, 62.

[39] Narveson, 'Publishing the Sole-talk', 113; White, *Tudor Books of Private Devotion*, 142. See, for example, Habermann, *Enimie of securitie*, sig. b7r–v.

quotation. Unpublished devotional texts, such as Grace Mildmay's meditations, follow the same pattern: editing, interlacing, and reassembling Biblical texts to sometimes vivid effect. But pure Biblical collage was a genre in its own right. A text in Henry Bull's *Christian praiers and holy meditations* mixed the psalms with verses from various Biblical prophets and from the books of Acts, Lamentations, Job, Judith, Wisdom, and Tobit. One of the most popular and ambitious sets of published collage psalms, Thomas Rogers' *A golden chaine*, spawned an unpublished imitation, called by its author 'The riche cheyne', which rearranged the books of Proverbs and Ecclesiastes.[40] Such projects were taken to a new height at the Little Gidding community in the late 1620s. Nicholas Ferrar and his neices spent a year assembling a huge, lavishly illustrated harmony of the Gospels, a literal cut-and-paste project divided into 150 chapters, and executed with such precision that the finished product could be mistaken for a printed book. Several more versions followed, partly because King Charles I made off with their first copy.[41] These books were produced for the community's use, but the effort was not merely functional. Undertaking any such Biblical project was not simply a job of work, nor a support for piety, but a labour of love. Part of the point of doing it was to do it. (Indeed, the literary or theological quality of the finished product was often dubious.) The endearing practice of Scriptural mathematics bears witness to this: counting the numbers of books, chapters, verses, words, and letters in the Bible, the longest and shortest chapters, or the most frequently occurring word ('and').[42] It is hard to imagine a more painstaking or, in worldly terms, a more pointless exercise, but to do this was to sing a love-song in numbers to the Word.

What was true of Scripture was also, to a lesser extent, true of uninspired texts. Commonplace books could be filled with edifying quotations. Students and divines frequently kept them, but commonplacing was not exclusively a scholar's practice.[43] Margaret Hoby and Grace Mildmay did it, and Elizabeth Isham's magpie collecting of 'spirituall flowers' in her childhood is recognizably the same thing. Elnathan Parr coached his readers on how to assemble such a book to support their prayers.[44] The chosen extracts ranged from soundbites to entire sermons. Some collections were thematically organized; others seem to be thrown together more randomly.[45] But we should not see the creation of these books as a merely passive recording. Copying was likened to digestion. Philip Melanchthon compared it to the hidden miracle of the bee who, by taking its pollen back to the hive's many compartments and subdivisions, is able to produce honey.[46] Even adapting

[40] Bull, *Christian praiers*, 288–91; FSL MS V.a.519.
[41] Margaret Aston, 'Moving Pictures: Foxe's Martyrs and Little Gidding' in Sabrina A. Baron et al. (eds), *Agent of Change: Print Culture Studies After Elizabeth L. Eisenstein* (Amherst, MA, 2007), 87, 90–4.
[42] Narveson, *Bible Readers*, 59–60; Sherman, *Used Books*, 202 n. 40.
[43] D'Ewes, *Autobiography*, 120; Clarke, *Collection*, 100.
[44] Hoby, *Diary*, e.g. 67; Isham, 'Confessions', fos 5r, 16v; Mildmay, 'Meditations', part II; Parr, *Abba Father*, 55–6.
[45] See, for example, LMA Guildhall MS 204; Saxby, 'Miscellany'; BL Egerton MS 2877; Bod. MS Eng c.2693.
[46] Peter Stallybrass, Roger Chartier, John Mowery, and Heather Wolfe, 'Hamlet's Tables and the Technologies of Writing in Renaissance England', *Shakespeare Quarterly* 55 (2004), 411.

a printed book for your own use could involve interleaving pages for notes, rearranging sections, inserting materials from elsewhere, adding or hand-colouring pictures, choosing binding-companions, and other forms of drastic customization which can, as William Sherman has pointed out, produce something amounting to a new book. If you were translating, that effort itself was a devotional act.[47] So too was the simple creation of a fair copy. Although obviously favoured by survival bias, it is striking how many extant commonplace books are beautifully and painstakingly produced: formal penmanship, ruled pages, marked margins, indexes, ornate title pages. These are treasured objects which represent an enormous investment of time and care, and sometimes considerable artistry.[48]

Turner's point about Merbecke—that he 'could not be unoccupied'—is important in itself. We shall return to this in Chapter 16, but for now we can note that exercises like transcribing, paraphrasing, or commonplacing could be means of basking in the Word's reflected glow, blamelessly filling your hours with something that was neither idolatry nor idleness.

PUBLIC AND PRIVATE WRITING

Pious writing was, however, more than a means of whiling away the years. Writing exists in order to be read. When Protestants wrote for devotional purposes, who were their intended readers, and why did they want to use the written word to reach them? Three broad readerships can be identified: other people, the writers themselves, and God.

Devotional writing was, potentially, a route to both fame and riches in early modern Britain. The market for pious books was lucrative, and even if few authors made their fortunes from sales, reputations made in print were often rewarded in career advancement, especially but not exclusively for the clergy. In the nature of things, however, no-one could admit that this was their motive for writing. Hence the polite fictions which all readers of early modern books know: this book is set forth humbly and reluctantly, because my friends found it and begged me to do so, or because someone else is about to rush into print with a corrupt or incomplete copy. As Arnold Hunt points out, this pretended reluctance was much mocked at the time, but was sometimes also perfectly real. Ministers and laypeople alike could be genuinely squeamish about publication, and the 'friends' urging publication were not always imaginary. Nehemiah Wallington and Jane Ratcliffe both repeatedly resisted friends 'earnestly importuning' them to publish their writings.[49] Similarly, the trope of the book which is rushed into print without permission from a second-hand copy of the author's manuscript is not merely fiction.[50] These

---

[47] Sherman, *Used Books*, 9; Habsburg, *Translations of the* Imitatio Christi, 127–8.
[48] See, for example, FSL MSS V.a.4, V.a.482; BL Egerton MS 2877; Bod. MS Eng c.2693; Bod MS Rawl C.473.
[49] Hunt, *Art of Hearing*, 120–8; Wallington, *Notebooks*, 264; Ley, *Patterne of Pietie*, 27.
[50] Gouge, *Short Catechisme*, sig. A3v.

things happened, and they could leave all parties feeling bruised. The best-selling *A Collection of certaine Promises out of the Word of God* was first published in 1629, in an anonymous and unauthorized edition. In 1631 the author, now identified but only as 'A.F.', oversaw a further edition, produced by another printer and complaining that the first was an inaccurate version of a text prepared 'for mine owne private vse'. The first printer replied with a third edition in 1633: its editor attributed it to the obviously pseudonymous 'Anne Phoenix' and complained that copies had had to be 'wrung' from the reluctant author, who 'neither deserves nor desires thankes'.[51] At least, 'Phoenix' clearly did not desire fame.

There were also more honourable motives for writing, which should not be dismissed entirely. It could, simply, be a means of giving glory to God. Like the psalmist, Elizabeth Isham wrote her *Confessions* as a 'memoriall of thine abundant Kindnes'. 'Not that I intend to have this published', she added in a marginal note; but she might circulate it within the family.[52] The avowed purpose of Anthony Gilby's 1548 polemic against Bishop Gardiner was, naturally, to refute Gardiner's doctrines, but he added that even if he could have done no more than blankly deny them, 'I iudge it my parte to publishe my faith, rather then by my silence to seame to consent to suche diuillishe doctrine'. This was the witness of the conscientious lookout, who announces coming perils simply to discharge a duty and regardless of whether or not anyone acts on his warning.[53] A similar approach invoked the Biblical parable of the talents, which teaches the duty to make use of whatever limited gifts you may have.[54] Perhaps that is too obviously a polite fiction, but it could be a joy as well as a duty. Gilby, thirty years later, explained that he had translated a book of Theodore Beza's because the book had so enriched him that he 'could not be silent'.[55] He was speaking not simply to be heard, but also—even principally—for the sake of speaking.

Others were more forthright about writing as a duty to their readers. Sometimes again this duty seems a little impractical. Half of Gabriel Powel's *The Resolued Christian* was addressed to criminals who were condemned to die but who remained 'vnpenitent and obstinate Malefactors', but we may guess that his words did not reach many of that rather specialist audience.[56] Most likely he never really meant them to. James Melville, by contrast, put money (if not *his* money) where his pen was. The title of *A Spirituall Propine of a Pastour to his People* conveys something of his sense of obligation; 'a maist godlie and loving friend' paid 500 marks towards the publication, but unhappily, sales recouped less than a fifth of the cost. The same sense of duty could also drive people to publish others' works. Edward Hake cited

---

[51] The author's identity remains uncertain but may be Anthony Fawkener. 'A. F.', *The Saints Legacies: Or, A Collection of certaine PROMISES out of the Word of God* (1631: RSTC 10635), sig. *2v; 'Phoenix', *Saints Legacies*, sigs *6v–*7r.

[52] Isham, 'Confessions', fo. 2r; Stephens, '"My Cheefest Work"', 194–5.

[53] Gilby, *An answer*, fos 2v–3r; see below, p. 402.

[54] See, for example, Hall, *Certayn chapters*, sig. A3r; Richard Bernard and 'R. A.', *Davids Musick* (1616: RSTC 1935.5), sig. A2r–v; Wither, *Preparation to the Psalter*, 2; Catharine Davies, *A religion of the Word: the defence of the reformation in the reign of Edward VI* (Manchester, 2002), xii.

[55] Beza, *Psalmes of David*, sig. A5v.

[56] Powel, *Resolued Christian*, 151.

the law of treasure-trove to justify his publishing an edition of Guilelmo Daman's psalm tunes: good discoveries belong to the commonwealth, not exclusively to the discoverer.[57] Nehemiah Wallington called his first book, a summary of God's law, 'the widdows mite': however worthless his offering might be, he was still compelled to offer it. He made a fair copy of another of his books because he had showed it to a 'poore distressed soule' who was comforted by it, and this fired his conscience. 'I colde not sleepe in quiet til I had written it out fairer and oh I could wish it was written in a Booke and graven with an yron pen in lead or in stone for ever.' His sense of his intended audience was vague, but his sense of duty to them was sharp. Like a preacher, Wallington had to give voice to the Word burning within him; and writing was his only means of doing so. The treatise of comfort in time of plague that he wrote to 'condole the woefull and heavy Inhabitants that remaine in and about the Citie' seems to have been trying to scratch this itch.[58] If voices were forced to be silent, pens would cry out.

Whether anyone heard their cries was another matter. But those who did not achieve or aspire to print publication could still circulate hand-copied texts. This could be something like formal 'manuscript publication', in which a more-or-less fully formed text was passed to a select circle of friends and patrons, as a precursor or a decorous alternative to print publication. Sometimes we can glimpse the process by which manuscript publication eventually led to printing: the sheer labour of producing multiple handwritten copies was a factor.[59] But even the most apparently private texts could find readers. Kate Narveson uses the term 'household publication' to describe the preparation of texts for family use, texts which might be circulated while still unfinished.[60] The most common form of such texts was parental legacies. Godly matriarchs and patriarchs might write, or dictate, edifying memoirs for their children. Rose Throckmorton, for example, aged eighty-four and meditating on her

> most mercifull deliverances . . . thought good to set down the same in writing and to leaue it to my children to moue them to continue that thankfullnes to allmighty god which I their old mother cannot acknowledge too much nor too often.

The resulting account was copied and re-copied by her descendants, one copy being kept in the family Bible.[61] Other legacies were more explicitly didactic. In 1647 Wallington sat down his new son-in-law to read through one of his earlier books with him, taking a portion daily for three months: it was a kind of initiation into the Wallington family. The Northamptonshire gentlewoman Katherine

---

[57] Melville, *Autobiography*, 12; Guilelmo Daman, *The Psalmes of David in English meter, with Notes of foure partes* (1579: RSTC 6219), sig. A2r–v.

[58] Wallington, *Notebooks*, 31, 52–3, 269; cf. Wither, *Preparation to the Psalter*, 19; Thomas Becon, *The iewell of ioye* (1550: RSTC 1733), sig. C7v; Ryrie, *Gospel and Henry VIII*, ch. 3.

[59] See, for example, Hutchins, *Davids Sling*, fo. 2v; Byfield, *The Signes*, sig. A7v; Richard Rogers, *The practice of Christianitie* (1618: RSTC 21221), sig. a4r.

[60] Narveson, *Bible Readers*, 70; Cambers, *Godly Reading*; Cambers, 'Reading, the Godly, and Self-Writing'.

[61] BL Additional MS 43827A fos 5v–6r; Branch, 'Practical Piety', 14. Cf., amongst many examples, Bruce, *Sermons . . . with Collections*, 7; Blair, *Life*, xxi, 3; Shepard, *God's Plot*, 33.

Fitzwilliam wrote a series of catechisms to use with her own children, which allowed for a powerful combination of theology and intimacy.[62] Some families produced devotional guides: Sir Edward Rodney wrote a form of preparation for communion 'for the vse of his Children', and Elizabeth Jocelin's unfinished address to her unborn baby, written in correct anticipation of her own death in childbirth, became a best-seller. Richard Waste advised his 'Deer Children' to use his meditations 'because your Fathers good Aduises & prayers maye worke more with you than those made by straungers'. Grace Mildmay's book of meditations takes the form of an extended testament to her beloved daughter and grandchildren. 'Thus have I given my mind unto my offspring as my chief and only gift unto them.' The London merchant John Parker outsourced the work, leaving funds in his will for 'two godly Divines' to edit 'all his spirituall journals, his meditations and remembrances' for the use of his children.[63] Whether they ever attempted such a daunting task is not known.

For a great many Protestant writers, however, readers were either a pretext or an afterthought. They wrote for themselves. Elizabeth Isham wrote of her *Confessions* that 'if it may doe my Brother or his children any pleasure I think to leave it them', but there was no mistaking that the book was a private spiritual exercise first and last. Her careful, reflective account of how she came to write is worth attending to. When her brother left the household in 1638, shortly after her thirtieth birthday, she found herself facing the enforced leisure of genteel spinsterhood. She used it as an opportunity to devote herself to prayer, reading, and meditation, but 'I also comforted my selfe with writing'. She set about writing a full spiritual autobiography, a task which took her a year and a half and which 'so wholly tooke me up that I did nothing or very little besides'. Near the end she confesses her dismay that soon she will have to 'leave my worke which I soe well loved'. The final sections of the account stretch out, as if she could not bear to finish it. There are layers of motivation here, but the simplest one was to fill time absorbingly and blamelessly. Isham had read Joseph Hall, who taught that 'if I doe but little good to others by my endeuours, yet this is great good to mee, that by my labour I keepe my selfe from hurt'.[64] Literary endeavours could serve this purpose admirably. To call a guide to letter-writing *The Enimie of Idlenesse*, as William Fulwood did, may seem incongruous to modern eyes, but it evidently made sense to the Elizabethan buyers who made it a best-seller. John Hayward wrote the first edition of his *Sanctuarie of a troubled soule* while imprisoned in the Tower of London, from the conviction that 'wee shal be much acomptable for all our time'; Nicholas Themylthorpe made a similar decision in more comfortable circumstances, spending his old age

[62] LMA Guildhall MS 204, flyleaf verso; Seaver, *Wallington's World*, 6, 200; Paula McQuade, 'Maternal Catechesis in the Manuscript Miscellany of Katherine Fitzwilliam (c. 1600)', paper delivered to the Sixteenth Century Conference, Cincinnati, Ohio, 27 October 2012.

[63] FSL MS V.a.520 fos 2r–3v; Jocelin, *Mothers Legacie*; Bod MS Rawl C.473 fo. 1r; Mildmay, *With Faith and Physic*, 24, 70–1; Thomas Gataker, *The Decease of Lazarus Christ's Friend* (1640: RSTC 11656), 47.

[64] Isham, 'Confessions', fos 2r, 34r; Isham, 'Diary', 1638, 1639; Hall, *Meditations...A third Century*, III no. 39, pp. 81–2; see below, pp. 434–5.

composing his *Posie of Godly Praiers* because his working life had been filled with
worldliness, and 'I am desirous to spend these latter dayes in godly and Christian
exercises'.[65] Pious writing could be nothing more or less than a form of godly time-
wasting.

Writing of this kind could take almost any form. Lady Margaret Hoby, as well as
keeping a diary, annotated her Bible, wrote in her commonplace book, made fair
copies of sermons, and sometimes referred simply to 'priuat praier and writinge'.
Jane Ratcliffe similarly left a miscellany of pious papers behind her.[66] Most of this
kind of writing was functional and ephemeral. Its simplest purpose was undergird-
ing the frailties of memory. Wallington wrote, he said, 'because my memory is so
bade'. Writing not only created a permanent record, but also, as contemporaries
were well aware, was an aid to concentration; as words were inked onto the page
they were also inscribed on the memory.[67] This could mean writing down prayers
which you had copied, adapted, or composed for your own regular use; making lists
of those for whom you intended to pray; writing down vows or covenants; or taking
notes while reading, often on the book itself.[68] It was a motive for autobiography,
especially as years accumulated. John Beadle cited the battle with forgetfulness as a
central motive for diary-keeping. Aged forty-eight, Richard Norwood one day
'endeavoured to call to mind the whole course of my life past, and how the Lord
had dealt with me', and found that 'some things began to grow out of memory,
which I thought I should scarce ever have forgotten'. This provoked him to write
his spiritual memoir, 'considering that as age came on, forgetfulness would increase
upon me'. Happily, he had kept some lists of his sins and of God's mercies, which
helped to jog his memory while writing.[69]

Beadle's battle with forgetfulness was not fought purely for the sake of accurate
record-keeping, however. Richard Bernard explained that writing not only 'con-
firmes meditation . . . and keepes things once thought of'; it also 'shewes the minde
to the senses';[70] that is, it permits self-observation over time. Richard Rogers kept
his diary in order 'that I may so observe mine hart that I may see my life in frame
from time to time'. Like many other diarists, he periodically re-read what he had
written. His grandson Samuel annotated key entries in his own diary with asterisks,
either when he re-read them or to guide future re-reading. Some people re-read
their diaries as a regular discipline.[71] In the last year of his life, Wallington added a
note at the end of the book which he and his son-in-law had read a decade earlier.

---

[65] Hayward, *Sanctuarie of a troubled soule* (1618), II.sig. ¶2r; Themylthorpe, *Posie of Praiers*, sig.
A5r.

[66] Hoby, *Diary*, 183; Ley, *Patterne of Pietie*, 45–52, 85–91.

[67] Wallington, *Notebooks*, 31; and see e.g. Bernard, *Faithfull Shepherd*, 21–2; Janeway, *Invisibles,
Realities*, 58–9.

[68] Parker and Carlson, 'Practical Divinity', 158; Wariston, *Diary*, 172; Brinsley, *True Watch* (1608),
sig. A3r; Walker, *Sermon at the funerals . . .* , 47; and see above, pp. 130–91.

[69] Beadle, *Journal or diary*, 170–1; Norwood, *Journal*, 3.

[70] Richard Bernard, *The Faithfull Shepheard* (1607: RSTC 1939), 83.

[71] Knappen, *Two Diaries*, 72, 81, 100; Cambers, 'Reading, the Godly, and Self-Writing'; Rogers,
Diary, 2 n. 6; Ambrose, *Media*, 71; Blair, *Life*, 31; Clarke, *Lives of thirty-two divines*, 191. Cf.
Winthrop, *Papers*, 211; Forbes, 'Diary', 77; Hoby, *Diary*, 216.

He had, he said, re-read it 'many times', but even on this most recent pass he had observed 'more then in former tim I did', and had marked it accordingly. The book's title was *A Record of Gods Marcys*.[72]

Divine mercy was inextricably linked with the sin that made it necessary. Perhaps the commonest form of Protestant pious writing was the simple sin-list, a diary in embryo. Few these survive in their unvarnished form, although the student 'diary' of Samuel Ward comes close,[73] but we know that plenty more existed. They were an aid to normal Protestant self-examination. If your role in the divine courtroom was to accuse yourself before God, a sin-list was the prosecutor's brief. In particular, it was invaluable for allowing accumulated sins to be reviewed weekly, monthly or annually.[74] The obvious problem was that an attempt to list all your sins, comprehensively, was both impossible and uncomfortably reminiscent of Catholic sacramental confession, hence the variant recommended in Nicholas Byfield's best-selling *The Marrow of the Oracles of God*. Although sins themselves are infinite, Byfield reasoned, the kinds of sin are not, and he suggested composing and regularly updating an exhaustive list of the sins to which you, individually, are prone, to be used as prompt for self-examination.[75]

Diaries and autobiographies, however, could be more than simple catalogues of sins and mercies. They could attempt to capture the uncatchable, to pin the butterfly of spiritual experience to the page. Recording the brief, dazzlingly intense, high watermarks of the Protestant life was not only about thankfulness and assurance, but about preserving the moments almost photographically, so that a brief flash of light might burn constantly in words which keep the experience alive. It is not unlike the struggle to cling on to the wisps of spiritually significant dreams.[76] Keeping 'a memoriall in write' of flashes of fervour, insight, or joy, Alexander Hume advised his readers, 'shal kindle and inflame thy spirit' when beset by 'coldnes & slug-gishnes'.[77] Patrick Simson did something of this sort after his first wife's death. She had been fearfully tempted but had eventually found peace, due—as he believed—to his prayers, and so he wrote himself the following note:

> Remember, Remember, Remember, and never forget the 10 of August 1601, and what consolation the Lord gave thee. . . . Is not this a brand plucked out of the fire?

When the note was shown to him on his own deathbed he vividly recalled the event. We have already heard a number of other such rapturous accounts, but as well as the testimony itself it is worth noticing the fact of their being recorded.[78]

[72] Wallington, *Notebooks*, 96.

[73] Todd, 'Puritan Self-Fashioning'.

[74] Dyke, *Mystery of selfe-deceiuing*, sig A5r–v; Isham, 'Confessions', fo. 11v; D'Ewes, *Autobiography*, 353–4; and see above, pp. 53–9.

[75] Byfield, *Marrow of the Oracles* (1622), 251–4, 627–9; Byfield, *Marrow of the Oracles* (1619), 28–37.

[76] Wariston, *Diary*, 52–3; Webster, 'Writing to Redundancy', 47; Ryrie, 'Sleeping, waking and dreaming'.

[77] Alexander Hume, *Ane Treatise of Conscience* (Edinburgh, 1594: RSTC 13493), 73.

[78] Tweedie, *Select Biographies*, 108; see above, pp. 83–91.

Even brief notes could capture moments of spiritual experience which might otherwise slip away into the stream of memory.

Writing could also do more than preserve moments: it could create narratives. We shall be returning to the wider subject of how early modern Protestants understood their own life stories, but for now it is enough to point out that writing was the ideal means of giving shape to those stories.[79] As well as examining the past for signs of progress in grace, an autobiographical account and the inevitable selection which it involved could be used to pick out the events in your life which you believed were the turning points, so interpreting God's providential action in your personal history. Learning to understand your life story was, for Beadle, one of a diary's key purposes.[80] Self-deception and wishful thinking were obvious dangers in this process.[81] We have already seen some makers of vows and covenants trying and, on the whole, failing to use writing to impose meaning and shape on their lives contemporaneously, by brute force of will.[82] It could also be done retrospectively, by re-reading and re-writing. Isaac Ambrose rigorously sorted the events he recorded in his diary into judgements, mercies, afflictions, and providences, choosing apposite Biblical verses for each entry, in order to interpret both the event itself and the response which God required of him.[83]

What unites all these attempts to give shape to lives is that they look back in order to look forward. As Catherine Brekus puts it: 'Ultimately all devotional writing led to the same goal: preparation for death.' Elizabeth Isham was explicit that that was the purpose of her *Confessions.* John Janeway kept a daily spiritual diary which

> left a sweet calm upon his spirits, because he every night made even his accounts; and if his sheets should prove his winding-sheet, it had been all one: for, he could say his work was done; so that death could not surprize him.[84]

This was not sacramental confession, but it was not entirely unlike it. As long as you lived, you might review the papers which gave your life shape. When you died, the documents which you had collected might be entered in evidence in another Book altogether.

For while Protestants wrote to edify others, and to discipline, encourage, and shape themselves, there was a third and vital audience. They wrote to God. Writing, like speech, song, or thought, was a medium for prayer. Again this has its practical element. Just as devotees prayed aloud in order to aid concentration and to organize their thoughts, they prayed in writing in order to make their prayers permanent. We should not assume, however, that the many handwritten Protestant prayers which survive from this period are simply dead records of live prayers.

---

[79] See below, p. 409.

[80] Beadle, *Journal or diary*, 102–5.

[81] As Richard Norwood acknowledged: Norwood, *Journal*, 87.

[82] See above, pp. 30–9.

[83] Ambrose, *Media*, 98–116.

[84] Brekus, 'Writing as a Protestant Practice', 25; Isham, 'Confessions', fo. 7v; Janeway, *Invisibles, Realities*, 59.

Writing them could in itself be an act of devotion. Some directions for prayer, like those for a 'young beginner' surviving in a 17th-century pious miscellany, could only be carried out by writing.[85] James Howell wrote that before communion 'commonly I compose som new prayers, and som of them written in my own blood'. He certainly did not mean that literally, but the image suggests how spiritually intense the writing process could be.[86] Sometimes we can glimpse this in real time. We have already met John Welsh's astonishing letter to Lilias Grahame, consumed with ecstatic prayer.[87] If we suspect that of being a perform-ance, consider John Winthrop's struggle one day in 1617. He was engaged in working out a new daily schedule for himself, balancing work, family duties, study, and prayer, when the Devil put it into his head to build in some time for worldly pleasure. His response was to keep writing: to resist temptation with his pen, to command Satan directly to be gone, and in the end to record that, for the moment, he was victorious. Winthrop was not so much keeping a record as sending a message.[88]

In this light, the business of pious writing takes on a different aspect. A sin-list, for example, ceases to be merely a prompt for personal prayers and becomes something more like an entry in God's eternal register. This was what John Fuller envisaged a spiritual diary doing:

> There is a book of three leaves thou shouldest read dayly to make up this Diary; the black leaf of thy own and others sins with shame and sorrow; the white leaf of Gods goodnesse, mercies with joy and thankfulnesse; the red leaf of Gods judgments felt, feared, threatned, with fear and trembling.

You did not write such a book, you read it: your own diary was merely a transcript of it.[89] Earthly paper and ink symbolized of the terrifying, ineradicable permanence of God's book. Samuel Rogers wrote after one wretched day that 'I am almost ashamed to set to writing concerning any thing. . . . What shall I then? spunge out, this day out of the booke of my remembrance . . . or scratch the eyes of this day out; with Jobs Nailes of cursing.' Wallington, similarly, feared that on the day of judgement, 'these my own hand writting shall be broght against mee'. He was tempted to burn his books for that reason. On one occasion, a difficult customer persuaded him to sign a fraudulent bill. This collusion in her dishonesty cost him pangs of guilt and a terrifying dream of the Devil coming into his study 'like a man all in blacke ready to destroy me'. What is striking about this is that his guilt focused on the act of signing his name. He feared that 'this sin is the gratter because it is in wrighting'.[90] What was written, was written.

As a form of prayer, however, writing has an arm's-length quality to it. Writing a love-letter can be, in its own way, as intense an experience as falling into a lover's arms, but the distancing is inescapable. This does not mean, however, that praying

---

[85] Bod MS Rawl D.1350 fos 117r–126v.
[86] Howell, *Epistolæ Ho-Elianæ*, VI.49.   [87] See above, pp. 75–6.
[88] Winthrop, *Papers*, 198.   [89] Beadle, *Journal or diary*, sig. b4r.
[90] Rogers, *Diary*, 6; Wallington, *Notebooks*, 153–4, 264.

aloud was necessarily preferable.[91] Given God's sometimes painfully felt absence during prayer, a form of prayer which acknowledged that distance may have been comforting. But this also meant that writing lent itself particularly to one pious genre: the meditation. Insofar as meditation was a form of prayer, it was a form peculiarly well-suited to being written. The mood was more composed than fervent, and it was frequently addressed, in exhortation or reproach, to the devotee's own soul rather than to God as such.[92]

The experience of writing meditative prayer could prove both intensely personal and intensely powerful. It could be a record—'a memorial of my thankfulnes to God', as William Cowper put it—but the act of making such a record entailed reliving the experience: hence Richard Rogers, in his record of one day's spiritual highs and lows, commenting that 'at the setting downe hereof I was well affected'. It could even be the experience itself. 'I will tell you what good writing of bookes doth', explained Dorothy Leigh: 'it maketh the way to Christ easie to those that desire to goe in it.' Those who do not love writing, she declared, do not love prayer.[93]

Our final witness to this is Grace Mildmay. Her 'book of my meditations written' was 'the consolation of my soule, the joye of my hart & the stabilitte of my mynde'—not merely the record of such consolations. The book 'hath been to me as Jacob's ladder and as Jacob's pillar, even a book of testimonies between God and my soul'. The claim that they are *testimonies* is important. These were words she herself had written, but they stood as proof from outside herself that God was at work through her. As she explained:

> When I began sometimes to set down any part thereof I found myself empty and void at that very instant of any one thought or disposition to pray or meditate or to apprehend heavenly things. Yet notwithstanding before I went from that place, the Lord did minister such plenty of divine matter unto my mind as I was not able to comprehend so that I was constrayned to leave off for that time. . . . For he that looketh too fixedly upon the sun is sure to be stricken blind.[94]

If the Spirit could speak through you when you knelt in prayer, he could also do so when you sat at your writing-desk. Mildmay was not the only early modern Protestant to discover that the calm and discipline of writing could contain the dazzling heat of God's presence. Taking up pen and ink could be a means to grace, and the act of writing an epiphany.

---

[91] Webster, 'Writing to Redundancy', 41.   [92] See above, pp. 109–18.
[93] Cowper, *Most Comfortable Dialogue*, sigs A4v–5v; Knappen, *Two Diaries*, 55; Leigh, *Mothers blessing*, 94, 99.
[94] Mildmay, *With Faith and Physic*, 71.

PART IV

THE PROTESTANT IN COMPANY

13

The Experience of Worship

'Faith is by hearing, & hearing by the worde of God.' *Romans 10:17.*

PUBLIC PRAYER

A true Christian church, John Calvin famously ruled, is one which enjoys true preaching and the correct administration of the sacraments. The principle was theologically sound, but in practice it was a little awkward. While all mainstream English and Scottish Protestants intensely valued both preaching and the sacraments, sermons were only patchily available to many believers and the sacraments were very occasional events. Much the most common acts of public worship were neither. In England and Wales, the Book of Common Prayer provided a structure for weekly and daily public worship. The Scottish church was institutionally more insistent on regular preaching, but even in Scotland, especially when ministers were in desperately short supply during the early years of the Reformation, 'readers' would lead public prayers on Sundays, following the forms in the Book of Common Order. Non-sacramental, non-homiletic public worship was the daily bread and butter of British, and especially English, Protestantism. And it remains mysterious.

The mystery is not so much what actually happened in churches, although there are still real puzzles. In about 1600, the Sunday morning service in an average English parish church (not that any such place existed) went something like this. The congregation would dribble in, with many—especially the cream of the parish, who wanted to make sure they were seen—arriving after the service had begun. Unless there was a metrical psalm, worship would begin with the Prayer Book service of Morning Prayer—including two Bible readings and a substantial chunk of the psalms—followed, without a break, by the Litany and Holy Communion. Normally, however, the sacrament itself was not celebrated, and so the communion service would break off midway, after two further Bible readings and the recitation of the Creed, a practice which was 'of some in derision called the drie communion'. If there was a sermon, it would follow at this point, normally topped or tailed with prayers and metrical psalms. Many of those present might leave as soon as the sermon itself was over, not waiting for the concluding psalms, prayers, and blessing. There might be one or more baptisms after the main service, but few would stay for that.[1]

---

[1] Holinshed, *Chronicles*, I.232–3, is one of the best contemporary accounts. More jaundiced views can be found in Thomas Harrab, *Tessaradelphus, or The foure brothers* (Lancashire?, 1616: RSTC

The main service, that Morning Prayer-Communion sandwich, might last around one hour: a sermon would typically add another hour. In theory, for most of that time the people would be sitting (if there were pews), kneeling, or standing in silence, facing the minister. The voices heard would be those of the minister and the parish clerk, who read the prayers and readings, and who said or sung the psalms, canticles, and responses, perhaps supported by a small choir. Formal congregational participation was supposed to be restricted to answering 'Amen' to the prayers. That in itself was a controversial Reformation-era innovation; but in fact participation seems to have spread beyond this. Quite aside from congregational singing of metrical psalms—undoubtedly the most popular feature of the service—some of the laity seem increasingly to have joined in the Lord's Prayer and Creed, the responses in Morning Prayer and in the Litany, the general confession, and no doubt other points too. Women and men would speak up in unison, which was particularly shocking to some traditional sensibilities.[2] Indeed, while we can generalize about patterns of worship, there was enormous local variation. Ministers tweaked or drastically altered the service, legally or illegally. The use of physical space, of music and responses, and of dress, posture, and a host of subtler rituals varied widely. Some bishops were permissive, others prescriptive. The controversies generated could be intense.[3]

But the deeper question remains: what did it all mean? One theme is consistent: throughout our period there was a surprising lack of positive interest in the liturgical service. As Catharine Davies has pointed out, the Book of Common Prayer is by far the most enduring and influential text created during the reign of Edward VI, and a centrepiece of the official Reformation, but the prolific Protestant writers of the reign had virtually nothing to say about it. The best that the Forty-Two Articles of 1553 could find to say was that the book was 'in no point repugnant to the wholesome doctrine of the gospel, but agreeable thereto, furthering and beautifying the same not a little'—pretty damning, as faint praise goes.[4] Patrick Collinson argued that there is very little evidence of Elizabethan clergy paying any attention to liturgy as such, and pointed out that advice-books for Protestant ministers took virtually no notice of it—despite the fact that 'a normally conscientious incumbent' might spend some ten hours a week conducting Prayer

---

12797), sig. E3r–v; Field and Wilcox, *Admonition*, sig. B4v. For modern summaries, see John E. Booty, *The Godly Kingdom of Tudor England* (Wilton, CT, 1981), 183–7; Sharon L. Arnoult, ' "Spiritual and Sacred Publique Actions": The Book of Common Prayer and the Understanding of Worship in the Elizabethan and Jacobean Church of England' in Eric Josef Carlson (ed.), *Religion and the English People 1500–1640* (Kirkville, MO, 1998), 28–9. On the perennial problem of latecomers and early leavers, see, for example, Cleaver, *[G]odly form*, 26–9, 283; Brinsley, *True Watch* (1608), 65–6; Bernard, *A Weekes Worke* (1616), 143; Fisher, *Defence of the liturgie*, 52; Fuller, *Holy State*, II.93; Herbert, *Works*, 232.

[2] Arnoult, ' "Spiritual and Sacred Publique Actions" ', 28–9, 38; Jewel, *Works . . . The first portion*, 333; Ryrie, 'Psalms and confrontation', 124–5; Fisher, *Defence of the liturgie*, 45–6; Herbert, *Works*, 231.

[3] For an early list of variations, see BL Lansdowne MS 8 fo. 8r. Cf. Maltby, *Prayer Book and People*, 38–44; Durston, 'By the book', 54–5; Collinson, 'Shepherds, sheepdogs and hirelings', 208.

[4] Davies, *A religion of the Word*, 118.

Book services.[5] We have, to the best of my knowledge, no pre-1640 visual depictions of these services at all, an omission which testifies to a pervasive lack of interest. The Catholic polemicist Thomas Harrab, describing the English liturgy, added that 'of this many make smale account, but all the reckoning is of a sermon'. 'The fashion is now', Thomas Tymme regretted, 'to aske if there be a Sermon: if there be none, then either they come not at all, or nothing so cheerefully as they ought.' One of the liturgy's defenders claimed that others found 'the Liturgie a Lethargie' whose effect was 'to quench all zeale in the people by the wearisome prolixitie thereof'.[6] Why then—other than obedience to the law, which was perhaps reason enough—did English Protestants sit through an hour of readings and prayers every Sunday?

A theological reason was, as Davies has pointed out, being advanced by Anthony Gilby as early as 1548. He hoped for a vernacular liturgy which would allow the people to 'worship god & gyue glorie to his name', and through which Christ would be 'renowmed, praised and sanctified in the congregration', so that

> the honoure of God maye be amplified, and we the better resemble that heauenly Hierusalem, where they do incessantly syng praise criynge wyth one voice, Sanctus, sanctus, sanctus.[7]

A rapturous vision of what Protestant worship might be, but one which found few echoes. Perhaps it was too dangerous: the English state valued order over ecstasy. Or perhaps it was too remote from the reality of trying to marshall a reluctant population into outward conformity. The idea does resurface occasionally, often among enthusiasts for church music, who echo Gilby's allusion to heavenly choirs.[8] Perhaps singing was the easiest part of the service to find joyful. Thomas Bentley's prayers for use on the way to church have a plaintive feel to them: praying to 'reioice to be there', he declared that 'I haue a great while sore longed, with so godlie affection as I could, to celebrate thee in the frequented assemblies of the godlie'.[9] That is, he knew he *should* enjoy going to church, but he was not quite there yet. For him and for many others, attendance was more duty than pleasure.

Indeed, it could be positively fearful. The Genevan-Presbyterian strand of Reformed Protestantism, which became dominant in Scotland and was strongly present in England, was distinguished by its scruples about public worship. The 'regulative principle' of worship, as later Presbyterians dubbed it, argues, with fearsome Biblical backing, that any form of worship which is not explicitly author- ized in Scripture is 'will-worship', the product of corrupt human invention, and thus damnable idolatry. From this perspective, public worship was a minefield to be navigated, not a celebration to be enjoyed. As Nicholas Bownde put it:

[5] Collinson, 'Shepherds, sheepdogs and hirelings', 193–5, 207–10.
[6] Harrab, *Tessaradelphus*, sig. E3r; Tymme, *Chariot of Devotion*, 49; Fisher, *Defence of the liturgie*, 7–8.
[7] Gilby, *An answer*, fos 140v–142r.
[8] See, for example, John Case?, *The Praise of Musicke* (Oxford, 1586: RSTC 20184), 134–5; Thomas Ford, *Singing of Psalmes the Duty of Christians* (1653: Wing F1516), 139–40.
[9] Bentley, *Monument of Matrons*, 405, 407.

It is a very hard thing to serue God, as we should, and therefore in all parts of his worship wee must vse great diligence, that they may bee done in that manner, that he may fauourably accept them.

The purpose of public worship became to complete the exercise successfully without committing idolatry.[10] You were then safe for another week. Nor was this a fringe view. It underpins the Prayer Book's famous essay 'of ceremonies, why some be abolished and some retained'. The essay is clear as to why some ceremonies are abolished—they are burdensome, superstitious, and corrupt—but much vaguer on why others are retained, arguing merely that 'without some ceremonies it is not possible to keep any order or quiet discipline in the church'.[11] It appears that the best a ceremony can hope for—and what is the entire liturgy if not a ceremony?—is to be an inoffensive means of fulfilling a duty.

That it *was* a duty, moral as well as legal, was unmistakable. It was a regular theme of Protestant moralizing: turn up on time, stay until the end, and bring your entire household with you. (Samuel Clarke would sometimes praise a particular paragon of godliness because 'he never kept any of his Servants from Church to dresse his meat'; evidently leaving someone to mind the kitchen was normal practice.)[12] Above all, you had a duty to resist the inner voice suggesting oh-so-reasonably that, rather than 'trudge through the winter mud to church', you would be better off staying at home in the warm to read and pray on your own.[13] Edmund Allen's Edwardian catechism, for example, warned that whoever misses church 'without a very iust and lawful cause, is worthy to be excommunicate and excluded out from the number of the faithful congregacion'. This theme—that attendance at public worship was a matter of mere obedience—echoes through the period. We are God's servants, Richard Kilby argued: we should attend on him patiently without asking why.[14]

Dorothy Leigh agreed, but also tackled the obvious objection: what if your minister is inadequate and you know the service will not edify you? Her answer, essentially that you should make the best of it, is not entirely satisfactory. Richard Rogers acknowledged the same difficulty, but argued that those who 'sequester themselues from being present at the seruice of God' show unacceptable spiritual pride.[15] Mere obligation, however, is a thin incentive to a tedious duty. Hugh Latimer, preaching on the subject in 1553, was too honest to evade the problem entirely. He urged his hearers to attend church, 'for it is a good and godly order, and God will have it so', but he then had to admit that he did not always do so himself. As he explained:

I have none other excuse but this, namely, that I shall go thither in vain. . . . The parson of the church is ignorant and unable to teach the word of God, neither beareth he any

[10] Bownde, *Medicines for the plague*, 134; Davies, *A religion of the Word*, 122.
[11] Ketley, *Two Liturgies*, 156–7.
[12] Clarke, *Lives of thirty-two divines*, 146; Clarke, *Collection*, 15, 102. Cf. Cleaver, *[G]odly form*, 19–23.
[13] Narveson, *Bible Readers*, 127.
[14] Edmund Allen, *A cathechisme* (1551: RSTC 360), sigs C3v–4v; Kilby, *Burthen*, 44.
[15] Leigh, *Mothers blessing*, 231–3; Rogers, *Seven treatises*, 222–3.

good will to the word of God; therefore it were better for me to teach me family at home, than to go thither and spend my time in vain, and so lose my labour.[16]

Good Protestants were not supposed to say such things. They certainly thought them.

There were other compelling reasons both to attend the service and to ensure that others did so, but not all of these reasons were high-minded. Clergy—even clergy as talented and reckless as Latimer—have a stake in the institutional Church. For them to insist on attendance at worship was mere professional self-interest. For the laity, there were profound but essentially secular issues of sociability and conformity.[17] Perhaps most importantly, there was the matter of doctrinal policing. The Elizabethan state may not have wished to make windows into its subjects' souls, but it did want their bodies in church. Protestant states were frightened of Catholic subversion, and the clergy were convinced of the godlessness of most of their people; both could agree that dragooning the population into church week by week was wise. It would expose the hardcore opponents of the regime for what they were, and expose their more tractable neighbours to an hour or more of propaganda every week. If the godly and well-meaning were therefore compelled to attend services which would do them little good, that was a small price to pay. If they were permitted to skip church on the basis that they were praying at home, Catholics and carnal Protestants would pour through the resulting loophole like a flood. There was nothing for it but to make the godly and godless sit there, equally reluctantly, but for very different reasons.

Indeed, one commonly cited reason for diligence in attending church was not that it would directly benefit you at all, but that it was a public demonstration. There was an uplifting side to this, which saw participation in public worship as a form of mutual encouragement.[18] But by the early 17th century it was commoner, at least outside ceremonialist circles, to stress the obligation. John Preston argued that 'when God is honoured before many...more honour is done to him, it is a greater honour'. A more pragmatic note creeps into William Perkins' insistence that public prayer is public profession of our separation from ungodliness.[19] Skulking at home to pray suggested that you were ashamed to be seen at church, and Christians who would not stand up and be counted could expect that Christ would disown them. This was often phrased explicitly as an obligation to neighbours. John Ball's popular catechism taught that we attend church not only to 'professe our selues to bee the seruants of Christ' but also to 'stirre vp others by our example'. John Brinsley, similarly, described the obligation to be early for church as being 'for the good ensample of others'. How persuasive such examples were, we may doubt. Richard Kilby put it negatively and more convincingly: if those who

[16] Latimer, *Sermons and Remains*, 156–7.
[17] Christopher Marsh, '"Common Prayer" in England 1560–1640: the view from the pew', *Past and Present* 171 (2001), 66–94.
[18] Bradford, *Godlie meditations*, sig. G2v; Kate Narveson, 'Piety and the genry of John Donne's *Devotions*', *John Donne Journal* 17 (1998), 112–13.
[19] Preston, *Saints Daily Exercise*, 83; Perkins, *Godly and learned exposition*, 235.

have a reputation for piety are seen to be absent from church, it sets a terrible example. Dorothy Leigh warned against allowing others' laxity to infect you. Yes, the churches may be half-empty, but 'let there be one the more for thee'.[20] You turned up, in part, to stand in the breach against the supposed tide of godlessness overwhelming the land. In other words, even if the service left you completely without nourishment, you could head home with a clear conscience, knowing that simply by being there you had done your bit.

Not that the liturgy's content was irrelevant. It was there, as the Prayer Book's compilers and defenders freely admitted, as propaganda for the Protestant cause—and also, of course, for the Protestant state. Above all, that meant propaganda for the Bible. The Prayer Book was designed, not so much as a liturgy in the normal sense, but as a Scripture delivery mechanism.[21] The book's preface, first printed in 1549 and unchanged thereafter, was emphatic on the point. The purpose of common prayers in the early church, this text argued, was 'that all the whole Bible (or the greatest part thereof) should be read over once in the year', in order both to edify the ministers themselves and to equip them to preach the Word to others. That wholesome order had been subverted by various innovations which 'did breaik the continual course of the reading of scripture', but it was now restored.[22] The Tudor state did not have radio transmitters, but it did have pulpits, and by establishing a uniform order for common prayer it could broadcast a rolling programme of Bible reading to the population, lightly packaged with other prayers. The Prayer Book's defenders regularly pointed out that it contained 'nothing else but the eternal word of God', 'no other than God's written word'. It was a polemical point, both anti-Catholic and anti-puritan, but it was also largely true. The Prayer Book's texts are a tissue of Biblical quotation, and the service itself consisted of 'a solid block of Bible reading'.[23]

For its compilers and early advocates, the purpose of the Book of Common Prayer was not so much to worship God as to teach his people. We have already seen how texts published for private prayer were often heavily didactic.[24] This was even truer of public worship, whether liturgical or otherwise. If the primary purposes of extempore prayers led by preachers were to invoke God and to stir up zeal in their hearers, they could hardly help doing a little teaching too, and sometimes more than a little. Some listeners took notes from the prayers as they did from the sermons.[25] The prayer at the end of John Foxe's 1570 Good Friday sermon even provided a potted history of the Church.[26] The same is truer still of fixed liturgical texts. The Scottish order for baptism, for example, consisted chiefly

[20] Ball, *Short treatise*, 138; Brinsley, *True Watch* (1608), 65; Kilby, *Burthen*, 44; Leigh, *Mothers blessing*, 234.

[21] Davies, *A religion of the Word*, 137 n. 275.

[22] Ketley, *Two Liturgies*, 17–18.

[23] Cranmer, *Miscellaneous Writings*, 180; Sandys, *Sermons*, 46; Arnoult, '"Spiritual and Sacred Publique Actions"', 29.

[24] See above, pp. 223–4.

[25] For example, BL Egerton MS 2877 fo. 18r.

[26] Foxe, *Sermon of Christ crucified*, sig. T2r.

of two long discourses to be read by the minister, expounding first the sacrament itself, and secondly the Apostles' Creed.[27] Catholic commentators singled out the overtly didactic nature of Protestant worship as one of its key flaws. John Christopherson lamented that under Edward VI, the people came to church 'to heare only, and not to pray our selues'. 'Yt was never ment', Stephen Gardiner pointed out, 'that the people should in dede here the Mattyns or here the Masse, but be present ther and praye them selues in sylence.'[28] Protestants profoundly disagreed. Suitors in court are frustrated when they cannot understand their own lawyers' pleas, Archbishop Cranmer argued, so why should the laity accept incomprehensible prayers being said to God on their behalf? The Elizabethan Homilies argued that all public prayer must edify those who hear it. John Whitgift defended the use of the Athanasian Creed in the liturgy by telling its opponents that 'your meaning is, that we know too much, and therefore now we must learn to forget'; that is, the text was used primarily to increase knowledge. As Calvin said, 'the main part of true and right worship is to hear God speaking'.[29] Worship is all but swallowed up by teaching.

Did it work? Some European parallels suggest that exposure to Protestant worship could indeed be formative.[30] In Britain, however, there is meagre evidence of people learning much from the liturgy, or from the Bible readings which it contained. The power of the English Bible, in particular, turned out to be the Reformation's great false hope. Exposed to great slabs of Scripture, most people remained stubbornly unreformed. They might find themselves memorizing some texts, but the ability to parrot Scripture was not quite what the reformers had hoped for. Puritan critics derided the Prayer Book service as 'bare reading of the word', an insult which would have been a compliment a generation earlier.[31] The exceptions prove the rule. John Foxe described how Joan Waste was converted during Edward VI's reign after she 'gaue her selfe dayly to go to the Church to heare Diuine seruice read in the vulgare tounge'. However, he added that 'Homelies and Sermons' were equally important to her; moreover, she was blind, and so could only encounter the Bible by having it read to her. By the early 17th century we are reduced to brave resolutions like Dorothy Leigh's. Against the objection that there was little to learn at church, she warned that with such an attitude, 'I feare that thou wilt not learne that little'. There were only scraps to be had, but they should be gathered nevertheless.[32] The theme largely faded from sight. Merely herding people together to read the Bible at them no longer seemed like an adequate justification for attending church.

---

[27] *The forme of prayers and ministration of the sacraments &c. vsed in the English church at Geneua, approued and receiued by the Churche of Scotland* (Edinburgh, 1565: RSTC 16577a), 63–80.

[28] Christopherson, *An exhortation*, sig. X5r; James Arthur Muller (ed.), *The Letters of Stephen Gardiner* (Cambridge, 1933), 356.

[29] Cranmer, *Miscellaneous Writings*, 169–70; *Certain Sermons or Homilies*, 317–19; Whitgift, *Works*, II.482; Richard, *Spirituality of John Calvin*, 118.

[30] P. J. Broadhead, 'Public Worship, Liturgy and the Introduction of the Lutheran Reformation in the Territorial Lands of Nuremberg', *English Historical Review* 120/486 (2005), 302.

[31] Field and Wilcox, *Admonition*, sig. B1r; Holinshed, *Chronicles*, I.233.

[32] Foxe, *Actes and monuments* (1570). 2137; Leigh, *Mothers blessing*, 232.

Other justifications had to be found, if only because maintaining a regular, public, and compulsory religious assembly was a political and social necessity. The most heartfelt justification can be seen in the terminology. What happened in church before the sermon was not usually described as liturgy, worship, or divine service, but as public prayers. The purpose of public worship, Thomas Tymme argued in 1618, was 'not to make it a Schoole of diuinitie for instruction by preaching there: but therein to poure forth prayers vnto God'.[33] Those who were uneasy about assembling merely to hear the Bible or a pre-printed homily would certainly approve of collective prayer. As one of those very homilies pointed out, 'although God hath promised to hear us when we pray privately... public and common prayer is most available [effective] before God'.[34] The point was repeated throughout our period. Ball's catechism taught that 'publique seruice [is] worth more then priuate, as a societie exceedeth the worthinesse of one man'. Henry Burton, no less, stole his Laudian opponents' rhetoric to argue that 'the publicke Ordinance is the most perfect beauty of holinesse, ever to be preferred before priuate deuotions'.[35] This was, perhaps surprisingly, a Protestant truism.

The surprise is both historical and theological. Historically, Protestantism had first emerged as an underground movement, whose adherents discovered or rediscovered the power of prayer alone or in small groups. Theologically, it emphasized the individual standing before God without intermediaries. This emphasis on public prayer, then, may seem odd. Understandably, some scholars have seen it as a ceremonialist innovation or used it to differentiate ceremonialists from puritans. But ceremonialists' claim that puritans valued preaching over prayer was (mostly) a slander. When asked to choose between preaching and prayer, puritans steadily refused to do so, insisting that both were essential.[36] As Perkins' disciple Thomas Tuke put it:

I wil preach for praying, & pray for preaching. He that can not finde in his heart to come to the church to heare nothing but praier, by my consent he should not be suffered to come into the Church to heare nothing but preaching. Gods house is the house of preaching, and of praying to.[37]

As that comment suggests, Protestants of all stripes not only valued public prayer, but sited public prayer *in a church building*. Of course, they all also accepted that Christians could pray anywhere, that they carried the true temple with them, even that (order permitting) 'a good preacher may declare the word of God sitting on a horse, or preaching in a tree', and they held that the prayer sanctified the place, not vice versa. But applying Christ's description of the temple as 'the house of prayer' to church buildings was a commonplace.[38] Laudians and ceremonialists made this

[33] Tymme, *Chariot of Devotion*, 65.
[34] *Certain Sermons or Homilies*, 315.
[35] Ball, *Short treatise*, 138; Burton, *Israels Fast*, 16; cf. Latimer, *Sermons by Hugh Latimer*, 338.
[36] Targoff, *Common Prayer*, 51; Ferrell, 'Kneeling and the Body Politic'; Gouge, *Whole-Armor of God*, 422.
[37] Tuke, *Practise of the faithfull*, 34.
[38] Latimer, *Sermons by Hugh Latimer*, 206; Tuke, *Practise of the faithfull*, 32; Matthew 21:13. Cf. Babington, *Profitable Exposition*, 69*; Narne, *Pearle of prayer*, 422.

point, of course. It is no surprise that the second, Elizabethan book of homilies began with a homily 'Of the right use of the church or temple of God, and of the reverence due unto the same', which urged the people 'reverently to use the church and holy house of our prayers'. It even, cautiously, cited Jewish zeal for the temple as an exemplar.[39] But unmistakable puritans sang the same song. Lewis Bayly wrote:

> As thou enterest into the Church, say, How fearefull is this place? this is none other but the House of God. . . . And prostrating with thy face downeward, being come to thy place, say, O Lord, I haue loued the Habitation of thy House.

George Webbe admonished those entering a church that 'the place thou art going into is Gods House; there thou goest to heare God speaking vnto thee by his Minister; and to speake vnto him by Prayer'. Philip Goodwin distinguished between daily devotions at home, and assembling on Sundays 'in the presence of the great God'.[40] We can find undoubtedly orthodox Calvinists in both England and Scotland not only arguing for the care and beautification of church buildings, but actually doing it.[41] So, since we have seen that these same Protestants viewed the public liturgy with a mixture of dutiful obligation, unease, disillusionment, and tedium, why this enthusiasm for collective prayers in church?

Two linked reasons stand out. First, a genuine conviction that collective prayer was qualitatively different from the individual variety. As the emphasis on worship as teaching faded during the later 16th century, this view emerged, and became a dominant truism in the 17th. 'If one string of an instrument make a sounde, many stringes make a greater sound.' 'A sparke of fire in the fire, keepes fire; by it selfe, of it selfe goes out.' Thomas Playfere cited the Biblical proverb that a threefold cord is not easily broken, adding, 'then much more a hundred-fold cord, or a thousand-fold cord'.[42] Collective prayer was stronger, then, but in what sense? Often this explicitly refers to mutual encouragement, as devotees take heart from one another's example, which is straightforward enough. But there is also a simple assertion that God is more moved by more voices. Perkins used (again) the analogy of human petitioning. Many voices carry more weight with God, he argued, as 'a priuate mans supplication is not so much respected, as when a whole incorporation, or a whole shire make petition to a Prince'. For William Gouge, 'the cries of many ioyned together make a loud crie in Gods eares, and moue him the sooner to open his eares'. Richard Sibbes brought in the ever-popular image of prayer as wrestling with God, asking 'if the prayer of one be a wrestling, and striving, and forcing of him, as it were, against his will . . . what are the prayers of many?' He cited the Biblical claim that ten righteous people would have been enough to save Sodom

---

[39] *Certain Sermons or Homilies*, 145, 150, 152; cf. Cooper, ' "As wise as serpents" ', 218; Cosin, *Collection of Priuate Devotions*, 17–18.

[40] Bayly, *Practise of pietie*, 464–5; Rogers, *Garden* (1616), sigs F7v–8r; Philip Goodwin, *Religio Domestica Rediviva: or, Family-religion Revived* (1655: Wing G1218), 307.

[41] Fincham and Tyacke, *Altars Restored*, 103, 248–9; Adams, *The white devil*, 14; Cowper, *Life and Death*, sigs A4v–B1r.

[42] Babington, *Profitable Exposition*, 72; Playfere, *Power of praier*, 2–3.

from destruction. Thomas Goodwin took that story's emphasis on numbers even more literally. 'God stands sometimes upon such a number of voices, and one voice casts it, as when hee named ten righteous persons to save Sodome.'[43]

Now Perkins, Gouge, Sibbes, and Goodwin were all sober theologians. None of them would seriously claim that God was a democrat, to be swayed by the number of votes received in prayer, nor that he could be pressed by sheer weight of opinion into acting against his better judgement. So perhaps this is mere hyperbole, aiming to encourage fervour in prayer by making expansive claims about its power. In some hands, there does seem to have been a crude mechanicity at work. Claims like Thomas Tymme's—that the prayer of 'many thousands must needes be much more powerfull, than that which is made by one, or a few'—seem to be informed more by blunt common sense than theological principle, and perhaps betray the extent to which Protestant talk of prayer being powerful had slipped its moorings.[44] More subtle principles, however, are also at work here. One is humility. Since God does not hear the prayers of sinners, devotees have every incentive to join their own faltering voices with those of saints greater than themselves:

> All the parish joyneth in praier with you, wherefore you shall be heard the sooner. Some that you make least reckoning of may bee in greater favour with God than your selfe, and then you shall speede the better in praying with them.[45]

Secondly, and more importantly, to unite in prayer is itself virtuous. It is an open witness of faith, forbearance, and charity at work. William Narne argued that in public prayer, unlike in private, there was 'concord, conspiration, a coniunction of loue and charitie'.[46] In practice, this concord meant listening silently to the minister's words and adding *Amen* when he had finished, but we find this described as 'a sweet harmonie sent vp to our Heavenly Father' or 'Gods best melodie'.[47] The musical imagery suggests that public prayers are more than the sum of their parts. Collective prayers were powerful not because they were louder, but because they were more harmonious. Similarly, those who stressed the added value of public prayer often drew attention to the presence of the entire community. The contrast then becomes less between the voices of one and of many, and more between private individuals and the entire Church speaking as one. The model was the fast which the prophet Jonah's preaching had provoked in Nineveh, where not only the entire population but even the cattle and sheep had joined in public mourning.[48]

In any case, whether for sophisticated and subtle reasons or for crude and anthropomorphic ones, early modern Protestants saw a distinctive value in public prayers in general, and in the prayers of the entire community gathered in church in particular. This was, amongst other things, one of the centripetal forces which

---

[43] Perkins, *Godly and learned exposition*, 235 (and see above, pp. 252–3); Gouge, *Whole-Armor of God*, 426; Sibbes, *Works*, VI.96; Goodwin, *Returne of Prayers*, 74–5.

[44] Tymme, *Chariot of Devotion*, 41; cf. Harris, *Peters enlargement* (1624), 4–7.

[45] Kilby, *Burthen*, 44; and see above, pp. 105–6.

[46] Narne, *Pearle of prayer*, 444.

[47] Hill, *Christs prayer expounded*, sig. A6r; Narne, *Pearle of prayer*, 444.

[48] Jonah 3:7–8; Hildersam, *Doctrine of Fasting*, 43.

guarded the broad national churches of England and Scotland against schism and separatism during our period. It also ensured that, even if Protestants expected to gain little by way of edification or learning from attending church, they might still feel the urgency of being there.

This brings us to the second reason for valuing collective prayers. If you are convinced that they are powerful, that power infuses the experience. The emotional impact of public prayer was widely attested. Archbishop Cranmer's justification for an audible, vernacular service was that 'the heart is not moved with words that be not understand'. A lifetime later Perkins was declaring that 'publike praier serues to stirre vp zeale in them that be cold and backward', and the 1644 *Directory for the Publique Worship of GOD*, which did not prescribe texts for prayers, required ministers to speak such 'that both themselves and their people may be much affected, and even melted thereby'.[49] There is some evidence that this reflected lay people's experiences as well as ministers' hopes. 'Who hath not felt his heart moued in a congregation' during public prayer, Gervase Babington asked rhetorically? Extempore prayers might have this effect: Samuel Rogers recalled an occasion when a preacher's 'mournefull prayer melted mee into teares', and Archibald Johnston of Wariston's heartfelt responses to preachers' prayers sometimes included substantial, unpremeditated donations to the poorbox.[50] But so might the use of set forms. George Herbert's country parson reckoned that 'a devout behaviour in the very act of praying' the service would move the people to more reverence than any sermon. Richard Baxter, the most generous of nonconformists, remembered how until the mid-1630s 'I had joyned with the Common-Prayer with as hearty fervency as afterward I did with other Prayers'.[51] If such fervency did not come naturally, there was always scope for effort. James Howell described how he aimed 'to apply evry title of the Service to my own conscience and occasions', meaning, for example, that during the psalms 'I listen to them more attentively, and make them mine own'; that during the Creed, he considered the Polish gentry's custom of standing for the Creed with swords drawn, 'intimating thereby, that they will defend it with their lives and blood'; and during the reading of the Ten Commandments, 'wheras other use to rise, and sit, I ever kneel at it in the humblest and trembling'st posture of all, to crave remission'.[52] Whether he really maintained this pitch of devotion every week, we may doubt, but it does not sound as if he found the service tiresome.

For earnest Protestants, then, the normal Sunday service, preaching aside, was a paradoxical business. Most of them accepted the need for a liturgy but had little interest in or enthusiasm for it. The service could be tedious and rarely taught them much. Yet they did not (openly) question the obligation to be present. They believed in a national Church at which all adults were compelled to attend: for

---

[49] Cranmer, *Miscellaneous Writings*, 170; Perkins, *Godly and learned exposition*, 235; *Directory for the Publique Worship*, 77.

[50] Babington, *Profitable Exposition*, 72*; Rogers, *Diary*, 2; Wariston, *Diary*, 48, 50, 70.

[51] Herbert, *Works*, 231; Baxter, *Reliquiae Baxterianae*, 13.

[52] Howell, *Epistolæ Ho-Elianæ*, VI.47–8.

political, social, and also for theological reasons. Only in such a Church could the voices of the whole people be joined together in common prayer, which God had commanded and through which he could be commanded. That experience, of joining their individual voices in that great petition, could make it all worthwhile.

But while we have been focusing our attention on the self-consciously earnest, we should spare a thought for their less zealous neighbours, as we might assume that even those who rarely gave their religion much thought might do so on a Sunday morning. For the space of an hour or two, the numbers of at least passably earnest believers increased markedly. What was these people's experience of public worship?

The practicalities are worth noticing. The noises: psalms, groans, and stray dogs, as John Craig has memorably pointed out; perhaps, God forbid, snoring; and the subtler noises, the whispering and muttering as the minister or clerk strained to be heard in a cavernous building without microphones or hearing aids. Children who had not yet learned to conceal their boredom could add another layer of noise. The Yorkshire schoolboy who allegedly 'did daunce in tyme of devyne Service in the churche and did plaie at coverpin' was perhaps unusually bold, but others will have sat in silence longing to do the same.[53] And then there were the smells. Cramming unwashed human bodies into a confined space had consequences, even in a less fastidious age. John Phillips described a London church on a hot summer's day:

> Their pews seem pasties, wherein they incrusted,
> Together bake and fry; O patience great!
> Yet they endure, though almost drown'd in sweat.
> It seem'd as if those steaming vapours were
> To stew hard doctrines in.[54]

During the winter, by contrast, shared bodily warmth might be one of the chief attractions of church attendance. On a cold Sunday evening, you might keep warm more cheaply and effectively in a solid stone building full of people than sitting at home watching your winter's fuel stock burn away. Nor, indeed, did you spend the whole period seated, with the attendant chills, numbness and stiffening joints. For Ambrose Fisher, 'the variable delight which commeth by hearing, singing, answering' was one of the attractions of the Prayer Book service.[55]

Perhaps *delight* was an exaggeration, but, as Judith Maltby has argued, the evidence for real popular attachment to the Prayer Book services is strong.[56] While that attachment drew variously on political, social, and aesthetic concerns, as well as mere habit, we should not discount real devotion—which could, of course, infuse all those other factors. It is perhaps unsurprising to find the Prayer Book services being valued by those in distress of one kind or another, from storm-tossed mariners to

---

[53] Craig, 'Psalms, groans'; David George (ed.), *Lancashire: Records of Early English Drama* (Toronto, 1991), 14. The problem of whispering in church is tackled in John Angier, *An Helpe to Better Hearts, for Better Times* (1647: Wing A3164), 82–3. On sleeping and audibility, see below, pp. 354, 356–7.

[54] Phillips, *Satyr*, 7.

[55] Hunt, *Art of Hearing*, 205–6; Fisher, *Defence of the liturgie*, 8.

[56] Maltby, *Prayer Book and People*.

those nursing hangovers: fear and pain sharpen many people's piety, and make familiarity more important than stimulating novelty.[57] But we should take seriously what some puritans feared: that for many people, the Prayer Book service was proving sufficient for their devotional life. George Gifford's Atheos defended his curate by saying that 'hee doth reade the seruice, as well as any of them all, and I thinke there is as good edifiyng in those prayers and homilies, as in any that the Preacher canne make'. Similarly, the 1644 *Directory* lambasted the 'Ignorant and Superstitious People' for their attachment to the Prayer Book service, 'pleasing themselves in their presence at that Service, and their Lip-labour in bearing a part in it'.[58] This, perhaps, is the awful truth about public worship in post-Reformation England: that its many flaws and failures were not enough to stop most people, the zealous and the lax alike, finding some real spiritual sustenance in it.

BAPTISM

The practice of baptism, one of the two sacraments which Reformed Protestants acknowledged, was thick with paradox. Each individual received it only once, normally very soon after birth (Figure 14). The standard Reformed aspiration was to administer the sacrament in church on a Sunday, in public—if any of the public bothered to stay. Most adults would have attended dozens of baptisms, either simply as part of the congregation or, perhaps, serving as godparents. (Fathers, in a post-Reformation innovation, also attended their children's baptisms; mothers, often still confined and in any case not yet 'churched', never did so.)[59] In all but the smallest parishes, baptism was administered much more frequently than the other sacrament, the Lord's Supper. It was also logically and chronologically prior to it. Yet baptism received much less attention, and naturally, no-one could remember their own baptism.

Moreover, Protestant theology complicated the sacrament considerably. For Catholics, it was a simple matter: baptism cleansed you from original sin and was an absolute prerequisite for salvation. However, this simple principle was compatible neither with Protestants' understanding of salvation nor with their doctrine of the Church. God could save the unbaptized if he wished, and if he had chosen his elect for salvation before all worlds, he could hardly be thwarted in his purpose by the negligence of a priest. Which was certainly a source of comfort to some grieving parents, but the problem was obvious. If baptism was not necessary for salvation, what was it for?

The radical solution—to dispense with it entirely—would not be entertained until the advent of Quakerism. Even aside from Biblical and patristic precedent, the spectre of so-called 'Anabaptism' had to be countered. Universal infant baptism was

---

[57] See, for example, Norwood, *Journal*, 30; Owen, 'Diary of Bulkeley', 28.

[58] Gifford, *Briefe discourse*, fo. 2r; *Directory for the Publique Worship*, 4.

[59] David Cressy, *Birth, Marriage and Death: Ritual, Religion and the Life Cycle in Tudor and Stuart England* (Oxford, 1997), 149.

Fig. 14. Richard Day, *A Booke of Christian Prayers* (1578: RSTC 6429), sig. M1r. A unique Elizabethan depiction of a post-Reformation baptism.
Bodleian Library, Oxford.

a vital social glue, which made a universal Church possible. But the sacrament clearly needed theological value too. Protestants tended to find it in two different— but entirely compatible—images.

One image had a very clear Scriptural and symbolic basis, and appealed especially to Lutherans. This described baptism as spiritual washing, a cleansing from sin which marked new birth from water and the Spirit. Reformed Protestants, by contrast, preferred another, less intuitively obvious image with a thinner Scriptural basis: baptism as the seal of the Holy Spirit on a Christian. In the post-sealing-wax era, that image is not as vivid as it once was, but its meanings—a mark of ownership, a trustworthy pledge—are plain enough. It is used several times in the New Testament, but never explicitly in connection with baptism. The closest we come is in Romans 4:11, where Abraham's circumcision is described as 'the seale of the righteousness of the faith which he had', and Reformed theologians saw circumcision as the Old Testament analogue of baptism. Scripture, then, hardly compelled them to describe baptism as a seal, and yet they did. We find the image used by England's most preeminent Protestant theologian, by its most popular Protestant author, and a great many besides.[60] For no image better encapsulated the Reformed doctrine of baptism. If baptism is a seal, it has no intrinsic power, but is a sign of a pre-existent spiritual reality. Elect infants 'are holy before baptisme, and baptisme is but a seale of that holinesse'. That seal's purpose is to guarantee the promised salvation. Baptism is 'a seale of Gods promises'. Through it, the 'Couenant of Grace and forgiuenesse of sinnes is sealed vnto vs'.[61] We will return to the obvious problem with this shortly, but first, it is time to look at the part baptism played in the Protestant life.

---

[60] Perkins, *Whole treatise*, 311; Bayly, *Practise of pietie*, 198.
[61] Perkins, *Whole treatise*, 311; Byfield, *Marrow of the Oracles* (1622), 538; Egerton, *Boring of the Eare*, 60.

The most natural and the most important use of baptism was to recall your own. Virtually no-one could in fact do this, but they had attended others' often enough to be able to imagine it, and they were routinely urged to do so. George Herbert's idealized country parson

> adviseth all to call to minde their Baptism often . . . It is the safest course for Christians . . . to meditate on their Baptisme often (being the first step into their great and glorious calling).

Herbert himself meditated on how 'on my infancie/Thou didst lay hold, and antedate/My faith in me'. Perkins' disciple Paul Baynes agreed that the believer's recollection of baptism 'must needs be a forcible meanes to help him forward in a christian course, as oft as hee doth duly consider it'. One way that this might work is illustrated by the Prayer Book catechism. Its opening question asks the child's name, and then asks who gave the name, the answer being the child's godparents— unlocking a series of questions on the child's baptism and what it means.[62] In other words, recalling baptism was a means of making abstract doctrines directly personal. *You* were baptized; your godparents, men and women whom you respected, made promises for you; your very name bore witness to it. Richard Greenham recommended using baptism to teach the doctrine of the Trinity, since everyone knew that babies were baptized in the threefold Name: it was a foothold of accessibility on a dauntingly sheer doctrine.[63] Whether these exhortations worked is another matter. Ezekiel Culverwell urged each Christian to consider 'what sensible good he hath received by his Baptisme'; but he also claimed to have 'demanded this question of many (who were of good esteeme in the Church) who had little to say in this point',[64] and we may question how vivid this unremembered event could actually be.[65]

What was the point of remembering your baptism? The imagery of cleansing and renewal appealed to some, perhaps especially those of with an anti-Calvinist tinge. John Cosin was characteristically unapologetic, giving thanks that God 'hast vouchsafed to regenerate me . . . by water and the Holy Ghost in the blessed Lauer of Baptisme, thereby receiuing mee into the number of thy Children'— which was alarmingly close to the traditional Catholic doctrine. Yet John Hayward used the same idea, this time in self-reproach: 'thou wert once washed cleane with the heauenly fountaine in Baptisme', but have now fallen back into sin.[66] Jeremiah Dyke, more subtly, saw exactly that kind of repentance as part of baptism's purpose. An infant cannot be moved by baptism. It is memory which gives the sacrament its power, years after the water has dried. In adulthood, when a sinner is first touched with repentance, 'the Lord quickens a mans Baptisme, and makes it as

---

[62] Herbert, *Works*, 44, 258; Baynes, *Briefe Directions*, 215; Ketley, *Two Liturgies*, 369.

[63] Parker and Carlson, 'Practical Divinity', 213.

[64] Culverwell, *Treatise of faith*, 371.

[65] It was certainly vivid for Elizabeth Isham, but as we shall see she ascribed an unusual spiritual significance to her childhood. Isham, 'Confessions', fos 2v, 27v; and see below, pp. 434–5.

[66] Cosin, *Collection of Priuate Devotions*, 103; Hayward, *Sanctuarie of a troubled soule* (1602), 39; cf. Mildmay, 'Meditations', II.163.

powerfull, and efficacious as if that very day ministred'.[67] It was a powerful line of argument, but those who followed it too far might find themselves entertaining Anabaptist thoughts.

It was much safer to dwell on baptism as a seal of election. This was very widely cited as a source of consolation.[68] John Bradford's meditations affirmed that 'the holy Sacrament of baptisme, wherin thy holy name was not in vaine called vpon me . . . shuld most assuredly confirme, and euen on all sydes seale vp my faith'. Thomas Becon pulled out all the stops, assuring a dying man that baptism is

> a sure token of the fauour of God toward you, and that you are predestinate vnto euerlasting life. . . . Baptisme is a continuall signe of the fauour of God towarde vs, of the fre remission of sinnes, of our reconciliation vnto God for Christes sake, and that we be by adoption the sonnes of God.

But forceful phrasing cannot conceal the basic problem. Obviously, the fact of baptism was *not* a guarantee of salvation. Some baptized people go to Hell. Becon attempted to evade this problem simply by assuring his dying man that he believed the faith into which he had been baptized.[69] Later and more precise commentators confronted it more plainly. For Perkins, baptism was 'a seale and pledge of Gods mercie'; that is, a guarantee that God is merciful—*not* a guarantee that all baptized persons will be saved by that mercy. Those worried about their salvation could, Nicholas Byfield assured them, ask, 'hath not the Lord prouided me the Arke of Baptisme to preserue me from the seas of his wrath?' But providing an ark is not the same as reserving everyone a berth on it.[70]

As a matter of logic, such sleight of hand renders the argument worthless. But there is more to piety than logic, and the argument's frequent repetition suggests that early modern Protestants—who were certainly aware of the problems—nevertheless derived some comfort from it. Baptism did at least suggest that mercy was possible, not simply for humanity in general, but for you in particular. Elizabeth Isham found succour of this kind in recalling her baptism. She compared herself to a son whose father provides a great inheritance for him, 'and doth give him such breeding that in time to come he might be fitted for it, provided that he performe some duties to settle his estate when he should come to age'.[71] The gift is not irrevocable, but the promise is in good earnest.

Much the commonest use of the 'memory' of baptism, however, takes us in a different and—to modern eyes—stranger direction. This concerned the baptismal vows, in which the godparents solemnly promise, on the infant's behalf, to renounce the Devil, and to keep God's commandments, and also make a profession of faith. When early modern Protestants were exhorted to recall their baptisms, it was usually in order to reproach themselves for failing to keep these promises— promises which they had not made, to which they had not consented, and of which

---

[67] Dyke, *Worthy communicant*, 595.
[68] For example, Rogers, *Seven treatises*, 218; Culverwell, *Treatise of faith*, 371.
[69] Bradford, *Godlie meditations*, sig. E8v; Becon, *Sycke mans salue*, 447–9.
[70] Perkins, *Whole treatise*, 331; Byfield, *Marrow of the Oracles* (1622), 539.
[71] Isham, 'Confessions', fo. 27v.

they could have no first-hand memory.[72] Neither early modern Protestants nor their medieval forebears seem to have found this at all awkward—although some puritans did baulk at godparents' making vows on an infant's behalf.[73] Popular books of prayers put words of repentance for breaking baptismal vows in their users' mouths, with jarring claims of agency such as praying to 'make good that vow, which I made vnto thee in baptisme'. Some private devotional collections echoed the sentiment. Christ's incarnation celebrated a marriage between God and the soul, argued Edward Hutchins, 'but at baptisme, we in our owne persons doe as it were ratifie it: protesting that Christ shal be our husband, and that from that time, we wil take our farewel of the diuel'. The concept of adult consent implicit in the image of marriage, and the extraordinary phrase 'we in our owne persons': the claim of direct responsibility could not be emphasized more.[74] There were, naturally, theological justifications for this incongruous claim, often involving the concept of the covenanted community, but there does not seem even to have been any unease about it. Whether it really had purchase on believers' consciences is harder to know, but for John Winthrop, at least, it did. Meditating on his backsliding into sin on one occasion, he declared that, 'I am resolved, I saye, to stand to the Covenant of my baptisme'.[75] If nothing else, baptismal vows were a mast to which sinners could lash their faltering virtues when temptation began to sing.

However, Winthrop also provides us with one clue as to how these abstract and unremembered vows might become more immediate. He remarked on how his baptismal covenant had been 'renued so often since'. John Ball's popular catechism, likewise, urged readers 'to renew the couenant and vow, which we made vnto the Lord in Baptisme'. The most obvious way to bring your own baptism alive in your imagination, and to recall and inwardly to renew your vows, was to attend baptisms in your own parish church. Divines regularly urged their readers to renew their vows 'whensoeuer we see that Sacrament administred', and indeed to be present specifically for that purpose. You ought to attend baptisms, Lewis Bayly insisted, in part so 'that thou maiest the better consider thine owne ingrafting into the visible body of Christs Church'.[76] Neither the English nor the Scottish order for baptism made any formal provision for the adults present to renew their baptismal vows, but we can well imagine that when godparents declared, 'I will', earnest souls would mouth the words with them.

The earnest souls might well be in a majority, because this was one of the few compelling reasons actually to turn up to a baptism. If we know one thing about

[72] See, for example, Manningham, *Diary*, 159; Herbert, *Works*, 258; Fleming, *Diamond of deuotion*, 13–14; Habermann, *Enimie of securitie*; Tymme, *Siluer watch-bell* (1605), 249; Kilby, *Burthen*, 33; Foxe, *Actes and monuments* (1563), 1348.
[73] See, for example, Erasmus, *Enchiridion*, 27, 35, 90; cf. Richard Hooker, *Of the Laws of Ecclesiastical Polity: Book V*, ed. W. Speed Hill (Cambridge, MA, 1977), 292–3.
[74] Hutchins, *Davids Sling*, fo. 4v, p. 5; Byfield, *Marrow of the Oracles* (1622), 540; Bod MS Rawl D.384 fo. 1r.
[75] Winthrop, *Papers*, 194.
[76] Ball, *Short treatise*, 171; Brinsley, *True Watch* (1622), I.175–6; Hieron, *Helpe vnto Deuotion* (1608), 61–2; Bayly, *Practise of pietie*, 472; cf. Wilhelm Zepper, *The Art or Skil Well and Fruitfullie to Heare the holy Sermons of the Church*, tr. T. W[ilcox?] (1599: RSTC 26124.5), sig. H5v.

baptismal practice in early modern England, it is that a Sunday morning baptism after the main service was a signal for most of the congregation to get up and leave.[77] When there is a baptism, George Webbe admonished,

> haste not foorth of the Church (as many doe) but continue thy presence, that there thou mayest aright (vnto thy comfort) consider with thy selfe thine owne receiuing, heretofore into the visible body of Christs Church.[78]

Believers were urged to stay, not only to meditate on their own baptisms, but to pray for the infant, and to celebrate the increase of the Church. We are told that 'at the baptisme of an Infant newly borne, the ioy of the godlye is . . . amplified', but there is not much direct evidence for this. Evidence of attendance at strangers' baptisms is thin. Margaret Hoby once 'went to the church because there was a child baptised, and a sermon'—and that on a Thursday; but presumably the sermon was the bait that hooked her. When Richard Stonley attended a baptism in his London parish church in 1581, he did so more to collect evidence of the minister's nonconformity than to celebrate a new member of God's kingdom.[79]

In other words, most of those attending baptisms were friends and family. This determined their experience. Godparents, we are told, 'take inwardly a close and hid pleasure touching the Rite and facion of the heauenlye mysterie, and of the water of Regeneration, and . . . reioyce on the childes behalfe'—an overstatement, perhaps, but godparenthood was certainly a privilege. Despite some scruples about the persistence of a popish practice, most Protestants accepted that being a godparent was 'a good Christian duety'.[80] But it was the parents, the supposedly present father and the bodily absent mother, for whom the sacrament was most important. When Robert Woodford's daughter Sarah was born in 1638, he recorded his prayers to 'sanctify my child for the ordinance of baptisme & sanctify the ordinance to the child, & make the Child thine owne by grace'. A year earlier he had given a detailed account of his newborn son's baptism:

> I and my deare wife prayed in private this morninge to beseech the Lord for his blessinge vppon the sacrament of Baptime to our poore child this day that the inward grace might goe along with the outward signe &c. and that the Lord would make it the Instrument of some service to him in his Church in time to come and a Comfort to vs the parentes and surely the Lord hath heard vs in mercye.

At the service, Woodford was 'much affected' by the sermon, but he had a momentary panic during the sacrament itself. The Prayer Book service followed the medieval pattern of asking the godparents formally to name the child, and indeed it had long been the practice for godparents actually to choose the name, but it was becoming increasingly common for parents to make the decision. The

---

[77] See, for example, Zepper, *Art or Skil*, sig. H5r; Bayly, *Practise of pietie*, 472–3; Egerton, *Boring of the Eare*, 59–60.

[78] Rogers, *Garden* (1616), sig. G2v.

[79] *Short and pretie Treatise*, sig. C5v; Hoby, *Diary*, 174; FSL MS V.a.459 fo. 30r.

[80] *Short and pretie Treatise*, sig. C6r; Leigh, *Mothers blessing*, 26; Will Coster, *Baptism and Spiritual Kinship in Early Modern England* (Aldershot, 2002), part I.

Woodfords had, in keeping with the new fashion, decided to name the child John, 'the name by which I and my wife vsed to call it before it was borne'. However, once it was too late, Woodford realized he had forgotten to tell the godparents. Apparently reluctant to make a scene, he decided to 'wayt on god'. Happily, the boy was christened John in any case. Perhaps Woodford's own mother, who was acting as godmother to her grandson, had kept matters on the rails.[81]

Rose Hickman had a more dramatic experience. Like many Protestant parents during the 1550s, she feared that Catholic baptism was intolerably idolatrous. When she had a child early in Mary I's reign, she sought theological advice as to whether she could accept popish baptism in good conscience. She was assured that she could—for while Protestant theologians saw the Catholic baptismal rite as corrupt, they generally accepted its validity. Hickman complied, reluctantly. She did surreptitiously exchange the salt used during the rite for sugar, 'bicause I would avoide the popish stuff as much as I could', but her decision weighed on her conscience. By the time her next child was born, she was in exile in Antwerp, and she determined not to compromise again. She hid the baby, even though this risked a charge of Anabaptism which could have had the entire family killed. Eventually, 'some godly weomen' conveyed the child to 'a secret congregation of protestants', where the baptism was performed clandestinely. She herself was of course not present—in any case the entire rite would have been in Flemish. She never met the godparents, and seems never to have had any other contact with this congregation.[82] It is a revealing tale. For Hickman, it was evidently a matter of life and death not only to avoid popish rites, but also to seek out good Protestant ones. She or her husband could have baptized the child themselves, which would have been valid, if irregular, but instead, she risked her own life and her family's lives to have the baptism performed in secret, by strangers, in a foreign language.

What Antwerp's beleaguered Protestants made of this Englishwoman, we can only guess. It was brave of them to do as she asked, but if they were like their British co-religionists, not many of them would have paid too much attention to the event, except perhaps as a means of recalling their own baptisms. This, it seems, was both the secret and the extent of this sacrament's emotional power: it was personal. For parents and godparents, it was a moment of life-changing importance. If it was just another mewling infant in an age well-supplied with them, the whole business could be a little tedious, unless you could personalize it by meditating on your own, irrecoverably lost baptism. But even if you had better things to do on a Sunday afternoon than to haul yourself to yet another baptism, there was power in the knowledge that once upon a time, out beyond the reach of memory, it had been you. Promises had been made, a name had been given, a seal had been sealed which bound you, as an individual, into the covenanted community. Small comfort, perhaps, but in the desert, even a memory of the promise of water is worth retaining.

[81] Woodford, 'Diary', 20.viii.1637 recto–verso, 29.viii.1638 verso.
[82] BL Additional MS 43827A fos 14r–v, 17r–18r.

THE LORD'S SUPPER

In most post-Reformation parishes, baptism was an everyday event to which little attention was paid. The other sacrament, most commonly called the Lord's Supper, was celebrated much more rarely but could hardly have been more prominent in Protestants' minds.[83] It was a sacrament of unity, amongst many other things, but was bitterly divisive. Many more people in 16th-century England and Scotland died for their views on this sacrament than for any other Christian doctrine. For Reformed Protestants, the Catholic Mass was intolerable idolatry; for Catholics, the Reformed view and practice were intolerable blasphemies.[84]

The sacrament's central place in Christian piety both changed and persisted across the Reformation divide. Where the Mass had been a weekly or daily part of people's lives, the Lord's Supper was a rarity: perhaps celebrated three times a year, perhaps once, perhaps—especially in Scotland—not even that.[85] That was the pattern, not of the medieval Mass, but of medieval communion: for now, unlike in pre-Reformation world, every celebration of the sacrament was to be public, and all the people were invited to participate (Figure 15). It was one of the persistent frustrations of Protestant ministers and theologians that they were unable to break the popular pattern of receiving communion once or at most thrice a year. Some aspired to monthly or even weekly communion—an aspiration which, as Arnold Hunt's seminal essay on this topic pointed out, united earnest puritans and ceremonialists. Some ministers imposed more frequent communions, but could not compel the people to take part. Even the thrice-yearly reception that the Book of Common Prayer formally required proved unenforceable. Most people did as their medieval forebears had done: they received once a year, at or near Easter, and no more.[86]

That said, it is fundamental to understanding the sacrament's place in Protestant piety to realize that the invitation was far from universal. Only competent, adult Christians were welcome at the holy table. 'Fooles and children' were excluded, on the grounds that they 'cannot examine themselves'. The question was quite who fell into those categories. What, for example, about 'ignorant persons'?[87] In the Scottish church, local kirk sessions controlled admission to communion, and so both education and morals were commonly used to assess would-be communicants.[88] However, England's rule, laid down by the Elizabethan visitation articles,

---

[83] There is no neutral term for this sacrament. 'Mass' and 'the sacrament of the altar' imply Catholic doctrines; 'Lord's Supper' or 'Holy Communion' imply Protestant ones. 'Eucharist'—literally, 'thanksgiving'—suits both Catholics and Reformed Protestants, for different reasons, but not Lutherans. I use 'Lord's Supper' here simply as the most common early modern British Protestant usage.

[84] Lee Palmer Wandel, *The Eucharist in the Reformation* (Cambridge, 2006).

[85] Andrew Spicer, '"Accommodating of Thame Selfis to Heir the Worde": Preaching, Pews and Reformed Worship in Scotland, 1560–1638', *History* 88 (2003), 408.

[86] Arnold Hunt, 'The Lord's Supper in Early Modern England', *Past and Present* 161 (1998), 41–55.

[87] Dyke, *Worthy communicant*, 109; Pemble, *Introduction to worthy receiving*, sig. A2v. Cf. FSL MS V.a.436 p. 73.

[88] Todd, *Protestant culture*, 74–83.

Fig. 15. Richard Day, *A Booke of Christian Prayers* (1578: RSTC 6429), sig. M1v. A unique Elizabethan depiction of the English communion service. Communicants kneel around an unrailed table.

Bodleian Library, Oxford.

admitted anyone who could recite the Lord's Prayer, Creed, and Ten Commandments in English. Several reforming bishops had pioneered this in the reigns of Henry VIII and Edward VI, but it quickly came to seem too bare a minimum. Archbishop Grindal's 1571 injunctions for the diocese of York applied that test to those aged over twenty-four, but he expected those aged between fourteen and twenty-four—that is, those who had come to maturity under Protestant rule—to be able to recite the entire Prayer Book catechism.[89] Seventeenth-century commentators routinely worried that communicants were simply parroting texts, and were taking part merely 'because they are now at yeares of discretion, and must doe as others doe'. Yet English ministers had no legal right to exclude those who reached the Elizabethan standard. Attempts to do so could become fiercely contentious—although we must assume that, in many parishes, ministers could impose subtly or even drastically stricter tests on their own authority, and make them stick.[90]

As to age, the implication of Grindal's injunctions is that fourteen was the normal age of first communion, but if so that was at best a rule of thumb. Susan Wright's careful study of the subject guessed that sixteen was the commonest age of first communion in the 18th century, but admitted that 'concrete evidence is hard to find'.[91] Arthur Wodenoth was fourteen when he came to London and took his first

[89] Frere and Kennedy, *Visitation Articles*, II.17, 20–1, III.3; Hooper, *Later Writings*, 132–3; Grindal, *Remains*, 125.

[90] Pemble, *Introduction to worthy receiving*, 21; Hunt, 'Lord's Supper', 63–8; Christopher Haigh, 'Communion and community: exclusion from communion in post-Reformation England', *Journal of Ecclesiastical History* 51 (2000), 721–40.

[91] Susan J. Wright, 'Confirmation, catechism and communion: the role of the young in the post-Reformation Church' in her *Parish, Church and People: Local Studies in Lay Religion 1350–1750* (1988), 216–17. The later Anglican practice of governing admission to communion through the rite of confirmation was scarcely observed in this period. Indeed, while confirmation was a topic of some limited controversy, it hardly registered in the Protestant devotional life. Hooker, *Laws . . . Book V*, 320–30.

communion, as was Thomas Goodwin when he went up to Cambridge and took his. But fourteen was a common age for leaving home, and that, rather than numerical age, may have been the decisive factor in their cases. Elizabeth Isham and her younger brother and sister all received their first communion together, when she was seventeen; her siblings' exact ages are not known. Again, the prompt seems to have been a change of life rather than the calendar: their mother had recently died. George Herbert, who opposed a simple age-based rule for admission to communion, worried that 'children and youths are usually deferred too long . . . for want of Instruction'.[92] The implication is that some ministers, unable to impose a rigorous test of knowledge, were using age as a proxy, and indeed, in Scotland, where kirk-session discipline allowed the old and ignorant to be excluded, the young and zealous were able to take their first communions rather earlier. Robert Blair was admitted at age eleven; James Melville and the newly married Jean Stewart at thirteen.[93]

Ministers, in other words, faced opposing problems. They had to police admission to communion, excluding those who wanted to receive, but also to encourage more frequent reception. The stereotypical lay person, apparently, clamoured for communion once a year, but had no interest in more. The rationale for this odd position takes us some way into the subject, because the paradox is echoed in ministers' exhortations. They urged their people to come to communion, and dismissed their qualms about doing so, but at the same time they stressed that it was not to be done lightly. Jeremiah Dyke wrote that

> a man should so prepare himselfe for the Sacrament, as he would prepare himselfe for his death, look how he would be loth to goe to his grave, so should he be loth to go to the Lords Table.[94]

This was hardly an appealing invitation, but Protestant preachers of every stripe, like their medieval predecessors, insisted that to receive communion was to take your life in your hands. For John Cosin, it was 'this dreadfull Sacrament'; Christopher Sutton warned that God would strike dead those who received unworthily; John Dod called it the 'bane and destruction of dogges and swine, that dare presume to meddle with the same'. These fears were not metaphorical. St Paul had warned that those who received unworthily might fall ill or die, and early modern Protestants were ready to believe that this meant them.[95]

No wonder, then, if, as Sutton claimed, some lay people decided that 'it seemeth more safe to abstaine from often communicating'.[96] One argument was that 'the often receiuing of this Sacrament may breede a disesteeme thereof', turning it into something everyday.

---

[92] Wodenoth, 'Expressions', 120; Goodwin, *Works*, II.lii; Isham, 'Confessions', fo. 20r; Herbert, *Works*, 258.

[93] Blair, *Life*, 6–7; Melville, *Autobiography*, 23; Wariston, *Diary*, 4–6.

[94] Dyke, *Worthy communicant*, 100.

[95] Cosin, *Collection of Priuate Devotions*, 296; Sutton, *Godly meditations* (1613), 180–1; Dod and Cleaver, *Ten sermons*, 2; cf. Bradshaw and Hildersam, *Direction*, 5–6; I Corinthians 11:30; and see, for example, Wodenoth, 'Expressions', 120.

[96] Sutton, *Godly meditations* (1601), 269.

Those which often communicate . . . come coldly and without deuotion, and as it were customarily to the holy table, and no more adoe, but they which come seldome, come with farre greater deuotion and reuerence.[97]

Protestant divines simply tended, unconvincingly, to deny that this was true, but much the more serious problem was personal unworthiness. Those who were conscious of their own sins, or believed that they were inadequately prepared, were often deeply reluctant to receive.[98] Some of our most earnest Protestants felt the force of these concerns. On Good Friday 1619, Anne Clifford 'found my mind so troubled as I held not myself fit to receive Communion this Easter', and the whole house's communion was duly postponed. There was a communion in August 1635 'to which', Samuel Rogers wrote, 'I dare not go'.[99] Nehemiah Wallington had more than one such crisis. As a young man, he once went to church on a communion day but was 'so troubled in my mind' that he could not receive: he burst into tears, ran home and shut himself in his chamber. Some twenty years later, sleeping with a troubled conscience the night before a communion, he dreamed of 'a thing like a man all in blacke ready to destroy me', and woke terrified. He concluded that 'now I was unfit to goe to the sacrament: which thought made me to watter my couch'. However, observing his grief, he eventually decided that he would go to communion after all, 'knowing it is apointed for true repenttant sinners'.[100]

The divines who addressed these problems were better at pouring scorn on them than at resolving them. Those who had scruples about receiving communion unprepared, or when conscious of sin, were not reassured that it was all right to do so. Rather, they were simply told that they should not be in those conditions. Being sinful was bad; being compelled to miss communion because you were sinful was worse, and so the best advice was, don't be sinful, or at least repent immediately. 'No man ought to come that finds himselfe vnprepared', Arthur Hildersam wrote, 'but this is no excuse' for those in that situation: they have chosen to be unprepared, or to remain in sin, and so condemn themselves. Indeed, there was an absolute duty to receive the sacrament 'without faile, as often as occasion is offered',[101] which was hardly helpful. If you were one of those ordinary mortals whose attention to your religion was somewhat intermittent, this was a sharp dilemma. You had a duty to receive, but might condemn yourself in so doing. The unspoken implication was that, if you were not one of the elect, it hardly mattered, since it only underlined your damnation. William Bradshaw's popular communion handbook taught that communicants had a duty 'neuer to giue ouer searching & trying our selues, vntill we finde . . . graces in vs', but never bothered

[97] Tozer, *Directions for a Godly Life*, 41–2; Sutton, *Godly meditations* (1601), 267–73.

[98] Tymme, *Siluer watch-bell* (1605), 273; Bradshaw and Hildersam, *Direction*, II.67; Dod and Cleaver, *Ten sermons*, 14, 123; Cowper, *Triumph*, 258–66; Tozer, *Directions for a Godly Life*, 43–50; Hunt, 'Lord's Supper', 48–50.

[99] Clifford, *Diaries*, 70; Rogers, *Diary*, 26.

[100] Wallington, *Notebooks*, 38, 153–4.

[101] Bradshaw and Hildersam, *Direction*, II.67; Tozer, *Directions for a Godly Life*, 28. Cf. Cowper, *Triumph*, 251; Perkins, *Whole treatise*, 336–8.

explaining what to do if you could not find such graces. Henry Tozer's communicants' guide similarly urged would-be communicants to consider 'whether wee be in the number of the faithfull or not', on the grounds that to receive faithlessly is damnable, but he did not consider what you should do if self-examination produced the answer 'no'.[102] Presumably, your obligation was to line up and to eat and drink your condemnation in an orderly fashion.

Unsurprisingly, then, most lay people seem to have stuck with something like the medieval pattern of annual reception, fulfilling their duty without courting needless danger. Their reward was scorn from the pulpit. Thomas Adams dismissed 'once a yeare renewing thy acquaintance with God in the sacrament' as contemptuous of God. Others mocked those 'who thinke it sufficient to liue precisely that day, in which they receiue'; or those 'ignorant Protestants', the 'ordinary sort of people', who when they come to receive

> cannot tell how to looke, which way to turne themselves about any holy meditations: many times their mindes are like a clocke thats over-wound above his ordinary pitch, and so stands still; their thoughts are amazed at the height of these mysteries, and for the time they are like a blocke, thinking nothing at all.[103]

But it seems only natural that these people—devout enough, at least for the time being—should be perplexed by the fearful wonder to which they were called.

Even their more zealous brethren might baulk at weekly or even monthly communion, simply because the recommended regimes of preparation were so arduous and time-consuming. A sustained effort was necessary to ensure that you did not come to communion, as Jeremiah Dyke's influential *A vvorthy communicant* put it, 'piping hot out of the world'. Instead, you should 'collect together all the powers and faculties of the soule, to attend upon the businesse now in hand', and soften the wax of your heart to receive the seal of the Spirit. To receive inadequately prepared, even if not actually damnable, was at best futile: you could expect to 'depart without all comfort and assurance of Gods fauour'.[104]

Enough Protestants took this seriously to generate a strong market for communion-preparation handbooks. Some popular treatises on the sacrament, such as William Bradshaw's *Direction for the weaker sort of Christians* (ten editions, 1609–36) focused exclusively on preparation. Dyke might claim, contemptuously, that 'the preparation, specially of the younger sort, is to put on their best dresse', and add that such people had 'not so much as a preparation-houre', but for those unused to heroic devotional exercises, an hour might seem pretty daunting. Even Dyke admitted that most people believed that 'that there must bee somewhat done before they come, and therefore there must bee at least some sorrow, or shew of sorrow'. Arthur Hildersam claimed than before a communion

---

[102] Bradshaw and Hildersam, *Direction*, 109; Tozer, *Directions for a Godly Life*, 65.
[103] Adams, *The white devil*, 33; Tozer, *Directions for a Godly Life*, 167; Pemble, *Introduction to worthy receiving*, 9.
[104] Dyke, *Worthy communicant*, 260, 266, 448; Dod and Cleaver, *Ten sermons*, 54.

men (if they have any spark of grace in them) are apt to find in themselves some stirrings of their affections unto goodnesse, some motions of Gods spirit, some dispositions unto devotion, and remorse for sinne.

At such times almost all Christian hearts are 'moire easie to be wrought upon'.[105] If you were ever serious about your religion, this was the time. Quite *how* serious was another matter. Sir Edward Rodney's instruction to devote a full week to conscious preparation is extreme, but it was not unusual to speak of spending 'som dayes before' in preparation, or of 'many daies of private humiliation and prayer'. William Cowper alluded in this context to the Jewish practice of spending four days in preparation for the Passover, although he did not explicitly recommend it as a model. Sutton recommended three days of preparation, although he also praised the regime followed by 'a certaine virgine' who spent two days. Archibald Johnston of Wariston recorded spending the Wednesday and the Friday afternoons before a Sunday communion in preparative prayer.[106] Not many people could spare the time, or muster the discipline, for such regimes. But those who prepared more briefly could nevertheless be very conscious of the coming communion as the date drew nearer. Anne Clifford described how 'all this Lent I intended' to receive at Easter. 'Ever against a Communion', John Winthrop wrote, 'the neerer it grewe, the more would Sathan labour . . . to steale from me all appetite unto it.'[107] Neither diarist is exactly describing a regime of preparation, but there is certainly an intense awareness of a coming red-letter day.

For most communicants, the serious business of preparation began, at best, 'towards the end of the foregoing day'—this was the minimum on which Dyke insisted.[108] Sutton recommended taking little or no supper on the Saturday night, and then withdrawing yourself from company 'to spende a good part of the night in preparing thy mind for the daye following'. Wariston, preparing for an admittedly special communion—it was the week before his wedding—spent much of the Saturday night in or near the church building, making a catalogue of his sins. After midnight he 'cryed to the Lord from 2 hours to 6 in ane old barne'. That was extreme, but early rising on a communion day was commonplace.[109] William, Lord Russell's funeral sermon recounted how he had received communion three days before his death:

> Hee rose out of his bed that day before Sunne-rising, albeit hee was very weake, and caused himselfe to be apparelled; and then did wee pray together all of vs . . . and spent some three or foure houres, in continuall eyther prayer or speech about the SACRAMENT.[110]

---

[105] Dyke, *Worthy communicant*, 43, 159; Hildersam, *Doctrine of Fasting*, 114–15.

[106] FSL MS V.a.520 fo. 3r; Howell, *Epistolæ Ho-Elianæ*, VI.49; Bolton, *Boltons last and learned worke*, sig. C1v; Cowper, *Triumph*, 309; Sutton, *Godly meditations* (1601), 244, 251; Wariston, *Diary*, 4.

[107] Clifford, *Diaries*, 70; Winthrop, *Papers*, 211.

[108] Dyke, *Worthy communicant*, 247; cf. Dyke, *Mystery of selfe-deceiuing*, sig. A5v.

[109] Sutton, *Godly meditations* (1601), 139, 249; Wariston, *Diary*, 8; Tozer, *Directions for a Godly Life*, 144; Knappen, *Two Diaries*, 116.

[110] Walker, *Sermon at the funerals . . .*, 52.

Whether this story is true or not, it was the model to which the pious aspired.

What did such 'preparation' actually entail? In brief, more of the same: the normal discipline of self-examination and repentance, pursued with redoubled zeal. It should, Cowper warned, be 'a singular and extraordinary triall, farre aboue that which euery day wee are to take'. The preparation which Sir Edward Rodney envisaged consisted of

> doubleing or trebleing our ordinary times of prayer hearing and reading of sermons . . . putting of[f] worldly buisnes as much as is possible; giuing more almes then at other times; and conferring with others about the meanes to become a worthy receauer.

So the period of preparation was, in effect, like a Sabbath, but 'more serious': extended and intensified.[111] It was the infrequency of communion which made this both possible and valuable: communions became a kind of punctuation to the year, in which the weekly round of devotions could be roused from its routine. Your 'habituall graces', John Preston urged—the oxymoron was deliberate—should, at communion time, 'be new whetted, new scowred, that they may be bright and shining upon such an occasion'.[112] Prayers specifically written for use before communion modelled this kind of repentance and stirring up of graces, with the hope, as always, that by putting the right words in a devotee's mouth, they might become true.[113] Alternatively, we may suspect that the busy but pious simply recited some of these texts in place of a more arduous and unstructured regime.

One particular preparatory practice is worth noticing: fasting. The Catholic practice had long been to fast before communion, a practice linked not only to penitence but to the doctrine of Christ's bodily presence: his body should not mingle with corruption in the gut. Reformed Protestants were no longer required to do this, and many of them did not. Lady Margaret Hoby, for example, on several occasions mentioned, as a matter of course, that she had had breakfast before receiving.[114] But many earnest Protestants either continued to observe pre-sacramental fasting, or had rediscovered the practice. Robert Blair's first communion took place when he was eleven, in 1604 or 1605: it was not premeditated, but during the service he

> was greatly ravished in my spirit . . . and desired earnestly to communicate; but having gotten my breakfast I durst not; for it was then a generall received opinion, that the sacrament behoved to be received fasting.

---

[111] Cowper, *Triumph*, 308; FSL MS V.a.520 fo. 3v; Brinsley, *True Watch* (1622), I.179; Dyke, *Worthy communicant*, 247.

[112] Preston, *Three Sermons*, 44; cf. Bradshaw and Hildersam, *Direction*, 111.

[113] See, for example, Day, *Booke of Christian Prayers*, fos 89v–93v; Hunnis, *Seuen Sobs*, 'Honeysuckles' 82–6; Norden, *Pensiue mans practise*, 236; Prid, *Glasse of Vaine-glorie* (1600), sigs G10v–11r; Hieron, *Helpe vnto Deuotion* (1608), 72–7; Sorocold, *Supplications of Saints* (1612), 203–7; Sutton, *Godly meditations* (1613), 320–1; Tuke, *Practise of the faithfull*, 144–8; Bayly, *Practise of pietie*, 565–76.

[114] Philip Benedict, *Christ's Churches Purely Reformed: A Social History of Calvinism* (New Haven and London, 2002), 493; Hoby, *Diary*, 64, 75, 76, 91, 148, 167, 168, 178, 192.

However, as he prayed the matter over, it occurred to him that Christ had instituted the sacrament after supper, and 'so at the next table I sat down and communicated'. In Ayrshire, then, fasting was a 'generall received opinion' but not an enforced rule. Elsewhere in Scotland, the decision might not have been down to Blair's conscience. St Andrews' kirk session enforced sacramental fasting.[115] In England, as usual, matters were laxer. 'It matters not, whether they come fasting or not', pronounced William Perkins, but this permissive attitude seems to have masked widespread observance. 'Are you bound to come fasting to this sacrament?', Robert Hill asked in his communicant's handbook, and answered no. But he added that 'I thinke it fit to come rather fasting, than feasting, to this banquet', since all of the spiritual benefits generally associated with fasting applied with additional force in this circumstance. Hildersam, while clear that requiring fasting would be 'meere ignorance and superstition', did believe that 'it be fit for such as may conueniently doe it'.[116]

The voluntary nature of Protestant sacramental fasting also allowed for heroic over-achievement. One Wednesday, in the midst of his spiritual crisis, Wariston heard that there was to be a communion at Kirkcaldy the coming Sunday, and vowed to fast for the entire intervening period. He had to cross the Firth of Forth to get there, and in his weakened state he was horribly seasick, but he had his reward, as his diary—addressed to himself—recorded:

> Quhen thou was sitting at the taible, saule, never forget hou al thy body trimbled, and thy reins and syds brunt the for heat, and pained the with paine out of an excessive ardoure quherwith thou prayed to the Almightie. . . . At the taking of the cupe both thy head and thy hand so tottered and trimbled as almost thou could not get drunken; al sau it and wondred at it. . . . God never so praepaired the to ane comunion; never so moved the at on.[117]

Respectable theologians—especially English ones—would have frowned on such an extreme fast, but the sacrament was a moment for extremity, and Wariston's self-imposed regime was distinctive only in extent, not in nature. Fasting to prepare for a sacrament of eating and drinking appealed to Protestantism's love of paradox. When Jane Ratcliffe received the sacrament, we are told, 'she felt such a sweet refreshing as might make amends for the severity of her frequent fasting'.[118] This fasting need not be immediately before the sacrament at all: increasingly, the Scottish practice was to hold a series of fast days in the run-up to a communion, commonly on the preceding Sunday and perhaps also on the intervening Wednesday or Friday.[119] The point was not to receive the body of Christ with an empty

---

[115] Blair, *Life*, 6–7; McMillan, *Worship of the Scottish Reformed Church*, 198.

[116] Perkins, *Whole treatise*, 342; Robert Hill, *Christs Prayer expounded. A Communicant prepared. A Christian directed in life* (1607: RSTC 13472.4), 137–9 (cf. Dyke, *Worthy communicant*, 492); Bradshaw and Hildersam, *Direction*, 118–19 (cf. Clarke, *Collection*, 309); and see above, pp. 195–9.

[117] Wariston, *Diary*, 89, 95–7.

[118] Clarke, *Collection*, 428.

[119] McMillan, *Worship of the Scottish Reformed Church*, 226–7.

stomach, but—as John Dod put it, in a passage which makes no explicit reference to fasting—to

> get a thirstie soule. . . . Those onely that feele their owne barrennesse and emptinesse . . . and heartily desire the mercies of God through the merits of Christ: they onely, I say, haue right vnto and shall haue a portion in the same.[120]

As ever, outward fasting was valuable solely as a means to inward devotion.

So its purpose was the purpose of all sacramental preparation: to plumb depths in order to scale heights.[121] As Dyke put it:

> A prepared heart is a vessell that shall be filled at the Sacrament. . . . Fill such mens hearts with spirituall blessings . . . says the Lord at the Sacrament, fill them with spirituall food as ful as they can hold, as much as they can carry. . . . The larger is our preparation; the larger our Vessell.[122]

The sacrament became a climax of relief, assurance, and joy. Fasting only made this plainer, as a morsel of bread fed a hungry mouth, but well-breakfasted believers too could, if they had meditated adequately on their sins, 'come with an hungring and thirsting soule vnto thy table . . . to receiue strength and growth of assurance'. Hence the archetypal pre-sacramental prayer 'to hunger & thirst after this holy supper of the Lord'.[123] If communicants could truly feel their desperate need for the sacrament, that made the moment of reception all the sweeter.

This process of deliberately working up a pitch of devotion peaked during the service itself, which was anyway a drawn-out affair. In an English church, there was all the normal business of morning prayer, and then typically a sermon, before the focus turned to the holy table more than two hours into the proceedings. There then followed a long series of prayers and exhortations, during which the elements were prepared and blessed. This interval was unique in the experience of early modern Protestant worship, in that the people were encouraged not simply to pray with the minister, but to use his prayer and actions as a basis for their own, independent devotions. In particular, they were to do so during the lengthy process of actually administering communion to a church full of people. There might be music during this interval,[124] or there might simply be shuffling feet, creaking knees, and the murmur of the minister's voice. In either case, most people were left to their own prayers for most of the time, in an echo of medieval practices. Books of prayers routinely provided devotions to be said at this point, suggesting that some individuals would bring their own private prayer-books with them to church, and sit or kneel murmuring over them.[125] Strikingly, these prayers—to be said in a

---

[120] Dod and Cleaver, *Ten sermons*, 138–9.
[121] See above, pp. 38–9.
[122] Dyke, *Worthy communicant*, 45, 47–8.
[123] Hieron, *Helpe vnto Deuotion* (1608), 75; cf. Brinsley, *True Watch* (1622), I.181–2; Mildmay, 'Meditations', II.151–2.
[124] Nicholas Temperley, *The Music of the English Parish Church* (Cambridge, 1979), I.49; cf. Goodwin, *Works*, II.lii.
[125] For example, Sutton, *Godly meditations* (1601), 178; Bayly, *Practise of pietie*, 593–4; Cosin, *Collection of Priuate Devotions*, 291–301.

building full of worshipping Christians celebrating a sacrament of unity—were frequently written in the singular. In Thomas Becon's *The Flour of godly praiers*, the prayers to be said at communion are the only prayers in a long book to be so written. Another prayer on this theme begins in the plural but slips into the singular during its course.[126] At this crux of Christian devotion, collective worship gave way to the individual soul standing before God to receive—or be denied—its own assurance.

This atomization of the congregation can also be seen before the actual communion, when the table, bread and wine were prepared. During this part of the service, we are, as John Brinsley taught, 'to labour . . . to bring our hearts to an inward feeling of all that which outwardly is done'. That did not mean listening to the words spoken by the minister as much as watching and mediting on the recreation of Christ's Passion being played out at the table.[127] As Robert Bruce told his Edinburgh congregation:

> Sa oft as yee looke on it, yee sall not sa soone see that bread with your eie, but the bodie of Christ sall come in your mind: Yee sall not sa soone see that wine, but . . . the bloode of Christ sall come in your mind.[128]

Every step of the action was allegorized. The offering of the elements recalls God's offer of his son; the peoples' hands receiving them recall the importance of faith. Above all, the breaking of the bread and pouring of the wine recall, or represent, Christ's Passion. 'We see Christ crucified before our eyes; now we see him hanging, and bleeding upon the crosse.' When you see the bread broken, William Pemble urged, 'thinke on Christ torne and rent in his precious body with stripes and wounds'.[129] The claim that the minister's actions were a compelling visual recreation of Christ's sufferings may seem implausible, but association, instruction, and sheer devotional willpower made it so. It may also seem profoundly medieval, and in one sense it is, but not uncomplicatedly. Rather, it was the absolute and (increasingly) untroubled Protestant rejection of any doctrine of bodily presence which allowed them to embrace such vivid symbolism. Since there was no danger of believing that Christ's body really was present, it was possible to use the elements to meditate with dazzling intensity on his true body's past sufferings and present glory.

The crescendo was supposed to come when you finally knelt, or sat, and received. No spoken response was required from early modern communicants, but several books of prayers provided prayers or meditations 'to bee sayed at the receiuynge' of the elements. Unless communicants were receiving with an open

---

[126] Becon, *Flour of godly praiers*, fos 111v–114r; Day, *Booke of Christian Prayers*, fos 89v–93v. Cf. Tuke, *Practise of the faithfull*, 114–18, 149–52.

[127] Brinsley, *True Watch* (1622), I.181–2; Hunt, 'Lord's Supper', 59–60.

[128] Bruce, *Sermons vpon the Sacrament*, sig. C7r.

[129] Dyke, *Worthy communicant*, 519; Pemble, *Introduction to worthy receiving*, 8. Cf. *This booke is called the Treasure of gladnesse*, fo. 68v; Bradshaw and Hildersam, *Direction*, 123–7; Dod and Cleaver, *Ten sermons*, 14–15, 133; Brinsley, *True Watch* (1622), I.183–5; Tuke, *Practise of the faithfull*, 148; Rogers, *Garden* (1616), sig. G3r; Bayly, *Practise of pietie*, 591–3, 599–606; Tozer, *Directions for a Godly Life*, 150–7; Valentine, *Private Devotions*, 181–2.

book in one hand, such prayers were presumably either memorized or, more likely, intended as models rather than texts to be used verbatim.[130] Some later works suggest broad topics for meditation rather than specific words to be said. The commonest theme of such meditations was the struggle to 'apply to our selues all the merits of Christs passion'. This might take the form of praying for particular graces or confessing particular sins, or of reflecting that through the communion 'surely Christ is made one with vs, and we with him, and then our soules shall be strengthned, and our hartes spiritually reuiued'.[131] But if some prayers were abstract and allegorical, others could be shockingly vivid. When receiving the wine, Lewis Bayly urged,

> in the instant of drinking, settle thy meditation vpon Christ, as he hanged vpon the Crosse . . . wishing thy mouth closed to his side, that thou mightest receiue that precious bloud before it fell to the dusty earth.[132]

If you were hungry and thirsty enough, you had 'applied' the sacrament already.

The reward could—when it worked—be overwhelming. Devotional writers lined up to promise their readers that, 'provided a man so come to it as he ought', the sacrament would bring 'sudden refreshings falling like the dew vponhis heart', 'great peace and tranquility of the minde', 'the ioies of Gods presence . . . inwardly sealing in his heart the perswasion of his interest in Gods promises'. These claims were clichés, and no doubt more joy was professed than was felt, but plainly much of it was very real.[133] Wariston's religious turmoil was punctuated by communions at which God 'delt wonderfully' with him. Robert Bruce cited what Protestant communicants regularly 'taisted and felt in their sauls' as evidence of the truth of their doctrines. Grace Mildmay had this to say on communion:

> Let us take our fill of this pleasure, let us enter into this paradise, let us lift up our eyes and stretch out our hands and eat our fill of the tree of life, which our Lord Jesus Christ presenteth unto us by the hand of his ministers.[134]

That is exhortation as well as description, but such exhortations create the reality they expect.

First communions could pack a particular punch. John Livingstone recalled that at his, 'there came such an trembling upon me thayt all my body shook'. Thomas Goodwin's 'greatly affect[ed] me . . . I felt my heart cheered after a wonderful manner, thinking myself sure of heaven'. (He later dismissed these feelings as self-deception.) James Melville looked back longingly at the 'reverence and sence, in my saull' which had accompanied his first communion, and which he had all too

---

[130] Becon, *Flour of godly praiers*, 112v–114r; cf. Norden, *Pensiue mans practise*, 239; Featley, *Ancilla Pietatis*, 100–1.

[131] Bradshaw and Hildersam, *Direction*, II.126; Dod and Cleaver, *Ten sermons*, 15; cf. Bayly, *Practise of pietie*, 600; Featley, *Ancilla Pietatis*, 100–1.

[132] Bayly, *Practise of pietie*, 603.

[133] Dyke, *Worthy communicant*, 167; Byfield, *Marrow of the Oracles* (1622), 177; Sutton, *Godly meditations* (1601), 52–3; Byfield, *The Signes*, 126; Hunt, 'Lord's Supper', 57–8.

[134] Wariston, *Diary*, 1; Bruce, *Sermons vpon the Sacrament*, H8r; Mildmay, *With Faith and Physic*, 77.

rarely recaptured.[135] Arthur Wodenoth's first communion, by contrast, was apparently a formalistic and lifeless affair, but having keenly repented of this, he did not have enough superlatives to describe his second:

> The highest pinnacle of Solomon's glory did noe more transcend the lowest depth of Job's misery, then the ioy I now had, did the greatest comfort which before I ever felt. . . . As they have not felt it cannot imagine it, so neither can they that have, fully express it.[136]

Lettice Cary even claimed that, for her, each communion was more intense than the last: 'at the receiving of the blessed Sacrament my heart is still more enlarged, and more elevated with heavenly comforts'. Like others, she measured that enlargement and elevation in her tears. Sutton, by contrast, called the sacrament 'an end of tears', a sentiment which evidently struck a chord in the reader who marked this passage in one copy. Perhaps this meant that the sacrament was, for Sutton and his reader, a moment of unalloyed rejoicing, or perhaps one (or both) of them was trying to explain away the awkward fact that receiving sometimes left them dry-eyed.[137]

Sometimes it could be an anticlimax. One of the purposes of the meditations for communicants seems simply be to aid concentration. A moment's distraction—paying attention to your neighbour's new coat rather than to your Lord's sacrifice—could undo all the work of preparation. Communicants prayed against 'idle and gadding thoughts' or 'an vnstayed or wandring minde' at the moment of reception. Sutton suggested such simple thoughts for communicants as 'O God thou art good! O Soule thou art happy!', which could achieve little more than keep your mind on the job by brute force.[138] Most divines chose to ignore this problem, but a few confronted it. Many even of the elect, Ezekiel Culverwell regretted, 'seldome or never attaine that comfort by the holy Sacraments, which indeede they ought and might'. Perhaps, Jeremiah Dyke suggested, you have come to communion but, instead of 'comfortable refreshment . . . thou hast gone away with a dead, a sad, a drooping, an uncomfortable spirit'? If so, it was your own fault. 'We come with dead, livelesse, formall, narrow, straight, and closed hearts', stoppered against the Spirit, and then have the audacity to complain that God has not filled them. Perkins was more forgiving. Sometimes, he accepted, 'in the very instant of receiuing', a believer will 'feele his heart so hard, that he cannot lift it vp vnto God', but he counselled that 'the benefit of the Sacrament, is not tied to the very instant of receiuing'. What mattered was not that moment, but what followed.[139]

[135] Tweedie, *Select Biographies*, 132; Goodwin, *Works*, II. lii; Melville, *Autobiography*, 23.

[136] Wodenoth, 'Expressions', 122–3.

[137] Duncon, *Returnes*, 8; cf. Mildmay, *With Faith and Physic*, 29; FSL STC 23494, p. 59. Issues of gender may have been at play here: see above, pp. 191–2.

[138] Hieron, *Helpe vnto Deuotion* (1608), 76; Huntington Library, San Marino, CA, MS 15369 fo. 6v; Sutton, *Godly meditations* (1613), 174.

[139] Culverwell, *Treatise of faith*, 370; Dyke, *Worthy communicant*, 27–8, 468; Perkins, *Whole treatise*, 348.

That might mean the remainder of the service, as you returned to your seat feeling the sacramental wine 'warming thy colde stomacke'. If you had struck emotional gold, this afterglow was the moment to try to coin it into more lasting spiritual treasure. 'Affect me with a taste of this heauenly food', prayed Daniel Featley, 'and continue the relish of it in the mouth of my soule.'[140] But it was also the moment to wring some real spiritual benefit from the sacrament when raptures had not come. Hieron's post-communion prayer begged plainly

> that I may as sensibly feele his death to be sweet vnto my soule, as I do these creatures of bread and wine, to afford a pleasing taste and refreshing to my body. O Lord euermore giue mee such a feeling.[141]

Others counselled that feelings were not what really mattered. For John Dod, the Lord's Supper was 'the seale of the euerlasting couenant of grace', and so utterly trustworthy: whether or not you feel it, you are freed from sin in God's eyes and your faith is strengthened. On this view, the sacrament worked at a deeper level than mere emotion, and that itself constituted its consolation, as the reader who emphasized this passage in one copy seems to have found. A post-communion prayer ascribed to Edward Dering asked for assurance on exactly these grounds.[142] Others were more practical still. Arthur Hildersam and John Brinsley both made willingness to give joyfully to the poorbox at the end of the service a test of the sacrament's effectiveness.[143] The Prayer Book required the collection for the poor to be made before the communion, but the implication is that this was sometimes changed, and if Hildersam and Brinsley were right, it is easy to see why. Those who were genuinely moved by the communion, and those who wished to convince their neighbours or themselves that they had been, might dig that little bit deeper.

Even this was mere froth, however. The real test was not whether the sacrament set off fireworks in your soul, nor whether you emptied your purse into the poorbox, but whether it changed your life. The point was not to experience a temporary high, but to depart 'as Christ went from Jordan, full of the Holy Ghost', 'to become a new Creature'.[144] The devotional literature was full of ample promises of how this ought to work, and of post-communion prayers begging that it should be so. 'I had but a little grip of Christ before', declared Robert Bruce, 'as it were, betwixt my finger and my thoumbe; nowe I get him in my haill hande.' You ought to see, Dod taught, a perceptible and durable improvement in your moral character, and to feel, added Brinsley, 'a further growth in grace, and so thereby, a further confirmation, that wee are in the couenant of grace'. Henry Valentine was exhaustive: the sacrament ought

---

[140] Bayly, *Practise of pietie*, 604; Featley, *Ancilla Pietatis*, 102; cf. Sparke, *Crumms of comfort*, sig. K9v.

[141] Hieron, *Helpe vnto Deuotion* (1608), 78–9.

[142] FSL STC 6945.8, p. 16; Dering, *Mr Dering, his godly priuate prayers*, 238–9.

[143] Bradshaw and Hildersam, *Direction*, II.127–8; Brinsley, *True Watch* (1622), I.185; cf. Bayly, *Practise of pietie*, 619.

[144] Dyke, *Worthy communicant*, 465; Huntington Library, San Marino, CA, MS 15369 fo. 6v.

to quiet my conscience, to increase my faith, to inflame my charity, to amend my life, to save my soul, & to assure me that I am in the number of those blessed ones, who shal eat at thy table.[145]

All too often, it did not.

The hours and days following a communion could all too easily prove a spiritual slump, as normal life reasserted its grip. Samuel Rogers regularly spent post-communion Mondays anxiously watching himself, and lamenting 'that so quickly after a sacrament; my heart should grow dull, and untoward'.[146] The young Thomas Goodwin felt himself trapped in a cycle:

> I still upon every sacrament set myself anew to examine myself, to repent, and to turn to God; but when the sacrament was over, I returned to a neglect of praying, and to my former ways of unregenerate principles and practices.

He had once believed 'that if I received that sacrament, I should be so confirmed that I should never fall away', as well he might if he listened to some of the more loose-tongued preachers. The reality was harsher.[147] Jeremiah Dyke gave a start-lingly frank description of this problem. In preparation for the sacrament, he wrote, we ought to have our 'affections by degrees wound up to some spirituall height . . . to more than an ordinary, and common pitch'. Our post-sacramental duty was, simply, to maintain that state for as long as possible. 'We cannot hold them up in that height, and pitch, to which we have wrought our hearts . . . in the heate of holy exercises, but yet wee should endeavour it what we can.'[148] Reformed Protestants are rarely so open about their emotional self-manipulation.

Others, however, dealt more subtly with the problem. One approach was to see the hours immediately after communion as a time of particular spiritual vulnerabil-ity. Christ had warned of being freed from one demon only to be possessed by seven more. Margaret Hoby seems to have understood her experience of being 'boffeted' by unexpected temptations the day after communion in these terms. Post-communion prayers and exhortations commonly have this sense of peril: 'keepe me that I slippe not', 'be carefull with ioy to carrie [Christ] home with thee'.[149] Sutton, magisterial in his impracticality, suggested that communicants 'vse much silence, and some solitarinesse' for the remainder of the day. His own practice was to 'betake mee to some secreate place that I may talke onely with my Lord' and carry out a thorough spiritual debriefing, as part of a well-paced re-entry to ordinary life.[150]

This assumed that you had some gains to consolidate. If not, the recommended course was to 'endeavour by after paines in prayer, and humiliation to quicken, and awaken the efficacy of the Sacrament'. This was not as hopeless as it sounds.

---

[145] Valentine, *Private Devotions*, 179; Bruce, *Sermons vpon the Sacrament*, sig. G3r; Dod and Cleaver, *Ten sermons*, 38; Brinsley, *True Watch* (1622), I.176–7.

[146] Rogers, *Diary*, 20, 157; cf. 12, for a slightly more successful experience.

[147] Goodwin, *Works*, II.liii.

[148] Dyke, *Worthy communicant*, 598.

[149] FSL MS V.a.394 fo. 5v; Hoby, *Diary*, 168; Sorocold, *Supplications of Saints* (1612), 207; Bayly, *Practise of pietie*, 608.

[150] Sutton, *Godly meditations* (1601), 198, 254–9.

'Sacraments doe not alwaies worke for the present', Dyke reassured his readers, 'but the efficacy may come afterwards.' God runs to his own timetable. 'The Lord doth not alwaies powre his gifts vpon vs, the same day that we come vnto him in his holy ordinances.'[151] It was true of baptism; why not also of the Lord's Supper? And while you were taking the long view, you might also wonder if that sacramental rhythm which so frustrated Goodwin—holiness before followed by relapse after— was as static as you feared. Communion's effects could be cumulative. Sutton compared it to the sun, which warms more us the more we are exposed; Dyke, to food, by which we grow imperceptibly but progressively. This was Grace Mildmay's experience:

> The benefitt of our often receiuing this holy sacrament [is] that we are drawn & holden vp vnto God thereby, & washed and tyed vnto him more & more, by the lynckes, strong chaynes & bands of his loue.[152]

If at one communion you did not succeed in breaking your stony heart, try again.

In other words, we are dealing here with layers of emotional and even physiological games, and of excuses and rationalizations constructed when the games failed to work. Regimes of preparation made the moment of reception an 'emotional release', and earnest prayers for change tended to be self-fulfilling.[153] Plenty of early modern Protestants were easily self-aware enough to know this. They also believed, however, that sometimes the sacrament made possible a genuine transformation, whether subtle or dramatic, and we have to recognize that sometimes such transformations happened. Nehemiah Wallington, who sometimes worried that the sacrament was fruitless for him, also recorded a post-sacramental Monday when he arose at four o'clock to pray, and found that there was 'more sweetnesse to tarry at home and solace my soule with the Lord then there could be in . . . all the delight and pleasure the world could aford mee'. The most dramatic religious revival of the entire period—in fact, arguably the first ever Christian 'revival' meeting in the modern sense—took place in Ayrshire in the summer of 1630, the day after an open-air communion festival.[154] More poignant testimony comes from Wariston. As we have seen, he spent the summer of 1633 overwhelmed with grief following his young wife's sudden death, and made repeated attempts to use vows and resolutions to jolt himself back onto an even keel. None of these worked; after a day or two, he was drowning in despair again. What worked, it seemed, was the communion at Kirkcaldy for which he fasted so severely.[155] He did not claim so, although he was certainly intensely aware of the sacrament's emotional power, but his reader cannot help noticing that it marks a genuine turning-point for him, not least because it was immediately followed by the first period of sustained

---

[151] Dyke, *Worthy communicant*, 592; Ball, *Short treatise*, 161; cf. Bradshaw and Hildersam, *Direction*, 131–3; Brinsley, *True Watch* (1622), I.186–7.

[152] Sutton, *Godly meditations* (1601), 73; Dyke, *Worthy communicant*, 401–2; Mildmay, 'Meditations', 30.

[153] Hunt, 'Lord's Supper', 58.

[154] Wallington, *Notebooks*, 160; Tweedie, *Select Biographies*, 346–7; Schmidt, *Holy fairs*, 21–2.

[155] Wariston, Diary, 97–100, and cf. p. 9; see above, p. 135.

contentment he had enjoyed since his bereavement. Perhaps he had finally succeeded in manufacturing a crisis big enough to break the pattern; perhaps time had simply done its work; or perhaps we should be wary of presuming too easily to plumb the depths of this mystery.

EXPERIENCING THE SERMON

The sermon was the defining event of early modern Protestant worship. The preacher, duly called to his—always *his*, of course—vocation by God and recognized by the Church, spoke the word of God to the people. Not that his words were directly inspired, but the faithful hearer's *response* to faithful preaching was a work of the Holy Spirit.[156] The sermon was not simply a means of instruction; it was, in a well-worn truism repeated by Arthur Hildersam, 'the onely ordinary meanes, whereby thou wilt worke Faith and repentance in thy children, and the principall meanes whereby thou wilt increase them'.[157]

That truism has recently been underlined by Arnold Hunt's ground-breaking monograph on preachers and their audiences. Hunt argues that early modern Protestants saw the preached Word as more powerful, even as more authentically the Word of God, than the written Word of the Bible, and that preaching was held to be absolutely necessary for salvation. Some preachers, he suggests, even doubted whether the deaf could be saved, since, as St Paul said, faith comes by hearing. However, these sweeping claims owed more to preachers' hyperbole than to theological rigour or pastoral caution. Hildersam's cliché, after all, came with an escape clause: if preaching was the only *ordinary* means of salvation, that did not preclude extraordinary means, and deafness was obviously an extraordinary situation. The preachers whom Hunt cites were careful to pity the deaf only for their inability to hear the saving Word, not for their inability to be saved. In practice, tales of deaf people who found grace despite their disability were celebrated.[158] That fact itself is telling. Modern readers might be interested in the human rights of the deaf, but early modern preachers used the deaf as rhetorical devices to display God's power—even the deaf can hear him!—and to reprove human sloth—the deaf hear more readily than you! Henry Smith—'Silver-tongued Smith', reputedly one of the finest preachers in Elizabethan London—made this clear in a famous sermon on 'the art of hearing'. Citing a series of Biblical healing miracles, he argued that while God might sometimes strike a person blind or mute as a judgement, he never inflicts deafness. Deafness comes only and always from the Devil.[159] Smith, of course, had almost no interest in literal deafness. It was a metaphor for those who closed their ears to preaching. Of course those who cannot hear can be saved,

---

[156] Mary Morrissey, 'Scripture, Style and Persuasion in Seventeenth-Century English Theories of Preaching', *Journal of Ecclesiastical History* 53/4 (2002), 691.

[157] Hildersam, *Doctrine of Fasting*, sig. b4r.

[158] Hunt, *Art of Hearing*, esp. 21, 24–5, 55.

[159] Smith, *Sermons*, 640.

although, as with those who cannot read, it may be difficult.[160] But those who *will* not hear are already in the mouth of Hell.

The point has a wider significance. Those who praised preaching's virtues were not describing but exhorting, and such exhortations had a very particular target in mind: the casual conformists, the carnal Protestants and the near-atheists who, in the clergy's fears, filled most of their pews. It was a minister's responsibility to bring such people to a more earnest godliness. Preaching was the principal weapon in his arsenal; and the reason such people remained carnal was because they were impervious to it. George Gifford's treatise on what he termed 'the Countrie diuinitie' diagnosed this as the key failing of 'the common sorte of Christians': until they are willing to learn, they cannot be taught. 'Where a man despiseth the word, there can be no fayth.' Arthur Dent's archetypal 'plaine man' longed to be saved 'without all this running to Sermons', but Dent insisted that he could no more be saved without preaching than he could grow fat without eating.[161] This may seem unimaginative, but when all you have is the preacher's hammer, every parishioner looks like a nail. Here is Hildersam again:

> Wouldst thou then have thy heart softned? Bring it to this fire [preaching], if it be as hard as iron it will soften it, and make it plyable; bring it to this anvile where the hammer smiteth, and it will breake it. . . . If this will not soften thy heart, I assure thee nothing will doe it.[162]

The note of despair there is authentic. Preachers extolled preaching as a means of conversion, not because it was exceptionally effective, but because there was no alternative.

Conversion, in other words, was preaching's primary purpose. This is problematic, not only because plenty of people endured numerous sermons without being converted, but also because plenty of people were converted with fairly limited reference to sermons.[163] But there is another difficulty. If preaching was for conversion, what was the role of preaching to the converted? For convinced and earnest believers were, naturally, much the most assiduous sermon-goers. Every earnest early modern Protestant had, or aspired to, a diet of preaching which varied from the routinely hearty to the positively gluttonous. What was their experience of this regime?

For the regenerate, those who had already received their effectual calling, sermons had two linked purposes: exhortation and education. The first was the more straightforward: calling backsliders to repentance and encouraging perseverance in the Christian life. Part of the appeal of sermon-going was the hope that the preacher's words might be, as Samuel Ward put it, bellows to blow on and rekindle the flame of zeal. Nehemiah Wallington 'best approue[d] of that Minister as is most powerfull against my Sinne'; Nicholas Byfield hoped that Christians would 'heare such doctrine daily as will search thy heart and ransacke thy life'.[164] Very similar

---

[160] See above, pp. 259–61.   [161] Gifford, *Briefe discourse*, fo. 31v; Dent, *Plaine mans path-way*, 24–5.

[162] Hildersam, *Doctrine of Fasting*, 104–5.   [163] See below, pp. 436–41.

[164] Ward, *Coal from the Altar*, 42; FSL MS V.a.436 p. 42; Byfield, *Marrow of the Oracles* (1622), 238.

aspirations were attached to the Lord's Supper, and the two were often linked together: 'the word leads vs to christ be the ear: the sacraments leads vs to Christ be the eie'.[165] The parallel with the sacraments could also explain why the bellows of preaching sometimes seemed to blow mere hot air. As with the Lord's Supper, so with the sermon: there might be a delay, sometimes a long delay, before the spiritual benefits were felt, much as a medicine might take time to begin to ease a sufferer's symptoms. 'A Sermon preached seven years before may prove the meanes of a mans conversion seaven yeares after.'[166] That was a powerful assertion of the Spirit's work, but it also tacitly acknowledged a problem: sometimes—usually—preaching of this kind had little immediate effect.

Educational preaching faced a different problem: diminishing returns. Given how highly Protestants valued learning, it is no surprise that they elevated the teaching function of the sermon. A key purpose of preaching was to dispel 'error and darknes about religion', to unlock the hearer's ear so that 'the spirit of knowledge and vnderstanding might passe into the heart'. For Archbishop Sandys, it was 'to nurse the church with wholesome food, till we all grow up to a perfect man in Christ Jesus'.[167] That, however, implies that preaching was something which Christians might eventually outgrow. Preachers, always wary of giving excuses to slug-a-beds, gave no quarter to such implications, but they were easier to denounce than to stamp out. Some Protestants simply did find more nourishment in private study and devotion than in hearing their minister reiterate themes on which they had already heard him preach a dozen times. As Thomas Tymme argued:

> When the Ship commeth to the shoare, the sailes must be stricken, and the Anchor cast. And when man haue attained a competent knowledge of the way and meanes to saluation, they ought to be staied therein, and so then heare lesse, and pray more, and not to shew themselues *Non-proficients*, euer learning, and neuer in practise.[168]

This is not an 'anti-puritan' view, except in the sense that puritans were reluctant to say such things in public. The concern, that as a teaching tool the sermon had progressively less to offer to more experienced Christians, was widely shared.

Worse, the two problems could combine. If the fundamental purposes of preaching were to call the profane to repentance, and to teach them the basics of the faith, what was there for more mature believers? Even if some sermons, such as afternoon or mid-week gatherings, were aimed at smaller, more zealous audiences and could take more for granted, preachers tended to use such opportunities more for exhortation and denunciation than for consolation and counsel.[169] Perhaps the sermon as a genre determined that. In any case, while early modern Protestants

---

[165] Bruce, *Sermons vpon the Sacrament*, sig. B1v; cf. Perkins, *Whole treatise*, 293.

[166] Linaker, *Comfortable treatise* (1595), 62–3, 171; Dyke, *Worthy communicant*, 593–4; and see above, pp. 349–50.

[167] Rogers, *Seven treatises*, 215; Robert Wilkinson, *A Iewell for the Eare* (c.1602: RSTC 25652.7), sig. A4v; Sandys, *Sermons*, 44.

[168] Tymme, *Chariot of Devotion*, sig. A3r–v.

[169] Hunt, *Art of Hearing*, 209–11, 221.

fully expected their faith to be joyful, and often experienced it as such, they rarely exhibited or communicated such joy in their preaching. 'The voyce of a preacher', Thomas Playfere taught, 'ought to be the voyce of a cryer, which should not pype to make the people daunce, but mourne to make them weepe.'[170] For these and other reasons, even the most zealous believer might find attendance at sermons becoming a duty. As Ezekiel Culverwell worried, 'woefull experience bewrayeth that too too many (and those not of the worst sort) doe finde small comfort in the ordinary ministery of the Word'.[171]

This was not only because of such structural problems. Some preachers were simply inaudible, or long-winded, or plain dull. They ran out of ideas: given that a conscientious minister might hold a benefice for decades on end, and preach three times per week or more throughout that period, his listeners might well find as they listened to his thousandth sermon (around seven years in) that they knew in advance exactly what he would say on any given subject. Some preached at too basic a level for their more learned listeners; others were too highfalutin. That last problem is particularly pervasive, since most people's first encounter with the sermon, as children, was probably one of boredom and incomprehension.[172] Richard Norwood, aged twelve, was occasionally moved by sermons but only in a 'very confused and uncertain manner'; Elizabeth Isham, at the same age, was troubled as to 'why I profited no more by others at Church', and concluded that 'I delighted not so much in it because I understood it not'. She later claimed that 'the first time that I aprehended . . . or gave heede to a sermon' was when she was twenty.[173] And these were educated young people of at least tolerably godly families. The incomprehensible sermon was neither exceptional or atypical; rather, it was almost everyone's first experience of preaching, an experience which some people never moved beyond and to which others returned. 'How many', Jeremiah Dyke despaired, 'have lived all their dayes, and are even growne gray under the Gospell, and yet what grace or goodnesse have all the Sermons that ever they have heard wrought in them?'[174]

Naturally, there is another side to this story. Some preachers could transfix congregations. Hugh Latimer could keep his open-air audience standing spellbound in the Devon rain; Robert Bruce 'made always ane earthquake upon his hearers, and rarely preached but to a weeping auditory', and supposedly once even made King James VI cry.[175] (Richard Rogers' feat, of making himself weep during his own sermons, is not quite so impressive.[176]) Although not everyone could be a Latimer, a Bruce, or a Henry Smith, there were celebrity preachers aplenty

---

[170] Playfere, *Meane in Mourning*, 14. For a (rare) contrasting view, see *Short and pretie Treatise*, sig. C3v.

[171] Culverwell, *Treatise of faith*, 354.

[172] 'R. R'., *The House-holders Helpe, for Domesticall Discipline* (1615: RSTC 20586), 24–5.

[173] Norwood, *Journal*, 9–10; Isham, 'Confessions', fo. 15r; Isham, 'Diary', 1628.

[174] Dyke, *Worthy communicant*, 307.

[175] Devon Record Office ECA Book 51 fo. 342r–v; James Kirkton, *The Secret and True History of the Church of Scotland from the Restoration to the Year 1678*, ed. Charles Kirkpatrick Sharpe (Edinburgh, 1817), 26; Tweedie, *Select Biographies*, 307.

[176] Knappen, *Two Diaries*, 75.

throughout our period, but more ordinary mortals struggled. Some blamed the audiences. 'If the Preacher doe passe his houre but a little', Gifford acidly told the lax, 'your buttokes beginne for to ake, and yee wishe in your hearte that the Pulpit woulde fall.' Stephen Egerton made a similar point in his book *The Boring of the Eare.* The title did not mean then what it would mean now, but others openly admitted that some preachers bored their audiences: indeed, that they preached interminably, 'as though they had forgotten the people had any bodies, who doe not so much edifie as tedifie'.[177] The Derbyshire minister Richard Kilby was thoroughly jaundiced about standards of preaching. 'The common sort is much neglected', he judged:

> Most people for some three quarters of an houre, if they understand the words . . . will give very diligent eare: But if the Preacher confound their understanding, or bee longer than ordinary, they leave all, and thinke thus; When will yonder man have done.[178]

And not just the common sort. Nehemiah Wallington confessed to having often 'thought longe till the sarment [sermon] was done: and looking on the houre glasse wishing it were rune out'.[179]

Even run-of-the-mill preachers could do something to help. For one thing, they could do as Kilby suggested and keep to time. A preacher ought in principle to be at liberty to go on as long as the Word demanded, but 'to prevent wearinesse and irkesomenesse in his hearers', he ought '(ordinarily) not to exceed his houre'.[180] Kilby himself had a more radical solution: to blend preaching with catechesis. He described how he conducted the Sunday evening service:

> After the second lesson, I asked a youth . . . three or foure questions touching the foundation of Religion. Then I made those short answers plain, and proved them out of the Bible in halfe an houres space.[181]

This had the twin merits of keeping the young people on their toes, and of comparative brevity. But while catechesis was widely recognized to be as valuable a teaching tool as the sermon, it could not stir the affections.[182] There was no substitute for the Word: and there was no short-cutting the preacher's obligation to preach well.

This meant it was up to the laity to endure as best they could. So, naturally, they played, they whispered, and they passed notes—both children and adults. John Phillips claimed that adults sometimes deliberately brought their children to church with them so that they themselves would have a distraction during an interminable sermon.[183] Keith Thomas even found a case of a man who discharged a gun during

---

[177] Gifford, *Briefe discourse*, fo. 26r; Egerton, *Boring of the Eare*, 6; Wright, *Summons for Sleepers*, 47.

[178] Kilby, *Hallelujah*, 101; cf. Culverwell, *Treatise of faith*, 355.

[179] Wallington, *Notebooks*, 46.

[180] *The drousie disease: or, an alarme to awake church-sleepers* (1638: RSTC 6913.5), 108. Cf. Egerton, *Boring of the Eare*, 52–3; Herbert, *Works*, 235.

[181] Kilby, *Hallelujah*, 100, 123.

[182] Culverwell, *Treatise of faith*, sig. 4r–v; Herbert, *Works*, 257.

[183] Phillips, *Satyr*, 8.

a sermon—not, apparently, aimed *at* the minister. More circumspect souls merely fidgeted, which for most ministers was quite bad enough. Henry Mason thundered against those who 'when they are hearing of Gods word . . . *smile* in secret, or . . . *looke about*, or . . . *laie one legg over an* other'. Robert Wilkinson looked out from his pulpit and saw 'a needelesse shifting and stirring of the bodie, a fumbling with handes, a shuffling with the feete'.[184] 'A wandering eye', Robert Bolton warned, 'is always a sure evidence of a wandering heart', especially if it wandered to members of the opposite sex; audiences should have 'eyes fixed most commonly on the Preacher' instead.[185] Or instead of looking around, they might read. Since many ministers encouraged their congregations to bring Bibles to church and follow them from text to text, it was an easy matter to tune out the preacher's drone and read your Bible instead. Ministers, of course, disapproved of this, but in practice readers might find themselves powerfully moved by it.[186] There was daydreaming too. John Winthrop felt guilty when he lapsed into it, but not everyone was so conscientious. In Phillips' satire, the women of the parish spend the sermon planning the dinner to which they will invite the preacher, or in one case, designing in her mind a pulpit-cloth with an embroidered cushion, 'being loth/When the fierce Priest his Doctrine hard unbuckles,/That in the passion he should hurt his knuckles'.[187]

Or sometimes they slept. Sleeping in church was a problem so ubiquitous as to deserve an entire polemical treatise denouncing it. Some sleepers, it seems, were shameless. Hugh Latimer's tale of the insomniac who sought out sermons because 'I never failed of a good nap there' sounds like a preacher's tall tale, but there is a ring of truth when the anonymous *The drousie disease* describes those who come to church and consciously 'set our selves to sleepe . . . holding downe our heads, and leaning them on our elbowes, as on pillowes, pulling our hats over our eyes lest wee should see'. Mason claimed that some settled themselves to rest so unashamedly that it was 'as if they meant to draw the curtains about the bed, and bid goodnight to the Preacher'. One Wiltshire girl claimed that when her zealous new minister began to speak, 'I can then sit down in my seat and take a good nap'.[188] This was of course roundly condemned. It was common to cite, as a warning, the story of Eutichus, who perched on a high windowsill to listen to St Paul preaching, dozed off, and fell to his death. Early modern sermon-sleepers were warned that the same judgement might befall them, without the miraculous deliverance.[189] I cannot

[184] Thomas, *Religion and the Decline of Magic*, 191; Henry Mason, *Hearing and Doing the Ready Way to Blessednesse* (1635: RSTC 17609), 658; Wilkinson, *Iewell for the Eare*, sig. B6v.

[185] Bolton, *Three-fold treatise*, I.175–6; Kilby, *Burthen*, 43; Rogers, *Garden* (1616), sig. G1v; cf. Hill, *Christs prayer expounded*, II.28; Bayly, *Practise of pietie*, 467.

[186] Wariston, *Diary*, 106; Zepper, *Art or Skil*, sigs F3v–4r; Hill, *Christs prayer expounded*, II. 28; Egerton, *Boring of the Eare*, 43.

[187] Winthrop, *Papers*, 162; Phillips, *Satyr*, 8–9.

[188] Latimer, *Sermons by Hugh Latimer*, 201; *Drousie disease*, 54; Ceri Sullivan, 'The art of listening in the seventeenth century', *Modern Philology* 104/1 (2006), 35; Martin Ingram, *Church Courts, Sex and Marriage in England, 1570–1640* (Cambridge, 1987), 121.

[189] Egerton, *Boring of the Eare*, 40–1; cf. Zepper, *Art or Skil*, sig. F1r; Cowper, *Triumph*, 7–8, Wilkinson, *Iewell for the Eare*, sig. B7r.

quite bring myself to believe the tale of the preacher who, faced with a dozing congregation, shouted, 'Fire! Fire!'; when the people jumped up, still half-dazed, and asked, where?, the preacher replied, 'in hell for sleepers at Church'.[190] But it is true enough that the godly were often unwilling to let sleeping neighbours lie. The duty to awaken your neighbours by 'privily pulling' at them was often preached, and as we might expect, such a ministry was not always welcome. Nehemiah Wallington recorded an incident in which the officious waking of a sleeping neighbour had sparked a vicious quarrel between two families. Eventually, he noted somberly, the sleeper had been struck providentially dead.[191]

Wallington himself, however, sometimes struggled to stay awake at church, and he was not alone. Some blamed the ministers: the official Homilies, John Field and Thomas Wilcox jeered, left the people not edified but 'nodifyed'.[192] But what could be done about it? Preachers tended simply to tell people not to fall asleep, exhorting them that the words at which they were glazing over 'may doe us more good, then all those we have yet heard. Yea, that they may be the last which we shall ever heare'. Sometimes they warned that it was the Devil who was casting sleep in your eyes. Wallington tried to use this to rouse himself, recognizing sleepiness as diabolical and, when it came upon him, praying, 'Strike home O Lord strik home to my poore Soule'. One prayer for use before a sermon asks explicitly for divine aid against drowsiness.[193] But Wallington also employed more practical solutions. Having experimented with biting his tongue, or pricking himself with a pin—no mere pinching yourself—he settled on taking some pepper, garlic, or cloves with him to church, to bite on when he felt a wave of sleepiness.[194] It was common to recommend standing up when battling to keep your eyes open, and perhaps some chose to stand throughout a sermon for that reason, but standing up mid-sermon cannot have been so attractive: who would want every eye in the building to turn to them at that moment? Yet we have some claims that people did just that, and in any case changes in posture definitely helped. One Massachusetts preacher in the 1640s admitted that one benefit of the Prayer Book service was that the responses and the need for periodic standing helped keep the congregation awake.[195] It helped if you did not come to church on a full stomach—Sunday lunch made afternoon sermons noticeably more somnolent—and if you went to bed early the night before. Or you could follow the example of the Suffolk nonconformist Richard Blackerby, and take a nap before church.[196]

[190] *Drousie disease*, 86.
[191] Zepper, *Art or Skil*, sig, F1v; Wallington, *Notebooks*, 103; cf. *Drousie disease*, 148; Robert Hill, *Christs Prayer expounded. A Communicant prepared. A Christian directed in life* (1607: RSTC 13472.4), 179, 181.
[192] Field and Wilcox, *Admonition*,sig. B1v.
[193] *Drousie disease*, 134; FSL MS V.a.436 p. 17; Sparke, *Crumms of comfort*, sig. F2r.
[194] Wallington, *Notebooks*, 46–7.
[195] Clarke, *Collection*, 455; Horton Davies, *The Worship of the American Puritans, 1629–1730* (New York, 1990), 105.
[196] *Drousie disease*, 47; Bayly, *Practise of pietie*, 451–2; Robert Hill, *Christs Prayer expounded. A Communicant prepared. A Christian directed in life* (1607: RSTC 13472.4), 178; Clarke, *Lives of sundry Eminent Persons*, 62.

Best of all, however, was to have something to do. Following the preacher in the Bible might not be enough—another of Phillips' satirical pen-portraits was of a serving-maid who 'feeleth drawziness upon her creeping,/Turns down one proof, and then she falls a sleeping./Then fell her head one way, her book another'.[197] The best solution of all was to take notes, a practice whose value went far beyond keeping sleep at bay—or, indeed, keeping schoolboys' hands where their master could see them.[198] The importance of sermon-noting for earnest, literate Protestants would be hard to exaggerate. Sermon notebooks were kept throughout our period, by people as varied as Richard Stonley, Margaret Hoby, Nehemiah Wallington, and King Edward VI. John Bruen, who noted sermons assiduously for over thirty-five years, left his heirs not a book but a library.[199] Surviving notebooks range from the scrappy and almost unreadable, through the workmanlike and organized, to careful fair copies.[200] Not everyone did it: it is a little surprising to find that Elizabeth Isham only began taking sermon-notes at the age of thirty-two.[201] (The practice was somewhat gendered: we know of plenty of sermon-noting women, but some did think 'shame upon our woemen for writing . . . in the Church'.[202]) For others it was essential. One of the resolutions which Robert Hill suggested for his readers was, 'I must write the sermon if I can'. When Simonds D'Ewes was a boy, his schoolmaster had not taught him to note sermons, an omission which fomented 'desperate atheism'; but happily, soon after he left school, he was 'first directed . . . to take notes in writing at sermons, and so to become a rational hearer'.[203]

It is worth pausing for a moment on the practicalities of this. It is not simply that relatively few were literate; nor, as James Melville once discovered, that the overwhelming emotion of a heart-piercing sermon was hardly compatible with careful note-taking.[204] There was also a basic problem of space. As Hunt has pointed out, schoolboys sometimes leaned on the communion table to make their notes, and stained the linens with ink.[205] In the quill era, a writing-surface was not an optional luxury. You needed somewhere to rest your ink, unless you attempted some foolhardy expedient like hanging an open inkhorn from your belt. Some pews were actually equipped with writing-desks, and Phillips describes women bringing writing-books and inkhorns to church.[206] But there were other

---

[197] Phillips, *Satyr*, 4.

[198] Egerton, *Boring of the Eare*, 42; Julia F. Merritt, 'The pastoral tightrope: a puritan pedagogue in Jacobean London' in Thomas Cogswell et al. (eds), *Politics, Religion and Popularity in Early Stuart Britain* (Cambridge, 2002), 148; Zepper, *Art or Skil*, sig. G8v; Brinsley, *Ludus Literarius*, 257.

[199] FSL MS V.a.459 fos 70r, 79v; Hoby, *Diary*, 62–3, 67, 101; Seaver, *Wallington's World*, 199–202; Diarmaid MacCulloch, *Tudor Church Militant: Edward VI and the Protestant Reformation* (1999), 23; Hinde, *Faithfull Remonstrance . . . of Iohn Bruen*, 102.

[200] For an example of each see, respectively, FSL MSS V.a.23, X.d.501; Saxby, 'Miscellany'; BL Egerton MS 2877.

[201] Isham, 'Diary'. 1640.

[202] Frances P. and Margaret M. Verney, *Memoirs of the Verney Family during the Seventeenth Century* (1907), I.501.

[203] Hill, *Christs prayer expounded*, II.28; D'Ewes, *Autobiography*, 62, 95.

[204] Melville, *Autobiography*, 26.

[205] Hunt, *Art of Hearing*, 97.

[206] Phillips, *Satyr*, 8.

solutions. Almost all the sermon notes that now survive are fair copies, written at leisure afterwards. Many people cultivated techniques for memorizing the words as they were preached, to write up later in the day, rather than attempting to write while actually in church. One technique was to turn down the corners of the pages of all the Biblical references the preacher used, so as to jog the memory later.[207] But there were also technological solutions. Archibald Johnston of Wariston used a 'killoveyne penne'; that is, a form of early pencil.[208] More common was the use of a table-book, or 'tables'; that is, a book whose pages had been treated with plaster and glue to make a surface on which you might write using a brass stylus, and which could then be wiped clean and reused. Joseph Hall described a sermon-goer who 'puls out his Tables in haste' to make a note; Phillips, one who 'writes short-hand with a pen of brass'.[209]

Note-takers put themselves to all this trouble for a reason. Scholars are now familiar with the practice of sermon repetition, by which sermons were recalled and recapitulated in the household afterwards.[210] Note-taking was essentially a support technique for repetition. The Exeter merchant Ignatius Jurdaine took notes 'not for his own benefit alone', but for use in the household, where 'he did constantly repeat the Sermons'.[211] Repetition tested the attentiveness and understanding of those who had attended, and conveyed the substance of a sermon to those—such as servants preparing Sunday lunch—who had not. It also allowed a deeper meditation on what had already been heard: some compared it to chewing the cud. 'It may be', Wilkinson suggested, 'that wil pearce into the head at a second repeting, which at the first report would not.'[212] Hence the carefully structured, subdivided approach to preaching which was common through the period, intended explicitly to aid memorization and repetition: the sermon was intended as much to be repeated as actually to be heard.[213] But importantly, repetitions were not verbatim. They might be very brief summaries of a long discourse, or, indeed, expansion on and exposition of what the preacher had said.[214] They could, as the young Ralph Josselin discovered, turn the listener into a preacher. He would meditate on the sermon on his way home from church, and on arriving home, enthusiastically repeat it to his father, passing on the gospel which he had heard; he claimed the old man found this an occasion of 'much joy [and] comfort'. The diarist Samuel Ward repented for his 'want of affections in hearing the sermons repeated'.[215] In

[207] Jocelin, *Mothers Legacie*, sigs a3v–4r; Saxby, 'Miscellany', fos 25v, 56r; Rogers, *Garden* (1616), sig. G1r–v; cf. Joseph Hall, *Meditations and Vowes, Diuine and Morall* (1621: RSTC 12684), 738; Earle, *Microcosmographie*, 11; Philip Caraman (ed.), *William Weston: The Autobiography of an Elizabethan* (1955), 164.

[208] Wariston, *Diary*, 132, 148.

[209] Stallybrass et al., 'Hamlet's Tables'; Joseph Hall, *Meditations and Vowes, Diuine and Morall* (1621: RSTC 12684), 738; Phillips, *Satyr*, 5.

[210] Hunt, *Art of Hearing*, 72–7.

[211] Clarke, *Collection*, 455.

[212] Wilkinson, *Iewell for the Eare*, sig. B8v; cf. Scudder, *Christians daily walke* (1628), 85.

[213] Egerton, *Boring of the Eare*, 49–50.

[214] Rogers, *Garden* (1616), sig. G1v; Brinsley, *Ludus Literarius*, 257; Hunt, *Art of Hearing*, 77.

[215] Alan Macfarlane (ed), *The Diary of Ralph Josselin 1616–1683* (1976), 3; Knappen, *Two Diaries*, 108.

repetition, both speaker and listener ought to find their encounter with God renewed and deepened.

The same, of course, is true of the sermon itself. Its ultimate purpose was not to produce neatly-written notes, accurate repetitions, or an attentive congregation, but to evoke a spiritual response. As Lewis Bayly put it, listeners should 'labour not so much to heare the wordes of the Preacher sounding in thine eare, as to feele the operation of the spirit, working in thy heart'.[216] This raises the perennial conundrum of what human labour could have to do with the sovereign workings of the Holy Spirit, but the experience of generations of Protestants was that the two were inseparable. Egerton had this advice for those taking their seats for a sermon:

> Let no man thinke with himselfe, I will now sit downe and take my place, and sit downe at ease, and heare at pleasure, but rather let him thus thinke, I will go now to an exercise indeed. . . . I must now buckle with Satan and mine owne corruption.

Henry Smith described the task of listening as 'eare-labour'. Good listening could, in principle at least, make up for bad preaching. Perhaps, Daniel Featley admitted, you are faced with 'the barrenest and . . . the dryest Preacher': but a diligent bee can gather honey even from the dryest herbs. There was nothing passive about listening of this kind.[217]

Indeed, 'listeners' did not always remain silent. The extent of audience participation in the early modern sermon is uncertain, but it certainly happened. At one extreme are the ecstatic outbursts of the revivalist meetings in south-west Scotland and in Ulster during the later 1620s and 1630s, when some would 'fall upon an high breathing and panting, as those doe who have run too long'—although our witness, who was generally in sympathy with these revivals, added that 'these people were alike affected whatever purpose was preached'. But it seems that more respectable Scottish congregations could also be pretty interactive, for example replying aloud to their preachers' rhetorical questions.[218] In England, such outbursts were more controversial. The royal injunctions required 'quiet attendance' in church. Archbishop Bancroft was scathing about puritan sermons at which 'the whole companye of that sect' cry out '*Amen, Amen*'; groanings and exclamations during sermons were associated with separatism and fanaticism. A hostile witness to a 1590s fast sermon describes the congregation looking up the preacher's texts in their own Bibles, discussing them with their neighbours, and sometimes even coming to blows about them.[219] John Donne claimed that such practices were now only found 'beyond the Seas', but he claimed that English sermons were still bedevilled by 'periodicall murmurings, and noises, which you make, when the Preacher concludeth any point. . . . Those impertinent Interjections swallow

[216] Bayly, *Practise of pietie*, 469.

[217] Egerton, *Boring of the Eare*, 7; Smith, *Sermons*, 645; Featley, *Ancilla Pietatis*, 67.

[218] Tweedie, *Select Biographies*, 146; Todd, *Culture of Protestantism*, 53–4; cf. Cowper, *Life and Death*, sig. B2v.

[219] Frere and Kennedy, *Visitation Articles*, III.21; Richard Bancroft, *Tracts Ascribed to Richard Bancroft*, ed. Albert Peel (Cambridge, 1953), 73; Craig, 'Psalms, groans', 111–12; Philip Caraman (ed.), *William Weston: The Autobiography of an Elizabethan* (1955), 164–5.

up one quarter of his houre'. He even claimed that those nearby who could not hear a sermon would judge its quality 'according to the frequencie, or paucitie of these acclamations'.[220] Unless we are to imagine that the Ayrshire revivals had come to Paul's Cross, we have to assume that Donne was exaggerating, but clearly early modern sermons were not heard in reverent silence. Still, Donne's assumption that a noisiness meant popularity may not be entirely correct. Making a 'short and sudden' exclamation during a sermon was one of the techniques recommended to keep sleepiness at bay.[221]

Listening, then, was an active and even energetic process. But it also had its pitfalls. One came with sheer exposure. Early modern Protestants became, willy-nilly, connoisseurs of the sermon. By the 1620s, most British lay people of a certain age had heard more hours of sustained oratory than almost anyone alive today. It was hard to be exposed to that much preaching without developing some critical sense, especially for those with a standard grammar-school training in rhetoric.[222] Moreover, Protestant theology actively encouraged critical attention. 'The people ought iudicially to examine the doctrine taught', Samuel Hieron warned, 'before they dare to entertaine it. . . . No one man is exempted from this dutie of examining.' To maintain otherwise was 'the opinion of poperie'.[223] But how were listeners simultaneously to be critical of falsehoods and meekly receptive of the truth? Numerous preachers and authors addressed this issue, none of them very satisfactorily. The normal approach was to urge listeners to assess their preachers, but to do so 'with Wisdome, Charitie and Sobrietie', 'with a good and godly heart'. Indeed, 'so soone as it shall appeare, that the things which are spoken are agreeable to Gods word, then presently all censure must cease'—as if a sermon whose beginning is orthodox cannot later turn heretical. Nicholas Byfield suggested that listeners simply take what in a sermon was of use to them individually, and discard the rest. Yet it was a commonplace that listeners should store up what seems unimportant in the memory, in case it proved its worth years later.[224] In other words, ministerial precept and long exposure nurtured critical faculties which inoculated congregations against preaching. Preachers regularly denounced the culture of sermon-tasting, which critically appraised the performance rather than meekly hearing the Word. 'Some come not to haue their liues reformed, but to haue their eares tickled as at a play.' For hearers to judge their preachers, Henry Smith warned, was 'as if the ground should complaine of the seed'.[225] But he and his colleagues had trained their audiences to do exactly that.

The Protestant theology of preaching also contained a trap for more passive listeners, which may be more significant. Since preachers were concerned above all

---

[220] Evelyn M. Simpson and George R. Potter (eds), *The Sermons of John Donne* (Berkeley and Los Angeles, 1962), X.132–4.

[221] *Drousie disease*, 141.

[222] Ceri Sullivan, 'The art of listening in the seventeenth century', *Modern Philology* 104/1 (2006), 35.

[223] Hieron, *Preachers plea*, 234–6.

[224] Zepper, *Art or Skil*, sigs E6v–7r, F7v–8v; Egerton, *Boring of the Eare*, 46–7; Byfield, *Marrow of the Oracles* (1622), 532–3; Hieron, *Preachers plea*, 258. Cf. Perkins, *Whole treatise*, 294–5.

[225] Wilkinson, *Iewell for the Eare*, sig. C3v; FSL MS V.a.1 fo. 12r–v; Smith, *Sermons*, 249.

never to give anyone an excuse to miss a sermon, they emphasized the absolute duty to attend, even if the preacher was ignorant or incomprehensible. This was partly because of preachers' confidence—justified or not—that their rhetoric was powerful enough to snare people who wandered in idly or unwillingly,[226] but it could easily be taken to mean that sermon-attendance was in itself a holy act, even something tending to salvation. As Robert Harris put it, 'the world sits still and thinks to be saued for hearing'. A woman whom we know only as E.C. recalled that, when she was sixteen, 'though I did not understand the word, yet I had a great desire to the word, and to go to heare, because they served God therein that did so'. Bayly taught that 'the preaching of the Gospell is the standard or Ensigne of Christ; to which all souldiers and elect people must assemble themselues'—implying that bodily presence matters more than understanding. Grace Mildmay thought children should be taught that 'whosoeuer readeth & meditateth in the word of God faithfully & diligently & heareth it Preached constantly & reuerently, shall be sure to finde the spirit of God', regardless of how much they understood.[227] This is not exactly orthodox, but it is not exactly heretical either: as Valentine Marshall argued, the Spirit is not hampered by our lack of understanding. 'Theres an immanent, wheres not a transient power to edifie. Something is a going when we little think it: If it be but to humble us.'[228] And of course, no-one could object to using your inability to understand a sermon to teach yourself humility. But what, then, are we to make of the case of Andrew Brown, who was caught up in the revivals in Ulster in the 1630s, and who wept copiously at sermons—despite the fact that he had been both deaf and mute from birth? Yet the ministers decided that the effect these sermons he could not hear had on him was a sufficient sign of grace that he could be admitted to communion.[229] Apparently he had earnestly desired this. And yet he seems already to have found something which can only be described as a sacrament.

---

[226] Latimer, *Sermons by Hugh Latimer*, 201; Smith, *Sermons*, 647.
[227] Harris, *Peters enlargement* (1624), A3r; Powell, *Spirituall Experiences*, 77; Bayly, *Practise of pietie*, 196; Mildmay, 'Meditations', fo. 16r.
[228] Capel, *Capel's Remains*, sig. b5r.   [229] Tweedie, *Select Biographies*, 153.

14

Prayer in the Household

'When he had broght them into his house, he set meat before them, and reioyced that he with all his housholde beleued in God.' *Acts 16:34*

Early modern Protestants and modern historians alike readily divide piety into public and private, but this neglects the crucial, fertile, common ground of the household. In the hierarchical worldviews which seemed natural to early modern minds, the household was a microcosm of human kingdoms and of the whole created order. It derived its authority from those analogies, and lent its authority to them: fathers were kings in their houses, and kings were fathers to their subjects. The commandment to honour father and mother was applied to all earthly authorities. Moreover, the household was not only a little kingdom, but also 'a little Church', and ideally, as such, a foreshadowing of God's kingdom, 'a kind of paradise vpon earth'. This referred to the physical space as well as to the family. When John Bruen inherited his father's house he resolved to make it 'a little Bethel, a house of God, a pledge of his presence, and place for his service'.[1]

One striking sign of this, whose extent is only now becoming clear, is the use of religious decoration in the Protestant home. Tara Hamling's wonderful survey of English and Scottish Protestant domestic religious art has revealed how some wealthy households were filled with improving and exhortatory images, from full-scale carvings or wall-paintings of Biblical scenes, to subtler plasterwork patriarchs gazing down from the ceiling with stern benevolence. The effect was to maintain a continuous sense of the presence of God. And as in most post-Reformation churches, texts were everywhere in Protestant domestic decoration, even down to panels of the Ten Commandments. Several divines recalled the Biblical injunction to inscribe the Word on your gateposts: one early evangelical actually inscribed that text itself over a fireplace.[2] Another early reformer, who worked as a cloth-painter, took a more dangerous step: he added 'certeine sentences of the Scripture' to hangings he was painting for an inn in Colchester, which eventually led to a heresy charge.[3] There was also the quicker, more ephemeral, and apparently more wide-spread phenomenon of simply writing on walls with chalk or charcoal, again

---

[1] Clarke, *Collection*, 7; William Perkins, *Christian Oeconomie* (1609: RSTC 19677), 8; Hinde, *Faithfull Remonstrance . . . of Iohn Bruen*, 50.
[2] Hamling, *Decorating the Godly Household*, esp. 106, 107–8, 225–6; Hamling, 'To See Or Not To See?', 186–90. Cf. Calvin, *Psalmes of David*, sig. *2v; Cleaver, *[G]odly form*, 15; Deuteronomy 6:6–9.
[3] Foxe, *Actes and monuments* (1583), 1026.

typically above a fireplace. This could be taken to surprising extremes. In 1541–2 Thomas Becon described an idealized Protestant home in which—as well as a table of the Commandments—apposite Scriptures were painted onto everything from the door ('I am the door', inevitably), to the chimney ('The fire shall not be quenched'), and the washbasin ('Be ye washed, be ye clean'). This was a literary device, not a description of decorative habits, but similar houses filled with improving inscriptions were imagined by Thomas Elyot and by Erasmus.[4] Unsurprisingly, some reformers began actually to do it. In 1551 John Redman deprecated the newfangled habit of writing of Scripture on church walls and 'in other houses', but the 'great fashion' for such painted texts both north and south of the border would not peak for another half-century. In the early 17th century, Christopher Sutton was recommending 'the placing of some sentence' on the walls of your house, and in George Herbert's ideal parsonage 'even the wals are not idle, but something is written, or painted there, which may excite the reader to a thought of piety'. Andrew Willet may not have been the only cleric to post pious rules for the household on the walls.[5] The surviving examples, inevitably, are from the houses of the wealthy, but the fashion was not exclusive to them. Pious and improving scenes and texts were a standard part of the decoration of inns and alehouses, and some visitors were moved by them. Ephemeral broadsheets could be pasted up in such establishments, or in private homes, and for those who could not rise to decorated walls, there were cheaper alternatives. Amongst Becon's inscribed godly furnishings were cups and dishes—'If anyone is thirsty, let him come to me and drink'. The so-called 'metropolitan ware' of the early 17th century brought this to life: pottery items bore simple messages such as 'FEARE GOD' or 'FAST AND PRAY AND PITTY THE POOR'. Joseph Hall described, proverbially, how the famished eat hungrily, while the replete 'begins to play with the dish, or to read sentences on his trencher'.[6]

In other words, when Protestants described their homes as churches, it was not idle talk. These were sacred spaces, in the sense that they could be filled with vivid reminders of God's presence and of the doctrines they professed. But recognizing a house as a church also has its problems. Was what happened behind closed doors in pious households simply a reflection of what happened publicly in parish churches? If so, did that mean that fathers (or others?) were arrogating a ministerial role to themselves? If not, did that mean that authorized public piety was being subverted? How closed were the doors in any case? And how did these idealistic injunctions measure up to the reality?

---

[4] Thomas Becon, *[A Christmas banquet]* (1542: RSTC 1713), sigs A6r–B5r (cf. John 10:7–9; Isaiah 1:16, 66:24); Fleming, *Graffiti*, 34–8, 139–40.

[5] Redman, *Complaint of grace*, 71; Hamling, *Decorating the Godly Household*, 108–9; Sutton, *Godly meditations* (1613), 417; Herbert, *Works*, 240; Willet, *Synopsis Papismi*, sig. b2v.

[6] Watt, *Cheap Print*, 194–211; Willis, *Mount Tabor*, 117–18; Becon, *[Christmas banquet]*, sigs B1v–2r; cf. John 7:37; Hamling, *Decorating the Godly Household*, 207; Fleming, *Graffiti*, 152–3; Hall, *Meditations . . . A third Century*, III.139.

PRESCRIPTION AND PRACTICE

The obligation on families to conduct regular devotions together was routinely taught by Protestant divines throughout our period, following the course charted by the Christian humanists, who in turn drew on still older traditions. (By contrast, post-Tridentine Catholics, and indeed some Laudians, were far more uneasy about a practice which might marginalize the clergy.)[7] With the pre-Reformation example of Richard Whitford's *A werke for housholders* (seven editions, 1530–7) at their back, Protestant presses churned out manuals of evangelical household management: from the hesitant *A glasse for housholders* (only one edition, in 1542), through best-sellers such as *A godly form of householde gouernement* (nine editions, 1598–1624), to compendia like the backbreaking *Of Domesticall Duties* (three editions, 1622–34). Far more common than these lengthy treatises, however, were set forms of prayer for family devotions. A few books were published explicitly to provide these, notably Edward Dering's *Godly priuate praiers, for houshoulders to meditate vppon, and to say in their famylies* (nine editions, 1574–1624). But it was much more common to append a short form for domestic prayer to another text, perhaps as part of a revised or expanded edition. Such forms crept into the ends of such texts as Arthur Dent's *The plaine mans path-way to heauen,* John Brinsley's *True Watch, and Rule of Life,* and the best-selling spiritual anthology *A Garden of Spirituall Flowers.* They are very often added to catechisms. The catechism in the Scottish Book of Common Order included 'a forme of prayers to be vsed in priuate houses'. The second-best-selling book of the entire period (after the Bible), the English *Whole Book of Psalmes,* also regularly included 'A forme of prayer to be vsed in priuate houses'.[8] If nothing else, publishers evidently believed that adding these brief texts could help to sell books.

The practices which these sources urge are fairly standardized. Family prayers should, it was agreed, be held twice daily, morning and evening.[9] However, in practice this was aspired to more than observed. Even Nehemiah Wallington, who from his youth 'went to prayr and reading morning and evening with my Father', needed as an adult to threaten himself with a one-penny fine if he did not pray 'euery morning and euening with my familie'. Twice-daily family prayer is mentioned in breathlessly hagiographical accounts of pious worthies as if it were a mark of exceptional piety.[10] Permissions to meet only once, by contrast, are unspoken but unmistakeable. A family's religious duty, Crashaw taught, is 'daily to meete together' for prayer and Bible-reading. Plenty of published forms provided both

---

[7] Margo Todd, 'Humanists, Puritans and the Spiritualised Household', *Church History* 49 (1980), 22–3; Davies, *A religion of the Word,* 120.

[8] *Forme of prayers ... approued and receiued by the Churche of Scotland,* III.149; Sternhold and Hopkins, *Whole Booke of Psalmes,* 395.

[9] Perkins, *Christian Oeconomie,* 6; Herbert, *Works,* 248.

[10] LMA Guildhall MS 204, p. 35; Wallington, *Notebooks,* 51. See, for example, Rogers, *Three Scottish Reformers,* 121; Walker, *Sermon at the funerals ...* , 46; Clarke, *Collection,* 7; Latimer, *Sermons by Hugh Latimer,* 228–9.

morning and evening prayers, but others provided texts for family use simply called, for example, 'A forme of Prayer, daylie to be vsed'. One 'forme of Thanksgiuing and Prayer, to be vsed of all godly Christians in their Families' explicitly allowed in its text for it to be used either morning or evening, with minor changes.[11] Perhaps daily was a struggle in itself. As so often in pious prescriptions, idealism and realism were not easy to reconcile.

If it was to be morning or evening, morning was both easier and more important.[12] Morning prayer was normally supposed to happen as soon as the family was dressed and had observed their individual devotions (if any): presumably servants engaged in preparing breakfast would have a free pass. Evenings were trickier. Before supper risked interruptions, or tardiness if some were working, and would exclude more servants. After supper, quite aside from the risk that serious meditation might upset the digestion, the family—especially children—would be cold, sleepy, or both. Post-prandial drowsiness was, Daniel Rogers claimed, 'the canker of most family duties'. John Winthrop found that a substantial supper meant that 'I was sleepye and unweeldye in my familye exercises', but chose to slim down his diet rather than rearrange his evening. The Woodford family preferred to pray before supper, 'because fresh from drowsines'—'vnlesse some waighty occasion forbid'. One October, Lady Margaret Hoby recorded her household's evening devotions shifting to before supper, 'in regard of mens dullnes after meat and being winter', perhaps that family's equivalent of the modern ritual of changing the clocks.[13] But it also suggests that finding the right time in the evening could be awkward, and that evening prayer could easily be squeezed out altogether.

As to how much time was needed, a quarter of an hour was the consensus. John Brinsley urged families 'to offer vnto [God] daily one quarter of an houre morning and euening', and the forms he provided would indeed have taken about fifteen minutes to read aloud.[14] Paul Baynes' family prayers were

> not usually above a quarter of an hour long, and having Respect to the Weakness, and Infirmities of his Servants and Children, he used to disswade others from tediousness in that Duty.[15]

A few disregarded such caveats,[16] but we may guess that it was more common to gabble through family prayers than to extend them. In a perennially popular sermon on spending your time wisely, William Whateley warned that if a household has 'an ouer great burthen of ordinary businesse', it will 'hinder them from taking conuenient time to pray'. The form for family prayers appended to William

---

[11] Crashaw, *Milke for Babes*, 8; Dering, *Godly priuate praiers*, sig. K4v; Bernard, *A Weekes Worke* (1628), 210–22; Sparke, *Crumms of comfort*, sig. G2r.

[12] As tacitly admitted in Scudder, *Christians daily walke* (1628), 56: there is no parallel prescription for the evening.

[13] Daniel Rogers, *Matrimoniall Honour* (1642: Wing 1797), 143; Bernard, *Faithfull Shepherd*, 26; Winthrop, *Papers*, 204; Woodford, 'Diary' 12.ix.1637 verso; Hoby, *Diary*, 81.

[14] Brinsley, *True Watch* (1622), II.182.

[15] Clarke, *Lives of thirty-two divines*, 24.

[16] For example, Hinde, *Faithfull Remonstrance . . . of Iohn Bruen*, 72.

Fig. 16. Memorial painting to Bishop James Pilkington, Auckland Castle, County Durham. An unusually vivid depiction of an English family at prayer.

Author photograph. Permission granted by Auckland Castle.

Gouge's catechism gives us one straw in the wind: evening prayer is barely a third of the length of morning prayer.[17]

The practical arrangements can only have reinforced this. We have no realistic contemporary visual images of families at prayer. What we do have, copiously, is depictions of the practice on funeral monuments—which in itself tells us how domestic prayer was linked both to respectability and to family identity. One of the most striking and apparently lifelike of these is on Bishop Pilkington's memorial in Auckland Castle (Figure 16). All those present are on their knees, as most texts would lead us to expect.[18] All of them, children included, also have kneeling-cushions, but only the bishop and his wife are able to lean on a table. For the others to hold their postures for fifteen minutes would have been an achievement.[19] Perhaps, as some monuments imply, it was sometimes possible for more than two people to lean on a prayer-desk at a time (Figure 17). Even so, brevity would be a physical necessity as well as a convenience.

How many people practised it at all? It was, as Ralph Houlbrooke points out, 'never generally instituted' in England, and even north of the border, kirk sessions struggled to make it common practice.[20] 'Many will praie in the Church, that neuer regard priuate praier at home', William Perkins feared; there are those, Robert Bolton claimed, who 'cannot remember the day when ever they . . . prayed with their families'. To Arthur Dent, this was a mark of particular godlessness, but John Dod saw it as more widespread than that. Urging his hearers to domestic prayer, he

---

[17] Whately, *Redemption of time*, 43; Gouge, *Short Catechisme*, sigs D5v–7r.

[18] See, for example, Bayly, *Practise of pietie*, 343; Herbert, *Works*, 248; Hinde, *Faithfull Remonstrance . . . of Iohn Bruen*, 72.

[19] On postures of prayer, see above, pp. 171–7.

[20] Ralph Houlbrooke, *The English Family 1450–1750* (1984), 112; Todd, *Culture of protestantism*, 311–13.

Fig. 17. Monument to Edward Dixon and family, Little Rollright, Oxfordshire. The three-sided prayer-desk is here symbolic, allowing Dixon to be depicted at prayer with both of his wives, but such arrangements may also have allowed families to gather around a single desk.
Permission granted by the photographer, Martin Beek

imagined their response: 'if we should . . . haue prayer in our families, and the like, this would make vs to be scoffed, and mocked at, and to be tearmed precise fooles for our paines'. When preachers did succeed in persuading people to try it, they regarded it as a 'great reformation' and a sign of profoundly changed lives.[21]

However, given certain puritans' rhetorical propensity to dismiss the world as hopelessly corrupt, we should not take this altogether seriously. Samuel Hieron's more level-headed judgement on his Devon parishioners is worth noticing. Having urged his flock to family prayer, he 'perceiued withall in some, a better inclination to it, then power to performe it'. He wrote a devotional guide, for 'those which haue as yet but stammering and lisping tongues'.[22] The problem was inability rather than unwillingness. That is a useful lens through which to read another vein of puritan scorn, for those who say family prayers but do so inadequately. Bolton attacked 'a kinde of out-side Christians' who, for fear that they be thought 'starke Atheists . . . suffer prayers to be read Evening and Morning in their houses'. But such prayers are performed with 'irreverence, coldnesse, and indevotion', by someone who 'knowes not how to speake to the present and particular wants, necessities and occasions of the family'. That does not sound terribly different from

[21] Perkins, *Godly and learned exposition*, 234; Bolton, *Three-fold treatise*, II.167; Dent, *Plaine mans path-way*, 248, and cf. 321; Dod and Cleaver, *Ten sermons*, 89; Shepard, *God's Plot*, 53; Blair, *Life*, 63.
[22] Hieron, *Helpe vnto Deuotion* (1608), sig. A8r–v.

what Hieron described. The same could be said John Bruen's contempt for his neighbours, who observed merely 'a forme of godlinesse' and 'slubber over their morning and evening service'. 'Many there are', Samuel Torshell claimed, 'that keepe a course, goe on in the round, keepe up the custome of Family-prayer, but breake not off any of their sinnes.'[23] Here is John Phillips' satirical account of what psalm-singing was like in such households:

> *Go too therefore ye wicked men,*
> *Depart from me* [Thomas] *anon*
> *For the* [Yes Sir] *commandments will I keep*
> *Of God* [Pray remember to receive the 100*l.* in Gracious-street to morrow] *my*
>   *Lord alone*
> *As thou hast promis'd to perform,* [*Mary,* anon forsooth]
> *That death me not assaile,* [Pray remember to rise betimes to morrow
>   morning, you know you have a great many cloaths to soap]
> *Nor let my hope abuse me so*
> *That through distrust I quaile.*[24]

This merciless portrait of piety overtaken by routine and business is all too credible. But if divines saved their real scorn for those who prayed inadequately, rather than for those who did not pray at all, perhaps matters were not quite so bleak as they feared.

However, some of these criticisms raise a different problem. The theory was that family prayers should involve the entire household, including children and servants, and be led by the senior male present, normally the father. This was not always possible, nor was it always observed when it was possible. There might be rival meetings under one roof: one such case in the 1630s, when a nephew and uncle divided over the legitimacy of set forms, 'wrought great discontent in the family'— as well it might.[25] Even leaving such unusual schisms aside, in a large house to assemble all servants was in effect to close down the whole establishment, allowing fires and meals to go cold. Babes in arms would bring their own disruptions, and if they were to be left out, then others would have to stay with them, or at least be ready to slip away. And no-one would think of dragging the ill or bedridden into the parlour and forcing them onto their knees. There was a wider problem of coercion. Ministers urged householders to compel all those who were sentient, able-bodied, and who could be spared to be present, but such a hard line was evidently unusual. Robert Cleaver warned 'sound professors of the Gospell' who 'talke of discipline, and stil complaine of the want of Church-gouernment' that their ambitions were in vain, 'vnlesse they wil begin this most necessarie discipline in reforming their own houses'.[26] Elizabeth Jocelin's precept for her unborn child, in the event that he or she entered service, gives us a rare glimpse of this from below stairs: 'be sure that

---

[23] Bolton, *Three-fold treatise*, II.172; Hinde, *Faithfull Remonstrance . . . of Iohn Bruen*, 52–3; Samuel Torshell, *The hypocrite discovered and cured* (1644: Wing T1938), 60.

[24] Phillips, *Satyr*, 12.

[25] Hamling, *Decorating the Godly Household*, 105.

[26] Cleaver, *[G]odly form*, sig. A4r. Cf. Bayly, *Practise of pietie*, 340–1; Cartwright and Wilcox, *Two treatises*, 3; 'R. R'., *House-holders Helpe*, 23–4; Robert Horne, *Points of instruction for the ignorant* (1617: RSTC 13824), sig. E7v.

you absent not your selfe from publike prayer, if it bee vsed in the house where you liue'.[27] That is, she expected that servants would have a choice.

Worse, family prayers might be led 'by some inferiour, not of the Master of the family'.[28] In wealthy households, that might mean a chaplain retained for the purpose, such as the Hoby family's Richard Rhodes, which was acceptable if not ideal. Bishop Lake's biographer praised him for leading family prayers every evening 'in his owne person', which he saw as unusual 'in a man of his place'.[29] But in lesser households, you might, so John Bruen claimed, find masters 'putting a shag-haired servingman to read a few cold prayers' to cover their own idleness. There was some theological cover for doing this. Under certain circumstances, Perkins allowed, a man may appoint a 'steward' for his household duties, spiritual and otherwise. Daniel Rogers, in a book published in 1643, agreed that a servant might be used in this capacity, if 'for parts and humblenesse' he is 'meete to take it upon him'.[30]

Unlike Perkins, Rogers also gave another, preferred option: that a woman might take on the role. For widows, who were 'natural' heads of household, this was almost straightforward, unless there were adult sons present. But Rogers also accepted that a wife could lead family prayers if neither her husband nor any other 'man of better sufficiency' were present. Indeed, it could even be done in his presence, if he suffered from 'utter insufficiency of . . . knowledge and understanding', 'invincible defects of expression and utterance', or 'when there is an utter loosenes and carelesnes in him'. In other words, if he could not or would not lead family prayers, she might; and we can imagine that that would be a common enough pattern. Going even further, Rogers expected that sometimes a husband would 'allow her . . . or request her to undertake it', even if he himself was capable. Rogers was not completely permissive: if a husband wished to lead prayers, even though he did so execrably, a wife 'must not encroach upon the office and disauthorise her husband', no matter how badly she felt the urge. But he was quite clear that this was a very unfortunate state of affairs. He counselled a wife whose husband would 'by no meanes endure her Service in this kind' to pray earnestly 'to seeke the releefe of this burden'. He did not explicitly address the question of whether a wife might lead family prayers when her husband neither permitted her to do so nor did so himself. Perhaps his conscience found the dilemma simply too keen.[31]

Rogers' enthusiasm for women's household ministry has a whiff of Civil War-era liberty about it, and writers before 1640 did not go so far. The standard line from men such as Gouge and Cleaver was that women might lead prayers only in their husbands' absence, and that if there were no family prayers they should restrict themselves to prayer in secret.[32] An earlier period of crisis and sharp choices had,

[27] Jocelin, *Mothers Legacie*, 47–8.
[28] Bolton, *Three-fold treatise*, II.172.
[29] Lake, *Sermons*, sig. ʃ3r.
[30] Hinde, *Faithfull Remonstrance . . . of Iohn Bruen*, 53; Perkins, *Christian Oeconomie*, 172; Rogers, *Matrimoniall Honour*, 270.
[31] Rogers, *Matrimoniall Honour*, 128–9, 268–70.
[32] Cleaver, *[G]odly form*, 53; Gouge, *Whole-Armor of God*, 429.

however, forced others into positions not unlike Rogers'. John Hooper's advice to a Protestant woman over when she might legitimately flee from her Catholic husband has many of the same themes; such dilemmas were all too common in the mid-16th century.[33] Even in calmer times, when we look at what women actually did rather than what male authorities told them to, something not unlike Rogers' picture emerges. Elizabeth Melville, Lady Culross, can be found leading an almost public gathering in prayer in her chamber in 1630, although the combination of her aristocratic status and the exceptional atmosphere of the Kirk o'Shotts revival make that an exceptional case. More strikingly, when Elizabeth Isham's mother died, her father asked her (at a mere seventeen) 'to read praires a mornings... which since I have done'; the implication is that her mother had done so before her.[34] To find women of status leading servants or children in prayer, or teaching them, was almost routine. Jane Ratcliffe's hagiographer insisted that she taught no-one except her own children and servants, 'although an *Apollos*... might not disdaine to learne of such a *Priscilla*': a comment which leaves us a little unsure whether to believe him. Margaret Hoby recorded herself instructing 'som of my famelie', which she found eased her of her troubles.[35] Catechizing children and servants was an accepted woman's role, and might easily blur into leading prayers. Micheline White has pointed out that Dorcas Martin's translation of a Huguenot catechism, which was printed in the voluminous *The Monument of Matrones*, makes a crucial change to her source text: the authority figure posing the questions is changed from 'minister' or 'father' to 'mother'.[36]

One form of household prayer in particular inevitably involved wives: the private prayers of a married couple together. Daniel Rogers, as we might expect, urged couples 'to conferre, read, pray, confesse, and give thanks... jointly and mutually'. However, he thought that even many earnestly pious couples neglected this duty. In the terms he put it, this is not altogether surprising:

> They are loth to utter their ignorance, barrennesse, ungroundednesse in the principles, or their spirituall forgetfulnesse, unthankfulnesse, lukewarmnesse, especially the defect in marriage duties each to other. These they are ashamed to make each other privy to.[37]

In other words, he envisaged conjugal prayer which is shockingly, perilously intimate. Not everyone went quite so far, but the sense of the urgency of conjugal prayer was widely shared. In particular, it was an ideal means of putting the spiritually explosive business of sex in a safe pious box. 'Prayer', Richard Capel taught, 'will make and keepe the bed undefiled, and encrease love and mutuall affection'. William Gouge warned against 'the naturall heat of lust which is in most:

---

[33] Hooper, *Later Writings*, 609–11; cf. Megan L. Hickerson, *Making Women Martyrs in Tudor England* (Basingstoke, 2005).

[34] Tweedie, *Select Biographies*, 346–7; Isham, 'Diary', 1625.

[35] Ley, *Patterne of Pietie*, 27 (cf. Acts 18:24–6); Hoby, *Diary*, 67–8.

[36] Bentley, *Monument of Matrons*, 221–52; Micheline White, 'A biographical sketch of Dorcas Martin: Elizabethan translator, stationer and godly matron', *Sixteenth Century Journal* 30/3 (1999), 776–7.

[37] Rogers, *Matrimoniall Honour*, 129, 133–5, 142.

which if it be not by prayer . . . asswaged, it may proue a defilement of the vndefiled bed'. (He too believed that conjugal prayer was 'rare'.) Cleaver did not dwell on that, but he did suggest that couples should pray together for matters as 'are not to be mentioned in their families, but priuately: as namely, for a godly posteritie, and that in the birth, the children bee comely, and not monstrous'.[38] While most published set prayers for conjugal use imply that the husband would pray and the wife would listen, there are hints of mutuality too. Such prayers might be described as the couple's 'ioynt request vnto God'.[39] 'I doubt not', Gouge wrote, 'but that the wife may pray in the husbands presence when they two are alone', not least because 'many wiues' were more adept devotees than their husbands. Cleaver urged wives not only to talk about Scripture to their husbands, but to admonish humbly them for their moral failings.[40]

How many couples actually prayed together is unknowable, but we can at least round up some of the usual suspects. John Forbes of Corse referred to 'my privat morning prayer with my wife in our bed' as if it were fairly routine. Robert Bolton's 'constant course', allegedly, was to pray twice daily with his wife.[41] It was not always so smooth. Robert Woodford frequently recorded praying with his wife, and sometimes found 'comfort' or 'gracious affecions' in doing so, but he tended only to mention such prayer at times of crisis, such as an illness.[42] John Winthrop was troubled when his first wife, Mary Forth, would not share her spiritual life with him, but this suddenly changed, which he saw as an answered prayer, and he was soon afterward vowing that he would 'often praye and conferre privately with my wife'.[43] Daniel Rogers' parents, Richard and Mary Rogers, regularly prayed together: before travelling, last thing at night, and Richard even waking his wife in the night to pray with him. However, his periodic resolutions 'to be more profitable togither' and repentances for having 'discontinued the keeping of some covenants betwixt us' also suggest that they found a regular rhythm of conjugal prayer difficult.[44]

The most detailed testimony comes from Archibald Johnston of Wariston. On his wedding night, while his very young bride waited in bed, he knelt and thanked God that until that hour he had been kept from 'outward pollution of lust quhrto thou haist bein so oft and so sairly tempted'. Then, while he was actually climbing into bed, he 'offred to preferre the sight of his [God's] faice unto al carnal suppose lauful contentments', although at least he had the tact to do this silently. During their all-too-brief marriage, they often lay in bed speaking of 'the principals of religion'. He recalled—as usual, addressing himself—how he tested her knowledge,

---

[38] Capel, *Tentations*, 394; William Gouge, *Of Domesticall Duties* (1622: RSTC 12119), 236; Cleaver, *[G]odly form*, 174; and see, for example, Thomas Becon, *The pomaunder of prayers* (1578: RSTC 1748), fos 58r–59v.

[39] Hieron, *Helpe Vnto Deuotion* (1610), 410–15; cf. Bernard, *A Weekes Worke* (1628), 234–40.

[40] Gouge, *Of Domesticall Duties*, 235–6; Cleaver, *[G]odly form*, 102, 174.

[41] Forbes, 'Diary', 41; Bolton, *Boltons last and learned worke*, sig. C1v.

[42] Woodford, 'Diary', e.g. 20.viii.1637 recto, 12.ix.1637 recto, 28.xi.1637 recto, 29.xi.1637 second verso, 17.xii.1637 recto, 25.iii.1638 recto.

[43] Winthrop, *Papers*, 163, 168.

[44] Knappen, *Two Diaries*, 58, 68, 80–3, 96.

and she answered 'so perfytly as thou kissed hir, blissed God, and rejoyced in thy heart for verry joy to seie sutch ane young creatur to knou God'. They read to each other in bed through the winter, and regularly confessed their sins and prayed for blessings together. They prepared for communion together, and 'I was forced to blisse God for thos present tears and softnes of heart he had given to us both'. When Wariston eventually remarried he found a similar pattern, describing on one occasion how they 'in prayer had our hearts spiritualy dissolved for ane houre and ane half'.[45]

This points to one of the few solid lessons to be learned from this fragmentary material. If we cannot tell how many families prayed together, or how closely they adhered to their preachers' models for doing so, we can at least ask *why* family prayers were, or were not, practised. For those who did not, the answers are obvious: lack of time, lack of inclination, and lack of compulsion. Those concerns also weighed on many who did it. John Brinsley actually wrote them into his text for a family's morning prayer, having them confess that 'the holy exercises of thy Religion are vsually a wearinesse vnto vs; and wee find . . . a drowsinesse in our performance of them'.[46] Samuel Rogers compared his experience of private prayer, when God 'pours down his love through my whole being', to that of leading household prayers, when 'he withdraws himself from me'. But neither he nor his employers would have thought of abandoning the practice. It is no coincidence that household prayers were often called 'family-duty': you might not be enthusiastic for them, but they had to be done.[47] There was social obligation: prominent families ought to be, and lowlier families might want to be, seen to be observing such pieties. There was an obligation to set an example to the young and impressionable in the family, and there was an obligation to honour God. Neither the content nor the experience of household prayers mattered as much as their brute fact. As Daniel Rogers' permission to incompetent husbands suggests, it was more important that family prayers be attempted than that they be done well. Merely by granting God this regular sacrifice of time and comfort in the midst of family life, you had done what was necessary.

But as Wariston and his wives remind us, some people, sometimes, found family prayers to be a joy. Woodford also described being 'greatly affected in publique prayer in the family', 'much affected', and having 'fayth & warmed affeccions', or 'comfort & enlargement' in his family prayers. Forbes found 'great joy, great boldnes towards God, & great peace' at his 'evening domestick prayer with my privat familie'. Isaac Ambrose twice mentioned how specific Bible readings in family prayers had 'refreshed and cheared my soul'.[48] John Winthrop recorded how, at the end of one of his spiritual slumps, 'in my familye exercises, I fealt my faithe beginne to revive as a man out of a dreame'. This was in part because it gave him a sense of purpose. He wrote that:

---

[45] Wariston, *Diary*, 10–11, 229–30.   [46] Brinsley, *True Watch* (1622), II.182*–183*.

[47] Rogers, *Diary*, 131; see, for example, Ambrose, *Media*, 78; Woodford, 'Diary' 2.xii.1637 recto.

[48] Woodford, 'Diary' 28.xi.1637 recto, 10.xii.1637 verso, 28.xii.1637 verso, 5.iii.1637–8 recto; Forbes, 'Diary' 41; Ambrose, *Media*, 78–9.

the conscionable and constant teaching of my familye was a speciall businesse, wherein I might please God, and greatly further their and mine own salvation . . . so I purpose by Gods assistance, to take it as a chiefe part of my callinge, and to intende it accordingly.[49]

Of course, what he and all of these enthusiastic comments have in common is that they are the views of those who *led* family prayers. Since they were also the ones who summoned their households, willingly or unwillingly, to the parlour every morning, it was their opinions that counted. Whether their families, kneeling unsupported around them for fifteen minutes every morning, found comparable comfort remains unclear. No-one troubled to ask them.

THEMES OF FAMILY PRAYER

Once a family had assembled to pray—morning or evening, all or some, willingly or unwillingly—what did they actually do?

The published forms suggest two main models. Much the more common of these was a single, lengthy prayer which the leader would read aloud, or perhaps extemporize, while the family listened in silence. Their audible participation would be limited to an 'Amen' and, most likely, joining in the Lord's Prayer at the end. A chapter of the Bible would typically be read aloud before this prayer; occasionally 'some godly Booke' might be used as well, or even instead,[50] and one or more metrical psalms might be sung at some stage of the proceedings, which would of course involve everyone present.[51]

The alternative model is much less well attested in print but was perhaps almost as common, in England at least: the use of the Book of Common Prayer's services of morning or evening prayer, or of a form derived from them.[52] The primer published under Edward VI explicitly made this possible, but any family equipped with a Prayer Book could make the adaptations themselves very easily. A large proportion of the literate population, then, had at least the opportunity to do this. We do not know how many took it. One reason not to do so was that, if families wanted the Prayer Book offices daily, and their parish had a conscientious curate, they could go to church; some did so.[53] Richard Stonley's household did not do this every day, but his diary sometimes notes, on significant feast days that fell during the week, 'This day for lacke of seruice at our parishe Churche by our obstinate Curate I red the seruice at home to my familie', or 'This morning I vsed morninge prayer at home by cause we had no seruice at our Church'.[54] How far families actively chose to do this at home is another matter. John Cosin's *Collection of Priuate Devotions* included versions of Prayer Book morning and evening prayer (the latter truncated) which could easily have been used collectively. John Clarke, a

[49] Winthrop, *Papers*, 158, 213–14.   [50] Rogers, *Garden* (1616), sig. F6r.
[51] Ryrie, 'Psalms and confrontation'.   [52] See above, p. 232–8.
[53] Openshaw, *Short questions*, sig. A5v; Willet, *Synopsis Papismi*, sig. A3v.
[54] FSL MS V.a.459 fos 10v, 83v.

less controversial figure, urged that 'noble families, which are more than a modell of a little Church', should make more use of the Prayer Book in their daily devotions.[55] Perhaps some did.

There might be hybrids. The responsorial mode of the Prayer Book office does not work very well when there is no parish clerk to utter the responses. So we read that one Elizabethan family used a series of prayers, all taken from the Prayer Book, but rearranged to make what amounted to a new service, entirely led by a single speaker.[56] A different approach is suggested by an Elizabethan compilation of medieval devotional texts, *The Treasure of gladnesse*. Its prayers rarely echo the Prayer Book's words, but they have a strongly liturgical style. There are prose 'Anthems'—with no indication of how they should be used—as well as lengthy sets of versicles and responses, apparently intended for family use. Sometimes these take the form of a litany, in which a long series of clauses are all met with the same, brief reply, which could work very well in that setting. But others are more vexing, with sequences of lengthy responses which are never repeated. How this would work in domestic setting is very unclear. Did a second person—a wife, a servant, an older son?—kneel next to the father, or have a second copy of the book? Or did one person voice all the parts? We must assume however that, somehow or other, these prayers were used—the book would not have run through twelve editions in Elizabeth's reign otherwise.[57]

The stereotype of a long, single-voiced prayer may be oversimplified too. It is not simply that sometimes, the chapter of Scripture might be read by someone else,[58] nor that the reading might be followed by a question-and-answer session, blending prayer with catechesis in order to establish how much the youngsters present had understood.[59] Thomas Becon's best-seller *The sycke mans salue* gives us a different glimpse of what domestic prayer could mean. His idealized description of four men praying for their dying friend begins with a phrase from the psalms, familiar from the old liturgy. 'Lord heare our praiers', says one; and his friend completes the verse—'And let our cry com vnto thee'. To begin with their prayer is very much a collective effort, each saying no more than a single sentence, and the next seamlessly picking up the thread. That psalmic couplet is reused repeatedly. Eventually the most learned of them embarks on a lengthier prayer, while the others chip in with periodic 'Amens'.[60] Even if no-one prayed quite like this in real life, the model of using familiar phrases to construct responses that could be said without prompts, and of different voices joining in extempore prayers, may have been an alluring one.

Some families succumbed to one temptation in particular. If the household was a little Church, and 'the Master of the family' was 'the Priest in his owne house'; if prayers were understood to be teaching tools for their hearers as well as petitions to God; if household devotions included reading aloud from printed sermons,

---

[55] Clarke, *Holy Incense*, sig. A12r.   [56] Openshaw, *Short questions*, sig. A5v.

[57] *This booke is called the Treasure of gladnesse*, esp. fos 40r, 42r, 47v–48v, 53r–55r, 61r–62r.

[58] Bayly, *Practise of pietie*, 343; Rogers, *Garden* (1616), sig. F6r.

[59] For example, Clarke, *Collection*, 7; Rogers, *Garden* (1616), sig. F6r.

[60] Becon, *Sycke mans salue*, 287–8, 344; Psalm 102:1.

repeating sermons which household members had heard preached, and not only repeating on them but elaborating on them in a manner which 'many men . . . in the Countrey' described as 'a *priuate Preaching*'—if all that was accepted, what could be more natural than for heads of household to extend this into teaching and exhorting their families in their own words? And how could that be separated from that most alarming phenomenon, clandestine preaching?[61]

Some pretended this was uncontroversial. Henry Scudder told heads of household to gather their families, to pray with and read to them, and 'to instruct them in the principles of religion, oft whetting the Word vpon them'.[62] Nehemiah Wallington wrote that

> I haue taken great delight to admonish and instruct my family, It hath sometimes been as my appointed food to talke and speake of God. . . . I doe delight to make others partake of what good I my selfe get by hearing or Reading.[63]

But the dangers were inescapable. Lewis Bayly suggested that householders could 'admonish' those under their charge after the Bible reading, but he knew he was courting controversy, and buttressed his claim with lengthy patristic citations. John Bruen was accustomed, in family prayers, to 'propounding and applying some wholesome doctrine, profitable for their godly edification . . . as a pastor and teacher in his owne house'. This practice was 'much maligned, reproached, opposed, and questioned', and like Bayly, Bruen spent some time assembling Scriptural and theological justifications. His hagiographer defended him, but was at pains to claim that he drew not on 'some private spirit of interpretation', but rather on his sermon notes and on 'good Expositors'.[64] We may or may not believe that. In any case, it is noticeable that contemporary evidence of this practice in normal English or Scottish homes is rare. John Welsh, in his 'family exercise . . . read a portion of Scripture, and discoursed upon it', but he was then in France, ministering to Huguenots. Francis Higginson recorded having 'constantly served God morning and evening by reading and expounding a chapter', but that was on board a ship bound for New England.[65] There is retrospective testimony about our period, too, written when the world had changed. Richard Blackerby—who was ordained, but stripped of his preaching licence—was said to have 'constantly Preached in his Family', a rare explicit use of the word. Others of Samuel Clarke's heroes did more or less the same. Even Jane Ratcliffe spoke of God 'with such affectionate force, as if her soul were ready to leap out at her lips into the ears of others'.[66] If she sounds like a repressed preacher, she was perhaps not alone. Bishop Earle's satirical

[61] Bolton, *Three-fold treatise*, II.172; Hunt, *Art of Hearing*, 171; 'R. R'., *House-holders Helpe*, 26; and see above, p. 359–60.

[62] Scudder, *Christians daily walke* (1628), 56; cf. Rogers, *Garden* (1616), sig. F6r.

[63] FSL MS V.a.436 p. 42.

[64] Bayly, *Practise of pietie*, 343; Hinde, *Faithfull Remonstrance . . . of Iohn Bruen*, 74–7.

[65] Tweedie, *Select Biographies*, 38; Francis Higginson, 'Higginson's Journal of His Voyage to New-England', *Proceedings of the Massachusetts Historical Society* series iii, 62 (1929), 299.

[66] Clarke, *Lives of sundry Eminent Persons*, 62; Clarke, *Collection*, 163, 427; Clarke, *Lives of thirty-two divines*, 149.

'she-puritan' was furious 'that women must not preach . . . but what she cannot at the church she dos at the Table'.[67] John Winthrop frankly tells us that, with his ministerial ambitions frustrated, he found that 'the conscionable and constant teaching of my familye' gave him 'as sufficient incouragement to my studye and labour therein as if I were to teache a publick Congregation'.[68] Protestantism aspired to set the Word burning within Christian souls; they could hardly then be expected to contain it in silence. Perhaps domestic 'preaching' was less a threat to the established churches than a safety valve.

What these 'preachers' may have actually said is of course lost, but in the printed forms, at least, the contents of family prayers are conventional to the point of banality. Morning prayer typically began with thanksgiving for surviving the preceding night, and, indeed, for surviving your entire life up to that point. This could lead into thanksgiving for creation, or into an extended prayer of repentance. Thanksgiving was often an entry point for a quick exposition of justification by faith or indeed of the entire Protestant gospel, in the guise of giving thanks for all of these mercies—from 'thy mercie in sparing vs still to liue, and in not consuming vs away from the earth' onwards.[69] Sometimes—as in Samuel Hieron's prayer which asked God to remind those praying of certain important doctrines, which were duly spelt out—the purpose was nakedly didactic.[70] Often these broad doctrinal issues would consume the bulk of the prayer, but normally, towards the end, attention would turn to the day ahead. Now the family would commit the day to God, asking for continual awareness of his presence, delivery from danger, and protection from sin. There might also be a prayer to 'imploy our selues faithfully, religiously, & industriously in our calling'.[71] This was why prayer first thing in the morning was seen as so important: not simply that God 'favours no mans sloth or dilation', so that if you want to be heard you need to be prompt, but that 'the morning is the foundation of the day, [and] all things succeed as their foundations are laid'.[72] Morning prayer was a moment of circumspection which was—for as long as it lasted—the still, central point of your life. From it you looked to God; to the past, with penitence and thanksgiving, and to the future, with supplication and resolution.

Evening prayer, book-ending the day, served a slightly different purpose. Penitence was a much more dominant theme, with the day's sins to account for, and sometimes it crowded out everything else. The prospect of night-time dangers, and the Biblical warning against letting the sun set on your sin, spurred devotees to 'presume not to sleepe, till thou haue vpon thy knees, made a particular reconciliation with God in Christ for the same'.[73] Retrospection on the day might also include thanksgiving and meditation on any particular mercies, providences, or spiritual insights. Occasionally this, rather than penitence, dominates. There is at least a hope that evening can be a moment of peace in a busy world. 'Night is a time

[67] Earle, *Microcosmographie*, 120.
[68] Winthrop, *Papers*, 213.
[69] Babington, *Briefe conference*, 133.
[70] Hieron, *Helpe vnto Deuotion* (1608), 5–8.
[71] Rogers, *Garden* (1616), sig. G6v.
[72] Bod MS Rawl D.384 fo. 1v.
[73] Bayly, *Practise of pietie*, 313; cf. Ephesians 4:26.

when the world leaues a man (as it were) for a while', Dorothy Leigh wrote: 'pray when the world is asleepe, for assoone as it is awake, it will cry and call on thee . . . to attend it'.[74] But peace is generally overshadowed by danger. The physical dangers of the night were real enough, and evening prayer often sought to remind devotees that they might die before they woke. Beyond that, sleep itself is a foreshadowing of death, and the bed of the grave. One writer even compared bedbugs to the grave's consuming worms.[75] Other menaces were less tangible. Edward Hutchins prayed 'keepe me this night from storming Satan, who is woont . . . by night, to vndermine man, when his senses are fettered in bands of rest'.[76] If you girded yourself for battle when you prayed in the morning, you did so all the more at night.

Amidst these platitudes, one recurrent theme of both published and unpublished family prayers is worth noticing: prayer for the public world, whether for the monarch and commonwealth, for the Church as a whole, or for international or national crises. This material deserves some attention, partly because it contrasts with the resolutely personal focus of most Protestant devotion, and also because it is politically charged. The Tudor and Stuart monarchies routinely used prayer as a political tool. The Book of Common Prayer's frequent intercessions for the crown never hint that state power could be anything other than benign, and those liturgies were reinforced by periodic and strongly politicized occasions for special worship, commemorating events such as Queen Elizabeth's accession or the Gunpowder Plot.[77] Domestic prayers could not be managed quite so directly, but successive regimes did their best. In the adapted version of the Prayer Book daily offices printed in the 1553 Primer, the three collects of the public service were followed by a lengthy fourth collect for the king. Senior clerics both taught the duty to pray such prayers, and provided them in their published works: Bishop Cowper's prayer not only for James VI & I, but also for a fictional entity which he called 'this Church of England, Scotland & Ireland', is only one of the more blatant of these.[78] The royal chaplain who preached at court the day before Queen Elizabeth's death, in the presence of the archbishop of Canterbury and other notables, prayed a 'fervent and effectuall' prayer for her. Our witness only attended the sermon because he wanted to know whether the queen had already died.[79] Prayers for politics and politicians are always political, but it is rarely quite so obvious.

So when we find, as we do, that printed prayers routinely lead families in prayers which reinforce the existing political order, we are entitled to smell a rat. It was politic at least to pretend to pray such prayers, and to be seen to encourage others to do so. Some published political prayers are plainly more about loyalist ostentation

[74] Leigh, *Mothers blessing*, 74–5.
[75] Babington, *Briefe conference*, 145; Bernard, *A Weekes Worke* (1616), 110; Ryrie, 'Sleeping, waking and dreaming'.
[76] Hutchins, *Davids Sling*, 11–12.
[77] John P. D. Cooper, 'O Lorde save the kyng: Tudor Royal Propaganda and the Power of Prayer' in G. W. Bernard and S. J. Gunn (eds), *Authority and Consent in Tudor England* (Aldershot, 2002); Natalie Mears, 'Special nationwide worship and the Book of Common Prayer in England, Wales and Ireland, 1552–1642' in Mears and Ryrie, *Worship and the Parish Church*.
[78] Ketley, *Two Liturgies*, 384–97; Cowper, *Triumph*, 366; cf. Sandys, *Sermons*, 79–80.
[79] Manningham, *Diary*, 205–6.

than about piety. Richard Day's *Booke of Christian Prayer* opens with a full-page frontispiece of Queen Elizabeth at prayer and devotes about a sixth of its entire length to prayers for the queen and realm, plainly there to be noticed as much as to be used.[80] English Protestants arrested under Mary I regularly insisted that they prayed for the queen and realm, keen to clear their religion of the taint of sedition even if this was not enough to save their own lives. When that public prayer the day before Elizabeth's death 'left few eyes drye', we might diagnose propriety and fear as much as grieving loyalty.[81] Even within private houses too, political prayers could be useful. If the household was a little church, it was also part of a larger web of hierarchy and obedience, and so to join in prayer for the monarch reinforced authority structures within the household itself.

Yet earnest English and Scottish Protestants genuinely believed in their monarchs' God-given authority (the latter perhaps not quite so much). The Cornish gentleman William Carnsew was an avid reader of Protestant books but was generally reticent in his diary: the only prayerful note it contains is on the anniversary of Elizabeth's accession in 1576. 'Quene Elyzabethe hathe raynynid full .18. yeris godd p(re)serve her'.[82] Similarly, Richard Stonley was devotedly loyal to the queen, even as he used his position in the Exchequer to gamble recklessly and fraudulently with her money. His comparably terse diary carefully records the accession anniversary each year, adding a comment such as 'God send her a prosperous gouernment with many yeres to reign over vs'. When the anniversary fell on a Saturday, he added that on the Sunday he had stayed in 'praying god to send her Maiestie a prosperous Reign of this next yeare', and he was indignant whenever a preacher did not pray for the queen before or after his sermon.[83]

If everyday loyalty could be heartfelt, gratitude for deliverance from catastrophes like the Spanish Armada and the Gunpowder Plot could be more so. Oliver Pigg's short book of devotions on the Armada crisis prayed that, after such a deliverance, 'daylie and continuallie, wee may stirre vp our selues to thankfulnesse, and to speake of it to our children, and they to their childrens children'.[84] In the 1630s, Samuel Rogers recorded experiencing 'great inlargement' of the heart in his annual commemoration of the Gunpowder Plot, and Robert Woodford was still giving heartfelt thanks for delivery from 'this hellish powder plott'.[85] Thomas Tuke's popular book of prayers includes, routinely enough, a prayer of thanksgiving for the safe birth of a child. Remarkably, and entirely gratuitously, the prayer manages to incorporate thanksgiving for the failure of the Gunpowder Plot.[86]

Although King James could not have expected that, he could hardly object. But political prayers could sometimes be more dangerous. Sir Robert Harley wrote a

[80] Day, *Booke of Christian Prayers*, fos 22r–47r.
[81] Hooper, *Later Writings*, 612; Manningham, *Diary*, 206.
[82] Pounds, 'William Carnsew', 54.
[83] FSL MS V.a.459 fos 19r, 21r, 31r, 87r; FSL MS V.a.460 fo. 40r–v.
[84] Pigg, *Meditations concerning praiers*, 36.
[85] Rogers, *Diary*, 34; Woodford, 'Diary' 5.xi.1637 verso; cf. Saxby, 'Miscellany', fos 56v–57r.
[86] Tuke, *Practise of the faithfull*, 184–6. Cf. the unnecessarily detailed thanksgiving in Tymme, *Siluer watch-bell* (1606), 289.

memorandum in 1625, prompting himself to pray for Charles I's 'personal safety' (which was fine), for his marriage (which was ticklish), and even for 'the state of the ministery'—although apparently he thought that praying for the 'free passage of ye gospel' in England was going too far, since he scratched the phrase out.[87] This was especially the case during fasts: public or semi-public fasts, arising from political events, could be openly seditious, and even private fasts might be connected to public affairs.[88] When Samuel Ward drew up a list of 'motyves to fasting and publick humiliation', provocative public concerns headed the list: fear of Queen Henrietta Maria's popish influence, and of Catholic victories in the Thirty Years' War.[89] Those distressed by England's aloofness from that war might express their frustration by praying for the royal family—and especially for Princess Elizabeth, James VI & I's daughter and the husband of the Elector Palatine.[90] This habit of using prayer as a form of political exhortation was an old one. In Henry VIII's reign, Thomas Becon had prayed that his king would finish the Reformation he had begun; in Elizabeth's reign, he prayed that the Queen 'may nayle the head of Antechrist so fast vnto the ground, that he shall neuer be able to recouer him selfe agayne', which was not quite how she would have expressed her political ambitions.[91] In the 1630s, Woodford, like many others, was unequivocally praying 'for the Kinges maiestye . . . to inlighten his eyes'.[92] Less openly provocative, but often covering much more troublesome views, were simple prayers for the realm which made no reference to the powers that be. When Gervase Babington prayed for England, asking God to 'lessen in it daily the number of blinde and wilfull Papists, prophane Atheists, & increase the number of thy true children', or when Edward Dering prayed for 'thy whole Church, especially such as be persecuted for thy worde', they at least followed it up with prayers for the queen.[93] When James Melville, on his deathbed, 'rememberit the kirk in generall, and Scotland in particular', and more so, when John Welsh prayed, 'Lord, wilt thou not grant me Scotland?'—it is pretty clear that the intention behind these prayers would not have pleased their king.[94]

The recurrence of public affairs in family and other private devotions sometimes tells us about individuals' political views, but it also demonstrates the inseparability of the personal and the political. The family, a commonwealth in miniature, was a part of the whole, with a duty and a right to support that whole by the most

[87] BL Additional MS 70089 fo. 1r.

[88] See, for example, D'Ewes, *Autobiography*, 414; Wallington, *Notebooks*, 271. On public and private fasts, see Ryrie, 'Fall and rise of fasting', and above, pp. 195–9.

[89] Knappen, *Two Diaries*, 122.

[90] See, for example, Johann Gerhard, *Gerards meditations written originally in the Latine tongue* (Cambridge, 1631: RSTC 11773), II.153; Saxby, 'Miscellany', fo. 69r.

[91] Thomas Becon, *Newes out of heauen* (1541: RSTC 1740), sig. A6v; Becon, *Newe pathway vnto praier*, sig. R6r; Thomas Becon, *The pomaunder of prayers* (1578: RSTC 1748), fo. 99r. This last was a posthumous edition and the new material added to it, such as this prayer, may not be of Becon's composition.

[92] Woodford, 'Diary', 12.ix.1637 recto.

[93] Babington, *Briefe conference*, 144; Dering, *Godly priuate praiers*, sig. C5r. Cf. Sparke, *Crumms of comfort*, sigs D10v–12v.

[94] Melville, *Autobiography*, lviii; Tweedie, *Select Biographies*, 11.

effective means in creation: prayer. The Prayer Book might channel this duty into simple obedience, but Protestantism's restless conscience was not so easily contained. John Hooper's early formulation was that families should 'pray unto God for the promotion of his holy word, and for the preservation of the governors of the commonwealth': a thoroughly laudable project, but it was obvious which of those two interests Hooper would prioritize when they came into conflict.[95] Prayer, in early modern society, was powerful, politically as well as spiritually. Petitioning God—indeed, arguing and wrestling with him, as Protestants were wont to do— was more effective than petitioning any earthly prince. For all that regimes tried to use prayer to bolster themselves, they could not escape the political power which Protestant patterns of prayer for public matters had placed in private hands. Reflecting on the Civil Wars, Richard Baxter famously commented that 'the Warre was begun in our streets before the King or Parliament had any Armies'.[96] If so, the weapons with which it was fought were forged in Britain's parlours.

TABLE-GRACES

Many professed Protestants in early modern Britain did not pray very much outside of church. For these occasional devotees, three kinds of prayer were the most common. There was the prayer of emergency, since even the most nominal of Christians tend to rediscover their faith in moments of dire need. There was prayer before bed, or in bed;[97] and there were table-graces, perhaps the most neglected form of devotion in early modern Protestantism.

Brief prayers at meal-times were a well-established Christian habit, and the medieval description of such prayers as 'graces' persisted unproblematically into Protestant use. How widely they were actually used is a different matter. One Scottish catechism worried that some Protestants had abandoned it as a 'Monkish hypocrisie'.[98] Puritan gloom-mongers were, naturally, convinced that their neighbours neglected it. Richard Kilby claimed that he had never said grace in his youth and believed that many of his readers would be equally negligent. He warned that if meal-time prayer should 'seeme uncouth unto you, as it doth to many people, be afraid': this is a sign that 'your heart is a stranger to God'. He imagined his readers objecting that table-graces were 'so out of use with most folke, that if I offer to say grace among them, they will thinke scornfully of me'. Lewis Bayly, similarly, imagined that 'it may bee, because thou hast neuer vsed to giue thankes at meales, therefore thou art now ashamed to begin'.[99] How true these sweeping claims are, we cannot know. Evidence of grace *not* being said is, understandably, thin on the ground, and hard to interpret when we find it. Samuel Rogers' diary notes that

---

[95] Hooper, *Early Writings*, 33.
[96] Richard Baxter, *A holy commonwealth* (1659: Wing B1281), 457.
[97] On which, see Ryrie, 'Sleeping, waking and dreaming'.
[98] Davidson, *Some helpes for Schollers*, sig F2r.
[99] Kilby, *Burthen*, 26–7; Bayly, *Practise of pietie*, 357.

when Charles Louis, the Prince Palatine, visited Stortford in 1636, there was 'no thanks to meate'. Rogers shows no apparent surprise: was this simply normal? Yet he bothers to record it, suggesting it was at least noteworthy. In isolation this does not mean very much.[100]

By contrast, some sources suggest that table-graces were, if not universal, at least routine. Catholic clergy accepted that post-Reformation English Catholics could be present when Protestants were saying grace. In other words, those who disliked the phenomenon might find it unavoidable.[101] Some Protestant voices implicitly agreed. Robert Bruce, urging his Edinburgh congregation to greater thankfulness, argued that thanksgiving sanctifies God's gifts to us; and to prove it, claimed 'that quhilk is true in meate and drink, it is true in all the rest of the benefites, quhilk are pledges of his mercy'.[102] That is, he took it for granted that his hearers accepted the value of table-graces—and in general, Bruce was not a man to flatter his audience's virtues. The sheer quantity of printed table-graces in circulation tells its own story. *A Groue of Graces*, one of the six 'books' in Abraham Fleming's best-selling devotional anthology *The diamond of deuotion*, consists simply of forty-two short graces.[103] A compendium of that size was a little quixotic, but graces were ubiquitous wherever prayers were collected: prayer books, primers, catechisms, communicants' hand-books, and squeezed into spare pages of devotional works of all kinds. If printed popularity is any guide, there was a seam of early modern Protestants who did not regularly observe family prayers, but who did at least say grace at table.

The rhetoric used on the subject is revealing. One image, and only one, was consistently applied to those who failed to say grace: they were bestial, guilty of 'swinish rushing' on their food.[104] Or as a popular verse put it:

> He that eateth and drinketh,
> and letteth grace passe,
> Sitteth downe like an Oxe,
> and riseth like an Asse.[105]

So this was not only about piety, but about manners and about hunger. In an age of self-conscious attempts to link restraint at table with civility and propriety, saying grace demonstrated a degree of refinement.[106] Richard Waste laid a choice before his children: to 'give Honor & Thanks to God, who giueth thee thy meat', or to 'goe to thy meat & feed like a Beast'—adding that 'the sight of the clean table-furniture vsed about thy Dyett' should remind them of their own sinful filthiness.[107] For those embracing the emerging fastidiousness towards food characteristic of the period, the problem was not so much grace as food itself. Eating is

---

[100] Rogers, *Diary*, 43.
[101] Alexandra Walsham, *Church Papists* (Woodbridge, 1993), 64, 68.
[102] Bruce, *Sermons Preached*, sig. L2r; cf. sig. T7v.
[103] Fleming, *Diamond of deuotion*, 283 (five editions, 1581–1608).
[104] Dyke, *Two Treatises*, 265.
[105] Hill, *Christs prayer expounded*, III.40; cf. a variant in BL Egerton MS 2877 fo. 84r.
[106] Paul Connerton, *How Societies Remember* (Cambridge, 1989), 82–3.
[107] Bod MS Rawl C.473 fo. 2r.

the most bestial thing humans do, Lewis Bayly believed, and anyone who is too preoccupied with it 'liueth but to fill priuies'.[108] It is a rhetoric which would lose some of its force if your immediate concern was an empty belly. In other words, criticisms of meal-time impiety may say more about social than prayerful graces.

Similarly, such criticisms were often concerned with inadequate table-graces rather than with their total neglect. Some Protestants set a high standard. Nehemiah Wallington vowed 'that before I drinke one drop of drinke or eate a crume of bread . . . I lift up my heart to God'. The discipline may have saved his life. During his most dangerous youthful attempt at self-harm, when he tried to make himself drink beer laced with ratsbane, he baulked and poured it away because 'I could not intreate the Lord to blesse it unto me'.[109] At meal-times themselves, the ideal was for grace to be said both before and after, and printed graces almost always come in pairs. Some editions of John Bradford's meditations even provided, as well as pre- and post-prandial graces, a prayer to be said 'in the meale tyme'. Something of the kind may be implied by George Webbe's instruction to 'put not a morsell of any thing into thy mouth in thy Meale, before thou hast desired Gods blessing vpon it', which could be taken to mean that you should pray before every mouthful.[110]

If that was the ideal, of course almost everyone fell short. Bayly, while enthusiastic for table-graces, made no attempt at anything like Wallington's or Webbe's rule: grace was to be said only before dinner and supper. Breakfast was simply to be eaten 'in the feare of God',[111] and indeed, while separate graces for dinner and supper were commonplace, I have yet to find an early modern breakfast-grace. A different gap between ideal and reality is on display in Richard Bernard's populist devotional dialogue *A Weekes Worke*, which reprimands those who leave the table before the closing grace. Bernard's penitent sinner admits that 'I haue risen without any true reuerent remembrance of God; a few prayers, perhaps, I haue made'.[112] Busy people could not always wait, and a quick muttered prayer might seem adequate. When exemplary individuals are praised for their piety at table, it is often their post-prandial graces which are singled out: it seems likely that they were more neglected.[113]

Grace before dinner faced a different problem: impatient hunger and, perhaps, food growing cold. It was proverbial that 'long graces do/But keep good stomacks off that would fall too'.[114] Surviving graces suggest a tug-of-war over length between piety and practicality. Grace Mildmay's meditation before eating runs to three manuscript pages, and would be one to use before dinner was actually on the table. The Teviotdale minister John Smith is said to have repeated a psalm, or 'part of a long psalm', as part of his pre-dinner grace, which must have tried some guests'

---

[108] Bayly, *Practise of pietie*, 354.

[109] LMA Guildhall MS 204, p. 41; Wallington, *Notebooks*, 36, 178.

[110] Bull, *Christian praiers*, 119–20; John Bradford, *Godly meditations vpon the Lords prayer* (1597: RSTC 3487), fos 202r–203r; Rogers, *Garden* (1616), sig. F5r.

[111] Bayly, *Practise of pietie*, 352.

[112] Bernard, *A Weekes Worke* (1616), 78–80.

[113] See, for example, Clarke, *Collection*, 306, 452–3.

[114] John Suckling, *Fragmenta aurea* (1646: Wing S6126A), 19.

Fig. 18. Antoon Claeissins, 'Family Saying Grace', *c*.1585. A rare 16th-century image of table piety, from the Netherlands. Contemporary English diners apparently stood to say grace.

Shakespeare Birthplace Institute, Stratford-upon-Avon.

patience. Some printed graces are also unhelpfully long. Thomas Broke, editing one such collection, half-apologized for the fact.[115] The graces appended to the 1562 *Whole Book of Psalmes* showed one way forward: beginning with a lengthy pair of graces—over 150 words apiece—it then added two more pairs, growing progressively shorter. By the 17th century, brevity had won. It is rare to find printed graces much longer than a hundred words, and Thomas Tuke's set of ten graces includes one minnow of merely thirty-three words, which would take scarcely ten seconds to recite.[116] Unsurprisingly, after-dinner graces are often a little longer.[117]

The different bodily postures of pre- and post-dinner graces perhaps reinforced this. The evidence here is shaky: no reliable depiction of an early modern British table-grace survives. A contemporary Dutch painting (Figure 18) shows a family seated at prayer, but it seems that, at least in England, it was more normal to remain standing for pre-dinner grace. The very earliest evangelical devotional work in

[115] Mildmay, 'Meditations', II.92–4; Tweedie, *Select Biographies*, 314; John Calvin et al., *The forme of the common praiers vsed in the churches of Geneua* (1550: RSTC 16560), sig. ¢7v, fo. 204r–v. Cf. *Forme of prayers . . . approued and receiued by the Churche of Scotland*, III.154–8.

[116] Sternhold and Hopkins, *Whole Booke of Psalmes*, 398–401; Tuke, *Practise of the faithfull*, 221–2; cf. Kilby, *Burthen*, 28; Sorocold, *Supplications of Saints* (1616), 398–412; Norden, *Pensiue mans practise*, 267–70.

[117] See, for example, Hill, *Christs prayer expounded*, III.40–3; Hieron, *Helpe Vnto Deuotion* (1610), 466–70.

English, George Joye's primer *Ortulus anime*, refers to saying grace 'standinge before' the table, 'handes eleuated and ioyned togither'. Eighty years later, Lewis Bayly was insisting, 'sit not therefore downe to eate, before you pray'.[118] If, as both Bayly and Thomas Becon urged, you lifted up 'thy harte, thy handes and thyn eyes vnto heauen' when you said grace, that perhaps worked better when standing. But after dinner, we might expect most to remain seated, and again Bayly's injunction ('rise not, before you giue GOD thankes') supports this.[119]

Another, perhaps more significant area of slippage between expectation and practice concerned who actually said grace. Most divines expected, or hoped, that the head of household would do the job. But extempore graces were very rare. Extemporizing on the subject of food twice a day, every day, is not easy. Even Thomas Cartwright believed that Christ himself had used a set form for table-grace.[120] This made it easier for other voices to be heard. Some of the earlier, longer printed graces include a responsive element, such as the Lord's Prayer or the Prayer Book doxology.[121] Some enthusiasts would sing a psalm after the meal, like the apostles at the Last Supper.[122]

In private households, grace was often not said by an adult at all, but by a child. John Bruen may have deplored his neighbours' habit of procuring 'a simple and silly childe to say grace', but a great many Protestants simply assumed that saying grace was a child's role. The grace provided in *Ortulus anime* was 'to be sayd of chyldrene'. The Huntingdonshire children who supposedly suffered at the hands of the 'witches of Warboys' were afflicted with seizures 'as soon as they did offer to say grace either before or after dinner'. One of the very first elements of a Christian education for children was, Robert Cleaver taught, 'to teach them to praise god before and after meales'. The graces in Thomas Sorocold's prayer-book were intended for use 'by Children and others'. The title-page of the expanded edition of William Crashaw's catechism advertises 'houshold Prayers for Families, and Graces for Children'.[123] If children had a role in family piety, this was it: hesitantly or proudly to read or recite a short form of words—sometimes a verse, which would be easier to remember—before and after a meal. It was a training both in piety and in table-manners. What it meant for the adults present is another matter. Presumably pride in, affection for, embarrassment about, or discipline of children often

---

[118] Joye, *Ortulus anime*, sig. H2v; Bayly, *Practise of pietie*, 359.

[119] Becon, *Gouernans* (1549), fo. 6v; Bayly, *Practise of pietie*, 359.

[120] Clarke, *Collection*, 255. Robert Harris was said to find subjects for his after-dinner grace in the meal-time conversation: Clarke, *Collection*, 306. John Davidson's catechism provided set forms, but also pointed out that the 'matter and substance' of a grace matter more than the exact words: Davidson, *Some helpes for Schollers*, sig. F2r.

[121] Joye, *Ortulus anime*, sig. H3r; *The Primer, in Englishe and Latyn, set foorth by the Kynges maiestie* (1545: RSTC 16040), sig. C3v; *Prymmer . . . set fourth by the kinges maiestie* (1553), sigs a7r–b2r; Melville, *Spiritual Propine*, 17.

[122] Knappen, *Two Diaries*, 115; Clarke, *Collection*, 453.

[123] Hinde, *Faithfull Remonstrance . . . of Iohn Bruen*, 52; Joye, *Ortulus anime*, sig. H2v; Philip C. Almond (ed.), *Demonic Possession and Exorcism in Early Modern England: Contemporary Texts and their Cultural Contexts* (Cambridge, 2004), 97; Cleaver, *[G]odly form*, 264; Sorocold, *Supplications of Saints* (1616), 398; William Crashaw, *Milke for Babes . . . With houshold Prayers for Families, and Graces for Children* (1622: RSTC 6021).

swamped prayerfulness, and it would also be natural to associate saying grace with childishness. Graces must be used, John Davidson warned, 'not onely by children, but also by the best and most able in the house'.[124] Perhaps those who neglected grace simply wanted to put away childish things.

All of this implies that what was actually prayed for in table-graces did not particularly matter. What mattered was simply that it was done. But the contents of the prayers themselves are also worth noticing. Simple thanksgiving for food is one obvious major theme, particularly after meals, but there are others. Some graces attempt spiritual allegory, as in Becon's prayer that, as well as the gift of food, 'thou wylte also gyue vs the meate of aungelles, the true heauenly bread, euen that euerlastyng worde of God our Lord Iesus Christ'.[125] Few graces were quite so preachy, but it was common for them to use food to remind us of our need for 'the spiritual fode of thy word'.[126] The fullest extension of this was in Bernard's *A Weekes Worke*, which suggested different spiritual meditations for every part of the meal: milk should remind diners of catechizing, salt of the ministry of the word, sauce of affliction, and chewing of meditation.[127]

Other graces were more worldly. In Edward VI's reign, the high watermark of 'commonwealth' preaching, several graces focused pointedly on those who cannot put food on the table. Becon wanted his readers to pray before eating that 'we … may shew merci & kindnes to our pore neighbours by distrybuting to them part of these thy gifts'.[128] The official Edwardian primer includes an after-dinner 'grace' which is not a prayer at all:

> Al ye whom God hath here refreshed with his sufficient repast, remember your poore and nedye brethren, of the which some ley in the streates sore sycke, naked, and colde, some by hungrye and soe drye, that they would be glad of the least draught of your dryncke, and of the smallest parynge of youre bread.[129]

In later periods, the poor are, however, reduced to the occasional mention.[130] In their place, we find prayers for the monarch, church, and realm, especially after dinner: perhaps this helped to train children in right obedience.[131] Sometimes such intercessions are part of a wider after-dinner attempt to lift the company's attention from the table back to the world and their duties within it. Henry Bull suggested meditating on and following the example of victuallers' productive labour. Richard

---

[124] Davidson, *Some helpes for Schollers*, sig. F2r.

[125] Becon, *Gouernans* (1544?), fo. 5v. This phrase was omitted from the 1560 and subsequent editions.

[126] Sternhold and Hopkins, *Whole Booke of Psalmes*, 399. Cf. John Calvin et al., *The forme of the common praiers vsed in the churches of Geneua* (1550: RSTC 16560), fo. 201r–v; *Forme of prayers … approued and receiued by the Churche of Scotland*, III.155–6; Bull, *Christian praiers*, 117–18.

[127] Bernard, *A Weekes Worke* (1616), 69–80.

[128] Becon, *Flour of godly praiers*, fo. 14r.

[129] *Prymmer … set fourth by the kinges maiestie* (1553), sig b1r–v.

[130] See, for example, Bayly, *Practise of pietie*, 359; Sparke, *Crumms of comfort*, sig. O5r.

[131] See, for example, Sternhold and Hopkins, *Whole Booke of Psalmes*, 401; *Godly garden*, sig. Z4v; Hunnis, *Seuen Sobs*, 26; Rogers, *Garden* (1616), sig. G5r; Bayly, *Practise of pietie*, 362–4; Sparke, *Crumms of comfort*, sig. O2r–v; Thomas Vicars, *The Grounds of that Doctrine which is according to Godlinesse* (1630: RSTC 24700), sig. B6r.

Kilby prayed before meals that he would be nourished 'to doe thee true service in my calling'. It was in this spirit that John Phillips imagined a gluttonous minister's prayer for the strength to waddle his over-stuffed body home.[132]

The commonest theme, however, especially in graces before eating and especially after 1600, was not thanksgiving but blessing of the food. Given the general Protestant aversion to consecrating material objects, this may seem surprising, but it was used across the spectrum. Thomas Tuke prayed, 'blesse these creatures [the food] vnto our vse, that they may be to our health, strength & comfort'; Henry Valentine echoed, 'Blesse these thy creatures to the use of our bodies'. James Melville apparently distinguished between prayer after food, which he called a 'grace', and prayer before, which he called a 'blessing'.[133] There are implicit rationales for such blessings. They connect the gift of food to the Christian's duties, asking God to use the former to fuel diners for the latter. They also acknowledge that food has no intrinsic power to nourish, but can only do so through the subtle miracle of digestion, for which diners ought to pray. In an age when a well-stocked table could as easily mean food-poisoning as sustenance, this was not an idle prayer, and under those circumstances, giving thanks before actually eating might seem premature. But this does not seem adequate. Old patterns were resurfacing here, perhaps only lightly Protestantized. Graces—as the very word's persistence reminds us—had, like many of the smaller fragments of medieval piety, made it through the Reformation filter relatively intact. It helped that they were strongly associated with that most conservative age-group, prepubescent children, and it also helped that they concerned eating, an animal activity which Christians of all kinds were concerned to tame. When good Protestants blessed their food, they did not (consciously) mean by it what their Catholic predecessors and contemporaries did, but they still reached for similar words.

Other medieval meal-time pieties persisted too; for example, the old monastic and collegiate habit of reading aloud during meals, so that diners might sit in silence, chewing on the Word. The Little Gidding community's practice of reading Scripture and other improving books at meal-times has been called an echo of monasticism, but if so it was an echo heard more widely. Reformers under Henry VIII and Edward VI commonly advocated meal-time Bible-reading. Bishop Lake 'neuer sate downe to his meale, but he had according to the auncient fashion of Bishops a Chapter of the holy Bible, read by one whom he kept for that purpose'. Archibald Johnston of Wariston referred to Scripture being read 'at' or 'befor' both dinner and supper as if it were routine.[134] The readers might be servants, as in one

<hr/>

[132] Bull, *Christian praiers*, 121; Kilby, *Burthen*, 28; Phillips, *Satyr*, 19.

[133] Tuke, *Practise of the faithfull*, 221; Valentine, *Private Devotions*, 418; Melville, *Spiritual Propine*, 13. Cf., amongst many other examples, Joye, *Ortulus anime*, sigs H2v–3r; Becon, *Flour of godly praiers*, fos 14v–15v; Sorocold, *Supplications of Saints* (1616), 408; William Crashaw, *Milke for Babes... With houshold Prayers for Families, and Graces for Children* (1622: RSTC 6021), 66; Gouge, *Short Catechisme*, sigs D7r–8r; Sparke, *Crumms of comfort*, sig. O2r–v.

[134] Aston, 'Moving Pictures', 85; Frere and Kennedy, *Visitation Articles*, II.29; Cranmer, *Miscellaneous Writings*, 161; Becon, *Dauids harpe*, sig. A8v; Lake, *Sermons*, sig. ʃ3r; Wariston, *Diary*, 166.

stylized account of an Elizabethan household, but this, too, could be a role for children or youths. In the 1630s, the noncomformist minister Herbert Palmer acted as tutor to a group of gentlemen's sons who boarded with him; he had them read a chapter aloud each meal-time. When servants ate in their own quarters, as was becoming more common during our period, they might escape being read to, but their eating spaces could at least be decorated with improving Biblical texts or images.[135]

One of Edward Dering's after-dinner graces gives us a glimpse of how meal-time reading worked. This is a thanksgiving 'after the receyuing of our bodily suste-nance, and reading of some part of Gods holie worde our spirituall foode', which only makes sense if it follows simultaneous eating and hearing. But it also gives thanks for 'thy Word...wherein we haue had our conference'.[136] The reading set the agenda for meal-time conversation, and indeed, religious table-talk was a widely accepted mark of holiness. We regularly find pious individuals praised for 'conference...at her table...which sauoured of religion', or for zeal to 'talke at his Table of what had been taught in the Church'.[137] Eusebius Pagit, author of a popular guide to the Bible, was said to follow the twice-daily meal-time Bible readings with a question-and-answer session on the chapter that the family had heard. If conversation turned to more mundane matters, those like Robert Harris or Ignatius Jurdaine would wrestle it back to God, taking 'occasion from earthly things to speak of heavenly'.[138] The point, Becon argued in the 1540s, was to replace the 'fylthy communicacion' at table with 'that whiche is good to edify', and when put like that, no-one could argue. The danger, however, was that instead of godly subject matter elevating table-talk, meal-time irreverence would drag religion down. At table, Bishop Earle's 'she-puritan' 'prattles more then any' against Antichrist and preachers she dislikes, 'till a Capon-wing silence her'. Stephen Egerton agreed that too many diners' after-sermon talk consisted of 'scoffing, and carping at the doctrine, or at the Teacher thereof'.[139] Naturally, experienced sermon-goers, who have sat through an hour of indifferent or predictable discourse and who are now safely at home with food and drink in their bellies, will want to have their say, but this only underlines why meal-time piety was so important. The preacher Samuel Ward alluded to how an angel told St John the Divine to eat a scroll: this was a model for bringing Scripture and food together. Instead, he feared, most preferred tasting Scripture 'onely with the tippe of the tongue...neuer chewing the cud and digesting their meat'. As such, they do not find true nour-ishment, merely 'a smackering for discourse and table-talke'.[140]

---

[135] Openshaw, *Short questions*, sig. A6r–v; Cambers, *Godly Reading*, 101–2; Clarke, *Lives of thirty-two divines*, 190; Hamling, *Decorating the Godly Household*, 125–6.

[136] Dering, *Godly priuate praiers*, sig. D4r–v.

[137] Denison, *Monument or Tombe-Stone*, 97; Walker, *Sermon at the funerals...*, 47. Cf. Mildmay, *With Faith and Physic*, 32; Rogers, *Three Scottish Reformers*, 121; Willet, *Synopsis Papismi*, sig. a4r.

[138] *ODNB*; Clarke, *Collection*, 306, 452.

[139] Becon, *Gouernans* (1549), fo. 7r–v; Earle, *Microcosmographie*, 120; Egerton, *Boring of the Eare*, 63.

[140] Ward, *Coal from the Altar*, 57; cf. Revelation 10:8–10.

Divines might have fretted about impropriety. Most Protestants, however, found table fellowship a vital part of Christian sociability. In the early days of the British Reformations, one crucial lubricant of religious change was Lent-breaking: gatherings of reformers, fellow-travellers, and of the curious who met to eat together in defiance of the Church's official fasts. By good fellowship, and by mutual implication in an alluring, venial offence, they both helped to bind evangelical networks together and to draw in outsiders.[141] In the more dangerous day of Mary's reign, Protestants 'did table together in a chamber keeping the doores close shut for feare of the promotors'. In the Elizabethan period, separatists and suspected separatists shared meals as part of their conventicling. For conformists, these patterns persisted in the widely-attested, and mocked, clamour after a sermon to see who would have the privilege of hosting the preacher to dinner.[142]

There is one final, tantalizing issue. Were these meals mere sociability, or could they be something more? Arthur Hildersam, in his Jacobean communicants' handbook, asked

> whether all bread and wine that is broken and powred forth, giuen and receiued, may not aswell serue to represent and confirme these things vnto vs as these elements & actions that are vsed in this Sacrament.

Absolutely not, was his answer: only the elements used in church were sacramental, and that was an end of it.[143] But the question will not go away. Perkins urged his readers to find mementoes of Christ's Passion all around them, and in particular to 'beholde him at thy table in meate and drinke, which is as it were a liuely sermon and a daily pledge of the mercie of God in Christ'.[144] In the stylized Christian household which Becon described in 1542, the dishes were inscribed with the words, 'He that eteth my flessh, & drinketh my bloud, he dwelleth in me, and I in him'. Becon explained that,

> This putteth vs in remembraunce when we eate oure meate of the breakynge of Christes moost blessed body and the shedding of his moost precious bloud & by the remembraunce of it, & the beleuyng of the same, our soules at that very present, are no lesse fed & susteyned, than oure bodyes are wyth the meate.[145]

Becon was not a Quaker, claiming that every meal was the Lord's Supper, although it would be possible to read his words that way. But he was claiming that, if it is done correctly, an ordinary meal is a holy event. If it is a sacrament of sorts, it is one in which everyone, from the child saying grace to the servant reading the Bible, to the guests debating the merits of the preacher, becomes, for the moment, a priest.

[141] Ryrie, 'Fall and rise of fasting'.

[142] BL Additional MS 43827A fo. 9r (cf. John 20:19); Dexter, *Congregationalism*, 257; BL Lansdowne MS 157 fo. 186r; Hunt, *Art of Hearing*, 191; cf. Phillips, *Satyr*, 8–9; FSL MS V.a.459 fos 38v–42r.

[143] Bradshaw and Hildersam, *Direction*, II.48–9.

[144] Perkins, *Declaration of the true manner*, 37.

[145] Becon, *[Christmas banquet]*, sig. B2r.

CONFERENCE AND FELLOWSHIP

Godly table-talk is a subset of the larger phenomenon of Protestant sociability, both within and beyond the household. Donald Lupton wrote this meditation on a dead coal:

> Remotenesse, and solitarinesse makes it die. But joyned to the whole Company how soone recovers it the former virtue. It's no otherwise with the Elect Children, want of good exercises, and Company may abate, and lessen their heat of zeale.[146]

One of early Protestantism's distinctive features was enthusiasm for spending swathes of time simply talking about religion with fellow believers. We can glimpse Protestantism's university roots in this: the experience of belonging to a company of earnest young men talking intensely into the small hours was formative for generations of ministers, and the apparent ambition to turn the world into a giant university[147] owed something to nostalgia for this unrecoverable stage of life. When the evangelical propagandist Thomas Garrett had to flee Oxford in 1528, his friend Anthony Dalaber embraced him, weeping, then knelt and prayed for him, and then rushed out to tell as many of his friends in Oxford as he could.[148] The community was how such people found both identity and security. In later, less dangerous times, godly conference could become a club-house meeting for those whose hobby was God, a place where believers could speak freely of their enthusiasm to others who would understand. Richard Norwood recalled the early months of his conversion, when he was entirely without Christian company: 'I was as one that had found some inestimable treasure which none knew but myself.' It simply seemed unnatural to be unable to speak. True faith, Nicholas Byfield believed, 'will speak to God by prayer, and to men by conference, it cannot be silent'.[149]

The value of godly sociability was universally recognized. We have already met the ingrained early modern suspicion of solitude.[150] There was an obligation to 'conferre with such as can open the Scriptures' and to 'be acquainted with the godlie'.[151] 'Conuerse with good men' was one of the four principles of keeping 'within Compasse' which John Trundle's moralizing best-seller taught (see Figure 1). There was a parallel duty to edify others with your own conference: Jane Ratcliffe's godly talk, we are told, was able 'to inkindle the same holy fire (in their hearts who heard her) which burned in her owne bosome'.[152] Conference separated the true from the hypocritical believer (up to a point): 'nothing giueth a more sensible euidence of your conuersion, and translation from death to life' than

---

[146] Lupton, *Obiectorum Reductio*, 66.   [147] See above, p. 262.
[148] Foxe, *Actes and momuments* (1583), 1195.
[149] Norwood, *Journal*, 83; Byfield, *The Signes*, 134.
[150] See above, pp. 156–71.
[151] *[Geneva Bible]* (1586), instructions for use; Tyrwhit, *Elizabeth Tyrwhit's Morning and Evening Prayers*, 102.
[152] Ley, *Patterne of Pietie*, 68; cf. Rogers, *Seven treatises*, 365.

'holy speech and conference'.[153] It could be a source of enduring spiritual enlightenment: conferring with a friend in 1624, the young Simonds D'Ewes 'learned more touching the nature, signs, causes, and effects of faith, that principal Christian grace, than ever I had done before', an experience which convinced him of 'the invaluable happiness of conversing with those who were good and virtuous'. Nicholas Byfield promised that 'by acquaintance with them [godly persons], thou wilt bee brought into acquaintance with God himselfe'.[154] Indeed, conference could be 'heavenly'.

> Nothing bringeth more feeling ioy, comfort, and delight (next the communion with God in Christ) then the actuall communion of Saints, and the loue of brethren. It is the beginning of that our happinesse on earth, which shall be perfected in Heauen.

John Andrewes' best-selling chapbook on 'the beauty of heaven' dwelt, not only on the beatific vision, but on the reunion of parted friends. 'What cryes and shouts will there be for ioy? what clapping of hands and sweete embracements one of another?'[155] Elizabeth Juxon, we are told, habitually spent her Sundays 'conferring of Gods word', and at such times 'heartily desired, neuer to go againe into the world', but rather to 'spend all her dayes in that blessed fellowship with God'.[156] For her, it seems, fellowship with other believers and with God dissolved into one another.

'Conference' embraced a wide range of different forms of sociability. The simplest was individual friendship. For young converts, or highly educated ministers stuck in rural isolation, a good friend who shared their religious temper might be a lifeline. When Richard Baxter was sent away to school, he made a godly friend who was,

> the greatest help to my Seriousness in Religion, that ever I had before, and was a daily Watchman over my Soul! We walk'd together, we read together, we prayed together. . . . He would be always stirring me up to Zeal and Diligence.[157]

That particular friendship later failed, but such bonds could be enduring. Richard Rogers and Ezekiel Culverwell conferred and prayed together regularly for decades. John Fuller, writing a preface to a book by his friend and fellow minister John Beadle, recalled how over many years 'we oft breathed and powred out our souls together in Prayer, Fasting, and conferences'.[158] But 'conference' often refers to larger gatherings. Sundays were a particular day for them: the strictest sabbatarian could not object to spending Sundays in godly conference, visiting neighbours to speak of God, or reconciling quarrels, and given that Sunday observance could

---

[153] Scudder, *Christians daily walke* (1628), 151, 156; cf. Dent, *Sermon of Repentance*, sig. B7v; Mather, *Magnalia*, III.109.

[154] D'Ewes, *Autobiography*, 249; Byfield, *Marrow of the Oracles* (1619), 18–19.

[155] Scudder, *Christians daily walke* (1628), 157; Knappen, *Two Diaries*, 99; William Tyndale et al., *The whole workes of W. Tyndall, Iohn Frith and Doct. Barnes* (1573: RSTC 24436), sig. B3r; Andrewes, *Celestiall looking-glasse*, 28. On Protestants' hopes for reunion in Heaven, see Peter Marshall, *Beliefs and the Dead in Reformation England* (Oxford, 2002), 215–20.

[156] Denison, *Monument or Tombe-Stone*, 105.

[157] Baxter, *Reliquiae Baxterianae*, 4.

[158] Beadle, *Journal or diary*, sig. a5v.

otherwise become a little austere, socializing in this way had obvious attractions.[159] For some, such as the group of London apprentices who met for an hour before the service every Sunday in the early 1630s, it was their only opportunity. Others met less frequently: John Winthrop belonged to a group of twelve who met annually for prayer. Some groups would be more ad hoc, such as the group of 'good frends and neighbours' whom Rose Hickman called to her house to pray when her young son was dangerously ill.[160]

This applied particularly to those who might join in another household's family prayers, a practice which was both inevitable and dangerous. Naturally if there were guests in the house, they would be part of family prayers. What if some guests came specifically for the purpose? Some ministers deliberately led 'open' family prayers; and not only ministers. When John Bruen led family devotions in rural Cheshire, 'many of his neighbours and friends ... joyned with him', and when he moved to Chester, 'many neighbours' came to evening prayers in his house, 'and some every morning'.[161] This was dangerous ground. In Scotland, the Book of Common Order provided some space for 'conference' by requiring weekly meetings akin to the later English 'prophesyings'. Even there, however, after the 1618 Perth Articles controversially required kneeling at communion, some Scots began to hold 'private meetings ... to deplore the iniquitie of the time', and found themselves denounced from the pulpit, stripped of their offices, and even expelled from their homes.[162] In England, as Patrick Collinson pointed out, private religious gatherings were 'extra-legal rather than illegal'. Archbishop Whitgift tried to ban religious gatherings of more than one family in 1583, and the 1604 canons prohibited some gatherings of the clergy, but neither ruling could be made to stick particularly well. It was hard to draw a distinction between seditious conventicling, praiseworthy furtherance of mutual faith, and 'a group of neighbours [who] sang a few psalms after supper'.[163] In March 1584, ten people from the Essex town of Braintree were arrested for having used 'vnlawefull exercises' in a private house. It emerged that they had simply met for supper, discussed what they had heard at a public catechizing, read to one another from Foxe's *Actes and monuments*, sung a psalm, and gone home. The magistrate released them 'as men, whose example was rather to be followed, then theire weldoing to bee reproved'—but he also informed Sir

[159] Bradford, *Godlie meditations*, sig. G2v; Bownde, *Doctrine of the Sabbath*, 236–7; Bayly, *Practise of pietie*, 478; Tweedie, *Select Biographies*, 8.
[160] Kiffin, *Remarkable Passages*, 11–12; Winthrop, *Papers*, 169; BL Additional MS 43827A fo. 19v.
[161] Cambers, *Godly reading*, 92; Rogers, *Matrimoniall Honour*, 142; Clarke, *Lives of thirty-two divines*, 149; Clarke, *Lives of sundry Eminent Persons*, 62; Hinde, *Faithfull Remonstrance ... of Iohn Bruen*, 72, 135.
[162] *Forme of prayers ... approved and receiued by the Churche of Scotland*, 20–1; David Calderwood, *The History of the Kirk of Scotland*, ed. Thomas Thomson (Edinburgh, 1842–5), VII.449; John Spottiswoode, *History of the Church of Scotland*, ed. M. Russell (Edinburgh, 1848–51), III.268–9.
[163] Collinson, *Religion of Protestants*, 248–51; Haigh, *Plain Man's Pathways*, 114; Patrick Collinson, 'Night Schools, Conventicles and Churches: continuities and discontinuities in early Protestant ecclesiology' in Peter Marshall and Alec Ryrie (eds), *The Beginnings of English Protestantism* (Cambridge, 2002). See also the discussion of lay Bible exposition in Kate Narveson, '"Their practice bringeth little profit": Clerical Anxieties about Lay Scripture Reading in Early Modern England' in Martin and Ryrie, *Private and Domestic Devotion*.

Francis Walsingham, just in case he had made the wrong judgement.[164] This was not a straightforwardly confessional issue. The celebrated London wit, William Austin, more ceremonialist than puritan, insisted that regular private meetings of Christians 'for the stirring up of *Charitie* and *Devotion* . . . are not *Separations* from the great *Congregation*; but *parts of it*, and (as it were) so many *Vnder-schooles*', who follow Christ's own example in gathering his disciples.[165]

What actually happened at such meetings? Sometimes, simply chat. Too many Protestants, John Phillips claimed, 'know not what/Religion is, unless it be to *prate*'. Calvin, in bleak mode, claimed that most people studied Scripture simply 'that they may haue somethyng to talke vpon in company', and even 'to get accesse to ther wemen & ladies'.[166] Religion could simply be fodder for the lost art of conversation. In which case, as is still proverbial, chat could quickly escalate into argument, which was one of the reasons governments disapproved. The consequence of too much religious talk in Edward VI's reign, John Christopherson lamented, had been that,

> in euery house, at euery mans table, in euery corner, in euery strete, at euerye tauerne and inne, at all times was there suche unreuerent reasonynge of Gods highe mysteries, that those that mette together frendes, departed enemyes.[167]

Protestants joined in the tutting. The Elizabeth homily against brawling and contentiousness warned against those who dispute about religion 'upon the ale-benches . . . to vain-glory, and shewing forth of their cunning'. This sort of rhetoric remained a staple of anti-puritan literature. The stereotypical puritan was defined as 'an everlasting Argument', and Arthur Wilson denounced his own youthful habit of 'disputing with the People often in Religion'. However, we should question Wilson's claim that such arguments were undertaken 'rather out of Contention than Edification'.[168] People argue about religion not only because it matters to them, or because they are argumentative, but also because the experience itself is enlivening and edifying. In the 19th century, James Hogg claimed satirically that theological argument was a higher form of Protestant discourse than prayer, a gibe that stung because it was uncomfortably close to the truth. Richard Rogers described religious conference as being a matter of 'whetting on one the other'.[169] Especially for those raised in an academic culture based on disputation, religious argument could be a spiritual experience in itself.

However, when our sources speak about 'conference', they usually mean something a little more self-consciously godly. One picture is painted for us by John

---

[164] BL Lansdowne MS 157 fo. 186r.

[165] William Austin, *Devotionis Augustinianae Flamme* (1637: RSTC 973), 226, 230.

[166] Phillips, *Satyr*, 24; John Calvin, *An admonicion against astrology iudiciall* (1561: RSTC 4372), sigs A2v–3r.

[167] Christopherson, *An exhortation*, sig. T7r–v.

[168] *Certain Sermons or Homilies*, 124; Arthur Wilson, 'Observations of God's Providence, in the Tract of my Life', in Francis Peck (ed.), *Desiderata Curiosa*, vol. 2 (1735), XII.7; Earle, *Microcosmographie*, 121.

[169] James Hogg, *The Private Memoirs and Confessions of a Justified Sinner*, ed. David Groves (Edinburgh, 1991), 104; Knappen, *Two Diaries*, 64.

Hooper, writing an open letter to England's embattled Protestants early in Mary I's reign. He urged them regularly 'to have assemblies together . . . and there to talk and renew among yourselves the truth of your religion. . . . Comfort one another, make prayers together, confer with one another'. We find a slightly different kind of mutual comfort in 1587, when a group meeting under Rogers' direction spent four days reflecting systematically on their own sins and their neighbours' virtues, 'with great inflameing of our hartes'.[170] Another half-century later, Henry Scudder gave this instruction in 'holy speech and conference':

> Let the matter of your talke be, either of God, or of his Word, and wayes wherin you should walke; or of his workes . . . and of his mercies. . . . Impart also each to other the experiments & proofes you haue had of Gods grace and power, in this your Christian warfare.[171]

Even if conference was not as formal as this suggests, we should expect a degree of self-conscious decorum.

We do not have transcripts of such edifying conversations, but we do have something not entirely unlike them: the hugely popular literary genre of the edifying dialogue, often styled as a conversation between two or more neighbours. The genre was pioneered by Thomas Becon. Did some of his readers try to emulate the stilted conversations between Philemon, Eusebius, Theophyle, and Christopher, paper-thin characters whose doctrinal adventures he followed for more than two decades? In detail, perhaps not, but a book like *The sycke mans salue*—the most successful of Becon's dialogues—was plainly trying to teach readers how to conduct themselves together, as well as what to believe. Its twenty-five editions suggest that some, at least, were keen to learn such lessons.

Conference did not consist solely of discussion. It might, as with the Braintree group, include psalm-singing,[172] and also reading aloud. 'I doe delight', Nehemiah Wallington wrote, 'to make others partake of what good I my selfe get by hearing or Reading.' The young Baxter and his godly friend read through a library of 'serious Practical Books of Divinity' together.[173] Some groups served as book clubs, sharing rare, expensive, and—in some cases—dangerous texts. This was happening amongst London evangelicals as early as the 1520s. It seems to have reached Cornwall by the 1570s: William Carnsew's diary repeatedly refers to theological books being passed from neighbour to neighbour, often very soon after their London publication.[174] Not that the reading was always resolutely godly. John Knox and Henry Balnaves both worried that early Scottish evangelical gatherings were reading 'prophane authors and humain lectures'.[175] As the ambiguity of the

---

[170] Hooper, *Later Writings*, 589–90; Knappen, *Two Diaries*, 64.
[171] Scudder, *Christians daily walke* (1628), 151–2.
[172] Amongst many examples, see Knappen, *Two Diaries*, 99; Parker and Carlson, 'Practical Divinity', 193; Bownde, *Doctrine of the Sabbath*, 236–7; Scudder, *Christians daily walke* (1628), 151.
[173] FSL MS V.a.436, p. 42; Baxter, *Reliquiae Baxterianae*, 4.
[174] Pounds, 'William Carnsew', 21, 33, 40, 51.
[175] Alec Ryrie, 'Congregations, Conventicles and the Nature of Early Scottish Protestantism', *Past and Present* 191 (2006), 69–70.

word 'lecture' suggests, reading could easily shade into comment. The early Scottish reformer Adam Wallace, accused of unlicensed preaching, admitted only that he had 'red the Scriptures, and had gevin such exhortatioun as God pleaseth to geve to him, to such as pleased to hear him . . . sometymes at the table, and sometymes in other prevey places'. William Tyndale's practice of reading Scripture in merchants' houses on a Sunday seems to have included exposition. Becon's *Sycke mans salue* describes the dying man's friends choosing a series of Biblical passages to read to him fit to his purpose, without exposition as such, but careful selection and juxtaposition is comment in itself. Hooper's advice to underground gatherings in Marian England was to 'have some learned man . . . out of the scriptures speak unto you of faith and true honouring of God'.[176]

Most of our references to such ad hoc preaching pre-date the establishment of legal Protestant churches. After 1559–60, instead of replacing preaching, private conference now supported it, as a venue for repeating sermons or recapitulating catechesis. This might be done as a formal discipline in a group that met regularly, whether recalling a sermon they had just heard or reheating an old favourite; it might be an exercise for a pious schoolboy to repeat to his betters, for his own education and their edification.[177] It might happen ad hoc. Margaret Hoby simply 'conferred of the sarmon with the Gentlewemen that were with me' after dinner, which suggests something informal. Robert Blair, travelling through Ulster with some fellow-Scots, 'by way of conference . . . discoursed to them the most part of the last sermon I had preached'.[178] Most intriguing is the London apprentices' conventicle in the early 1630s, who resolved to spend their meetings 'in prayer, and in communicating to each other what experience we had received from the Lord; or else to repeat some sermon which we had heard before'. Reflection on their own spiritual experience and the recollection of others' teaching were two sides of a coin. And naturally, what fused them together was the experience of collective prayer. Such groups are invariably described as spending their time 'in conferrence and prayer'. We are rarely told any more than that, and as Collinson suggests, it seems likely that extempore prayer was normally used in this setting. The example of the young David Dickson, who led a group of Scottish ministers in prayer for two hours, is perhaps extreme,[179] but we can assume that 'conference' was always punctuated by, and often soaked in, collective prayer.

This was particularly so of one important, specialized variety of conference: confession and spiritual counsel. The Reformation had abolished sacramental confession, as theologically wrong-headed and liable to corruption, but from the beginning there was regret that the pastoral baby was being thrown out with

[176] Knox, *Works*, I.238; William Tyndale et al., *The whole workes of W. Tyndall, Iohn Frith and Doct. Barnes* (1573: RSTC 24436), sig. B3r; Becon, *Sycke mans salue*, esp. 8–9, 74; Hooper, *Later Writings*, 590.
[177] Hinde, *Faithfull Remonstrance . . . of Iohn Bruen*, 212; Kiffin, *Remarkable Passages*, 12; Clarke, *Collection*, 160.
[178] Hoby, *Diary*, 126; Blair, *Life*, 54.
[179] Kiffin, *Remarkable Passages*, 11–12; Tweedie, *Select Biographies*, 134; Collinson, *Religion of Protestants*, 266; Kirkton, *Secret and True History*, 17–18.

the sacramental bath-water.[180] Some Lutheran territories retained compulsory confession, shorn of its sacramental content.[181] The Reformed did not, but they were aware that a critical opportunity for private counselling and spiritual solace had been lost. 'In times past', Richard Greenham reflected, 'men were too far gone with *Auricular confession*, now men come too short of christian conferring.' But denouncing corrupt popish practices while trying to promote the pastoral virtues of 'right and true confession' was an almost impossible trick to pull off.[182] Although post-Reformation clergy continued formally to offer the opportunity to confess your sins, the practice was all but abandoned. (To some extent its place was taken by new practices such as catechizing, self-examination and diary-keeping.)[183] In practice, the regular Protestant use of confession was confined to a single setting: the deathbed, to which we shall return.[184]

Yet ministers continued to recommend individual spiritual counsel, for two main reasons. The first was teaching: one-to-one instruction could be much more effective than the kind broadcast from the pulpit. It was, in Samuel Fairclough's image, like filling a bottle with a funnel rather than simply leaving it out in the rain.[185] In particular, ministers taught that those who had questions on any matter of doctrine should ask their betters—notably, wives should ask their husbands. Whether anyone actually did this is another matter. All we have are airy claims by hagiographers.[186] Henry Smith preached that, if you did not grasp what he or a colleague had said, 'you should inquire, and they should instruct you againe'.[187] But that is the kind of offer preachers only make if they do not expect to be overwhelmed by pestering parishioners, and the mood could change rapidly. John Downame warned against disturbing ministers with 'slight and triuiall' questions, describing seeking their counsel as a last resort once the believer's own researches had been exhausted. 'It is not fit that their Pastour . . . should spend too much of his time in giuing satisfaction to euery particular man . . . in euery vselesse doubt.'[188] So if the offer of pastoral counsel was ever seriously taken up, it was swiftly withdrawn.

It was more common to seek out spiritual counsel when troubled by sin or fear of damnation. 'In the troubles of conscience', William Perkins advised, 'it is meete and conuenient, there should alwaies be vsed a priuate Confession', and others echoed the sentiment.[189] The problem was finding an appropriate counsellor.

---

[180] Ryrie, *Gospel and Henry VIII*, 32; Davies, *A religion of the Word*, 101; Thomas, *Religion and the Decline of Magic*, 186–7.

[181] Susan Karant-Nunn, *The Reformation of Ritual* (1997), 96–7; Mary Jane Haemig, 'Communication, consolation and discipline: two early Lutheran preachers on confession' in Katherine Jackson Lualdi and Anne T. Thayer (eds), *Penitence in the Age of Reformations* (Aldershot, 2000), 46–7.

[182] Parker and Carlson, 'Practical Divinity', 203; Latimer, *Sermons and Remains*, 13, 180.

[183] The writing of a book or letter is occasionally described as a confession, with the reader cast in the role of the confessor. Kilby, *Burthen*, 1; Howell, *Epistolæ Ho-Elianæ*, VI.46.

[184] See below, pp. 460–8.

[185] Clarke, *Lives of sundry Eminent Persons*, 162; cf. Dod and Cleaver, *Ten sermons*, 56.

[186] See, for example, Walker, *Sermon at the funerals . . .* , 47; Ley, *Patterne of Pietie*, 26.

[187] Smith, *Sermons*, 658.

[188] Downame, *Guide to Godlynesse*, 645–6.

[189] Perkins, *First part of The cases of conscience*, 5; cf. *Short and pretie Treatise*, sig. C3v; Byfield, *Marrow of the Oracles* (1622), 183; BL Egerton MS 2877 fo. 83v.

When Richard Norwood sought one, he first found a minister whose 'imperious strain' alienated him; on another occasion, he found two ministers who gave the impression they were keen to be rid of this 'confused and distracted' young man. He also feared being too open with his counsellors, lest they conclude that he was damned.[190] Those who advised seeking counsel invariably warned that confidants should be chosen with extreme care. Unlike Catholic confession, Protestant spiritual counsel was not sacramentally sealed. Richard Capel saw seeking spiritual counsel as a desperate last resort: for principled reasons—you ought to turn to God first—but also for practical ones. 'It is dangerous to tell our veriest friend' secrets; you never know who may turn out to be a 'blab'. Often, he suggested, women make better confidantes than men—unless they cannot keep secrets from their husbands.[191] No wonder that those struggling with temptation often kept their troubles to themselves, as Elizabeth Isham did. Her rationale was that, since her need was not for doctrinal advice, no-one else could help her: 'I was not troubled with any point of Religion but onely thus strongly tempted, which I knew was by God's permishion and that it was his triall of me.' In restrospect she saw this as an error, but she, at least, was apparently least likely to ask for help when she most needed it.[192] Good fellowship between godly neighbours, or structured collective exercises, were all very well, but the more intimate and potentially powerful conference became, the more it ran up against a grave problem, that of opening yourself up to other sinners.

KEEPING COMPANY WITH SINNERS

Letting other human beings into your religious life was both inescapable and deeply dangerous. The final section of this chapter will consider how early modern Protestants tried to navigate these dangers.

Should they, for example, compare themselves to other people? Normally the answer was no. The proper measure of virtue is God, not fallen humanity. Lewis Bayly warned, 'think not that thou art a Christian good enough, because thou dost as the most, and art not so bad as the worst'. Measuring yourself by others is a mark of the hypocrite who cares more of their opinion than for God's.[193] And yet that would not quite do. As Leif Dixon has pointed out, certain preachers' tropes, such as the warning that not one in a thousand would be saved, almost begged listeners to compare themselves to their neighbours in the pews. Conscience-literature consoled worried believers by pointing out that 'you are not alone. . . . There bee a number of Gods deere children, who are as much and as often troubled with the

---

[190] Norwood, *Journal*, 34, 100–1.
[191] Capel, *Tentations*, 179–80, 184, 192–3.
[192] Isham, 'Confessions', fo. 22v.
[193] Bayly, *Practise of pietie*, 232; Bolton, *Discourse about happinesse*, esp. 61. This is also the central argument of William King, *The Straight Gate to Heauen* (1616: RSTC 14997.3) (six editions, 1616–36). Cf. Knell, *Godlie and necessarie Treatise*, sig. A3v.

same griefe of minde aswell as you'.[194] Arthur Hildersam even recommended receiving the Lord's Supper along with the virtuous, since that joins you with them in communion, leading you 'to become more and more like vnto them both in faith and conuersation'.[195] In other words, Protestants were supposed to switch between carefully assessing others' virtues and vices, and studiously ignoring them, according to the needs of the particular moment. The trick is easier described than performed.

Matters only worsened when you actually interacted with others, for company could be as dangerous as it was beneficial. The obvious path was to shun 'the company of damned hel-hounds, and hellish miscreants', 'the seruants of a strange God',[196] and instead cleave to like-minded individuals who shared something of your own religious experience. If you are trying to attain true repentance, Henry Tozer and John Dod suggested, you should seek out 'other men, who are themse-lues touched with a feeling in this kinde'; those who have broken hearts themselves 'are more able and skilfull to pierce and wound the soules of others'.[197] But the problems with this are legion. To modern eyes, the most obvious is its cliquish exclusivity, which can sometimes be startling: against the Augustinian injunction to hate sin but love sinners, Byfield urged his readers to hate not only sin but also 'sinners, because they hate God'.[198] But as Patrick Collinson has pointed out, we should not be fooled by the rhetoric. Real social separatism was rare in our period.[199] For one thing, sinners do not normally wear labels identifying them-selves as such. In any case, companions did not have to be notorious sinners in order to be dangerous. Mere 'idle and unprofitable Talk' was, to John Rogers, 'a Canker that consumeth all Good'. Believers could be as dangerous as scoffers. Keeping company with 'lukewarm professors', Henry Scudder warned, produces 'an insensible chilling of your spirits, and . . . taking off the edge of your zeale'.[200] Richard Kilby shows us what this might mean. His agonized account of his struggle with sin—and with kidney-stones—in the spring of 1614 is punctuated by his spending time in company, which seemingly inevitably turned his mind from God. 'I cannot call to minde that ever I was in company with any, and drawne into a familiar communication, but that I was also drawn into sinne.' By *sin*, he meant 'idle talk' and distraction.[201] Perhaps he simply lacked a local soulmate, but perhaps not: Richard Rogers recorded an occasion when 'wandringe by litle and litle in needlesse speech' with his wife drew them both away from God.[202] To be in company was, inevitably, to be exposed to others' sins. The question was not how to avoid this encounter, but how to deal with it.

[194] Dixon, 'Calvinist Theology', 185; Linaker, *Comfortable treatise* (1595), 2–3.
[195] Bradshaw and Hildersam, *Direction*, II.13.
[196] Greenwood, *Workes*, III.22; Byfield, *Marrow of the Oracles* (1622), 515.
[197] Tozer, *Directions for a Godly Life*, 89; Dod and Cleaver, *Ten Sermons*, 10.
[198] Byfield, *The Signes*, 121.
[199] Collinson, *Religion of Protestants*, 269–71.
[200] Mather, *Magnalia*, III.110; Scudder, *Christians daily walke* (1628), 142–3.
[201] Kilby, *Hallelujah*, esp. 88–90, 93, 95–6, 102–3, 135, 137–40, 152.
[202] Knappen, *Two Diaries*, 58.

Early modern Protestants tackled this problem in three broad ways. The first was to confront and rebuke others' sins. Some Protestants at least aspired to the grace of 'telling my neighbours their faults without dissimulation'. To be still in the face of sin was 'vnchristian sufferance. . . . Our conniuance is sinfull, our silence banefull, our allowance damnable'. Instead, you should give sinners 'apparent signes of thy dislike': which meant rebuking them 'not as some do, with a smiling countenance: but as our Sauiour did with an angrie countenance, mourning also, as he did, for the hardnesse of their hearts'.[203] The trouble was that few people took such rebukes kindly. This kind of thing gave puritans a reputation for hypocrisy, and gave busybodies free rein. Richard Sibbes, who was as clear about this duty as anyone, also warned against the over-enthusiastic censure which is too ready to 'unchurch and unbrother' fellow Christians. Robert Harris' rule of thumb—that you should 'vse no more words against mens sinnes, then thou wilt make prayers for their soules in secret'—possibly curtailed some excesses.[204] A more regular solution was to make criticism reciprocal, emphasizing the duty to take others' rebukes of your own failings in good part. We find the young Nehemiah Wallington vowing to take his wife's, siblings', and parents' reproaches kindly, and he took it as a sign of his election that 'I count him a freend that will reprove me'.[205] But even he clearly found it difficult, and we might imagine that those whose sins most needed rebuking would be the least willing to accept rebukes.

We should notice, however, that some such reproaches raised fewer hackles in early modern society than they would today. There was an accepted—although not unlimited—right for superiors to correct their inferiors' sins: parents rebuked their children, husbands their wives, ministers their congregations. When moral reprimands truly struck to the heart, they usually had hierarchy behind them in this way. When James Melville received his first communion, aged thirteen, an elder of his parish 'gaiff me an admonition concerning lightness, wantonnes, and nocht takin tent [paying attention]', which he remembered all his life. The seven-year-old Thomas Goodwin was pulled aside by a servant, 'who observing some sin in me, reproved me sharply, and laid open hell-torments as due to me, whither, he said, I must go for such sins, and was very vehement with me'. Again, it stayed with him.[206] Nor was it only children. Richard Greenham once told a recently bereaved widower that he had feared God would bury something that belonged to him, 'beecause I saw you often bury mine instructions made unto you'. If, as it seems, he got away with this jaw-dropping tactlessness, it was because of his office. Compare the Somerset layman Henry Bindon, who in 1626 told a dying neighbour to repent of her former adultery. The outraged woman, who had less than an hour to live, threw him out, and he was later accused of having usurped 'the office of a priest'.[207]

[203] Sparke, *Crumms of comfort*, sig. E12r; Adams, *The white devil*, 9; Clarke, *Holy Incense*, 145; 'R. R.', *House-holders Helpe*, 29–30.

[204] Sibbes, *Bruised reede*, 85, 96; Harris, *Peters enlargement* (1624), sig. A4v; cf. Ward, *Coal from the Altar*, 12–15.

[205] Hildersam, *Doctrine of Fasting*, 106; LMA Guildhall MS 204 p. 39; Wallington, *Notebooks*, 285.

[206] Melville, *Autobiography*, 23; Goodwin, *Works*, II.lvii.

[207] Parker and Carlson, *'Practical Divinity'*, 184; Haigh, *Plain Man's Pathways*, 127–8.

In other words, a social norm of hierarchical moral discipline trumped a theological principle of universal brotherly reproach. Wallington gives us a glimpse of this in practice. He vowed both to reproach and to be reproached by his wife and siblings, but he baulked at the idea of reproaching his parents. Sibbes' description of how 'private Christians' are guilty of 'usurpation of censure towards others' reveals similar scruples.[208]

George Gifford's fictionalized account of his encounter with his parishioners' religious assumptions gives us a finer-grained view of this problem. His plain man, Atheos, dislikes having his sins rebuked, but not under all circumstances. 'It woulde not greeue me to be reproued by those which are learned, but now euery Iacke wilbe medling'. And he cites the Gospel warning against attending to the mote in another's eye, rather than the plank in your own. 'Zelotes' (Gifford's mouthpiece) replies with the revealing claim that those who hate discipline 'doe euer alleadge that saying of Christe'. Christ, he argues, did not mean to outlaw spotting motes in others' eyes as such. 'What if I see ye are blinde and ready for to fall into the pit of eternall destruction?' Should he not act to save his neighbour then?[209] Christians are supposed to be their brothers' keepers. As such, John Brinsley argued, the Christian obligation to 'admonish, reproue, exhort' others was a universal one. 'Meeknesse', Henry Scudder stated bluntly, 'is not to be shewed in the matters of God.'[210] The Elizabethan gentlewoman Katherine Stubbes was said to be so gentle that 'she was neuer knowne to fall out with any of her neighbours . . . much lesse to scold or brawle'. Yet if those neighbours were indulging in scurrilous, blasphemous, or bawdy talk, she 'woulde rebuke them sharpely, shewing them the vengeaunce of GOD due for such deserts'.[211] This made sense in its own terms, but the distinction between rebuking and scolding may have been lost on the neighbours.

The second approach to conferring with sinners was almost the opposite: to aspire to reconciliation and pacification. Sometimes this was spurious, especially in theological matters, but as we have seen, there was real unease about polemic and confrontation, and devotion could indeed be a means of circumventing division.[212] 'If we must needs contend', a prayer of Richard Bernard's asked, 'let it be . . . to see who can excell others' in 'zeale for thy truth, thy worship, thine honor and glory'.[213] More to the point, healing worldly quarrels was generally recognized as virtuous. Reconciliation with neighbours was an appropriate way to spend the Sabbath.[214] Ministers, at least, had a duty and right to heal not only their own but others' quarrels. In England, this was down to the tact and energy of individual clergy; to be called a 'promoter of Peace and Concord amongst his Neighbours' was

---

[208] LMA Guildhall MS 204 p. 39; Sibbes, *Bruised reede*, 96. Cf. Robert Cleaver's careful argument that a wife may rebuke her husband's sins if she has 'sufficient reason': Cleaver, *[G]odly form*, 174.

[209] Gifford, *Briefe discourse*, fos 18v–19r, 65r, 79v; cf. Matthew 7:3–5.

[210] Brinsley, *True Watch* (1608), 155; Brinsley, *True Watch* (1622), II.182*; Rogers, *Garden* (1615), II sig. F5r; cf. Genesis 4:9.

[211] Stubbes, *Christal glasse*, sigs A2v–3r.

[212] See above, pp. 290–2.

[213] Bernard, *A Weekes Worke* (1628), 226.

[214] Bayly, *Practise of pietie*, 478.

high, but not unusual praise.[215] In Scotland, the ministry of reconciliation was institutionalized in kirk sessions, which, like Calvinist consistories across the early modern world, devoted much of their energies to dispute resolution. That expectation underpinned what John Welsh achieved when he first came to Ayr as minister, and found a town riven by feuding.

> His manner was, after he had ended a skirmish amongst his neighbours ... to cause cover a table upon the street, and there brought the enemies together; and beginning with prayer, he persuaded them to profess themselves friends, and then to eat and drink together.[216]

The echo of the Lord's Supper was no accident. The threat of excommunication was the kirk sessions' final sanction against inveterate quarrellers. In both England and Scotland, unresolved quarrels could deter neighbours from communion, and communion-season made the need for reconciliation seem urgent.[217]

The third approach to handling sinners bypassed their sins altogether and aimed instead at their conversion. This is a little unexpected. Early modern Protestants, especially Reformed Protestants, showed relatively little interest in serious missionary activity, a quirk which is often linked to the doctrine of predestination and the fatalism it supposedly engenders.[218] Gifford's dialogue ends with the countryman, Atheos departing, obstinate in his errors. Zelotes, entirely unsurprised, comments: 'I looke for none other rewarde from ye: the blacke More can not change his hewe, nor the Cat of the mountayne her spots.'[219] And indeed, there was nothing of the missionary zeal of the 18th century; but nor was there total neglect.

At the simplest level, Protestants were supposed at least to notice the fate of the unconverted. Prayers for the conversion of Jews, Turks, and pagans were pretty abstract in islands where all three were in short supply. But these easily extended to prayer for 'all misbeleeving people', or even for 'them whiche as yet do not perfectly knowe the'.[220] The trouble was, again, a certain half-heartedness. It is not merely the effect of predestination, although we can feel that hobbling Robert Saxby's prayer for the Gospel to enjoy 'a free and Ioyfull passage thorow the world ... for the conversion of those who belong to thine Elecion'.[221] Many devotees simply did not believe it would or could happen. Oliver Pigg's prayer for the Spanish at the time of the Armada is typical. He begins with five lines asking for God to bring them to the truth, and then spends nearly two full pages praying, 'or else (Lord) ... curse them in all their actions ... as the fire burneth the forests'. Edward Hutchins' prayer 'against the enimies of the truth' similarly briefly acknowledged

---

[215] Parker and Carlson, '*Practical Divinity*', 83; cf. Willet, *Synopsis Papismi*, sig. b3v.

[216] Tweedie, *Select Biographies*, 6.

[217] Hunt, 'Lord's Supper', 62.

[218] For an acknowledgement, and valiant defence, of the distinctive 'Puritan type of evangelism'—consisting entirely of preaching by ministers to captive audiences—see Packer, *Quest for Godliness*, 291–308.

[219] Gifford, *Briefe discourse*, fo. 83r.

[220] Kilby, *Burthen*, 31; Heyden, *Bryefe Summe*, sig. N8v. Cf. Becon, *Newe pathwaye unto praier*, sig. N1v; Pinke, *Tryall of a Christians loue*, II.26.

[221] Saxby, 'Miscellany', fo. 69r.

the possibility of their conversion, before asking God to 'mowe them downe like haie'. He even reworked the Gospel parable of the lost sheep: in his version, the wanderer should be devoured by a lion, 'least turning to thy little flocke, she corrupt the rest'.[222]

This does not rule out declaring the Gospel to the unconverted, but it changes the mood. You do it, such prayers imply, because it is an obligation, and because it justifies God's punishment of those who stop their ears, not because you expect it to work. A proverb had it that the apostles had been fishers of souls, who 'caught many at one draught', but their modern successors were instead huntsmen, 'that with much toil and clamour running up and down all day, scarce take one Deer or Hare e're night'. When an Italian Jew visited Andrew Willet's vicarage in Hertfordshire, Willet welcomed him and spent a month trying to convert him. However—and, Willet's biographer implied, inevitably—the visitor's fair words were empty, and he disappeared when a baptism was threatened. It was to be expected. Evangelism was a duty, but a fruitless one. The prophet Ezekiel compared himself to a lookout warning of approaching danger, whose obligation was to sound the alarm regardless of whether the people chose to act on it. In this sense, the duty to warn of the coming judgement could be perfectly fulfilled even if there was not a single convert.[223] That duty was at its keenest in the dangerous days of the mid-16th century, when, amidst sore temptations to dissemble their beliefs, Protestants were urged 'plainely to professe the Lord'. They did so for the sake of doing so, not in order to convert others. The witness of Marian martyrs who sang psalms in prison, or who read 'certayne chapters of the Bible . . . with so hye an loud a voyce, that the people without in the streetes, might heare', was intended less to win over their hearers than to declare their own faithfulness.[224] The imperative continued when the persecution ceased. In the 1620s, Nehemiah Wallington was vowing to 'declare and speake of the mercies and goodnes of God vnto others', conceived as an obligation to God rather than to the hearers.[225]

But of course the two cannot be separated. In the next breath, Wallington also resolved to 'lead such a life as others seing my holy life and conuersation may be wonne thereby'. That wish recurs throughout our period. An Edwardian prayer asks for holiness of life so 'that al men may therby bee drawen vnto the, and se that we are thy disciples and followers'. By faithfully receiving the sacrament, Henry Tozer believed, we not only declare our faith to others, but 'also by our example stirre them vp to the performance of the same duty'.[226] The appeal of this approach was that it offered a way of spreading the faith while avoiding the awkward business of *talking* about it. Believers could simply focus on their own holiness and hope

[222] Pigg, *Meditations concerning praiers*, 15–17; Hutchins, *Davids Sling*, 58–9.

[223] Willet, *Synopsis Papismi*, sig. c1r–v; Samuel Clarke, *The Lives of Two and Twenty English Divines* (1660: Wing C4540), 80; Hooper, *Later Writings*, 67; cf. Ezekiel 33:2–9.

[224] Gilby, *An answer*, fo. 3r; Foxe, *Actes and monuments* (1563), 1629, 1656; Foxe, *Actes and monuments* (1570), 1735.

[225] LMA Guildhall MS 204, p. 42.

[226] LMA Guildhall MS 204, p. 42; Heyden, *Bryefe Summe*, sig. O1r; Tozer, *Directions for a Godly Life*, 38. Cf. Bernard, *A Weekes Worke* (1616), 93–4; Brinsley, *True Watch* (1608), 58–9.

that would do the trick. Hugh Latimer used, and inverted, the Biblical precept that doing good to enemies heaps coals on their heads. This meant, he claimed, that by patient suffering, 'thou shalt heat him; for he is in coldness of charity. At length he shall remember himself, and say, "What a man am I!" '—and reform himself.[227] It is an appealing idea, but not, perhaps, very likely to have been effective.

The problem, then, was not so much that early modern Protestants were indifferent to evangelizing, but that they found it socially awkward and practically unsuccessful. Richard Rogers, who earnestly urged his readers to spread the faith, admitted that many people found the attempt to be 'toyle and tediousnes'; that it often seemed 'vnciuill, and vnseasonable, either among straingers, or their owne neighbours', and that even when it is done, 'we seeme to preuaile little'. One Jacobean preacher urged the duty, but also warned against casting pearls before swine, and against speaking 'tediously' or 'beat[ing] the hearers with repetitions'.[228] So forms of proselytism which did not involve direct engagement with its targets (like the attempt to attract converts through holy living), or which did not aim at success (like the Marian martyrs' demonstrative witness), had an obvious attraction. The actual speaking could be left to the minister, safely in his pulpit. Even those who did counsel ordinary Christians to speak about the Gospel to their neighbours usually recommended doing so cautiously, 'whensoever occasion serveth' or 'as occasion is offered'. The Biblical precept to be ready to answer those who question your faith could become a principle of not speaking until you are spoken to.[229] The young lawyer Andrew Kingsmill apparently spent much of his time in study, readying himself 'to teach other if at any time God shoulde call him therevnto'; John Hooper likewise called believers to 'study to have a thorough knowledge' of the faith, so that they might 'to be ready to make answer for the same'.[230] These were not idle or evasive exhortations, but they did mean that believers could sit reading in their studies and persuade themselves that they were spreading the Gospel.

That is not quite the end of the matter. 'It is our dutie being conuerted our selues to strengthen others', Rogers taught, but for some *duty* was not quite the word. 'There is no greater joy', Thomas Goodwin wrote, 'then . . . to see soules converted by us.'[231] And indeed, it might be the seeking as well as the success that was joyful. According to Jeremiah Dyke, the Christian soul

> having once tasted, and found the sweetnesse and goodnesse that is in Christ, and in the wayes of God, it cannot rest, but it must seeke others, to bring them to participate of the same goodnesse with it selfe.

He took this zeal to be one of the signs of true faith.[232] This kind of ecstatic, almost involuntary proclamation is a recurrent phenomenon. Arthur Wodenoth wrote that one immediate effect of his conversion was a 'desire that others might partake

227 Latimer, *Sermons by Hugh Latimer*, 439; Proverbs 25:21–2, Romans 12:20.
228 Rogers, *Seven treatises*, 63; FSL MS V.a.347 fo. 14v.
229 Latimer, *Sermons and Remains*, 196; Rogers, *Seven treatises*, 63; I Peter 3:15.
230 Kingsmill, *Viewe of mans estate*, sig. A2v; Hooper, *Later Writings*, 572.
231 Rogers, *Seven treatises*, 63; Goodwin, *Returne of Prayers*, 28.
232 Dyke, *Worthy communicant*, 323–4; Byfield, *The Signes*, 134.

of that grace and mercy which God had shewed unto mee'. John Winthrop, as a
new convert, had 'a great striveling in my heart to draw others to God'.[233] The
Word burns within the heart. It burned with particular intensity in the first
generations of the Reformation, when converts were most liable to be thunder-
struck by the evangelical message's novelty. Miles Coverdale wrote that the true
convert 'shall be compelled by the Spirit of God to break out into praise and
thanksgiving', and 'shall not be content . . . till other men know also what God hath
done for him'.[234]

The Catholic reformer Nicholas Harpsfield had had a bellyful of this. The typical
early convert, he wrote, was not content simply to 'whisper' the faith, but 'thirsted
very sore to publishe his newe doctrine and diuulge it', and had 'an ytche of
preaching'. Such callow evangelicals believed that they could out-argue any scholar
and out-preach any cleric.[235] It is undeniable. Some Protestants' eagerness simply
to speak of their faith regardless of circumstances, and their zeal for theological
argument in and out of season, swept aside all propriety. Katherine Stubbes'
husband claimed that

> if she chanced at any time to be in place where either Papists, or Atheists were . . . she
> would not yeeld a iote, nor giue any place vnto them at al, but would most mightily
> iustifie the truth of God, agaynst their blasphemous vntruths, and conuince them, yea,
> & confound them by the testimonies of the word of God.[236]

Harpsfield would have said that she was scratching an itch.

This third approach to dealing with sinners—actively trying to convert
them—was in practice the rarest. Some Protestants, sometimes, prayed for it,
others tried—or told themselves that they were trying—to do it by setting an
example of godliness, by preparing for occasions to speak which might or might not
ever come, by blurting out testimonies of their own faith, or by plunging into
arguments with those who disagreed. Occasionally, however, something more
constructive might happen. Social norms, again, eased it. Ministers were expected
to try to win souls, either in the pulpit or in person; masters and landlords might
require servants and tenants to hear them out. Lady Margaret Hoby repeatedly
refers to having 'had som speach with the poore and Ignorant of the som princeples
of religion' or to spending time in conference with 'a yonge papest maide'. Ben
Jonson imagined a pious and learned prisoner who converted an illiterate and ill-
mannered sergeant.[237]

Or take the stylized but not entirely unrealistic scenario which opens Arthur
Dent's *The plaine mans path-way to heauen*. The two godly heroes of the dialogue
are in a meadow. When they see the other two, godless characters approaching, the
godly layman, Philagathus, says, 'It were good for vs to take some occasion to

---

[233] Wodenoth, 'Expressions', 123; Winthrop, *Papers*, 156.
[234] Coverdale, *Remains*, 536.
[235] Nicholas Harpsfield, *The life and death of Sr Thomas Moore,* ed. Elsie Vaughan Hitchcock
(Early English Text Society o.s. 186, 1932), 84, 86.
[236] Stubbes, *Christal glasse*, sig. A2r–v.
[237] Hoby, *Diary*, 62, 66, 105; Ben Jonson et al., *Eastward hoe* (1605: RSTC 4970), sig. H4r–v.

speake of matters of religion; it may be we shall doe them some good.' They greet each other, and it turns out that the two newcomers are on their way to buy a cow. Philagathus replies, 'Leaue off this talking of kine, and worldly matters; and let vs enter into some speech of matters of religion, whereby we may doe good, and take good one of another.' Whereupon they all sit under a tree, and after some 350 pages of dialogue, one of the two is converted.[238] Of course, this makes no more pretence to realism than do the characters' names, yet in the long days and long nights during which our early modern forebears had to make their own entertainment, the offer of some extended religious chat may not have been unwelcome. If nothing else, Dent's book offered a model to which to aspire. If you wanted to know how to have religious conference with sinners without consenting to, or being corrupted by, their sin, and without merely denouncing it either, this was one way to do it. Not a very realistic or plausible one, perhaps, but then, what were the alternatives?

[238] Dent, *Plaine mans path-way*, 2–4.

PART V

THE PROTESTANT LIFE

15

The Meaning of Life

'It is now time that we shulde arise from slepe: for now is our saluation nere, then when we beleued it.' *Romans 13:11*

Historians often use the phrase 'life cycle' to describe the social changes associated with birth, childhood, adulthood, death, and mourning.[1] For our purposes, however, this image—with its implications of continuity, and of rhythms larger than the individual—is inappropriate. Early modern Protestants did not have a life cycle. They had life courses: each individual's own personal pilgrimage through life and death to their ultimate, pre-ordained destiny. There are of course patterns, which is what makes the final section of this book possible: shared experiences of childhood, adulthood, ageing, and dying. But in the end it was individual believers, not a society, who would have to stand before God.

More importantly, this was how early modern Protestants understood their lives. They were incubating the novel idea that every Christian life story was, in fact, a story: a coherent and progressive narrative in which the Spirit providentially led the believer on a winding but sure path to Heaven. Understanding that narrative in any individual case was not easy, especially when the particular story was not yet over, but the principle that every life lived under God must have a coherent meaning of this kind was unshakeable. The effort to discern those meanings was one of the wellsprings of the diaries, biographies, and autobiographies which began to flourish in our period.[2] It was one of Protestantism's greatest sources of consolation: even disasters and failures were embraced within God's plan. And it gave the Protestant life the distinctive, restless dynamism which this book argues is one of its most pervasive qualities. So to examine the Protestant life-course is not only to ask what a Protestant childhood, or a Protestant deathbed, was actually like. First of all, it is to listen to the stories which Protestants told about their lives.

PROGRESS AND REPENTANCE

For much of this book we have been asking questions about the normal or the routine experience of being Protestant. However, early modern Protestants were not terribly interested in normality, stasis, or rhythm. To develop and remain

---

[1] For example, Cressy, *Birth, Marriage and Death*.
[2] Williams, 'Religious experience', 581–2.

within a set of religious habits was, in their eyes, a kind of death. They looked for a spiritual life which was linear, not cyclical. Rather than moving through the rhythms of the old sacramental system, they expected to move on from conversion, through higher and greater knowledge and holiness, until death. Spiritual progress thus becomes essential, and backsliding—a very Protestant word—fatal. As Archbishop Sandys put it:

> Walk on, go forward. For if ye be in the way of life, not to go forward is to go backward. . . . Take heed, I say, of backsliding. . . . Go on from strength to strength, from virtue to virtue. . . . God grant that there be not a retiring from strength to weakness, from virtue to sinfulness![3]

Those whose lives did not reflect this kind of progress had a problem.

The Protestant theology of sanctification underpinned this. One of the keys to Luther's theological breakthrough was his separation of justification (the declaration that a sinner is righteous in God's eyes) from sanctification (the life-long process of actually becoming righteous). This distinction requires that the justified person will in fact progress towards virtue. Overlay this with Calvinist predestination, and the implication is that anyone whose progress stalls or reverses may in fact never have been justified at all.

This meant that the redeemed sinner's life should have a very distinctive shape. As the puritan agitator Thomas Wilcox put it, 'if you be not now, as in regarde of spirituall graces, in better estate then you were longe a go, feare your condition'. Those who are not growing are as good as dead. 'Standing water putrefies and rots.'[4] Stagnation was potentially even worse than a spectacular fall into sin, which might at least spark appalled repentance. John Brinsley repeatedly warned against 'standing at a stay, least for not going forward, I goe backeward in thy iustice, and become an Apostate'. He recommended weekly self-examination on the point. Elizabeth Melville, in her *Godlie Dreame*, describes wanting to rest for a moment, but being told by Christ, 'Nay, thou mayst not sit nor stand./Hold on thy course'. It was a commonplace that Christians should 'leaue euery daie some synne', 'daily procede further and further, from vertue to vertue', 'euery day grow vntil we come to perfection'.[5] Daily progress was accepted as a sign of election.[6] This is, in other words, unremittingly relentless.

The obvious result was fear of backsliding, and unceasing self-discipline. Sin, as Anthony Maxey preached before James I, was a slippery slope: the slightest misstep could start a cascade which would sweep you into Hell. Nipping any burgeoning

---

[3] Sandys, *Sermons*, 233.

[4] Thomas Wilcox, *A right godly and learned Exposition, vpon the whole Booke of Psalmes* (1586: RSTC 25625), sig. A2v; Dyke, *Worthy communicant*, 401–2; Cowper, *Triumph*, 179; Andrewes, *Celestiall looking-glasse*, sig. A8r.

[5] Brinsley, *True Watch* (1608), 10; Brinsley, *True Watch* (1622), II.203; Melville, *Godlie Dreame*, sig. A5v; Dering, *Godly priuate praiers*, sigs A3v, E1r, F3v; Dent, *Sermon of Repentance*, sig. B7r; Brinsley, *True Watch* (1608), 162; Bod MS Rawl C.473 fos 6v–7v.

[6] See, for example, Cancellar, *Alphabet of prayers*, sigs A5v–6r; Norden, *Pensiue mans practise*, 75; Rogers, *Seven treatises*, sigs A3r–v; Perkins, *First part of The cases of conscience*, 89; Dod and Cleaver, *Ten sermons*, 11; Crashaw, *Milke for Babes*, 60; Bayly, *Practise of pietie*, 255; Hoby, *Diary*, 67.

sin in the bud—or, as he put it, 'the nipping of a Serpents head'—was essential: the Devil was always ready to seize his opportunity. Richard Sibbes agreed that the Christian 'is no farther safe, than watchfull' against sin.[7] Nor was this simply a matter of avoiding sin. Nicholas Byfield insisted that the Christian must 'carefully perseuer in his first loue'; that is, maintain the spiritual and emotional heights of conversion undimmed throughout life. He did not explain how this was to be done. But Richard Rogers wrote his enormous *Seven treatises* in part to explain how to 'fall not from our first loue'. He was appalled by the slapdash ways of his contemporaries who 'doe not think this possible to keepe, yea and increase it from day to day', and who therefore scarcely enjoy the fruits of the Spirit. To 'waxe cold', he wrote, is 'an intollerable trecherie'.[8]

In fact this merely acknowledged the problem: that a theory of steady, progressive sanctification was a poor fit with real life. Squaring this circle was a major preoccupation of Reformed Protestant piety. There were several possibilities. One was to set the right pace. Progressive sanctification was a lifetime's work, not a day's or a year's. Saints could afford to take their time, and might even be wise to do so. 'If wee had learned but euery yeare one vertue since we were borne', Thomas Tymme lamented, 'we might by this time haue bin like saints among men.' That at least seems a manageable tempo.[9] I have found no suggestion of Protestants avoiding tackling their sins too quickly, so as to leave themselves some headroom in the future, but it would not surprise me if the temptation were there.

A second approach was to emphasize that even the weakest Christian would progressively grow in strength. Tymme promised that, while the Christian life may be difficult at the beginning, it grows progressively easier as sanctification gathers pace. This claim defies both long-standing Christian tradition and common sense, but Rogers agreed. His assurance that 'the beginning is the hardest' was underlined by one relieved (or sceptical) reader. Richard Sibbes used the Biblical image of a smouldering flax: barely alight, but capable, if blown into life by the Spirit, of producing 'glorious fireworkes of zeale and holinesse'.[10] To be daunted by the thought of having to improve day by day was to make the mistake of thinking that it was a matter of effort. Sanctification was the Spirit's work.

A third, related possibility was to distinguish between perception and reality. Whether or not we feel holy, William Cowper argued, is unimportant. 'Wee haue our owne vicissitudes of feeling, and not feeling: wee are changeable, but the Lord remaineth the same.' If we feel ourselves to be far from God, we should remember the perseverance of the saints and trust him. Indeed, feelings might be the polar opposite of the reality, rather than merely disconnected from it. John Dod comforted those who felt 'their corruptions stirring more violently, and temptations rushing vpon them more fiercely then euer before' after receiving the sacrament.

[7] Maxey, *Golden chaine*, sigs G7v–H1v, H4r; Capel, *Tentations*, sig. ¶10r.
[8] Byfield, *Marrow of the Oracles* (1622), 464–5; Rogers, *Seven treatises*, 57, 69–70, 257, 432–3. Cf. Revelation 2:4.
[9] Tymme, *Siluer watch-bell* (1605), 45; Bod MS Rawl C.473 fos 7v–8r.
[10] Tymme, *Siluer watch-bell* (1605), 109–11; Rogers, *Seven treatises*, 344 (underlining in FSL STC 21215); Sibbes, *Bruised reede*, 46–9, 134.

That was not a sign of backsliding, but the opposite: 'now that their sinne hath had a deadly blow, it beginneth (like a madde Bull in the same case) to rage more furiously'.[11] The argument that the Devil only pays attention to those who are threatening to escape him had a long pedigree.

All of these arguments, however, maintained the essential claim that sanctification was a continuous, unbroken process. For a great many, it was plainly not. Backsliding was an unavoidable pastoral reality. Rogers acknowledged in the *Seven treatises* that even amongst the elect, 'many . . . do yet lose and fall from their first loue', and well he might, for he had spent some years mercilessly diagnosing this failing in himself. It was a commonplace that the once-fervent were all too likely to grow 'formall and cursorie', 'cold and heauy'.[12] The sense of being becalmed during the long years of middle age was particularly prevalent. Margaret Hoby expressed her frustration with it, in her terse way: 'I Continewe in my accostomed exercises but my increasinges in goodes waies is not as I thirst for.' Nehemiah Wallington, in 1644, thought it applied not only to him but to the whole nation. 'We are no better for hearring and praying now then we ware a yeare agoe, as proud as could & dead in dutys as then.'[13] The experience of sanctification did not match the theory.

Thus the theory was adjusted, in two main ways. The first was to overlay an element of rhythm, or undulation. This applied in particular to the quixotic attempts to maintain the emotional pitch of first conversion. It was a commonplace that the Church had been given unusual gifts in the apostolic age, which were then withdrawn when it was no longer in its infancy. The indulgent but condescending way in which some Protestants looked back on the naïve ardour of their first conversions has something of that air to it. First love was a stage to be passed through as faith matured.[14] Henry Greenwood's bestelling treastise on Judgement Day imagined the Devil accusing the believer of having 'left thy first loue', as Rogers and others warned he would. But Greenwood rejected the accusation, and on experimental rather than theological grounds: 'Shew me any one of gods elect, that feeleth his loue at al tymes alike: it is not the manner of graces working.' George Herbert longed that 'what my soul doth feel sometimes,/My soul might ever feel!'—but he, too, knew that that was simply not the way things were.[15]

One comforting notion was that of a regular rhythm to the spiritual life. Perhaps it was like the tide: Christians might expect 'the flowing and ebbing of heavenly joy', 'an accesse and recesse of the Spirit'; or the seasons: 'fayth hath not onely a Spring time, and a Sommer season; but also a Winter, when it beareth no fruite'.[16]

---

[11] Cowper, *Triumph*, 69; Dod and Cleaver, *Ten sermons*, 18. Cf. Rous, *Mysticall Marriage*, 324; FSL MS V.b.214 fo. 92r.

[12] Rogers, *Seven treatises*, 432; Knappen, *Two Diaries*, 56–8, 70, 72, 89–90; Bolton, *Discourse about happinesse*, 94; Brinsley, *True Watch* (1611), II.11.

[13] Knappen, *Two Diaries*, 83–4; Hoby, *Diary*, 205; FSL MS V.a.436 p. 112; Cohen, *God's Caress*, 13.

[14] See, for example, Winthrop, *Papers*, 156; Norwood, *Journal*, 77, 86–7; Kiffin, *Remarkable Passages*, 6–7.

[15] Greenwood, *Treatise of . . . Iudgement*, sig. F2r-v; Herbert, *Works*, 55.

[16] Rogers, *Diary*, 131; Rogers, *Garden* (1616), sigs C7r, D1v.

So if you were not progressing, you were perhaps not dead, but merely hibernating. Herbert marvelled:

> Who would have thought my shrivel'd heart
> Could have recover'd greennesse? It was gone
> Quite underground.[17]

This might also colour the experience of the good times. Francis Rous cited the proverbially provident ant: 'learne of him in the summer of consolation, to provide for the winter of desertion'.[18]

Unfortunately, such regularity could be just as poor a fit to lived experience. Wallington made no such implicit promises to himself:

> Gods children finde such unevennesse in their lives that they are so off, and on: so out and in, now in good frame, but by and by sinsibly distempered, and alltogether unlike themselves. Sometimes how we are hoysed up to the very skies . . . other while againe cast downe into the very deepes of hell, not able to pray.

He did, however, have an explanation. God permits such changeability 'to the intent . . . we may take the faster hold when we return againe: that the tast of his love may be the sweeter'. John Bradford had made the same point a lifetime earlier, arguing that when God withdraws from us it is not 'to our owne losse, but to our luker and aduantage: euen that thy holy spirit with bigger portion of thy power and vertue, may lighten & chere vs'.[19]

Which brings us to the second way of adjusting expectations of sanctification: but first it is worth noticing that what is happening here is the shaping of narratives. The simple claim to relentless sanctification was a life story. The claim to rhythms of sanctification, seasonal or otherwise, was a life story. So too, in a much more fine-grained—and therefore more satisfying—way, was the second means of handling sanctification's problems, which grew to prominence as predestinarian orthodoxies hardened around the turn of the 17th century. This concentrated not on feelings of distance from God but on actual sin. Sanctification, obviously, ought to mean becoming less sinful. But in practice Christians continue sinning, and in principle they expect always to do so. This tension was usually dealt with by arguing that, while the elect continue to sin, that they are sinful in a different way from the reprobate. Richard Baxter, as a young convert, believed that while the elect could sin, they could not do so 'deliberately and knowingly' (a point of view he later firmly disavowed). John Preston argued, similarly, that 'a particular offence doth not offend [God] so much . . . as if we grow to a generall rebellion against him'. In other words, when the elect sin it is out of character; the reprobate, on the other hand, make a habit of it.[20] This is very close to the traditional Catholic distinction between mortal and venial sins, which early Protestants had derided, but by the

---

[17] Herbert, *Works*, 166.
[18] Rous, *Mysticall Marriage*, 214.
[19] Wallington, *Notebooks*, 52; Bull, *Christian praiers*, 217; cf. Scudder, *Christians daily walke* (1628), 587–8.
[20] Baxter, *Reliquiae Baxterianae*, 7; Preston, *Saints Daily Exercise*, 77; cf. Rogers, *Seven treatises*, 296.

17th century we find that distinction creeping back into Protestant usage, sometimes in those very words.[21]

A variant on this emphasized repentance rather than sin. Everyone sins, but the elect, 'if they stumble ... yet they will not lye down, and wallow in the mire'. They match daily sin with daily repentance, whereas the reprobate simply pile sin upon sin. Impenitence, one pious miscellany notes, 'is wors than sinning'; believers may be surprised or tempted into sin against their better judgement, but failure to repent can only be deliberate obstinacy.[22] Thus is all very well, but it could too easily become a licence to sin, as Protestants believed the Catholic sacramental system had been. To repent, return to the same sins, and repent again is to be stuck 'like a horse in a mill', always turning but never really moving. Thomas Hooker called this 'the mill of prayer'.[23] To repent and repeat was simply to mock God. As the author of one commonplace book put it:

> I am weary of repenting; the often vowes & promises of amendment in our priuat & publique humiliations, and our as often relapses into the same and worse iniquities makes God weary of repenting.[24]

Such relapses were particularly shocking after receiving the sacrament, a problem which Protestants across the spectrum identified.[25] Thomas Goodwin remembered having been stuck in such a pattern in his own youth, and in retrospect he saw the whole cycle as steeped in sin.[26] No-one wanted their life story to be a tale of a dog returning to its vomit.

There was only one approach which recognized the reality of recurrent sin but was also able to maintain a satisfying and plausible life narrative. This was to make repentance a transformative rather than a routine event. For every step back, there must be two steps forward. Repentance must be an occasion of closing one chapter and opening another. If you sin, George Abbot wrote in the 1650s, 'then know, that sin is thine advantage or opportunity, which thou art to improve to mount thee to a higher rise of Gospel-ground, and step forward towards more grace'. If you fall, ensure that you always bounce back higher.[27] So this was the perennial struggle of Protestant repentance: to keep it from sinking into mere routine, and to ensure that it led to a redoubling of efforts, because only that would mark it as true repentance. It was a struggle which only grew harder.

[21] For example, Andrewes, *Conuerted Mans New Birth*, 25–6; Isham, 'Confessions', fo. 22v. Cf. Hildersam, *Doctrine of Fasting*, 22.

[22] Scudder, *Christians daily walke* (1628), sig. A8v, p. 266; Preston, *Saints Daily Exercise*, 132; Bod MS Rawl D.384 fo. 1v.

[23] Webster, 'Writing to Redundancy', 52; Rogers, *Garden* (1615), II.D4r; Thomas Hooker, *The Soules Humiliation* (1637: RSTC 13278), 68; cf. Samuel Torshell, *The hypocrite discovered and cured* (1644: Wing T1938), 60.

[24] FSL MS V.a.280, II fo. 14r.

[25] Christopher Sutton, *Godly meditations upon the most holy sacrament of the Lords Supper* (1630: RSTC 23494), 341; Dyke, *Worthy communicant*, 158–61; Tozer, *Directions for a Godly Life*, 165–7.

[26] Goodwin, *Works*, II.lviii–lix.

[27] George Abbot, *Brief Notes upon the whole Book of Psalms* (1651: Wing A65), sig. A7r.

We can follow the battle in Protestantism's prayer-books, which produced texts ostensibly intended for repeated use but which would be almost impossible to use routinely. Take, for example, the prayer of confession from the early versions of Thomas Becon's *Gouernans of vertue*:

> In these wycked synnes, oh Lorde God, haue I hytherto walked according to the wyl of the prynce of this world, while I did that, that was pleasaunt to the fleshe. . . . Ah wretche that I am this came to passe, bycause that I dyd neuer earnestly stryue agaynste the suggestions of Satan, nor the concupiscences of the worlde, nor yet the lustes of my fleshe. . . . In thys tyme of grace & mercy, I myserable synner come nowe vnto the.[28]

There is a great deal more in this vein, but the flavour is clear enough. 'Hitherto'; 'this came to pass'; 'this time of grace'—this is a one-off prayer of conversion masquerading as a prayer for daily use. Like similar prayers in some of Becon's other works, it was plainly intended to guide new converts rather than to feed regular devotions.[29] In each case he put these prayers at the very beginning of the book. This focus on new converts made particular sense in the Reformation's heroic age, and it did fade thereafter. In the 1560 edition of the *Gouernans of vertue*, the prayer of confession was toned down.[30]

Throughout our period, however, we find exceptionally intense prayers of repentance, which it is hard to imagine being used routinely. So we have Miles Coverdale: 'I tremble & quake at myne owne vnaduised wilfulnesse . . . & dooe vtterly altogether myslyke myself, neither is there any thyng present before myne iyes but helle fyer.' Or John Norden: 'Yea, Lord, I doe vnfainedly condemne all my former life to be most vile, determining in my heart, by thy grace to forsake sin, & cleaue vnto godlines.'[31] That particular theme—asserting that the moment of prayer is a decisive turning-point in your life story, and that today is the first day of the rest of your life—is a recurrent one, in private papers as well as published books. Whenever she received the sacrament, apparently, the countess of Huntingdon prayed for 'a stedfast resolution to leade a new life, & to become a new Creature'. Grace Mildmay prayed:

> I doe confesse that I am not worthy of the least benefitt which thou oh God hast bestowed on me from my byrth vnto this daye. And that I haue neglected my seruice & myne obedience vnto thee continually, in all the whole course of my life passed. . . . I doe most humbly presente my selfe before thee, with a full purpose & intent by thy grace from this time forward, to secke & learne to knowe my blessed sauiour Jesus Christ.[32]

In isolation this reads like a turning-point, a new conversion, but it is an unremarkable passage in her writings. Every day was supposed to be a new beginning.

Sometimes the regularity of these turning-points is even plainer. John Gee's best-selling *Steps of Ascension vnto God* required its readers to pray thus every Monday morning:

---

[28] Becon, *Gouernans* (1549) fos 3v–4v.
[29] Becon, *Flour of godly praiers*, fos 3r–7v; Becon, *Pomaunder of prayer*, fos 2v–3v; cf. Heyden, *Bryefe Summe*, sigs N1r–2r.
[30] Becon, *Gouernaunce* (1560), 2–4.
[31] Coverdale, *Devout meditacions*, sigs D1v–2r; Norden, *Pensiue mans practise*, 70.
[32] Huntington Library, San Marino, CA, MS 15369 fo. 6v; Mildmay, 'Meditations', II.89.

Wee are beginning the weeke, but alas we begin not to be reformed in our liues and conuersations, but the more weekes passe ouer our heads, the greather burthen of sin we take vpon our backes.[33]

This defies any tendency to allow devotions to slip into routine, but a weekly jolt of spiritual crisis was not enough for some. Tymme instructed his readers each night to review their sins, 'with this resolution in thy selfe, to spend the remainder of thy life after a better manner, (and with a better conscience) than heretofore thou hast done'.[34] And then to make the same resolution the following night, and the night after that. One Elizabethan prayer-book provided a pair of confessions which describe the devotee's sins as

> so odious, detestable and greuous vnto my harte, that without the hope of thy greate mercie . . . I shoulde vtterly fall into desperation, and be damned for euer in hell fire. . . . But this is my hope, O father, that thou wilt giue me the grace of true repentaunce. . . . Make me . . . ioyfully to runne with the lost sonne vnto the lappe of thine euerlasting pitie.

These texts were 'to be said euery day, and at all times'.[35]

On one level, this is merely silly. It is an attempt to keep repentance from hardening into routine by sheer intensity of rhetorical bombardment, but even the most overblown language can be made banal by repetition. The better prayer-books, especially later in our period, recognized this, and provided calmer texts better suited to regular use.[36] Others recognized that renewed repentance had a different flavour from the initial kind. Michael Sparke's *Crumms of comfort* compared the Christian's daily struggle for renewal to the supposed way 'the Eagle reneweth his Age by grinding of his Bill', and had the weary sinner pray, 'I . . . presume once againe after my sinne, to returne home vnto thee'. This was a long haul.[37] But if the attempt to kick-start repentance by hyperbole was unlikely to succeed for very long, there is no mistaking the need to do so. How else were sinners to escape being imprisoned in routine, deluding themselves that they were progressing while in fact trapped in the mill of prayer?

NURTURING CRISIS

All forms of Christianity share the aspiration to maintain a continuous sense of the presence of God. Protestants' need to see the narratives of their own lives leading towards God made this aspiration particularly keen for them. The Christian is called, Henry Scudder wrote, to walk with God: meaning 'that by the eye of faith

---

[33] Gee, *Steps of Ascension*, 28. For other examples of scheduled, weekly spiritual crises, see Bayly, *Practise of pietie*, 458; Sparke, *Crumms of comfort*, sigs B8v–9r.

[34] Tymme, *Watch-bell* (1640), 294–5.

[35] *Godly garden*, fos 57r–58r, 79r.

[36] For example, Hieron, *Helpe vnto Deuotion* (1608); Sorocold, *Supplications of Saints* (1612).

[37] Sparke, *Crumms of comfort*, sigs C6v, E7v.

he see God present before him in all his actions, thinking of him oft vpon all occasions'. And he did mean *all*:

> The Commandment to walk with God is indefinite, without limitation . . . at all times, in all companies, and in all changes, conditions, and estates of your life whatsoeuer. . . . You are not dispensed with for any moment of your life: but all the dayes of your life, and each day of your life, and each houre of that day, and each minute of that hour; you must passe the time, the whole time of your dwelling here in feare.[38]

This was useful as a weapon against sin. The thought of God's presence ought to blunt most temptations, or, as John Bradford more positively put it, 'there is nothinge that maketh more to trewe godlynes of life then the persuasion of thy presence'.[39] But it was less a technique than an end in itself. Grace Mildmay prayed, 'Oh glorious Lord, which way so ever I turn . . . let me continually taste, feel and find thee, retain, hold and keep thee, in all things and above all things.' To be always gazing on God was to be in Heaven, as well as a means of evading Hell.[40]

Maintaining that gaze was, however, a constant struggle. Richard Kilby, whose record of this battle is particularly agonized, all too often thought of God 'as of a thing at the furthermost end of all the world'.[41] How was this concentration on the invisible God, rather than the mundane world, to be achieved? Mere urgings to do it were common. Persons' *Christian Directory* was essentially one long exhortation to this effect.[42] But such exhortations were subject to diminishing returns. Others had more practical suggestions, such as 'occasional' or 'extemporal' meditations, arising from such simple daily sights and events as a sunrise or a morning wash. By relentlessly allegorizing the mundane world to draw spiritual lessons from it, these could keep the mind and heart in Heaven rather than on earth. God is, after all, everywhere. 'I cannot see how a wise Christian, can let any thing passe him', Donald Lupton claimed in his meditations, 'without some benefit by it.'[43] Similarly, the habit of decorating Protestant homes with edifying mementoes, and even of adorning everyday articles with improving texts, could surround believers with reminders that God's eyes were fixed on them.[44]

But here we are concerned with a different approach: the cultivation of a sense of crisis. This is close to the heart of what it meant to be Protestant. Protestantism was born in crisis and in conflict, and it was through those experiences that Protestants found their identity and met their God. It is not simply that Protestantism of all kinds 'thrived on anxiety'.[45] More specifically, Luther's so-called theology of the Cross mined a seam which runs abundantly through the New Testament and the early Fathers: the claim that persecution is a sign of God's favour, and martyrdom

---

[38] Scudder, *Christians daily walke* (1628), 7, 16–17, 56.
[39] Bradford, *Godlie meditations*, sig. M2r; Sparke, *Crumms of comfort*, sig. L2v.
[40] Mildmay, *With Faith and Physic*, 74.
[41] Kilby, *Hallelujah*, 34, 93; see above, p. 135.
[42] Gregory, '"True and Zealouse Seruice"', 255–7; cf. Rogers, *Garden* (1616), sig. B3v.
[43] See above, pp. 112, 115–16; Lupton, *Obiectorum Reductio*, 158.
[44] Hamling, *Decorating the Godly Household*.
[45] David Hempton, *The Church in the Long Eighteenth Century* (2011), 142.

the Christian's highest calling. The first generations of English and Scottish Protestants took this up with fervour. In the 1520s Thomas Bilney wrote that

> I haue often bene afrayde, that christ hath not bene purely preached now a long tyme. For who hath bene now a long season offended through hym? Who hath now thys many yeares, suffred any persecution for the Gospells sake? Where is the sworde which he came to send vpon the earth?

The old church was discredited by its own stability. False prophets, Bilney recalled, cried 'Peace, peace', when there was no peace: and it does not really matter whether he knew that in citing this text to this effect he was directly echoing Luther.[46] William Tyndale was more forthright. From his exile, he wrote that those seeking assurance of salvation should consider their personal circumstances. 'By sofringe art thou sure. . . . Tribulation is a blessynge, prosperite is a curse.'[47]

During the perilous early years of the Reformation, this claim was invaluable. Evangelicals were excoriated as seditious innovators who deserved whatever persecution they got. By claiming that opposition was a sign of God's favour, evangelicals could turn these accusations on their heads. Thomas Becon claimed that Christ had been called 'a heretyke . . . an enemy to our mother the holy chyrch', and argued that 'it is therefore no newe thyng for the prechers of goddes worde & the earnest louers of the holye Scripture to be thus rayled vpon'. He and the many others who advanced these arguments turned their worldly weakness into their greatest strength.[48] It was a logically almost impregnable position. By inverting common sense, reading defeats as victories, political failures as spiritual successes, and martyrdoms as triumphs, this argument prepared early Protestants for almost anything which the early modern state could throw at them.

Anything, that is, except victory. When English Protestants unexpectedly came into their kingdom in 1547, the result was not only elation but also disorientation. Their reliance on persecution was such that they responded much like a hypochondriac who is given a clean bill of health—that is, with confusion and suspicion. Protestant preachers under Edward VI began to cast themselves as Jeremiah, warning of coming judgement if England did not grasp the offered moment of redemption. As Catharine Davies' seminal article pointed out, Edwardian Protestants preferred thinking of themselves as a poor, persecuted little flock than as the leaders of a Christian commonwealth; and they spent much of the reign expecting the sky to fall on their heads. This was not a political forecast but a theological deduction. Even when the young king was in good health, in 1551, Anthony Gilby wrote that Hugh Latimer, Thomas Lever, John Hooper, Thomas Becon, and Robert Horne were all now England's Jeremiahs, warning of the coming wrath,

---

[46] Foxe, *Actes and monuments* (1570), 1182; cf. Jeremiah 6:14.

[47] William Tyndale, *The obedience of a Christen man* (Antwerp, 1528: RSTC 24446), fos 3r, 7r–8r, 21r–22r.

[48] Becon, *Dauids harpe*, sigs C8v–D1v. Cf. John Bale, *A mysterye of inyquyte contayned within the heretycall genealogy of P. Pantolabus* (Antwerp, 1545: RSTC 1303), fo. 78v; George Joye, *The exposicion of Daniel the prophete* (Antwerp, 1545: RSTC 14823), fo. 239r; BL Harleian MS 425 fo. 4r; Ryrie, 'Afterlife of Lutheran England', 227–9.

and he added, remarkably, 'when these are gone others cometh of their ashes'—which could mean only one thing.[49]

Perhaps time could have allayed such fears. Instead, it vindicated them, through Mary's persecution in England, and the briefer but comparably grim experience of civil war in Scotland in 1559–60. Those traumas passed, but the fires of Smithfield and of Edinburgh baked the expectation of (and need for) crisis and persecution into British Protestants' identity. They embarked on what would, in the event, be eighty years of settled Protestant hegemony convinced not only that the sky was about to fall on their heads, but also that imminent disaster was a welcome vindication of their own faithfulness.

As disaster steadily failed to materialise, however, British Protestants confronted an awkward problem. How could they maintain the sense of constant crisis in a settled, peaceful life? They feared that stability would foster formalism and complacency. 'As standing waters turne into mud, and breed frogges and toads; so a long peace begets a crue of uglie and noysome vices.'[50] Reformed Protestantism was, as Leif Dixon puts it, a religion 'built for the pyrotechnics of revolution, not for the long, slow slog'. Once the crises of the mid-century were past, 'there were no trials of faith left'.[51] And so it was necessary to invent them.

The easiest way of doing so was to take advantage of real or plausible dangers. We have already seen how the perils of the Thirty Years' War found an echo in domestic prayers.[52] Other dangers were even easier fodder: most obviously, the plague. William Crashaw wrote his *Londons Lamentation for her Sinnes* from the midst of the terrible epidemic of 1625, during which he had ministered heroically. He urged his readers to feel 'touched with the sense of this hand of our God' and 'put in mind of our mortality'. The crisis was an occasion for renewed repentance, fasting, and moral renewal. Crashaw laid out a glorious prophetic vision of a post-plague commonwealth of justice, peace, and plenty. He and others claimed that this was not simply another epidemic, but 'such a plague as our ancients neuer heard of, and our posterity will scarce belieue'.[53] No doubt all such visitations seem so to those in their midst, but in fact they had a ghastly regularity to them. The apocalypticism was less sober judgement and more rhetorical trick.

The same trick could be attempted in the absence of a specific threat. Ordinary life was dangerous enough. Thomas Knell's 1581 treatise on prayer opens with these words:

> The dangerous daies and troublesome times, with the imminent and present perils that now and dailie doe hang ouer our heads readie to fall on vs, do greatlie require, and as it were compel vs to giue our selues vnto praier.[54]

---

[49] Catharine Davies, '"Poor Persecuted Little Flock" or "Commonwealth of Christians": Edwardian Protestant concepts of the Church' in Peter Lake and Maria Dowling (eds), *Protestantism and the National Church in Sixteenth-Century England* (1988), 85. The list was not exhaustive: cf. Knox, *Works*, III.167.

[50] Primrose, *Christian Mans Teares*, 153–4.

[51] Dixon, 'Calvinist Theology', 185–6.

[52] See above, pp. 380.

[53] Crashaw, *London's Lamentation*, sigs A3v, A4v–5r, C2v–3r; Featley, *Ancilla Pietatis*, sig. a1r.

[54] Knell, *Godlie and necessarie Treatise*, sig. A2r.

Quite what these dangers and perils were is neither clear nor important. They were only a ploy to catch the reader's attention. The simplest way of doing this was to remind an audience of the incontrovertible fact that death might come at any time. John Andrewes urged both young and old to

> imagine that the Spring of our dayes are past, our Summer is spent, and that wee are arriued at the Autumne, or fall of the leafe . . . the Lamp of our liues lyeth twinckling vppon the snuffe.[55]

As that warning implies, Reformed Protestantism gave this perennial Christian theme a subtly different meaning: less the imminence of judgement—that, after all, was foreordained—and more the need for the story of your life to turn towards God before it reached the last page.

This all makes excellent sense, and we have already seen how some individuals used thoughts of imminent death in this way. In the depths of his despair, Archibald Johnston of Wariston sung Psalm 116 'as if thou wer in the hinmist hour of thy lyfe'; in his agonizing illness, Richard Kilby's conviction that he was 'at the doore of death, and the gate of hell; terrified with the sight of Gods wrathfull judgement' gave him a transforming view of his own sins.[56] But in times of good health and security, such shocks were harder to come by. Life is indeed both short and unpredictable, but it is also full of false alarms. People are liable to become accustomed to not dying. It can even begin to seem normal. How could Protestants stop themselves settling into—dread word—'security'?[57]

The trouble was that any technique to shock themselves into awareness of their spiritual state could be dulled by repetition.[58] The repentance which is accompanied by hot tears one day can become part of the mill of prayer by the next. As preachers ratchet up their rhetoric, audiences become progressively more inured to its effects. Arthur Dent urged, 'although wee could neuer bee moued with any Sermon hetherto, yet let vs now bee moued once at last': a powerful appeal, to be sure, but what then was the next preacher supposed to say?[59] Similarly, it was a commonplace to urge audiences and readers that *now*, the present moment, was the time for repentance, that it should and could be a moment of crisis in their lives. Throughout the published text of Gilbert Primrose's 1624 fast sermon *The Christian Mans Teares*, the word 'NOW' was capitalized to emphasize the urgency of his call to repent.[60] But how many such calls could an audience hear before they suspected their preachers of crying wolf?

This problem came to a sharp point over the matter of deathbed repentance, a recurring theological headache for Protestant pastors. Protestants held that good

[55] Andrewes, *Conuerted Mans New Birth*, 11–12. Cf. Bentley, *Monument of Matrons*, 365; *Drousie disease*, 134.
[56] Wariston, *Diary*, 44; Kilby, *Burthen*, sig. A3v; cf. Blair, *Life*, 17–18.
[57] See above, pp. 23–4.
[58] Apart, perhaps, from fasting: on which see above, p. 199.
[59] Dent, *Sermon of Repentance*, sig. C4r.
[60] Primrose, *Christian Mans Teares*.

works were unnecessary for salvation, and sometimes cited the example of the penitent thief crucified with Christ to prove that mere faith was sufficient.[61] But the story also teaches that it is possible to live a wicked life and be saved by repenting at the final hour, and that was not a life-plan which Protestant ministers wanted their people to adopt. So while they admitted that deathbed repentance was possible, they insisted that repentance could not safely be postponed. The standard approach was to point out, as William Perkins did, that 'it is not in the power of man to repent when he himselfe will': it depends on God's gace. You may plan to repent at leisure in later life, but not be able to do so when the time comes.[62] William King, in a sermon delivered in King's Bench prison which became a best-seller, took this a little too far: God, he claimed, has appointed for everyone a time for repentance, 'and he which mispendeth that time and is not made Christian then, can neuer be saued'.[63] Others were more pragmatic. The dying may be 'too much troubled with the greife of the body' to repent—and merely saying 'crie God mercie' was not enough, or 'so should euery foole repent'. Or perhaps their hearts will simply be too hardened with sin by then. Robert Bolton's begrudging comment that 'I do not go about . . . absolutely to exclude repentance from the deaths bed' captures the mood: deathbed repentance did happen, but it was rare, and often false.[64] 'Though true repentance be neuer too late, yet late repentance is seldome true.'[65] Kicking repentance down the road was thus the height of folly. 'The more we Judge our selves Daily', resolved John Rogers, 'the less we shall have to do . . . when we come to die. Oh! That is an unfit Time for This!'[66]

The reason that this argument was so often repeated was, of course, that it was not being heard. Ingrained sinners, Thomas Tuke claimed, would 'say that they care not, so they may haue halfe an houre before their death to repent them of their sinnes, and to pray to God for mercie'. Divines regularly went out of their way to deny that the penitent thief gave permission to postpone repentance. Those like George Gifford and Arthur Dent who wrote explicitly to expose the errors of 'carnall Protestants' regularly confronted the belief that repentance could safely be postponed.[67] The possibility of being saved without works had, it seems, been half-understood widely enough to be misleading.

Richard Norwood gives us a characteristically thoughtful reflection on the whole problem. He remembered consciously thinking that it was too soon to repent: not

---

[61] *Certain Sermons or Homilies*, 43; Luke 23:40–3.

[62] Perkins, *Salve for a sicke man*, 33. Cf. Bruce, *Sermons Preached*, sigs Y1v–2r; Preston, *Three Sermons*, 62; Andrewes, *Conuerted Mans New Birth*, 13; Dent, *Sermon of Repentance*, sigs C4v–5r; Bayly, *Practise of pietie*, 175–6.

[63] William King, *The Straight Gate to Heauen* (1616: RSTC 14997.3), 33–4; cf. Goodwin, *Works*, II.liv.

[64] Lancelot Langhorne, *Mary Sitting at Christs Feet* (1611: RSTC 15197), 28; Dent, *Sermon of Repentance*, sig. A6v; Bolton, *Discourse about happinesse*, 62.

[65] Dent, *Plaine mans path-way*, 277; Dyke, *Two Treatises*, 155–7.

[66] Mather, *Magnalia*, III.113; cf. Perkins, *Salve for a sicke man*, 45.

[67] Tuke, *Practise of the faithfull*, 44; Gerhard, *Meditations*, 27–8; Bayly, *Practise of pietie*, 181; Persons, *Booke of Christian exercise*, ed. Bunny, 368–71; Dent, *Plaine mans path-way*, 125, 277; Gifford, *Briefe discourse*, fo. 70r.

because of sloth or wantonness, but because he doubted he could keep it up. He knew that the life of an earnest Reformed Protestant was one of progressive, relentless sanctification, and feared embarking on that journey too soon. He said to himself:

> It is not best to make too much haste, lest I should return again to my sinful delights. It will be better when the unbridled fury and heat of youth is somewhat assuaged.... Take thy fill a little and be a little satisfied in worldly pleasures before we part and must come together no more.[68]

The echo of Augustine's famous prayer for future chastity is no accident, since Norwood knew the *Confessions* well, and by the time he wrote this, he was well aware that it was theological nonsense. But it was also compelling. Like taking communion unworthily, repenting inconstantly might simply redouble God's wrath.[69] Better to think that, if God has appointed a time for your repentance, it has not yet come. It was common enough for a misspent youth to be followed by conversion and respectability. If you thought your whole life was ahead of you, as most young people do, why not wait a little longer? The best inoculation against the preachers of urgent repentance was the thought: yes, but not yet.

ASPIRING TO MARTYRDOM

For those who had already taken that first step of repentance, the struggle to maintain a continual sense of crisis took a different shape. Their preachers' terrifying rhetoric, and the shrill self-administered warnings they read from published prayers, were inevitably subject to diminishing returns. A subtler strategy was to weave a constant awareness of crisis into the substance of the Protestant devotional life itself. Two forms in particular are worth noticing here. The first was the use of the psalms. As we have repeatedly seen, the psalms were ubiquitous in early modern Protestant devotion: said or sung in church, in the family, in conference, and in private prayer; read, transcribed, paraphrased, memorized. Protestant devotion was, we might say, psalmic, and the psalms' themes therefore helped to define the vocabulary of Protestant piety. Those themes are distinctive. A great many of the psalms allude, in the first person, to situations of pressing danger, and in particular to the scorn and malice of enemies. I have argued elsewhere that the enthusiastic Protestant embrace of these psalmic priorities helped give Protestant piety its distinctively aggressive tinge.[70] But it also helped to keep a sense of crisis simmering in day-to-day Protestant practice, since the psalms' threats and dangers were easily interpreted allegorically. Devotees might be daily encouraged to think of, for example, their backache or their money troubles as an assault from spiritual enemies: that is, as crises and as persecution. Every cloudy day could be the valley of the shadow of death. We can see this happening in the psalm paraphrases and pastiches written by Protestant poets: from Elizabeth Hastings'

---

[68] Norwood, *Journal*, 60.   [69] See above, pp. 338–40.
[70] Ryrie, 'Psalms and confrontation'.

collection of 'Psalms of judgement' and Anne Southwell's psalm-poems—'Let not my life with shame be stayned/nor foes triumph on me'—to the collage psalms which Richard Kilby assembled in order to interpret his own predicament as a spiritually fruitful crisis.[71] Kilby's enemies were the Devil, his own sin, and his kidney-stones, but with the help of a psalmic framework, that could seem as much like persecution as anything endured by Foxe's martyrs.

Which brings us to the second means of using regular Protestant piety to promote a regular sense of crisis: borrowing crises from the past. The care with which Protestants treasured and burnished the memories of their martyrs is well known, and is usually seen as a matter of building an anti-Catholic identity. But the purpose of commemorating the martyrs was not simply to remind Protestants who their enemies were. John Foxe's *Actes and Monuments*, for example, was not only read very widely, but sometimes unmistakably used as a devotional text. Reading the text aloud was the centrepiece of the proceedings at a suspected conventicle denounced in 1584. At the other end of the Protestant spectrum, in the Little Gidding community, Foxe's book was read aloud during supper on Sundays, and was treated as 'second only to Scripture'. Samuel Ward, urging its use, promised that 'the very pictures of the fires, and Martyrs, cannot but warme thee'.[72] This did not principally mean the heat of indignation against popish tyranny. Foxe's gruesomely memorable villains may be the liveliest characters in his book, but they were not what readers most sought out in the generation after his own death in 1587. The first commercially successful abridgement of Foxe's book, Clement Cotton's *The mirror of martyrs* (six editions, 1613–37), jettisons all Foxe's narrative and historical material, to focus exclusively on the martyr-narratives themselves: and in particular, on the martyrs' constancy immediately before (and during) their deaths, their prayers, their words of comfort to one another and to their loved ones, and their general spiritual readiness for suffering. There are no doctrines, and no villains, simply people showing courage in the face of death. If you were warmed by this, it was by the heat of your own imagined martyrdoms, through a kind of pious fantasizing. To read these martyr-stories was almost inevitably to ask yourself: what if it were me?

This kind of vicarious suffering brought a thrill of fear to Protestant readers. In the 1580s, Gervase Babington set out to dispel the anxieties with which he thought Protestants were most often troubled, the last of which was, 'I feare my nature if persecution should arise for religion'. His description of how he dealt with it 'whensoeuer I thinke of this matter' makes it sound like an almost everyday event, and for some it may have been.[73] Satirists might lampoon those who wished 'to become a martyr . . . like those in Foxe's book', but for some it was no joke. One seven-year-old girl in the early 17th century, finding herself tempted to deny her faith, consequently

[71] Huntington Library, San Marino, CA, MS 15369 fo. 15v; FSL MS V.b.198 fo. 7r; Kilby, *Hallelujah*, 71, 115–18.
[72] BL Lansdowne MS 157 fo. 186r; Aston, 'Moving Pictures', 83–5; Ward, *Coal from the Altar*, 55.
[73] Babington, *Briefe conference*, 113–14.

began to examin my self on this manner, what wouldest thou doe ... if thou shouldest be tempted to deny Christ, and be called to suffer for his sake, as some of thy kindred were in Queen Maries time?[74]

The effect of reading martyr-stories, Grace Mildmay believed, was to encourage believers 'manfully to suffer death and to give our lives for the testimony of the truth of God'. John Forbes of Corse described 'meditating in my bed in the morning vpon the persecutions of the saints of God', praying that God 'would vphold vs, & bear vs through all our tryalls, & make vs faithfull & joyfull to the death'. Elizabeth Juxon was said to have been

> very mindfull of the fiery triall which might come vpon vs: and she for her part looked for it, and prepared for it: Yea, she was minded rather to burne at a stake, then euer ... to betray the truth of the Gospell.[75]

The real danger of such a fiery trial was pretty distant, but its value to Protestants struggling against routine and hypocrisy was unmistakable.

This fearful fascination with hypothetical dangers was underpinned by the much-repeated truism that all Christians must suffer martyrdom. William Pinke taught that 'none are saved but Martyrs; Martyrs either actually or habitually'— that is, it is not necessary actually to be killed, but in that case, believers need to make their own inner martyrdoms.[76] When Patrick Simson was on his deathbed, some children whom he had baptized were brought to him for a blessing. He roused himself to warn them that they might 'be baptized with the baptism of affliction and martyrdome, as the bairnes of Bethlehem'. Someone protested that he was scaring them, but he declared, 'None enters in heaven bot martyres: he who hes it rooted in his heart to suffer for the truth is already a martyre for God'. When Richard Corbett's caricatured 'distracted Puritane' is tied up by his friends for fear of his sanity, he comforts himself: 'Whilst this I endure,/Faith makes me sure,/To be one of Foxes martyrs.'[77]

Not everyone found these thoughts comforting, and preachers recognized the problem. Pinke, for example—having told his audience that they must be martyred—urged them to 'afflict not thy selfe with such sad supposals, what if Queene Maries dayes should come a gaine; what if I should be brought before such a fellow as Bonner', and quoted Christ's cold comfort that each day has evil enough of its own. Gabriel Powel argued, less helpfully, 'that burning aliue is not so extreame a torment as commonly it is thoughte to be', on the grounds that Christ would give his elect courage.[78] One of Foxe's stories in particular was much-repeated: the tale of Laurence Saunders and Dr Pendleton, who were imprisoned

[74] Elizabeth Evenden and Thomas S. Freeman, *Religion and the Book in Early Modern England* (Cambridge, 2011), 186; Powell, *Spirituall Experiences*, 162.

[75] Mildmay, *With Faith and Physic*, 23; Forbes, 'Diary', 62–3; Denison, *Monument or Tombe-Stone*, 111.

[76] Pinke, *Tryall of a Christians loue*, I, 21; cf. Bayly, *Practise of pietie*, 772–84.

[77] Tweedie, *Select Biographies*, 107; Corbett, *Poems*, 244.

[78] Pinke, *Tryall of a Christians loue*, I.27; Powel, *Resolued Christian*, 264. Cf. Harris, *Peters enlargement* (1624), 15.

together. Pendleton swore he would stand firm; Saunders feared he would waver; but in the event, it was Pendleton who crumbled and Saunders who went to the fire. So the fearful should be confident and the confident fearful—exactly the kind of paradox Protestant theology cherished.[79] For those who would not be so easily reassured, there was more practical advice. Some writers cited the example of Thomas Bilney, who 'first tried his finger by himselfe in the Candle, before he tried his whole body in the fire'.[80] But even that was no substitute for the inner strength given by grace. What better test of that than to meditate upon and try yourself against the stories of the martyrs?

This was partly a matter of keeping the memories of past troubles fresh and bleeding. The Scottish Book of Common Order, for example, included three lengthy prayers dating from 1559–60, from 'the tyme of our extreame troubles', 'the time of... persecution by the Frenchmen'. One of these, as a text first published in 1565 claims, is 'yet commonly vsed in the Churches of Scotland, before the sermon'. These texts were reproduced in virtually all editions of the book until the early 17th century, and some even in the 1630s. So throughout our period, Scottish congregations were at least formally encouraged to recall, with vivid specifics, 'that iustely thou hast punished vs by the tyrannie of strangers, & that more iustelie thou mayest bring vpon vs againe the bondage & yoak which of thy mercy for a ceason thou hast remoued'.[81] The threat especially was kept lively, because while British Protestants enjoyed some security after 1560, many of their Continental brethren did not. Elizabethan prayer-books regularly included prayers for persecuted Christians, and especially for the French and Dutch churches, 'which are almost consumed with these fierie tryalles'.[82] In London and a few other southern English towns, the French and Dutch exile churches regularly held public fasts, in response to the calamities at home and also because 'the wrath of God threatens the whole earth together'. Even in St Andrews, the scholars gathered to sing psalms, apparently spontaneously, when they heard reports of the St Bartholomew's Day Massacre.[83]

Repeated invasion scares brought such fears home. During the Armada crisis, Gilbert Frevile's neighbours were boasting—from the relative safety of County Durham—of English valour and Spanish cowardice, but he knew that it might 'please the Lord to giue our landes to the conquest of the spaniards', and that if this

[79] See, for example, Pinke, *Tryall of a Christians loue*, I.26; Culverwell, *Treatise of faith*, 416; cf. Foxe, *Actes and monuments* (1570), 1671.

[80] Dyke, *Worthy communicant*, 290; Webbe, *Practise of qui[e]tnes*, 36; Perkins, *Salve for a sicke man*, 47–8.

[81] *Forme of prayers... approued and receiued by the Churche of Scotland*, 27, 53; William Cowan, *A Bibliography of the Book of Common Order and Psalm Book of the Church of Scotland: 1556–1644* (Papers of the Edinburgh Bibliographical Society vol. 10, 1913).

[82] Dering, *Godly priuate praiers*, sigs C5r, E4v–6r; Hutchins, *Davids Sling*, 23–6; Norden, *Pensiue mans practise*, 55.

[83] O. Boersma and A. J. Jelsma (eds), *Unity in Multiformity: The Minutes of the Coetus of London, 1575, and the Consistory Minutes of the Italian Church of London, 1570–1591* (Publications of the Huguenot Society 59, 1997), 85; Melville, *Autobiography*, 27.

happened he should accept it as a just judgement on England's sins.[84] In 1617 invasion talk frightened the eight-year-old Elizabeth Isham, who remembered that

> Those of the presiser sort was the most aprehensive of it. . . . I will remember that at this time heareing sum talke of there cruelty . . . and hearing of the joys of those Marters that suffered for the Prodistant Religion, I was at this time very apprehensive of there Blessednes.

As well she might be. As an adult, Isham rather disapproved of such scaremongering, fearing that concentrating on exotic dangers distracted from more everyday judgements.[85] That was an unusual scruple, although the repeated failure of such fears to materialize was certainly a problem. In the 1590s John Norden, having detailed the sufferings of the French church, had to admit that there was no immediate sign of such things happening in England, but linked it back to 'the remembrance of our little persecution in the time of Queene Marie'. His marginal note—'the persecution in Queen Maries time, a meane to praye now'—makes the devotional purpose of such remembrance unmistakable. Others looked forward, urging, 'Let vs in the time of our greatest tranquillity meditate of the euill to come', and insisting that this temporary peace should be used to prepare for the coming persecution.[86] Lewis Bayly covered all eventualities. If God calls believers to the 'honour to suffer Martyrdome', he warned, it might be by 'open burning' (as under Mary); by 'secret murdering' (as under the Spanish Inquisition); by 'outragious massacring' (as in France); or by 'being blowne vp with Gun-powder' (which needed no explanation). However it came, what mattered was living in readiness for it, so 'that wee may seale with our deaths the Euangelicall trueth which we haue professed in our liues'.[87]

Those who did not wish to contemplate being burned, massacred, or blown up could use martyr-stories analogically. Foxe himself envisaged this, believing that the martyrs' example ought to encourage readers 'to stand more stoutly in battaile agaynst our aduersaries', by which he meant temptations to sin and worldliness in the present.[88] When Sessilia Dewes died in 1618, her husband wrote a long account of her exemplary pious death 'at the beginning of a large Book of Martyrs', setting her struggles and triumph alongside those of Cranmer, Latimer, and Ridley. Foxe himself described the victims of plague as martyrs. Not even death was necessary. Richard Sibbes said that simple struggles with temptation 'make the life of many good Christians almost a Martyrdome'.[89] But traditionally martyrdom requires a persecutor, and this mentality helped to make Protestants unusually ready to interpret any opposition as persecution. A Jacobean treatise on household

[84] BL Egerton MS 2877 fo. 87r–v.
[85] Isham, 'Confessions', fo. 9r–v.
[86] John Norden, *A progresse of pietie* (1596: RSTC 18633), fo. 37v; Gouge, *Whole-Armor of God*, 110; Wither, *Preparation to the Psalter*, 131.
[87] Bayly, *Practise of pietie*, 783–4.
[88] Foxe, *Actes and monuments* (1570), 1541.
[89] D'Ewes, *Autobiography*, 111; Prid, *Glasse of Vaine-glorie* (1600), sigs H12v–I8v; Sibbes, *Bruised reede*, sig. G12r.

piety warned that those who were mocked for sermon-repetition 'must not . . . be daunted with such scorning, though it bee a persecuting'.[90] Puritans both revelled in such 'persecution' and, sometimes, actively sought it out. 'All the house against mee as too strict; but I have comfort in it', wrote Samuel Rogers in his diary. When George Gifford's 'Atheos' wished mildly that puritans would become better sub-jects, 'Zelotes' responded with a disproportionately self-righteous response: 'I must suffer your reproch, for if they haue called the good man of the house Beelzebub, howe much more those which be of his houshold.'[91] Richard Hooker mocked this puritan tendency to interpret 'the least degree of most mercifullie tempered severitie' as martyrdom, although in the wake of the arrests and executions of the early 1590s that has a sinister ring to it. Hooker, however, also shows that all sides could play this game. Ridiculing Thomas Cartwright's argument that those who are forced to behold popish ceremonies are 'martyred in their mindes', he retorted: 'they that judge them selves Martyrs when they are grieved, should thinke withall what they are whom they grieve'.[92] For earnest Protestants of all stripes, the chance to interpret even the most minor insults, afflictions, and difficulties as martyrdom was immensely tempting. What better way to give instant meaning to their lives?

[90] 'R. R.', *House-holders Helpe*, 26.
[91] Rogers, *Diary*, 71; Gifford, *Briefe discourse*, fo. 83r.
[92] Hooker, *Laws . . . Books I–IV*, 19–20, 305–6.

16

The Stages of Life

'Take hede therefore that ye walke circumspectly, not as fooles, but as wise, redeming the time: for the dayes are euil.' *Ephesians 5:15–16*

CHILDHOOD

The history of childhood has become a lively area of scholarly study in recent decades. The fruitfully provocative theses of Philippe Ariés and others who questioned whether pre-modern and modern experiences of childhood had anything in common have now been pretty much overturned, but the resulting debates have taught us a great deal about early modern childhood.[1] It now seems unmistakable, for example, that early modern parents loved and valued their children, even if they did not always love them according to our own age's norms. Childhood religion, however, remains both opaque and under-studied. Much of what we know relates to such revealing but exceptional cases as child martyrs or the supposed victims of demonic possession.[2] Throughout this book, children have had walk-on parts: making vows, memorizing prayers, weeping for religious or worldly reasons, being excluded from communion and baffled by sermons, participating in family prayers, and leading their households in saying grace at table. This section will pull some of these themes together.

Childhood is the most vital and most mysterious stage of the early modern Protestant life. Vital not only because it shaped all that followed, but because, probably, the majority of baptised Protestants in our period never lived beyond it. Mysterious, because our sources show us so little of childhood religion. The diaries

---

[1] Philippe Ariés, *Centuries of Childhood* (1960); Hugh Cunningham, *Children and Childhood in Western Society since 1500* (1995); Cressy, *Birth, Marriage and Death*; Houlbrooke, *English Family*.

[2] See the pioneering studies in Diana Wood (ed.), *The Church and Childhood* (Studies in Church History 31, 1994); also Sarah Covington, ' "Spared not from tribulation": Children and Early Modern Martyrologies', *Archiv für Reformationsgeschichte* 97 (2006), 165–83; Anna French, 'Spiritual Narratives of Childhood in Early Modern England', University of Birmingham PhD thesis, 2008; Anna French, 'Possession, Puritanism and Prophecy: Child Demoniacs and English Reformed Culture', *Reformation* 13 (2008), 133–6. I am grateful to Dr French for drawing my attention to this subject and for many discussions around it. Some pioneering studies have looked at the roles of 'youths', the people we would now call teenagers and young adults: notably Susan Brigden, 'Youth and the English Reformation', *Past and Present* 95 (1982), 37–67; Alexandra Walsham, 'The Reformation of the Generations: Youth, Age and Religious Change in England, c. 1500–1700', *Transactions of the Royal Historical Society* 6th ser. 21 (2011), 93–121.

and autobiographical accounts which we have used throughout this book are all written by adults: Wallington's papers, the earliest of which date from his twenty-first year, are about as early as we get. Some of them then tell us a little about their earlier lives, but—with two major exceptions, to whom we shall return—this material is frustratingly scanty. Wallington, for example, for all his enormous written output, tells us almost nothing about his early childhood.[3]

As Patrick Collinson pointed out, adult Protestants paid very little attention to children's religious practice. We know almost nothing about the provision for children in public worship, and we have to assume that this was because there was not much of it.[4] The religion of children younger than ten or twelve was rarely taken very seriously. It was often said that the children of faithful parents were likely to be predestined to salvation, but this was most often applied to babies, and was in any case intended more to comfort grieving parents or to flatter a household's piety than to praise a real live child.[5] But while parents might have a rosy view of their cherubs, children themselves were consistently told that they were firebrands of Hell. The difference is plain in a contrasting pair of prayers in Edward Hutchins' best-selling *Davids Sling against great Goliah*. A mother's prayer for her children's education asks God to 'hew and square the rough table of their harts, of stonie make them fleshie, that being softened by the dew of thy blessings, they may beare the seale of adoption in thy sonne'. Although hardly dewey-eyed, this is at least compassionate. The prayer for schoolchildren's own use, however, asks God 'to crop the crooked boughes off, and to mowe downe the ripe haruest of wicked nature': a far more brutal view of the child, immersed in original sin, whose nature had to be suppressed, and whose will had to be broken.[6]

When adult Protestants looked back on their childhoods, that is what most of them saw. The theme of John Winthrop's brief account of his youth was his utter depravity. Only when he was ten did he begin to have 'some notions of God', and even so 'it made mee no whit better'. Thomas Goodwin dismissed his childish prayers as mere hypocrisy. Richard Kilby lamented 'the evill seasoning of mine heart in my tender yeares'. He had had a dog and a cat whom he loved, along with 'other vaine things . . . when mine heart should have been taken up, and filled with the love of God'. Lewis Bayly's meditation on childhood asked, 'what is youth but an vntamed Beast? . . . Ape-like, delighting in nothing but in toyes and baubles?'[7] Most Protestant autobiographers neglected childhood because they assumed it was a bestial swamp of sin.

As we have seen, constructing and interpreting life-narratives was an important part of the early modern Protestant mindset, so this neglect of childhood may seem surprising. The answer lies in part in the genres used to give shape to these narratives. The obvious model, Augustine's *Confessions*, had, as we have seen,

---

[3] Seaver, *Wallington's World*, 28.

[4] Collinson, *Religion of Protestants*, 229–30.

[5] Perkins, *How to live*, 82–3; Rogers, *Garden* (1615), II sig. D1r.

[6] Hutchins, *Davids Sling*, 104–6; Morgan, *Godly Learning*, 145–6.

[7] Winthrop, *Papers*, 154; Goodwin, *Works*, II.lvii–lviii; Kilby, *Hallelujah*, 35; Bayly, *Practise of pietie*, 63.

surprisingly little influence during this period, chiefly because no English translation was widely available until 1631.[8] The *Confessions* were well-known, but mostly at second-hand, so while certain episodes might be widely quoted, its overall model of childhood has as little influence as its model of autobiography. As Laura Branch has suggested, the most widely available alternative narrative form was the martyr-narrative—which was in any case one of the key prisms through which Protestants interpreted their identities.[9] This developed into the full-blown Protestant hagiography, a genre later given canonical form by John Bunyan, in which conversion is merely the beginning of a story which culminates in death.[10] The contrast with the *Confessions*, whose drama peaks at the point of conversion, is sharp. In martyr-narratives and hagiographies, childhood—like all life before conversion—is rarely granted much attention.

A short digression on fruit-trees. The best-known single incident in the *Confessions* describes the young Augustine and his friends stealing pears from a tree, an event which, for Augustine, became a symbol of his own youthful depravity. The incident was certainly famous in the early modern period.[11] It has become common to see echoes of that claim in other accounts, sometimes justifiably. When Elizabeth Isham, who knew the *Confessions*, relates a childhood theft of pears, it is no coincidence.[12] But the connection is not always so plain. The alleged echoes usually relate simply to the theft of fruit, while Augustine's account focuses on the sheer malice of the act and his hope to impress his friends. Margo Todd has argued that Samuel Ward's repeated mentions in his student diary of overindulgence in cherries, plums, or pears are an Augustinian trope.[13] Perhaps so, but the problem is that our sources, scant as they are, are full of childhood pilfering, often of fresh food. Richard Baxter and Samuel Fairclough both ascribed their conversions to guilt after raiding neighbours' orchards. Nehemiah Wallington recalled stealing carrots from a grocer's cart. The young James Melville had the fear of Hell put into him when his beloved elder sister caught him in some petty stealing. Elizabeth Walker remembered an incident from her childhood in which she had been sent to fetch something from the room where apples were stored, on the grounds that she was more trustworthy than her sisters. She actually took an apple, but, conscience-stricken, went back and returned it rather than tasting it.[14] If some of these contain Augustinian allusions, they also point to a different truth: children tend to swipe things, and in pre-modern Britain, fruit was much the most obvious thing to swipe. It tends to arrive in sudden gluts which may rot if not eaten; its appearance simply hanging on—or falling off—a tree teases the boundary between private property and communal resource; and for children who might well be hungry, especially for

---

[8] See above, p. 301.

[9] See above, pp. 423–7; Branch, 'Practical Piety', 5.

[10] Campbell, *Religion of the Heart*, 52.

[11] See, for example, Blair, *Life*, 6.

[12] Isham, 'Confessions', fo. 10r; Stephens, '"My Cheefest Work"', 198.

[13] Todd, 'Puritan Self-Fashioning', 247.

[14] Clarke, *Lives of sundry Eminent Persons*, 154; Baxter, *Reliquiae Baxterianae*, 3; Seaver, *Wallington's World*, 28; Melville, *Autobiography*, 18–19, 28; Walker, *Holy Life*, 13.

rare sweet foods, the temptation could be overwhelming. And gorging on fruit of dubious ripeness is a sure road to indigestion, which can be relied upon to waken the conscience. In other words, the stolen-fruit motif may recur so frequently, not because these authors are emulating Augustine, but because they, Augustine, and almost every other child of the pre-modern period shared the experience of scrumping fruit.

Yet there was more to Protestant childhood than depravity. Catechisms could sometimes simply be tools for stamping orthodoxy onto young sinners, but could sometimes be more: the texts Katherine Fitzwilliam composed for her young children's use have a tender, child-centred intimacy to them. Some children tried in earnest to be Protestant, and some divines admitted that the normal strictures on childhood depravity did not apply to those 'who in their tender yeeres by meanes of religious nurture haue beene seasoned with the grace of God, dropping by little and little into them'.[15] John Bruen claimed to have received his effectual calling as a child, and recalled finding 'unexpressible joys' in reading and prayer when aged six or seven. His biographer was clearly uneasy about this, but made the best of it, invoking the *Confessions* to argue that God may 'put some good motions of his Spirit even upon the hearts of children'. But he added that at best this only happens 'upon occasion now and then'.[16]

It was not perhaps quite so rare as conventional wisdom assumed. Robert Blair was six when he had his first conversion. He was sick, and so left alone in the house while everyone else went to church one Sunday. Alone in a silent town, 'the Lord caused my conscience to reflect upon me with this query, Wherefore servest thou, unprofitable creature?'—a query which a visiting preacher soon after helped him to answer.[17] Alice Wandesford reckoned she experienced 'the first dawning of God's Spirit in my heart' when she was four. Hearing that God had made the stars moved her to 'a forceable consideration of the incomprehencable power and infinite majestie of Allmighty God', which 'caused in me a sincere love to Him for His goodnesse to me'.[18] John Livingstone's less vivid recollections of 'when I was but very young' capture a different truth. He could not remember precisely when 'the Lord at first wrought upon my heart', merely that 'I would sometimes pray with some feeling, and read the word with delight, but thereafter would very often intermitt any such exercises . . . and again begin and again intermitt'. The seven-year-old Thomas Goodwin was similarly changeable, to his own later disapproval.[19] Repeated, episodic conversions do not fit at all well with early modern Protestant life narratives. Yet they do ring true to the nature of childhood experience.

Such early faith could certainly seem profound enough. Richard Willis gives a heartwarming cameo of how, while he was at his desk one morning, 'my little grand

---

[15] Paula McQuade, 'Maternal Catechesis in the Manuscript Miscellany of Katherine Fitzwilliam (c. 1600)', paper delivered to the Sixteenth Century Conference, Cincinnati, Ohio, 27 October 2012; Dyke, *Two Treatises*, 25.

[16] Hinde, *Faithfull Remonstrance . . . of Iohn Bruen*, 7–9.

[17] Blair, *Life*, 4–5.

[18] Thornton, *Autobiography*, 6–7.

[19] Tweedie, *Select Biographies*, 132; Goodwin, *Works*, II.lvii–lviii.

child came into the roome where I was, falling downe upon her knees, and desired me to pray to God to blesse her'. He did so in silence, and she, trusting that it was done, went forth happily, 'assureing her selfe of the blessing shee desired'.[20] Such tenderness is perhaps a grandparent's prerogative. A woman known to us as I.B. had a sharper-edged experience. Her six-year-old son refused to play with the foul-mouthed neighbouring children. She tried to persuade him that he ought simply to forgive them, but he replied solemnly, 'Mother, with great repentance God can forgive, for his mercies are great; but good Mother, let us forbeare that which is evill'. The implicit reprimand brought her to renewed repentance herself.[21]

Slightly older children, aged around ten to fourteen, might achieve a more mature piety. Nehemiah Wallington was ten 'the first time that ever I prayed in privat myselfe'. Thomas Shepard was the same age when his father fell ill and 'I did pray very strongly and heartily' (and vainly) for his life. Alice Wandesford spent her twelfth birthday meditating on the story of Christ in the temple when he was the same age, and measuring herself against him: 'although I daily read the word of God, yet [I] was of a weake capacity to know the way to salvation'. At twelve even John Winthrop 'began to have some more savour of Religion'.[22] One reason for isolating this age-group—the years before and on the cusp of puberty—is that, for boys of a certain social class, it marked a distinct life-stage: grammar school. This, for William Cowper and for a good many others, was when God began 'to acquaint my heart to seek him: . . . he put this prayer in my heart euery day in the way, Lord, bow mine eare, that I may heare thy Word'.[23] It was no coincidence. Since godliness and good learning were so intimately connected, it was a truism that the best means of nurturing one was to fill a child's head with the other. As boys learned catechisms and repeated sermons, mind and soul were trained together. Published prayers for schoolboys' use ask God for 'so much learning and know-ledge, as may best fit me to be thy faithfull servant' or to 'grow to be learned & godly men', blending education and piety seamlessly.[24] Some girls shared a com-parable experience. Grace Mildmay gratefully remembered her mother teaching her prayers and setting her to daily Bible reading, and advised her daughter that all children should be exposed constantly and diligently to Scripture, 'vntill they be brought to the perfection of knowledge, faith & holynes'. A woman whom we know as M. K. was singled out from her eleven siblings when she was seven, as the most fit for learning, and set to work on the Bible and Erasmus' Gospel para-phrases. 'About this time', she remembered, she took up a serious discipline of self-examination, such that 'whatsoever I was about, still my heart was praying'.[25]

---

[20] Willis, *Mount Tabor*, 211.

[21] Powell, *Spirituall Experiences*, 53.

[22] Wallington, *Notebooks*, 267 (see above, p. 166); Shepard, *God's Plot*, 39; Thornton, *Autobiography*, 13; Winthrop, *Papers*, 155.

[23] Cowper, *Life and Death*, sig. A3v. Cf. Wariston, *Diary*, 1; Sibbes, *Works*, I.cxxxv.

[24] Alexander Nowell, *A Catechisme, or Institution of Christian Religion* (1625: RSTC 18736), sig. G3v; Kilby, *Burthen*, 99; Day, *Booke of Christian Prayers*, fo. 89v.

[25] Mildmay, *With Faith and Physic*, 29; Mildmay, 'Meditations', fo. 16r; Powell, *Spirituall Experiences*, 161–3.

These snapshots, while distorted by memory, do suggest something of what a pious Protestant child was like. Young children, from perhaps four to eight, might have bouts of intense piety and prayerfulness. If the level of understanding varied, the sincerity and intensity of the intentions and experiences are not to be doubted, at least for as long as they lasted. Older ones might develop a faith which a generous adult could recognize as authentic. Education was often a trigger for this. So too was a troubled conscience, especially if there was fruit on the trees.

There would be little more to say if it were not for two exceptional accounts written in the 1630s. Richard Norwood and Elizabeth Isham's spiritual autobiographies are quite unlike any others from our period, for both of them had read and been deeply influenced by Augustine's *Confessions*. This, apparently, is how Norwood came to believe that the Holy Spirit was preparing the ground through the 'childish piety' which pre-dated his actual conversion.[26] In his early youth, before the age of ten or twelve, he tells us, 'the Lord was pleased by means of my parents, school-dame, school-masters and sermons, to plant in my heart some seeds of religion and the fear of God'. Those seeds did not yet bear fruit, and yet he was keen to recall them, in part because they did keep him from gross sin for some years thereafter. He described these childish impulses to piety as 'praeludia, offers or essays of the Holy Spirit of God, as it is said our Savior took little children in his arms and blessed them'.[27]

He also tells us something of what this 'childish piety' consisted. 'When I was a child going in long coats to school', he learned to sing the psalms 'with great facility and delight', and was 'much affected' by them, especially the psalms of praise. Aged seven or eight, he was assiduous in reading Scripture, and was 'taken with great admiration of some places'. He was 'frequent in private prayer,' and sometimes made vows to God which I was careful to observe'—although as an adult he reckoned that these prayers were mere attempts to barter with God. He was sometimes moved by sermons. He rarely understood them, but like many a quick-witted ten-year-old, he badly wanted to understand, even if it meant working things out for himself. He remembered—and counted as a sin—'at several times reasoning . . . about whether there were a God'. Adults assured him that God loved him, but he was not sure 'how they could know it was so'. When he tried to share his enthusiasm for Scripture with his parents, 'they made me little answer (so far as I remember) but seemed rather to smile at my childishness'. This made him wonder whether what the preachers taught was really true,

> or whether elder people did not know them to be otherwise, only they were willing that we children should be so persuaded of them, that we might follow our books the better and be kept in from play. And thus did atheism show.[28]

[26] Norwood's childhood religion is discussed, from a different perspective and with perhaps excessive psychohistorical confidence, in Stachniewski, *Persecutory Imagination*, 110–16.
[27] Norwood, *Journal*, 5–6.
[28] Norwood, *Journal*, 5–10.

Norwood was that rare thing: an adult who could recall what it was really like to be a child. We should take seriously his reminder that early modern children listened closely to what their elders said and did not say about religion, and that they did not always hear it in quite the way they were meant to.

Elizabeth Isham's two accounts of her life—a brief 'diary' with annual entries and a much more involved account which she referred to as her *Confessions*—have an even more detailed and textured account of her childhood religion: perhaps because, unlike Norwood, she had not experienced a dramatic fall into sin and subsequent conversion. She attributed her religious formation chiefly to her mother and her grandmother: 'even when I begun to speake they taught me to pray'. In early childhood, she 'aprehended thee to be Glorious in thy selfe that thou wert God' and 'thought thee to have a celestiall being from all eternity and . . . knew that thou wast of all power that thou knewest our thoughts'. When she was about eight years old, however, 'I came to a fuller knowledge of thee', a change she ascribed to education but also to her parents' discipline. Her first earnest prayers were 'to avoyde my mothers displeasure', a problem which made a matter as trivial as a lost needle seem desperate. When the needle was found 'I rejoysed much at it supossing it to be thy doeing'. God was her protector against her mother's wrath. 'In these dayes feareing my parents I had no other refuge but to flie unto thee.' The fear was not idle. In her fury, Judith Isham used to have a servant hold her daughter down, the better to beat her. For a time at least, Elizabeth seems to have feared God in the same way. If she saw a red sun or moon, 'I feared that the day of Christ was at hand'. She interpreted any mishap as a judgement, and set herself to frequently repeating her prayers, Commandments, Creed, and catechism. The catechetical training was her father's contribution. He trained his children to memorize it, and was much 'offended with me' that she could remember ballads better than the set text. She worked each night for the dread moment on a Sunday when the recitation would be demanded of her, and adds that 'I more feared my father then my mother'.[29]

Looking back on this phase, she was tempted to dismiss those memorized prayers as worthless, 'talking like a parrit rather of custom then devotion'. But

> upon consideration I thinke better of this early serving of thee my God; perceiving the inclination of Children to be apt to learne that which is not so good and to rejoyce in it; therefore now I thinke it better by way of prevension to season them in the best.

And indeed, as her religion blossomed in her ninth and tenth years, there quickly came to be much more to it than fear. Her grandmother showed her another way. She gave the children psalters and taught them to sing, in which Elizabeth 'much delighted . . . thinking I did well'. Their mother, however, put a stop to that, on the grounds that the children could not sing sufficiently reverently: even as an adult Elizabeth still felt the sting of that denial. A happier memory was her visits to the old lady during an illness, when she herself was eight or nine. Struck by the delight

---

[29] Isham, 'Confessions', fos 3r–4r, 7r, 9v, 10r–v.

her grandmother took in her devotional books, Elizabeth took to reading and copying from them.[30]

For her, as for so many other children before and since, books were her liberation. Aged ten, she 'delighted' in reading the Sermon on the Mount, and thereafter her Biblical and devotional reading only accelerated. Her prayers began to have less worldly themes, asking for 'faith and grace' and 'striving to weepe'. Whether because of her increasing earnestness, or simply because of increasing age, the conflicts with her parents gradually receded. When she was sixteen, she and her siblings abandoned the recitations of the catechism, against their father's wishes— although she added that she continued to repeat it to herself daily. Her mother died the following year, but not before making peace with her daughter. Again, a book had been crucial: the exposition of the Ten Commandments written by John Dod, who was a family friend and a spiritual counsellor to the older woman. She took to heart Dod's warning that children should be disciplined in love rather than in anger. Her new technique, when she saw Elizabeth misbehave, was not to fly into a rage but to 'holde her fan afore her face', praying for patience and judgement. This gave Elizabeth time to reflect on her error, so that as soon as the fan was lowered she would go and ask forgiveness, and would be set a penitential task, 'which I performed with the more dilligence she having delt so well with mee'. Our sources rarely let us come so close to a happy ending.[31]

What do these two subtle accounts of Protestant childhoods add to our overall picture? They remind us of some obvious truths. Children are individuals, and neither happy nor unhappy families all resemble one another; and children take their own lives, including their religion, immensely seriously, and can be very finely attuned to managing the loving, unpredictable, condescending, inattentive and sometimes incomprehensibly punitive adult world. But there are also some more specific lessons. Early modern Protestantism's twinning of faith and intellectual understanding fostered an assumption that until you were old enough to under-stand doctrines, you could not be properly Protestant. Children's religious provi-sion therefore consisted largely of training: providing the building blocks with which they could build a mature faith in adulthood. So there were texts to memorize, warnings of hellfire to internalise, and simple doctrines about the power of God and the utility of prayer. Isham, generous as ever, gives us a positive reading of this. She did not understand much of what she learned by rote, she admitted, but it had 'since come flowing into my mind to my better instruction'. If such lessons do not help the child, they may help the adult to whom the child is parent.[32] Or they may not. Some children, like Norwood, might be alienated by the simplicity and (sometimes) insincerity of the religious instruction they received. Others might never graduate from it, and remain reciting prayers, making vows and hoping to be saved by good intentions all their lives. Divines lambasted this kind of religion as mere country divinity and carnal Protestantism. But the principles of

---

[30] Isham, 'Confessions', fos 5r, 6v–7r.
[31] Isham, 'Confessions', fo. 10v; Isham, 'Diary', 1618, 1619, 1620, 1624.
[32] Isham, 'Confessions', fo. 7r.

child-rearing which they themselves taught fostered it, and perhaps the doctrines they believed meant that no fundamentally different approach was possible.

CONVERSION

'Conversion' may seem an odd word to use of post-Reformation Britain. In the first generations of the Reformation there were many 'converts'; that is, individuals who self-consciously changed their religion to something new. But while conversions of that kind certainly continued, in all directions, after 1560 most—not all—English and Scottish people were reared in conformity to the newly established churches and did not need to 'convert' to Protestantism. The word therefore reverted to something like its medieval meaning. Conversion, for second- and even for many first-generation Protestants, was conversion not from error to truth, nor from unbelief to faith, but from formal or hypocritical Christianity to a more sincere and earnest kind. It was not about changing your beliefs, but owning them: a 'penitential reorientation' or moral renewal.[33]

It may seem odd to class conversion as one of the stages of life, since a first conversion could in theory and even in practice take place at any age. But by far the commonest pattern, after the first generations, was to be converted in the teens or early twenties.[34] This, like conversion itself, was strongly gendered. Women and girls were, of course, converted, but we have many fewer conversion-narratives, and more cases in which their conversions were gradual and seamless. The dramatic changes, the sudden renunciations of sin and sharp redirecting of lives, tend to come from boys and men. Given the double standard of sexual morality, it was easier for men than for women to leave a sinful past behind them; female unchastity could not be shrugged off by mere repentance. Nor was it so easy for women to assert their spiritual individuality. And there is also a connection between male conversions and education. Boys learned *about* religion when they were at grammar-school, but they discovered its power for themselves while at university. Protestantism was, in its bones, a religion of universities. Those weird communities—filled with youths, liberally populated with older men, entirely devoid of women and of children—were its natural habitat.

Consider, for example, the case of Christopher Love. Love was brought up in Cardiff by well-to-do parents, and took to his schoolwork with enthusiasm, but was—so his biographer claimed—entirely godless in his childhood. In 1633, however, a new minister came to town, and the fifteen-year-old Love turned up for 'the novelty of it': he had supposedly never heard a sermon before. The preacher confronted him with 'his Sins, and . . . his vndon Condition', and he went home

---

[33] Peter Marshall, 'Evangelical conversion in the reign of Henry VIII' in Peter Marshall and Alec Ryrie (eds), *The Beginnings of English Protestantism* (Cambridge, 2002), 19–22; Cohen, *God's Caress*, 5–7. Cf. Michael Questier, *Conversion, Politics and Religion in England, 1580–1625* (Cambridge, 1996).

[34] Cohen, *God's Caress*, 203 n. 5.

'with an Hell in his conscience'. His father, dismayed by 'the great Sadnesse of Spirit which did lye vpon him', locked him in his room to prevent him attending any more sermons. Like any self-respecting fifteen-year-old, he climbed out of the window and went anyway. At this second sermon, we read that he experienced 'a blessed Convertion', reinforced by spiritual counsel from the minister. This supposedly sparked a wave of conversions amongst his schoolfellows. The father, however, continued to oppose his son's new direction. He was trying to secure the boy an apprenticeship, but for Christopher, only one destination now had any appeal: Oxford. And there he eventually went, almost penniless and much against his father's better judgement. He providentially found an appropriately godly mentor and worked prodigiously hard: the conversion was complete.[35]

It does not particularly matter how much of this story is true. The stylization tells its own tale. Childhood simply dismissed, as usual; conversion as a teenager, triggered by preaching, and by the means of conviction of sin; and a resolution which involved an assertion of independence from worldly ways and the ever more earnest pursuit of godly learning. This is Protestant conversion as it was supposed to be; not, however, as it always was. Two particular aspects of this mismatch deserve our attention. First, the means of conversion, and second, the process.

As we have seen, most Protestants believed that 'the word preached is the only ordinarie meanes to beget faith'.[36] Often it was true. William Kiffin was set on the road to conversion by a sermon which 'made a very great impression on my heart'. He resolved to attend 'the most powerful preaching', and a series of further sermons marked the stages of his crisis. Thomas Goodwin, to whose sermons Kiffin eagerly listened, was himself converted after being dragged unwillingly to a sermon by his friends in Cambridge: 'I thought myself to be as one struck down by a mighty power.' Samuel Rogers similarly claimed to have attended a sermon in 1627 merely for novelty, and found that 'the whole sermon melted mee, and made mee come sobbing home'.[37] This trope, of the scornful or casual listener caught unawares by the power of the Word, might raise our suspicions. Rogers, scion of one of England's greatest puritan families, must have known that this was expected to happen to him sooner or later. What might raise our suspicions more is that so many of the airy claims about the power of preaching to convert relate to the illiterate masses, churchfuls of whom are sometimes said to be converted at a time. People of that status are not usually granted the complex, multistaged processes which, as we shall see, better-educated Protestants took as the norm. The woman who 'burst out into desperate crying, that *shee was a damned soule*' during a sermon of Richard Greenham's; the crowds converted by Robert Blair's preaching at Stewarton; 'the remarkable conversion' that happened at the Kirk o'Shotts revival in 1630—seen from the pulpit, these were stand-alone events, but to the individuals concerned they will have been part of a larger process which is now

[35] BL Sloane MS 3945 fos 80r–82v.
[36] Brinsley, *True Watch* (1608), 52; see above, pp. 351–2.
[37] Kiffin, *Remarkable Passages*, 2, 4–5, 8–9; Goodwin, *Works*, II. liii–lv; Rogers, *Diary*, 2.

irrecoverable.[38] Robert Bruce, so the story went, was one approached after a sermon by a 'poor Highlander', so moved by what he had heard that he 'offered him his whole substance (which was only two kowes) upon condition Mr Bruce would make God his friend'.[39] That story tells us much more about learned Protestants' condescension to their uneducated countryfolk, and about their concepts of preaching, than it does about the Highlander, his religion, or his cattle.

Protestant divines had an ulterior motive for emphasizing conversion by sermon: to discredit alternatives, in particular conversion by reading. For every one person 'won to the Christian faith and true godlines by priuate reading', Daniel Featley claimed, there are 'many thousands that haue bin added to the Church by publike Sermons'—although the only example he could cite was St Peter's Pentecost sermon. He compared sermons and books respectively to rain and snow; snow is more enduring, but rain warmer and more nourishing.[40] Such arguments are driven, as Arnold Hunt has pointed out, by a theological bias in favour of the preached rather than the printed word.[41] However, there is also practical and professional interest. Preachers would emphasize the importance of sermons, wouldn't they? Not merely to fill pews, but also to squelch any attempts by non-attenders to make unverifiable claims that they were sitting at home reading. And yet in reality private reading was enormously important in sparking conversions. We cannot quantify the matter as Featley tried to, but we do have plenty of examples. Some of those are people who had no access to preaching at the time. In the 1530s, Rose Throckmorton's mother 'came to some light of the gospell by meanes of some english books sent privately to her . . . from beyond sea'; nearly a century later, Richard Norwood, deprived of regular preaching while in Bermuda, found that it was when reading Augustine that 'Christ began to be formed in me'.[42] But we cannot so easily write off Elizabeth Wilkinson, converted in the early 1620s by reading Lewis Bayly's *Practise of pietie* and Calvin's *Institutes*. Nor Elizabeth Isham, whose emergence into a mature faith was made possible 'by bookes'. Richard Baxter's father was converted 'by the bare reading of the Scriptures in private, without either Preaching, or Godly Company'; young Richard himself was converted chiefly by a series of books, in particular Persons' *Book of Resolution*. By the Civil War era, the weight of examples was such that claims like Featley's simply became unsustainable.[43]

But the polemical opposition between preaching and reading conceals the fact that the two usually reinforced each other. There was not one ordinary means of grace, but many. Simonds D'Ewes' conversion crisis in 1624 was triggered by

[38] Parker and Carlson, *'Practical Divinity'*, 252; Blair, *Life*, 19; Bruce, *Sermons . . . with Collections*, 140.

[39] Kirkton, *Secret and True History*, 26.

[40] Featley, *Ancilla Pietatis*, 65–6; Acts 2:41. Cf. a slightly more extreme claim made in almost identical terms by Edward Vaughan: *Plaine and perfect Method*, 42.

[41] Hunt, *Art of Hearing*, 19–59.

[42] BL Additional MS 43827A fo. 3v; Norwood, *Journal*, 71.

[43] Clarke, *Collection*, 516–17; Isham, 'Confessions', fo. 8r (and see above, p. 435); Baxter, *Reliquiae Baxterianae*, 2–4; Hunt, *Art of Hearing*, 165–6.

hearing a sermon, but sealed by reading Samuel Ward's *The life of faith* the following day. Thomas Shepard, whose conversion was punctuated by a series of sermons, also credits Richard Rogers' *Seven Treatises*. In addition, his friends' talk of God's wrath 'did much awaken me'. Private conversation was vital for D'Ewes too, as—like Christopher Love—he conferred with the preacher who had moved him. The young John Bruen was brought back from a dalliance with popery by conversations with a fellow-student, an achievement which made Bruen's biographer question the truism that sermons were the ordinary means of salvation.[44] Consciences could be stirred by rebukes, illnesses, worldly misfortune, even a pounding hangover.[45] And some could not or would not explain the earthly cause of their conversions at all. Robert Bolton was converted by 'the LORD . . . laying before him the ugly visage of his sins', having spent months assailed by foul—and unspecified—temptations. Conversion, after all, was God's work. Goodwin insisted that in his conversion it was God 'with whom only and immediately I had to do. . . . I . . . myself was merely passive'.[46] The wind blows where it wills.

When—as it often did—preaching did have an essential part to play, it was not always the part which its advocates scripted. We have already noticed the wide but not complete consensus that conversion must begin with an appalled confrontation with the horror of sin.[47] However, that was only the beginning, and since we are dealing with Reformed Protestants, that end involved enlightening the mind as well as easing the heart. Conversion was readily understood as understanding. Norwood's experience, after the first crisis of his conversion, was that his thoughts were clarified and his misconceptions melted away.[48] And it was here, naturally enough, that preaching truly came into its own. Shepard's drawn-out conversion experience was not sparked by a sermon, but it was more or less concluded by one. We have already met I. B., whose conversion was prompted by a rebuke from her solemn six-year-old; it was cemented by a sermon. John Cotton was first convicted of his sin when he realized with horror, that the news of William Perkins' death made him feel relieved; but it took Richard Sibbes' preaching to finish the job. Richard Rothwell was convicted by a rebuke for playing bowls with papists on a Saturday—he should have been preparing for the Sabbath; it was a sermon the following day which turned this into a proper conversion.[49] Nicholas Byfield acknowledged the pattern. To find assurance, he advised, first pray for it, and then 'waite vpon the preaching of the Gospel'.[50] Those who turn up to a sermon desperate for relief, or thirsty for enlightenment, are after all much more likely than

[44] D'Ewes, *Autobiography*, 249–50; Shepard, *God's Plot*, 41, 43; Hinde, *Faithfull Remonstrance . . . of Iohn Bruen*, 16–18.
[45] See, for example, Clarke, *Lives of thirty-two divines*, 68, 168–9; Winthrop, *Papers*, 155; Shepard, *God's Plot*, 41.
[46] Bolton, *Boltons last and learned worke*, sigs b5r–v; cf. Bruce, *Sermons . . . with Collections*, 8; Goodwin, *Works*, II.lvi.
[47] See above, pp. 36–7.
[48] Norwood, *Journal*, 74.
[49] Shepard, *God's Plot*, 45; Powell, *Spirituall Experiences*, 53; Clarke, *Collection*, 58; Clarke, *Lives of thirty-two divines*, 68.
[50] Byfield, *Marrow of the Oracles* (1622), 247.

the passive or sceptical to find what they need: they will hunt for the specks of gold in a sermon where most of the audience will simply hear dross. If sermons did not trigger the process of conversion as they should have done, they often completed it.

This view of the *process* of conversion does, however, bring us to the other mismatch between theory and experience in this area. It was acknowledged that conversion was indeed a process.[51] Perkins, with characteristically schematic clarity, discerned three stages. First, a 'liuely sense of our misery' brings us to consider God's promises. There follows a desire to believe, expressed in earnest prayer for mercy, which leads, lastly, to 'a setling and quieting of the minde touching Christ and his benefits vpon some assurance therof, wrought and conceiued in the minde by the spirit of God'.[52] Experiencing this could, however, be messier than that implies, and as time wore on divines became readier to acknowledge this. Moving from simple repentance to real conversion, Robert Bruce warned, was 'not wrought in ane instant of time'. Conversion 'comes not all on the sudden, but vsually by certaine steppes and degrees', warned Daniel Dyke—even suggesting that a too-rapid conversion was 'an ill signe, a presage of no durable soundnesse'.[53] Some people could pin down a precise narrative or even a date of their conversions, and some divines advocated doing so. The young Richard Baxter was troubled that he did not know 'the Time of my Conversion, being wrought on by . . . Degrees'.[54] But thunderclap conversions were strictly for Saul on his road or Augustine in his garden. For real early modern Protestants, and indeed for most of the idealized ones too, the business was drawn out—sometimes agonizingly so. If they chose to elevate a particular moment, they recognized that that was not the whole story. Even Norwood, whose turning away from sin was far from imaginary, did not notice what was happening to him at the time. 'But afterwards . . . I began to think . . . surely there is a great change wrought in me.'[55] It was not the stereotypical experience, but it did reflect a basic Reformed Protestant truism: conversion was God's work, and happened on his initiative.

Simply blurring conversion into a seamless process will not do, however. Conversion was like sanctification: the silent workings of grace might be steady and continuous, but human awareness of and response to that grace was punctuated. Conversion as consciously experienced and narrated was neither process nor event, but a series of events, a staccato sequence of episodes, sometimes extending over many years. This did not fit terribly well with the sharp dichotomies of later Reformed Protestant theology, in which everyone either had or had not received an effectual calling. Those using that framework tended to write off earlier experiences retrospectively as false starts, and to see later ones as qualitatively different. Samuel Rogers' explicit description of one crisis as '(as it were) a second conversion' is unusual.[56] However, it is hard to see some accounts in any other way. Simonds D'Ewes described how, during a visit home when he was fifteen, the 'blessed

---

[51] Webster, 'Writing to Redundancy', 42–3.   [52] Perkins, *How to live*, 20–1.

[53] Bruce, *Sermons Preached*, sigs Z6r–7r; Dyke, *Mystery of selfe-deceiuing*, 85–7.

[54] Baxter, *Reliquiae Baxterianae*, 6. Cf. D'Ewes, *Autobiography*, 249–50; Beadle, *Journal or diary*, 48, 50.

[55] Norwood, *Journal*, 72.   [56] Rogers, *Diary*, 3.

example' of his mother's piety 'did admirably strengthen and settle me in the love and exercise of the best things: so as now I began to perform holy duties feelingly and with comfort'. Seven years later, a sermon on grace, and the conversation and reading it prompted, led him not only to 'the use and comfort of that grace' but also to 'a certain hope and assurance of mine own salvation'. Or again, John Bruen's biographer, who strived mightily to fit him into a classic conversion-narrative, dated his effectual calling to age twenty-six, when his father died, but also tells us that Bruen himself claimed to have received his calling as 'a child, little'. He also describes Bruen's reconversion from popery as a seventeen-year-old student.[57] It seems futile to ask which of these events was the 'true' conversion.

In the 17th century, such repeated conversions might be interpreted by separating calling from the gift of assurance, as in D'Ewes' case; and as also in John Winthrop's. Aged eighteen, and newly married, Winthrop 'first found the ministry of the word to come to my heart with power' and 'could no longer dally with Religion'. But aged thirty, he found himself laid 'lower in myne owne eyes then at any time before' by knowledge of his sins; and was thereafter 'filled with joy unspeakable, and glorious and with a spirit of Adoption'. However, he was careful not to exaggerate this second change. He did not pray with any more 'fervency or more enlargement of heart' than before, simply 'with more confidence'. What made that first conversion unsatisfactory was not its incompleteness but its inconstancy. He had been pious 'by fits only'.[58] Likewise, the newly converted Thomas Shepard was, in his own memory, 'blind and unconstant' in affections, repeatedly 'shook...off' wholesome admonitions and repeatedly took up and abandoned habits of prayer.[59] The echo here of the dismissive language used about childhood piety is striking. Winthrop, Shepard and others thought that their greater constancy betokened a deeper conversion. It may simply reflect the universal experience that human beings grow set in their ways as they age.

With their need for crisis, and their focus on the importance of the present moment, Protestants were in some sense aspiring to be converted afresh every day. Yet some individuals do seem to have successfully moved to a more settled and—so they told themselves, at least—deeper faith, a stage associated, for some of them, with the peace they called assurance. Perhaps this was the result of a genuine spiritual breakthrough; perhaps it was the result of age, habit, and responsibility dulling the mercurial spirits of youth; perhaps it was sheer conversion fatigue, as living your life at a pitch of crisis for decades on end simply became impossible. They would have said that grace could work through any of these.

THE PASSAGE OF TIME

Once past the turbulence of conversion(s), early modern Protestants then embarked on the long, slow, slog of the middle years. The task was disconcertingly

---

[57] D'Ewes, *Autobiography*, 104, 249–50; Hinde, *Faithfull Remonstrance . . . of Iohn Bruen*, 9, 16–18, 42–5.
[58] Winthrop, *Papers*, 155–6, 158–9.   [59] Shepard, *God's Plot*, 40–1.

simple: to grow holier day by day, while being mindful of God, never backsliding, and preparing for death.

One obvious way of doing this was through a life devoted wholly to religious exercises; yet—as well as being impossible for most people—this was not an ideal to which Reformed Protestants aspired. Naturally they rejected anything which smacked of monastic practices. But divines also had little taste for the 'disordered excesse' associated with some new converts, whose 'first love' was not yet tempered, who 'reade daily for diuers houres' and who 'thinke it religion to heare . . . all the Sermons [that] can be come vnto'. Such people 'vpon pretence of seeking continuance of comfort . . . neglect their lawfull businesse'.[60] That last was a serious charge, and it did not apply only to new converts. It was an accepted truth, Richard Rogers believed, that zealous Protestants 'of all other are most negligent in their businesse'. In particular, he worried that pious servants 'when their minds should be vpon their worke, are found oftentimes at their booke and at prayer', whereas the worldly, driven by avarice and fear, work much harder. He claimed that some masters refused to hire openly religious servants for this reason, and that lazy servants might claim piety as a cloak for their sloth.[61] Nehemiah Wallington shows us this kind of pious time-wasting at first hand. He admitted that he had 'lost much time and necklected my calling' through his obsessive writing, a 'delight' which led him to 'still [steal] time when I should not'.[62] That double concern—neglect of calling and theft of time—takes us to the heart of this question. The emphasis on secular work as a divine vocation has long been seen as one of Protestantism's most distinctive innovations. But underlying that is the more fundamental question of the use of time. For as the spiritual dynamism of conversion ebbed, a new dynamic took its place in the Protestant life.

The Scylla and Charybdis of Protestant ethics were hypocrisy and idleness, false action and inaction. We have seen how formative the fear of hypocrisy could be, but the fear of idleness, the 'rust and canker of the soule', was also pervasive. 'The idle man', Joseph Hall warned, 'is the diuels cushion, on which hee taketh his free ease: who as hee is vncapable of any good, so he is fitly disposed for all euill motions.' Idleness, in John Trundle's diagnosis, 'dulleth vnderstanding, nourisheth humours, choaketh the braine', and he added, 'hee is not worthy of the name of man that spends a whole day in pleasure'. For, as Henry Scudder put it, 'God neuer made any man for play, or to doe nothing'.[63] The bedridden could still read and write, as the books described as a 'poore Exercise of my sicknesse' testify. John Foxe told of a blind girl who learned rope-making because she 'in no case would be idle'. The young and unmarried were particularly vulnerable to idleness, but anyone

---

[60] Byfield, *Marrow of the Oracles* (1622), 249; Baynes, *Briefe Directions*, 103.

[61] Rogers, *Seven treatises*, 361–2.

[62] Wallington, *Notebooks*, 265.

[63] Bolton, *Some generall directions*, 70; Hall, *Meditations . . . A third Century*, III.81; Trundle, *Keepe within Compasse*, sigs C5v–6r; Scudder, *Christians daily walke* (1628), 57; cf. Thomas Scott, *The Belgicke Pismire: Stinging the slothfull Sleeper, and Awaking the Diligent* (Holland, 1622: RSTC 22069), 1.

could be at risk.[64] To lie abed in the morning was to court moral disaster. James Melville's poetic 'Morning Vision' described a cold, wet April morning in which 'sweete Lady *Lasines*' urged him to stay in bed, promising to 'take you in my armes' and to be joined by her daughters Lust, Vainglory, and Envy. Even idle thought when lying awake at night was a 'rouing and frisking of the phantasie . . . a fretting worme that eats out a great deale of most mens time'.[65]

Idleness' evils, then, were legion. Some of them were nakedly political. Ruling classes like hardworking taxpayers, and from the beginning of the Reformation evangelicals had contrasted their industriousness with Catholics' supposed indolence. For Henry VIII, this had a particular appeal, and it undergirded his assault on monasticism. Edward VI's primer asked God 'to graue in the heartes of all labourers and workemen a wyllynge dispocion to trauayle for their lyuynge', which seems to have the good order of the realm more in view than the prosperity of the labourers' souls or bodies. The theme was canonized in the Elizabethan Homily 'against Idleness', which warned the English population at large 'always [to] be doing of some honest work'. In particular, wage-earners should consider idleness at work to be theft from their employers.[66] This is ethics by the rich and powerful, for the rich and powerful.

Yet it was never merely that. Idleness was not simply another sin. It 'is never alone, but hath always a long tail of other vices hanging on'. It was 'the mother and nurse of euil'; it 'openeth the doore for the diuell to enter into vs with ful swing'. The idle have time to listen to the Devil and nothing with which to crowd him out. They never rouse themselves to pray.[67] Like sleep itself, idleness is a form of spiritual death, a 'dangerous dulness' into which the soul can, fatally, be lulled.[68]

Quite what constituted idleness was a vexed point. The problem of Sabbath observance meant that, especially latterly, British Protestants were divided on this. But as Kenneth Parker's invaluable analysis has established, the question cut across the supposed division between puritans and conformists. It was rather, like so much else, a division between the earnest clerics of all parties who—after the first generation—favoured a restrictive and counter-intuitive definition of Sabbath 'rest', and the wider population whose notion of a godly Sabbath had room for some recreation.[69] Behind this lay the wider issue of whether recreation could be a legitimate use of time. Most Protestants admitted that it could, but with diminishing enthusiasm. Hugh Latimer could preach that 'it is lawful for poor men

---

[64] Francis Bacon, *The Translation of Certaine Psalmes into English Verse* (1625: RSTC 1174), sig. A3r (cf. above p. 303); Foxe, *Actes and monuments* (1570), 2137; Latimer, *Sermons and Remains*, 64; cf. Cleaver, *[G]odly form*, 331.

[65] Melville, *Spiritual Propine*, 54; Whately, *Redemption of time*, 36; cf. Bod MS Rawl D.384 fo. 1v.

[66] Ryrie, *Gospel and Henry VIII*, 152; *Prymmer . . . set foorth by the kinges maiestie* (1553), sig. P8r–v; *Certain Sermons or Homilies*, 463–6.

[67] *Certain Sermons or Homilies*, 463; Norden, *Pensiue mans practise*, 14; Cleaver, *[G]odly form*, 331; Leigh, *Mothers blessing*, 218; cf. Sandys, *Sermons*, 117; Dod and Cleaver, *Foure Sermons*, 29; Sibbes, *Bruised reede*, 309.

[68] Hayward, *Sanctuarie of a troubled soule* (1602), 38; Sheltco à Geveren, *Of the ende of this world, and seconde commyng of Christ*, tr. Thomas Rogers (1577: RSTC 11803a.7), tp. verso.

[69] Kenneth L. Parker, *The English Sabbath* (Cambridge, 1988), esp. 70–1.

sometimes to be merry', and could even organize a sermon around the image of a card-game, but his generation's emphasis on liberty would soon feel like libertinism. Authorities tended grudgingly to permit 'idle pleasures and sports', and then instantly to hedge them about with warnings against their abuse.[70] Richard Norwood eventually came to believe that God 'doth not forbid us taking delight in that wherein there is indeed true delight', but his view as a new convert—that worldly pleasures were 'stolen things which God did not allow of'—was perhaps more typical.[71]

Other than such near-prohibitions, Protestants found two more constructive ways of handling recreation. One was to treat it as medicinal. 'It is healthfull to stir your bodies', Richard Kilby advised his readers, at least in 'honest sports'. James Melville remembered approvingly that when he went to university, his father gave him bows and arrows, and golf clubs and balls—it was St Andrews, after all—but not money to play catchpull. Martial sports such as archery, in particular, were good not only for the individual's body but for the defence of the entire commonwealth.[72] The other approach was to spiritualize it. In William Perkins' phrase, 'Christian men and women should with their earthly recreations ioyne spirituall meditation of the death of Christ'. Ideally, this meant that religious exercises should actually be your recreation, although that argument was usually part of a tortuous attempt to explain how a Sunday spent exclusively on such exercises could meaningfully be described as a day of rest.[73] Back in reality, the priority was instead to pursue *godly* recreation. Dicing, dancing, perhaps hunting were excluded. Other pastimes could be rescued at a stretch. John Bruen kept a pious commonplace book which he called 'his Cardes being 52 in Number', but any resemblance to cards is not obvious to its modern reader.[74] Music-making, by contrast, was far more easily redeemed. Protestants were widely encouraged to sing psalms 'for thy recreation, and not so much for thy recreation, as for thy profit'.[75] Grace Mildmay saw her daily lute playing and singing as part of her devotions. She also spent a good deal of time in sketching or embroidery, exercises which 'did greatly recreate my mind', but in which she also 'found in myself that God wrought with me in all'. Elizabeth Isham, who was unapologetic about her love for needlework, did not explicitly describe it as a devotional exercise, but she certainly chose pious subjects, from a psalm text to a picture of Adam and Eve. Bishop Earle's 'she-puritan' did 'no good works but what are wrought on the Sampler'.[76] Masculine recreations were less easily spiritualized, although, somewhat after our period, Izaak

[70] Latimer, *Sermons by Hugh Latimer*, 8; Latimer, *Sermons and Remains*, 162; Sandys, *Sermons*, 118; Leigh, *Mothers blessing*, 171, 176; Scudder, *Christians daily walke* (1628), 67–8.
[71] Norwood, *Journal*, 74–5; cf. Winthrop, *Papers*, 198, 205.
[72] Kilby, *Burthen*, 101; Melville, *Autobiography*, 30; Scott, *Belgicke Pismire*, 13; cf., classically, Roger Ascham, *Toxophilus, the schole of shootinge* (1545: RSTC 837).
[73] Perkins, *Declaration of the true manner*, 11; Scudder, *Christians daily walke* (1628), 66–7; cf. Perkins, *Whole treatise*, 460–1; Bayly, *Practise of pietie*, 446; Byfield, *Marrow of the Oracles* (1622), 123.
[74] BL Harleian MS 6607 fo. 1r; Cambers, *Godly Reading*, 104.
[75] Fleming, *Diamond of deuotion*, 249.
[76] Mildmay, *With Faith and Physic*, 35; Isham, 'Diary', 1621, 1631; Isham, 'Confessions', fo. 9v; Earle, *Microcosmographie*, 118.

Walton made the case for fishing, 'the contemplative man's recreation'. He claimed that Dean Alexander Nowell had been a 'constant practiser of Angling', a past-time which produced food which he could give to the poor, and which allowed him to spend his time 'harmlessly, and in a recreation that became a churchman'.[77]

Recreation was acceptable, in other words, only if it was a means to a worthwhile end. This instrumentalist approach is implicit in the very word *recreation*, whose early modern meaning was, as Elaine McKay has suggested, closer to 'regeneration' than 'relaxation'. Recreation might be fun, but it was also purposeful.[78] This was partly a matter of proportion. 'Rest', Sandys allowed, 'but rest *a little*', and even then not before earning it. William Whateley's rule of thumb was to spend no longer each day in 'pastime' than in 'religious exercises'. But if you can only rest once you have worked, you only rest in order to work. The only legitimate reason for rest was 'to quicken and reuiue the spirits, and to fit men for matters of greater importance'. Whately compared recreation to sharpening a scythe; that is, it is necessary, but labourers who did nothing else would not only be idle but would also damage their tools.[79] So recreation may be permissible or even necessary, but the one thing you must not do during recreation is to relax.

Underpinning all this, indeed providing a constant drumbeat of urgency to the Protestant life, was a very particular view of time. Richard Greenham, commenting on recreation, deplored the whole concept of 'past-time'. It is wrong simply to while away time which God has given you.[80] The proof-text was Ephesians 5:16, which speaks of 'redeming the time'—which, according to the Geneva Bible's marginal note, meant 'selling all worldlie pleasures to bye time'. In Whateley's best-selling sermon *The Redemption of time*, he argued that it meant 'to win all the time wee possibly can, for the duties of Religion and Godlinesse'. The wise Christian 'must not suffer any of these bargains of time to passe him but must buy vp, & buy out, all the minutes therof', and will not willingly allow 'any houre, or minute . . . to bee layd out in any thing but matters that may fit him for a better life'. The particular force of the image of *redemption* was that, in this struggle for time, everyone started from behind, like a runner slow off the blocks. Everyone could look back at their childhood and see a mere wasteland of squandered time. Even sleep was 'a Culler, or rather devourer of time'. And the relentless 'sliding of minutes' into the past never stopped.[81]

The principle of redeeming time was being preached from at least the 1580s, but the terms grew ever more exacting.[82] Earlier reformers were content with vague

[77] Walton, *Complete Angler*, 9, 36.

[78] Elaine McKay, '"For refreshment and preservinge health": the definition and function of recreation in early modern England', *Historical Research* 81/211 (2008), 61–3.

[79] Sandys, *Sermons*, 336–7; Whately, *Redemption of time*, 15–19; Dod and Cleaver, *Ten sermons*, 70–1; Latimer, *Sermons by Hugh Latimer*, 120.

[80] Parker and Carlson, 'Practical Divinity', 181–2.

[81] Whately, *Redemption of time*, 1, 3, 5, 10, 46 (six editions, 1606–34); Green, *Print and Protestantism*, 219; Scudder, *Christians daily walke* (1628), 18–19; *Drousie disease*, 84–5.

[82] See, for example, Parker and Carlson, 'Practical Divinity', 160; Rogers, *Seven treatises*, 334; John Monipennie, *A Christian Almanacke* (1612: RSTC 18019), sig. A2v; Rogers, *Garden* (1616), sig. F4v; Rogers, *Garden* (1615), II sig. A7v.

principles such as 'lose as little time as ye may'. In the 1570s we can find the Cornish gentleman William Carnsew, an earnest enough Protestant, unselfconsciously describing spending 'all daye playinge and tryfflynge the Tyme awaye'.[83] That kind of view would not last. The Jacobean orthodoxy was that 'euery houre requireth a religious imployment'. Elnathan Parr's 'godly Admonitions concerning Time' emphasized that every stroke must be redeemed. 'On this moment', and therefore on every moment, 'depends eternity'. Henry Scudder warned that,

> You are not dispensed with for any moment of your life: but all the dayes of your life, and each day of your life, and each houre of that day, and each minute of that hour.... You are accountable vnto God for losing and misspending all that precious time wherein you doe not walke in his wayes.[84]

That peculiarly unremitting view was distinctively puritan, but more conformist Protestants did not fundamentally disagree. Christopher Sutton argued, not that we owe every second of time to God, but rather that time is all we ever truly own. 'Man is Lord of the time.' Yet this came to the same thing. If time is all we have, spending it wisely is essential. 'Seeing that time is granted vs to dispose well of our future condition, let not any houre passe without fruit.'[85]

These exhortations had their effect. We can find Protestants of all kinds, especially after 1600, trying, and, inevitably, failing, to discipline their time. Wallington's personal covenant included a vow to 'stand not Idle at any time'; John Rogers', a vow to 'lose no Time . . . but be doing some Good'.[86] Margaret Hoby spent a journey with a stranger who had nothing edifying to say, 'and therfore the time, as ill bestowed, I greeued for'. When Mary Swain spent any time in 'ordinary recreation', she supposedly remarked, 'This is a passing away of the time, but no redeeming of the time'. The same principle supported the practice of very early rising: those who had fallen behind in the race of life could at least steal a march on the day.[87]

So, if idleness was to be feared, and every moment to be redeemed, but not by devoting an entire life to explicit piety, how were the long hours to be filled? For most Protestants there was a simple answer: to labour in their vocation. But that idea is important enough to deserve our attention at a little more length.

VOCATION

More than a century ago, Max Weber used the concept of vocation to link the 'Protestant ethic' to the 'spirit of capitalism'. The argument he started shows little

---

[83] Pounds, 'William Carnsew', 35, 40, 58; cf. Tyrwhit, *Elizabeth Tyrwhit's Morning and Evening Prayers*, 102; Perkins, *Salve for a sicke man*, 48.

[84] John Monipennie, *A Christian Almanacke* (1612: RSTC 18019), sig. A3v; Parr, *Abba Father*, 106–32, esp. 106, 111; Scudder, *Christians daily walke* (1628), 17–18. Cf. Tweedie, *Select Biographies*, 121.

[85] Sutton, *Godly meditations* (1613), 422–3.

[86] Wallington, *Notebooks*, 47; Mather, *Magnalia*, III.111.

[87] Hoby, *Diary*, 131; Lancelot Langhorne, *Mary Sitting at Christs Feet* (1611: RSTC 15197), 19; Ryrie, 'Sleeping, waking and dreaming'.

sign of dying down, but fortunately, here we have to do no more than skirt around its edges. Weber discerned two distinct Protestant concepts of vocation: an early, static version and a later, more dynamic one. It is now pretty clear that his dynamic concept had not fully emerged in our period—if, indeed, it ever existed at all. But while Weber argued that that static view implied 'absolute acceptance of things as they were', it remained a powerfully revolutionary idea.[88] And it directly affects our concern in this section, which is how early modern British Protestants understood the way they spent most of their adult lives.

For almost (not quite) everyone in early modern Britain, secular work was a necessity of life. The Reformation did not change this, although the steadily worsening economic climate across our period did make it more pressing. What the Reformation did do was to change how secular work was understood, in two linked ways. First, it emphasized that work, in the abstract, was a moral good. One strain of Christian thought, drawing on classical models, had always been inclined to see labour as an evil: as Keith Thomas points out, 'everyone knew that there would be no work in heaven'. But another strain, running through monasticism and Christian humanism, argued that in this world, work was a moral duty. Protestantism made this argument its own, adding the anti-clerical twist that those who do not work are parasites.[89] Where Robert Persons' *Book of Resolution* described the saints living an austere life 'in fastinge, prayenge, punishinge there bodyes, and the lyke', the Protestantized edition added the phrase 'in painful labour, profitable to others' to the beginning of the list.[90] The obvious target of these barbs was the religious orders, mere leeches in Protestant propaganda, but the idle rich were also implicitly—or explicitly—included. None of this necessarily meant that work was seen as fulfilling or rewarding, although some found it so. What it meant was simply that work was a universal obligation. 'He that hath no honest businesse about which ordinarily to be employed', Samuel Hieron preached, 'cannot please God.'[91] Adam's curse—'in the sweat of thy face shalt thou eat bread'—was much cited. As Archbishop Sandys put it:

> Man is born unto service and labour, as birds unto flight. We were not redeemed and bought with a price to be idle and do nothing . . . but to walk every one in that vocation wherewith he is called.[92]

It is an arduous enough vision, but it does at least make it clear that there is no shame in working.

---

[88] Weber, *Protestant Ethic*, esp. 85, 160–2.

[89] Keith Thomas, *The Ends of Life: Roads to Fulfilment in Early Modern England* (Oxford, 2009), 78–97, esp. 79.

[90] Bunny also amended Persons' discussion of sloth to add direct criticisms of how the slothful 'take no pains in their several callings'. Persons, *Christian Directory*, ed. Houliston, 19, 305–6; Persons, *Booke of Christian exercise*, ed. Bunny, 13, 385–6.

[91] Samuel Hieron, *All the Sermons of Samvel Hieron* (1614: RSTC 13378), 246.

[92] Genesis 3:19; Sandys, *Sermons*, 117, 182. Cf. Heyden, *Bryefe Summe*, sig. L4v; Latimer, *Sermons and Remains*, 37–8; Scott, *Belgicke Pismire*, 1; Gee, *Steps of Ascension*, 119; Bolton, *Some generall directions*, 49.

Hence the other, more revolutionary Protestant claim, originating with Luther: that all honest work was of equal spiritual dignity. Outwardly, William Tyndale admitted, 'there is difference betwixt washing of dishes, and preaching of the word of God; but as touching to please God, none at all'.[93] To some extent this was a by-product of anticlerical polemic. Hugh Latimer repeatedly told the tale of how St Anthony, living as a hermit, was told by God that there was a cobbler in Alexandria whose life was more perfect than his own. The indignant saint hastened to find the cobbler, who, surprised, denied having any heroic virtue. He simply described how he began each day with prayer, then spent the whole day 'in getting my living', all the while living honestly and instructing his family in godliness as best he could. The story was told to deprecate the religious life as much as to elevate the secular one. But Latimer was also keen to praise secular work in its own right. He liked to argue that Christ, by labouring as a carpenter, 'did sanctify all manner of occupations'. 'Let no man disdain or think scorn to follow him in a mean living.'[94]

This concept of secular work could be liberating, but it could also, as Weber pointed out, be strongly socially conservative. This was certainly part of Latimer's meaning. Citing the apostles' original calling to be fishermen, he warned that 'every man hath his vocation: as these men here were fishers, so every man hath his faculty wherein he was brought up'. It was only legitimate to change your vocation if, like the apostles, you were explicitly called by God to do so. 'God would have every man to live in that order that he hath ordained for him.' Latimer had a (dubious) Biblical warning for those who disliked their vocations: Lot's wife, who 'would not be content with her good state, but wrestled with God's calling, and she was for that cause turned into a salt stone'.[95] Richard Greenham had an anecdote of a man who 'began through the temptation of Sathan to mislike his calling and chaunged it', but then became discontent with his new calling and changed again and again. Eventually, having a pain in his leg, he read Christ's command to cut off the limb that offends you, hacked off his foot with an axe, and died. This, Greenham implied, is where itchy feet will take you. In the 1620s, Robert Bolton was still lambasting the 'hollownesse and hypocrisie', even the 'coozening', of those who aspire to change their vocations.[96] 'Suite thine owne Calling', the title page of the moralizing best-seller *Keepe within Compasse* commanded (see Figure 1). There were genuine spiritual concerns here: humility, obedience. But the attempt at social control is plain. Since labour was dignified, labourers should remain labourers. Religious authority in general, and the pulpit in particular, continued to be monopolised by appropriately trained and institutionally approved men. The Edwardian primer's prayer to 'be contente with oure callynge [and] quietlye lyue in the same' was a transparent plea for submissive good order.[97]

[93] Tyndale, *Doctrinal Treatises*, 102.
[94] Latimer, *Sermons and Remains*, 94, 158–9; Latimer, *Sermons by Hugh Latimer*, 214, 392–3. Cf. Hieron, *Helpe Vnto Deuotion* (1610), 95–6; Sibbes, *Works*, VI.101.
[95] Latimer, *Sermons and Remains*, 29–34, 37–8, 94; Latimer, *Sermons by Hugh Latimer*, 165.
[96] Parker and Carlson, *'Practical Divinity'*, 245; Bolton, *Some generall directions*, 48–9.
[97] *Prymmer . . . set fourth by the kinges maiestie* (1553), sig. R2v.

This consensus did not break during our period, but it did come under pressure. Quite aside from its weak Biblical basis, changes of occupation were often a matter of necessity in turbulent economic times. Richard Rogers admitted that while a Christian 'ought not hastily nor lightly' to abandon a legitimate calling, 'the decay of his former trade' or 'other sufficient and waightie considerations' sometimes left little choice.[98] This was Richard Norwood's experience. Having left his family's land, which could not support him, he was berated by a minister for leaving his calling. He replied that in fact he was 'destitute of a calling', and asserted that the seafaring life he now desired was 'an honest, necessary and commendable calling'.[99] Those criteria were important. A calling was not simply work, but work worth doing.

This had implications both for choice of a trade—when choice was possible— and for conduct within it. As Tyndale put it:

> Let every man ... whether brewer, baker, tailor, victualler, merchant, or husbandman, refer his craft and occupation unto the common wealth, and serve his brethren as he would do Christ himself.[100]

Christians should not only live within their callings but 'study to do good vnto all men by the true & diligent exercise therof'.[101] The purpose of work was not to fill the belly or to 'gape ... greedily after riches', but (as prayers for workers' use insisted) to labour 'for the Church and Commonwealths good', 'to loue our Neighbour as our selues, and to doe to euery one as wee would haue them doe to vs'.[102] Work should be 'profitable to the societie of mankind', not simply to the worker. That meant keeping work in its rightful place—no 'ouergreedy busying of our selues in vnnecessary businesse'.[103] It meant working conscientiously: Dorothy Leigh suggested that Christians should not only labour for six days, as God did in creation, but also 'looke ouer thy worke, and see that it bee good' as he did. And it meant working honestly, 'without fraude or deceit', even without driving hard bargains.[104] These were hard strictures to obey. Arthur Wodenoth was a gold-smith's apprentice when he first converted, and steeled himself to disobey when ordered to do something he thought was dishonest. The result was to 'render myself obnoxious to the severest punishment of my Master (and sometimes it was severe)'. Nor did such troubles cease with apprenticeship. Nehemiah Wallington's regular dilemmas are a reminder that remaining pure in a cut-throat business climate was not easy.[105]

[98] Rogers, *Seven treatises*, 362.   [99] Norwood, *Journal*, 33.

[100] Tyndale, *Doctrinal Treatises*, 102.

[101] Becon, *Pomaunder of prayer*, fo. 23v; Perkins, *Whole treatise*, 526; Rogers, *Garden* (1615), II sig. F4r.

[102] Rogers, *Seven treatises*, 325; Webbe, *Practise of qui[e]tnes*, 371; Sparke, *Crumms of comfort*, sig. B9v; Crashaw, *Milke for Babes*, 56.

[103] Cleaver, *[G]odly form*, 56; Webbe, *Practise of qui[e]tnes*, 371; cf. Hieron, *Helpe Vnto Deuotion* (1610), 100–1.

[104] Leigh, *Mothers blessing*, 220; *Forme of prayer ... approued and receiued by the Churche of Scotland*, III.180; Tyndale, *Doctrinal Treatises*, 102–3; Rogers, *Garden* (1615), II sig. F4v.

[105] Wodenoth, 'Expressions', 123; Wallington, *Notebooks*, 153.

Some crafts and occupations were not legitimate at all. As William Perkins put it, only 'offices and callings which serue to preserue the good estate of any familie, Church, or common-wealth, are lawfull'.[106] Craftsmen, Thomas Fuller insisted, ought to make things which are either 'necessary for mankind', or else 'contributeth to mans lawfull pleasure'. To manufacture items which merely 'pander to mans lust', such as jewellery, or which are actively evil, such as guns, is no Christian's calling. Lawyers, too, were regarded more as a self-interested guild than as the fearless guardians of justice.[107] Whether anyone's career choices were actually determined by these concerns is another matter. But Weber would have been intrigued to know that merchants largely escaped godly disapproval. The prayers for various occupations in Thomas Becon's *The Flour of godly praiers* mostly focus on the corruptions and temptations to which they are prey, but Becon's account of merchants purrs with approval. They travel, he wrote, not only to bring one country's goods to another, but so 'that al kindes of men shuld be knit together in vnity & loue'. And he prays for merchants' safety in their travels, so that through their 'prosperous iournyes . . . the common weale may prospere & floryshe wyth the abundaunce of worldli things thorow their godly & ryghteous trauaile'. Others took a slightly more jaundiced view, but claims both for the necessity of commerce and for its role in furthering international goodwill persist through our period.[108] Many merchants had been early and staunch supporters of the Protestant cause; perhaps ministers knew which side their bread was buttered.

Or perhaps not, for there was no such mercy for the landed classes. Ministers throughout our period deprecated rack-renting landlords, along with all others— usurers, monopolists, simoniacs—who make their livings from others' losses. Even the official primer of Edward VI's reign was bleakly realistic about how noble and gentle the nobility and gentry really were.[109] 'There be too many' of the landed classes, Arthur Dent lamented,

> which follow no honest calling, liue to no vse, no body is the better for them. . . . They are like drone bees: they are vnprofitable burdens of the earth. God hath no vse of them, the Church no good, the Common wealth no benefit, their neighbours no profite, the poore no reliefe.[110]

Richard Sibbes even bracketed gentlemen and beggars together as those without callings, who burdened the commonwealth. Others had more positive suggestions to make. The landed classes' true vocation was to govern their estates wisely, serve

---

[106] Perkins, *How to live*, 40.

[107] Fuller, *Holy State*, II.120; John Denison, *A Three-fold Resolution, verie necessarie to saluation* (1608: RSTC 6596), 64; *Prymmer . . . set fourth by the kinges maiestie* (1553), sigs P7r–8r; Scott, *Belgicke Pismire*, 34–5.

[108] Becon, *Flour of godly praiers*, fo. 30v; Latimer, *Sermons by Hugh Latimer*, 214; Clarke, *Holy Incense*, 198–203; *Prymmer . . . set fourth by the kinges maiestie* (1553), sigs P6r–v; Immanuel Bourne, *The Godly Mans Guide with a Direction for all, especially, Merchants and Tradsmen* (1620: RSTC 3417), 26–8; Scott, *Belgicke Pismire*, 95–6; Baxter, *Reliquiae Baxterianae*, 89.

[109] *Prymmer . . . set fourth by the kinges maiestie* (1553), sigs P4r–5v. Cf. Dent, *Plaine mans pathway*; Scott, *Belgicke Pismire*, 27–35.

[110] Dent, *Plaine mans path-way*, 171.

the commonwealth unstintingly, defend the poor mercifully, and study Scripture diligently. And 'if they can finde nothing to doe, let them giue themselues much to priuate praiers, and reading of the scriptures, that they may be able to instruct and exhort others'.[111]

These comments focused principally on men's vocations, but women's consciences were not exempt. Women's vocations were multilayered, and some were gender-specific. Silence, for example, which for 'a woman is a great virtue'. That might not seem like much of a vocation, but some (male) authorities presented it as an active good, setting an example of godly and ordered obedience to the household. In reality, the Protestant conscience could make women speak up at least as readily as it silenced them.[112] Silence's counterpart, chastity, was accepted by men and women alike both as the summit of feminine virtue and the keystone of a Christian woman's vocation.[113] But women also had less passive vocations. A prayer for a new mother's use after childbirth, added to later editions of Thomas Becon's *The pomaunder of prayers*, had her look forward to the rest of her life and ask 'that I . . . may both faithfully liue & walke in my vocation'.[114] For most users, that vocation would consist largely of secular work to support themselves and their families. Or there might be a focus on family responsibilities, especially that of childrearing—although Becon's prayer, strangely, makes no mention of the newborn child at all.

Again, it is amongst the landed classes that the question of women's vocations becomes most vexed, precisely because they had a degree of choice about whether and how much to work. Pious gentlewomen like Elizabeth Hastings and Grace Mildmay readily applied the word 'vocation' to their lives.[115] But what did women of this status understand their vocations to be? Some elements were obvious. They should manage their households so 'that all be frugally and thriftily done', in keeping with the much-cited Biblical model of the 'vertuous woman'. This applied particularly to a new social category, the minister's wife, who should make her household both a model of good order and a fountain of charity to her neighbours.[116] Or there was childrearing. Following the Christian-humanist model, Protestant commentators consistently disparaged the practice of wet-nursing, insisting that Christian women ought to suckle their own children. The knot of medical, spiritual, social, and patriarchal opinions behind this advice is not easy to

---

[111] Thomas, *Ends of Life*, 89; Latimer, *Sermons and Remains*, 37; Latimer, *Sermons by Hugh Latimer*, 486; Rogers, *Seven treatises*, 359–60; Dent, *Plaine mans path-way*, 178; Bod MS Rawl C.473 fo. 3r.

[112] Latimer, *Sermons and Remains*, 93; Cleaver, *[G]odly form*, 53; Stubbes, *Christal glasse*, sigs A2r–3r; see above, p. 400.

[113] See, for example, Ketley, *Two Liturgies*, 463–4; Leigh, *Mothers blessing*, 30–1; John Foxe, *Acts and Monuments of matters most speciall and memorable* (1641: Wing F2035), sig. (a)6v.

[114] Thomas Becon, *The pomaunder of prayers made by Thomas Becon* (RSTC 1748. London: John Day, 1578), fo. 27v.

[115] Huntington Library, San Marino, CA, MS 15369 fo. 2v; Mildmay, 'Meditations', II.89. Cf. Mildmay, *With Faith and Physic*, 84.

[116] Proverbs 31:10–31; Rogers, *Seven treatises*, 324; Cleaver, *[G]odly form*, 53, 81–91; Holinshed, *Chronicles*, I.233; Herbert, *Works*, 239.

untangle. But when, for example, Elizabeth Juxon marked her conversion by stopping the use of wet-nurses for her own children, the decision has to be read in vocational terms.[117] For the wider vocation of motherhood, consider Elizabeth Jocelin's posthumous best-seller *The Mothers Legacie*. It was written during her pregnancy, which followed six years of childless marriage during which she had prayed for a child with increasing urgency. During the pregnancy, however, she came to fear—correctly, as it turned out—that she would herself die from the complications, which would 'preuent mee from executing that care I so exceedingly desired, I mean in religious training our Childe'. So she set to writing her advice down 'to expresse my motherly zeale'. It was the only means she had of fulfilling a vocation which was to be taken from her at the very point of being realized. She died leaving it uncompleted, and it is still heart-wrenching to read.[118]

Jocelin's thwarted hopes to teach her child also point to another vocation for gentlewomen: teaching those under their authority. Margaret Hoby read to her 'workwemen'; Margaret Corbet prepared her servants for catechism and communion; Elizabeth Isham taught a maid to read.[119] Or, as we have already seen, there was sewing or other textile work. Arthur Dent recommended that women 'make shirtes, smockes, coates, and garments, and giue them to the poore'. Lettice Cary, as a girl, made a purse for herself, so that she could fill it with pennies begged from her parents and then give them to the poor.[120] Or there was medicine. George Herbert saw skill at healing as an essential qualification for a minister's wife. Hoby's occasional references to dressing wounds and to attending 'my patients' suggest that this was a regular part of her life too. Isham set herself to studying herbs, in part to make medicines for her sister. All of them are left behind, however, by Grace Mildmay, whose cutting-edge medical research became her life's work, work in which she found 'that God wrought with me in all'. It was shown not only in a vast legacy of medical papers and ingredients, but also in her expert and wide-ranging medical practice for the poor of the district.[121]

The repeated emphasis on charity is no accident. Early modern Protestantism was highly ambiguous about wealth. On one hand, it denounced riches as a snare and a delusion. 'It is a most difficult thing', Richard Rogers warned, 'to possesse them without great daunger to our soules. . . . The more a man hath of these earthly commodities, the lesse he is inriched with spirituall grace.' One reader underlined that last sentence—perhaps troubled in conscience, since this was not a cheap book.[122] The orthodoxy in Edward VI's reign was that it was nearly—but not quite—impossible to be both rich and righteous. More than a century later,

---

[117] Herbert, *Works*, 239. See, for example, *A glasse for housholders, wherin thei maye se, howe to rule theim selfes and ordre their houshold* (1542: RSTC 11917), sigs D5r–E5v; Denison, *Monument or Tombe-Stone*, 113.

[118] Jocelin, *Mothers Legacie*, sigs B1v–3v, p. 1.

[119] Hoby, *Diary*, 81; Clarke, *Collection*, 506; Isham, 'Confessions', fo. 17r.

[120] Dent, *Plaine mans path-way*, 178–9; Rogers, *Seven treatises*, 324; Duncon, *Returnes*, 145–6.

[121] Herbert, *Works*, 239; Hoby, *Diary*, 100, 105; Isham, 'Confessions', fo. 28r; Mildmay, *With Faith and Physic*, 35, 102–3; ODNB.

[122] Rogers, *Seven treatises*, 385–6; underlining in FSL MS 21215.

Richard Baxter's view was that 'usually the Rich are Proud and Obstinate', and he quoted George Herbert to much the same effect. Daniel Dyke warned that 'prosperity to religion, is as the Iuie to the oake, it quickely eates out the heart of it'.[123] Yet Protestant divines were seldom willing to leave it there. The Edwardian texts which castigated the rich also warned the poor not to 'enuye, murmure or grutche' against them, even praising Lazarus, 'which chosed rather paciently, and godly to die, then vniustly or by force to gette anye mans goodes'. Nor would Protestants countenance wilful poverty, of the kind vowed by professed religious in the Catholic world. 'Neither riches nor poverty of themselves help us any thing at all unto the kingdom of God', warned Becon. The Biblical strictures against the rich, he claimed—without much backing from the text—apply only to 'that kind of rich men which have their hearts glued vnto their riches'.[124] Being rich was not in itself an obstacle to salvation. What mattered was how you went about it. Protestants' theology of justification made this possible; their commitment to the social hierarchy and their need for friends in high places made it prudent. And so wealthy Protestants could, quite literally, have the best of both worlds.

The strictures applied to rich Christians were not imaginary, however. 'The rich man', a Jacobean anthology taught, 'must know himselfe to be, not a Lord, but a Steward of Gods blessings.' This had an intangible, inner element: 'not to trust in vncertaine riches but in the living lord', and to 'vse our prosperitie . . . soberly'.[125] It also had a practical consequence, in the obligation to be charitable. 'It is a worthy thing', Arthur Dent accepted, 'to be a good rich man which doth much good with his riches, which keepeth a good house, relieueth the poore, ministreth to the necessity of the Saints, and giueth cheerefully.' If the rich were indeed 'stewards', Becon prayed, they should 'liberalli & cherefulli bestow part of such goodes as thou hast committed vnto them vpon their pore neighbors'.[126] No-one could disagree, but the half-heard words 'part of' in Becon's prayer testify to a certain limited liability. Early modern Protestants could certainly be generous. Archibald Johnston of Wariston, for example, periodically gave impressively large sums to the church poorbox. He, and perhaps some others, also practised voluntary tithing, giving a tenth of a certain set of incomes to the poor.[127] But shaving off 10 per cent of his income would not have beggared him, nor did anyone think that it should have done. Almsgiving should be limited by prudence. The rich should give to the poor, not—as some medieval idealists had argued—join their number. Riches, a preacher at Paul's Cross taught in 1602, are for almsgiving, for glorifying God, for rewarding the virtuous—but, before all those, they are 'to serve our owne necessity'. In 1643, Nehemiah Wallington, whose own generosity was real enough, met a mentally

---

[123] *Prymmer . . . set fourth by the kinges maiestie* (1553), sigs Q1r–2r; Becon, *Flour of godly praiers*, fo. 32r; Baxter, *Reliquiae Baxterianae*, 94 (cf. BL Harleian MS 6607 fo. 8r); Dyke, *Two Treatises*, 319.

[124] *Prymmer . . . set fourth by the kinges maiestie* (1553), sig. Q2v; Becon, *Flour of godly praiers*, fo. 33v; Becon, *Catechism*, 388–9; cf. Luke 16:20–3.

[125] Rogers, *Garden* (1615), II sig. F4r; BL Additional MS 43827A fo. 7v; Rogers, *Seven treatises*, 334; cf. Nicholas Breton, *A Solemne Passion of the Soules Loue* (1598: RSTC 3696), sig. B4r.

[126] Dent, *Plaine mans path-way*, 177; Becon, *Flour of godly praiers*, fo. 32v.

[127] Wariston, *Diary*, 32, 48, 70, 122; Walton, *Complete Angler*, 36.

troubled gentlewoman. Amongst other things, 'she would give above her ability not thinking when she hath given that she hath given enough so that often shee would goe back and give them more'.[128] To him, this was evidence of a disturbed mind, not a saintly one.

The wealthy early modern Protestant is not Max Weber's imaginary Calvinist capitalist, but the two bear some resemblance. Protestants were willing to be rich, as long as they did it right. That meant earning their money justly, spending it thriftily, and practising prudent liberality. To claim that you may do what you like with your own money, Arthur Dent argued, is like claiming that you may kill your own child with your own axe.[129] But if riches were spiritually dangerous, nobody seems actually to have shunned them on that basis. On the contrary, there was a tendency to see them as a blessing. Not many went so far as the preacher who claimed that God saved the tax-collector Zacchaeus in part 'by his riches, which to the good are sacramentes of his favor'. However, those who worried that religious duties ate into their worldly work were often promised that God would in fact reward religious diligence with worldly prosperity. 'Though it seem to hinder you . . . no, saith the Lord, it will increase your store.'[130] The same logic was applied to almsgiving. Latimer preached, 'Have ye heard of any man that came to poverty, because he gave unto the poor? . . . Give, and you shall gain. . . . Give twenty pence, and thou shalt have forty pence.' He even described this as godly usury. This may seem incautious, but half a century later Richard Rogers was agreeing with him. By giving our riches to the poor, he argued, we 'do lend them vnto the Lord . . . and so whatsoeuer we lay out, shall plentifully be payed vs againe'. (He did admit that this repayment was 'not alwayes in riches', but might be in, for example, inner peace.)[131] Sometimes this kind of talk does seem to be merely metaphorical. When Thomas Goodwin calls Christians to engage in 'this thriving trade of entercourse with God; the returns whereof are better than the merchandise of silver', or when Anthony Fawkener commends 'the greatest (and yet lawful) vsury of all others, to part with one outward blessing, and to receiue an hundreth for it', the returns and blessings they mean are clearly spiritual. But metaphors tend to rub off on their intended meanings, and Fawkener was happy to link being 'diligent in thy calling' to outward prosperity. John Dod, at least, was unmistakably literal. 'Obedience to Gods commandments . . . brings the blessing of God vpon vs for outward things, as well as for inward.' A marginal note emphasizes that this means 'outward prosperity'.[132]

These comments depart significantly from one of Protestantism's original theological themes: Luther's so-called theology of the Cross, which, as we have seen, argued that the Christian life ought to be one of suffering and outward humiliation.

---

[128] Manningham, *Diary*, 198; Wallington, *Notebooks*, 211.
[129] Dent, *Plaine mans path-way*, 178.
[130] Manningham, *Diary*, 136; Preston, *Saints Daily Exercise*, 32; cf. Gifford, *Briefe discourse*, fos 43v–44r; Pemble, *Introduction to worthy receiving*, 49.
[131] Latimer, *Sermons by Hugh Latimer*, 408–10; Rogers, *Seven treatises*, 462.
[132] Goodwin, *Returne of Prayers*, sig. A11r; Fawkener, *Collection of Promises*, 141, 157–61; Dod and Cleaver, *Ten sermons*, 100.

From the 1570s onwards there was a revival of English interest in Luther, led by John Foxe and picked up by Perkins, Bolton, and others. These theologians were outspoken in opposing the perceived slide towards a prosperity gospel. 'The end of Christs passions', Foxe insisted, 'was not to make vs rich in this earth.' He denied that Christ has brought his people 'a peny more of possessions'. Perkins emphasized that 'care for heauen and heauenly things' should eclipse any concerns about worldly prosperity. For Bolton, the self-satisfied equation between worldly good fortune and God's favour is hypocritical. In fact, he warned, it is the wicked who prosper, while the elect 'sticke fast in the mirie clay of pouertie and contempt'.[133] These were not exactly voices crying in the wilderness, but they were swimming against a tide. There was a mood abroad in English Protestantism—it is hard to discern any equivalent in Scotland—which was ready to interpret worldly prosperity as a sign of divine favour.

Was that mood Weber's Protestant ethic? It was not entirely unlike it. It was an ethic requiring Christians to work. It distinguished between good workers (artisans or merchants) and bad (landowners or lawyers); permitted riches to be accumulated and seen as a mark of divine approval; and did not permit excessive consumption or generosity, a caveat which, as Weber pointed out, leads willy-nilly to the accumulation of capital. But the differences are striking too. *Choosing* a vocation still, in this period, seemed like a contradiction in terms. Obedience in accepting and remaining within a calling remained key values, even as economic riptides eroded them. And even if the paralyzing, isolating salvation-anxiety which Weber attributed to the doctrine of predestination existed, it certainly did not drive economic activity as he imagined.

One other, simple but neglected factor did drive early modern Protestantism's work ethic, which takes us back to our starting point: idleness, and the fear of idleness. Bolton, who had no patience with his contemporaries' dalliance with a prosperity gospel, did not therefore doubt the value of good labour, but he had different, and more straightforward motives. 'A seasonable imployment in a ciuill Calling', he wrote, 'is a Soueraigne preseruatiue, and curbe for preuention of infinite swarmes of idle, melancholike, and exorbitant thoughts.' Moreover, by following 'an honest Calling'—whatever it might be—the Christian practises a slew of virtues: 'Faith, Obedience, Patience, Meekenesse, Constancie, Truth, Fidelitie, Inuocation, Thanksgiuing, experience of Gods prouidence, &c.'[134] The occupation itself did not matter a great deal: it was simply a stage on which these spiritual battles could be fought. And perhaps the most widely accepted godly motive to work was that it starved the Devil of opportunities. As the Elizabethan Homilies put it:

> Let us therefore always be doing of some honest work, that the Devil may find us occupied . . . for he that diligently exerciseth himself in honest business is not easily catched in the Devil's snare.[135]

---

[133] Ryrie, 'Afterlife of Lutheran England', esp. 231–3; Foxe, *Sermon of Christ crucified*, fo. 25r; Perkins, *How to live*, 45; Bolton, *Discourse about happinesse*, 50–2; and see above, pp. 241–2.

[134] Bolton, *Some generall directions*, 49.

[135] *Certain Sermons or Homilies*, 463. Cf. Themylthorpe, *Posie of Praiers*, 9; Ralph Venning, *Milke and Honey* (1653: Wing V206), 25.

The value of labour was a negative one: it soaked up time harmlessly.

This was not simply a theory. Real Protestants found it worked in practice and were grateful for it. Margaret Hoby wrote one day, 'all the after none I was buseed about takinge of accountes and other thinges so that through Idlenes, distractions had no aduantage'. Nehemiah Wallington saw 'painfulnesse in my calling' as a vital weapon in his personal battle with sin. Richard Norwood deliberately kept himself constantly employed, so that 'Satan . . . found little place or entertainment'. Elizabeth Isham reckoned that one of the chief benefits of writing her *Confessions* was that 'this worke so wholy tooke up my delight with the thought of it, that there vanished those idle vaine and proud thoughts'. 'What a sweet Life it is', John Rogers wrote, 'when every part of the Day, hath some Work or other allotted unto it.'[136] We have already met the Protestant conviction that relentless spiritual progress was the only way to avoid backsliding. It is matched, and Protestantism's endless, restless dynamism was equally driven by, the conviction that relentless labour was the only way to crowd out sin. What exactly that labour might be was a secondary issue, as long as 'we spend not our time vainelie, or idlie'.[137] The point was simply that there was a great void of time from which the Devil had to be excluded by intensive and innocent activity. And secular work, however tedious, back-breaking, or indeed futile it may be, does have this great merit: it takes up a great deal of time. The roots of the Protestant work ethic may lie less in Calvinism's theological crises than in the simple need blamelessly to pass the long, long wait until death.

MARKING THE YEARS

To navigate the middle years of life, it helps to have milestones. Traditional Christianity generously provided these in the liturgical calendar, but that calendar's place in everyday life and devotion was directly challenged by the Reformation. St Paul's polemic against observing 'dayes, and moneths, and times, and yeres' fitted well with Reformed Protestants' wariness of treating any time or place as holier than any other. The Geneva Bible's marginalia applied this verse to feasts such as Easter and Whitsun, adding that such 'beggerlie ceremonies are moste pernicious to them which haue receiued the swete libertie of the Gospel'.[138] In Reformed Scotland, all the traditional feasts and holy days were in theory swept away, at least until the Perth Articles attempted to restore some of them. In England, most of the principal traditional feasts were retained throughout our period, with their status hotly contested. The opponents of such commemorations in both countries wanted one day only to be observed: Reformed Protestantism's Sunday Sabbath.[139]

---

[136] Hoby, *Diary*, 109; Wallington, *Notebooks*, 43; Norwood, *Journal*, 85; Isham, 'Confessions', fo. 35v; Mather, *Magnalia*, III.111.

[137] Cowper, *Triumph*, 363.   [138] Galatians 4:10.

[139] Harrab, *Tessaradelphus*, sig. E4r.

Yet, like so many other divisive issues, this dispute does not map cleanly onto any puritan/conformist divide. English conformists naturally used the Prayer Book's calendar, and ceremonialists and Laudians were certainly keen to restore holy days to their former glory. But plenty of those with a puritan tinge also observed them. Part of this was simply pragmatic. Critics of traditional holy days had often focused, not on their basic legitimacy, but on their encouragement of sloth and lawlessness. When Hugh Latimer claimed that 'the Devil hath more service done unto him on one holiday, than on many working days', he meant dicing and drinking, not inappropriate devotions.[140] The 1559 Injunctions insisted that holy days were to be spent 'in hearing the Word of God read and taught, in private and public prayers'—in effect, as additional Sabbaths: and it was hard even for puritans to dislike that. Richard Greenham thought that holy days were 'the fittest and most convenient times for fasting daies', since no-one would take offence. That was wishful thinking: when John Ball led some of his Cheshire neighbours in an Ascension Day fast, the bishop hauled them in for fasting on a feast day. But at least they were not ignoring the day. Nor did the foreign Protestant churches in Elizabethan London, which regularly held their fasts on major feast days. Likewise, John Bruen sponsored preachers for the local festivities around St Andrew's day— to the discomfort of his more precisionist biographer.[141]

Others were happy to embrace feast days more fully. Thomas Becon praised their godly institution; a treatise appended to the 1568 translation of the *Imitation of Christ* celebrated how 'they stirre vs vp vnto the Remembraunce of Gods wonderfull actes and miracles wrought for the saluation of mankinde'. Elizabeth Isham knew that some Protestants rejected holy days, but she disagreed. 'Surely it is a good thing to rejoyce in these Feasts; and in the holydayes which are keept in memory of the Apostles.' She took comfort from the fact that her sister's death fell on All Saints' Day.[142] Brilliana Harley, whose puritan credentials are unassailable, saw the Ember week fasts which her former (and aggressively anti-Laudian) minister had set up as a highlight of the year.[143] Laudians wanted to claim holy days as their own, but many puritans were not willing simply to give them up.

Whether they added their own to the list is another matter. Several scholars have commented on the appearance of Protestant calendars of saints, which listed Protestantism's heroes and martyrs on the anniversaries of their deaths, along with other notable anniversaries in Biblical or ecclesiastical history. The very first English evangelical primer did this, in 1530. There does not seem to have been any

[140] Latimer, *Sermons by Hugh Latimer*, 52–3.

[141] Frere and Kennedy, *Visitation Articles*, III.15; Parker and Carlson, *'Practical Divinity'*, 160; Samuel Clarke, *The Lives of Two and Twenty English Divines* (1660: Wing C4540), 171; O. Boersma and A. J. Jelsma (eds), *Unity in Multiformity: The Minutes of the Coetus of London, 1575, and the Consistory Minutes of the Italian Church of London, 1570–1591* (Publications of the Huguenot Society 59, 1997); Hinde, *Faithfull Remonstrance . . . of Iohn Bruen*, 90–6.

[142] Becon, *Fruitful treatise of fasting*, sigs H8v, I3v–4r; *Short and pretie Treatise*, sigs C4v–5r; Isham, 'Confessions', fos 8v, 30v. She cited Featley, *Ancilla Pietatis*, in her support: see sig. A9r–v, pp. 115–17.

[143] Brilliana Harley, *Letters of the Lady Brilliana Harley*, ed. Thomas Taylor Lewis (Camden Society old series 58: 1854), xvi, 15.

devotional intent in any of this, however. Such calendars were essentially almanacs or even curiosities. The calendar in Henry Bull's *Christian praiers* included the anniversaries of Nebuchadnezzar's siege of Jerusalem, the sending of the quails to the Israelites in the wilderness, and the reformation of Geneva in 1535. There is no sense that readers were supposed to do anything with this information. The best-known English calendar, that appended to some editions of John Foxe's *Actes and monuments*, seems to have been put there without Foxe's own involvement, and the best scholars of the subject see it as an attempt to market the book to churches by making it look liturgical.[144] I know of no evidence of such 'feasts' actually being observed in any sense, although no doubt readers were sometimes edified by recalling martyrs who had suffered on a particular day. If there were new Protestant commemorations, they were of more recent coinage. Local anniversaries might be celebrated in worship: this at least happened in puritan Dorchester, where the town's deliverance from the great fire of 1613 was marked annually for at least twenty years. On the national scale, we have already seen the enthusiasm of some Protestants for the anniversaries of Elizabeth I's accession—'the Quens day', as Margaret Hoby called it—or the Gunpowder Plot.[145]

Much more importantly, Protestants—puritan and conformist alike—were developing new ways of marking time. The most prominent of these, the Sabbath, is a subject so large it is impractical to examine it in detail here, and so well treated elsewhere that it is unnecessary.[146] One aspect of Sabbath devotion is worth noting, however, which is the Sabbath as punctuation to the preceding week. By the early 17th century it was becoming routine for earnest Protestants to take a retrospective look at the week's sins and successes as part of their Sabbath observance, often on the Saturday afternoon or evening.[147] John Brinsley commended 'this weekly practice of considering our wayes and obseruing how wee growe'. For Dorothy Leigh, the Sabbath served as a kind of safety net: if you should 'ouerslip' yourself, and fail to settle your accounts with God one night, the Sabbath's review of the week would correct the omission.[148]

Weekly reviews could blur into routine almost as quickly as the daily kind, however. There was also a need for more considered reviews at longer intervals. William Pemble encouraged Christians to review their lives 'every weeke, moneth, and yeare'. The ferocious anti-Arminian Thomas Taylor, citing the practices of the Levitical priesthood, recommended an annual 'day of humiliation in serious fasting and prayer, to make atonement for our owne and others sinnes'. Isaac Ambrose

[144] Elizabeth Evenden and Thomas S. Freeman, 'Red Letter Day: Protestant calendars and Foxe's "Book of Martyrs"', unpublished paper consulted with permission of the authors, 2011; cf. Andrew Pettegree, *Reformation and the Culture of Persuasion* (Cambridge, 2005), 207–8. Joye, *Ortulus anime*, sig. A3v; Henry Bull, *Christian praiers and holie meditations* (1596: RSTC 4032); cf. Bull, *Christian praiers*, where the calendar consists almost exclusively of Biblical events.
[145] Underdown, *Fire from Heaven*, 93; Hoby, *Diary*, 192. Cf. Bayly, *Practise of pietie*, 520–1; and see above, pp. 378–9.
[146] Above all, Parker, *English Sabbath*.
[147] Sparke, *Crumms of comfort*, sigs D3v–4v; Clarke, *Holy Incense*, 140–1.
[148] Brinsley, *True Watch* (1608), 172; Leigh, *Mothers blessing*, 230–1. Cf. Scudder, *Christians daily walke* (1628), 85; Bernard, *A Weekes Worke* (1616), 130–4.

seems to have seen his annual woodland retreats in this light. But while Ambrose simply took his retreats 'about that pleasant Spring time', others were more specific about dates.[149] Birthdays, for example: we have already met Alice Wandesford meditating on the twelve-year-old Christ on her twelfth birthday. Nehemiah Wallington revised his personal convenant and adding more articles on his twenty-sixth birthday. Thomas Larkham even counted the years from his birthdays. At the other end of the spectrum, John Cosin's prayer for birthday use asked for grace 'that I may bewaile my sinfull yeeres past, and spend the rest of my time heere in a godly, righteous, and sober life'. No puritan could possibly object.[150]

It was more common, however, to use a date which amounts to a major, unacknowledged Protestant feast day: New Year's Day. If Wallington revised his covenant on his birthday once, he did so on 1 January on at least three occasions, resolving 'to begine a new life' or to 'take another corsse with myselfe'. On 1 January 1634 Archibald Johnston of Wariston meditated 'on al Gods blissings bestoued on me al the last year, beginning at the first of Januar until this present houre', which implies that this was a regular discipline for him. Robert Saxby composed a meditation for New Year's Day, asking 'that 'now, with this new year, wee may Become new creatures Indeed . . . And be borne agayne'.[151] Nor was this only a 17th-century pattern. Richard Stonley ended the first extant volume of his diary on 31 December 1582, with the words 'So ended this day and the yere with thankes to Almighty god for preservinge me to this day And humbly besech hym to graunt me grace to procede in this next yere in his feare & Love'. A tantalizing account by John Hooper records the arrest of a Protestant conventicle during a clandestine meeting in the small hours of 1 January 1555. They had assembled to repent collectively for their previous outward conformity to Catholicism, and the date will have been no coincidence. The successful raid suggests that the Marian authorities expected to find Protestants busy that night.[152]

Daniel Featley, arguing for a good Protestant use of traditional feast days in the 1620s, closes the circle for us. He provides a prayer for use on 1 January, which, as he notes, the Prayer Book observes as the feast of the circumcision of Christ: yet the prayer is described as one 'for New-yeeres day'. It seamlessly moves from asking for spiritual circumcision and thanking God for the first-fruits of Christ's blood to praying, 'Thou hast begunne a new yeere, beginne in mee a new reformation'. If Protestants were happy to make use of the Church's feast days, it was more individual concerns which made the marking of time urgent. The long monologue of the Protestant life needed punctuation. A new year offered the tantalizing possibility of a new start: perhaps, this time, you could leave your sins behind,

[149] Pemble, *Introduction to worthy receiving*, 50; Taylor, *Christ Revealed*, 150; Ambrose, *Media*, 74, 76; see above, p. 166.
[150] Thornton, *Autobiography*, 13 (see above, p. 432); LMA Guildhall MS 204, p. 43; Susan Hardman Moore (ed.), *The Diary of Thomas Larkham, 1647–1669* (Woodbridge, 2011), xi; Cosin, *Collection of Priuate Devotions*, 411.
[151] LMA Guildhall MS 204, p. 38, 41; Wallington, *Notebooks*, 32, 48–9; Wariston, *Diary*, 189–90; Saxby, 'Miscellany' fo. 140r.
[152] FSL MS V.a.459 fo. 99r; Hooper, *Later Writings*, 612.

and take a decisive step towards sanctification. It was possible, at least at that moment, to pray in earnest, 'Let mee . . . from this day to my old age and death walke in newnesse of life'.[153]

THE DEATHBED

Late medieval piety had had a distinctive focus on preparation for death and the so-called art of dying. Protestantism had a different theology but the same preoccupation.[154] It was and remained a truism for pious Christians on all sides, throughout our period, that life was a preparation for death. Thomas Playfere was exaggerating when he wrote that 'the wicked neuer think of death; but the godly think of nothing els', but only a little. Death 'cannot too oft be thought vpon', pressed Richard Rogers; you should, urged Christopher Sutton, wake from your sleep and break off from your food to maintain your constant meditation on the subject.[155] Actually living this way was not easy, but Nehemiah Wallington, at least, made a serious effort. During 1621 he bought a string of books on death—including Sutton's—and moreover

> I was at grate charge in bying Anatomie of Death[156] and a littel black coffin to put it in, and upon it written Meemento Mory And this I had to stand on a ginstoul by my bedsid every night and some meals to stand upon or by my Table.[157]

He desisted after a friend suggested this was superstitious.

This was indeed probably not very helpful to the young Wallington, but it was more practical than it seems. To be constantly reminded of death was to keep your mind on what mattered—God, judgement, sin, and sanctification—rather than on the clamouring irrelevancies of this passing world.[158] But as well as contemplating death, Protestants aspired actively to prepare for it. 'The more we Judge our selves Daily, the less we shall have to do on our Sick-beds, and when we come to die.' The ideal was exemplified in a preacher's anecdote of a mortally wounded soldier who is told not to fear death, and answers, 'I thanke God, I feare not death, and these thirty yeeres together, I neuer arose at the morning, that euer I made account to liue till night'. The point was pre-emptively to deprive death of its sting. Those who prepared aright would find 'true peace and comfort upon thy death bed'.[159]

---

[153] Featley, *Ancilla Pietatis*, 441, 447.

[154] The best treatment of cultures of dying across this period remains Ralph Houlbrooke, *Death, Religion and the Family in England 1480–1750* (Oxford, 1998), 147–219; cf. Cressy, *Birth, Marriage and Death*, 379–95; Danae Tankard, 'The reformation of the deathbed in mid-sixteenth-century England', *Mortality* 8/3 (2003), 251–67.

[155] Playfere, *Meane in Mourning*, 61; Rogers, *Seven treatises*, 390; Sutton, *Disce mori*, 5.

[156] Apparently a miniature skeleton, death's-head, or some similar image.

[157] Wallington, *Notebooks*, 270–1.

[158] For example, Prid, *Glasse of vaine-glorie* (1585), 25.

[159] Mather, *Magnalia*, III.113; Rogers, *Sermon preached . . . . at the funerall*, sig. C3r; Perkins, *Salve for a sicke man*, 39–41; Pemble, *Introduction to worthy receiving*, 49.

In other words, Protestants prepared for the moment of death because that moment had enduring consequences.[160] Thomas Tymme described death as a race for which training was essential, both because it is difficult to run and because 'they which slip and stumble in it, shal neuer more find any hope of saluation'. Using an old cliché, he warned that 'as the Tree falleth, so it lyeth: as death leaves thee, so shall judgement find thee'. Henry Valentine used the same image to warn that 'to dye well is a point of the greatest consequence in the world, because eternity depends upon it'.[161] As has often been pointed out, this is a somewhat surprising view for Reformed Protestants. Doctrines of assurance and the perseverance of the saints ought to have quenched the deathbed's supposed spiritual dangers.[162] If pressed on the point, most Protestants accepted that the manner of dying was not a foolproof test of spiritual status. An outwardly 'good' death did not guarantee salvation, and—the more pressing point—those who died badly might still be holy. If sickness or temptation led otherwise godly people to die 'as men forsaken of God vttering some words vnbeseeming their holy profession', this did not, Wallington noted, prove anything: 'the Lord knoweth who are his. . . . We must not therefore iudge of men by their death, but rather by their life'.[163] But the tone of this and similar comments demonstrates the tide of opinion against which they swam. John Cosin provided a prayer anticipating the possibility of raving or blaspheming during death throes, and pre-emptively disowning any such sentiments, which is pretty clear testimony to the worries around this subject. Elizabeth Isham was troubled by her mother's unquiet death, although she eventually managed to explain it to herself. In particular, to die suddenly and unprepared was still seen as a damning judgement from God, and left any hagiographers with a difficult case to make.[164] Sudden death was prayed against just as it had been before the Reformation. It is not actually a token of damnation, Arthur Hildersam warned, but it is 'a temporall judgement, and a signe of GODS anger'.[165]

Persistent medieval patterns are obviously at work here, but there were Reformed theological justifications too. One no-nonsense approach was to argue that, providentially, the elect always die well. Valentine insisted that 'a good life cannot have a bad death. Such as the premisses are, such will be the conclusion'.[166] In practice, however, this meant either damning large numbers of otherwise godly individuals, or extravagantly stretching the definition of a good death. A subtler approach focused on the perennial Protestant fear of hypocrisy. The point of death—when

---

[160] Richard Wunderli and Gerald Broce, 'The Final Moment Before Death in Early Modern England', *Sixteenth Century Journal* 20/2 (1989), 259–75.

[161] Tymme, *Siluer watch-bell* (1605), 31; Tymme, *Watch-bell* (1640), 295; Valentine, *Private Devotions*, 262–3.

[162] Karant-Nunn, '"Christians' Mourning"', 124–5.

[163] Houlbrooke, *Death, Religion and the Family*, 203–4; LMA Guildhall MS 204, p. 369; cf. Perkins, *Salve for a sicke man*, 96; Sutton, *Disce mori*, 252–4.

[164] Cosin, *Collection of Priuate Devotions*, 370; Isham, 'Confessions', fo. 19r–v; Houlbrooke, *Death, Religion and the Family*, 208–10. See, for example, Hinde, *Faithfull Remonstrance . . . of Iohn Bruen*, 106–9; Capel, *Capel's Remains*, sig. b4r.

[165] Hildersam, *Doctrine of Fasting*, 10; Norden, *Pensiue mans practise*, 23.

[166] Valentine, *Private Devotions*, 265–6.

there is no longer any point in trying to fool anyone, but God must be confronted directly—was seen as one of the truest tests of sincerity. William Perkins warned that 'many ancient professors' died in spiritual confusion, because in their lives, 'they more respected men then God; and therefore in the time of death, when they must needs deale with God indeed, they know not what to doe'.[167] So for those who died suddenly, or in delirium, this test was useless. But the classic early modern death—that is, in bed, over a period of hours or days, and more or less of sound mind—could reveal a believer's true self as never before.

For all that, that the early modern Protestant deathbed was a highly structured cultural site. Dying was too important a business to be improvised. The dying were plentifully provided with scripts to follow. The first English Protestant guide to the art of dying, *A myrrour or glasse for them that be syke*, was printed in 1536. It, and Thomas Becon's best-selling *The sycke mans salue*, which imitated and expanded on it, gave an idealized model of the Protestant deathbed. Books like Philip Stubbes' even more successful *A christal glasse for christian vvomen* provided scarcely less idealized reports of a 'real' case. By the turn of the 17th century, moderately attentive Protestant patients will have known what was expected of them. Most of the features of the good Protestant death have been thoroughly examined by scholars such as Ralph Houlbrooke. Matters such as the obligation to make a will, the need to maintain outward peace, the chance to reconcile quarrels, the opportunity to receive spiritual counsel, and the vexed question of whether or not to receive the sacrament do not need to detain us here.[168] But dying was also the last act of the Protestant life narrative, bringing the struggles of many years to a climax. The deathbed was the ultimate place of crisis and self-definition. Two particular aspects of that crisis illustrate how life-stories were brought to a close there.

The first is the literal matter of life and death. Our sources routinely speak of 'deathbeds', but obviously a sickbed only becomes a deathbed retrospectively. It was never easy to be sure whether someone really was mortally ill, or how long they were likely to last. The result was a dilemma for both patients and companions: to hope and pray for recovery, or to prepare for death? The two are not exclusive, but they are in tension. It is hard to fight to remain in this world if you are already turning your mind to the next, and it is harder to prepare for death if you are still nourishing a fierce hope of life. The dying Judith Isham, for example, was deeply distressed when a minister came to speak to her about death: she threw him out, 'saying you would have me die whether I will or can. death is terrable to mee . . . O let me live with my husband and my Children'.[169] How, then, ought patients to pray during a serious illness?

As we have seen, the conventional Protestant wisdom was that prayers for worldly goods—such as recovery from illness—ought to be made conditionally, asking for recovery only if it is God's will. Published prayers for use by the sick

[167] Perkins, *Godly and learned exposition*, 234.
[168] Tankard, 'Reformation of the deathbed', 256–7; Houlbrooke, *Death, Religion and the Family*, 81–109, 184–204.
[169] Isham, 'Confessions', fo. 19v.

commonly do this.[170] But as we have also seen, sometimes this broke down, and especially at the sickbed. Close to the end, with their souls stripped bare of the constraints of hypocrisy, the dying might attain almost supernatural perception.[171] One repeated feature of Protestant death-narratives is the patient who achieves a prophetic assurance of imminent death. James Melville, suffering from an abscess, correctly concluded that it was mortal and would not listen to any doctors' equivocations.[172] Intriguingly, this kind of certainty is most commonly associated with death in childbirth. Elizabeth Jocelin, during the later stages of her pregnancy, was overcome with 'almost . . . a propheticall sense of her dissolution', so much so that she 'secretly tooke order for the buying a new winding-sheet'—although she did claim that 'I despaire not of life, nay, I hope and daily pray for it'. During her pregnancy, Katherine Stubbes supposedly told virtually everyone she met 'that, that child should be her death, & that she should liue but to bring that child into the world'. Her husband regarded this accurate prediction as a 'prophesie . . . reuealed vnto her by the spirit of God'. During her illness, she refused to pray for health, conditionally or otherwise, but always prayed 'absolutely, that God would take her out of this miserable world'.[173]

It is a cliché of Christian devotion that, like St Paul, Christians ought to long for death. When we find Jane Ratcliffe, in perfect health, writing a short treatise on why she desires to die, that may seem like an abstract exercise. And when we find the sick lamenting on their deathbeds, 'I desire to be dissolued and to be with Christ', we may suspect—as some contemporaries disapprovingly did—that their desire is as much for an end to suffering as anything else.[174] Yet it seems implausible to dismiss prophetic certainty about impending death either as a pious pose or as a wish to be put out of your misery. Pregnant women, of all people, might hope both to return to good health and to have something to live for if they escaped the present danger. Two other readings of this phenomenon seem more plausible. First, certainty was more spiritually manageable than doubt. Clinging onto desperate hopes for life led to something like Judith Isham's disorderly end. (In the event of an unexpected recovery, it would be easy enough to thank mercy unlooked-for.) In this case, certainty of death was not a pose, but a technique: a means to embrace what might otherwise be feared, and to become, as the Edwardian primer put it, 'ioyfull and glad to dye'.[175] Secondly, we have to recognize that sometimes death truly was desired, not only as an end to suffering but as a positive good. Stubbes broke into laughter during her illness, describing 'a vision of the ioyes of heauen, and the glory that I shal go too'. John Welsh, writing from prison of his desire for

---

[170] See above, pp. 122–7; Sutton, *Disce mori*, 256–7; Sparke, *Crumms of comfort*, sigs E1r–2v.

[171] See, for example, Edward Dering, *M. Derings workes* (1614: RSTC 6678), sig. I4v; Rogers, *Three Scottish Reformers*, 126; Tweedie, *Select Biographies*, 107.

[172] Melville, *Autobiography*, lvi–lvii.

[173] Jocelin, *Mothers Legacie*, sigs a4v–a5r, B10r; Stubbes, *Christal glasse*, sigs A3v–A4r; cf. Shepard, *God's Plot*, 71; Winthrop, *Papers*, 184.

[174] Ley, *Patterne of Pietie*, 85–91; Prid, *Glasse of vaine-glorie* (1585), 57–60; Walker, *Sermon at the funerals . . .*, 51; Stubbes, *Christal glasse*, sig. A4r; Winthrop, *Papers*, 193; Sutton, *Disce mori*, 2; Perkins, *Salve for a sicke man*, 70; cf. Philippians 1:23.

[175] *Prymmer . . . set fourth by the kinges maiestie* (1553), sig. V3r.

death, went into transports, longing 'for the fruition of thy blessed presence . . . my glory, my joy, and my gain, and my crown'.[176] On your sickbed, with such a vision before your eyes, and with a realistic chance of departure from this tawdry world in prospect, how could you not hope that this was the path down which God was at last calling you?

The deathbed's greatest drama, however, was the fate of the soul, not the body. Alongside the crowd of family, neighbours, ministerial comforters, and anxious would-be heirs who gathered around the deathbed were some less tangible visitors: devils and angels battling for the dying person's soul. Their presence has long been recognized, and a valuable essay by Peter Marshall has analysed the role played by angels in particular, but it was the Devil who drove the crisis.[177] The deathbed was, and was universally expected to be, the arena for the last and greatest spiritual confrontation of the Protestant life.

His role at the deathbed was, naturally, to tempt. However, the deathbed temptations of early modern Protestants had a very particular flavour. Occasionally we find temptations to false confidence and self-righteousness: Perkins, ever wary of conventional wisdom, warned against this. Or there were temptations to atheism, doubting the reality of your faith when the crunch came. Judith Isham was 'temted with blasfemous thoughts . . . doubtings . . . and want of reverent beleeving' during a lengthy illness—from which she in fact recovered. William, Lord Russell, endured a 'spiritual desertion' on his deathbed which led him to doubt his faith for a time.[178] But one temptation above all was feared and experienced. As Becon put it, 'Satan at the hour of death . . . wolde plucke the from thyne assurance & stedfast fayth in Christes blode & persuade the that thou art but a damned wretche'.[179] The Devil's main, almost exclusive argument at the deathbed was: despair, for you are too sinful to be saved.

This became an invariable stereotype of the Protestant death. Becon laid it out in a dramatized dialogue. After a long discussion with his counsellors, the dying man, Epaphroditus, suddenly and with no apparent provocation falls into despair for his sins. 'Me thinke I fele a very hel within my brest.' The reader is jarred by this non sequitur, but the counsellors are unsurprised. It is normal, comments Becon's mouthpiece Philemon, for the dying to be so assaulted by Satan that 'he shall see nothing but the fearce wrath, & terrible iudgement of God against sinners. . . . Whome of Gods elect hath he let pas vnassailed, vntempted, or vnproued?' They go on to counsel Epaphroditus through his struggle over the course of some forty pages.[180]

A scarcely more realistic account is given in the highly stylized report of Stubbes' death. Again the temptation comes out of a clear sky. She made a confession of her

[176] Stubbes, *Christal glasse*, sig. A4v; Tweedie, *Select Biographies*, 20–1.
[177] Peter Marshall, 'Angels around the deathbed' in Peter Marshall and Alexandra Walsham (eds), *Angels in the Early Modern World* (Cambridge, 2006), 83–103.
[178] Perkins, *Salve for a sicke man*, 109–110; Isham, 'Confessions', fo. 11r–v; Walker, *Sermon at the funerals . . .*, 53.
[179] Becon, *Gouernans* (1544?), fo. 93r.
[180] Becon, *Sycke mans salue*, 348–50 et seq.

faith, and 'she had no sooner made an end ... but Sathan was ready to bid her the combat, whome shee mightely repulsed'. Having been peaceful a moment before, now 'she bent the browes, shee frowned, and looking, as it were, with an angry, sterne, and fierce countenaunce ... burst forth ... in contempt of him to whom shee spake'. A long monologue delivered to the Devil followed—'Get thee packing, thou damned Dog'—which again makes clear that the temptation she faced was to doubt whether her sins could be forgiven.[181] On the deathbed, John Hayward assumed, 'then shall the conscience sharply accuse. ... Scarce is there any seuere sentence in all the bible against sin, which the diuell will not bring into mind'.[182] Lewis Bayly warned that a literal trial is held inside every dying Christian:

> Reason sits as Iudge, the Diuell puts in a Bill of inditement ... wherein is alleaged all thy euil deeds, that euer thou hast committed. ... Thine owne conscience shall accuse thee, & thy Memory shall giue bitter euidence, and Death stands at the Bar ready, as a cruell Executioner to dispatch thee. ... Now the Diuels, who are come from Hell to fetch away thy soule, begin to appeare to her; and wait, as soone as shee comes foorth, to take her, and carrie her away.[183]

The only escape from such condemnation was an appeal to the throne of mercy.

This is a literary cliché, but it was one which both reflected and determined real deathbed experiences. The dying, and their friends, were advised earnestly on how to combat this temptation.[184] Prayers written for the use of the dying routinely expect that they will face this trouble.[185] John Donne's deathbed sonnet describes how

> Despaire behind, and death before doth cast
> Such terrour, and my feeble flesh doth waste
> By sinne in it, which t'wards hell doth weigh.[186]

Real deathbed accounts agree—although strikingly, most of the most detailed of them relate to women. Hostile rumours claimed that Katherine Brettergh had died in despair; a book was written to deny it, but it admitted that for some time she was daunted by 'the seueritie of Gods iustice, and the greatnes of her sinnes', which had made her 'a pray to Satan'. Anne Sharington, twelve hours before her death, seemed troubled; she explained that 'the Devil was busy with his temptations but she thanked God she had overcome all'. When Patrick Simson's wife was dying, she was overcome with 'distrust of God's mercies': just like 'many hundreds of God's best children before their death', her brother-in-law added. Thomasine Winthrop spent much of her last day

---

[181] Stubbes, *Christal glasse*, sigs C2v–3r.
[182] Hayward, *Sanctuarie of a troubled soule* (1602), 107; cf. Norden, *Pensive mans practise ... The second part*, 129.
[183] Bayly, *Practise of pietie*, 76–7.
[184] See, for example, Perkins, *Salve for a sicke man*, 111; Hieron, *Helpe vnto Deuotion* (1608), 154–6; Featley, *Ancilla Pietatis*, 677–96; Sibbes, *Bruised reede*, 180.
[185] See, for example, FSL MS V.a.482 fos 42r–44r; *Godly garden*, fos 143r–144v; Norden, *Pensiue mans practise*, 241–5.
[186] Donne, *Poems*, 322.

defyinge Satan, and spitting at him, so as we might see by hir setting of hir teethe, and fixinge hir eyes, shakinge hir head and whole bodye, that she had a very greatt conflict with the adversarye.

Her trump card in this conflict was the insistence that God 'would not take away his lovinge kindnesse from hir'.[187]

It is in fact hard to find Protestant deathbed narratives which do not include this temptation. When John Bruen was dying, he apparently commented, as if it were a remarkable mercy, that God 'hath given me so strong evidence of his favour and love in Christ, that I am not troubled in mind nor conscience'.[188] Perkins was careful to point out that, on the deathbed, 'some are not tempted, and some are'. As he pointed out, there are no good Biblical precedents for it.[189] But in practice this temptation seems to have been a standard expectation and a very common experience.

I would suggest three different ways of reading this pattern. First, temptation was a script to be followed. That is not to say that the dying were simply going through the motions, but sometimes it is at least clear that their companions fully expected it to happen. Josias Welsh, a Scot who died in Ulster in 1634, was capable of no more than disjointed words in his final struggles. Once he cried out, 'Oh for hypocrisie!'—whereupon the minister attending him commented, 'See how Satan nibbles at his heel when he is going over the threshold to heaven'. A little later, hearing one of those present use the word 'victory', Welsh cried out, 'Victory! Victory! Victory for evermore!', and died a few moments later. From these outbursts his friends constructed a textbook struggle with temptation.[190] It is not at all clear that they were right to do so, but textbook patterns can become self-fulfilling. Moreover, since defeating temptation was a sign of godliness, there was a strong incentive to conform to the pattern; not least since that pattern ended with deliverance. When Stubbes' tirade against the Devil was ended, 'she fell suddenly into a sweete smiling laughter, saying: Now is hee gone, now is he gone: doe ye not see him flie like a coward?' In Becon's dialogue, once the counsellors have had their say, Epaphroditus comments, 'Nowe me thinck I am in heauen so great quietnes, rest, ioy, and confort do I finde in my conscience'.[191] Those who sought such quietness, who sought to fool others into thinking they enjoyed it, or who sought to fool themselves might be well-advised to have a quick bout of temptation to despair. Perhaps they would come out the other side.

Unfortunately, not everyone did. To die before resolving a battle with temptation was to risk becoming a byword, like the Hackney blasphemer who died in 1573, supposedly 'confessing in deede gods omnipotent power' but lamenting that 'he coulde not pray for grace'.[192] Since the speed of death's approach is

[187] Harrison, *Deaths aduantage*, III.11–12; Mildmay, *With Faith and Physic*, 29; Tweedie, *Select Biographies*, 108–9; Winthrop, *Papers*, 185–9.
[188] Hinde, *Faithfull Remonstrance...of Iohn Bruen*, 223; cf. Melville, *Autobiography*, lvi–lxiv.
[189] Perkins, *Salve for a sicke man*, 18.
[190] Tweedie, *Select Biographies*, 149–50.
[191] Stubbes, *Christal glasse*, sig. C3v; Becon, *Sycke mans salue*, 384.
[192] Edmund Bicknoll, *A swoord agaynst swearyng* (1579: RSTC 3049), fo. 34v.

unpredictable, this called for fine judgement. Henry Greenwood provided 'a short death-bed Dialogue' between the Devil and the soul over this matter, and it is indeed short: three-quarters of an octavo page, in which the soul ends by refusing to listen to the Devil anymore and by turning to silent prayer.[193] Fictional characters could afford long speeches: in reality the dying often could not. Yet they could not always snap themselves out of despair in time. Some were paralyzed by it. Some accounts are very drawn-out: a Mr Throgmorton who despaired of God's grace in the early 17th century was attended by the celebrated divine John Dod, but it took days of counsel, prayer, Bible study, confession, absolution, fasting, and vigils before he found mercy in the nick of time.[194] Such people do not seem simply to have been following a script. Their despair was real.

So perhaps—the second possibility—despair was merely a reaction to the prospect of a painful death. That dying people should be frightened is hardly surprising. Thomas Tymme explicitly linked bodily and spiritual suffering. Death is 'that last agonie': an agony of body in which 'the speech groweth hoarse, faint, and hollowe ... the countenance waxeth pale, the feet die, and the Arteries send forth a colde sweat', and an agony of temptation and of the approach of the day of judgement, all of which 'vehemently terrifieth'. To find peace while life is perceptibly ebbing away is not necessarily easy, and the less so if bodily suffering is taken as a sign of spiritual tribulation. John Norden lamented in prayer that 'the grieuous sicknes which hath taken hold vpon me, hath dried vp all my bones, and consumed my poore carkas euen to nothing', which we might think sounds bad enough; but worse, the Devil 'perswadeth me, that thou thus visitest me of meere malice'.[195] So the more intense your physical sufferings, the more you might doubt God's mercy, and fear that the deathbed was not a pathway to Heaven but a foretaste of Hell.

Which brings us to the third reading of these temptations: less medical or psychological than theological. If medieval Christians, too, had found deathbed despair troubling them in similar ways, Reformed Protestants had their own reasons for it. It is not only that, as Robert Bolton warned, the Devil 'reserues his fieriest dart, his deadliest poison, his sharpest sting, his Gunpouder-plot vntill he meete vs on our deaths bed': that would explain the fact of temptation, but not its particular manifestation. If you had a strong sense of assurance, as Bruen apparently did and as Perkins recognized some others might, then no doubt you could escape it. But if you did not, then at the point of death it would be only natural for any doubts about your salvation to surface. This was when hypocrisy and self-delusion were liable to be laid bare: 'when vpon his deaths bed hee awaketh', Bolton said of the hypocrite, 'and hath ... his particular sinnes reuealed vnto him ... he graspeth nothing but feare and amazement, anguish and sorrow'.[196] The same applies to elect Christians who fear that they may be self-deluding.

---

[193] Greenwood, *Treatise of ... Iudgement*, sig. F3r.
[194] FSL MS V.a.248 fos 2r–8r.
[195] Tymme, *Siluer watch-bell* (1605), 38; Norden, *Pensiue mans practise*, 245.
[196] Bolton, *Discourse about happinesse*, 38, 101.

So is this the point at which the despair of which Reformed Protestants were connoisseurs finally breaks its shackles? For some, yes, but as we have seen, while early modern Protestants recognized how intimate their relationship with despair could be, they also insisted that despair was a step on the way, rather than the end of the process.[197] The stereotypical deathbed temptation provided not only for confronting despair in all its horror, but also for finally, decisively despatching it. Those who had sought assurance all their lives might now at last attain it. Throgmorton, at the end of his struggles, declared that 'the Ioy & comfort of gods grace which I haue labored for this 37 yeares together is now com to my soule'.[198] Even for those with some experience of assurance, a few moments gazing into the abyss was not a bad way to reinforce it. The deathbed's great advantage, after all, is that nothing needs to be sustained for very long. The relentless battle against backsliding was almost over. Like all the best crises, this final one could propel the believer to victory, ready promptly to depart in peace and indeed in triumph. Many early Christians sought baptism on their deathbeds; their medieval successors looked to the sacramental trio of extreme unction, penance, and death-bed communion. The viaticum which early modern Protestants sought was assurance, and the sacrament which delivered it was a full-dress battle with, and final victory over, despair.

[197] See above, pp. 38–9.
[198] FSL MS V.a.248 fo. 8r.

Conclusion

A long book deserves a short conclusion. The argument running through this book has been that, to understand what it meant to be Protestant in Reformation Britain, we have to understand the intensity, the dynamism, and the broad-based quality of this religious culture. The intensity is a matter of the emotional experience sought, in private, in public, and through many different means and stages of life. The ongoing attempt to seek and maintain that intensity, to keep the eyes fixed on something too bright to be seen, gave the Protestant life its restless, unwearying dynamism, as believers chased the promises which God had given them. It was a long chase, but they had enough experience of brief moments of grasping those promises, and enough grounds for hoping that they would do so again, to make it a life's pursuit which left all else behind it. This is why, for all the many contradictions and pathologies of the early modern Protestant experience, it appeared true, right, and beautiful to those who lived within it.

But if I have not already persuaded you that intensity and dynamism are indispensable categories of analysis, it is now too late. Here I want to comment on my third claim: that this was in important ways a broad, unified, religious culture.

Early modern British Protestants were obviously different from one another, not only as individuals but across a whole range of categories. Yet there were also striking commonalities. When viewed from the perspective of devotional experience, the classic chronological, geographical, confessional, and even social boundaries are trampled by free passage.

Chronologically, Protestantism certainly changed during our period, and not merely through the almost inevitable process of developing doctrine, refining practice, and bedding down of habits. Some old devotional patterns which the first generations of Protestants reviled crept back into their children and grandchildren's practice, from the making of vows to the use of fasting. The early priority on Christian liberty came to seem less important and more double-edged. Some echoes of the old ways gradually died away, such as the resonances of the primer tradition. The crystallizing of Calvinist orthodoxies in the final half-century of our period provided some hard edges to devotional practice, although this usually only made explicit what had already been implicit. Political change had its effects: the pious meaning of martyrs and martyrologies, for example, changed dramatically across our period, and the Laudian innovations sparked some novel responses. Some genuinely new forms of pious practice appeared during our period, such as diary-keeping. But for all that, the unity of Protestant piety across the period *c.*1530–1640 is more striking. The changes are shifts in mood, refinements, and developments rather than radical discontinuities or innovations. Repeatedly, we have been able to trace pious phenomena back to the 1540s, 1530s or even earlier. One enormous difference between the beginning and end of our period is the quantity of surviving sources, but we should not allow this to distract us. Where we can see what was happening in the earlier period, it is recognizably akin to, and often virtually the same as, the picture that can be painted in much more detail a century later. A 1530s evangelical who was stranded in the 1630s by a careless time-traveller would not have taken too long to acclimatize.

This chronological unity is worth noticing for two reasons. First of all, it suggests that 'early modern Protestantism' is a meaningful category. William Perkins did not spring fully formed from Martin Luther's neck, but something which we can recognize without anachronism as Protestantism took form very early on. It is customary for historians of the early British Reformations to talk of 'evangelicals' rather than 'Protestants', on the grounds that the movement was then too fluid for an anachronistic confessional label, which is true enough. But this should not distract us from the fact that later Protestantism was present in all its essentials in this early evangelicalism. Nor should this be surprising. Scholars sometimes assume that ideas need to 'develop' or 'mature' over decades, as if they were trees. Sometimes we even dispute an early date for a particular text or argument on the grounds that it was too early for such thoughts to be thought. But in times of crisis, ideas can 'develop' very quickly. Not that a decade is quick, except when subject to historical foreshortening. In our own world, and in our own lives (especially when young), a decade may as well be an age, and our forebears' lives were no less intense than our own.

Secondly, the unity of Protestantism across our period shows us that it is part of a wider web of Christian practice. Medieval (and older) patterns of piety persisted everywhere in Protestantism: from the use of set forms of prayer, through the value attached to weeping, to the meanings given to the deathbed. Often these were given new theological dress, which sometimes—as in the treatment of Bibles as holy objects—went more than skin deep. Reformed Protestantism's extreme self-consciousness about ritual meant that there was always an explanation for retaining or reinventing a medieval practice, but sometimes these were *ex post facto* explanations rather than real reasons. Similarly, many of the patterns laid down during our period endured long after it was over. One of Christianity's most enduring myths is its claim to be timeless, and habit and repetition are themselves sacralizing forces. So it should be no surprise that these patterns persist. While the discontinuities at either end of our period are very real, ordinary believers often did their best to ignore or minimize the impact of events such as a Reformation or a Civil War, to continue pursuing what they knew as holiness and to pass it on to their children. Periodization is necessary, but it tears a seamless garment. By which I mean that my claims throughout this book that early modern Protestants did something should not be taken to mean that their ancestors or their descendants did not.

Much the same can be said of the geographical unity of British Protestantism. We have had a great many invaluable local studies of the British Reformations. Yet this book has paid virtually no attention to regional differentiation within England, on the simple grounds that Protestantism—a culture which incubated in universities and was propagated in London's print-shops—did not take on very much local colour. The most significant difference was between those areas where self-consciously earnest Protestants could feel like an establishment and those where they were aware of being embattled. Regional differences within Scotland were more pronounced, as a distinct, revivalist culture sprung up in the south-west in the early 17th century, whence it spread to Ulster—albeit it was part of a nationwide network. The other great Scottish regional difference, between Gaelic and Scots-speaking Protestantism, deserves more attention, as does the distinctive but elusive Protestantism of Welsh-speakers: but this is a book about Anglophone Protestant culture, and it is already long enough.

The differences between England and Scotland cannot be effaced. Their Reformations were dramatically different, and so was their post-Reformation experience of worship. Scotland's break with its medieval past was more abrupt, although never absolute. The English Church's retention, in its liturgy and polity, of some medieval trappings gave it a distinctive flavour, where the Scottish Church was in some ways closer to the European Reformed mainstream. But Scotland too was distinctive, in its incubation of a form of Protestantism that was much more relaxed about forays into the prophetic and miraculous: some Scottish reformers were much readier to hear God speaking to them directly through dreams and special providences, and were much less cagey about the potentially literal power of prayer. The similarities are also very real. We have repeatedly observed the same pious phenomena on both sides of the Border. The two countries' Reformations had been interwoven from the beginning, and it was the vision of a shared Reformation which turned 'Britain' from a humanist pipedream into a serious cultural and political project. Individuals crossed back and forth, and Scotland's Protestant print culture was almost as London-based as England's. The union of the crowns was only an additional bond. English and Scottish Protestants were not the same, but they were brethren, close enough that their contrasts can be as instructive as their similarities.

Confessional unity is the most controversial area. Even if we exclude separatists and Laudians, as I largely have, English Protestants were self-consciously divided into puritans and conformists for more than half our period. These divisions were real and bitter, but throughout this book I have suggested that they can be overdone, or rather, that they were confined to particular issues which often had little to do with personal piety. Again and again, on the questions which are supposed to define them, we find individuals straying heedlessly across the boundaries. Puritans used set forms unproblematically both in public and private devotion. They noted and observed holy days. They valued public and private prayer and denied that it was in competition with preaching. They revered the sacraments. They observed fixed times of prayer. They made and kept vows. Their 'conformist' neighbours, those who were earnest rather than conventional about their religion, valued preaching. They wept and groaned in their devotions. They meditated and sought ardour and zeal. Protestants in both 'camps' promiscuously read one another's books, and indeed also read Catholic books, medieval or contemporary, edited or unedited.

Patrick Collinson famously argued that the differences between puritanism and conformity were 'differences of degree, of theological temperature so to speak, rather than of fundamental principle'; that puritans were merely the 'hotter sort of protestants'.[1] Which is true on two different levels. First, what distinguished puritanism from conscientious conformity was a certain scrupulousness, political rashness, and anti-popish zeal, all of which were matters of degree rather than of definition. But secondly, it suggests that 16th-century Christians cannot be ranged along a single spectrum. There were doctrinal and ecclesiological distinctions: between Catholic and Protestant, and to a much lesser and subtler extent between puritan and conformist Protestants. But there were also differences of temperature which cut across party lines. Edmund Bunny was right to spy a kindred spirit in Robert Persons, for all their disagreements: both 'were trying to persuade readers to become rigorous Christians', and that common commitment to rigour and earnestness united them despite their profound disagreements.[2] Nor, as Judith Maltby has reminded us, will it do to assume that conformist Protestants were puritans who lacked the courage of their convictions. This has been a book about *earnest* Protestants of all parties, all of whom could be said to be the hotter sort of Protestants. Their earnestness, their rigour, was what united them, and what set them apart from a large chunk of the population. From the point of view of devotion, the key difference among British Protestants was not doctrine, but ardour.

Soon enough, of course, the Civil Wars would force most British Protestants to choose sides. It is all too easy to read those divisions back into the earlier period, even labelling individuals as puritan or otherwise on the basis of which way they jumped in the 1640s. But this misses the genuine force which tied mainstream English and even Scottish Protestants together throughout our period: the universal loyalty to the national, all-inclusive Protestant church. However bitter the disagreements over specific issues, for most Protestants they were a family quarrel within that framework. Puritans' and conformists' devotional patterns united them, and they also insisted that, despite everything, they were united. Perhaps we should believe them.

Some of the social divisions of Protestantism can also be overemphasized. Gender, for example: as Kate Narveson has argued, Protestant piety tended to efface rather than emphasize gender distinctions. 'There is greater truth in the early modern commonplace that "souls have no sexes" than is often recognized'.[3] Of course gender affected piety in a great many ways, some obvious, some subtle. Some of the language of Protestant emotion, notably the loaded term 'ravishing', was specific to men. Pious weeping came more easily to most women than to many men. There were distinctive, although overlapping, masculine and feminine spaces

---

[1] Patrick Collinson, *The Elizabethan Puritan Movement* (1967), 26–7.
[2] Gregory, '"True and Zealouse Seruice"', 254.
[3] Narveson, *Bible Readers*, 132–3, 179–80, 194.

for prayer, and indeed privacy and solitude had different meanings and values for men and for women. Pious men's and women's approaches to death were distinct. But, given how deep the gender differentiation of early modern society ran, these differences are surprisingly limited. Of course Protestantism was caught up in wider patterns: women, most obviously, were no more permitted to preach after the Reformation than before. Yet Protestant practice tended to soften rather than to emphasize such differences. Women were not supposed to lead family prayers, but in practice many did. They were not supposed to preach, but they could and did write. Early modern Protestantism was not a liberating force. Some early modern Protestant women, however, found liberation within it.

Much the same could be said of a key division within the adult male population, between lay and ordained. Protestant clericalism was different from the Catholic variety, but not necessarily less intense. The clergy guarded their status and responsibilities vigilantly. And yet, for comparably educated laymen, the difference in their authority did not extend very far beyond the walls of the parish church. Laymen could not preach, but they could publish, and they could exhort household gatherings which might extend beyond the immediate family. Ian Green has made the distinction between lay and ordained writers a part of his framework for analysing Protestant print, but for the pre-Civil War period the evidence for this is mixed.[4] A certain strain of populist moralizing is perhaps distinctively lay; the sermon is of course distinctively clerical. Clergy, perhaps, more naturally teach with a note of authority. And yet a great many devotional works do not make the author's status plain, and in some cases we would be hard-pressed to guess if we did not know from other sources. Clerical devotion does not seem to have been markedly different from laypeople's. Perhaps that testifies to the success of Protestant clergy in forming their people in their image, or perhaps it is an illusion caused by the dominance of clergy and of clericalized rhetoric in our sources, but more likely it suggests that educated Protestants, whether ordained or not, were formed by a common culture.

That points us to a much deeper social division, linked with but not identical to the division between earnest and tepid believers. The educated few and the uneducated mass were in different worlds. In particular, the illiterate were largely excluded from self-consciously Protestant culture, and also from most of our sources, where they appear mostly as jaundiced caricatures of 'carnal Protestants'. No doubt this was often the case, but we have enough evidence to suggest that some such people did take their Protestantism every bit as seriously as their social superiors. For some, that was itself an educational lever. For the rest, all we have are glimpses of a sermon-heavy and strongly ritually patterned Protestantism, some of whose preoccupations (fear of over-frequent communion, for example) seemed bafflingly impious to the educated elite. They were not; but their religious cultures, while recognizably Protestant, are strikingly different. Protestantism was

---

[4] Green, *Print and Protestantism*.

a university religion, and the experience of formal education of some kind or another was fundamental to what its preachers understood it to be.

This applies with particular force to one important subgroup of the not-yet-educated: children. The under-twelves made up a third or more of the population of early modern Britain, but are as neglected by modern historians of religion as they were by early modern divines. We, at least, have the excuse of a dearth of sources. Throughout this book we have tried to catch glimpses of children's religion: making vows, mouthing first prayers, haltingly leading their families in saying grace, reading to their elders, sitting baffled through interminable sermons, and trying to feel their way through the religious world around them. There is much more work to be done in this field, but for the moment we can say this much. Many Protestant children took their religion immensely seriously, but it was a religion different from that of their earnest, well-educated elders. They were usually assumed to be lumps of unregenerate sinfulness, to whom the heights of faith and grace were as yet inaccessible. Establishment Protestantism dealt with children like it dealt with the uneducated: by aspiring to liberate them from their undesirable condition. It did not engage seriously with the subterranean Protestantism of childhood, with its own vivid preoccupations and habits. It is up to us to recognize this distinct Protestantism's existence, and also its enduring influence on those who had passed through it, whether or not they permitted themselves to remember it.

This briskly superior attitude towards the young and the unlettered is one of many features of early modern Protestantism which seem unattractive to modern eyes. The pervasive doctrine of predestination may not have marooned as many believers in despair as has sometimes been claimed, but it is still something few of us nowadays find appealing. The relentless intensity of the quest for sanctification, the need to nurture a permanent sense of crisis, and the fear of idleness, together imply a dynamism which is positively exhausting to contemplate. The pious regimes to which earnest believers sometimes subjected themselves can only be called punitive, and the guilt which accompanied the inevitable failure to maintain them was a part of the package. Whatever intensity early modern Protestants found in their religious practice, they paid a high price for it.

Yet some pearls are worth a great price. The reason many early modern Protestants were in earnest about their religion was that they were convinced that this was such a case. The point is not that the experience of Protestantism was a happy one. Sometimes it was, and those voices are too easily ignored; but often it was not. The unhappy, however, laboured, struggled, wrestled, and redoubled their efforts. They did this, of course, because they believed that the doctrines which had been preached to them were true, and therefore that this course of action was rational. But that was not all. They knew that well enough that that kind of transactional religion was a mere story-faith, the faith that makes devils tremble. They pursued and persisted in their arduous religion because it enlarged them—or at least because they hoped it might. They had glimpsed enough to trust that it was worth persisting. They sought out and nourished despair, self-loathing, tears, and martyrdom because of a basic truth that all lovers know: it is better to feel pain than to feel nothing. Whatever else can be said of their religious experience, there is no doubting its force or its profundity.

From the modern world, for most of us at least, the problems with these believers' all-embracing religion are too apparent. The distance which separates them from us is too great, nor we would have it any other way. But if we wish to understand our forebears and the world they made, we can at least still press our noses against the glass. Through it, we can still glimpse their world—and, for a moment, feel something of the harrowing, searing, intoxicating, and ravishing intensity of being Protestant.

Select Bibliography

MANUSCRIPTS

Cambridge University Library, Cambridge
Additional MS 3117. Pious miscellany of Robert Saxby

Devon Record Office, Exeter
ECA Book 51. Commonplace book of John Hooker

British Library, London
Additional MS 43827A. Autobiographical account of Rose Throckmorton (als. Lock)
Additional MS 70089. Remembrances of Sir Robert Harley
Egerton MS 2877. Commonplace book of Gilbert Frevile, c.1583–91
Harleian MS 425. John Foxe papers
Harleian MS 1026. Commonplace book of Justinian Pagett
Harleian MS 6607. John Bruen's 'Cards'
Lansdowne MS 8. Early Elizabethan ecclesiastical papers
Lansdowne MS 157. Letterbook of Sir Julius Caesar
Royal MS 17.A.xvii. Prison writings of Thomas Smith, 1549–50
Royal MS 18.B.xix. 'The praise of Musick', c.1610
Sloane MS 3945. Seventeenth-century miscellany, including the 'Life' of Christopher
  Love

London Metropolitan Archives, London
Guildhall MS 204. Nehemiah Wallington, 'A record of Gods Marcys'

John Rylands Library, Manchester
English MS 958. Diary of John Forbes of Corse, 1624–48

Central Library, Northampton
Northamptonshire Studies Collection. Lady Grace Mildmay's Meditations

Bodleian Library, Oxford
MS Eng. c.2693. Commonplace book of Walter Boothby, c.1632–1665
MS Rawl C.113. Collection of metrical Scriptures, 17th century
MS Rawl. C.473. Private devotions of Richard Waste, 1640s
MS Rawl. D.384. Abingdon miscellany, temp. Charles I
MS Rawl D.1350. Theological miscellany, 1640s

New College, Oxford
MS 9502. Diary of Robert Woodford, 1637–41 (unpaginated)

Huntington Library, San Marino, Calif.
MS 15369. 'Certaine Collections of the right honble Elizabeth late Countess of Huntingdon for her owne private vse', 1633

Folger Shakespeare Library, Washington, DC

Add. 1266. Caroline collection of the Pauline epistles

V.a.1. Five Laudian sermons, *c.*1633–6

V.a.4. 'Certaine collections taken out of Dr [Richard] Sibb[e]s his sermons preached by him att Grayes Inne in London and elsewhere', *c.*1634.

V.a.23. Henry Borlas' notes on ten sermons heard at Oxford, *c.*1605

V.a.248. Commonplace book of John Eaton and others, *c.*1638–50

V.a.280. Collection of sermons and notes, *c.*1640–50

V.a.347. Sermon book of Dorothy Phillips, 1616–17

V.a.394. Arthur Lake, bishop of Bath and Wells: six sermons on Christ's temptation, 1612–13

V.a.399. Commonplace book, late 16th/early 17th century

V.a.436. Nehemiah Wallington, 'An Extract of the passages of my Life or the Booke of all my writting books', 1654

V.a.459, V.a.460, V.a.461. Journals of Richard Stonley, 1581–2, 1593–4, 1597–8

V.a.482. 'A Booke of certeine devoute and godlie Praires', 1564.

V.a.519. 'The riche cheyne, conteyning all the parables & sentences wrytten in the two bokes of Salomon', 1589.

V.a.520. Sir Edward Rodney and others, prayers and meditations

V.b.198. Commonplace book of Lady Anne Southwell, ca.1588–1636

V.b.214. Miscellany on religion and state affairs, 1559–1601, compiled *c.*1601

X.d.475. Commonplace book, *c.*1625

X.d.501. Notes of two sermons preached by Jean Veron, 1559/60

PRINTED PRIMARY SOURCES

Adams, Thomas, *The white deuil, or The hypocrite vncased* (1613: RSTC 131)

Ambrose, Isaac, *Media: The Middle Things* (1650: Wing A2958)

Andrewes, John. *A celestiall looking-glasse: to behold the beauty of heaven* (1621: RSTC 592)
—— *The Conuerted Mans New Birth* (1629: RSTC 595)

'Augustine' [ps.], *Certaine select prayers gathered out of S. Augustines meditations* (1574: RSTC 924)

Babington, Gervase, *A briefe conference betwixt mans frailtie and faith* (1584: RSTC 1082)
—— *A profitable Exposition of the Lords Prayer* (1588: RSTC 1090)

Ball, John, *A short treatise contayning all the principall grounds of Christian religion* (1631: RSTC 1316)

Baxter, Richard, *Reliquiae Baxterianae, or, Mr. Richard Baxters narrative of the most memorable passages of his life and times*, vol. I (1696: Wing B1370)

Bayly, Lewis, *The Practise of pietie. Directing a Christian how to walke that he may please God* (1620: RSTC 1604)

Baynes, Paul, *Briefe Directions vnto a godly Life* (1618: RSTC 1626)

Beadle, John, *The journal or diary of a thankfvl Christian* (1656: Wing B1557)

Becon, Thomas, *[A Christmas banquet]* (1542: RSTC 1713)
—— *A newe pathwaye unto praier* (1542: RSTC 1734)
—— *Dauids harpe ful of moste delectable armony* (1542: RSTC 1717)
—— *The gouernans of vertue, teachyng a Christen man, howe he oughte dayely to lede his life* (1544?: RSTC 1724.5)

Becon, Thomas, *The Gouernans of vertue, teaching a christen man, howe he oughte dayly to lede his lyfe* (1549?: RSTC 1725.3)
—— *The Flour of godly praiers* (*c.*1550: RSTC 1719.5)
—— *A fruitful treatise of fasting* (1551: RSTC 1722)
—— *The Gouernaunce of Vertue, teching al faithful Christians, howe they oughte dayly to leade their lyfe* (1560?: RSTC 1726)
—— *The sycke mans salue* (1561: RSTC 1757)
—— *The pomaunder of prayer* (1565: RSTC 1747)
—— *The Catechism of Thomas Becon: with other pieces*, ed. John Ayre (Cambridge, 1844)
Bentley, Thomas (ed.) *The Monument of Matrones* (1582: RSTC 1892)
Bernard, Richard. *A Weekes Worke. And a Worke for every weeke* (1616: RSTC 1964.3)
—— *The Faithfull Shepherd* (1621: RSTC 1941)
—— *A Weekes Worke. And a Worke for every weeke* (1628: RSTC 1964.7)
Beza, Theodore, *The Psalmes of David, truly opened and explaned by Paraphrasis* (1581: RSTC 2034)
Blair, Robert, *The Life of Mr Robert Blair, Minister of St. Andrews, containing his Autobiography from 1593 to 1636*, ed. Thomas M'Crie (Edinburgh, 1848)
Bolton, Robert, *A discourse about the state of true happinesse* (1611: RSTC 3228)
—— *Some generall directions for a comfortable walking with God* (1626: RSTC 3251)
—— *Mr. Boltons last and learned worke of the foure last things* (1632: RSTC 3242)
—— *A three-fold treatise: containing the saints sure and perpetuall guide. Selfe-enriching examination. Soule-fatting fasting* (1634: RSTC 3255)
Bownde, Nicholas, *The Doctrine of the Sabbath, Plainely layde forth, and soundly proued* (1595: RSTC 3436)
Bownde, *Medicines for the plague that is, godly and fruitfull sermons* (1604: RSTC 3439)
Bradford, John, *Godlie meditations vpon the Lordes prayer, the beleefe, and ten commaundementes* (1562: RSTC 3484)
—— 'An exhortacion to the carienge of Chrystes crosse', in Miles Coverdale, *Remains of Myles Coverdale*, ed. George Pearson (Cambridge, 1846), misattributed to Coverdale
Bradshaw, William, and Arthur Hildersam, *A Direction for the weaker sort of Christians* (1609: RSTC 3510)
Brinsley, John, *The True Watch, and Rule of Life* (1608: RSTC 3775.5)
—— *The True Watch, and Rule of Life* (1611: RSTC 3777)
—— *Ludus Literarius: Or, The Grammar Schoole* (1612: RSTC 3768)
—— *The True Watch, and Rule of Life* (1622: RSTC 3782.5)
Browning, John, *Concerning publike-prayer, and the fasts of the Church* (1636: RSTC 3919)
Bruce, Robert, *Sermons Preached in the Kirk of Edinburgh* (Edinburgh, 1591: RSTC 3923)
—— *Sermons vpon the Sacrament of the Lords Supper* (Edinburgh, 1591?: RSTC 3924)
—— *Sermons . . . with Collections for his Life*, ed. William Cunningham (Edinburgh, 1843)
Bull, Henry, *Christian praiers and holy meditations* (1570: RSTC 4029)
Burton, Henry, *Israels Fast. Or a Meditation vpon the Seuenth Chapter of Joshuah* (1628: RSTC 4147)
—— *A Tryall of Private Devotions* (1628: RSTC 4157)
—— *A narration of the life of Mr. Henry Burton* (1643: Wing B6169A)
Byfield, Nicholas, *The Signes or An Essay Concerning the assurance of Gods loue, and mans saluation* (1614: RSTC 4236)
—— *Directions for the private readeing of the Scriptures* (1618: RSTC 4214)
—— *The Marrow of the Oracles of God* (1619: RSTC 4219.5)
—— *The Marrow of the Oracles of God* (1622: RSTC 4220.5)

Calvin, John, *The Psalmes of David and others. With M. John Calvins Commentaries*, tr. Arthur Golding (1571: RSTC 4395)

Cancellar, James, *The alphabet of prayers, verye fruitfull to be exercised and vsed of euerye Christian man* (1573?: RSTC 4560)

Capel, Richard, *Tentations: their nature, danger, cure* (1633: RSTC 4595)

—— *Capel's Remains*, ed. Valentine Marshall (1658: Wing C471)

Cartwright, Thomas [?], and Thomas Wilcox, *Two treatises. The holy exercise of a true fast, described out of Gods word. . . . The substance of the Lordes supper* (1610: RSTC 4314)

Certain Sermons or Homilies Appointed to be Read in Churches in the time of the late Queen Elizabeth (Oxford, 1844)

Christian Prayers and Meditations in English French, Italian, Spanish, Greeke, and Latine (1569: RSTC 6428)

Christopherson, John, *An exhortation to all menne to take hede and beware of rebellion* (1554: RSTC 5207)

Clapham, Henoch, *A Tract of Prayer* (1602: RSTC 5346.5)

Clarke, John, *Holy Incense for the Censers of the Saints* (1635: RSTC 5358)

Clarke, Samuel, *A Collection of the Lives of Ten Eminent Divines* (1662: Wing C4506)

—— *The lives of thirty-two English divines* (1677: Wing C4539)

—— *The Lives of sundry Eminent Persons in this Later Age* (1683: Wing C4538)

Cleaver, Robert?, *A [g]odly form of householde gouernement* (1598: RSTC 5382)

Clifford, Anne, *The Diaries of Lady Anne Clifford*, ed. David J. H. Clifford (Stroud, 1990)

Corbett, Richard, *The Poems of Richard Corbet*, ed. Octavius Gilchrist (1807)

Cosin, John, *A Collection of Priuate Devotions: in the Practice of the Ancient Church* (1627: RSTC 5816.4)

Coverdale, Miles, *Devout meditacions, psalmes and praiers* (1548: RSTC 2998.5)

—— *Remains of Myles Coverdale, Bishop of Exeter*, ed. George Pearson (Cambridge, 1846)

Cowper, William, *A Most Comfortable and Christian Dialogue, betweene the Lord, and the Soule* (1611: RSTC 5929)

—— *The triumph of a Christian* (1618: RSTC 5939)

—— *The Life and Death of the Reverend Father and faithfull Seruant of God, Mr. William Cowper* (1619: RSTC 5945)

Cranmer, Thomas, *Miscellaneous Writings and Letters of Thomas Cranmer*, ed. John Cox (Cambridge, 1846)

Crashaw, William, *Londons Lamentation for her Sinnes* (1625: RSTC 6017.5)

Culverwell, Ezekiel, *A treatise of faith* (1623: RSTC 6114)

—— *The way to a blessed estate in this life* (1623: RSTC 6118.3)

—— *A ready way to remember the Scriptures* (1637: RSTC 6111)

Davidson, John, *Some helpes for young Schollers in Christianity* (Edinburgh, 1602: RSTC 6324.5)

Day, Richard, *A Booke of Christian Prayers* (1578: RSTC 6429)

Denison, John, *The Monument or Tombe-Stone* (1620: RSTC 6603.7)

Dent, Arthur, *A Sermon of Repentance* (1582: RSTC 6649.5)

—— *The plaine mans path-way to heauen: Wherein euery man may cleerely see, whether he shall be saued or damned* (1607: RSTC 6629)

Dering, Edward, *Godly priuate praiers, for houshoulders to meditate vppon, and to say in their famylies* (1581: RSTC 6689.2)

—— *Mr. Edward Dering, his godly priuate prayers for Christian families* (1624: RSTC 6690)

D'Ewes, Simonds, *The Autobiography and Correspondence of Sir Simonds D'Ewes*, ed. James Orchard Halliwell, vol. I (1845)

A Directory for the Publique Worship of GOD (1644: Wing D1544)

Dod, John, and Robert Cleaver, *Foure Godlie and Fruitful Sermons* (1611: RSTC 6938)

—— *Ten sermons tending chiefly to the fitting of men for the worthy receiuing of the Lords Supper* (1611: RSTC 6945.4)

Donne, John, *The Poems of John Donne*, ed. Herbert J. C. Grierson (Oxford, 1912)

Downame, John, *A guide to Godlynesse or a Treatise of a Christian Life* (1622: RSTC 7143)

The drousie disease: or, an alarme to awake church-sleepers (1638: RSTC 6913.5)

Duncon, John, *The Returnes of Spiritual comfort and grief in a Devout Soul* (1648: Wing D2605)

'Dwalphintramis' [i.e. John/Richard Bernard?], *The Anatomy of the Service-Book* (1641?: Wing B1998)

Dyke, Daniel, *The mystery of selfe-deceiuing. Or A discourse and discouery of the deceitfullnesse of mans heart* (1614: RSTC 7398)

—— *Two Treatises. The one, Of Repentance, The other, Of Christs Temptations* (1616: RSTC 7408)

Dyke, Jeremiah, *A worthy communicant. Or A treatise, shewing the due order of receiving the sacrament of the Lords Supper* (1636: RSTC 7429)

Earle, John, *The Autograph Manuscript of Microcosmographie* (Leeds, 1966)

Egerton, Stephen, *The Boring of the Eare* (1623: RSTC 7527.5)

Erasmus, Desiderius, *Christian Humanism and the Reformation: Selected Writings*, ed. John C. Olin (New York, 1965)

—— *Enchiridion Militis Christiani: an English version*, ed. Anne M. O'Donnell (Early English Text Society 282: 1981)

Featley, Daniel, *Ancilla Pietatis: Or, the Hand-Maid to Priuate Devotion* (1626: RSTC 10726)

F[awkener?], A[nthony?], *A Collection of certaine Promises out of the Word of GOD* (1629: RSTC 10634.7)

Fenner, William, *A Treatise of the Affections; Or, The Soules Pulse* (1642: Wing F707)

Field, John, and Thomas Wilcox, *An Admonition to the Parliament* (Hemel Hempstead?, 1572: RSTC 10848)

Fisher, Ambrose, *A defence of the liturgie of the Church of England* (1630: RSTC 10885)

Fleming, Abraham, *The diamond of deuotion* (1581: RSTC 11041)

The forme of prayers and ministration of the sacraments &c. vsed in the English church at Geneua, approued and receiued by the Churche of Scotland (Edinburgh, 1565: RSTC 16577a)

Foxe, John, *Actes and monuments of these latter and perillous dayes* (1563: RSTC 11222)

—— *The ecclesiasticall history contaynyng the Actes and monuments* (1570: RSTC 11223)

—— *A sermon of Christ crucified, preached at Paules Crosse* (1570: RSTC 11242)

—— *Actes and monuments of matters most speciall in the church* (1583: RSTC 11225)

Frere, Walter, and William Kennedy, *Visitation Articles and Injunctions of the period of the Reformation* (Alcuin Club Collections 14–16, 1910)

Fuller, Thomas, *Thomas Fuller's The Holy State and the Profane State*, ed. Maximilian Graff Walten (New York, 1938)

Gee, John, *Steps of Ascension vnto God, or, A Ladder to Heaven* (1625: RSTC 11706.4)

[Geneva Bible] The Bible (1586: RSTC 2145)

The Geneva Bible: a facsimile of the 1560 edition, ed. Lloyd E. Berry (Madison, W.I., 1969)

Gerhard, Johann, *The meditations of Iohn Gerhard*, tr. Ralph Winterton (Cambridge, 1627: RSTC 11772)

Gifford, George, *A Briefe discourse of certaine points of religion, which is among the common sort of Christians, which may bee termed the Countrie Diuinitie* (1581: RSTC 11845.5)

—— *A Short Treatise against the Donatists of England* (1590: RSTC 11869)

Gilby, Anthony, *An answer to the deuillish detection of S. Gardiner* (1548: RSTC 11884)

A godly garden out of the which most comfortable herbs may be gathered (1574: RSTC 11555)

Goodwin, Thomas, *The Returne of Prayers* (1641: Wing G1253A)

—— *The Vanity of Thoughts Discovered* (1643: Wing G1264)

—— *The Works of Thomas Goodwin, D.D.*, vol. II (Edinburgh, 1861)

Gouge, William, ΠΑΝΟΠΛΙΑ ΤΟΥ ΘΕΟΥ. *The Whole-Armor of God* (1616: RSTC 12122)

—— *A short Catechisme* (1627: RSTC 12128)

Greenwood, Henry, *A Treatise of the great and generall daye of Iudgement* (1606: RSTC 12337)

—— *[Greenwoods workes]* (1616: RSTC 12327)

Grindal, Edmund, *The Remains of Archbishop Grindal*, ed. William Nicholson (Cambridge, 1843)

Habermann, Johann, *The enimie of securitie or A daily exercise of godlie meditations*, trans. Thomas Rogers (1583: RSTC 12582.6)

Hall, John, *Certayn chapters taken out of the Prouerbes of Salomon* (1550: RSTC 12631)

Hall, Joseph, *Meditations and Vowes, Diuine and Morall* (1605: RSTC 12679.5)

—— *Meditations and Vowes, Diuine and Morall: A third Century* (1606: RSTC 12680.5)

—— *The Arte of Divine Meditation* (1606: RSTC 12642)

Harrab, Thomas, *Tessaradelphus, or The foure brothers* (Lancashire?, 1616: RSTC 12797)

Harris, Robert, *Peters enlargement vpon the prayers of the Church* (1624: RSTC 12839.7)

—— *Peters enlargement vpon the prayers [sic] of the Church* (1627: RSTC 12842)

Harrison, William, *Deaths aduantage little regarded, and The soules solace against sorrow Preached in two funerall sermons* (1602: RSTC 12866)

Hayward, John, *The sanctuarie of a troubled soule* (1602: RSTC 13003.7)

—— *The sanctvarie of a troubled soule* (1618: RSTC 13006.5)

Herbert, George, *Works*, ed. F. E. Hutchinson (Oxford, 1941)

Heyden, Cornelius, *A Bryefe Summe of the whole Byble*, tr. Antony Scoloker (1550?: RSTC 3018)

Hieron, Samuel, *The Preachers Plea* (1604: RSTC 13419)

—— *A Helpe vnto Deuotion* (1608: RSTC 13406.3)

—— *A Helpe Vnto Deuotion* (1610: RSTC 13406.5)

Hill, Robert, *Christs prayer expounded, A Christian Directed, and a Communicant prepared* (1606: RSTC 13472)

Hildersam, Arthur, *The Doctrine of Fasting and Praier, and Humiliation for Sinne* (1633: RSTC 13459)

Hinde, William, *A Faithfull Remonstrance of the Holy Life and Happy Death, of Iohn Bruen* (1641: Wing H2063)

Hoby, Margaret, *The Diary of Lady Margaret Hoby, 1599–1605*, ed. Dorothy M. Meads (1930)

Holinshed, Raphael, *Holinshed's Chronicles of England, Scotland and Ireland* (1807)

Hooker, Richard, *Of the Laws of Ecclesiastical Polity: Preface, Books I to IV*, ed. Georges Edelen (Cambridge, Mass., 1977)

—— *Of the Laws of Ecclesiastical Polity: Book V*, ed. W. Speed Hill (Cambridge, Mass., 1977)

Hooper, John, *Early Writings of John Hooper*, ed. Samuel Carr (Cambridge, 1843)

Hooper, John, *The Later Writings of Bishop Hooper* (Cambridge, 1852)

Howell, James, *Epistolæ Ho-Elianæ. Familiar Letters Domestic and Forren* (1645: Wing H3071)

Hunnis, William, *Seuen Sobs of a Sorrowfull Soule for Sinne* (1583: RSTC 13975)

Hutchins, Edward, *Davids Sling against great Goliah* (1581: RSTC 14010)

Janeway, James, *Invisibles, Realities, Demonstrated in the Holy Life and Triumphant Death of Mr. John Janeway* (1673: Wing J470)

Jewel, John, *The Works of John Jewel, Bishop of Salisbury. The first portion*, ed. John Ayre (Cambridge, 1845)

Jocelin, Elizabeth, *The Mothers Legacie, To her vnborne Child* (1624: RSTC 14624)

Joye, George, *Ortulus anime. The garden of the soule* (Antwerp, 1530: RSTC 13828.4)

Ketley, Joseph (ed.). *The Two Liturgies, A.D. 1549, and A.D. 1552: With Other Documents Set Forth by Authority in the Reign of King Edward VI* (Cambridge, 1844)

Kiffin, William, *Remarkable Passages in the Life of William Kiffin: Written by Himself*, ed. William Orme (1823)

Kilby, Richard, *The Burthen of a Loaden Conscience* (1635: RSTC 14594.3)

—— *Hallelujah. Praise yee the Lord* (1635: RSTC 14956.7)

Kingsmill, Andrew, *A Viewe of mans estate, wherein the great mercie of God in mans free iustification by Christ, is very comfortably declared* (1574: RSTC 15003)

Kirkton, James, *The Secret and True History of the Church of Scotland from the Restoration to the Year 1678*, ed. Charles Kirkpatrick Sharpe (Edinburgh, 1817)

Knappen, M. M. (ed.), *Two Elizabethan Puritan Diaries by Richard Rogers and Samuel Ward* (Chicago, 1933)

Knell, Thomas, *A godlie and necessarie Treatise, touching the vse and abuse of praier* (1581: RSTC 15033.33)

Knox, John, *The Works of John Knox*, ed. David Laing (Edinburgh, 1846–64)

Lake, Arthur, *Sermons with some religious and diuine meditations* (1629: RSTC 15134)

Latimer, Hugh, *Sermons by Hugh Latimer*, ed. George Elwes Corrie (Cambridge, 1844)

—— *Sermons and Remains of Hugh Latimer*, ed. George Elwes Corrie (Cambridge, 1845)

Leigh, Dorothy, *The mothers blessing* (1616: RSTC 15402)

Ley, John, *A patterne of Pietie. Or The Religious life and death of that Grave and gracious Matron, Mrs. Jane Ratcliffe* (1640: RSTC 15567)

Linaker, Robert, *A comfortable treatise for such as are afflicted in conscience* (1595: RSTC 15638)

—— *A comfortable treatise, for the reliefe of such as are afflicted in conscience* (1620: RSTC 15641)

Lupton, Donald, *Obiectorum Reductio: Or, Daily Imployment for the Soule* (1634: RSTC 16945)

Manningham, John, *The Diary of John Manningham of the Middle Temple, 1602–1603*, ed. Robert Parker Sorlie (Hanover, N.H., 1976)

Mason, Henry, *Christian Humiliation, Or, A Treatise of Fasting* (1625: RSTC 17602)

Mather, Cotton, *Magnalia Christi Americana* (1702)

Maxey, Anthony, *The golden chaine of mans saluation . . . 4. seuerall sermons before the King* (1610: RSTC 17687)

Mayer, John, *Praxis Theologica* (1629: RSTC 17743)

Melville, Elizabeth, *A Godlie Dreame* (Edinburgh, 1620: RSTC 17814)

Melville, James, *A Spirituall Propine of a Pastour to his People* (Edinburgh, 1598: RSTC 17816)

—— *The Autobiography and Diary of Mr James Melvill*, ed. Robert Pitcairn (Edinburgh, 1842)

Mildmay, Grace, *With Faith and Physic: The Life of a Tudor Gentlewoman, Lady Grace Mildmay 1552–1620*, ed. Linda Pollock (1993)

Narne, William, *The Pearle of Prayer, Most Pretious, and Powerfull* (Edinburgh, 1630: RSTC 18360)

Norden, John, *A pensiue mans practise, verie profitable for all persons* (1598: RSTC 18617.7)

—— *A pensive mans practise. Or the pensiue mans complaint and comfort. The second part* (1609: RSTC 18626a.5)

Norwood, Richard, *The Journal of Richard Norwood, Surveyor of Bermuda*, ed. Wesley Frank Craven and Walter B. Hayward (New York, 1945)

Openshaw, Robert, *Short questions, and answeares, contayning the Summe of Christian Religion* (1633: RSTC 18828.5)

Owen, Hugh (ed), 'The Diary of Bulkeley of Dronwy, Anglesey, 1630–1636', *Anglesey Antiquarian Society and Field Club Transactions* (1937), 26–172

Parr, Elnathan, *Abba Father: Or, a plaine and short direction concerning Priuate Prayer* (1618: RSTC 19312)

Parr, Katherine, *The lamentacion of a sinner* (1547: RSTC 4827)

Pemble, William, *An introduction to the worthy receiving the sacrament of the Lords Supper* (1628: RSTC 19579)

Perkins, William, *An exposition of the Lords prayer* (1593: RSTC 19700.5)

—— *A salve for a sicke man* (Cambridge, 1595: RSTC 19742)

—— *A Declaration of the true manner of knowing Christ Crucified* (Cambridge, 1596: RSTC 19685)

—— *The first part of The cases of conscience* (Cambridge, 1604: RSTC 19668)

—— *The whole treatise of the cases of conscience* (Cambridge, 1606: RSTC 19669)

—— *A godly and learned exposition of Christs Sermon in the Mount* (Cambridge, 1608: RSTC 19722)

—— *Christian Oeconomie* (1609: RSTC 19677)

—— *How to live, and that well* (1611: RSTC 19729)

Perrott, James, *Certaine Short Prayers and Meditations vpon the Lords Prayer and the Ten Commandements* (1630: RSTC 19772)

Persons, Robert, *A booke of Christian exercise, appertaining to resolution*, ed. Edmund Bunny (1584: RSTC 19355)

—— *The Christian Directory (1582): The First Booke of the Christian Exercise, Appertayning to Resolution*, ed. Victor Houliston (Leiden, 1998)

Phillips, John, *A Satyr against Hypocrites* (1655: Wing P2101)

'Phoenix, Anne' [ps. for Anthony Fawkener?], *The Saints Legacies: Or, A Collection of certaine PROMISES out of the word of God* (1633: RSTC 10635.3)

Pigg, Oliver, *Meditations concerning praiers to almighty God, for the safety of England* (1589: RSTC 19916.3)

Pinke, William, *The Tryall of a Christians syncere loue vnto Christ* (1631: RSTC 19942)

Playfere, Thomas, *The Meane in Mourning. A Sermon* (1596: RSTC 20015)

—— *Hearts delight. A sermon* (Cambridge, 1603: RSTC 20010)

—— *The power of praier* (Cambridge, 1603: RSTC 20025)

Pounds, N. J. G. (ed), 'William Carnsew of Bokelly and his Diary, 1576–7', *Journal of the Royal Institution of Cornwall* new series 8/1 (1978), 14–60

Powel, Gabriel, *The Resolued Christian, exhorting to Resolution* (1600: RSTC 20150)

Powell, Vavasor, *Spirituall Experiences, Of sundry Beleevers* (1653: Wing P3095)

Preston, John, *The Saints Daily Exercise. A Treatise concerning the whole dutie of prayer* (1629: RSTC 20251)

—— *Three Sermons vpon the Sacrament of the Lords Supper* (1631: RSTC 20281)

Prid, William, *The glasse of vaine-glorie* (1585: RSTC 929)

—— *The Glasse of Vaine-glorie* (1600: RSTC 931)

Primrose, Gilbert, *The Christian Mans Teares, And Christs Comforts* (1625: RSTC 20389)

A prymmer or boke of priuate prayer . . . auctorysed and set fourth by the kinges maiestie (1553: RSTC 20373)

'R. R.', *The House-holders Helpe, for Domesticall Discipline* (1615: RSTC 20586)

Redman, John, *The complaint of grace, continued through all ages of the world*, ed. William Crashaw (1609: RSTC 20826.5)

Rogers, Charles (ed.), *Three Scottish Reformers* (1874)

Rogers, Daniel, *Matrimoniall Honour* (1642: Wing 1797)

Rogers, Francis, *A sermon preached . . . at the funerall of William Proud* (1633: RSTC 21175)

Rogers, Richard, *Seven treatises, containing such direction as is gathered out of the Holie Scriptures, leading and guiding to true happines* (1603: RSTC 21215)

—— et al. *A Garden of Spirituall Flowers* (1615: RSTC 21213.3)

—— *A garden of spirituall flowers* (1616: RSTC 21207)

Rogers, Samuel, *The Diary of Samuel Rogers, 1634–1638*, ed. Tom Webster and Kenneth Shipps (Church of England Record Society 11: 2004)

Rous, Francis, *The mysticall Marriage. Experimentall Discoveries of the heavenly Marriage betweene a Soule and her Saviour* (1631: RSTC 21342.5)

Sandys, Edwin, *The Sermons of Edwin Sandys*, ed. John Ayre (Cambridge, 1841)

Scott, Thomas, *The Belgicke Pismire: Stinging the slothfull Sleeper, and Awaking the Diligent* (Holland, 1622: RSTC 22069)

Scudder, Henry, *The Christians daily walke in holy securitie and peace* (1628: RSTC 22116)

—— *The Christians daily walke in holy securitie and peace* (1631: RSTC 22117)

Shepard, Thomas, *God's Plot: The Paradoxes of Puritan Piety, Being the Autobiography and Journal of Thomas Shepard*, ed. Michael McGiffert (Amherst, Mass., 1972)

A short and pretie Treatise touching the perpetuall Reioyce of the godly, euen in this lyfe (1568: RSTC 24230)

Sibbes, Richard, *The bruised reede, and smoaking flax* (1630: RSTC 22479)

—— *The Complete Works of Richard Sibbes*, ed. Alexander B. Grosart (Edinburgh, 1862–4)

Smith, Henry, *The Sermons of Master Henrie Smith* (1592: RSTC 22718)

Smith, John, *Essex Dove, Presenting the World with a few of her Oliue Branches* (1633: RSTC 22799)

Smith, Samuel, *Dauids blessed man. Or, A short exposition vpon the first Psalme* (1617: RSTC 22840)

Sorocold, Thomas, *Supplications of Saints. A Booke of Prayers* (1612: RSTC 22932)

—— *Supplications of Saints. A Booke of Prayers and Prayses* (1616: RSTC 22933)

Sparke, Michael [?], *Crumms of comfort, the valley of teares, and the hill of ioy* (1627: RSTC 23015.7)

Sternhold, Thomas, John Hopkins et al, *The Whole Booke of Psalmes, collected into Englysh metre* (1562: RSTC 2430)

Stubbes, Philip, *A christal glasse for christian women* (1592: RSTC 23382)

Struther, William, *Scotlands Warning, or a Treatise of Fasting* (Edinburgh, 1628: RSTC 23370)

Sutcliffe, Matthew, *An Answere Vnto a Certaine Calumnious letter published by M. Iob Throkmorton* (1595: RSTC 23451)

Sutton, Christopher, *Disce mori. Learne to die* (1601: RSTC 23475)

—— *Godly meditations vpon the most holy sacrament of the Lordes Supper* (1601: RSTC 23491)

—— *Disce viuere. Learne to liue* (1602: RSTC 23483)

—— *Godly meditations upon the most holy sacrament of the Lordes supper* (1613: RSTC 23492)

Taylor, Thomas, *Christ Revealed: or The Old Testament explained* (1635: RSTC 23821)

Themylthorpe, Nicholas, *The Posie of Godly Praiers* (1618: RSTC 23934.5)

This booke is called the Treasure of gladnesse (1574: RSTC 24193.5)

Thornton, Alice, *The Autobiography of Mrs Alice Thornton*, ed. Charles Jackson (Surtees Society 62, 1873)

Torshell, Samuel, *The Saints Humiliation* (1633: RSTC 24142)

Tozer, Henry, *Directions for a Godly Life: Especially for Communicating at the Lord's Table* (1628: RSTC 24161)

Trundle, John?, *Keepe within Compasse* (1619: RSTC 14898.5)

Tuke, Thomas, *The Practise of the faithfull* (1613: RSTC 24314)

Tweedie, W. K. (ed.), *Select Biographies Edited for the Wodrow Society, vol. I* (Edinburgh, 1845)

Two treaties the first concerning the Holy Scriptures in generall (Hamburg, 1640: RSTC 24260)

Tye, Christopher, *The Actes of the Apostles, translated into Englyshe Metre* (1553?: RSTC 2983.8)

Tymme, Thomas, *A siluer watch-bell* (1605: RSTC 24421)

—— *A siluer watch-bell* (1606: RSTC 24422)

—— *The Chariot of Devotion* (1618: RSTC 24415a)

—— *A silver watch-bell* (1640: RSTC 24434)

Tyndale, William, *Doctrinal Treatises and Introductions to Different Portions of the Holy Scriptures*, ed. Henry Walter (Cambridge, 1848)

Tyrwhit, Elizabeth, *Elizabeth Tyrwhit's Morning and Evening Prayers*, ed. Susan M. Felch (Aldershot, 2008)

Valentine, Henry, *Private Devotions, Digested into Six Letanies* (1635: RSTC 24576.3)

Vaughan, Edward, *A Plaine and perfect Method, for the easie vnderstanding of the whole Bible* (1617: RSTC 24600)

Walker, Anthony (ed.), *The Holy Life of Mrs Elizabeth Walker* (1690: Wing W305)

Walker, William, *A sermon preached at the funerals of the Right Honourable, William, Lord Russell* (1614: RSTC 24964)

Wallington, Nehemiah, *The Notebooks of Nehemiah Wallington, 1618–1654: A Selection*, ed. David Booy (Aldershot, 2007)

Walton, Izaak, *The Complete Angler and The Lives of Donne, Wotton, Hooker, Herbert and Sanderson*, ed. A. W. Pollard (1906)

Ward, Samuel, *A Coal from the Altar, to Kindle the holy fire of Zeale* (1615: RSTC 25039)

Wariston, Archibald Johnston of, *Diary of Sir Archibald Johnston of Wariston, 1632–1639*, ed. George Morison Paul (Scottish History Society, 1911)

Warwick, Arthur, *Spare-Minutes; or, resolved meditations and premeditated resolutions* (1634: RSTC 25097)

Webbe, George, *The practise of qui[e]tnes: directing a Christian how to liue quietly in this troblesome world* (1618: RSTC 25166.3)

Wetenhall, Edward, *Enter into thy Closet, or a Method and Order for private Devotion* (1666: Wing W1495B)

Whately, William, *The Redemption of time* (1606: RSTC 25318)

Whitgift, John, *The Works of John Whitgift*, ed. John Ayre (Cambridge, 1851–3)

Wilkinson, Robert, *A Iewell for the Eare* (*c*.1602: RSTC 25652.7)

Willet, Andrew, *Synopsis Papismi, That is, a generall view of Papistrie* (1634: RSTC 25700a.5)

Willis, Richard, *Mount Tabor. Or Private Exercises of a Penitent Sinner* (1639: RSTC 25752)

Winthrop, John, *Winthrop Papers, vol. I: 1498–1628* (Boston, Mass., 1929)

Wither, George, *A Preparation to the Psalter* (1619: RSTC 25914)

Wodenoth, Arthur, '1645, Expressions of Mr. Arthur Wodenoth', ed. Harold Spencer Scott, in *The Camden Miscellany X* (Camden Society, s.3 vol. 4: 1902)

Wright, Leonard, *A Summons for Sleepers* (1589: RSTC 26034.3)

Zepper, Wilhelm, *The Art or Skil Well and Fruitfullie to Heare the holy Sermons of the Church*, tr. T. W[ilcox?] (1599: RSTC 26124.5)

SECONDARY SOURCES

Arnoult, Sharon L., '"Spiritual and Sacred Publique Actions": The Book of Common Prayer and the Understanding of Worship in the Elizabethan and Jacobean Church of England' in Eric Josef Carlson (ed.), *Religion and the English People 1500–1640* (Kirkville, M.O., 1998)

Aston, Margaret, 'Moving Pictures: Foxe's Martyrs and Little Gidding' in Sabrina A. Baron et al. (eds), *Agent of Change: Print Culture Studies After Elizabeth L. Eisenstein* (Amherst, Mass., 2007)

Bozeman, Theodore Dwight, *The Precisianist Strain: Disciplinary Religion and Antinomian Backlash in Puritanism to 1638* (Chapel Hill, N.C., 2004)

Branch, Laura, 'Practical Piety: The Spiritual Autobiography of Rose Throckmorton (*c*.1526–1613),' University of St. Andrews M.Litt dissertation (2007)

Brekus, Catherine A., 'Writing as a Protestant Practice: Devotional Diaries in Early New England' in Laurie P. Maffly-Kipp et al. (eds), *Practicing Protestants: Histories of Christian Life in America* (Baltimore, 2006)

Brümmer, Vincent, *What Are We Doing When We Pray? A Philosophical Inquiry* (1984)

Cambers, Andrew, 'Reading, the Godly, and Self-Writing in England, circa 1580–1720', *Journal of British Studies* 46/4 (2007), 796–825

—— *Godly Reading: Print, Manuscript and Puritanism in England, 1580–1720* (Cambridge, 2011)

Campbell, Ted. A, *The Religion of the Heart: a Study of European Religious Life in the Seventeenth and Eighteenth Centuries* (Columbia, S.C., 1991)

Carruthers, Mary, 'Sweetness', *Speculum* 81/4 (2006), 999–1013

Christian, William A., Jr, 'Provoked Religious Weeping in Early Modern Spain' in John Corrigan (ed.), *Religion and Emotion: Approaches and Interpretation* (Oxford, 2004)

Clutterbuck, Charlotte, *Encounters with God in Medieval and Early Modern English Poetry* (Aldershot, 2005)

Cohen, Charles Lloyd, *God's Caress: the psychology of Puritan religious experience* (New York, 1986)

Collinson, Patrick. *The Religion of Protestants* (Oxford, 1982)

—— 'Shepherds, sheepdogs and hirelings: the pastoral ministry in post-Reformation England' in W. J. Shiels and Diana Wood (eds), *The Ministry: Clerical and Lay* (Studies in Church History 26, 1989)

Como, David, *Blown by the Spirit: Puritanism and the emergence of an antinomian underground in pre-Civil-War England* (Stanford, 2004)

Cooper, Trevor, '"As wise as serpents": the form and setting of public worship at Little Gidding in the 1630s' in Natalie Mears and Alec Ryrie (eds), *Worship and the Parish Church in Early Modern Britain* (Aldershot, 2012)

Craig, John, 'Psalms, groans and dogwhippers: the soundscape of worship in the English parish church, 1547–1642' in Will Coster and Andrew Spicer (eds), *Sacred Space in Early Modern Europe* (Cambridge, 2005)

—— 'Bodies at prayer in early modern England' in Natalie Mears and Alec Ryrie (eds), *Worship and the Parish Church in Early Modern Britain* (Aldershot, 2012)

Cressy, David, *Birth, Marriage and Death: Ritual, Religion and the Life Cycle in Tudor and Stuart England* (Oxford, 1997)

Davies, Catharine, *A religion of the Word: the defence of the reformation in the reign of Edward VI* (Manchester, 2002)

Davies, Natalie Zemon, *The Gift in Sixteenth-Century France* (Oxford, 2000)

Dexter, Henry Martyn, *The Congregationalism of the Last Three Hundred Years as Seen in its Literature* (New York, 1970: facsimile of 1880 original)

Dixon, Leif, 'Predestination and pastoral theology: the communication of Calvinist doctrine, c. 1590–1640' (University of Oxford DPhil thesis, 2007)

—— 'Calvinist Theology and Pastoral Reality in the Reign of King James I: the Perspective of Thomas Wilson', *Seventeenth Century* 23/2 (2008), 173–97

Durston, Christopher, 'By the book or with the spirit: the debate over liturgical prayer during the English Revolution', *Historical Research* 79/203 (2006), 50–73

Ferrell, Lori Anne, 'Kneeling and the Body Politic' in Donna B. Hamilton and Richard Streier (eds), *Religion, Literature and Politics in Post-Reformation England, 1540–1688* (Cambridge, 1996)

Fincham, Kenneth, and Nicholas Tyacke, *Altars Restored: The Changing Face of English Religious Worship, 1547–c.1700* (Oxford, 2007)

Fleming, Juliet, *Graffiti and the Writing Arts of Early Modern England* (2001)

Green, Ian, *Print and Protestantism in Early Modern England* (Oxford, 2000)

Gregory, Brad S., 'The "True and Zealouse Seruice of God": Robert Parsons, Edmund Bunny, and The First Booke of the Christian Exercise', *Journal of Ecclesiastical History* 45/2 (1994), 238–68

Habsburg, Maximilian von, *Catholic and Protestant Translations of the* Imitatio Christi, *1425–1650* (Aldershot, 2011)

Haigh, Christopher, *The Plain Man's Pathways to Heaven: Kinds of Christianity in Post-Reformation England, 1570–1640* (Oxford, 2007)

Hamling, Tara, 'To See Or Not To See? The Presence Of Religious Imagery In The Protestant Household', *Art History* 30/2 (2007), 170–97

—— *Decorating the 'Godly' Household: Religious Art in Post-Reformation Britain* (New Haven and London, 2010)

Houlbrooke, Ralph, *The English Family 1450–1750* (1984)

—— *Death, Religion and the Family in England 1480–1750* (Oxford, 1998)

Hunt, Arnold, 'The Lord's Supper in Early Modern England', *Past and Present* 161 (1998), 39–83

—— *The Art of Hearing: English Preachers and their Audiences, 1590–1640* (Cambridge, 2010)

Karant-Nunn, Susan C, '"Christians' Mourning and Lament Should Not Be Like the Heathens": the Suppression of Religious Emotion in the Reformation' in J. M. Headley et al. (eds), *Confessionalization in Europe, 1555–1700* (Aldershot, 2004)

—— *The Reformation of Feeling: Shaping the Religious Emotions in Early Modern Germany* (Oxford, 2010)

Kaufman, Peter Iver, *Prayer, Despair and Drama: Elizabethan Introspection* (Urbana and Chicago, 1996)

Kendall, R. T. *Calvin and English Calvinism to 1649* (Oxford, 1979)

Longfellow, Erica, '"my now solitary prayers": *Eikon basilike* and changing attitudes toward religious solitude' in Jessica Martin and Alec Ryrie (eds), *Private and Domestic Devotion in Early Modern Britain* (Aldershot, 2012)

Leverenz, David, *The Language of Puritan Feeling: An Exploration in Literature, Psychology and Social History* (New Brunswick, N.J., 1980)

McKay, Elaine, 'English Diarists: Gender, Geography and Occupation, 1500–1700', *History* 90/298 (2005), 191–212

McMillan, William, *The Worship of the Scottish Reformed Church, 1550–1638* (Dunfermline, 1931)

McQuade, Paula, 'Maternal Catechesis in the Manuscript Miscellany of Katherine Fitzwilliam (c. 1600)', paper delivered to the Sixteenth Century Conference, Cincinnati, Ohio, 27 October 2012

Maltby, Judith, *Prayer Book and People in Elizabethan and early Stuart England* (Cambridge, 1998)

Martin, Jessica, and Alec Ryrie (eds), *Private and Domestic Devotion in Early Modern Britain* (Farnham, 2012)

Martz, Louis L., *The Poetry of Meditation: A Study in English Religious Literature* (New Haven and London, 1962)

Mears, Natalie, and Alec Ryrie (eds), *Worship and the Parish Church in Early Modern Britain* (Aldershot, 2012)

Morgan, John, *Godly Learning: Puritan Attitudes towards Reason, Learning and Education, 1560–1640* (Cambridge, 1986)

Narveson, Kate, 'Publishing the Sole-talk of the Soule: Genre in Early Stuart Piety' in Daniel W. Doersken and Christopher Hodgkins (eds), *Centered on the Word* (Newark, N.J., 2004)

—— *Bible Readers and Lay Writers in Early Modern England* (Farnham, 2012)

Nuttall, Geoffrey F., *The Holy Spirit in Puritan Faith and Experience* (Oxford, 1946)

Orlin, Lena Cowen, *Locating Privacy in Tudor London* (Oxford, 2007)

Packer, J. I, *A Quest for Godliness: the Puritan Vision of the Christian Life* (Wheaton, Ill., 1990)

Parker, Kenneth L., *The English Sabbath* (Cambridge, 1988)

—— and Eric J. Carlson, *'Practical Divinity': the Works and Life of Revd Richard Greenham* (Aldershot, 1998)

Paster, Gail Kern et al. (eds), *Reading the Early Modern Passions: Essays in the Cultural History of Emotion* (Philadelphia, P.A., 2004)

Patterson, Mary Hampson. *Domesticating the Reformation* (Madison, W.I., 2007)

Quitslund, Beth, *The Reformation in Rhyme: Sternhold, Hopkins and the English Metrical Psalter, 1547–1603* (Aldershot, 2008)

Reinburg, Virginia, 'Hearing Lay People's Prayer' in Barbara Diefendorf and Carla Hesse, eds, *Culture and Identity in Early Modern Europe (1500–1800)* (Ann Arbor, Mich., 1993)

Richard, Lucien Joseph, *The Spirituality of John Calvin* (Atlanta, 1974)

Ryrie, Alec, *The Gospel and Henry VIII* (Cambridge, 2003)

—— 'The Psalms and Confrontation in English and Scottish Protestantism', *Archiv für Reformationsgeschichte* 101 (2010)

—— 'The Afterlife of Lutheran England' in Dorothea Wendebourg (ed.), *Sister Reformations: The Reformation in Germany and England* (Tübingen, 2011)

—— 'The fall and rise of fasting in the British Reformations' in Natalie Mears and Alec Ryrie (eds), *Worship and the Parish Church in Early Modern Britain* (Farnham, 2012)

—— 'Sleeping, waking and dreaming in Protestant piety' in Jessica Martin and Alec Ryrie (eds), *Private and Domestic Devotion in Early Modern Britain* (Farnham, 2012)

Schmidt, Leigh Eric, *Holy Fairs: Scottish Communions and American Revivals in the Early Modern Period* (Princeton, 1989)

—— *Hearing Things: Religion, Illusion and the American Enlightenment* (Cambridge, Mass., 2000)

Schwanda, Tom, *Soul Recreation: The Contemplative-Mystical Piety of Puritanism* (Eugene, Ore., 2012)

Seaver, Paul S., *Wallington's World: a puritan artisan in seventeenth-century London* (Stanford, 1985)

Shamir, Avner, 'Bible burning and the descration of bibles in early modern England', Roskilde University PhD thesis (2010)

Sherman, William H., *Used Books: Marking Readers in Renaissance England* (Philadelphia, 2008)

Stachniewski, John, *The Persecutory Imagination: English Puritanism and the Literature of Religious Despair* (Oxford, 1991)

Stallybrass, Peter, Roger Chartier, John Mowery, and Heather Wolfe, 'Hamlet's Tables and the Technologies of Writing in Renaissance England', *Shakespeare Quarterly* 55 (2004), 379–419

Stephens, Isaac, '"My Cheefest Work": The Making of the Spiritual Autobiography of Elizabeth Isham', *Midland History* 34/2 (2009), 181–203

Tankard, Danae, 'The reformation of the deathbed in mid-sixteenth-century England', *Mortality* 8/3 (2003), 251–67

Targoff, Ramie, *Common Prayer: the language of public devotion in early modern England* (Chicago and London, 2001)

Thomas, Keith, *Religion and the Decline of Magic* (1971)

—— *The Ends of Life: Roads to Fulfilment in Early Modern England* (Oxford, 2009)

Todd, Margo. 'Puritan Self-Fashioning: The Diary of Samuel Ward', *Journal of British Studies* 31/2 (1992), 236–64

—— *The Culture of Protestantism in Early Modern Scotland* (New Haven and London, 2002)

Underdown, David, *Fire from Heaven: Life in an English Town in the Seventeenth Century* (New Haven and London, 1992)

Walsham, Alexandra, *Providence in Early Modern England* (Oxford, 1999)

—— *The Reformation of the Landscape: Religion, Identity, and Memory in Early Modern Britain and Ireland* (Oxford, 2011)

Watkins, Owen C., *The Puritan Experience* (1972)

Watt, Tessa, *Cheap Print and Popular Piety* (Cambridge, 1991)

Weber, Max, *The Protestant Ethic and the Spirit of Capitalism*, tr. Talcott Parsons (1992)

Webster, Tom, 'Writing to Redundancy: Approaches to Spiritual Journals and Early Modern Spirituality', *Historical Journal* 39 (1996), 33–56

White, Helen C., *English Devotional Literature (Prose) 1600–1640* (Madison, W.I., 1931)

White, Helen C., *The Tudor Books of Private Devotion* (Madison, W.I., 1951)
Williams, Rowan, 'Religious experience in the era of reform' in Peter Byrne and Leslie
Houlden, *Companion Encyclopaedia of Theology* (1995)

ONLINE RESOURCES

Early English Books Online: http://eebo.chadwyck.com/
English Short Title Catalogue: http://estc.bl.uk
The Acts and Monuments Online: http://www.johnfoxe.org/
Oxford Dictionary of National Biography: http://www.oxforddnb.com/
Elizabeth Isham, 'My Booke of Rememberance', *c.*1639, ed. Elizabeth Clarke and Erica
Longfellow: http://www.warwick.ac.uk/english/perdita/Isham/index_bor.htm
Elizabeth Isham, Diary, ed. Elizabeth Clarke and Erica Longfellow, at http://www.warwick.ac.uk/
english/perdita/Isham/index_yr.htm

Index

Note: Numbers in italics refer to illustrations

Abbot, George 414
Adams, Thomas 242–3, 293, 340
aggravation 53–4, 68, 311
Alcock, John 234–5
Allen, Edward 320
alms, almsgiving 138, 196, 261, 296, 327, 342, 348, 445, 452–4
America, *see* New England
Ambrose, Isaac 84, 107, 166, 188, 274, 301, 304, 312, 373, 458–9
Andrewes, John 60, 86, 190, 244–5, 391, 420
Andrewes, Lancelot, bishop of Winchester 203–4
Angier, John 79
Anglicans, *see* conformist Protestants
antinomianism 36, 129
apocalypse, apocalypticism 193
Aristotelianism 18–19, 20–1
Armada, *see* Spanish Armada
Arminians, Arminianism 7, 8, 9
asceticism 54–5, 195–9
assurance 23–4, 39–41, 44–8, 59, 65, 81–2, 190, 332, 344–5, 439, 441, 461, 467–8
atheism, atheists 33, 80, 119–20, 123, 128, 352, 358, 368, 380, 404, 433, 464
Augustine of Hippo 21, 82, 99, 105, 110, 120, 224, 398, 422, 438
  Confessions 301, 422, 429–31, 433
Austin, William 393

Babington, Gervase 66–7, 72, 170, 210, 276, 327, 380, 423
Baker, Richard 146, 211
Bale, John 287
Ball, John 73, 104, 204, 321, 324, 333, 457
Balnaves, Henry 394
Bancroft, Richard, archbishop of Canterbury 360
Baxter, Richard 139, 156
  as a youth 21, 34, 192, 233–4, 282, 327, 391, 394, 413, 430, 440
  quoted 31, 218, 263, 381, 438, 453
Bayly, Lewis, bishop of Bangor, *Practise of Piety* of 35, 57, *183*, 222, 262, *264*, 290, 330
  importance of 22, 283–4
  on household piety 376, 381–3, 385
  on prayer 24–5, 69, 127, 148, 153, 165, 170, 173, 178, 182, 185, 187, 199, 201, 209, 212, 218, 238, 275, 325
  quoted 22, 46–7, 50, 78, 263, 279, 333, 346, 360, 362, 397, 426, 429, 465
  readers of 35, 220, 296 n., 438
Baynes, Paul 156, 331, 366

Beadle, John 142, 298, 300, 310, 312, 391
Becon, Thomas 242, 364, 457
  Flour of godly praiers 220, 223–4, 225, 293, 345, 450
  Gouernans of vertue 51 and n., 52, 224, 233, 291, 385–6, 388, 415
  on prayer 99, 109, 150, 200–1, 206–7, 209, 451
  reputation and impact 5, 285, 394
  quoted 81, 119, 130, 197, 219, 243, 261–2, 276, 380, 389, 418, 453
  Sycke mans salue 79, 220, 244, 285, 332, 375, 395, 462, 464, 466
Bentley, Thomas 159, 319
Bernard, Richard 164, 171, 310, 383, 386, 400
Bernher, Augustine 108
Bicknoll, Edmund 182
Bilney, Thomas 38, 241, 418, 425
Blackerby, Richard 167, 294, 357, 376
Blair, Robert
  biography 84–5, 133–4, 338, 342–3, 431
  devotional experience 25–6, 43, 88, 93, 106, 134–5, 142, 166, 168, 195, 202, 206, 265, 300–1
  ministry 37, 195, 267, 395, 437
Bolton, Robert 372
  conversion 36–7, 439
  on despair and assurance 32, 35, 38, 72, 81, 84
  on hypocrisy and self–deception 73–4, 93, 105, 368, 467
  quoted 42, 64, 78, 86, 89, 117, 149, 187, 218, 356, 367, 421, 448
  theology of the cross in 55, 62, 455
Book of Common Order 215, 237 n., 317, 322–3, 392, 425
Book of Common Prayer 8
  hostility to 203, 215, 232, 234, 323
  in private and domestic devotion 214, 232–8, 268, 275, 293, 374–5, 378, 380, 385, 459
  in public worship 317–18, 320, 322–3, 327–9, 334, 336, 348, 357
Bownde, Nicholas 68, 71, 75, 78–9, 206–7, 260, 319–20
Bradford, John 64, 97, 99, 110, 112, 175, 209, 213, 227–9, 234, 237, 240, 282, 285, 289, 299, 332, 383, 413, 417
Bradshaw, William 339–40
Braithwaite, Richard 287
Branch, Laura 430
Brekus, Catherine 61, 312
Bretterh, Katherine 65, 84, 103, 160, 188, 232, 271, 294–5, 465

Brinsley, John 45–6, 55, 80, 89, 106, 108, 150,
    152, 207, 221–2, 277, 321, 345, 348,
    365–6, 373, 400, 410, 458
Broke, Thomas 384
Browne, Thomas 169
Browning, John 100, 116, 173, 196–8, 201,
    210–11
Bruce, Robert
    biography 37, 244, 294–5
    devotional practice 152, 211
    ministry 354, 438
    quoted 33, 36, 60, 67, 100, 103, 121, 132,
        154–5, 161, 192, 208, 345, 346, 348,
        382, 440
Bruen, John 260, 457
    death of 466–7
    devotional life 88, 141, 159, 173, 177, 188,
        238, 254, 293, 376, 392, 444
    quoted 59–60, 363, 369–70, 385
    reading and writing of 115, 234, 238, 274,
        284, 302, 303–4, 358
    youth 169, 431, 439, 441
Brümmer, Vincent 120
Brunfels, Otto 226
Bulkeley, Robert 273
Bull, Henry 61, 66–7, 108, 204, 214, 285, 295,
    305, 386, 458
Bullinger, Heinrich 296
Bunny, Edmund 55, 269, 285–8, 290–1,
    447 and n., 472
Bunyan, John 167, 225, 430
Burton, Henry 45, 143, 148, 154, 196, 225,
    261, 272, 275, 286, 304, 324
Byfield, Nicholas 28 n., 277
    on assurance 39, 189–90, 332, 439
    on emotion 42, 65, 72, 75, 88, 189, 267, 411
    on prayer 24, 102, 190, 204, 248
    on repentance 57, 311
    quoted 278, 280, 352, 361, 390–1, 398
    readers of 220

Calvin, John 18, 89, 177, 205, 317, 323, 393, 438
Cambers, Andrew 11 n., 160, 270
Campbell, Ted 266
Cancellar, James 149
Capel, Richard 23, 105, 131–4, 137–9, 175,
    246, 249, 279–80, 371, 397
Carnsew, William 299, 379, 394, 446
Carter, John 158, 211
Cartwright, Thomas 54–5, 122, 124, 196, 203,
    385, 427
catechisms, catechesis 224, 229, 259, 268, 277,
    331, 337, 355, 365, 371, 375, 381–2, 388,
    395–6, 431, 434–5
Cary, Lettice 8, 25, 94, 159, 175, 181, 188,
    193, 347, 452
Catholics, Catholicism 109, 187, 284–92, 382,
    413–14
    devotional life of 1–2, 113–14, 222, 243

Charles I, king 207, 305, 380
charity, *see* alms
children, childhood 133–4, 189, 191–2,
    260–2, 267–8, 272, 296, 305, 328,
    337–8, 354–5, 366, 371, 385–8, 395,
    399, 427–36, 474
Christopherson, John, bishop of
    Chichester 269, 323, 393
church buildings 169, 324–5, 341
Clapham, Henoch 101–2, 217
Clarke, John 75, 106, 201–2, 213 n., 222, 226,
    374–5
Clarke, Samuel 11, 320, 376
Cleaver, Robert 92, 280, 296–7, 369–70,
    372, 385
Clifford, Anne 162, 166, 188, 221, 289, 293,
    339, 341
Clutterbuck, Charlotte 92, 227
Collinson, Patrick 2, 318, 392, 395, 398, 429, 472
Commandments, *see* Ten Commandments
commonplace books 11, 61, 234, 278, 303,
    305–6, 310, 414
communion, *see* Lord's Supper
confession (of sins) 56–8, 311–12
    confession to human confidantes 58, 395–7
confirmation 337 n.
conformist Protestants 6–8, 203–5, 233, 287, 457
conscience-literature 31, 33, 37, 45, 52, 92, 106
Constantine, George 230
conversion 36–8, 42–3, 82–3, 263, 352, 401–5,
    415, 431, 436–41
Cooper, Thomas, bishop of Winchester 134–5
Corbet, Margaret 452
Corbett, Richard 29, 31, 424
Cosin, John 90, 147–8, 203, 215, 221, 244,
    275, 331, 338, 374, 459, 461
Cotton, Clement 423
Cotton, John 439
Coverdale, Miles 51, 82, 217, 223, 228, 404
Cowper, William, bishop of Galloway
    devotional experience 38–9, 43, 314, 432
    on prayer 89, 101, 117, 122, 124, 156, 189,
        203, 248, 252, 254
    quoted 45, 47, 64, 68, 85, 91, 245, 263, 266,
        341–2, 378, 411
Craig, John 185–6, 212–13, 328
Cranmer, Thomas, archbishop of
    Canterbury 294, 323, 327
Crashaw, William 51, 128, 133–4, 144–6, 242,
    271, 365, 385, 419
creed, creeds 150, 218, 230, 232, 317–18, 323,
    327, 337, 434
Cromwell, Thomas, vicegerent in spirituals 237
Culverwell, Ezekiel 48, 57, 73, 104, 106,
    131–2, 139, 168, 248–9, 272, 277–8, 284,
    331, 347, 354, 391

Dalaber, Anthony 201, 390
Davidson, John 132, 385 n., 386

Davies, Catharine 318, 418
Day, Richard 90, 119–20, 187, 202, 220, 228, 289, 379
death, dying 103, 127, 180, 185, 188, 208–9, 212, 237, 244, 282, 294–5, 311–12, 399, 420–2, 460–8
  grief for the dead 79, 125–6
Denison, John 284
Denison, Stephen 35, 50
Denley, John 180
Dent, Arthur 23, 52, 56, 58, 150, 164, 259, 263, 352, 365, 367, 404–5, 420–1, 450, 452–4
Dering, Edward 41–2, 134, 209, 239, 241, 265–6, 348, 365, 380, 388
despair 18, 24, 27–32, 38–9, 46, 157, 162, 464–8
Devil 23, 24, 28, 32–3, 37, 42, 52–4, 93, 103, 157, 189, 244–7, 252, 254, 292, 313, 351, 357, 378, 412, 455–6, 464–7
D'Ewes, Simonds 39, 261, 299, 358, 391, 426, 438–41
diaries 11, 29, 82, 298–301, 310–13, 396, 409, 469
Dickson, David 43, 247, 395
Directory for the Publique Worship of God (1644) 215, 228, 273, 327, 329
Dixon, Leif 9, 66 n., 397, 419
Dod, John 36, 54, 57, 61, 101, 106, 136–7, 203, 240, 262, 265, 296–7, 338, 344, 348, 367–8, 398, 411–12, 435, 454, 467
Donne, John 58, 64, 91, 93–4, 105–6, 167, 187, 301, 360–1, 465
Downame, John 84, 111 n., 115, 274–5, 396
Drexelius, Jeremias 34, 285
Duncon, John 79
Dyke, Daniel 35, 53, 56, 59, 60–1, 70, 72–3, 82, 86, 129, 137, 145, 194, 209, 246, 280, 300, 440, 453
Dyke, Jeremiah 65, 69, 76, 150, 262–4, 290, 331–2, 338, 340–1, 344, 347, 349–50, 354, 403

Earle, John, bishop of Salisbury 51, 212, 225, 246, 283, 376–7, 388, 444
Edward VI, king 358, 418
Egerton, Stephen 267, 284, 355, 360, 388
Elizabeth I, queen 140, 378, 380
  celebrating the accession of 304, 378–9, 458
Elizabeth of Bohemia, princess 380
Elyot, Thomas 364
Erasmus, Desiderius 1, 18, 112, 243, 263, 267, 276, 294–6, 364
Eucharist, *see* Lord's Supper
Euler, Carrie 296 n.
evangelism 401–5
exorcism, *see* possession

Fairclough, Samuel 140, 271–2, 295, 396, 430
fasts, fasting 8, 24, 25, 54, 62, 131, 138, 188, 195–9, 251–2, 256, 326, 341–4, 380, 389, 391, 419, 457, 469
Fawkener, Anthony 307 and n., 454
Featley, Daniel 7, 19, 93–4, 116–17, 155–6, 184, 188, 204, 206, 212, 220, 222, 224, 250, 267, 348, 360, 438, 459
Fenner, William 19, 72
Ferrar, Nicholas 139, 305
Field, John 357
Fisher, Ambrose 150, 171, 207–8, 217, 228, 232–3, 327
Fitzwilliam, Katherine 308–9, 431
Fleming, Abraham 25–6, 167, 265, 382
Forbes of Corse, John 44, 85, 160, 163–4, 178, 188, 252, 372–3, 424
Forbes of Corse, Patrick, bishop of Aberdeen 254
Ford, Thomas 79–80
Foxe, John 46, 55, 92, 289, 322, 426, 455
  Actes and Monuments 11, 182, 184, 209, 237, 260–2, 271, 283, 287, 323, 392, 423–7, 442, 458
Freese, Edward 302, 363
Frevile, Gilbert 149–50, 425–6
Fuller, John 391
Fuller, Thomas 77–8, 313, 450
Fulwood, William 157, 309

Garden of Spiritual Flowers 39, 60–1, 72, 365, 453
Gardiner, Stephen, bishop of Winchester 307, 323
Gardiner, William 293
Garrett, Thomas 201, 390
Gee, Edward 38
Gee, John 194, 271, 415–16
gender 74, 91, 158, 160, 166, 185, 191–2, 268, 274, 318, 329, 358, 370–1, 397, 432, 436, 444–5, 451–2, 463, 465–6, 472–3
Geneva Bible 8, 148, 159, 181, 193, 252, 445, 456
Gerhard, Johann 143
Gilby, Anthony 263, 307, 319, 418–19
Gifford, George 31, 111, 228, 232, 259, 263, 269, 329, 352, 355, 400–1, 421, 427
Glendinning, James 178
Glover, Robert 46–7
Goodwin, Philip 325
Goodwin, Thomas
  childhood 192, 338, 346, 349, 399, 414, 429, 431
  conversion 42–3, 51–2, 437, 439
  ministry 36
  on prayer 71, 101, 103–4, 122, 124, 127, 147, 207, 250, 326, 454
  quoted 19, 41, 83, 193, 265, 278, 403

Gosnold, Paul 303
Gouge, William 22, 65–6, 102, 132–3, 147,
  160–1, 171, 173, 180, 187, 193, 204, 210,
  216, 220, 235, 243, 271, 277, 325, 366–7,
  370–2
Granada, Luis de 113, 284–5
Green, Ian 10, 291, 296, 473
Greene, Robert 34
Greenham, Richard 46–7, 71, 78–9, 111–12,
  117, 128, 138, 141, 148, 197, 212, 245–6,
  252, 267, 273–4, 331, 396, 399, 437, 445,
  448, 457
Greenwood, Henry 35, 45, 67, 189, 228, 412, 467
Grindal, Edmund, archbishop of
  Canterbury 271, 337
Gunpowder Plot 86, 140 n., 378–9, 426, 458

Habermann, Johann 108, 237
Habsburg, Maximilian von 288
Hacket, William 74, 178, 209
Haigh, Christopher 9
Hake, Edward 307–8
Hakewill, George 131
Hall, Joseph, bishop of Exeter 18, 78, 87,
  113–16, 157–9, 170–1, 201, 216, 245–6,
  266, 291, 303, 309, 359, 364, 442
Hamling, Tara 5 n., 186, 363–4
Harding, Thomas 269
Harley, Brilliana 457
Harley, Robert 215, 379–80
Harpsfield, Nicholas 404
Harrab, Thomas 319
Harris, Robert 68, 102, 109, 120, 140, 169–70,
  177, 206, 208–9, 213, 230, 246, 254–5,
  362, 385 n., 388, 399
Hastings, Elizabeth, countess of Huntington 59,
  115, 228, 265–6, 280, 415, 422–3, 451
Hayward, John 22, 24, 34, 47, 64–5, 76, 89–90,
  116, 164, 174, 249, 290, 309, 331, 465
Henrietta Maria, queen 380
Henry VIII, king 234–5, 380, 443
Herbert, George 20–1, 45, 63, 69, 81–2, 85,
  93, 100–1, 139, 148, 176–7, 186, 198,
  212–14, 219, 251, 261, 271, 280, 327,
  331, 338, 364, 412–13, 452–3
Heywood, Oliver 155
Hickman, Rose, see Throckmorton, Rose
Hieron, Samuel 56, 111, 134, 173, 213–14,
  218–19, 223, 240, 348, 361, 368–9,
  377, 447
Higginson, Francis 376
Hildersam, Arthur 19, 54–5, 102, 198, 205, 248,
  339–41, 343, 348, 351–2, 389, 398, 461
Hill, Robert 254, 343, 358
Hoby, Margaret 21, 23, 83, 97, 111, 159, 247,
  282, 300, 305, 310, 334, 342, 349, 358,
  366, 370–1, 395, 404, 412, 446, 452, 456

Hogg, James 393
Holinshed, Raphael 234
Homilies 50, 55, 99–100, 119, 122, 124, 201,
  204, 207, 208, 242, 263, 271, 280, 294,
  323–5, 329, 357, 393, 443, 455
Hooker, Richard 6, 9, 77, 157, 213,
  291, 427
Hooker, Thomas 414
Hooper, John 55, 92, 120, 128, 239, 243, 263,
  279, 371, 381, 393–5, 403, 418, 459
Houlbrooke, Ralph 367, 462
Howell, James 138, 148, 163, 200–1, 313, 327
Hudson, Thomas 46, 145
Hume, Alexander 298, 311
Hunnis, William 179, 188, 224, 236, 302
Hunt, Arnold 185, 269, 306, 336, 351, 358, 438
Huntington, countess of, *see* Hastings, Elizabeth
Hutchins, Edward 224, 241, 290, 333, 378,
  401–2, 429
hypocrisy 4, 61, 70–4, 104–5, 129, 155, 188,
  190–1, 213, 228, 461–2

idleness 4, 129, 146, 148, 157, 303, 306, 309,
  442–6, 455–6
Imitation of Christ 70, 285, 287–8, 457
Ireland 5, 37, 128–9, 163, 167, 178, 195,
  362, 471
Isham, Elizabeth
  biography 86–7, 138, 272, 331 n., 338, 371,
    397, 430, 434–5
  devotional experience 75, 188, 332, 354
  devotional practices 32, 138, 145–6, 148,
    165, 188, 218, 220, 230, 232, 234, 236,
    444, 457
  household of 260–1, 273, 452, 461
  quoted 30–1, 426
  reading 115, 234, 268, 272, 274, 280, 282,
    294–5
  writings 300–1, 305, 307, 309, 312,
    358, 456
Isham, Judith 31, 218, 267–8, 289, 300, 371,
  434–5, 438, 462–4

James VI and I, king 354
Janeway, John 299, 312
Jesuits, Jesuit spirituality 39, 113–14, 289
Jewel, John, bishop of Salisbury 269
Jocelin, Elizabeth 182, 221, 252, 268, 309,
  369–70, 452, 463
Josselin, Ralph 359
Johnston of Wariston, Archibald 11 n., 189,
  193, 236
  childhood 189, 272
  devotional experience and practices 40, 62,
    75, 83–4, 109, 117–18, 138, 154, 160,
    177, 194, 211, 227, 232, 236, 249, 252,
    327, 341, 420, 453, 459

marriage and bereavement (1633–4) 29, 126, 135, 141–2, 230, 300, 343, 346, 350–1, 372–3

reading and writing 220, 274, 279, 300, 359, 387

Jonson, Ben 260, 404

Joye, George 385

Jurdaine, Ignatius 88, 271, 359, 388

Juxon, Elizabeth 50, 74, 159, 162, 273, 391, 424, 452

Karant-Nunn, Susan 177, 205, 289

Kaufman, Peter Iver 119, 217

Kendall, R. T. 66

Kiffin, William 36, 279, 437

Kilby, Richard 7, 220–1

cited 156, 216, 227, 276, 283, 320, 321–2, 381, 444

devotional practices and ambitions 71–2, 135–7, 148, 176, 188, 197, 228, 238, 386–7, 423

ministry 355

sin, despair and repentance 25, 50, 69–70, 106, 129, 381, 398, 417, 420, 429

King James Bible 159, 180

King, John, bishop of London 240

King, William 421

Kingsmill, Andrew 60, 277–8, 403

Kirk o'Shotts, revival at (1630) 94, 350, 371, 437

Knell, Thomas 72–3, 99, 106, 120–1, 124, 207, 250–1, 419

Knox, John 103, 275, 287, 394

Lake, Arthur, bishop of Bath and Wells 18, 370, 387

Lake, Peter 10 n.

Lanyer, Aemilia 193

Larkham, Thomas 459

Latimer, Hugh, bishop of Worcester 5

cited 38, 80, 205, 241, 244, 293, 320–1, 356, 403, 443–4, 457

on paradox and 'contrary grace' 92, 242–3, 248–9

on prayer 105, 121, 124, 126, 140, 146, 151, 166–7, 200, 227, 228–9

on vocation 448, 454

reputation 141, 175, 354, 418

Laudians, Laudianism 6, 90, 180, 324–5, 331, 365, 457

Leigh, Dorothy 56, 81, 104, 120–1, 146–7, 149, 160, 178, 261, 276–7, 282, 314, 320, 322–3, 378, 449, 458

Ley, John 158, 251

Linaker, Robert 36, 44–6, 52, 92, 103, 105, 213, 216, 280

Little Gidding 139, 278, 305, 387, 423

Livingstone, John 94, 142–3, 163, 197, 211, 247, 346, 431

Loarte, Gasper 285

Lollards, Lollardy 163, 287–8, 296

Lord's Prayer 124, 150, 153, 222, 227–32, 242, 318, 337, 374, 385

Lord's Supper 163, 172, 188, 266, 317, 336–51, 353, 373, 398, 401–2, 414–15

admission to communion 150, 336–8

frequency of communion 336, 338–40

the Mass 178, 180

Love, Christopher 436–7

Lupton, Donald 115–16, 390, 417

Luther, Martin 32, 38, 40, 91, 166, 204–5, 241–2, 250, 280, 286, 410, 417–18, 448, 454–5

Lutherans, Lutheranism 108, 110, 143, 161, 284, 330, 396

McKay, Elaine 445

Maltby, Judith 328, 472

Manningham, John 300

marriage 87, 138–9, 141–2, 296, 371–3

Marsh, George 234

Marshall, Peter 464

Marshall, Valentine 273, 295, 362

Martin, Dorcas 371

Martz, Louis 286

Mary I, queen of England 126

Mason, Henry 58, 170, 196, 198–9, 356

Maxey, Anthony 74–5, 410

Mayer, John 194

meditation 68–9, 87, 109–18, 171, 201–2, 223, 276–7, 314, 417

Melanchthon, Philip 305

Melville, Elizabeth 154, 158, 194, 197 n., 212, 371, 410

Melville, James 43–4, 57, 87, 133–4, 161, 168, 182–4, 212–13, 217, 307, 338, 346–7, 358, 380, 387, 399, 430, 442, 444, 463

memorization 214, 221–2, 260, 272, 277–9, 346, 359, 434

men, *see* gender

Merbecke, John 301–2

Merritt, Julia 7

Middleton, Thomas 34

Mildmay, Grace 432, 451–2

and prayer 116–18, 238, 415, 417

cited 362, 424

devotional experiences 236, 265, 281, 314, 346, 350

devotional practices 57, 152, 173, 175, 185, 383, 444, 451–2

reading 273–4, 277, 281

writings 111, 299–300, 302, 305, 309, 314

Milton, John 207, 215

Mombaer, Jean 113–15

monasticism 148, 150, 166, 279, 303, 381, 387, 442–3, 447, 453

Monipennie, John 304

Montagu, James 44

Moray, William 303

More, Thomas 41, 273
music 88, 196, 318–19, 328, 344, 444; *see also* psalm-singing

Narne, William 25, 176, 189, 194, 206, 208, 252–3, 326
Narveson, Kate 8, 222, 270, 308, 472
New England 167, 216–17, 252, 357, 376
Norden, John 22, 54, 69, 87–8, 106–7, 120, 125, 145, 177–8, 187, 229, 265, 426, 467
Norwood, Richard 34, 51
    childhood and youth 31, 35, 124, 133, 167, 354, 433–4, 449
    conversion 34, 84, 137–9, 421–2, 438–40
    devotional experience and practices 82–3, 124, 133–4, 137–9, 147, 149, 168, 185, 188, 213, 218, 250, 397, 456
    quoted 86, 163, 390, 444
    reading and writing 272, 279, 301, 310, 433
Nowell, Alexander 445

Openshaw, Robert 233–4
Owen, John, bishop of St Asaph 221

Pagit, Eusebius 277, 388
Palmer, Herbert 272, 388
paradox 35, 37–8, 49, 65–6, 86, 91–5, 207, 242, 250, 267, 329, 343, 425
Parker, Kenneth 443
Parker, John 309
Parker, Matthew, archbishop of Canterbury 303
Parr, Elnathan 24, 97, 104, 116, 147, 185, 206, 214, 217, 219, 222, 249, 305, 446
Parr, Katherine, queen 110, 265, 288–9, 293
Parry, Henry, bishop of Worcester 131
Pascal, Blaise 46, 76, 84
Pasfield, Robert 260, 267, 277
Passion, Christ's 18, 116, 161, 166–7, 175, 249, 289–90, 345–6
Paternoster, *see* Lord's Prayer
Patterson, Mary Hampton 8, 282–3
Pemble, William 61, 151, 263, 345, 458
Perkins, William 226, 283, 439, 455
    on assurance 44, 129–30, 440
    on prayer 66, 100, 108–9, 119–20, 122, 127, 147, 159, 170–1, 187, 198, 200, 206, 208, 210, 228, 230, 235, 321, 325, 327
    pastoral advice 22, 24, 37, 47, 52, 91, 131, 191, 241, 266, 343, 347, 370, 396, 421, 444, 450, 464, 466–7
    quoted 41, 62, 64, 69, 81, 196, 242, 245–6, 250, 290, 330, 332, 367, 389, 440, 462
    readers of 282
Perrott, James 150, 220–1
Persons, Robert 34–35, 55, 70, 82, 89, 269, 282–8, 290, 417, 438, 447, 472
Perth Articles (1618) 172, 392, 456
Phillips, John 211, 260, 328, 355–6, 358–9, 369, 387, 393

Pilkington, James, bishop of Durham 173, 367
Pinke, William 94, 263, 424
Pigg, Oliver 223, 379, 401
plague 19, 128, 140, 242, 251, 271, 304, 308, 419, 426
Playfere, Thomas 61, 75, 78, 80, 161, 189, 193–4, 210, 250, 255, 325, 354, 460
possession 32, 292, 385, 428
Powel, Gabriel 46, 240–2, 284–5, 307, 424
Powell, Vavasor 41
preaching 37–8, 64, 88, 351–62, 375–7, 394–5, 437–40, 473
predestination 7, 27–32, 38–41, 44, 65–7, 91, 410, 413–14, 429, 455
Preston, John 24, 42, 68, 71, 73–4, 100, 104–5, 107, 120, 146, 152–3, 202–4, 205 n., 321, 342, 413
Prid, William 110
primers, primer tradition 63, 71, 110, 166–7, 178, 181–2, 209, 226 n., 238, 285, 288–9, 385, 457, 469
    Edward VI's primer (1553) 201, 223, 226, 233, 237, 374, 378, 386, 443, 448, 450, 463
Primrose, Gilbert 19, 76, 189–93, 195, 290, 420
privacy 97–8, 154–8, 188, 209–10
Proud, William 160, 233
psalms 32, 79, 88, 110, 138, 188, 216, 226–7, 249, 275–6, 278, 302–3, 327, 422–3
    'collage psalms' 225, 226, 304–5, 422–3
    psalm-singing 57, 88, 154, 168, 180, 208, 261, 317–18, 369, 374, 385, 392, 394, 402, 420, 425, 433–4
puritans, puritanism 12, 77–8, 100–2, 203–5, 211, 215–18, 230, 235, 237–8, 252, 292–3, 333, 353, 368, 393, 399, 446, 457
    definitions and scope 6–9, 324

Ratcliffe, Jane 158, 204, 251, 304, 306, 310, 343, 371, 376, 390, 463
reading 14, 111–12, 201–2, 223, 259–97, 403, 435, 438
    aloud 322–3, 375–6, 387–8, 394–5, 423
recreation 443–5
Redman, John 152, 159, 364
Reinburg, Virginia 205, 219
Rich, Richard 171–2
Robartes, Lucy 162
Rodney, Edward 194–5, 309, 341–2
Rogers, Daniel 366, 370–3
Rogers, Francis 244
Rogers, John 136, 151, 160, 197, 223, 398, 421, 446, 456
Rogers, Richard 29, 391
    devotional experience and practices 69, 107, 131–2, 134, 154, 168, 188, 194, 196–7, 354, 372, 394, 398
    diary 299, 310, 314

on prayer 108, 112–13, 121, 145–6, 151, 160, 204, 221, 244, 320
quoted 23, 51, 62–4, 69, 78, 89, 92, 261, 265, 274, 285, 393, 403, 411–12, 442, 449, 452, 454, 460
Seven Treatises, reception of 51, 121, 135–6, 283–4, 302, 411, 439
Rogers, Samuel 21, 23, 85, 95, 137, 299, 310, 313, 327, 339, 349, 373, 379, 381–2, 427, 437, 440
Rogers, Thomas 221, 305
Rothwell, Richard 439
Rous, Francis 39, 44, 47, 75, 85–6, 88, 90, 162, 242, 413
Russell, William, Lord 341, 464

Sabbath, observance of 3, 196–7, 205, 224, 262, 342, 391–2, 400, 439, 443–4, 456–8
preparation for 138, 177
Samuel, William 303
Sandys, Edwin, archbishop of York 108, 123 n., 169, 187, 266, 353, 410, 445, 447
Sandys, Sir Edwin 285
Satan, *see* Devil
Saunders, Laurence 424–5
Saxby, Robert 61, 146, 275 n., 401, 459
Schmidt, Leigh Eric 13, 42
Scotland, Scots 5, 43–4, 131–2, 134, 163, 172, 178, 196, 211, 237, 252, 338, 360, 471
Scrimger, John 126–7
Scudder, Henry 44, 47–8, 61, 65, 67–8, 81, 116–17, 124–5, 153, 157, 196, 200, 220, 240–1, 255, 279, 376, 394, 398, 400, 416–17, 442, 446
Seaver, Paul 302
security 23–4, 27, 62, 63, 73, 265, 420
separatists, separatism 6, 163, 214, 215, 217, 223, 360, 389
sermons, *see* preaching
servants 158, 160, 229, 260–1, 272, 282, 320, 359, 366, 369–71, 375, 387–8, 404, 434, 442, 452
Shakespeare, William 105
Shamir, Avner 294
Sharington, Anne 465
Shaxton, Nicholas, bishop of Salisbury 277
Shell, Alison 187
Shepard, Thomas 36, 125, 133–4, 140, 143, 149, 251, 283–4, 432, 439, 441
Sherman, William 306
Sibbes, Richard 33, 38, 52–3, 67, 69, 93, 103, 106, 121, 129, 145, 202–3, 241, 249–51, 262, 267, 282, 325, 399–400, 411, 426, 439, 450
Simson, Archibald 73, 80
Simson, Patrick 180, 311, 424, 465
Smith, Henry 33, 54, 268, 279, 351, 360–1, 396
Smith, John, minister in Essex 190–1, 193

Smith, John, minister in Teviotdale 383
Smith, Samuel 115, 150, 152
Sorocold, Thomas 76, 128, 223–4, 289, 385
Southwell, Anne 423
Southwell, Robert 192, 284
Spanish Armada 86, 140, 223, 379, 401, 425
Sparke, Michael 23, 24 n., 45 and n., 61, 68–9, 90, 109, 129, 147–8, 157, 168, 206, 233, 238, 245, 275, 290, 416
Speed, John 277
Stallybrass, Peter 274
Sternhold, Thomas 302
Sterry, Peter 42
Stewart, Jean 141–2, 160, 230, 274, 338
Stoicism 18, 20, 72, 81, 125
Stonley, Richard 8, 273–4, 299, 334, 358, 374, 379, 459
Stubbes, Katherine 84, 270, 400, 404, 463–6
Stubbes, Philip 462
Struther, William 62, 156, 178, 245, 255–6
suicide 27–31, 295
Sutcliffe, Matthew 204
Sutton, Christopher 23, 42, 76, 112–13, 116–17, 192, 252, 267, 289–90, 294, 338–9, 341, 347, 349–50, 364, 446, 460
Swain, Mary 446

Taverner, Richard 110
Taylor, John 293
Taylor, Thomas 458
tears 59, 61, 156, 187–95, 213, 255–6, 279, 290, 339, 347, 362, 435
Ten Commandments 57, 150, 177, 205, 218, 230, 232, 268, 282, 327, 337, 363–4, 434–5
Themylthorpe, Nicholas 50, 187, 219, 309–10
Thirty Years' War 140, 251, 380
Thomas, Keith 13, 355–6, 447
Thornton, *née* Wandesford, Alice 164, 267, 431–2, 459
Throckmorton, Job 74
Throckmorton, alt. Hickman, Rose 126, 300, 308, 335, 392, 438
Todd, Margo 430
Torshell, Samuel 196, 198, 251, 369
Tozer, Henry 232, 340, 398, 402
Treasure of gladnesse 277, 288, 375
Trinity, Trinitarianism 224, 235–8, 268, 331
Trundle, John 155, 208, 390, 442, 448
Tuke, Thomas 92, 102, 128, 192, 209, 216, 238, 250–1, 324, 379, 384, 387, 421
Turner, Richard 301–2
Tyacke, Nicholas 7
Tye, Christopher 271
Tymme, Thomas 23–4, 35, 45 n., 87, 117, 171, 206, 269–70, 319, 324, 326, 353, 411, 416, 461, 467
Tyndale, William 5, 63, 99, 268–9, 395, 418, 448–9

Tyndale, William (*cont.*)
　Biblical translations of 159
Tyrwhit, Elizabeth 236 n., 240, 293, 296

Ulster, *see* Ireland

Valentine, Henry 34–5, 348–9, 387, 461
Vaughan, Edward 274
Verney, Sir Ralph 268
Vicars, Thomas 25
Vives, Juan Luis 112, 115, 209, 285

Walker, Elizabeth 430
Walker, William 47
Wallace, Adam 395
Wallington, Nehemiah 21–6, 33, 59, 62, 72,
　83, 85, 93, 102 n., 126, 136–7, 139, 177,
　193, 241 n., 245, 255–6, 295–6, 306, 339,
　350, 352, 355, 357–8, 399–400, 412–13,
　429–30, 432, 442, 449, 453–4, 456, 461
　devotional practices 147, 149, 152–4, 162,
　164, 166, 187, 197, 235, 251, 272, 281–2,
　293, 308, 310–11, 365, 376, 383, 394,
　402, 446, 459, 460
　and despair 27–8, 30–1, 85, 156–7, 159
　as a writer 145, 299, 302–3, 308, 310–11,
　313, 442
Walsham, Alexandra 7
Walton, Izaak 444–5
Wandesford, Alice, *see* Thornton, Alice
Ward, Samuel, Cambridge diarist and
　theologian 50, 52n, 68–9, 311, 359, 380,
　430
Ward, Samuel, Ipswich preacher 52, 72, 115,
　146, 197, 291, 352, 388, 423, 439
Wariston, *see* Johnston of Wariston
Warwick, Arthur 115
Waste, Joan 323
Waste, Richard 146, 151, 165–6, 216, 221,
　239, 309, 382
Webbe, George, bishop of Limerick 18, 80–1,
　206 n., 274, 290–1, 325, 334, 383
Weber, Max 29, 446–8, 450, 454–5
weeping, *see* tears

Welsh, John 75–6, 140, 151, 157, 161, 166,
　211, 376, 380, 401, 463–4
Wesley, Susanna 160
Wetenhall, Edward 149, 157–9, 161–2, 171,
　233, 273–5
Whateley, William 79, 153, 366, 445
Whitaker, Jeremy 261, 271
White, Helen C. 109–10, 116, 226 n., 285, 289
White, John 133
White, Micheline 371
White, Rawlins 260
White, Thomas 116
Whitgift, John, archbishop of Canterbury 7,
　123, 203–4, 323, 392
Whitford, Richard 156, 160–1, 365
Wight, Sarah 295
Wilcox, Thomas 357, 410
Wilkinson, Elizabeth 35, 438
Wilkinson, Robert 356, 359
Willet, Andrew 136, 364, 402
Williams, Jean 77
Willis, Richard 272, 431–2
Wilson, Arthur 393
Winthrop, John 203
　conversion and youth 73, 83, 429,
　432, 441
　devotional experience and practices 21, 31,
　40, 73, 83, 84, 87, 94, 104, 107, 117,
　135–6, 137–8, 139, 140, 152, 168, 177,
　188, 279, 283, 333, 341, 356, 366, 372,
　373–4, 377, 392, 404
　diary 300, 313
Winthrop, Thomasine 185, 465–6
Wither, George 225, 245, 281
Wodenoth, Arthur 7–8, 82, 337–8, 347,
　403–4, 449
women, *see* gender
Woodford, Robert 80–1, 125, 134, 168, 229,
　334–5, 366, 372–3, 379–80
Woodman, Richard 294
work 153
Wright, Leonard 186
Wright, Susan 337
Wright, Thomas 267

26904757R00282

Printed in Great Britain
by Amazon